SAMUEL READ HALL LIBRARY
LYNDON STATE COLLEGE
LYNDONVILLE, VT. 05851

1995

S0-BBE-261

Essays in
Ancient Greek Philosophy

SAMUEL READ HALL LIBRARY
LYNDON STATE COLLEGE
LYNDONVILLE, VT. 05851

Essays in Ancient Greek Philosophy

Volume Two

Edited by John P. Anton
Professor of Philosophy
University of South Florida
and Anthony Preus
Professor of Philosophy
State University of N.Y., Binghamton

State University of New York Press
Albany

180
Es73
v. 2

Published by
State University of New York Press, Albany

© 1983 State University of New York

All rights reserved

Printed in the United States of America

No part of this book may be used or reproduced
in any manner whatsoever without written permission
except in the case of brief quotations embodied in
critical articles and reviews.

For information, address State University of New York
Press, State University Plaza, Albany, N.Y., 12246

Library of Congress Cataloging in Publication Data

Main entry under title:

Essays in ancient Greek philosophy.

  Papers originally presented at the annual meetings of
the Society for Ancient Greek Philosophy, 1953-   .
  Vol. 2 edited by John P. Anton and Anthony Preus.
  Includes bibliographical references and indexes.
  1. Philosophy, Ancient—Addresses, essays, lectures.
I. Anton, John Peter, 1920–   . II. Kustas, George L.
III. Preus, Anthony. IV. Society for Ancient Greek Philosophy.
B171.A56   180   69-14648
ISBN 0-87395-050-X (v. 1)   AACR2
ISBN 0-87395-623-0 (v. 2)
ISBN 0-87395-624-9 (v. 2 pbk.)

Contents

v

CONTENTS

Preface

THE papers printed in this volume offer the reader a clear view of the scope and quality of the work that the Society for Ancient Greek Philosophy continues to sponsor through annual meetings in conjunction with the American Philosophical Association and the American Philological Association. But aside from the invited papers presented at the annual meetings, important contributions by members of the Society for Ancient Greek Philosophy have been made through participation in a number of international conferences, including the World Congress on Aristotle in 1978, in Thessaloniki, Greece.

The Society for Ancient Greek Philosophy was formed in the early 1950s by a group of scholars interested in the systematic study of classical thought. The first meeting was held with the support of the Eastern Division of the American Philosophical Association on December 28, 1953, in Rochester, New York. To date, the following scholars have served as presidents: Gregory Vlastos, 1954; Glenn R. Morrow, 1955; Ludwig Edelstein, 1956; Raphael Demos, 1957; Philip Merlan, 1958; Friedrich Solmsen, 1959; J. B. McDiarmid, 1960; Philip Merlan, 1961; John H. Randall, Jr., 1962; Phillip DeLacy, 1963 and 1964; Leonard Woodbury, 1965 and 1966; E. L. Minor, Jr., 1967 and 1968; G. E. L. Owen, 1969 and 1970; Joseph Owens, 1971 and 1972; Rosamond Kent Sprague, 1973 and 1974; William W. Fortenbaugh, 1975 and 1976; Charles H. Kahn, 1977 and 1978; Martin Ostwald, 1979 and 1980; John P. Anton, 1981 and 1982. The office of secretary-treasurer has been held by Rosamond K. Sprague, 1953–56; J. M. Robinson, 1956–57; R. K. Sprague, 1957–63; R. W. Hall, 1963–72; John P. Anton, 1972–80; Anthony Preus, 1980– .

Of the fifty invited papers presented to the Society since 1968, only twenty-seven appear in this volume. A number of important papers have not been included here because they have become available as chapters in monographs or collections.

The papers selected for publication are arranged in four thematic groups centering around the major periods of ancient Greek philosophy: (1) pre-Socratics, (2) Plato, (3) Aristotle, (4) post-Aristotelian Philosophy.

PREFACE

We are grateful for permission to reprint the papers that have been published in the following periodicals: *Apeiron*; *Arion*; *Canadian Journal of Philosophy*; *Greek, Roman and Byzantine Studies*; *Isis*; *Journal of Hellenic Studies*; *Journal of the History of Ideas*; *Nature and System*; *Paideia*; *Philosophical Inquiry*; and *Phronesis*; we also thank The Walter de Gruyter Company for permission to reprint from *Arktouros*. Full references are given in footnotes on the first page of each paper. Thirteen papers appear here for the first time; in several instances their authors have made extensive revisions and additions, for which we express our appreciation.

We wish to thank Dr. Ellen Miskiewicz, Dean of the Graduate School of Emory University, and the University of South Florida for travel grants; the acting Dean of the School of Arts and Sciences at the State University of New York at Binghamton, Dr. Robert Melville, for secretarial assistance and other services in preparing the manuscript; and the Director of the State University of New York Press, Dr. William D. Eastman, who has earned our deep gratitude for his continuous support and concern for this publication.

Introduction

THIS collection of essays, selected from those presented to the Society for Ancient Greek Philosophy from 1968 through 1979, is intended to stimulate interest in the major accomplishments of classical philosophers. The essays have been grouped in roughly chronological sequence from the pre-Socratics through post-Aristotelian philosophers; this ordering makes sense to historians of philosophy and permits the reader to trace certain themes through several writers in an intelligible manner.

Each paper in this volume explores a concrete problem or set of interconnected questions in terms of the answers made possible by the textual evidence and corroborative facts. The papers are all pieces of independent research; their authors were invited to present papers to the Society on the basis of their previously published work and were given a free hand in choice of theme and methodology. The reader will not fail to notice that there is no dominant doctrine, no uniformity of methodology, that the essays in this volume may be said to represent. Undoubtedly it is this variety of philosophical sources and systematic approaches that accounts for the fruitful directions taken recently by scholarship in classical philosophy. The Introduction to the first volume summarizes several of the major types of interpretation developed during the previous decades; we need not repeat that material here.

In the ten years or so since that volume appeared, continued careful scholarship and philosophical analysis have increased our understanding of texts and interpretations. We would not want to characterize the decade as one of radical departures in methodology or of revolutionary discoveries, but there have been some noteworthy changes in emphasis. A significant number of younger scholars, some of them represented in this volume, have published works notable for the depth and maturity with which they have handled highly complex issues; their teachers have also continued to be vigorously and impressively productive. We may particularly note a shift in accent from a predominant preference for the application of linguistic methods in the study of texts to a more intensified concern for the contextual examination of philosophical concepts; the essays printed here show a more liberal, although still controlled, use of historical and cultural elements in interpretation.

The significant gains in the treatment of ancient Greek philosophy and the increasing reliability of recent interpretations are by no means isolated phenomena. The great strides made in recent decades owe much of their momentum to invaluable contributions from adjacent fields of Greek studies. A number of books and articles dealing with mythical thought and methodological problems of mythology, published since the mid-century, have opened as many new vistas as they have removed defects due to cultural bias and limited perspective. A better understanding of the transition from oral tradition to literal and literary forms for the preservation and communication of attitudes, ideas, values, and attainments has led to fruitful explorations of the cultural role that poetry in all its diverse forms had played in ancient times. Scholars have taken a closer look at the function of language in its diverse cultural and literary uses and have thus discovered much that was previously hidden deep under the surface of the surviving texts of the epic, lyric, and dramatic poets. Historical, papyrological, and archaeological investigations have provided no less assistance for the corroboration of textual interpretations. Taken together, the collective work of dedicated scholars in this and other countries is patiently paving the way for a more secure travel of the philosophical interpreter, lessening the risk of falling into the speculative temptation that bogged down many, even great, scholars in the past.

II

John Ferguson's paper offers a general introduction to pre-Socratic philosophy from the angle of a single concept. He shows how, from a discussion of the texts, we are able to reconstruct the various meanings of δῖνος and δίνη in the early philosophies of nature. In pursuing his topic, he moves from Aristotle and Plato back in time to the views of Anaximenes and Anaximander, citing as he treats each system the sources and authorities. Perhaps one of the more startling findings is that the vortex is a concept explicated by a surprisingly divergent set of models; not only the whirlpool or the tornado but also the winnowing sieve is a *dinos*, and these and other models are used for contrasting cosmological schemes.

In the view of the increase of recent scholarship in the complex problems of the surviving fragments of the Eleatic texts, it is not surprising that several of the essays in Part I are concerned with Xenophanes, Parmenides, and other writers related to the Eleatic school. This strong interest is in line with emphases in recent publications elsewhere, including a special issue of the *Monist* (January 1979, vol. 62, no. 1). A similar interest may be discerned in relation to Anaxagoras, whose thought has recently been much investigated both in America and Europe. The two essays on the Sophists reflect renewed interest in investigation of problems common to rhetoric and philosophy and show how much scholarship has gained by incorporating results of historical research in the last two decades.

James H. Lesher approaches the issue of the scope and nature of Xenophanes' skepticism by placing the question within a more generally critical framework. He argues that the type of skepticism that Xenophanes sought to establish is best understood in the context of a controversy that pits the poet's approach against that of traditional religion. The controversy was generated by religious beliefs attributing perfect knowledge to the divine; is there a way for man to tap divine knowledge? Xenophanes particularly attacks divination as a way to truth; in making this point, Lesher cites sources that support his view that there are many precursors of Xenophanes' position within the literary tradition. Thus it should be clear that Xenophanes need not have drawn his conclusions from a purely philosophical tradition. The skepticism of this poet rests on grounds considerably different from those of the skeptics of the Hellenistic period, but Xenophanes set in motion investigations into issues of belief and knowledge that constituted the beginning of a revolutionary way of thinking.

Parmenides' poem has challenged many a thinker both in its entirety and in its fragmentary parts. Jackson P. Hershbell undertakes to determine where the critical and puzzling fragment B16 belongs in the poem. Burnet and many others have placed it in the second part, the Way of Opinion; Hershbell, like J. H. M. Loenen, puts it in the first part, the Way of Truth, arguing that it is intended to affirm a close relationship between thought and being. He translates thus:

> As each man has a union of the much-wandering limbs
> of the body, so is mind present to men.
> For it is the same thing which the constitution of
> the limbs (mind) thinks, both in each and every man.

The concepts in this fragment do not, he argues, need to belong to a theory of knowledge, nor to a critique of sense-perception; B16 actually gains philosophical importance as a substantive part of the Way of Truth. Hershbell contributes a high degree of philological sophistication to the interpretive work this fragment requires to place it in its proper context.

Alexander P. D. Mourelatos, somewhat like Lesher, turns to literary texts for much-needed information concerning ways of thinking reflected not only in Plato but also, quite importantly, in Parmenides. He also relies heavily on an analysis by G. E. L. Owen of the relationships between the use of the existential quantifier and such expressions as "what is not," "nothing," and "not-being." Owen argued that the assumption that Plato is talking about "Non-Being" in, for example, the *Sophist*, just because he uses the phrase "what is not," is "mischievous." Mourelatos shows that Owen's attack can be pursued on a broader plane and that literary contexts support and refine Owen's philosophical analysis as applied to the thought of the pre-Socratics as well as of Plato. He concludes that the "dialectic of being in classical Greek speculation focuses not on 'what there *is*' but on '*what* it is' or '*how* it is'; not on existence but on *physis*, constitution, or form." Mourelatos's essay, together with his well-known book, *The Route of Parmenides* (Yale University Press, 1970), give an important perspective on recent discussions of Eleatic philosophy and on the subsequent developments that generated the great debates about "being," "nothing," and "not-being."

It is well established that the teachings of Parmenides became the object of speculative investigation. Their theoretical importance was due not only to the celebrated defense of a motionless universe but perhaps more to the fact that Parmenides made subsequent thinkers aware of the intellectual criteria any counter-theory must satisfy if plurality and motion are to be recognized as ultimate facts and cosmic principles. David Furley's essay shows with admirable clarity how complex the problems in speculative cosmology had become for the pluralists who sought to meet the Parmenidean challenge. Since not all that Parmenides had taught could be ignored with impunity, the way to proceed with the issue of Anaxagoras' response calls for a careful identification of those Parmenidean positions accepted by each pluralist, and those rejected, and for what reasons. The analysis of the extant fragments, Furley argues, allows a contrast between the method of Anaxagoras and that of Empedocles; by following the development of subsequent discussions we can conclude that the Anaxagorean philosophy of nature stands firmly in the line that continues from Parmenides to Plato.

Anaxagoras occupies a place in Greek philosophy not only as a thinker of acknowledged originality but also as a seminal cosmologist; this is well presented by Margaret E. Reesor's essay, "Anaxagoras and Epicurus." Focusing on several similarities between the two thinkers, Reesor is more concerned with ways in which Epicurus departed from the atomism of Democritus than she is with any direct Anaxagorean influence on the philosophy of the Garden. Reconstructing the philosophical position of Anaxagoras concerning truth and error, sense-perception and mind, Reesor goes on to compare the Epicurean interpretation of these concepts. One may recognize in Epicurus a tendency to move away from earlier atomism toward a refinement of a position resembling that of Anaxagoras; this movement would also help to explain some of the characteristics of later Epicureans such as Lucretius.

It is most instructive to read the essays by Furley and Reesor together, since both invite reconsideration of the standard ways of viewing the place of Anaxagoras in pre-Socratic thought, and both provide some of the background necessary for an assessment of the innovations of later atomism, and of later epistemological and physical speculation generally.

Arthur Adkins and Philip Ambrose examine the contributions of the Sophists to the philosophical tradition; both rely on works taken to be primarily from the literary rather than the philosophical tradition, but their examinations of these works are fundamental for an understanding of intellectual developments in late fifth-century Athens. Arthur Adkins's essay rigorously examines the *Helen* and *Palamedes* of Gorgias. These show-pieces of rhetoric constitute the longest connected pieces of argument that we have from the Sophists, yet have been relatively little explored by historians of philosophy. Inspired by the renewed interest in the development of an unbiased assessment of the Sophistic movement, Adkins cautiously explores the rhetorical practice of these pieces in relation to reports of Sophistic philosophical positions. The essay is, as a consequence, a contribution to the history of "ordinary logic" as much as to the history of rhetoric, and it challenges our interpretations of the conceptual structure of early Greek philosophy on a number of important issues. Gorgias helped to develop the tools for effective argumentation—how did he put them into practice? Adkins lucidly discusses the merits of the arguments in the *Helen*, fully exposing the grounds for determining whether they have any philosophical merit. He also compares some of the arguments in the *Palamedes*, particularly as they concern freedom and responsibility; in this respect the essay is an extension of his well-known study *Merit and Responsibility* (Oxford University Press, 1960). Even if we find that some of the arguments in the *Helen* and the *Palamedes* are rather ad hoc, they remain instructive in that they rely upon presuppositions shared by fifth-century Greeks in their consideration of moral issues; consequently Adkins's essay may also assist in our understanding of the ethical standpoint of Socrates, Plato, and ultimately, Aristotle.

Philip Ambrose notes how it is generally believed that Aristophanes mixes freely aspects of the historical Socrates and selected features of the Sophists in the composition of the *Clouds*. Ambrose focuses on an exploration of the extent to which the character of Socrates in that play reflects the philosophical developments introduced by Prodicus rather than, for example, Diogenes of Apollonia. After showing that the linguistic studies of Prodicus have influenced the contents of the play more than surface effects allow us to discern at first sight, Ambrose draws conclusions manifestly at variance with those of K. J. Dover. (*Aristophanes' Clouds*, Oxford University Press, 1968.) He defends the claim that there is a partial conflation of Socrates and Prodicus as *personae*, and hence that the *Clouds* contributed to the popular confusion prevailing in the minds of Athenians down to the time of the trial of Socrates. Part of his defense of this thesis rests on the fact that several ancient references to the play are best understood according to this interpretation.

Adkins and Ambrose deal with "co-Socratic" rather than "pre-Socratic" problems. More particularly, Ambrose's essay, concerned as it is with one of the main sources of the "Socratic problem," serves well as a transition to the first essay of the next section.

III

Having noted that scholarship since World War II "ended in a dilemma of contradiction," Eric Havelock has re-opened the search for the historical Socrates. The first part of his essay challenges the accepted criterion implied in the use of the classificatory terms "early" and "Socratic" as a period of Plato's compositions; taking a hint from Aristotle, he argues that perhaps it would be more fruitful to see the Socratic *logoi* as mimetic. Havelock joins this to his well-known thesis that Plato wrote at a time when the technology of communication was passing rapidly from oral to literary methods. A new literary genus, the Sophistic *logos*, emerged; the Socratic *logos* is a species of that genus which offers novel educational instruments and forms. Plato was an active participant in this new wave of written prose formulations. From all this Havelock concludes that "Socrates" in Plato's writings "is a mask for his own thinking." It is therefore impractical as well as impossible to extricate a biography of Socrates from what are essentially Plato's own works in style and substance. Havelock's position, cogently argued in this essay, will receive further attention in larger works scheduled for publication.

Robert S. Brumbaugh shifts attention to the internal references in Plato's dialogues that might hold evidential significance for correlating doctrines and dramatic dates. Brumbaugh takes issue with the unsatisfactory results of interpretations that ignore the interlocking between the literary and logical aspects of the dialogues; in addition, he advances a metaphysical reason for his exploration, which if overlooked adds to an already unacceptable split between two Platonic traditions, the "formalist" and the "process" views. Applying his method to what is regarded as an acceptable grouping of the dialogues into periods, Brumbaugh arrives at three general conclusions: the connective tissue of the early works is that they are setting straight the record of the Socratic doctrines, providing thereby the only true defense against the charges of his accusers; the final justification of the philosophical vision of life, as lived by Socrates, is the dominant perspective in the middle dialogues; in the final period, Plato sets his sights on three fundamental strategic targets, completing his analysis and investigation of logical, cosmological, and ethical problems, the great themes announced in the *Republic*.

Diskin Clay brings fresh insights into comedy and tragedy, tracing the elements assumed in the *Symposium* to the fuller articulation they receive in the *Republic* and *Laws*. Clay's graceful and elegant essay shows how response to literary nuance in the *Symposium* can yield valuable results for the philosophical understanding of Plato's thesis, despite the elliptical presentation of the concluding episode. There can be no doubt about Plato's determination to assign to poetry a new function, one that serves both moral aspirations and political ideals by encouraging the imitation of persons at once good, intelligent, and noble. Since the function of poetry and all art is to serve the city well, dramatic poetry, whether it be that of the tragedian or of the comedian, is validated only when it is subordinate to the overarching objectives of political wisdom. Clay brings to his reader the powerful suggestion of a paradoxical Socrates who, as Eros, brings comedy and tragedy together in his philosophical wholeness.

L. A. Kosman, concentrating on the first definition of *sophrosyne* in the *Charmides*, provides a deeper understanding of this cardinal virtue; a more inclusive objective of the essay is a detailed examination of the search for understanding of "temperance" in this dialogue. Going beyond Helen North's fundamental work (*Sophrosyne*, Cornell University Press, 1966), Kosman questions the adequacy of Socrates' argument. His detailed analysis leads him to declare also that "no Socratic fallacy is *eo ipso* a Platonic fallacy." The *Charmides* provides Kosman with a fine opportunity to initiate a contextual exploration of the technical and logical subtleties present in the Platonic method of definition. One of the most helpful procedural tools in this case is that of keeping in the foreground the purpose of definition in functional perspective, or to state the issue more plainly, in relationship to what the dialogue wants us to understand. In the case of the *Charmides*, Kosman is convinced that the procedure he has employed is especially rewarding in bringing us closer to the goal of identifying the specific elements associated with "quietness" that enter the virtue of *sophrosyne*.

Although the intricacies of argument and counter-argument for and against the immortality of the soul have elicited extensive commentaries since the subject became a centerpiece of Platonic studies, the logic of the argument has once again been investigated by another generation of scholars. It is not so much the fascination the doctrine holds as it is the challenge of ascertaining the merits of the arguments that motivates recent studies. C. C. W. Taylor's painstaking scrutiny of the proofs in the *Phaedo* relative to the thesis that the soul is a *harmonia* anticipated, when the paper was presented in 1970, arguments also to be found in David Gallop's commentary on the *Phaedo* (Oxford, 1975). The student of Plato's works will surely notice the importance attached to the concept of *harmonia*, particularly when the situation demands its philosophical employment; its appearance in the discussion of immortality is more problematic. Taylor examines anew the validity of Socrates' objections to a theory that may seem *prima facie* fatal to the theory of immortality, that the soul is an example of a *harmonia*. Taylor, with meticulous care, first notes the disagreement among commentators in their interpretations of Socrates' counter-argument and then looks at the meaning of the refuted thesis, defending the position that the arguments are not fatal to the thesis because they fail to cover all its versions.

No concept in Plato's ontology or epistemology, or even ethics or politics, is more central and yet more obscure than that of the Form of the Good. G. Santas focuses attention on the problems and difficulties that inevitably arise in the mind of the reader who wishes to interrelate the diverse statements Plato makes in the course of the middle books of the *Republic* concerning *to kalon*. Santas complicates his task by granting that Plato's *Phaedo*, *Symposium*, and *Timaeus* also presuppose the privileged position of the Good in the explanations set forth in those dialogues. A close reading of the text allows us to interpret Plato as holding a two-fold thesis about the supreme position of the Form of the Good, namely that it is both the final cause of all action and the ultimate condition of the intelligibility of all the other Forms. Santas uses recent discussions of self-predication and marshalls evidence that distinguishes two sorts of attributes of the Forms, ideal and proper, to support his thesis that "the theory of the Form of the Good in the *Republic* is truly the center-piece of the canonical Platonism of the middle dialogues"; it is just that feature of Plato's theory that justifies his being called "the first grand philosophical synthesizer."

Edward M. Galligan turns his attention to the refutation of the "Dreamed Theory" in the *Theaetetus* in order to assess critically the theory's view of *logos*. This is a serious issue in the interpretation of Plato's epistemology and is the turning point between the *Theaetetus* and the *Sophist*. Galligan's discussion is based on an analysis of the whole-part problem as related to *logos*, whereby *logos* is understood as disclosing the nature of the whole but not of parts. The reason given for this limitation is that parts identified as genuinely elemental remain unstatable. Only wholes *qua* complexes have a *logos*; the elemental parts do not. The "Dreamed Theory" in the *Theaetetus* develops a test case for this distinction. When Galligan turns to an examination of the place of *logos* in the *Sophist*, he finds that this dialogue provides a vantage point that may be used to determine whether Plato changed his position at all, in particular how Plato "might have been able to loosen the dilemma which refutes the theory." Galligan points out that the theory is important not only epistemologically but also ontologically, since it provides the conditions of giving true accounts of complexes in the world.

Robert G. Turnbull summarizes much of the thematic material that relates Plato to his tradition; philosophical conflicts demanded resolution. Turnbull identifies the challenge to Plato as one of synthesis of the apparently antithetical cosmic visions of Heraclitus and Parmenides—the one a world that "is and is not," the other a world that only "is." Placing the Platonic task within the parameters of *episteme* and *doxa*, Turnbull proceeds with a systematic analysis of the relevant texts to point up unnoticed features of the two types of cognition. The epistemological analysis leads to possible resolutions of the apparent ontological impasse. Seen in perspective, the present essay amplifies the research presented in its author's 1978 presidential address to the meeting of the Western Division of the American Philosophical Association.

The reader will have noticed that the essays in this part of the volume especially emphasize the middle period. This may indicate a trend; in the previous decade a greater emphasis upon the later period dialogues, *Parmenides, Theaetetus, Sophist*, and *Timaeus*, could be ascertained, but we now expect more attention to the *Phaedo, Republic*, and other earlier dialogues.

IV

Most of the papers on Aristotle included in this volume deal with either psychological or biological issues, rather than with logic or metaphysics. Although this partially reflects a recent trend in Aristotelian studies, we must also acknowledge that several of the papers on other aspects of Aristotle's philosophy, otherwise qualified for inclusion, have since become chapters in monographs. Interest in Aristotle's ethics continues unabated and is reflected in the essays by Fortenbaugh and Preus, but most particularly in Keyt's essay.

William W. Fortenbaugh examines the origins of Aristotle's bipartite psychology. He compares two common theories of that origin: first, that the roots of Aristotle's psychology are to be found in the Platonic three-fold division of the soul, later collapsed into emotion and reason; second, that the tragic poets, by refining a popular psychology, provided Aristotle with a distinction between emotional and deliberative responses. Fortenbaugh, relying on his knowledge of Euripides, shows that the bipartite moral psychology is already present in the *Medea* and *Hippolytus*; further elaboration and theoretical refinement provided what was needed for Aristotle's distinction between moral virtue and practical wisdom. Fortenbaugh's significant findings, besides accounting for origins, offer an attractive solution to the puzzle commentators have created by supposing that Aristotle's critical remarks on what turns out to be an Academic version of the bipartite soul could also have been a phase of self-criticism. We may add that this essay, like several others in the volume, benefits importantly from the author's keen interest in texts not always investigated by historians of philosophy.

Theodore Tracy develops a theme in the biological theory of the soul, the central role of the heart. (Another recent treatment is C. R. S. Harris, *The Heart and Vascular System in Ancient Greek Medicine*, Oxford University Press, 1973.) Besides its intrinsic interest for the interpretation of Aristotle's theory of the nature of life, the role of the heart in Aristotle's psychology is also crucial evidence for the relative dating of his various works. F. Nuyens (1948) argued that the definition of the soul in *de Anima* II and the theory that the heart is the seat of the soul are absolutely incompatible theses and thus could not have been held simultaneously. Tracy summarizes some of the debate since that time and concludes that the question has not been settled. If one refrains from a "chronological solution" of the sort proposed by Nuyens, one must all the more find a satisfactory philosophical solution to the apparent incompatibility. Tracy points out that these supposedly "irreconcilable" Aristotelian theses appear side by side in the same text, so Aristotle could not himself have supposed them to be incompatible. Taking his lead from an article by Charles Kahn (AGP, 1966) on Aristotle's psychology, Tracy shows that the physiological model used in the *de Anima* is also used in the biological works to cover not only the faculties of the sensitive soul but also the entire animal soul. Thus Tracy arrives at a conclusion opposed to that of Nuyens, arguing that the texts make sense when we begin to understand how and why Aristotle thought it necessary to postulate a dominant organ.

Anthony Preus reexamines the method and motivation of Aristotle's classification of animals and shows how other problems are approached with similar means. The essay reviews the central role the concept of *eidos* plays in Aristotle's investigations, but in determining its meaning Preus finds it necessary to diverge from some previous commentators. One such divergence is the widely accepted characterization of *eidos* in terms of a rigid essentialism; although some biologists ascribe to Aristotle a typological taxonomic theory, Aristotle's writings offer no uncontrovertible support of that interpretation. The theory of species developed in the context of the biological works can also assist in the interpretation of some passages in the normative works, in particular the classification of pleasures in the *Nicomachean Ethics* and the taxonomy of constitutions in the *Politics*. Throughout, Preus argues that the selection of classificatory criteria remains functional; this is perhaps his fundamental answer to those who attribute a later form of essentialism to Aristotle.

Critics have studied Aristotle's ethical and political writings not only for his powerful analyses of the ends and ideals of human life, but often more for the challenge that his arguments and formulations present to those working on substantive current problems. Aristotle's theory of happiness has never failed to arouse interest or to invite fresh interpretations and vigorous debate. David Keyt seeks to understand the sharp contrasts Aristotle makes between two ways of life, both in accordance with virtue, open to those who seriously aim at achieving human excellence: the philosophical life, concentrating upon theoretical activity, and the practical-political life, sustained by practical wisdom and the moral excellences. Keyt examines the merits of the argument for the theoretical life as perfect happiness against the background of two contrasting interpretations, both of which have found strong support in recent years. The "exclusive" interpretation claims that the attainment of happiness in no way depends on the coordinate securing of subordinate ends; the "inclusive" interpretation says that happiness includes the activities involved in both sorts of virtue. Keyt attributes the difference to rigid conceptualizations of the problem, forcing a decision between strict intellectualism and a moderate one. His essay should be read as an eloquent defense of the latter alternative, in opposition to the interpretation of, for example, John Cooper, *Reason and Human Good in Aristotle* (Harvard University Press, 1975). We may note that Cooper presented his position to the Society, but his paper is now part of that book.

Chung-Hwan Chen turns to the *Metaphysics* for Aristotle's argument that Plato cannot account for change in terms of the theory of ideas. Following C. J. de Vogel and I. Düring, *contra* Werner Jaeger, Chen claims that Aristotle had never accepted the theory of transcendent ideas, separate from both particulars and from the mind of God. Working with these and other related senses of "transcendent," Chen evaluates Düring's version of the thesis to determine the truth of its claims. One significant observation he makes is that the *Categories* should, if written by Aristotle, be regarded as an early writing—but it contains no indication of acceptance of transcendence. Other earlier books contain evidence that could be used in support of some version of Jaeger's thesis, although even there the theory must have been modified to suit Aristotle's pursuits at the time. Chen argues that Jaeger is right in his assessment that the problem of change is what led Aristotle to reject the transcendence of the Forms, even though he was tempted to regard them as ideal values.

David E. Hahm's discussion of the fifth element in Aristotle's *de Philosophia* leads rather directly to the Hellenistic and Roman periods, since evidence concerning the contents of that early piece is gathered in the writings of later philosophers. Hahm carefully analyzes the many fragments, and their sources, in an attempt to develop a critical appraisal of a doctrine attributed to Aristotle by some ancient writers, that of the "fifth element." The essay is a substantial contribution to the systematic examination of the evidence that must be used in reconstructing the original treatise and Aristotle's views of cosmology. A valuable aspect of the paper is the employment of philological tools to assess the two traditions stemming from the *de Philosophia*: Cicero's account and the doxographic evidence. Hahm shows that the fragments accepted as belonging to the treatise do not allude to a five-element cosmology; if the doctrine is to be accepted as authentic, it must belong to some other phase of Aristotle's career. Clearly Aristotle's physical treatises contain several undecided issues deserving of future study.

V

David Konstan's essay combines a critical discussion of Epicurean physics with an extended treatment of technical issues. His analysis of Epicurean science should suffice to convince the reader of the great interest in the contributions of ancient philosophers to the development of physical thought. Recently historians of science have rejected the intellectually naive appraisal that atomism was nothing more than an appendix to the ethics of withdrawal and tranquility. As Konstan says, "Some surprising and ingenious propositions have been attributed to Epicurus, and to some extent to Democritus, in modern interpretations of ancient atomic theory. These propositions betray a serious involvement by the atomists with the physical and philosophical implications of their doctrines on matter and void." Recognizing how recent discussions illuminate otherwise obscure points in Epicurean texts by establishing a clear lineage of concepts from the Eleatics to Epicurus through Aristotle, Konstan amplifies the reconstruction and rehabilitation of Epicurean physics by looking again at concepts like collision, contact, and weight, placing them in the framework of Epicurus' theoretical model, which he defends as representing "a major achievement in the history of mechanistic world models."

John M. Rist's essay contributes to ongoing investigations of Stoic ethics. Recent publications by Rist, as well as by A. A. Long and others, have considerably increased our understanding of the ways in which the Stoics dealt with complex problems concerning the nature and function of such fundamental notions as virtue, impulse, and happiness, and the high place they occupy in the practice and theory of Stoicism. Rist's present essay, although generally concerned with the problem of consistency in ethical theory, may be read as a lucid introduction to the early Stoic point of view. He alerts the reader to the fact that the idea of *eudaimonia*, as the end of the moral life, became much more complicated after the early Stoics introduced a number of distinctions, redefining the relation between virtue and happiness. Since the Stoics decidedly granted more significance to the role of virtue, they created an anomaly in the priority of ethical objectives, with the inescapable consequence of posing a demand for the reconsideration of traditional notions in order to preserve consistency in their ethical theory. Rist has adroitly laid bare the philosophical significance and implications of the new element in the early Stoics.

Josiah B. Gould examines another important and influential feature of the Stoics: their concern with determinism. Looking at Alexander of Aphrodisias' arguments against the Stoic views of fate, Gould shows the ground on which the Stoic position can be defended. Noting that the idea of fate appears explicitly for the first time in the writings of Chrysippus (Gould has written an important book on that philosopher, State University of New York Press, 1970), he proceeds to show how the Stoic theory of causality lies at the basis of the notion, since according to the Stoics, both natural and ethical events are universally determined. Only on this ground, Gould insists, can the Stoic concept of fate make sense; universal determinism, in its historical setting, constituted an astounding departure from the philosophies of Plato, Aristotle, and Epicurus. The Stoic treatment of fate includes an impressive, if not altogether consistent, account of the attendant key notion of human responsibility within a system containing no basis for an escape from rigid causality.

The philosophy of Plotinus, especially the systematic aspects of his metaphysics, his extension of Plato's dialectical method to accommodate the blendings and cross-currents of Hellenistic synchretistic visions as well as his own brand of Neoplatonic logic, and his place in late antiquity as a seminal thinker, have recently received considerable attention from scholars with a sharp eye for historical detail and textual difficulties. In his essay, Richard T. Wallis, whose earlier work on Neoplatonism alerted many students to the multifarious character of this movement and the great variety of thematic material it encompassed beyond strictly philosophical topics, has discussed Plotinus' treatment of paranormal phenomena, chiefly his concern with astrology. Unless the reader is already familiar with Plotinus' *Enneads*, he would be unlikely to suspect what seriousness Plotinus attached to astrological phenomena and how his system does in fact stretch the principles of philosophical investigation into the universe as a whole to encompass paranormal occurrences and events. By enlarging the contours of the self and recasting the genealogy of the soul beyond traditionally recognized boundaries, Plotinus came to allow for an intelligibility of events beyond and above the domain governed by deterministic ways, as distinguished from those in the sensible world. As Wallis ably points out, it is the self's affinity to the supra-sensible order that enables Plotinus to connect the paranormal phenomena with rational explanations.

John M. Dillon focuses attention on a controversy in later Greek ethics. His analysis of *metriopatheia* provides a needed opportunity to compare

Stoic and other philosophers on an ethical issue concerning whether one ought not feel emotions, or have the right amount of emotions. The arguments advanced properly belong to the branch of ethics dealing with the theory of passions in relation to the soul and its parts, on the one hand, and their place in the pursuit of virtue and the good life, on the other. The diverse answers given to the issues were vigorously defended in the ethics of Plato, Aristotle, and the early Stoics. Some later philosophers took an essentially Aristotelian line, looking for a mean in respect of the emotions; others believed that an orthodox Stoic position demanded total impassivity as a necessary precondition for the Sage. Dillon explains the controversy about *metriopatheia* and *apatheia* as one concerned with moral psychology; whether it could be characterized as a verbal dispute or not, the debate was regarded as central by several ancient schools.

VI

The brief remarks given in the preceding sections will, we hope, assist the general reader in identifying issues, trends, problems, and approaches as they emerge in each essay. We wish to suggest some profitable paths, opened by recent scholarly interpretations, for a critical understanding of the classical mind and its relevance to our own philosophical methods and objectives.

Journal and Standard Reference Abbreviations

AGP	Archiv für Geschichte der Philosophie
AJP	American Journal of Philology
Ant Cl	Antiquité Classique
APQ	American Philosophical Quarterly
BICS	Bulletin of the Institute of Classical Studies
CP	Classical Philology
CQ	Classical Quarterly
CR	Classical Review
CW	Classical World
DK	Hermann Diels and Walter Kranz, *Die Fragmente der Vorsokratiker*
HSCP	Harvard Studies in Classical Philology
JHP	Journal of the History of Philosophy
JHS	Journal of Hellenic Studies
LSJ	Liddell, Scott, and Jones, *Greek-English Lexicon*
MH	Museum Helveticum
NYR	New York Review of Books
PAS	Proceedings of the Aristotelian Society
PQ	Philosophical Quarterly
PR	Philosophical Review
RE	Pauly-Wissowa: *Real Encyclopädie der Klassischen Altertumswissenschaft*
REA	Revue des études anciennes
RFIC	Rivista de Filosophia e d'Instruzione Classica
RhM	Rheinisches Museum für Philologie
RPhL	Revue Philosophique de Louvain
SB	Sitzungsberichte der Bayerischen Akademie der Wissenschaften
YCS	Yale Classical Studies

Abbreviations of works by ancient authors as listed in LSJ, unless explained in the text.

Part I

PRE-SOCRATICS

Dinos[1]

I

ἶνος and δίνη are terms related to movement. It is true that δῖνος is applied to round, static objects such as a threshing-floor and a drinking-cup, and the scholiasts on *The Clouds* suggested that such an earthenware pot had displaced the familiar statue of Hermes at the entry to the phrontisterion (cf. Aristophanes *Clouds* 1473). But though the ancient world knew working-models (a working astronomical model with epicyclic gearing has been recovered from a shipwreck and leads us to give credence to the stories of Archimedes' working-models, and even to wonder whether after all Plato may have had something such in mind in the *Republic* myth), and though Empedocles uses a mobile image in the cup of water which does not spill as you whirl it round (DK 31 A 67), we shall not be surprised to find a static model of a dynamic event. When Euripides, philosophy-orientated as he was, writes of οὐράνιαι δῖναι νεφελας δρομαίου (*Alc.* 244) he shows that δίνη is a dynamic term. The basic meaning of δῖνος or δίνη seems to be a whirlpool or eddy in water, and it is this analogy which is applied somehow, somewhere, to movement within the universe. But how? and where?

"Dinos" was presented to the 1968 Toronto meeting of the Society for Ancient Greek Philosophy and was revised and published in *Phronesis* 16, no. 2 (1971): 97–115; we thank the editors and Royal VanGorcum Ltd for permission to reprint.

John Ferguson is President of Selly Oak Colleges in Birmingham, England.

[1]I follow the example of Norman O. Brown in offering after each section the principal sources I have drawn upon, as an alternative to laborious and distracting footnotes. The references are not of course exhaustive: they include all views referred to, and any others I have found especially useful. The following books have been constantly consulted:

Burnet, J. *Early Greek Philosophy*. London, 1920.
Diels, H. and Kranz, W. *Die Fragmente der Vorsokratiker* (cited as DK). Berlin, 1954.
Gomperz, T. *Greek Thinkers*, vol. 1. London, 1901.
Guthrie, W. K. C. *A History of Greek Philosophy*, vols. 1–2. Cambridge, 1962–5.
Heath, T. L. *Aristarchus of Samos*. Oxford, 1913.
Kirk, G. S. and Raven, J. E. *The Presocratic Philosophers*. Cambridge, 1957.
Skemp, J. B. *The Theory of Motion in Plato's Later Dialogues*. Cambridge, 1942.
Tannéry. P. *Pour l'histoire de la science hellène*. Paris, 1930.

II

Ἐκ Διὸς ἀρχώμεσθα. To trace the story of δῖνος we shall have to move backwards in time, starting with Aristotle. In *De Caelo*, he is arguing to a fifth element. He assumes that natural bodies have a principle of motion within them. All locomotion is either straight or circular or a combination of the two. The four elements of earth, air, fire, and water naturally move in a straight line in a vertical plane; if there were no fifth element, circular motion would have no natural place in the cosmos. But circular motion must be primary: (a) the circle is complete and finite, the straight line infinite and incomplete (269 a 20); (b) circular motion is continuous and eternal (συνεχῆ καὶ ἀίδιον 269 b 8). The case is argued at greater length in *Physics* 8. He has already defined nature as "the principle and cause of motion and rest to those things only in which she inheres primarily as distinct from incidentally" (2, 192 b 20). In *Physics* 8, 9 he argues the primacy of circular motion (a) because a circle is finite and a straight line is not, (b) because complete motion in a straight line, returning to its starting-point, requires two movements, up and down again, (c) because circular motion is eternal, (d) because in circular motion there is no beginning, middle, and end definable, (e) because the determinative point of a circle is the centre, and when a sphere rotates it is in one sense in motion, but in another, through its determinative point, at rest, (f) uniform rotation with its unit of the completed circuit is the standard of all measurement of time and motion, being the easiest to calculate (cf. 4, 223 b 18), (g) circular motion is the only uniform motion; motion in a straight line changes velocity, accelerating as it removes itself from the place of rest. From the primacy of circular motion among other forms of locomotion, he passes to the primacy of locomotion among other forms of κίνησις, adducing Empedocles, Anaxagoras, the Atomists, the Milesians (whom Aristotle treats as a group, cf. 1, 187 a 12), and the Platonists. The passage is important: it makes it unlikely that κίνησις in Anaximander and Anaximenes is other than locomotion.

In *De Caelo* 2, 13 he starts from various theories of the mobility or immobility of the earth. He goes on to show that motion must be discussed not in relation to a single element but in relation to the total cosmos. Is motion natural (φύσει) or enforced (βίᾳ)? There cannot be enforced motion unless motion exists in nature; the same is true of rest. It follows that if the earth is at rest βίᾳ the enforced rest must arise from some natural rest or motion. This will be the vortex (τὴν δίνησιν). Aristotle is assuming his proof of the primacy of circular motion, but he is also speaking historically, for he goes on: "This is the cause that all allege, reasoning from what happens in liquids and in the air; for in these the larger and heavier objects are always carried towards the middle of the whirl (δίνῃ)" (295 a 11) (Guth-

4

rie must be wrong in "This is the name which all agree in giving . . . ,"
since the name does not seem to have been used by the Milesians, if they
held such a theory, or by Anaxagoras, who certainly did). The earth remains
at the centre of the vortex, either by reason of its flatness and size or on the
Empedoclean notion of the cup of water swung swiftly round (which we
shall discuss later). Aristotle subjects these views to some criticism, on the
following grounds: (a) There is no account of the earth's natural motion. (b)
The immobility of the Earth in the rule of Strife in Empedocles is not to be
explained by the vortex at that point. (c) "Even if in the past it is through the
vortex that the parts of the earth were carried to the centre, through what
cause is everything that has weight still carried towards it? Surely the vortex
is not drawing closer to us" (295 a 33). (This is precisely what Anaxagoras
seems to have said.) (d) Why does fire move upwards? Not through the vortex! If fire has a natural motion, so may earth. (e) Heaviness and lightness
are not defined by the vortex; they must have existed before the vortex.
Aristotle does not follow out this criticism, but he means a doctrine of natural positions which does away with the need for a vortex.

There is one other important relevant passage in Aristotle. This is *De
Anima* 1, 3. Aristotle is discussing the κίνησις of the soul, and isolates
four forms of κίνησις, locomotion, change of state, decay, and growth.
The discussion which follows is not very clear, but Aristotle rejects movement in a straight line for the soul on *a priori* grounds; if its natural movement were up it would be fire, if down it would be earth. He also rejects the
circular movement which Plato postulated in *Timaeus*. νόησις is not
περιφορά, nor will circular movement do as a model for thought,
since it is the essence of thought to move to a conclusion. Plato had linked
the motion of the soul with the motion of the heavenly bodies. Aristotle
comments that the reason why the heavenly bodies move in a circle is obscure (407 b 6), but there is nothing in the essential nature of the soul to
link it with circular movement, nor any profession that circular movement is
better.

Aristotle is important as a source for earlier views on the vortex and for
his criticisms of them; he is also important because while rejecting the
model of the whirlpool or whirlwind in favor of his own theories of natural
position and natural movement, he offers interesting theoretical justification
of the primacy of circular motion. Some of the analysis is no doubt original
with him, but it is unlikely that none of the arguments had occurred to earlier thinkers.

Cherniss, H. *Aristotle's Criticism of Presocratic Philosophy*. Baltimore, 1935.
Guthrie, W. K. C. *Aristotle: On the Heavens*. London, 1939.
Wicksteed, P. and Cornford F. M. *Aristotle: The Physics*, 2 vols. London,
1934.

III

Plato need not long delay us: the problems are fascinating, but of limited relevance to the present enquiry. In *Laws* 10 (893 b 1) he isolates ten kinds of motion: (i) circular motion round a fixed centre, (ii) locomotion in a straight line by gliding or rolling, (iii) combination, (iv) separation, (v) increase, (vi) decrease, (vii) coming into being, (viii) destruction, (ix) the capacity to move another object and be moved by another, (x) the capacity for self-movement and moving other objects. Of these the last is supreme. But a little later (898 a 2) he asserts that uniform circular motion, as of a spinning globe, is the best model for the revolution of reason, and argues from this to a link between the circular movement of the sky and a guiding intelligence. The argument picks up *Timaeus*. There the Divine Artificer constructs the cosmos as a single unit (33 c ff.), a living creation, in the most appropriate shape, namely a sphere, and assigns to it the form of motion appropriate to reason and intelligence, namely revolution round a fixed point. This motion is a rotation of the whole universe with all its contents. The rectilinear motions which disturb the simple picture of rotation, up, down, backwards, forwards, left, right, are irrational and intrusive. Somewhat later (46 c ff.) Plato picks out a contrast between νοῦς and ἀνάγκη, linking νοῦς with αἰτία and ἀνάγκη with ξυναίτια; ἀνάγκη here refers to physical causes which serve no rational end. In *The Laws*, in interpreting the atomists, he links ἀνάγκη with τύχη in the explicit phrase κατὰ τύχην ἐξ ἀνάγκης (10,889 c); to the atomists φύσις and τύχη are responsible for the greatest things, τέχνη for the slighter. νοῦς is associated with uniform circular motion, ἀνάγκη with random movement. It follows that Plato rejects the idea of an irrational vortex, since that would for him be a contradiction in terms; this passage is clearly directed against the atomists. It is interesting that later Plato uses the model of the winnowing-fan (52 e ff.).

Cornford, F. M. *Plato's Cosmology*. London, 1937.
Skemp, J. B. *The Theory of Motion in Plato's Later Dialogues*. Cambridge, 1942.
Taylor, A. E. *Commentary on Plato's Timaeus*. Oxford, 1928.

IV

In Democritus the doctrine of the vortex is explicit and familiar. The elements are stated to be perpetually moving in the void ἀεὶ κινουμένων τῶν ὄντων ἐν τῷ κενῷ (DK 68 A 40). The motion is random, like the motes in a sunbeam (cf. Arist. *de An.* 1, 403 b 31). Here clearly, perpetual

6

movement is not identified with movement in a circle, but this may be original with the atomists. Aëtius states that Democritus regarded vibration as the basic motion (68 A 47): παλμός. He may be reading Epicurean thought back into the earlier atomists; yet we are still dealing with thought based on analogy, and the image of winnowing is of some importance. Then for some reason not stated, a whirl or vortex was separated off from the whole, of all kinds of shapes (68 A 67; B 167). Simplicius attributes this to chance (cf. Arist. *Phys.* 2, 196 a 24); and some modern interpreters have identified this with statistical probability; Democritus would not have so put it, but it may not be too far from his intent. In the vortex there is the repulsion of unlike atoms (68 A 37) and the attraction and entanglement of like to like. An important fragment explains this first in terms of the familiar "Birds of a feather flock together" and then of the tendency of seeds in a sieve to come together in their kinds κατὰ τὸν τοῦ κοσκίνου δῖνον or pebbles under the action of waves (68 B 164). The most important aspect of this for our concern is πάντα τε κατ᾽ ἀνάγκην γίνεσθαι, τῆς δίνης αἰτίας οὔσης τῆς γενέσεως πάντων, ἣν ἀνάγκην λέγει "everything happens according to necessity, the vortex being responsible for the coming-into-being of all things, and he calls this necessity" (D.L. 9, 45 = DK 68 A 1). "This" can grammatically refer to vortex or coming-into-being, but it is clearly the former; compare the phrase κατ᾽ ἀνάγκη μὲν καὶ ὑπὸ δίνης (68 A 83), or Aëtius's definition of ἀνάγκη in Democritus as the resistance, locomotion and impact of matter (68 A 66). Necessity then means physical or natural law, and that is identified with the vortex which initiates the process. One additional point: the δίνη continues: at least it is reasonable to see it in Lucretius' *caeli turbine* (5, 624 cf. 510) where it is associated with the view that the closer stars move more slowly than those more distant: it is thus present as well as primal, astronomical as well as cosmogonical. Some have thought on the basis of a passage in Epicurus' *Letter to Pythocles* (92) that Democritus held a whirl within a stationary rim. I can see nothing in this mutilated and obscure passage which applies to Democritus, and Lucretius did not so understand him.

Alfieri, V. E. *Gli Atomisti.* Bari, 1936.

Bailey, C. *The Greek Atomists and Epicurus.* Oxford, 1928.

———.*Titi Lucreti Cari De Rerum Natura Libri Sex*, 3 vols. Oxford, 1941.

Ferguson, J. "The Date of Democritus" *Symb. Osl.* 40 (1965) 17–26.

Hammer-Jensen, I. *Den Aeldste Atomlehre.* Copenhagen, 1908.

Liepmann, H. C. *Die Mechanik der Leucipp-Democritischen Atome.* Leipzig, 1885.

Lowenheim, L. *Die Wissenschaft Demokrits und ihr Einfluss auf die moderne Wissenschaft.* Berlin, 1914.

Schreckrenberg, H. *Ananke.* München, 1964.

V

Behind Democritus stands the obscure figure of Leucippus. The picture we have of his thought is not essentially different from that of Democritus. The only surviving sentence of Leucippus is "Nothing comes into being at random; everything in accordance with a principle and by necessity" (67 B 32). This accords with the use of necessity in Democritus, which is identified with the vortex. The words do not mean, as they are often translated, "Nothing happens"; Leucippus would not have written χρῆμα for that (cf. οὐδὲν χρῆμα γίνεται in Anaxagoras 59 B 17, from whom the phrase is borrowed) they are thus not incompatible with an originally random movement but until the vortex is produced, no thing comes into being. We have two other words which must come from Leucippus; he spoke of χιτῶνα καὶ ὑμένα, a covering or membrane which formed *in a circle* round the universe (67 A 23): the circle is important. In Aëtius' summary of *The Great World-System* again we find the indivisible bodies in continual motion, which is explicitly said to be ἀπρονόητον καὶ τυχαίαν. In the summary in Diogenes Laertius there are some important passages (which Kirk, whose treatment of the atomists is curiously perfunctory, does not excerpt) τὴν γῆν ὀχεῖσθαι περὶ τὸ μέσον δινουμένην; the earth (which is in the shape of a tambourine) is supported as it rotates around the centre (D.L. 9, 30 = DK 67 A 1). He proceeds to speak of the production of a vortex in which like came to like, the fine atoms passed outwards, as if they had been sieved out; the rest remained and became entangled, forming a spherical structure (the membrane above), which enclosed all kinds of bodies. "As these were whirled round in accordance with the resistance of the centre (κατὰ τὴν τοῦ μέσου ἀντέρεισιν) the surrounding membrane became thin, as the continuous bodies unceasingly flowed together in accordance with their contact with the vortex. In this way the earth came into being, as the things which had been carried towards the centre remained together there" (D.L. 9, 32 = DK 67 A 1). Thus we see in Leucippus no explanation of the origin of the vortex. Since the vortex was set up there is a tendency of like to come together with like; this is taken from Anaxagoras, but for Leucippus likeness is of shape and size, not of sort and substance, and it is this that sieves out the fine atoms and leaves others forming a spherical membrane. What happens then has been well explained by Burnet; it puzzled Gomperz. Gomperz wrote (1, 339 E.T.): "these effects were the precise contrary of what they should have been by the laws of physics. The centrifugal force which is released by a rotatory movement is doubtless admirably adapted to sift an agglomerated mass of matter. But, as every centrifugal machine would show, it is the heaviest substances which are hurled to the greatest distance." Gomperz's

8

constructive explanation merits reconsideration. The motion of a whirlwind or "twister" or even of slighter eddies will carry off lighter objects but leave heavier, and because of the friction as it approaches the ground does in fact deposit matter at its centre. Gomperz suggests a false extrapolation from observed phenomena. It is even more likely that Leucippus had in mind the tendency of a maelstrom to suck boats to its centre. What Burnet has shown is that Leucippus offered a physical explanation of this in terms of the contact between all parts of the vortex, so that the motion of the outer membrane is communicated (and, we may add, in a closed system) to all inside. The speed of revolution is of course slower towards the centre, and this is what Leucippus means by the resistance of the centre. We now understand more clearly residual rotation of the earth, and its equilibrium in the centre, there being no "up" and "down" in the void for the early atomists, as there was for Epicurus, and the rotation of the vortex being horizontal in relation to the earth.

VI

Diogenes of Apollonia reaffirmed a monism based on air, against the pluralism of Empedocles and Anaxagoras, and accepted from Anaxagoras the doctrine of a divine intelligence which he identified with air. In general the formation of the world was due to the rarefaction and condensation of air. He stated that everything is in motion, though we have no evidence of his speaking of unceasing motion. Kirk took the view that this motion was rotatory, but he depended in part for his view on an emendation by Kranz. The MS reading makes sense: "where the dense ran together it made a solid mass" (συστροφὴν ποιῆσαι: Kranz συστροφῆι γῆν ποιήσας, which Kirk renders "centripetally" 64 A 6). Rotation is, however, to be seen in the heavenly bodies (64 A 12). The words δῖνος and δίνη do not appear in our sources, so that it is dangerous to be dogmatic: with his debt to Anaxagoras, Diogenes may have derived his image of the rotation from him rather than from Empedocles or Leucippus.

VII

Anaxagoras is more important. After his general account of Νοῦς he proceeds: "Mind controlled the whole revolution, so as to revolve from the beginning. It began to revolve first from a small beginning, and now revolves to a greater extent, and will revolve to a greater extent in the future. Mind knows all the things which were mingled together, separated out or divided off. Mind organized all that was going to exist, and that existed in the past but does not exist now, and all that exists now or will exist in the future, in-

9

cluding this revolution, the present revolution of stars, sun, moon, air and fire (all in process of being separated off). This revolution produced the process of separating off: the dense is separated off from the rare, the hot from the cold, the bright from the dark, and the dry from the moist" (DK 59 B 12). To this we may add two more passages: "When Mind initiated motion, there was a process of separating off from the totality in motion, and all that Mind set in motion was divided out. As things were set in motion and divided out, the revolution greatly increased the process of division" (59 B 13) ". . . as these things revolved in this way and were separated out by the force and speed. Speed produces force" (59 B 9). The interpretation of this has occasioned less controversy than other parts of Anaxagoras, but it is extremely difficult to interpret and even to translate. In the first quotation ἔγνω is most easily rendered "knows," and Simplicius so understood it (*Cael.* 608, 27 ff.), but Lämmli argued forcefully for the meaning "determined." αἰθήρ is clearly "fire," as Aristotle understood (*Cael.* 270 b 24; 302 b 4; *Meteor.* 369 b 14). The MSS in the next sentence have αὕτη, but some editors prefer to emend to αὐτή, "the actual revolution." In the next quotation it is not clear whether ἀπεκρίνετο is impersonal, as I have taken it, or whether Mind is separated off (so Heidel, Diels-Kranz, Guthrie). I take ἀπὸ τοῦ κινουμένου παντὸς to mean not "all that was moved," which could be unambiguously expressed by a different word order, but "the all in motion." This might be contradicted if ἀπό του σμικροῦ and ἐπὶ πλέον in 59 B 12 refer to the areas affected, but they seem to me vaguer than that. In any case once the outer part of the universe is in motion it is easy to speak of "the universe in motion." We may reasonably postulate increasing acceleration. The word for revolution is not δῖνος or δίνη, which nowhere appears, but περιχώρησις; the verb is used of Thales journeying round Greece (D.L. I, 44), of kingship coming round in succession (Hdt. I, 210), or of a waiter going round with the water (Aristophanes *Birds* 958): it is noncommittal and suggests no clear image. Anaxagoras may have believed (so Cleve) that lifeless bodies of themselves move only along a vertical axis. Any other motion requires an explanation. Νοῦς therefore, so to say, put itself into orbit and that revolution has gradually been transmitted to the whole universe, and the universe has changed in accordance with centrifugal force. This is why Anaxagoras does not use δίνη (which was available to him from Empedocles); his model is different; the appearance of δῖνος in a vague passage from Clement is hardly to be pressed to the contrary (59 A 57). Hence the flinging out of stones to form sun, moon, and stars (59 B 16; A 71 and especially A 12). It is just here that we must insist on the fact that δίνη is not a vortex, but an eddy, whirlpool, or whirlwind; it would be impossible to describe the motion as a δίνη flinging things *outwards*.

Anaxagoras' view however is not a simple one. He evidently thought that Νοῦς imparted its revolution first at the outer edges of the universe, and tended to pick up the lighter bodies, leaving the heavier towards the centre (59 A 42 cf. 59 A 1 = D.L. 2, 8). Then comes a second stage when the centre is in motion and tending to fling its heavier parts outwards, though Anaxagoras thought of them being sucked out. This must be emphasized. Anaxagoras understood the results of centrifugal force, but not the cause; hence Guthrie is clearly right against Burnet and Cleve in claiming that the earth is not itself revolving, though he is wrong in applying the model of the vortex or eddy. In addition Anaxagoras had in mind a model derived from Empedocles, of a cup of water whirled round without losing the water, and seems to have thought that really violent revolution holds the objects in its sweep tight, so that they do not fly outwards or fall inwards (59 A 12). Guthrie seems to me wrong in his interpretation of the increasing revolution: "The notion that the rotating cosmos was at first small, and is continually growing by drawing in more of the infinite surrounding it, is interesting, particularly in the light of some recent cosmogonical theory" (2, 296). I can see nothing of this at all. The revolution started at the outside of the cosmos, and the increase refers to the spread of the revolution from the periphery towards the centre, which it has not yet reached. One last point. The famous Socratic criticism that Anaxagoras made no practical use of Νοῦς in arranging the details of his cosmos (P. *Phd.* 98 b 7) shows that Anaxagoras forms the bridge between the identification of physical law (ἀνάγκη) with Love and Strife in Empedocles and with the vortex in the atomists.

Cleve, F. M. *The Philosophy of Anaxagoras.* New York, 1949.

Gershenson, D. E. and Greenberg, D. A. *Anaxagoras and the Birth of Physics,* pp. 348–49. New York, 1964.

Heidel, W. A. "On certain fragments of the Pre-Socratics." *Proc. Am. Ac. Arts and Sci.* 48 (1913):681–734.

Lämmli, F. *Vom Chaos zum Kosmos.* Basel, 1962.

Raven, J. E. "The Basis of Anaxagoras's Cosmogony." *C.Q.* N.S. 4 (1954):123–37.

Zafiropulo, J. *Anaxagore de Clazomène.* Paris, 1948.

VIII

So far as we can see it was Empedocles who coined the concept of the δίνη. The word comes in two of the fragments. One from *Purifications* (DK 33 B 115) tells of the tossing of the sinful soul from air to sea, sea to land, land to the sun's rays, and from the sun to "the eddies of air" (αἰθέρος ἔμβαλε δίναις). This need not be a technical term. The other is more important (33 B 35).

> when Strife has reached the lowest depth
> of the vortex, and Love is at the centre of the rotation,
> by her power all these things come together to be one single thing.

As far as we can see Empedocles describes the formation of the world out of a homogeneous unity under the influence of Strife. The original change is one of separation; air is separated off, surrounds the world, and solidifies to enclose it; fire follows, so that two hemispheres are formed, one of fire and one of fire and air. These begin to revolve because of the preponderance of fire in one region (31 A 30). Further the constriction of the earth by the force of the rotation (τῇ ῥύμῃ τῆς περιφορᾶς) squeezed water out (31 A 49). Aristotle adds that Empedocles used the model of a cup whirled round without the water spilling to explain the immobility of the earth (31 A 67 = *De Caelo* 2, 295 a 13); and again that "the earth remains at the centre because of the vortex" (300 b 3). All this is difficult of interpretation. That an imbalance of the elements first separated off might produce motion is reasonable, but there seems no reason why it should produce rotatory motion; probably we must say that Empedocles adduces his explanation of the origin of motion, and accepts the observed fact of rotatory motion, but fails to bring the two fully together. We may accept the accumulation of the heavier bodies at the centre, and their constriction, in terms of the whirlpool or whirlwind. But the cup in motion not at the centre seems a curious model to explain the immobility of the earth at the centre. Some interpreters allege misunderstanding by Aristotle, Mugler of the model, which he suggests was a solid body floating in liquid in a cup, Cherniss of the thing to be explained, which he suggests was why the water, air, and fire outside do not fall on the earth. Either of these is ingenious; both make Aristotle ingenuous. Gomperz may be right in suggesting that Empedocles had a keen scent for analogies which he applied over-hastily: "Set the goblets revolving quickly, and their contents will not escape; set the firmament revolving quickly, and the earth at its centre will not slip" (1, 242). Aristotle (*Cael.* 295 a 31) says that the earth cannot be held at the centre by the vortex because it is impossible to adduce the vortex once the elements are separated. I do not see this. Once the initial separation has been produced by Strife, and the vortex set in motion, Empedocles plainly thinks that the vortex will continue the process of separation with the heavy bodies tending to the centre and the light to the periphery; when the separation is complete, the vortex will maintain the same conditions. Then in fr. 35, which represents the advance of Love, Love ousts Strife from the centre of the vortex; we must with Diels-Kranz, Raven, and Guthrie insert fr. 36 in place of the doublet 35, 7. The result, as O'Brien says, must be that as Love's power increases and the elements begin to commingle again the heavy things have to move outwards, contrary to the action of the vortex, and this paradox accounts for the precise mention of the vortex here. One final point about Empedocles. He evidently did not identify the vortex with necessity, but made necessity identical with his motive powers Love and Strife, which are, as we have seen, independent of the vortex (31 A 45). This shows that the identification of the vortex with necessity was original with the atomists.

Bignone, E. *Empedocle*. Torino, 1916.

Cherniss, H. *Aristotle's Criticism of Presocratic Philosophy*, p. 204. Baltimore, 1935.

Millard, C. E. *On the Interpretation of Empedocles*. Chicago, 1908.

Mugler, C. *Devenir cyclique et pluralité des mondes*. Paris, 1953. 129–45.

Munding, H. "Zur Beweisführung des Empedokles." *Hermes* 82 (1954): 129–45.

O'Brien, D. "Empedocles fr. 35, 14–5" *C.R.* N.S. 15 (1965): 1–4.

Pfligersdorffer, G. *Studien zu Poseidonios*, p. 110. Wien, 1959.

IX

It is however necessary to look behind Empedocles. On the one hand there is the tradition of Pythagoras and the Eleatics, on the other Ionian physical speculation. Most of us move uneasily in the world of the early Pythagoreans. There are two points to single out. The first relates to the celebrated columns of opposites. There, rest and straight are in the good column, motion and curved in the evil. Such an analysis stands squarely in the path of the perfection of circular motion, and almost justifies Burnet's over-schematic and overdogmatic statement that Pythagoras broke with the vortex-theory. The Pythagoreans were in fact fascinated by figures formed of straight lines, equating for example the pyramid with fire, the cube with earth, the octahedron with air, and the icosahedron with water, and these are of course important factors in the cosmogony in which the world is generated out of numbers, the point 1 flowing into the line 2 which flows into the plane 3 and that into the solid 4. This is a very different world-picture from any we have examined so far; as evidence it is negative but not valueless. But, secondly, the Pythagoreans did hold to a spherical universe, and in Alexander Polyhistor's analysis, which Raven has carefully examined, the cosmos is formed from fire, water, earth, and air: "and from these comes into being a cosmos, endowed with life, intelligent, spherical in shape, encircling the earth in the centre (itself spherical in shape and inhabited round about)" (D.L. 8, 25 = DK 58 B 1 a). So that among the Pythagoreans, despite the columns of opposites, there was some idealization of circularity, though not of circular motion. It is just here that Parmenides is important. Raven has argued that Parmenides was exploring the logical consequences of accepting the first column and rejecting the second. The result is, interestingly, the acceptance of sphericity, and of a ball as the model for the universe (εὐκύκλου σφαίρης ἐναλίγκιον ὄγκῳ surely means "like the mass of a well-rounded ball" not "like the mass of a well-rounded sphere" and is not to be taken as a verbal attempt to escape spatial extension: DK 28 B 8, 43), but the rejection of motion.

Alcmaeon is in all this the most important figure. He apparently used the analogy of circular motion and psychic function; indeed he probably devised it, and it was from him that it passed to Plato (*Ti.* 40 a; *Laws* 10, 895). According to Aristotle (DK 24 A 12), he stated that all divine things are forever in continuous motion (κινεῖσθαι γὰρ καὶ τὰ θεῖα πάντα συνεχῶς ἀεί), moon, sun, stars, and the whole sky, and he used this as the model to show the immortality of the human soul. Another passage from Aristotle quotes Alcmaeon as saying that men die because they cannot join the beginning to the end (24 B 2). Michael Apostolius, who also cites the passage, adds κύκλος γὰρ ἂν ἦν (*Corp. paroem.* 2, 674). We are not here concerned with the human soul. The continuous motion, however, must be κυκλοφορία, and (though we cannot be certain about relative dates) it looks as if Empedocles devised the model of the δίνη, but theories of circular motion in the cosmos antedate him, and we may infer a possibility that earlier theories of continuous or increasing motion do refer to motion in a circle.

Cardini, M. T. "Il cosmo di Filolao." *Riv. di Stor. della Fil,* I (1946): 322–33).

Cornford, F. M. "Mysticism and Science in the Pythagorean Tradition," *C.Q.*16 (1922):137–50; 17(1923):1–12.

———. *Plato and Parmenides.* London, 1939.

Heidel, W. A. "Qualitative Change in Presocratic Philosophy." *Arch. Gesch. Phil.* 14 (N.F. 7)(1906):333–79.

Raven, J. E. *Pythagoreans and Eleatics.* Cambridge, 1948.

X

Anaximenes has always been a shadowy figure alongside the other pre-Platonics. Here there is no indication of a primal vortex in our sources, apart from a general statement by Aristotle in talking of the vortex that all who generate the sky claim that the earth comes together at the centre (*De Caelo* 2, 295 a 7); as Kirk says, the statement would have been enough to make Theophrastus explicit, had there been anything to be explicit about. The cause of change in Anaximenes is the rarefaction and condensation of the primal air (DK 13 A 5). But Theophrastus does attribute to Anaximenes a

doctrine of eternal motion. In pseudo-Plutarch the statement appears immediately after the doctrine of rarefaction and condensation: "the movement,"
i.e., the process of change, "exists from eternity" (13 A 6). In Hippolytus
the statement is expounded: "it" sc. air "is always in motion; for it would
not be reproducing all the changes it does if it were not in motion" (13 A 7).
(Kirk treats this as a generalization: "things that change do not change unless
there be movement.") (It is not clear whether μεταβάλλειν is transitive
or intransitive: I have essayed an equally ambiguous translation.) Heidel
equates this eternal movement with the vortex, on the basis of a further passage from Hippolytus which suggests that the heavenly bodies move round
the earth with a circular motion, like a turban round a head; the image must
come from Anaximenes, but it is not clear whether he was referring to the
wrapping of the turban in the first place, or the twirling of the completed
turban; probably the former. He regarded the heavenly bodies as leaves
floating on the air; the only passage to tell against this —ἥλων δίκην
καταπεπηγέναι τὰ ἄστρα τῷ κρυσταλλοειδεῖ (13 A 14)—can-
not mean "fixed the stars like nails in the substance like ice," which would
be an odd thing to do, and does not accord with the other evidence; we must
accept Guthrie's physiological explanation of a spot on the viscous membrane. The image of leaves on air (13 A 7; 14; 15) does suggest that the air
is in motion carrying the leaves; and Aëtius suggests that the stars bend
their courses when opposed by condensed air (13 A 15). The general motion
is certainly circular (συμπεριφερόμενα (13 A 14). It follows that
in Anaximenes (a) the image of the vortex or whirlpool was not explicitly
found, (b) there is a circular movement of the air round the earth, (c) we are
not justified on the evidence before us in equating this with the eternal process of condensation and rarefaction and postulating a primal cosmopoietical
vortex.

Guthrie, W. K. C. "Anaximenes and τὸ κρυσταλλοειδές." C.Q. N.S. 6
(1956):40–44.
Heidel, W. A. "The ΔINH in Anaximenes and Anaximander." C.P. 1
(1906):279–82.

XI

So to Anaximander. Here we face the same problem as in Anaximenes.
There is no doubt that the heavenly bodies are regarded as cartwheels encircling the earth (DK 12 A 21; 22), tubes full of fire which appears through
an aperture. Nothing else is completely clear; there is in fact curiously little
reference to motion in our sources, though the word περιφέρεται
does appear once (12 A 21). Probably, however, the image of the wheel is
meant to suggest that the whole tube is rotating. There is an important sen-

tence in Aëtius which neither Kirk nor Guthrie discusses, and Diels-Kranz classify under Anaximenes: (13 A 12) οἱ δὲ τροχοῦ δίκην περιδινεῖσθαι. This must refer to Anaximander. The appearance of a word in our doxographic sources is of no final moment; still it is sufficient indication that the δίνη may be astronomical as well as cosmogonical. As to the cosmogony, the opposites are separated off through the eternal motion, ἀποκρινομένων τῶν ἐναντίων διὰ τῆς ἀϊδίου κινήσεως (12 A 9). Each unit within the phrase is controversial; so is the whole phrase. I agree with Kirk against Hölscher that we can rely on this as authentically based on Theophrastus, in the light of pseudo-Plutarch (12 A 10). Aristotle has ἐκκρίνεσθαι (Phys. I, 187 a 20); Theophrastus is likely to represent Anaximander's intention more accurately; the separation is *off* not *out*. But what is the eternal motion, which is also mentioned by Hippolytus (12 A 11)? Here we are confronted with two main schools of thought. One is vitalist, the other mechanistic. One stresses a general statement by Aristotle (Phys. 8, 250 b 11), which identifies a motion which exists deathlessly and unceasingly with a kind of life, and emphasizes the divinity of the indefinite as inevitably involving the power of movement; it also draws attention to biological analogies in Anaximander's cosmogony. The other stresses the obvious physical facts: eternal motion is circular; circular motion does produce centrifugal force and the tendency to "separate off"; it is true that Theophrastus does not speak of δίνη in connection with Anaximander, but that may be merely that he did not find the actual metaphor, which Empedocles seems to have coined. It is not correct to identify all circular motion with a vortex or whirlpool, which is a particular model. I incline to believe that circular motion must be intended, but that it was not developed into a vortex-theory for another century.

Baldry, H. C. "Embryological Analogies in Presocratic Cosmogony." *C.Q.* 26 (1932):27–34.

Burch, G. B. "Anaximander the First Metaphysician." *Review of Metaphysics* 3 (1949–50):137–60.

Heidel, W. A. "The ΔΙΝΗ in Anaximenes and Anaximander." *C.P.* 1 (1906):279–82.

Hölscher, U. "Anaximander und die Anfänge der Philosophie." *Hermes* 81 (1953):257–77, 385–417.

Kahn, C. H. *Anaximander and the Origins of Greek Cosmogony.* New York, 1960.

Neuhauser, J. *Anaximander Milesius.* Bonn, 1883.

Seligman, P. *The Apeiron of Anaximander.* London, 1962.

Tannéry, P. *Pour l'histoire de la science hellène.* Paris, 1930.

Vlastos, G. "Equality and Justice in the Early Greek Cosmogonies." *C.P.* 42 (1947):156–78.

XII

Can we go back further? Not with any certainty. The Orphic—or non-Orphic—primal egg is hardly to the point, even if it can legitimately be placed in the earlier period of Orphism; in any event it is curiously infrequent in the Near East though common in other parts of the world. But eggs do not rotate. More important is Oceanus. Oceanus in primitive Greek thought is a river which encircles the world. It flows of course, so that there is circular movement round the earth; the epithet ἀψόρροος presumably means "flowing back into itself." The myth of Oceanus is in the background of Thales, and it is possible that it suggested the model of the whirlpool. It is curious that, so far as I can see, in the surviving creation-epics and hymns of the Near East there is no mention of the rotation of the sky or of the whole cosmos as part of the process of creation, not even in Mesopotamia with their astronomical preoccupations, either in *Enuma Elish* or in the more fragmentary accounts or in Berossus. The cosmological vortex is a Greek concept.

Guthrie, W. K. C. *Orpheus and Greek Religion.* London, 1952.
Heidel, A. *The Babylonian Genesis.* Chicago, 1951.
Linforth, I. M. *The Arts of Orpheus.* Berkeley, 1941.
Nilsson, M. P. *Geschichte der griechischen Religion*, vol. I. München, 1955.

XIII

A little science, which is curiously difficult to track down, as vortex-theory is frequently omitted from general handbooks of physics, and related to specific problems in textbooks of hydrodynamics and aerodynamics; further, when articles appear, they tend to be highly technical. The great investigator of vortex-theory was the German Helmholtz, who wrote comprehensively on the subject, but the importance of aerodynamics in the twentieth century has led to new discoveries.

The concept popularly called centrifugal force (it is not really *centrifugal*) is relatively easy for the layman to understand. A point on the surface of a spinning wheel has at any given moment an angular momentum tangential to the wheel, and if it is not held to the centre by the forces inherent in a rigid structure it is in that direction that it will tend to move. The phenomenon is familiar observationally. Place a pebble on a potter's wheel, rotate the wheel, and the pebble will be flung off. This is the model which Anaxagoras is using.

The vortex is more complex. Hydrodynamics uses the concepts of irrotation (flow in a given direction without any rotational element) and vorticity. Vorticity arises in water or air from the meaning of two currents.

In a stream with smooth, regular bottom and sides the flow is irrotational, but irregularity will set up cross-currents and a tendency to vorticity. A vortex can most easily be considered in a closed system, say the stirring of a glass of water: the fact that in whirlpools and whirlwinds the container is more water and more air does not affect the principle involved. Here two phenomena may be noticed. The first is that where the velocity is highest the pressure is lowest: hence the fact that the water at the centre is lower than at the rim. The principle may be shown experimentally by forcing water through a pipe of irregular diameter and inserting tubes into the pipe at right angles to the direction of flow. Where the pipe is narrower and the velocity of flow consequently greater the water will rise less high in the tube than where the pipe is wider and the velocity smaller. Bernouilli identified the formula $p + kv = $ constant, where p is the pressure, v the velocity, and k is constant. The other phenomenon is that of boundary-layer flow. This is a flow in a vertical plane from the surface-centre to the outside, down the outside, along the base to the centre and up. It is this that in a whirlwind tends to draw loose objects on the surface of the earth to the centre, from which it may lift them, unless the pull of gravity is too strong, in which event there is a tendency for them to accumulate at the centre.

There is a further point. We are sufficiently familiar through Jules Verne with the concept of the maelstrom which sucks boats down and into the centre. The picture was familiar to the Greeks through Charybdis in *The Odyssey,* though there is a reverse process of regurgitation as well. The effect of the boundary-layer flow and centrifugal tendency is for the denser bodies to move towards the circumference and the lighter bodies towards the centre. As a boat is lighter than water (or it would sink) there is a natural tendency for boats to move towards the centre of a whirlpool. It is possible that this is accentuated by gravity, since by Bernouilli's Principle the centre is lower than the circumference and the pressure at the centre less. It is likely, however, that ancient belief about whirlpools would not discriminate between a vortex in a channel, and a vortex in a container like a bath, when the plug blocking the outflow is removed. Plainly in this last there is an additional force of suction drawing objects within the bath down and towards the point of outflow. It is even possible that in some maelstrom effects there is a drainaway of some kind creating a suction. At any rate the Greeks would observe the movement of solid bodies along the surface of the earth to accumulate at the centre during a whirlwind or eddy of air, and they were familiar with the maelstrom effect which is in fact the obverse of the same coin. These are the models used by those who postulate a vortex or eddy.

Private communications from Prof. Murray Braden, Prof. Charles Coulson, Mrs. Elnora Ferguson, and Mr. John Holding.

XIV

Some general conclusions:

1. Speculation on a circular movement as part of cosmogony is Greek: it is part of the general process of replacing mythology by science and mathematics. Dinos did indeed kick Zeus out (Aristophanes *Clouds* 828).

2. That the primal movement was circular was suggested by observation of the sky and the heavenly bodies: a further factor was the apparently continuous nature of circular motion by contrast with rectilinear which to the Greeks tended to a goal or limit. The theoretical perfection of the circle or sphere plays a small part.

3. There are various models for circular motion. Anaximander uses a wheel spinning. The model of the whirlpool or whirlwind starts with Empedocles, who scatters his analogies freely, is rejected by Anaxagoras, and is taken up again by the Atomists. The different models offer different emphasis and even different implications; it is important to stress that the concept of cosmic rotation does not of itself imply the thought of vortical flow. In general, although I have used it, the mathematical term "vortex" is not a true representation of δῖνος or δίνη, which would be better rendered "eddy." Among the most persistent models involved in cosmogony is the sieve of winnowing-fan. Sometimes this is a model for random movement producing orderly results: at least once the word δῖνος is explicitly applied to it.

4. The Atomists equate the δίνη with ἀνάγκη or natural law. This in turn is equated, at least by the time of Plato and Aristotle, with τύχη.

JAMES H. LESHER

Xenophanes' Scepticism

XENOPHANES of Colophon (fl. 530 B.C.) is thought to have been the first sceptic in the history of western philosophy, but the character of his scepticism was the subject of dispute as early as the fourth century B.C., and the central statement of his position, Fragment 34,[1] has been variously interpreted ever since. Much of recent discussion has concerned the severity and scope of his sceptical thesis, but it would be of equal philosophical interest to know what Xenophanes' reasons were for maintaining scepticism, or what features of Xenophanes' life and times may have contributed to his sceptical outlook. It is the contention of this paper that Xenophanes' scepticism is best understood as a response to traditional religious and poetic ways of thinking, and is therefore closely tied to his criticism of Homeric religion, and that the key to a proper understanding of his sceptical remarks lies in an often mentioned but seldom discussed aspect of his writings: the attack on divination.

I. Ancient Accounts

The following extract from Xenophanes' poetry was widely quoted and discussed in antiquity (B 34):

> καὶ τὸ μὲν οὖν σαφὲς οὔτις ἀνὴρ ἴδεν οὐδέ τις ἔσται
> εἰδὼς ἀμφὶ θεῶν τε καὶ ἄσσα λέγω περὶ πάντων·
> εἰ γὰρ καὶ τὰ μάλιστα τύχοι τετελεσμένον εἰπών,
> αὐτὸς ὅμως οὐκ οἶδε· δόκος δ' ἐπὶ πᾶσι τέτυκται.[2]

While a full translation requires argument and cannot be assumed at the outset, it is clear that the basic elements of Xenophanes' view are (in some sense of these terms): truth (τὸ σαφὲς), knowing (ἴδεν, εἰδὼς, οἶδε), speaking of the real (τετελεσμένον εἰπών), and belief or

This paper was presented to the 1975 New York meeting of the Society for Ancient Greek Philosophy and published in *Phronesis* 23 (1978):1–21; we thank the editors and Royal VanGorcum Ltd for permission to reprint.

James Lesher is Professor of Philosophy at the University of Maryland at College Park.

seeming (δόϰος). Any adequate interpretation of Xenophanes' scepticism, while it can be supplemented by reference to other fragments and background information, must make sense of these notions, and their interconnections. Sextus mentions two alternative interpretations: in the first,[3] Xenophanes is thought to have held that everything is incomprehensible (πάντα ἀϰατάληπτα), and this is supported by reading σαφές as 'true' or 'known':

> Yet the true and known—at least in respect of non-evident things—no human being knows; for even if by chance he should hit upon it, still he knows not that he has hit upon it but imagines and opines.

As the context of Sextus' discussion (VII, 46–52) makes clear, the sceptical dispute concerns not so much the attaining of true belief, but a criterion (ϰριτήριον) for determining which beliefs are true or which appearances are veridical. Xenophanes is taken here to be denying the existence of a criterion since he holds that even if someone were to say what is real or true, he would not know that he had done so, and hence would have only belief or opinion.

But this interpretation of the fragment is implausible. Not only does it restrict, without justification, the scope of the sceptical thesis to what is 'non-evident', but it translates Xenophanes' simple "he knows not" (οὐϰ οἶδε) into "he knows not that he has hit upon it" (οὐϰ οἶδεν ὅτι ἐπιβέβληϰεν αὐτῶι), and requires that we attribute to Xenophanes the rather subtle doctrine that knowing the truth entails knowing that one knows the truth, or at least that knowing the truth entails being convinced that what one believes is true. It is doubtful, at least in English, that either entailment holds, but they are not so far fetched as to exclude being attributed to Xenophanes. The difficulty is simply that both are more complex formulations than the original "even if he says what is true, he does not know." Further, since σαφές and ἀληθής are not synonyms,[4] Xenophanes' scepticism could be directed toward 'certain,' 'absolute,' or 'sure' knowledge, rather than knowledge of the truth *simpliciter*.

Sextus mentions a second, less sceptical, interpretation of this sort: Xenophanes does not deny all comprehension or apprehension (ϰατάληψις) of the truth, but only that which is ἐπιστημονιϰήν and ἀδιάπτωτον (Bury: "cognitive and inerrant"). Men can apprehend the truth, even if they cannot attain it with certainty—or without reservations (παγίου)—and we can adopt probable reasoning as a criterion for determining what is true (VII, 110). This reading gains some support from Fr. 35: "let these things be believed as resembling the truth (ἐοιϰότα τοῖς ἐτύμοισι)." Yet we must still assume that Xenophanes' concern was also that of the later sceptics: the existence of a criterion for distinguishing be-

ESSAYS IN ANCIENT GREEK PHILOSOPHY

tween truth and falsity (or reality and deceptive appearance) and we also are required to attribute to Xenophanes some general notion of apprehension of which knowledge and belief are distinct species. Both interpretations given by Sextus constitute expansions in the language of a later period, and in the context of a dispute of which, for all we know, Xenophanes may have been wholly ignorant. So far we may reasonably conclude only that Xenophanes denies that men have knowledge (or perhaps that men have knowledge of τὸ σαφὲς) while he allows that men have beliefs which, in some cases, may resemble what is true or real (ἐτύμοισι).

Later writers tell us that Xenophanes coupled the distinction between knowledge and mere belief with a contrast between divine and human capacities: god knows the truth, but belief is alloted to men,[5] and Alcmaeon begins his work with a similar remark, perhaps following Xenophanes: "concerning the non-evident, concerning things mortal, the gods have a clear understanding (σαφήνειαν), but men merely conjecture from signs."[6] As Snell has shown in detail, there was by Xenophanes' time a well-established poetic tradition contrasting divine knowledge and human ignorance,[7] and the attribution of this view to Xenophanes is supported by the frequent, and often disparaging, remarks about the beliefs of *mortals* (B14: βροτοί, B18, B36: θνητοῖσι), and by his conception of the one God, superior to gods and men, unlike them in body and mind (B23), who moves things by his mind (B25), and who enjoys, in some sense, a whole or complete seeing, thinking, and hearing) (B24). We have so far no reason to think that B34, taken by itself, reflects this religious context (although I shall argue for this in Section III following), but we can reasonably conclude on the basis of the evidence already cited, that Xenophanes' scepticism has this feature: as Guthrie puts it, "men could have no certain knowledge, that was reserved for God" (*A History of Greek Philosophy*, p. 398).

II. Recent Accounts

In Karl Popper's famous "Back to the Pre-Socratics,"[8] Xenophanes is alleged to have held that "all our knowledge is guesswork, yet that we may nevertheless, by searching for that knowledge 'which is the better' find it in the course of time." Popper sees Xenophanes, as did the early Greek sceptics, as an early proponent of his own theory of knowledge: "that knowledge proceeds by way of conjectures and refutations," and not according to the Baconian myth of induction. Popper concedes that it may sound incredible, but asserts anyway, that there is a clear recognition of this "theory of rational knowledge almost immediately after the practice of critical discussion had begun." But even conceding for the moment that Xenophanes did think of human understanding as progressing toward but never attaining knowledge of the 'final truth,' we are still very far from being told that knowledge is obtained not simply from observation and experiment, but from the construction and criticism of theories.[9] According to Diogenes Laertius, Xenophanes held opinions which were opposed to (ἀντιδοξάσαι) those of Thales and Pythagoras, and we know that he criticized the accounts given by Homer and Hesiod. There is no evidence that he held, as Aristotle clearly did hold, that inquiry was best conducted by a review and criticism of previous doctrines and theories.[10] Nor do the remaining fragments reveal that he implicitly followed this principle; apart from one allusion to the Pythagorean doctrine of metempsychosis (B7) and a suggestion that he admired Thales for his ability to predict eclipses (B19), there is no sign that he practiced, much less preached, Popper's principle of 'rational knowledge.'

Yet Popper's account raises an issue that has clear relevance for an interpretation of Xenophanes' scepticism: how can Xenophanes be a proponent of scepticism if he holds also (in B18) that "mortals in time, through seeking, discover what is better (or the better)"? Can one consistently deny the possibility of knowledge and at the same time affirm that discovery is possible? Further, as Fränkel asks, how can we consistently think of Xenophanes, "this investigator and portrayer of reality who took delight in the gathering and contemplation of facts" as one who was also "a sceptic, a tired doubter or a deft but unconvinced dialectician, and that he had no real confidence in the reality of the world of appearances?" (p. 122). Neither of these considerations poses an unavoidable dilemma. Xenophanes does not say, as Popper has it,[11] that men find "that *knowledge* which is the better," but only that they discover what is better, and as Guthrie explains, the replacement of divine revelation with human inquiry, which is the full thesis of Fr. 18, may represent Xenophanes' rejection of a primitive 'golden race,' and the promotion of a conception of human progress or improvement 'both morally and in the conditions of life' (p. 400). In any event, there is no inconsistency generated by holding that men fall short of certain knowledge, or even knowledge *simpliciter,* while also conceding that men discover arts, skills, values, or beliefs which are better than previous ones. Similarly, one need not, in order to be justly termed a sceptic, affirm a universal doubt, or a rejection of the evidence of the senses. Fränkel's argument rests on the frequently adopted but mistaken assumption that a sceptic, worthy of the name, must be a pyrrhonian sceptic, that is, must call for a suspension of belief, or perhaps even a rejection of all beliefs as false. There have however been sceptics, as ancient as Carneades and as recent as Keith Lehrer, who deny that we ever know anything, but insist nonetheless that much ought to be believed as true, not the least of which are the beliefs about the world based on the obvious evidence of sense experience. There is no contradiction in asserting that p is true, or ought to be believed, even though p is not something which should be claimed to be known, or known with certainty.[12] Consequently, we cannot hope to show that Xenophanes was not really a sceptic simply on the grounds that *one* form of scepticism would be incompatible with other aspects of his philosophy.

Fränkel's interpretation is however based largely on linguistic considerations involving B34 itself, and since Fränkel's account is shared, at least in part by Snell, Guthrie, and Untersteiner, and presents a detailed exegesis, it deserves careful consideration.

Fränkel views B34 as an expression of a 'robust empiricism,' and, far from denying the possibility of knowledge, it holds that knowledge which is empirically grounded, based on first-hand observation and experience, can be certain and exhaustive (σαφές). To know, as can be seen in Herodotus' notion of ἱστορία, is to have seen, and this close connection of knowing with seeing is borne out by the etymology of οἶδα, literally "I have seen," but commonly simply "I know." Thus Xenophanes is not rejecting knowledge, but only the pretensions to knowledge of one who has not seen things for himself (αὐτὸς οὐκ οἶδε). Since we have no first-hand experience of divine attributes and operations, we can have no reliable knowledge of them, but there are plausible suppositions that can be made.

This interpretation makes *some* sense, and we are indebted to Fränkel for his careful rendering of the subtle nuances of many of the terms in the fragment (e.g., τὰ μάλιστα τύχοι) which went unnoticed in earlier commentaries, but his rendering is not without difficulties. Let us assume for the sake of argument that ἴδεν in line 1 (καὶ τὸ μὲν οὖν σαφὲς οὔτις ἀνὴρ ἴδεν οὐδέ τις ἔσται) does mean seeing, and in particular non-metaphorical 'seeing'—i.e., visual sense perception,[13] and also that this justifies reading εἰδὼς in line 2 (εἰδὼς ἀμφὶ θεῶν τε καὶ ἄσσα λέγω περὶ πάντων) as "designating only a knowing rooted in vision" (p. 123).[14] We must then take Xenophanes' thesis to be that 'what is clear or precise (σαφές) no man has ever perceived, nor will there ever be anyone who knows on the basis of empirical observations about the gods and about everthing else of which I speak.' We can understand why Xenophanes might have held that the gods could not be perceptually known, and hence why it was not possible to have perceptual knowledge about *everything* of which he spoke, but why should he have thought that no man has ever had perceptual knowledge of what is σαφές, especially if he is willing to allow that sense perception is the source of that knowledge which is certain and exhaustive? The problem is that while the second line discusses knowledge specifically about the gods and everything else of which Xenophanes speaks, the first line is unrestricted: no man has ever seen τὸ σαφές. To repair the interpretation, and to over-rule what is the prima facie sense of the passage, we must find some basis for thinking that Xenophanes wishes to restrict his scepticism to σαφές knowledge of some particular province, and Fränkel maintains that it is the non-evident or supersensible that is the implicit subject throughout. Apart from the suggestion that the preceding context might have already supplied a concrete referent and content for σαφές, the only *argument* that Fränkel gives is that the "closely resembling postscripts in the quotations by Arius Didymus and Varro give a good indication of the wider context: 'but God has a genuine knowledge even of transcendent things'" (p. 128). But what these postscripts provide is simply a contrast of divine knowledge with human opinion, and as Guthrie notes, the dichotomy between transcendent and non-transcendent things is "not in the originals" (p. 396n.).

A similar difficulty for Fränkel's interpretation emerges from the generality of Xenophanes' conclusion in line 4: δόκος δ' ἐπὶ πᾶσι τέτυκται: belief (or supposition) is allotted to all things. This remark is at odds with Fränkel's contention that Xenophanes is concerned to deny only knowledge of the supersensible world, and counts as well against thinking that Xenophanes allows for the possibility of knowledge based on sense experience. If Xenophanes meant to deny only knowledge of the supersensible, one would expect him to claim that belief is allotted to *these* things (and not *all* things), and if he did think that men could gain reliable knowledge in some manner, one would not expect him to conclude "but belief is allotted to all things." In short, although lines 2 and 3 might by themselves suggest that Xenophanes' scepticism was directed only against second-hand 'knowledge' of the supersensible world, lines 1 and 4 indicate a general scepticism about the capacity of human beings to see the clear and certain truth, and a willingness to concede only that men can attain true beliefs. Xenophanes was probably not the extreme sceptic that Sotion took him to be, but he still seems more of a sceptic than Fränkel would have us believe.[15]

III. Xenophanes and Early Greek Religion

We have so far been thinking of Xenophanes as the originator of a cryptic epistemological theory, and have considered that theory through the accounts given by later writers, both ancient and modern. It is however very unlikely, as Charles Kahn has observed, that either of these ways of viewing a pre-Socratic philosopher, will provide a complete picture:

> The very possibility of understanding sixth-century ideas, where the documentation is so sadly lacking, depends upon our fuller knowledge of the older poetic outlook. It is only by placing the Milesians in between two regions of light provided by archaic poetry on one hand and classical philosophy on the other—by thus illuminating them, as it were, from above as

well as from below—that we may have any hope of seeing a bit deeper into this dark period of transition and creation.[16]

It is true that Kahn's inquiry concerns the origins of Milesian cosmology, and he may not have intended these remarks to apply to other pre-Socratics, but there is ample justification for adopting this approach in our investigation of Xenophanes' scepticism. Xenophanes was after all a wandering poet who criticized the stories about the gods told by Homer and Hesiod (A1, B11), and testified to the extent of Homer's influence on common opinion (B10: ἐξ ἀρχῆς καθ' Ὅμηρον ἐπεὶ μεμαθήκασι πάντες . . .). In what ways might the poetic tradition of Homer and Hesiod have influenced Xenophanes' thinking, and especially, how might the religious outlook of the older poets link up with his views on human knowledge?

We have already noted that B34 probably embodies, or at least is connected with, a traditional poetic contrast between divine wisdom and human ignorance, but there are other features of Homeric religion which were repudiated by Xenophanes. He rejects the conception of gods in human form (B11, B14) and conceives of one god, greatest among gods and men who is unlike men both in body and mind (B23). One insufficiently appreciated feature of Xenophanes' critique of religion is his repudiation of religious practices, and not simply religious conceptions. He expresses scorn for the practice of placing pine branches around the house in the belief that these branches are somehow themselves βάκχοι—divine powers (B17, and we are told by Diogenes Laertius that he rebuked (καθάψασθαι) Epimenides, a man who enjoyed a reputation as a prophet and miracle worker.[17] According to Aetius[18] and Cicero[19] Xenophanes denounced the practice of divination (μαντική), the attempt to acquire knowledge through the use of omens and portents of various sorts.[20] This feature of Xenophanes' writings, the attack on divination and related superstitious practices, furnishes, I believe, a basis for a coherent account of his general philosophical outlook, and his scepticism. If I am right about this, then we can not only make sense of some troublesome fragments, we can also appreciate the origins of his sceptical outlook, and the significance of the intellectual revolution which was effected by Xenophanes, and by the pre-Socratic philosophers generally.

Xenophanes' rejection of divination is, first of all, not unconnected with other aspects of his thought. It is a reasonable inference from his conception of god as unlike mortals in raiment, voice, or body, that the gods do not appear in mortal form, nor do they speak directly to us. Nor, since it is unfitting for the god to be in different places at different times (B14, 26), is it possible for god to 'come or go in our midst' (μετέρχεσθαι in B26). Yet, as Flacelière states ". . . genuine μαντική, in the original sense of the word (mania: madness) [is] caused by possession, by the literal presence of the god in the soul of the prophet or prophetess, who thus receives the revelation direct from heaven." Fränkel observes that in the attack on divination, Xenophanes "made the chasm between the here and the beyond unbridgeable" (p. 130), but the chasm had already been provided for in Xenophanes' positive account of the one god.

Nor is the attack on divination unconnected with Xenophanes' cosmology in which celestial phenomena are explained in terms of water and earth (B29), or perhaps simply earth (B27). Nilsson's account of the conflict between religious and philosophical ways of thinking which was a general feature of pre-Socratic philosophy, and which led to the diminished influence of seers and oracles, serves equally well as an explanation of the connection between Xenophanes' critique of divination and his cosmology:

> The real clash took place between that part of religion which interfered most in practical life and with which everyone came into contact every day, namely, the art of foretelling the future, and the attempts of natural philosophy to give physical explanations of celestial and atmospheric phenomena, or portents, and other events. Such explanations undermined the belief in the art of the seers and made it superfluous. For if these phenomena were to be explained in a natural way, the art of the seers came to naught.[21]

That Xenophanes' cosmology had this anti-divinational flavor is indicated by several isolated remarks about traditional portents, as well as the subjects of his cosmological interest. So far as I know, only Dodds has noticed the connection: "[Xenophanes gives] naturalistic explanations of the rainbow (Fr. 32) and St. Elmo's fire (A39), both of which are traditional portents."[22] Rainbows are among the most striking and suggestive of all natural phenomena, and have been taken as harbingers of good fortune, but for Xenophanes, "she whom they call Iris, she too is actually a cloud, purple, and flame red, and yellow to behold" (B32). St. Elmo's fire, the freak electrical phenomenon sometimes seen on ships' masts during storms, was considered a portent of good fortune, and was thought of in antiquity as two brothers (Dioscuri, later Cabiri) who were the guardian saints of mariners in distress,[23] but to Xenophanes, "those which some call the Dioscuri are little clouds glimmering in virtue of the kind of motion that they have" (A39, Guthrie trans.).

Flacelière presents the following brief summary of the phenomena which were taken as omens or portents:

> Atmospheric phenomena, meteora, were obviously signs of the will of the gods; especially of Zeus, the god of the atmosphere and the sky. The weightiest presage of all, the one that could negate or confirm all others, was thunder. In the Iliad, whenever Zeus wishes to encourage one of the

Greek or Trojan heroes he does so by hurling a thunderbolt to the right of him. Rain also comes from Zeus, and was regarded as a sign of his will, a diosemeion. But beyond the clouds and all other atmospheric phenomena were the stars: in Homer, Sirius, 'Orion's Dog,' was a star of ill-omen; the Spartans would never embark on a campaign before the full moon, which appears to be the reason why they did not arrive at Marathon until the battle was over.[24]

Among other celestial phenomena thought of as omens or portents were eclipses, shooting stars, and the phases of the moon. The industrious mantic seer could find significance in dreams, sneezes, volcanic eruptions, the sounds of gongs and rustling branches, the entrails of sacrificed animals, birds, and the casting of dice or bones.[25] While the explanations which Xenophanes gives are neither detailed nor always consistent, they do focus on many phenomena involved in the practice of divination:

1. "He says that the sun and the stars come from clouds" (A32, Plu. *Strom.* 4, cf. A33, 38, 40).

2. "Xenophanes said there are many suns and moons according to regions, sections, and zones of the earth, and that at a certain time the disc is banished into some section of the earth not inhabited by us, and so treading on nothing, as it were, produces the phenomenon of an eclipse" (A41a, Aetius, *Placita*, II, 24, 9).

3. "Eclipses occur by extinction of the sun (σβέσιν ἡλίου) and the sun is born anew at each of its risings" (A41, Aet. II, 24, 4).

4. "The moon disappears each month because it is extinguished" (A43, Aet. II, 25, 4).

5. "Comets (κομήτας) are groups or motions of burning clouds" (A44, Aet. III, 2, II).

6. "Lightnings (ἀστραπάς) take place when clouds shine in motion" (A45, Aet. III, 3, 6).

7. "The phenomena of the heavens come from the warmth of the sun as the principal cause. For when the moisture is drawn from the sea, the sweet water separated by reason of its lightness becomes mist and passes into clouds, and falls as rain when compressed, and the winds scatter it" (A46, Aet. III, 4, 4).

Epicurus, whose naturalistic explanations of these phenomena resemble both in content and terminology those given by Xenophanes,[26] states explicitly what seems to me to be an implicit conclusion of Xenophanes' account:

> We are bound to believe that in the sky revolutions, solstices, eclipses, risings and settings, and the like, take place without the ministration or command, either now or in the future, of any being who at the same time enjoys perfect bliss along with immortality.[27]

In short, Xenophanes' cosmology, as well as his conception of the one god, probably served to support his attack on divination through signs. Men personify natural phenomena and think of them as visible signs of the will of the gods, but they are in reality only changes due to the motion of clouds and the kindling and extinction of fires. The true divinity exists elsewhere.

These inter-connections do not, taken in isolation, show that Xenophanes' epistemological remarks have anything to do with the practice of divination, but they do suggest that his rejection of divination was not devoid of philosophical importance. Further, since divination is essentially a means for acquiring knowledge we ought at least to consider the possibility (though this has never, to my knowledge, been attempted) that these two aspects of Xenophanes' thought are related in some important way to one another. The crucial question is whether B34 is itself illuminated by drawing attention to the attack on divination, and to the significance attached to divination in the poetic tradition.

We can begin by considering Xenophanes' *reason* for concluding that no man has seen or known what is σαφές (and that there never will be anyone who knows about the gods and everything else of which he speaks):

εἰ γὰρ καὶ τὰ μάλιστα τύχοι τετελεσμένον εἰπών, αὐτὸς ὅμως οὐκ οἶδε.

As Fränkel has argued, we need not think of τύχοι (εἰπών) simply as 'chanced' (to say) or 'accidentally' (said), but rather as 'succeeded' (in saying), or 'correctly' (saying). Thus (taking τὰ μάλιστα as 'especially' or 'more than others') τὰ μάλιστα τύχοι εἰπών means 'succeed above others in saying.'[28]

What then can be made of τετελεσμένον: "for even if someone should succeed above all others in saying what is τετελεσμένον, still he would not know?" Τετελεσμένον has been understood as the 'complete truth' or 'what is completely true' (Kirk and Raven, Freeman, Burnet) or simply as 'true' (Guthrie), or 'what is really present' (Fränkel), but the literal meaning of τετελεσμένον, 'what is completed, accomplished, brought about' (from τελέω) has been largely ignored.[29] So far as I can determine, τετελεσμένος occurs twenty-three times in Homer.[30] In eighteen of these passages, it is linked with speaking or saying, and the following passages illustrate this repeated formulaic expression, "speaking of that which has been brought about or will be brought about" (Murray trans.):

1. "for this will I speak and verily this thing shall be brought to pass" (τὸ δὲ καὶ τετελεσμένον ἔσται), *Il.* I, 212 = II, 257; VIII, 401, VIII, 454; *Od.* II, 187, XVII, 229, VIII, 82.

2. "He arose and spoke a threatening word, that hath now been brought to pass" (ὃ δὴ τετελεσμένος ἐστί), *Il.* I, 388.

3. "I will declare to thee as it verily shall be brought to pass" (ὡς καὶ

29

τετελεσμένον ἔσται), *Il.* XXIII, 410 = XVI, 440, XXIII, 672, XIX, 487.

4. "I would that this word of thine might be fulfilled" (ἔπος τετελεσμένον εἴη), *Od.* XV, 536 = XVII, 163, XIX, 309.

This passage from the *Odyssey* (XVII, 153 ff.) gives an indication of the sort of context in Homer in which someone speaks of what is τετελεσμένον:

> Then among them spoke also the godlike (θεοειδής) Theoclymenus, saying:
> 'Honored wife of Odysseus, son of Laertes, he truly has no clear understanding (οὐ σάφα οἶδεν); but do thou hearken to my words, for with certain knowledge will I prophesy to thee (ἀτρεκέως γάρ σοι μαντεύσομαι), and will hide naught. Be my witness Zeus above all gods, and this hospitable board and the hearth of noble Odysseus to which I come, that verily Odysseus is even now in his native land, resting or moving, learning of these evil deeds, and he is sowing the seeds of evil for all the wooers. So plain a bird of omen did I mark as I sat on the benched ship, and I declared it to Telemachus' [*Od.* XV, 536].
> Then wise Penelope answered him: 'Ah, stranger, I would that this word of thine might be fulfilled (ἔπος τετελεσμένον εἴη).'

These passages, and others in Homer[31] provide ample justification for reading τετελεσμένον εἰπών as "speaking or saying what is brought to pass." This fits well in the context of line 3 of B 34, since it is obvious that one kind of thing that one might succeed in saying is a true prediction about future events. One can also connect this with τὰ μάλιστα since some persons might be thought to 'succeed above all others in saying what comes to pass.'[32] The full message of lines 3–4 is that even if one succeeded above others in speaking of what is brought to pass, still he himself does not know, but belief or opinion is allotted to all things.

It is not yet clear whether B34, in its entirety, espouses a general scepticism or simply scepticism about the claims to knowledge of those who succeed in correctly predicting events, but this latter scepticism is present in lines 3–4 and does serve as the basis for Xenophanes' claim in lines 1–2. Xenophanes' scepticism then involves, at least in part, an implicit repudiation of a central figure in Greek religion, the oracle or prophet, and a repudiation as well of the stature enjoyed by these figures in the Homeric epic. Yet doubts about the infallibility of prophets had already appeared in Homer, and the trustworthiness of divination was a recurrent theme in classical literature.[33] So while Xenophanes' scepticism about divination is revolutionary as a repudiation of the entire enterprise, it is not wholly without precedent.

It should also be noted that the passage quoted at length from *Od.* XVII, 153 ff. not only links up prophecy with saying what is τετελεσμένον, but also displays a connection, found elsewhere in Homer, between the gift of prophecy possessed by the mantic seer and 'sure' or 'clear' knowledge (Theoclymenus claims that Telemachus οὐ σάφα οἶδεν, but that he himself will give an exact or certain [ἀτρεκέως] prophecy). The form σαφές which appears in line 1 of B34 does not appear in Homer, but σάφα knowing and σάφα speaking do occur. To say or know in a way which is σάφα is, at the very least, to say or know what is *true* (cf. *Il.* IV, 404: "Son of Atreus utter not lies (μὴ ψεύδε᾽) when thou knowest how to speak truly (σάφα εἰπεῖν)," but it commonly carries a special emphasis on knowing or saying the full, clear, and detailed truth (cf. *Od.* XVII, 106: "tell me σάφα of the return of thy father"). On occasion it serves to characterize not what is known but rather the manner in which something is known, and designates a knowing that is sure, certain or expert (cf. *Il.* XV, 632: "unskilled [οὐ σάφα εἰδώς] to fight a wild beast"; *Il.* XX 201 = 432: "I know well of myself [σάφα οἶδα καὶ αὐτός] how to utter taunts"; *Il.* VII, 226: "Hector, now verily shalt thou know of a surety [σάφα εἴσεαι] man to man what manner of chieftains there be among the Danaans"). It is such certain knowledge that is claimed by Poulydamas (*Il.* XII, 228 ff.: "on this wise would a soothsayer interpret, one that in his mind had clear knowledge [σάφα θυμῷ εἰδείη] of omens, and to whom the folk gave ear"). Athene, disguised as Mentes, speaks to Telemachus (*Od.* I, 200 ff.): I will now prophesy to thee as the immortals put it in my heart, and as I think it shall be brought to pass (τελέεσθαι), though I am in no wise a soothsayer (μάντις), nor one versed in the signs of birds (οἰωνῶν σάφα εἰδώς). Although Athene is not portrayed as claiming to be σάφα εἰδώς in such matters (indeed any claim of prophetic wisdom would be at odds with her disguise in purely mortal form), the fact that she claims to be neither a prophet nor one skilled in signs of birds indicates that such skill is typically claimed by the prophet.[34] Thus when Xenophanes asserts in B34 that no man has seen or know τὸ σαφές it is quite possible that he had in mind a sure or certain knowledge of this sort. Since lines 3–4 concede that someone might succeed in saying what comes to pass, it is unlikely that Xenophanes wishes to deny that men sometimes attain truth. Since these lines serve as Xenophanes' reason (γάρ) for denying that men apprehend what is σαφές, or in a manner which is σαφές,[35] it is likely that he intends to deny that men ever enjoy sure or certain knowledge of the truth, even if they do sometimes succeed in saying it (and can, as in line 4, believe or suppose that it is true).

It is now possible, I believe, to see Xenophanes' remarks as a reflection of, and in part as a reaction against, some basic ways of thinking that were embedded in archaic poetry and religion. While adopting the traditional con-

31

trast between human and divine capacities, especially the capacity to know, he rejected the belief that this gulf is bridged by the intervention of divine beings in mortal form, or that the gods somehow speak to men through signs or inspired prophets. Xenophanes' repudiation of divination was probably based on his own positive theology and his de-anthropomorphized cosmology, and is one facet of his attack on the religion of Homer and Hesiod. He denied that men who correctly predict events thereby possess knowledge, and this repudiation of knowledge by divination seems to have led him to adopt a general scepticism about the capacity of mere mortals to attain sure or certain knowledge about the gods and everything else of which Xenophanes speaks.

But there is a remaining problem. The inference is monumentally fallacious: diviners who claim to know the future really do not know, therefore no man has had certain knowledge of the truth nor will there ever be anyone who has knowledge about the gods and everything else of which I speak. How could Xenophanes have reached a general sceptical position simply from the failure of *some* men to know *some* things?

IV. The Grounds for Xenophanes' Scepticism

Since σαφήνεια was thought to be possessed by the gods alone (as in Alcmaeon B1), it might be argued that B34 does not reject the possibility of *all* human knowledge, but simply asserts that no man ever enjoys the clear and certain knowledge, possessed by the gods, especially the one god who is greatest above gods and men. If so, then the failure of seers and oracles to gain knowledge even when they speak truly, could be viewed as a reasonable basis on which to doubt that any man ever shares in the synoptic and certain knowledge of the gods. So the argument is not: since some men don't know some things, no one knows anything, but rather: since those who could be most expected to share in the knowledge of the gods fail to do so, then no man ever does so (even if they can acquire knowledge by their own inquiry).

This proposal has some merit, but it falls short of being a convincing account, for reasons that became clear in our discussion of earlier attempts to restrict the scope of Xenophanes' scepticism: while line 1 denies knowledge of what is σαφες, line 2 denies knowledge (without specification of type) of the gods and everything else of which he speaks; line 4 asserts only that belief or seeming is allotted to all things, and B18 does not say that men acquire *knowledge* through their own seeking. It is simply unreasonable to think that a man who says *no* man knew or will know with respect to *everything,* and that belief or seeming is assigned to *everything* means to say implicitly that some men do know something. The proposal must be rejected. What is useful however in this first attempt to mitigate the

fallaciousness of Xenophanes' inference is its recognition of seers and oracles as paradigms of a sort: they, if anyone, could be expected to share in
the knowledge of the gods.[36] To complete the account, we must explain
how, in two different respects, Xenophanes argues for a general sceptical
thesis on the grounds that since the conditions necessary for knowledge are
not met even in the most promising or favorable circumstances, they are
never satisfied.

The first paradigm is referred to in line 3 of B34—even if someone
should succeed above others in saying what is brought to pass, still he does
not know. What must be remembered is the rather obvious point that the
most favorable or promising case that could be made for the art of divination
is its track record, i.e., a citation of instances where the predictions made by
seers and oracles turned out to be right. This was in fact the kind of 'proof'
supplied on occasion by those who claim to possess prophetic powers.[37]
Thus, although μαντική is not explicitly mentioned in line 3, Xenophanes
is challenging what is in fact the most favorable case to be made for knowledge through divination, and claiming that even when someone succeeds in
saying truly what comes to pass, he still does not know. His reason for this
claim is not stated but as I have already suggested, it is likely tied to his own
conception of the gods and his alternative naturalistic explanation of omens
and portents of various sorts. Since divination does not supply knowledge,
given even the most favorable outcome, it can be reasonably concluded that
we cannot acquire knowledge by means of its techniques.

It should also be noted that while foreknowledge was perhaps the most
characteristic claim of the diviner, and successful prediction its strongest
support, divination was by no means confined to the future. The most famous seer in Homer, Calchas, is described as "the best of diviners who
knows things that were, and were to be, and that had been before" (Il. I,
70). We do not generally know the sorts of questions put to the famous oracles at Delphi and elsewhere, but the leaden tablets excavated at Dodona
display a variety of topics on which the oracle was consulted. These include
questions about the past and present, as well as the future.[38] Epimenides,
who received Xenophanes' rebuke, is described by Aristotle as one "who
did not practise divination about the future, only about the obscurities of the
past" (Rhet., 1418 a 21 ff.). Thus, a repudiation of μαντική would result
not only in a scepticism about the diviner's capacity to know the future, but
an equal scepticism about their capacity to penetrate the obscurities of the
present and past.

But why would it follow from the failure of these men to know anything, that no man has known or will know anything? The answer lies in the
status of seers and oracles as paradigm cases, and in the background assumptions about knowledge which were well established in the poetic tradition both preceding and enduring after Xenophanes' time. Part of this back-

ground has been already stated: 'men could have no certain knowledge, that was reserved for God.' What needs to be added is only, as Guthrie puts it, "a commonplace of poetry, expressed in invocations to the muses and elsewhere, that mankind had no sure knowledge unless the gods chose to reveal it."[39] This conception of knowledge through divine revelation or inspiration is explicit in Homer (e.g., in the introduction to the Catalogue of Ships at *Il.* II, 484–93: the gods know everything and mortals know nothing unless the gods choose to reveal it) and Hesiod (*Theogony*, 26 ff.), and it occurs in the writings of later philosophers. Parmenides presents his way of truth as a revelation from "the goddess who leads the man who knows through every town" and Parmenides "will learn all things" even though "there is no truth in the beliefs of mortals" (*D-K* B1). Empedocles also dismisses the claims of mere mortals to have comprehended the truth (*D-K* B2), but he invokes the muse to lead him on to the heights of wisdom (*D-K* B3). Not uncharacteristically, Empedocles linked his special insight with the attainment of semi-divine status (*D-K* B112). In short, given the 'poetic epistemology' of Xenophanes' time, the attainment of certain knowledge requires either an ascent of mortals to the level of the gods or a descent of the gods into human affairs, and Xenophanes denies that either of these ever occurs. The first of these is made clear by Xenophanes' refusal to think that someone could be both mortal and immortal (cf. A13: if they are gods, do not lament for them, if they are men, do not sacrifice to them), and the second possibility is ruled out as 'unfitting' for the true divinity. If one views certain knowledge as the prerogative of the gods, and makes, as Fränkel puts it, "the chasm between the here and the beyond unbridgeable" ("Xenophanesstudien," p. 130), a scepticism concerning human knowledge becomes logically inescapable.

Given these assumptions, B34 becames clear and coherent: mankind has no certain knowledge unless the gods impart it to us, or some men succeed in attaining the status of the gods. But the gods do not come among us and they do not speak to us either in their own voices or through signs and oracles. Those who might be most thought to enjoy revealed knowledge of the truth do not do so, for even if they succeed above others in saying what comes to pass, still they do not know, and belief is allotted to all things. So the certain truth no man has seen nor will there ever be anyone who has knowledge about the gods and everything else of which I speak.

I have argued that a clear, consistent, and coherent interpretation of Xenophanes' scepticism can be provided by attending to the religious and poetic tradition in which he stood, and we can now also gain a more realistic appreciation of his achievements. His scepticism is not likely to appeal to contemporary philosophers; it rests on assumptions about knowledge and divine revelation which are no longer widely believed, and it is closely tied to aspects of Homer's religion which are now mainly of historical interest. Nor can he, without exaggeration, enjoy the status of being an early proponent of the theories of later Greek sceptics or modern philosophical views of the nature and growth of scientific knowledge. There are similarities between his sceptical thesis and the conclusions of the later sceptics, but the grounds for his scepticism are very different from theirs, and there is no good reason to think that he espoused Popper's 'principle of rational knowledge.'

What is noteworthy in Xenophanes' thought is his articulation of the contrast between belief and knowledge, and his contention that whatever truth is to be gained must come as a result of human initiative and inquiry. While he remained too much a traditionalist to think that this could result in certain knowledge, for that was reserved for the gods, he did believe that men could discover what resembled the truth, or what was at least likely to be true. None of this, it seems to me, constitutes the emergence of a 'robust empiricism.' But Xenophanes' call for investigation, his repudiation of divination, and his related demythologized cosmology, constitute a departure from earlier ways of thinking that is justly thought of as revolutionary.[40]

NOTES

[1] Except where noted to the contrary, the Greek text of the fragments is taken from Diels, *Die Fragmente der Vorsokratiker*, 6th ed. rev. W. Kranz, 3 vols. (Berlin, 1952). Hereafter cited as *D-K*. Selections from Xenophanes are cited by number and letter (A: Leben und Lehre, B: Fragmente).

[2] It is quoted by Sextus Empiricus in this form on three occasions (*Adv. Math.* VII, 49, 110; VIII, 326, and δόκος δ᾽ ἐπὶ πᾶσι τέτυκται is quoted at *Pyrrh. Hyp.* II, 18). Plutarch has γένετ᾽ for ἴδεν in the first line, but this has been rejected in *D-K*, following Fränkel's argument in "Xenophanesstudien," *Hermes* 60 (1925) since γένετ᾽ requires a separation of τὸ σαφὲς from εἰδὼς that is impossible in genuine Archaic style. Further textual sources are listed in Guthrie, *A History of Greek Philosophy* vol. I, (Cambridge, 1967), p. 395. Fränkel's paper has been translated by M. R. Cosgrove and A. P. D. Mourelatos and included in the latter's *The Pre-Socratics: A Collection of Critical Essays* (New York, 1974), pp. 118–31. Subsequent references to Fränkel are to this translation of this paper.

[3] According to Diogenes Laertius (*Lives* IX, 20), "Sotion says that he was the first to maintain that all things are incognizable, but Sotion is in error" (Hicks trans.).

[4] See, for example, Fränkel: "σαφές unites the notion of completeness . . . with that of reliable, faithful, and unadulterated apprehending" ("Xenophanesstudien," p. 127). A fuller discusssion appears later in this paper (Section III).

[5] *D-K* A24 (Arius Didymus in Stobaeus, *Ecl.* II, 1, 17) ὡς ἄρα θεὸς μὲν οἶδε τὴν ἀλήθειαν, δόκος δ᾽ ἐπὶ πᾶσι τέτυκται, and Varro in Augustine, *De Civ. Dei* 7, 17: *hominis est enim haec opinari, Dei Scire*.

⁶ *D-K* 24B1; περὶ τῶν ἀφανέων, περὶ τῶν θνητῶν σαφήνει αν μὲν θεοὶ ἔχοντι, ὡς δὲ ἀνθρώποις τεκμαίρεσθαι. The text is not certain. While a contrast between divine knowledge and mortal conjecture is clear, it might be read with equal sense, "concerning the non-evident, the gods have a clear understanding, concerning things mortal, men merely conjecture from signs," or perhaps "concerning things mortal, the gods have a clear understanding, concerning things non-evident, men merely conjecture from signs."

⁷ Bruno Snell, *The Discovery of the Mind,* trans. T. G. Rosenmeyer (Oxford & Boston, 1953), esp. Ch. 7 "Human Knowledge and Divine Knowledge Among the Early Greeks." See, for example, the prelude to the 'catalogue of ships' in the *Iliad*: "for you are goddesses, you are at hand and know all things, but we hear only a rumor and know nothing" (485–86); Theognis, *Elegiac Poems* (141–2): "we men practise vain things, knowing nought, while the gods accomplish all to their mind." For further examples, see Guthrie, pp. 398–99. This contrast, coupled with a conception of λόγος as human contrivance, forms the basis for Untersteiner's view of B34 (cf. Mario Untersteiner, *Senofane* (Firenze, 1967), esp. pp. ccix–ccxxvi.

⁸ Karl Popper, "Back to the Pre-Socratics," in *Studies in Presocratic Philosophy*, ed. D. J. Furley and R. E. Allen (London, 1970), p. 152. Popper's paper appeared originally in *P.A.S.* (N.S.) 59 (1958–59); a similar account is given in his *Conjectures and Refutations* (London, 1963).

⁹ To make Popper's thesis even remotely plausible, we must read τετελεσμένον εἰπών in B34, as 'saying the final or complete truth,' but (as will be developed in detail later) τετελεσμένον has an ordinary sense of that which is completed, made actual, or brought about, and perhaps also, following Fränkel, that which is real or present. In neither case can τετελεσμένον εἰπών be taken as 'saying that which is the complete or final explanation or theory.'

¹⁰ Even so, Aristotle's view is that knowledge is gained not through the *refutation* of previous conjectures, but, so far as possible, their *confirmation*. Just prior to the discussion of incontinence Aristotle states, "Here as in other cases we must set down the phainomena and begin by considering the difficulties, and so go on to vindicate if possible all the common conceptions about these states of mind, or at any rate most of them and the most important" (*NE* VIII 1 1145 b 2–6). We are indebted to G. E. L. Owen's "Tithenai ta Phainomena" in *Aristote et les problèmes de la methode* (Louvain, 1961) for an appreciation of the extent to which *phainomena* means not 'the observed facts," but "common conceptions" (ἔνδοξα).

¹¹ Popper, "Back to the Pre-Socratics," p. 152. Snell (*The Discovery of the Mind*) also assumes that what men discover is knowledge, and, though he seems not to realize it, this makes his characterization of Xenophanes' doctrine dangerously close to an explicit inconsistency. He attributes the following views to Xenophanes "human knowledge is in its essence deceptive" (p. 139), "only apparent knowledge" (p. 140), "fallacious" (p. 141), *and* "men acquire knowledge through their own striving" (p. 140), "man's own initiative, his industry and zeal, become crucial for the acquisition of knowledge" (p. 140), "knowledge consists of the data gained from inquiry and search" (p. 140). I find his one attempt to reconcile these two positions exceptionally opaque: "knowledge as such is obscure, but it is illumined by searching" (p. 140).

[12] See, for example, Lehrer's "Why Not Scepticism?" *Philosophical Forum* 2 (1971): 283–98.

[13] I do not think we can exclude the possibility of ἴδεν being a kind of 'mental seeing.' Homer had already spoken of 'mental seeing' (ἰδέσθαι ἐν φρεσίν) and what is σαφές (clear, certain, true) is more naturally thought of as propositions, accounts, stories, rather than the objects of sense perception.

[14] It is at least worth noting that εἰδέναι, although etymologically connected with verbs of seeing, had already by the time of Homer acquired a broader sense in which one could consistently say, "I know (οἶδα) even though I have not seen." The following passage is from Bk. XX of the *Iliad*, 203 ff.

. . . we know (ἴδμεν) each other's parents and lineage, for we have heard tales told in olden days by mortal men, but with sight of eyes hast thou never seen my parents nor I thine (ὄψει δ' οὔτ' ἴδες) (Murray trans.).

Cf. also, Heitsch, "Das Wissen des Xenophanes," *Rheinisches Museum für Philologie* 109 (1966): 193–235, and *Iliad* VI, 150; Hesiod, *Theogony* 53–62, 915–17.

[15] Fränkel's later paraphrase indicates that he does not adhere to his early translation ("and what is precise no man has seen") and adopts the expansion I have suggested: "τὸ μὲν σαφὲς ἄνθρωπος οὐδεὶς γνοίη ἂν πάντων γε πραγμάτων πέρι: a reliable knowledge with respect to all of the objects spoken of here, particularly concerning the gods, is not possible for men" (p. 128).

[16] Charles H. Kahn, *Anaximander and the Origins of Greek Cosmology* (New York, 1960), p. 134.

[17] Plato tells the story of Epimenides' visit to Athens and his prophecy about the Persian invasion (*Laws*, 642d-e). Aristotle also refers to him as a seer at *Rhet.* 1418 a 21 ff.

[18] "Ξενοφάνης καὶ Ἐπίκουρος ἀναιροῦσι τὴν μαντικήν," Aetius, *Placita*, V, 1, 1 (*D-K* A 52).

[19] "Of these—to mention the most ancient—Xenophanes of Colophon, while asserting the existence of gods, was the only one who repudiated divination in its entirety (*divinationem funditus sustulit*)," Cicero, *De Divinatione*, Falconer trans. (Loeb), I, iii, 5.

[20] The most detailed and comprehensive study of Greek divination is still Bouché-Leclercq, *Histoire de la Divination dans l'Antiquité*, 4 vols. (Paris, 1879–82). His discussion of Xenophanes (vol. I, 33–34) treats the attack on divination as a consequence of Xenophanes' conception of god's majesty, and influential primarily in the Sicilian comedians' (Aristoxenes, Epicharmus) attacks on *les devins de carrefour*. Other valuable accounts of the extraordinary techniques employed by professional and amateur seers are provided by W. R. Halliday, *Greek Divination* (Chicago, 1913); R. Flacelière, *Greek Oracles*, D. Garman, trans. (New York, 1965); and M. P. Nilsson, *Greek Folk Religion* (New York, 1948), esp. "Seers and Oracles," pp. 121–39.

[21] Nilsson, *Greek Folk Religion*, 136. Sophocles expresses a scepticism about divination (*O.T.*, 499–512) which closely parallels what I think is Xenophanes' thesis: the gods have perfect knowledge, but there is no sure test (χρίσις ἀλη-

θής) that a mortal seer (μάντις) attains knowledge even if he excels above others in his skill of interpreting omens (σοφία). Cf. the summary by J. C. Kamerbeek, "The contrast between divine and human knowledge [μὲν—δέ] explains their scepticism as to the truth of Teiresias' words, based on their faith in Oedipus." (*The Plays of Sophocles* [Leiden, 1967], p. 120.) The summary statement of 499–512 given above is based on the translation by Richard Jebb, *Sophocles, The Plays and Fragments* (Amsterdam, 1966).

²² E. R. Dodds, *The Greeks and the Irrational* (Berkeley, 1951), p. 196, n. 7.

²³ Nilsson, *Greek Folk Religion*, pp. 92, 121.

²⁴ Flacelière, *Greek Oracles*, p. 18.

²⁵ Cf. Flacelière, *Greek Oracles*, "Divination by Signs." Xenophanes is said to have visited Etna and commented on the periodic frequency of volcanic eruptions (Aristotle, *De Mirab.*, 833 a 15). We are also told, though the reason is not given, that Xenophanes disapproved of dice (A16). These fragments are however not obviously related to his attack on divination.

²⁶ Epicurus' naturalistic explanations of celestial phenomena consistently follow those given by Xenophanes, though he is not mentioned by name: "the rising and setting of the sun, moon, and stars may be due to kindling and quenching (ἄναψιν καὶ σβέσιν)"; or it may be due to "their coming forward above the earth or by its intervention"; eclipse of the sun may be due to the quenching of its light (κατὰ σβέσιν); lightning may be due to the motion of atoms in the clouds; comets are due to fires in the heavens, etc. (Diogenes Laertius, *Lives*, X, 91–93, 96–98, 101, 111). While Epicurus concedes that the facts allow for a plurality of explanations, he insists that the exclusion of myth is a necessary condition (μόνον ὁ μῦθος ἀπέστω) for understanding and peace of mind (103).

²⁷ Letter to Herodotus in Diogenes Laertius, *Lives*, X, 76. Following Epicurus, Lucretius attacks religious superstition on the basis of alternative physical explanations of the motions of heavenly bodies, eclipses, lightning, clouds, rain, volcanic eruptions, the seasons, plagues, rainbows, etc. (*De Rerum Natura*, V, VI).

²⁸ Fränkel, "Xenophanesstudien," p. 126.

²⁹ At one point Fränkel translates τετλεσμένον εἰπών as "saying something which turns out to be true," but he later discards this in favor of 'articulating what is really present' ("Xenophanesstudien," 126–27). Guthrie (*A History of Greek Philosophy*, p. 395, n. 4) characterizes τετελεσμένον as 'a typically Homeric word' but does not indicate what it typically means in Homer.

³⁰ Cf. R. J. Cunliffe, *A Lexicon of the Homeric Dialect* (1924), 337. A great many more examples could be provided by broadening the criterion to include variant verbs for 'speaking' (e.g., ἀγορεύω—to speak publicly) and other forms of τελέω (e.g., the prediction of Calchas at *Il.* II, 330).

³¹ Cf the predictions of Melantheus (*Od.* XVII, 299). Antinous (*Od.* XVIII, 82), Odysseus (*Od.* XIX, 547).

³² Seers and oracles are of course the paradigm cases, but the description could refer to anyone who succeeds in correctly predicting the future. According to Diogenes Laertius (*Lives*, I, 23) Xenophanes admired Thales for his ability to predict eclipses and set the solstices. B. L. van der Waerden (following an explanation given by M. Schramm) accounts for Thales' prediction by pointing out that Thales predicted only that an eclipse would occur in a certain *year* (Herodotus, I, 74) and,

given enough background information about preceding lunar and solar eclipses, it was possible to discover that in some years solar eclipses were likely to occur (*Science Awakening II: The Birth of Astronomy* [New York, 1974], pp. 120–22). Xenophanes' admiration for Thales (assuming the accuracy of the story) need not be at odds with his scepticism about divination, since he may have credited Thales with 'skill in conjecture,' not knowledge. Euripides adopts this position when he says that "the good prophet is the man skilled in conjecture" (*Hel.*, 744–57); Plato credits the oracles and prophets with 'well-aimed conjecture' (εὐδοξία) but insists that this is still only true opinion, not knowledge (*Meno*, 99c).

³³ In Book II of the *Odyssey*, Eurymachas tells the prophet Halitherses to go home and prophesy to his children, for 'many are the birds who under the sun's rays wander; not all of them mean anything' (181–82), "Nor do we care for any prophecy (θεοπροπίης), which you, old sir, may tell us, which will not happen, and will make you even more hated" (μυθέαι ἀκράαντον, ἀπεχθάν-εαι δ' ἔτι μᾶλλον, 202). See also Hector's scorn for the prophecy from birds given by Poulydamas (*Il.* XII, 228 ff.: "one bird only is best, one omen—to fight for our country"). Aristophanes was later to ridicule the sooth-sayers in *The Knights* and *The Birds*. Sophocles' *Oedipus Rex* contains occasional sceptical remarks about the reliability and legitimacy of prophecy (lines 500–15) but since Teiresias' prediction is ultimately confirmed, one cannot suppose that Sophocles' intention was to undermine confidence in divination. Divination was not repudiated by either Plato or Aristotle, at least not in all its forms, and it was defended by the Stoics. The most extensive criticism among later philosophers was provided by the Epicureans, as can be seen in the remarks of the Epicurean Boethos in Plutarch's dialogue, *On the Pythian Oracles:* ". . . the Sibyls and Bakis have foretold every sort of event and misfortune: if it so happens that a number of them have come to pass, nonetheless at the time they were uttered their prophecies were lies, even if fortuitous circumstances should eventually appear to make them true." (Quoted in Flacelière, *Greek Oracles*, p. 81.)

³⁴ So characteristic in fact that it becomes natural to speak of the prophets themselves as σαφής—sure or unerring (cf. Liddell and Scott: σαφής; for example, the description of Teiresias in Sophocles' *Oed. Rex,* 286: σαφέσ-τατα).

³⁵ The syntax of σαφές (direct object of ἴδεν, accusative of respect, or adverbial accusative) is unclear, but I do not see that a reasonable interpretation of the fragment presupposes a definitive answer. What is σαφές may be what is not known, or it may be the respect in which one does not know, or the manner in which one does not know. The important point is that σαφές, ἴδεν and εἰδώς in lines 1–2 are set in clear contrast (μὲν—δέ) with δόκος in line 4. Denniston cites this fragment as an example of an οὖν (in τὸ μὲν οὖν σαφὲς) emphasizing a prospective μέν (*The Greek Particles* [Oxford at the Clarendon Press, 1954], p. 473). This contrast makes it unlikely that τὸ σαφές functions as an independent sentence as, for example, in Cleve's: "and this is sure by all means" (*The Giants of Pre-Sophistic Philosophy* , p. 28).

³⁶ The great importance of seers and oracles in both public and private affairs is perhaps sufficiently well known to need any further argument. One need only point to the great popularity of the traditional oracles at Delphi, Dodona, and Claros (near

Colophon), and according to Herodotus, the incessant use made of seers in military matters as the clearest evidence of the exalted position which they enjoyed. The major role played by diviners in Greek religion is explained in detail by Nilsson, *Greek Folk Religion*, 123–39.

[37] In Book II of the *Odyssey*, Halitherses predicts the fate that is to befall Penelope's suitors, and then argues:

"I who foretell this am not untried, I know what I am saying. Concerning him, I say that everything was accomplished in the way I said it would be at the time the Argives took ship for Ilion, and with them went resourceful Odysseus. I said that after much suffering, with all his companions lost, in the twentieth year, not recognized by any, he would come home. And now all this is being accomplished (νῦν πάντα τελεῖται)." (170–76. Lattimore trans.)

A similar defense is offered by Euthyphro, the self-proclaimed theological expert in Plato's *Euthyphro* (3c), when he complains of his reception in the assembly: "When I tell them in advance what will occur they laugh at me, and yet I have never made a prediction that did not come true."

[38] Included among those questions recorded were these: whether a man's wife will bear him a child, whether the child which his wife is carrying is actually his, whether a man will do well by breeding sheep, and, my favorite, "Agis asks Zeus Naios and Dione whether he lost the blankets and pillows himself or whether they were stolen by someone outside the household." For other examples see C. Carapanos, *Dodone et ses ruines* (Paris, 1878) 68 ff., and the *Bulletin de Corr. Hell.*, 83 (1959) 669–73.

[39] Guthrie, *A History of Greek Philosophy*, p. 398. It has been thought that Xenophanes rejected the view that mortals derive their knowledge from the gods, and held instead that men gain knowledge through their own inquiry (Snell, *The Discovery of the Mind*, pp. 139–44; John Robinson, *An Introduction to Early Greek Philosophy* [New York, 1968], pp. 55–56). But this is not implied by the fragments. Xenophanes denies that the gods revealed all things to mortals from the beginning and he repudiates divination, but he nowhere rejects the assumption that if *knowledge* is to be attained at all by mortals, it must come by divine revelation. What man can discover through seeking is 'the better' (B18) which can easily be the δόκος of B34, and which may resemble or be similar to what is true (B35). One relevant fragment on this issue is the tantalizingly brief B36: ὁππόσα δὴ θνητοῖσι πεφήνασιν εἰσοράασθαι, "as many as they have revealed to mortals to look upon." But it does not say anything about *knowledge*. The major obstacle in the path of thinking that Xenophanes espouses knowledge gained through inquiry is one of consistency. Like Snell, Robinson seems untroubled by attributing to Xenophanes the following: "only through patient inquiry does the truth come to be known" and "the truth itself is known only to god" (p. 56).

[40] I am indebted to William Fortenbaugh, David Glidden, G. B. Kerferd, David Konstan, Martha Nussbaum, and Gregory Vlastos for their criticism of earlier drafts of this paper. I would also like to thank A. P. D. Mourelatos, Carl Brumbach, William Sewell, and Ronald Swigger for their assistance during the early stages of my research on this topic.

JACKSON P. HERSHBELL

Parmenides' Way of Truth and B16

A T least three interpretations have been given to B16 of Parmenides' poem. It has been taken for a fragment of his theory of knowledge, of his doctrine of sense perception, and of his views on sensing *and* knowing.[1] Evidence for these interpretations is taken from Aristotle's *Metaphysics* and Theophrastus' *De Sensibus*. The fragment is usually assigned to the second part of the poem, the Way of Seeming or Opinion.

In this study it will be argued that B16 comes from the first part of the poem, the Way of Truth, and that it is a statement neither of a theory of knowledge nor of sense perception, but an affirmation of the close relationship between thought and Being:[2] there can be no thought without that which is, or in Parmenides' words, ". . . neither can you recognize that which is not (that is impossible) nor can you speak about it" (B2, 7–8).[3]

Regardless of the motives for the second part of Parmenides' poem, no guarantee of truth is given for its content. In B1, 28–30, for example, the goddess who is addressing Parmenides, invites him to inquire into the nature of truth, and the beliefs or "guesswork" of mortals:

> I bid you to inquire into all things, both the steadfast heart of persuasive (well-rounded?) truth, and the opinions of mortals in which there is no genuine conviction (πίστις ἀληθής).[4]

In B8, 50 f. the goddess concludes the first part of her presentation and introduces Parmenides to the Way of Opinion:

> I now cease my reliable discourse and reflection concerning truth. Henceforth you must learn the opinions of mortals, listening to the deceptive order of my words.

If B16, then, belongs to a part of the poem declared false or unreliable by Parmenides' goddess, how can it be considered a piece of positive doctrine? For if the Way of Opinion is false or unreliable, it would seem that all theo-

This paper was presented at the 1970 New York meeting of the Society for Ancient Greek Philosophy and published in *Apeiron* 4, no. 2 (1970):1–23; we thank the editors and Monash University for permission to reprint.

Jackson Hershbell is Professor of Classics at the University of Minnesota.

ries or teachings found in it are equally unreliable. Moreover, it is not certain that the teachings in the Way of Opinion originated with Parmenides or were proclaimed by him as his own.[5] Whatever its interpretation, if B16 contains a positive or reliable teaching, it should belong to the Way of Truth.

The foregoing conclusion could be avoided, of course, if it be argued that the Way of Opinion is partially true, a "likely story" designed to explain the world of appearance. For example, in B8, 60–61, Parmenides' goddess declares:

> I tell you this arrangement (διάκοσμον), fitting in all respects (ἐοικότα πάντα) so that no mortal will ever surpass you in opinion.

On the basis of this passage it has been maintained that the goddess is about to offer the best description of empirical reality, a description having a high degree of probability or likelihood of being true. Such an interpretation seems *prima facie* plausible, given the word ἐοικότα. But on closer inspection, whatever the meaning of ἐοικότα,[6] the crux of these verses is found in B8, 61, and they cannot be interpreted to mean that the "arrangement" proclaimed by the goddess is the best and most probable account of the phenomenal world. Verse 61 only means that the goddess will instruct Parmenides so that no one can surpass him in mortal opinion concerning the world. An interpretation of the Way of Opinion as partially true or as a probable cosmology seems irreconcilable with the basic outlook of Parmenides' goddess for whom Being and non-Being, truth and falsity, always remain in sharp contrast. There are no degrees of reality for her and Parmenides.[7]

Despite the fact that no truth is claimed for the Way of Opinion, several interpreters place B16 in it and consider this fragment part of Parmenides' theory of knowledge or his doctrine of sense perception. L. Tarán, for example, maintains, "for Parmenides the phenomenal world is non-existent, and therefore there is no sense in supporting one theory about it against another."[8] Nevertheless, he maintains that Parmenides is developing a theory of knowledge in B16 and that this fragment does not belong to Parmenides' Way of Truth.[9] How a theory of knowledge can be seriously proposed which is considered false by its author, is not explained by Tarán. Such a procedure is like the attempt to think A and not-A simultaneously (an impossible task for Parmenides or for anyone who attempts to think). In order to avoid such difficulties, it is necessary to maintain either (a) that B16 contains a positive teaching or theory and therefore belongs to the Way of Truth, or (b) that B16 is not a true or reliable doctrine and therefore belongs to the Way of Opinion. If the latter is correct, then B16 together with the other opinions in the Way of Opinion, is unimportant for understanding Parmenides' own views concerning reality. In other words, B16 would have no genuine philosophical meaning and must be considered only one of the many false opinions a mortal can entertain concerning the phenomenal world.

But there are important reasons for concluding that B16 has philosophical significance, and that it does not belong to the Way of Opinion, but to the Way of Truth. These will now be examined.

The only evidence that B16 formed part of the Way of Opinion is based on the accounts of Aristotle and Theophrastus, but neither of them gives a clear or wholly unambiguous indication to which part of the poem the fragment originally belonged. Aristotle quotes it in the *Metaphysics* (1009b) while discussing those philosophers who believe that thought (φρόνησις) and sense perception (αἴσθησις) are the same, and that impressions given through sense perception are necessarily true. Like Empedocles, Parmenides believed that changes of thought (μεταβάλλειν τὴν φρόνησιν) are dependent on changes of bodily condition. Aristotle then quotes B16 without further explanation or indication of its original context in Parmenides' poem.

Theophrastus attempts to explain the fragment in some detail in *De Sensibus*, and in order to determine, if possible, the original place of B16 in Parmenides' poem, it is necessary to consider his comments.[10] Having initially placed Parmenides with those thinkers who believe that sense perception involves the principle of likeness, Theophrastus proceeds in sections 3–4 to comment specifically on Parmenides' views and quotes B16. Although it is not explicitly acknowledged to be part of the Way of Opinion, Theophrastus' commentary, which describes the dependence of the understanding (γνῶσις) on "hot" and "cold," strongly suggests B16 came from the second part of the poem. For "hot" and "cold" seem to be nothing but the peripatetic interpretations of light and night which figure so predominantly in the Way of Opinion. Moreover, some of Theophrastus' observations may rely on Aristotle's discussion of the same fragment in the *Metaphysics* (1009b) where Aristotle maintained that Parmenides, together with Democritus and Empedocles, supposed that thought and perception were the same. So in *De Sensibus*, Theophrastus asserts that thinking (τὸ φρονεῖν) and perceiving (τὸ αἰσθάνεσθαι) were considered identical by Parmenides. At this point, both interpretations are in agreement and appear to justify the belief that B16 belongs to the Way of Opinion. For since the Way of Opinion is usually interpreted as being somehow concerned with the world of phenomena or appearance, it would seem that a discussion of sense perception also belongs to it. Or at least why would Parmenides discuss sense perception in a part of his poem, viz., the Way of Truth, which deals with an unchanging, unbegotten, and indestructible reality?

But the decision to place B16 in the Way of Opinion on the basis that Parmenides identified thought and sense perception is premature, especially since it is not clear that B16 has anything to do with the senses, Theophrastus' (and Aristotle's) interpretation notwithstanding. Moreover, Theophrastus' observation that Parmenides considered thought and sense perception identical, though it comes immediately after B16, is hardly supported by the fragment. In fact, several interpreters think that Theophrastus made a major mistake in attributing the doctrine of the sameness of perception and thought to Parmenides.[11]

Another reason for assigning B16 to the Way of Opinion is Theophrastus' ascription to Parmenides of the view that understanding depends on two elements, "hot" and "cold"; as their amount varies in the individual, his understanding changes, a better or more refined understanding being dependent on the "hot." But even understanding requires a certain proportion or συμμετρία (perhaps Theophrastus' interpretation of Parmenides' κρᾶσις).[12] At this point, Theophrastus quotes B16.[13]

ὡς γὰρ ἕκαστος (ἑκάστοτ') ἔχει κρᾶσιν
μελέων πολυπλάγκτων (πολυκάμπτων)
τὼς νόος ἀνθρώποισι παρέστηκεν (παρίσταται)· τὸ γὰρ αὐτό
ἔστιν ὅπερ φρονέει μελέων φύσις ἀνθρώποισιν
καὶ πᾶσιν καὶ παντί· τὸ γὰρ πλέον ἐστὶ νόημα.

If the fragment is read, however, without peripatetic or other presuppositions, there is no explicit mention of "hot" or "cold," or the more genuine Parmenidean light and night. Also there is no specific indication in the fragment that the mind (νόος) or object of thought (νόημα) depends on the balance of "hot" and "cold" or light and night; unless, of course, some deduction is made that the krasis consists of light and night. A reader of the fragment itself can only come to the conclusion that some kind of relationship between the krasis of limbs, presumably the limbs of the human body, and the human mind, is affirmed in the fragment. Moreover, the concluding phrase of B16, τὸ γὰρ πλέον ἐστὶ νόημα (lit. "for the full (or more) is thought") looks much like one of the conclusions reached in the Way of Truth where the close affinity between *that which is* and thought, is constantly stressed, e.g., B2, 3–4, B8, 34–36, and in B8, 21 ff. *that which is* is considered indivisible and "full of existence" (ἔμπλεον ἐόντος).[14]

Before the conclusion of his discussion of Parmenides in *De Sensibus*, Theophrastus also remarks that "absolutely everything that is has a certain kind of understanding" (καὶ ὅλως δὲ πᾶν τὸ ὂν ἔχειν τινὰ γνῶσιν), and this seems to be a loose summary statement of fragments from the Way of Truth, e.g., B8, 35–36, "for not without that which is . . . shall you find thinking" (οὐ γὰρ ἄνευ τοῦ ἐόντος, ἐν ὧι πεφατισμένον ἐστιν, εὑρήσεις τὸ νοεῖν), and B3 in particular, "for the same thing exists for thinking and being" (. . . τὸ γὰρ αὐτὸ νοεῖν ἐστίν τε καὶ εἶναι). That Theophrastus' remark may be based on these or other fragments from the Way of Truth is suggested by the following: (a) Theophrastus' use of τὸ ὄν, a key term in Parmenides' Way of Truth, cannot be legitimately extended to the changing phenomena of the Way of Opinion; (b) B3 . . . τὸ γὰρ αὐτὸ νοεῖν ἐστίν τε καὶ εἶναι especially could be taken to imply not only that everything which thinks exists, but also that everything which exists thinks.[15] In any case, there is no other extant fragment or anything in the Parmenidean tradition to support Theophrastus' statement.

Since Theophrastus' discussion of Parmenides nearly concludes with such an observation, possibly based on the fragments in the Way of Truth, there is some indication that he was not sure where B16 was located in Parmenides' poem. In fact, he may not have been working with a complete text of the poem and was strongly under the influence of Aristotle in his interpretation of Parmenides.

In view of J. B. McDiarmid's careful study of Theophrastus on the Presocratics, the previous supposition cannot be disregarded. According to McDiarmid, for example, there is no indication that Theophrastus made use of much more of presocratic original writings than he quotes in *Physicorum Opiniones*, and some of these are taken from Aristotle's writings, or perhaps from a collection of excerpts for use in the Lyceum.[16] This could also be true of B16 in *De Sensibus* where Theophrastus fails to indicate its original context and surprisingly overlooks the distinction he made in *Physicorum Opiniones* between the two parts of Parmenides' poem. As a result, he fails to hint that the views he is stating are not Parmenides' own, or that B16 must come from the Way of Truth if it is to be taken seriously as a correct formula for either perception or knowledge.[17]

In fact, Theophrastus' repeated complaint about Parmenides, ὅλως οὐδὲν ἀφώρικεν and οὐδὲν ἔτι διώρικεν, may be based on lack of information about Parmenides' poem. Apart from Theophrastus' not very detailed reference in *De Sensibus* to memory and forgetfulness, and the brief discussion of the perceptions of the dead, there is no clear evidence that he was working from a complete text of Parmenides' poem. Contrary to J. Mansfeld, the phrase ἐν οἷς φησι does not prove that Theophrastus had a complete copy of the poem.[18] It only indicates that B16 and other unquoted passages (even in his treatment of other philosophers, Theophrastus seldom quotes the passages he is discussing) were known to him. Mansfeld's contention that Aristotle quoted B16 from memory, whereas Theophrastus had a copy of the whole poem, is difficult to understand.[19] Given the evidence, one can as convincingly maintain that Theophrastus quoted B16 from memory whereas Aristotle had a full copy of the poem.

45

The other explanation, of course, for Theophrastus' complaints about Parmenides is that he is raising questions and employing categories not relevant to Parmenides. For example, there is no doubt that Parmenides did discuss memory and forgetfulness, and the perceptions of the dead, but were they discussed in the contexts and in the terms that Theophrastus suggests? As Vlastos correctly points out, the corpse-like passivity of sense perception should not surprise a reader of Parmenides, but all these references, e.g., the "undiscriminating hordes" whose eyes are sightless, and ears full of noise, are found in the Way of Truth, not in the Way of Opinion.[20] In any case, Theophrastus is not always a careful interpreter of his predecessors, and even such a sympathetic critic as G. M. Stratton admits that Theophrastus "was not always of clearest judgment."[21]

It must also be added that there is little in Theophrastus' discussion of B16, apart from his own doctrine that sense perception involves a certain correspondence or composition suited to the object, which could not have been derived from Aristotle's *Metaphysics*. For example, Aristotle claims there (1009b) that Parmenides identified thought and perception, making thought dependent on bodily changes. In an earlier section (986b) Aristotle mentioned that Parmenides placed "hot" under Being and "cold" under non-Being:

> For, claiming that non-being in contrast to Being, does not exist, he thinks it necessary that Being be one and that nothing else be. . . . But being forced to conform to phenomena, and believing that these are one according to formula but many according to sensation, he now posits two causes or two principles, the Hot and the Cold, as if speaking of fire and earth; and he classifies the Hot as the principle with respect to being but the Cold as the principle with respect to non-being.[22]

Since Theophrastus was no doubt familiar with the *Metaphysics* he could assume from Aristotle's brief discussion of B16 that it was somehow concerned with the body and thought or perception. And since, according to Aristotle's interpretation of Parmenides, "hot" and "cold" were the two elements of the phenomenal world, perception would somehow be connected with these. Identifying the term *krasis* in B16 with his own concept of συμμετρία, Theophrastus concluded that "knowledge" required a certain proportion of the elements. At the same time, however, Theophrastus seems to have understood that B16 concerns a higher grade of knowledge. For knowledge (γνῶσις) in general depends on the predominant element, and in the case of the higher kind of knowledge, this is assumed by Theophrastus to be the "hot." As J. Loenen has correctly remarked, genuine νόος can only arise when "hot" predominates.[23] But returning to the *Metaphysics*, "hot" is the principle with respect to Being. It is, therefore, tempting to conclude that Theophrastus himself regarded B16 part of the Way of Truth, and not primarily concerned with sense perception except insofar as it was mistakenly taken to be identical with thought.

In general, there are no overwhelming reasons for accepting Theophrastus' interpretation of B16 or for claiming that B16 belonged to the Way of Opinion. There are other equally plausible ways of interpreting B16. It cannot be assumed that since Theophrastus was closer in time to Parmenides, he was also closer in spirit, especially since his purpose in *De Sensibus* is not to give a detailed analysis of Parmenides, but a textbook survey of previous thought on sense perception. Moreover, in view of the ambiguity, paucity, and even inaccuracy of Theophrastus' comments on B16, one does well beginning with Parmenides' *ipsissima verba*.

In order to demonstrate the compatibility of B16 with the Way of Truth, the meaning of two important terms must be determined, that is, κρᾶσιν and μελέων in the first verse. If "limbs" is taken in its usual sense as the limbs of the human body, there seems little room for Theophrastus' interpretation that the *krasis* is a blend or mixture of "hot" and "cold," or light and night.[24] The grammatical construction indicates that whatever the meaning of *krasis*, it somehow involves the limbs of the body: χρᾶσιν μελέων. There are, however, two ways to avoid this conclusion. One could deny that μέλεα refers to the limbs of the body, but instead to the elements of the cosmos, the *maxima membra mundi*, light and night.[25] Hence the mind is dependent on the mixture of the cosmic limbs. The other argument shows that μέλεα refers to the human body. But since all things consist of light and night (cf. B9), these are also the ingredients of the human body. Hence the phrase should be interpreted as referring to a mixture of light and night which, in turn, compose the bodily limbs.[26]

But these two explanations of μέλεα are not convincing. Nowhere in the fragments does Parmenides refer to light and night as "limbs." At best, these are the "shapes" or "forms" (μορφαί) mentioned in B8, 53–54. Why does Parmenides not use this term in B16 if he wanted to say that men's minds are dependent on the mixture of light and night? Parmenides is normally very consistent in his terminology. The second possibility takes μέλεα in its common meaning, but expects the reader to understand that, nonetheless, a mixture of light and night underlies the human limbs. This is stretching a point, for can it safely be assumed that *all* things, including the human body, are composed of light and night? Does the *all* in B9, for example, "since all things have been named light and night," refer to everything in the cosmos, or primarily to celestial phenomena? There is reason for thinking that light and night do not form the basis of all things in the Way of Opinion, but that these are only *examples* of difference or opposition.[27]

In general, it cannot be safely assumed either that *melea* means more than "human limbs" or that light and night are the underlying components of these. But more important, κρᾶσιν μελέων makes perfectly good sense if the *melea* are the limbs of the human body.

Various meanings of *krasis* are cited in Liddell and Scott; for example, the temperament of the mind or body, temperature, harmony, union. Often the word refers to the mixing of water and wine, not a random mixture, but one based on a certain proportion of water to wine, usually 3:1.[28] The word also seems to have something to do with the sequence in which water and wine are mixed. Consider, for example, Xenophanes B5:

> Nor would anyone mix wine (κεράσειε) first pouring it into the cup, but rather the water and then the wine.

Similarly *krasis* sometimes appears in combination with ἁρμονία. For example, in Plato's *Phaedo* (86b) the soul is a κρᾶσις καὶ ἁρμονία of the elements of the body, and in *De Anima* (407b31) Aristotle reports the view of those who hold that the soul: τὴν ἁρμονίαν κρᾶσιν καὶ σύνθεσιν ἐναντίων εἶναι.[29]

If one keeps in mind, then, that *krasis* has the sense of intentional, artful, or even harmonious blending, what is a κρᾶσις μελέων? It is probably nothing more than a way of saying that the limbs of the human body function together or in a harmonious or unified fashion. The limbs though individually having a tendency to "wander" (note πολυπλάγκτων), function together as a whole. The literal meaning of κρᾶσις as a "mixture," therefore, should not mislead one into thinking that this clearly links B16 with the Way of Opinion. In this section of the poem Parmenides does use μῖξις, but here he is probably thinking of the mingling of the sexes, a symbol perhaps of the whole cosmological process. And unlike *krasis*, it does seem to be a technical term.[30]

Against the previous observations, it could be objected that interpreting κρᾶσις μελέων as a way of saying that the limbs of the human body function harmoniously, is to reduce *krasis* to the level of a metaphor. If one keeps in mind, however, the meanings given in Liddell and Scott, it seems clear that *krasis* was not always understood in its root sense of a simple mixture or blending. Among the English meanings assigned are "temperature" of the air, temperament, combination or union (cf. the passage in *Phaedo* 86b cited above), and the combination of two vowels into one long. These examples do not, of course, show how Parmenides understood the term. But they do suggest that any literal rendering of *krasis* as "mixture" or "blend" is by no means certain. A metaphorical meaning of *krasis* is possible, and given the interpretation of μελέων as the limbs of the human body, almost necessary.

B16, 1–2 then seems to affirm that each man has a coordinated body which is formed or "mixed" of much-wandering limbs. And just as every man has a unified body, so mind is present to men. In interpreting these verses, two possibilities exist: (a) these first two lines are a simile, just as "men have similar bodies, so they have similar minds,"[31] or (b) some kind of relationship between mind and body is being affirmed. But the nature of the relationship remains unclear. Do the verses mean that mind is dependent on the body for its existence, i.e., "just as each man has a body . . . so mind is present"? Or do the verses mean the existence of a coordinated or unified body is dependent on mind? In order to understand the full meaning of lines 1–2, it is necessary to consider lines 3–4.

The grammar of B16, 3–4 has been much discussed, but Tarán, to some extent following Hölscher, has given probably the best and simplest explanation.[32] According to him, φύσις μελέων is the subject of φρονέει, and ὅπερ, accusative: the object of φρονέει. Since τὸ αὐτό is the subject of ἔστιν and ὅπερ is correlative with it, lines 3–4a can be translated:

> For it is the same thing which the constitution (φύσις) of each and every man's limbs thinks. . . .

The term φύσις in B16, 3 needs some explanation. In a now old but important study, Περί φύσεως, W. A. Heidel argues convincingly that the primary sense of φύσις is "growth." But according to him, it also has the sense of the end or result of a process. Viewed from without, it is "the outward constitution or frame of a thing"; considered from within, "it is its inner constitution or character."[33] Without pursuing Heidel's discussion in detail, it is important to note his observation that as interest in the microcosm grew, φύσις understood as the *mental* constitution assumed great importance. It comes to have the meaning of endowment, talent, or instinct, e.g., Protagoras B3; Democritus B33, B278. Or following Kirk's more recent analyses of φύσις in Heracleitus, the word means the constitution or essence of a thing, that which governs a thing's behaviour.[34] Whether one agrees wholly with Heidel's or Kirk's analyses, it seems clear that φύσις, like *krasis*, is by no means a simple concept. In the fragments of Parmenides' poem, the word φύσις occurs only in B16 and in one other fragment, B10, where it probably means something like "stuff" or "essence" (*Äther-Wesen* in DK18, p. 241). Now if it is true that φύσις in B16 can mean something like mental constitution, or that which governs a thing's behaviour, there is nothing which prohibits the identification of this φύσις μελέων with νόος; viewed from within, mind is the constitution of the bodily limbs; i.e., controls the body's movements. To understand φύσις in another sense, as a physical component of the body or the body itself, is difficult. What thinks (φρονέει) is νόος, not the body. Any other interpretation of φύσις would seem at variance with common sense as well as the rest of Parmenides' thought where what apprehends or thinks is always νόος, not σῶμα. This is not to say, of course, that Parmenides regarded νόος as the φύσις of *all* things. It is the φύσις only of the human body. Whether he would have asserted, à la Berkeley, that all reality is at root "mental" or somehow dependent on mind is not clear, and at best doubtful.

If the previous observations are correct, it would seem that lines 3–4 further explain the relationship between mind and body suggested in 1-2: the *krasis* of the body which is similar in all men is dependent on the presence of mind. Mind is the φύσις μελέων precisely in the sense that it enables the limbs to work together so that there can be a living, functioning body at all. And this mind which controls the body also thinks the "same thing" in all men:

> As each man has a union of the much-wandering limbs of the body, so is mind present to men.

> For it is the same thing which the constitution of the limbs (mind) thinks, both in each and every man.

The word γάρ is often used to confirm or strengthen an assertion.[35] In this case, it suggests that the relationship between these verses is as follows: men have similar minds just as they have similar bodies, indeed it being the mind that governs the body. That men's minds are similar is shown from the fact that they think the same object, the nature of this object being given in 4b.

The meaning of 4b τό γὰρ πλέον ἐστὶ νόημα, is not clear at first. Literally it can be translated, "for the full (or more) is thought."[36] "Full" rather than "more" is the correct translation since the lines are probably meant to recall the notion that thought is an apprehension of what is "whole" or "all together" (cf. οὐλομελές and ὁμοῦ πᾶν in B8, 4–5). What is, is full of being (ἔμπλεόν ἐστιν ἐόντος in B8, 24). In view of the references then to the "fullness" or "completeness" of Being, it is not surprising to find Parmenides maintaining that thought which has Being for its true goal, is itself fulfilled or realized. There may, in fact, be a connection between the πλέον ἐστὶ νόημα, of B16, 4 and the description of τὸ ἐόν in B8, 42 as being τετελεσμένον. For both πληρόω and τελέω have the sense of accomplishment or fulfillment, the former sometimes referring to the realization of what a man's θυμός desires, a psychological fulfillment (cf. πληρόω in Liddell and Scott). Taken in itself, of course, B16, 4b is an incomplete statement, but since Parmenides claims that there can be no thought without *that which is* (non-Being is unthinkable, e.g., B2, 7–8), "the full" must be existence or Being: genuine thought is full of *that which is*.

There is, moreover, little doubt that 4b further emphasizes or clarifies "the same thing" of verse 2. What is the "same thing" which the constitution or mind of all men thinks? The obvious answer is *that which is* or Being. All men, no matter how conceptually confused, think Being: "for you cannot recognize that which is not (that is impossible) nor could you express it," B2, 7–8. Likewise, the path of non-existence is "unthinkable and unnamable, for it is not a genuine way," B8, 17–18. This is the Parmenidean axiom, and any attempt to interpret B16 must consider this axiom.

Though it is dangerous to speculate in the absence of Parmenides' own words, the foregoing interpretation of B16 is not incompatible with the passage about the dead. According to Theophrastus' report on this, the dead man does not perceive light or warmth since the fire has left him. Recalling Aristotle's mistaken ordering of "hot" under Being, is it possible that the passage was originally an argument to the effect that the dead do not think at all? Theophrastus claims the dead perceive the cold, *that which is not*; this is impossible. The dead, then, have no minds and since νόος is absent from them, there can be no *krasis* of the limbs. One of the most obvious characteristics of the dead is the absence of coordinated bodily movement, or, for that matter, any movement at all. Possibly Parmenides, reflecting on this, concluded mind was absent from the dead.

But if B16 belonged to the Way of Truth, where was its original place in the poem? Loenen, who also believes that B16 is a fragment of the Way of Truth, places it after B3.[37] This seems to be correct, especially in view of Theophrastus' remark, "absolutely everything which is, has a certain kind of understanding." Moreover, both fragments contain the expression, τὸ αὐτό, and that this is a reference to *that which is* or τὸ ἐόν, is strongly suggested by B8, 29, ταὐτόν τ᾽ ἐν ταὐτῶι τε μένον καθ᾽ ἑαυτό τε κεῖται. As Loenen and Hölscher have indicated, "the same" (das Selbige) was probably used by Parmenides in B3 and B8, 29 to indicate an abstract concept as such.[38] Probably B16 also has some connection with B4:

λεῦσσε δ᾽ ὅμως ἀπεόντα νόωι παρεόντα βεβαίως
οὐ γὰρ ἀποτμήξει τὸ ἐὸν τοῦ ἐόντος ἔχεσθαι
οὔτε σκιδνάμενον πάντηι πάντως κατὰ κόσμον
οὔτε συνιστάμενον.

There are no convincing reasons for assigning this fragment to the Way of Opinion.[39] In B8, 25 Parmenides asserts ἐὸν γὰρ ἐόντι πελάζει (so in B4, 2 τὸ ἐὸν τοῦ ἐόντος ἔχεσθαι). Moreover, the whole point of B4 is to emphasize the unity of *that which is*; it cannot be affected by spatial or temporal distances, but is all one. Assuming then, that B4 belongs to the Way of Truth, what relationship exists between it and B16? As in B16 the limbs are given the epithet "much-wandering" (πολυ-πλάγκτων), so in B4

51

Parmenides speaks of a sundering and scattering of *that which is*. But he is quick to add that it is not possible to separate and scatter *that which is*; for "things absent" are present to the mind. In B16 the mind of man, which controls the *krasis* of the much-wandering limbs, always thinks the same thing. It is as if Parmenides meant that wherever men have wandered or strayed, they can only think one thing: *that which is*. The connection of ideas in B3, 4, and 16 appears then as follows: the nature of human thought is basically the same, no matter how different men's opinions may be. Moreover, it makes no difference where men find themselves: "As the mind of a man darts quickly, he who has travelled over far lands, and thinks in his heart, would I were here, or there . . ." so men can only think and speak about *that which is*.[40]

Two objections can be made against the previous interpretation of B16. First, if it is correct, is B16 not a fragment of a theory of knowledge? It appears as if Parmenides dealt with the relationship between knowledge (or thought) and Being. Second, does this interpretation not translate Being into terms of Becoming, i.e., the human body? Can the mortal frame, *qua* mortal, think Being?[41]

It is possible, of course, to regard B16 as part of a theory of knowledge provided that it is not assigned to the Way of Opinion. As such, it must belong to the Way of Truth. But more important, it is questionable whether a category such as theory of knowledge or epistemology can be applied to Parmenides' thought. There is, for example, no concern in the extant fragments with defining knowledge or with usual epistemological problems, e.g., the justification of claims to knowledge, the limits of knowledge, or the relationship between sense perception and the external world. It is not until Plato's *Theaetetus* that such problems are considered. Parmenides' primary concern seems to be metaphysical, that is, with the relationship between Being, language, and thought, and the implications of denying intelligibility to non-Being. Is it not, therefore, anachronistic or misleading to look for a theory of knowledge in the fragments of Parmenides' poem?

The second objection has been framed in the traditional antithesis between Being and Becoming, which cannot, however, be found in Parmenides' thought: Being is not the antithesis of Becoming, but of non-Being. The human body either exists or it does not exist, and for Parmenides there are no degrees of reality.[42] Accordingly body exists as much as mind. It either exists or it doesn't exist: ἔστιν ἢ οὐκ ἔστιν. Why cannot this mind, despite its bodily associations, think *that which is*? Parmenides' mind could and did even though it required divine aid.

In its entirety, B16 affirms a connection between mind and body, and a close relationship between mind and Being. There is no explicit evidence either in the fragment itself or in Aristotle's *Metaphysics* and Theophrastus'

De Sensibus that it came from the Way of Opinion. Moreover, if it is read without peripatetic presuppositions as to what is or is not implied in it, there are no convincing reasons for considering B16 part of a doctrine of sense perception or theory of knowledge. It simply follows from the initial axioms of Parmenides' goddess, and affirms her conviction that non-Being cannot be thought or expressed. All men, even those who try to follow the backward-turning path of Being and non-Being, think the same thing, viz., *that which is*.

NOTES

[1] According to Burnet, "this fragment of the theory of knowledge which was expounded in the second part of the poem of Parmenides must be taken in connection with what we are told by Theophrastus in the 'Fragment on Sensation.' " J. Burnet, *Early Greek Philosophy* (reprint, New York, 1957) p. 178, note 1. Many interpreters of Parmenides' poem follow Burnet in assigning B16 to the second part. See also W. K. C. Guthrie *A History of Greek Philosophy*, vol. 2 (Cambridge, 1965), p. 67; L. Tarán, *Parmenides* (Princeton, 1965), pp. 253–63; J. Mansfeld, *Die Offenbarung des Parmenides und die menschliche Welt* (Assen, 1964), p. 175 ff.; and U. Hölscher, *Anfängliches Fragen* (Göttingen, 1968), p. 112 f.

G. Vlastos, "Parmenides" Theory of Knowledge," *Transactions of the American Philological Association* 77 (1949): 66–77, argued that B16 is part of Parmenides' doctrine of sense perception, not of his theory of knowledge.

Finally, an interpretation of this fragment as Parmenides' views on sensing and knowing has been offered by H. Fränkel, "Parmenidesstudien," *Göttinger Nachrichten* (1930): 153–92, especially 170 and 174. See also H. Fränkel, *Wege und Formen frühgriechischen Denkens* (Munich, 1955): 173–79. In *Anfängliches Fragen*, Hölscher also maintains (p. 113) that Parmenides' teaching in B16 concerns ". . . Erkenntnis im allgemeinsten Sinne . . . . , ohne zwischen Wahrnehmung und Denken, zwischen Trug und Wahrheit zu unterscheiden."

[2] This thesis is not wholly new. It is proposed, for example, by J. H. M. Loenen in *Parmenides, Melissus, Gorgias* (Assen, 1959). He writes (p. 58): "As to the place of fr. 16 we can by no means be sure that this really formed part of the *doxa*. On the contrary, there are good reasons for holding that fr. 16 belonged to the first part." My reasons for assigning B16 to the first part are, however, different. Moreover, we do not agree concerning particular details or the interpretation of Parmenides' poem as a whole.

[3] The expressions "that which is," "Being," and "existence" are used interchangeably in this study without any attempt to give them a more precise meaning. "That which is" is a translation of the substantive participle τὸ ἐόν used occasionally in the fragments, e.g., B4, 2 and B8, 35. The most convincing interpretation of Parmenides' thought is that of G. E. L. Owen, "Eleatic Questions," *CQ* 54 (1960): 84–102. According to him, the subject of Parmenides' poem is "what can be talked or thought about" (pp. 94–95). I have accepted Owen's general interpretation for the purpose of this study.

[4] In "Well-rounded Truth and Circular Thought in Parmenides," *Phronesis* 3 (1958): 15–30, G. Jameson argues in favor of the reading εὐπειθέος ("persuasive"). His discussion strikes me as εὐπειθής.

[5] Tarán, *Parmenides*, p. 228. Tarán writes: "The arrangement as a whole is, most probably, Parmenides' own, but the details come from various sources."

[6] From the meanings of ἐοικότα which have been proposed by various scholars, see Mansfeld, *Offenbarung*, 146–47, and Tarán, *Parmenides*, p. 225.

[7] This interpretation of Parmenides' thought is supported by Montgomery Furth. See his "Elements of Eleatic Ontology," *Journal of the History of Philosophy* 6 (1968): 111–32. Tarán also convincingly maintains that ". . . Parmenides did not believe in degrees of error. . . .," *Parmenides*, p. 207. Hölscher's interesting interpretation of B8, 53–54:

μορφὰς γὰρ κατέθεντο δύο γνώμας ὀνομάζειν

τῶν μίαν οὐ χρεών ἐστιν—ἐν ὧι πεπλανημένοι εἰσίν—

and his translation of the first half of verse 54, τῶν μίαν οὐ χρεών ἐστιν as "zwei Formen, von denen nur eine einzige zu nennen unmöglich, oder unzulässig ist," does not prove that the Way of Opinion is partially true. Whatever the meaning of B8, 54 may be, it is clear that the opinions of mortals (and therefore the Way of Opinion) are false: they have decided to name two forms . . . in this they have gone astray (ἐν ὧι πεπλανημένοι εἰσίν). See Hölscher, *Anfängliches Fragen*, p. 103 ff., especially 107.

[8] Tarán, *Parmenides*, p. 227.

[9] Tarán, *Parmenides*, pp. 209, 253ff.

[10] For the text of Theophrastus' discussion, see G. M. Stratton, *Theophrastus and the Greek Physiological Psychology before Aristotle* (London, 1917, pp. 68–69. Or see H. Diels and W. Kranz, *Die Fragmente der Vorsokratiker*, 7th ed. (Berlin, 1954), p. 226 (A46).

[11] For example, Tarán and Guthrie. According to Tarán, "his [Theophrastus'] major mistake consists in attributing to Parmenides himself the doctrine that thought and perception are the same, as Aristotle had already done." Tarán, *Parmenides*, p. 262. See also Guthrie, *History*, vol. 2, p. 25.

[12] For the meaning of συμμετρία, see Stratton, *Theophrastus*, p. 157. Tarán appears to consider συμμετρία as Theophrastus' interpretation of Parmenides' τὸ πλέον. Tarán, *Parmenides*, p. 257. But this is not correct. Τὸ πλέον is interpreted by Theophrastus as ὑπερβάλλον.

[13] Readings not accepted by me have been placed in parentheses. Contrary to Mansfeld, *Offenbarung*, p. 176 and Tarán, *Parmenides*, p. 169, ἕκαστος and not ἑκάστοτε must be read. First, the word ἑκάστοτε is not known before Herodotus (Fränkel, "Parmenidesstudien," p. 172, note 1). Second, if ἑκάστοτε is accepted, κρᾶσιν (accusative) must be changed to κρᾶσις (nominative); otherwise there is no subject for B16, 1. Manfeld's proposal that the subject of ἔχει is the goddess (he reads ἑκάστοτε) is not convincing. For if this interpretation is accepted, ἔχει κρᾶσιν must be taken as being equivalent to κεράννυμι. Moreover, the parallels cited by Mansfeld are weak (for example, Semon. fr. 1, τέλος μὲν Ζεὺς ἔχει κτλ. is not relevant). See Mansfeld, *Offenbarung*, p. 179 ff., (especially 182–84). Third, ἕκαστος agrees quite well with πᾶσιν καὶ παντί in verse 4. Hölscher

has most recently argued in favor of ἑκάστοτε. He writes, *Anfängliches Fragen*, p. 113, "Das Zeitadverb ἑκάστοτε ist ebenso von der Überlieferung wie durch die parellelen Formulierungen desselben Gedankens, besonders bei Empedokles, geboten, und damit hängt wohl auch das Präsens παρίσταται zusammen." In support of this observation, he refers to *Od.* 18, 137, Archil. 68(D), and Empedocles B108. The verb παρίσταται is confirmed perhaps by Empedocles B108 and the other parallels, if they are parallels. But the adverb ἑκάστοτε appears neither in Empedocles B108 nor in the other passages cited by Hölscher. One can argue equally as well that the reading ἑκάστοτε is based on a mistaken interpretation of Empedocles B20 and B108. See Loenen, *Parmenides*, p. 54, note 106. Moreover, Hölscher does not explain how κρᾶσιν (accusative) can be the subject of ἔχει if the reading ἑκάστοτε is accepted.

Most interpreters accept Theophrastus' reading πολυπλάγκτων and not πολυκάμπτων. See Tarán, *Parmenides*, p. 170. παρίσταται instead of παρέστηκεν, seems to be an incorrect variant. For metrical reasons it cannot be accepted. But on the whole, Loenen's observation is correct:

> If the arguments based on the philosophical meaning of the fragment as a whole are left out of account for a moment, it may safely be said that no conclusive philological arguments can be given for the correctness of any one of these readings. No one will therefore dispute that the decision which of these readings is the correct one has to be based on the interpretation.

Loenen, *Parmenides*, p. 51.

[14] Mansfeld's objection to Loenen's discussion of the word is not completely accurate. He writes (*Offenbarung*, p. 190), "Loenen deutet, *ohne Anschluss an Fr. 9. 3 in Erwägung zu ziehen,* πλέον im Sinne von ἔμπλεον ἐόντος und nimmt dies in der Bedeutung des absoluten Seienden, *als ob Fr. 8. 24 die einzige Parallelstelle wäre*" (italics mine). But Loenen does mention B9, 3 specifically. See Loenen, *Parmenides,* p. 53: "Indeed, it is not at all probable that this word here means 'more,' considering that πλέον in fr. 9, 3 means 'full'. . . ." See especially note 100 on the same page.

[15] In fact, a contemporary interpreter of Parmenides drew this very conclusion from B3 (incorrectly, I think). See E. D. Philips, "Parmenides on Thought and Being," *Philosophical Review* 64 (1955):546–60.

[16] See J. B. McDiarmid, "Theophrastus on the Presocratic Causes," *Harvard Studies in Classical Philosophy* 61 (1953):85–156, especially 133. J. A. Philip, "Parmenides' Theory of Knowledge," *Phoenix* (1958):63–68, is not as cautious as McDiarmid. He writes (p. 63): "Theophrastus is quoting a fragment he found in the *Metaphysics* in the sense in which Aristotle quoted it; and Aristotle, even if he was quoting with the whole poem of Parmenides before him, chose a singularly obscure and inconclusive passage to illustrate his point."

[17] McDiarmid, "Theophrastus," p. 122.

[18] Mansfeld, *Offenbarung,* p. 177.

[19] Loenen also maintains that Theophrastus had a copy of the whole poem. He does not, however, give reasons for this view. Loenen, *Parmenides,* p. 55.

[20] See Vlastos, "Parmenides' Theory," p. 69.

[21] Stratton, *Theophrastus,* p. 60. Interestingly enough, Vlastos, who bases

much of his interpretation of B16 on Theophrastus, also admits that Theophrastus was not always correct. For example, statements such as ". . . Theophrastus himself was far from clear about the precise reference of this formula . . ." or ". . . on any interpretation this last remark is thick-headed . . ." do not suggest confidence in Theophrastus. Vlastos, "Parmenides' Theory," p. 71, note 38. Fränkel also seems to think (*Wege und Formen*, p. 176) that Theophrastus' interpretation is "willkürlich." There is a tendency to accept Theophrastus' remarks insofar as they support one's own interpretation; otherwise to reject them.

[22] The translation is that of H. G. Apostle. See his translation and commentary, *Aristotle's Metaphysics* (Bloomington, 1966), p. 22.

[23] Loenen, *Parmenides*, p. 57.

[24] For the meaning of μέλεα, see Guthrie, *History*, vol. 2, p. 67, Tarán, *Parmenides*, p. 170, and Mansfeld, *Offenbarung*, p. 189. Mansfeld writes: "Die Verwendung von μέλεα, in der Bedeutung 'Elemente' ist, dem älteren Sprachgebrauch gegenüber, offenbar ein Novum. Wir halten deshalb daran fest, dass μέλεα 'Glieder' in der Bedeutung 'Glieder des menschlichen Körpers' bedeutet."

[25] See, for example, H. Schwabl, "Sein und Doxa bei Parmenides," *Wiener Studien* 66 (1953):70.

[26] Tarán, *Parmenides*, pp. 170, 253 f.

[27] For further discussion, see Furth, *Journal of the History of Philosophy* 8, pp. 127–29. Tarán also believes that the principal error of the Way of Opinion is "difference." He writes concerning light and night: "Whether what mortals name are these two principles or any others, they are equally mistaken." Tarán, *Parmenides*, p. 225.

[28] See the discussion under "Meals" in O. Seyffert, *A Dictionary of Classical Antiquities* (reprint, New York, 1959):384.

[29] H. G. Liddell and R. Scott, *A Greek-English Lexicon*, ed. H. S. Jones (Oxford, 1961). See the entries under κρᾶσις. The verb κεράννυμι is also closely associated with the concept of harmony. See, for example, Plato's *Laws*, 835b. Under the verb κεράννυμι in H. Ebeling, *Lexicon Homericum* (photographic reproduction, Hildesheim, 1963), the following note is found (p. 763): "wenn μιγνύναι eine zufällige, natürliche Vermengung bez., mit dem Nebenbegr. der Unordnung, *conturbatio*, so ist κέρασθαι eine beabsichtigte, kunstmässige Mischung mit dem Nebenbegr. der Verbesserung, *temperatio*." J. A. Philip, "Parmenides' Theory", pp. 64–65, also interpreted the first verse of B16 as having something to do with harmony. But he found this meaning not in κρᾶσιν, but in μελέων. He translates the latter "musical members or harmonies" and cites *Phaedo* (68B). But such an interpretation seems especially speculative. The meaning of "harmony" or "union" must be found in *krasis*, and Philip's own reference suggests this.

[30] See Loenen, *Parmenides*, pp. 58–59, note 116.

[31] Loenen, *Parmenides*, p. 60.

[32] See Tarán, *Parmenides*, p. 256. He translates "for the same thing is that the φύσις μελέων thinks in each and in all men." For a survey of the interpretations given to verses 3–4, see Tarán, *Parmenides*, pp. 225–56. It must be noted that Tarán's and Hölscher's constructions of the sentence are similar. Hölscher initially argued in "Grammatisches zu Parmenides," *Hermes* 84 (1956):397, that the sentence simply means "Ebendas ist es, was die Beschaffenheit des Körpers denkt"

and "Erst so gelesen wird das Relativum als Akkusativ verstanden." See also Hölscher's discussion in *Anfängliches Fragen*, 115–16. In both works, Hölscher interprets τό as a demonstrative and translates B16, 2b–4 accordingly: "Denn dies ist es eben, was die Beschaffenheit . . . denkt . . .: das Überwiegende ist der Gedachte." In support of his opinion that τό is a demonstrative, he writes in *Anfängliches Fragen*, p. 116, note 58: "Demonstrativa mit Formen von αὐτός sehr häufig, z. B Platon *Polit.* 267c τοῦτο αὐτό ἐστιν ἤδη τὸ ζητηθέν." But his example does not prove that τό in B16, 2 is a demonstrative. It only shows that τοῦτο with αὐτό is a demonstrative. Tarán maintains, without further explanation, that τό is not a demonstrative. Tarán, *Parmenides*, p. 256, note 77. Loenen interprets the τό of B16, 4b as a demonstrative. He translates τὸ γὰρ πλέον ἐστὶ νόημα as "for that (τό) is full thought" and explains ". . . in fact, this τό refers back to the preceding sentence. . . . The τό of l.4 thus refers back to the object or content of thought (ὅπερ φρονέει) which is identical in all men (τὸ . . . αὐτό). . . ." Loenen, *Parmenides*, pp. 53–54. In homeric usage τό can have a demonstrative meaning, but there are also cases in which it is used like the Attic article (see, for example, R. Kühner and B. Gerth, *Ausführliche Grammatik der griechischen Sprache*, part 2, vol. 2 (photographic reproduction, Hannover, 1966), 575–98, esepcially 579. Usually the article is placed before forms of αὐτός. In any case it can be maintained that the meaning of τό in B16 does not depend wholly on grammatical considerations.

[33] W. A. Heidel, "Περὶ φύσεως. A Study of the Conception of Nature among the Pre-Socratics," *Proceedings of American Academy of Arts and Sciences* 45 (1910):110.

[34] G. S. Kirk, *Heraclitus, the Cosmic Fragments* (Cambridge, 1954), pp. 42–43, 228 ff. Kirk cites B16 of Parmenides' poem and explains that "what thinks is φύσις μελέων." Kirk, *Heraclitus*, p. 230.

[35] Loenen, *Parmenides*, p. 60, note 118.

[36] Both Mansfeld and Tarán translate τὸ πλέον "the full." See Mansfeld, *Offenbarung*, pp. 189–94 and Tarán, *Parmenides*, p. 258. Hölscher's translation of τὸ πλέον as "das (jeweils). Überwiegende" in "Grammatisches," p. 397 and *Anfängliches Fragen*, p. 116, is not convincing. First the adverb "jeweils" is not found in the Greek text (in "Grammatisches zu Parmenides" it is placed in brackets but not in the book) but belongs to Hölscher's interpretation. Secondly, that τὸ πλέον means "das Überwiegende" in Parmenides' poem appears doubtful in view of B8, 24 πᾶν δ' ἔμπλεόν ἐστιν ἐόντος and B9, 3 πᾶν πλέον ἐστὶν ὁμοῦ φάεος. In these verses it can only mean "full."

[37] Loenen, *Parmenides*, p. 58.

[38] See Hölscher, *Anfängliches Fragen*, p. 101 and Loenen, *Parmenides*, p. 59. Hölscher, however, offers a different interpretation of τὸ αὐτό in B16.

[39] Hölscher follows J. Bollack in assigning B4 to the Way of Opinion. *Anfängliches Fragen*, p. 124 ff.

[40] Hölscher and Fränkel quote these verses from *Il.* 15. 80 f. although for different reasons. See Hölscher, *Anfängliches Fragen*, p. 123.

[41] In order to make the objection, Vlastos' own words have been paraphrased. See Vlastos, "Parmenides' Theory," pp. 68, 71 ff.:

It would be wrong to jump to the conclusion that this preponderance provides also the physical formula for the knowledge of Being. No such formula could be given without translating Being into terms of Becoming. . . . The mortal frame, *qua* mortal, cannot think Being. Yet the "knowing man" can and does think it. . . . To resolve this paradox is impossible, for it is only the epistemological counterpart of the ontological dualism of Being and Becoming.

But Vlastos' own proposal, that every true judgment of Being has as its basis not only "more" light, but "all" light, seems, in fact, to be a translation of knowledge of Being into Becoming.

[42] There is no reason to think Parmenides would have denied the existence of the human body, and fallen into his own trap. If Owen's interpretation of the poem is accepted, it is clear that the body exists for I can both think and speak about it. See note 3.

ALEXANDER P. D. MOURELATOS

"Nothing" as "Not-Being": Some Literary Contexts That Bear on Plato

I T has often been noticed that Plato, and before him Parmenides, assimilates "what is not" (τὸ μὴ ὄν) to "nothing" (μηδέν or οὐδέν).[1] Given that the central use of "nothing" has important ties with the existential quantifier ("Nothing is here" = "It is not the case that there is anything here"), it has widely been assumed that contexts that document this assimilation also count as evidence that both within them and in cognate ontological contexts the relevant sense of "being" or "to be" is that of existence. That this assumption is not to be granted easily, has been compellingly argued by G. E. L. Owen.[2] His main concern was to show that the assumption is particularly mischievous in the interpretation of the *Sophist,* where he found it totally unwarranted. My own concern is to attack the assumption on a broader plane. "Nothing" in English has uses that do not depend on a tie with the existential quantifier. So too in Greek: *mēden* or *ouden* can be glossed as "what does not exist," but it can also be glossed as "not a something," or in Owen's formulation, "'what is not anything, what not-in-any-way is': a subject with all the being knocked out of it and so unindentifiable, no subject."[3] In effect, the assimilation of "what is not" to "nothing" may—in certain contexts—work in the opposite direction: not from "nothing" to "non-being" in the sense of non-existence; rather from "non-being" as negative specification or negative determination to "nothing" as the extreme of negativity or indeterminacy. To convey the sense involved in this reverse assimilation I borrow Owen's suggestive translation "not-being" for *mē on,* a rendering which makes use of an incomplete participle, rather than the complete gerund, of the verb "to be."

To make alternatives clear, I begin with an exploration of the relevant English uses. The semantic spectra of "nothing" and of the personal form

This paper was presented at the 1977 Atlanta meeting of the Society for Ancient Greek Philosophy and published in *Arktouros, Hellenic Studies Presented to Bernard M. W. Knox,* edited by G. W. Bowersock, Walter Burkert, and M. C. J. Putnam (Berlin and New York, 1979); we thank the editors and Walter de Gruyter for permission to reprint.
Alexander Mourelatos is Professor of Philosophy at The University of Texas at Austin.

"nobody" are, of course, wider than logic books might suggest. Only two uses concern us, and these can be quickly formulated if we take the expressions "nobody" and "nothing" as answers to two types of questions.

(a) 1. Who is in the house now?—Nobody.
    2. What is in the box?—Nothing.
(b) 1. Who is the gentleman over there?—Nobody.
    2. What is that shape over there?—Nothing.

The one-word answers in exchanges (a) are clearly equivalent to more perspicuous expanded paraphrases of the form "There is no K in L," where K can be replaced by an appropriate classifier or natural-kind expression and L can be replaced by a locative word or phrase. This is the use of "nobody" or "nothing" that is closest to the negative existential quantified expressions in formal logic, $\sim(\exists x)Fx$. For suggestive convenience, in spite of some infelicity—since (a)-type sentences are tensed, whereas the existential quantifier imports no time implications—I shall call (a) the "existential" use of "nobody" and "nothing."

It is not as easy to give a single perspicuous paraphrase of the one-word answers in type (b). The respondent may intend to dispute the interrogator's presupposition that there actually is something, let alone a gentleman or a shape, in the region referred to. In that case, the question receives in effect a type (a) answer. A distinct type (b) is defined in the case in which the respondent does not dispute the interrogator's existential presupposition. He says, roughly: "I notice who you are referring to, but he's nobody," or "I notice what you're referring to, but it's nothing." In that sort of case the respondent may be using the words "nobody" or "nothing" to convey the following message:

(i) The subject is "of no account": he or she or it lies outside the interlocutors' scope of interests, in whatever way and however broadly these interests are defined by the interlocutors' current endeavor.

Thus the snobbish respondent might say "He's nobody" with reference to someone of inferior status; or "It's nothing" may be the reassuring response of a doctor to a patient concerning certain physical changes in the patient's body they have both observed.

With the term "nothing," but in reference either to a thing or to a person, the respondent can also convey this message:

(ii) The subject is an extremely poor, worn out, or reduced specimen of the kind it prima facie appears to be.

The point is that the subject is extensively deprived of the normal character-istics of its kind, so it can "barely" or "hardly" be called, as for example in exchanges (a) and (b), a "gentleman" or a "shape." One can more aptly speak of what the subject "is not" rather than of what he, she, or it "is." In the limiting case, to borrow one of the definitions in *Webster's Third New International Dictionary,* the subject is "something that is characterized by utter absence of determination: perfect indistinguishableness." Let me refer to (b) in either of its two subtypes as the "characterizing" use of "nobody" or "nothing."

What underlies type (a), the existential use, is a conception of non-being as *emptiness:* I search the house and find that it is vacant; or I open the box and find that it is empty. What underlies type (b), the characterizing use, is a conception of non-being, or properly not-being, as (i) *lack of stand-ing* (almost in that juridical sense in which someone may have "no standing" in a particular court and case) or (ii) *privation* or *attenuation.* Just as the ex-istential use of "nobody" or "nothing" corresponds to the existential use of "to be," the characterizing uses correspond to copulative "to be." The person or thing deprecated as a "nobody" or a "nothing" is certainly no fictive or non-existent entity.

One might object at this point that there is no need to import a copula-tive construction in the analysis of the characterizing use. For may we not explain the use by leaning on the possible paraphrase, "the subject is treated *as though* he, she, or it did *not exist*"? The answer is that the paraphrase just given is really an elaboration, not an analysis, of the characterizing use. For it suppresses an important implication the characterizing use proclaims: the reason why the person or thing disparaged as "of no account" may be said not to exist is that he or she is a "no-body," or it is "not-a-thing": the subject *is not* identical with any particular person/thing we are prepared to deal with, nor classifiable under any of the kinds of persons/things that are of concern to us. Similarly to speak of a person or thing as a "nothing," in the sense that the subject is a very impoverished, enfeebled, or attenuated speci-men of its kind admittedly could be paraphrased by "might just as well not exist." But the paraphrase will not do as an analysis of the locution in the characterizing use. For the latter alludes to the rationale of the "just as well" version: the subject is no-thing, not-being in that it is "not-F_1," "not-F_2," "not-F_3," and so on, where the Fs stand for characteristics familiar to us, and which the subject normally ought to have.

The characterizing use of *mēden* and cognate negative terms, such as *ouden* and the personal forms *mēdeis, oudeis,* has been studied in detail by A. C. Moorhouse.[4] Let me review some of his major points and expand with my own comments on two of his most suggestive examples.

In Homer the characterizing sense[5] is served by the adjective of disparagement *outidanos,* "a no-somebody-fellow," a person "of no account, worthless, sorry, good for nothing." The Homeric indefinite pronoun *outis,* from which *outidanos* is derived, has only the existential sense of "nobody," never the characterizing sense.[6] The usual forms *oudeis* and *mēdeis* are also restricted to existential uses in Homer. But beginning in the Archaic period first *oudeis, ouden,* and then also *mēdeis, mēden,* expand their use by taking over the characterizing sense of Homer's *outidanos,* now in reference both to persons and to things.

A remarkable early example of the developing new use of *oudeis* is in the opening of Pindar's Sixth Nemean Ode:

> There is one race of men, one race (*genos*) of gods; both have breath of life from a single mother. But a power that has sundered itself through and through holds us divided (διείϱγει δὲ πᾶσα κεϰϱιμένα δύναμις), so that the one (scil. *genos,* 'race') is nothing (*ouden*), while for the other the brazen sky is established their sure citadel forever. Yet we have some likeness (*prospheromen*), either in great intelligence (*megan noon*) or in strength (*physin*), to the immortals, though we know not (*ouk eidotes*) what the day will bring, what course after nightfall destiny has written that we must run to the end.[7]

The race of men is certainly not a "nothing" in the sense of non-existence. It is a "nothing" in the sense of lacking many of the attributes the gods have, and exemplifying poorly or marginally those attributes that the two races possess in common. Pindar illustrates with reference to one such attribute: "Like the gods we have intelligence, and yet we do *not know.* . . ." It is relevant to note here that in another ode Pindar conveys this not-being of humanity using the very image and turn of phrase that Plato was to use in formulating a metaphysics of degrees of reality:

> ἐπάμεϱοι· τί δέ τις; τί δ᾽ οὔ τις; σϰιᾶς ὄναϱ ἄνθϱωπος.
> We are things of a day. What are we? What are we not? Man is the shadow of a dream. (*Pyth.* viii. 95–96)

The characterizing use, amply attested in other fifth-century authors, including Aeschylus and Aristophanes, becomes especially prominent in Sophocles and Euripides. Most instructive for our purposes is a passage from Sophocles, *Electra* 1163–67:

> Dearest one, how you have destroyed (ἀπώλεσας) me! Surely (δῆτα) you have destroyed me, beloved brother! So then receive me into this your shelter (ἐς τὸ σὸν τόδε στέγος), me who is nothing into that which is nothing (τὴν μηδὲν ἐς τὸ μηδέν), that I may dwell with you below from now on.

Electra is here addressing the urn she thinks contains the ashes of her dead

brother Orestes. A recent critic confesses bewilderment (I append translations of the lines he cites):

> Electra seems to assert in 969 that the dead are living ["you'll win the
> praise of piety from your dead father below"]; then she seems to deny it in
> 1166 ["nothing to nothing," quoted above] and 1170 ["dead men do not
> suffer pain"] . . . [t]he problem of the ontological status of ghosts in this
> play seems to me very obscure.[8]

I believe there is no such problem; the supposed obscurity and the critic's
bewilderment arise simply from a failure to appreciate a certain natural or
inevitable, but logically transparent, semantic complication, one that is inherent in discourse about the dead—in Greek or in English. The point is
worth a digression, for it has implications for an understanding of the concepts of "nothing" and "non-being" that go beyond the *Electra* passage.

What, in the event of a person's death, makes semantically possible the
locutions "he is no more," "he does not exist," "he is nothing (existential
sense)," and their respective counterparts in Greek, is the *absence* of that
person from the world of the living.[9] But if we should picture a world of the
dead, to which persons who are no longer alive recede, and where they take
permanent abode, denizens of that world can be said "not to exist" only by a
sort of semantic legerdemain: a linguistic transposition, a metonymy. For
that world is one of (existential) non-being not on that world's own terms
and from the perspective of its denizens, but on the terms of the living, and
in the perspective of the living. So the Underworld is the domain of "nothing" (existential) even though it has quite a large population, the members of
which, however shadowy in their texture and however reduced they be in
their powers, are involved in trials, in acts of expiation or purification, and
who relish or loathe, praise or censure, the acts of their survivors in the
world above.

This metonymy holds only with respect to the existential use of "non-
being" and "nothing." In the characterizing use there is uninterrupted continuity between the two worlds. Indeed it is the characterizing use that permits
us and even encourages us to picture the world of the dead as an extension
of the world of the living. The characterizing use mediates, in effect, the
metonymous and hyperbolic uses of "non-being" and "nothing." For while
there is no sense to the idea of degrees of *existence*[10] or degrees of *nothingness* (in the existential sense), there is no conceptual bar to thinking of degrees of "not-being" (not of "non-being") or of "nothing" in the characterizing sense. Thus it is possible for a living person to employ an effect of hyperbole by saying "I am dead already," "I do not exist," "I am
nothing" (existential) because without hyperbole and with no recourse to
metonymy he perceives himself as privatively or negatively characterized to
a degree that verges on what is appropriate for someone in the realm of the

dead. In a nutshell: the dead can call themselves "nothing" (existential) by metonymy; the living can call themselves "nothing" (existential) by hyperbole. But both the dead and the living can quite properly call themselves "nothing" in the characterizing sense; for in *that* sense it is simply a matter of more and less.

So now let us go back to the *Electra* passage. Critics, including Moorhouse, have failed to notice an important syntactic ambiguity. The expression *to mēden* may well be understood as "the nothing" or "nothingness," as a synonym of "extinction" or as an abstract name of the Underworld pictured as the domain of non-existence. Preserving parallelism of sense, the meaning of 1165–66 would then be: "receive me, the one who (already) does not exist (τὴν μηδέν) into (the realm of) non-existence (*to mēden*)," a strongly emotional utterance in which the hyperbolic and metonymous uses of "nothing" are juxtaposed.

But there is also another way of understanding *to mēden*, by construing the neuter article *to* not as introducing an abstract noun but simply as referring to the neuter noun that occurs in the preceding line, *to stegos*, "the shelter," Electra's metaphor for the funerary urn. That construction is ready to hand, as is clear from the parallelism ". . . me . . . to this shelter here; . . . the one who is nothing to this (urn) that is nothing." Both Electra and Orestes, the latter as embodied by the ashes contained within the urn, as well as by the urn itself as container, are a "nothing" in the characterizing sense. The supposed nothingness of Orestes is obvious: he does not speak, he does not move, he cannot come to Electra's help—and so on and so forth with the many "not-*F*"s implied in Orestes' utterly deprived state. It is precisely in that sense that Electra, at the beginning of this scene (1129), calls Orestes—again identified with the ashes in the urn—a "nothing": "Now I hold you in my hands as a nothing (οὐδὲν ὄντα)."[11] In fact, Sophocles does not leave us to imagine Orestes' "not-*F*"s; as though to confirm the sense of "nothing" in line 1129 and prepare us for the second half of the "nothing to nothing" of line 1166, he has Electra recite a whole string of Orestes' deprivations beginning at line 1136:

> Out of (ἐκτός) your home, an exile on alien (ἄλλης) soil, you died wretchedly (κακῶς ἀπώλου), without your sister near (δίχα); nor (κοὔτε) did I wash you . . . nor (οὔτε) did I get to pick you up off the blazing pyre . . . but tended by the hands of strangers you have come back a diminutive mass (σμικρὸς ὄγκος) in a diminutive receptacle (σμικρῷ ἐν κύτει) . . . [your] nurture unavailing (ἀνωφελήτου). (1136–45)

The nothingness of the urn itself is not simply its diminutive size; the urn is hardly a "shelter" (as it is called at 1165); the oxymoron figure, "a shelter that is not a shelter," is here very close to the surface.[12]

In this same speech Electra gradually identifies her own fate with that of Orestes. At one point the rhetoric goes even beyond identification, picturing the dead Orestes not merely as the one totally deprived but as one who is actively depriving Electra "of everything," "like a storm" (1150–51). So we are already inclined to think of Electra as a "nothing" in the characterizing sense before we finally hear her climactic hyperbole, "I am dead" (1152, cf. 1164). Even before this scene Sophocles has spelled out Electra's privative nothingness: from the first scenes the play has been studded with Electra's remarks of self-pity, in which she characterizes her predicament by using negative phrases and privative *a-* or *apo-* compounds.[13]

To attempt to determine whether at 1166 it is the existential or the characterizing sense of *mēden* that constitutes the primary semantic layer would seem gratuitous. In Electra's speech of desolation a line that packs together the characterizing, the hyperbolic (with respect to Electra), and the metonymous (with respect to the Underworld) use of "nothing" is just what we would expect from the pen of a tragic poet.

The evidence alluded to and discussed so far is certainly adequate to establish that the characterizing use of *mēden/ouden* and *mēdeis/oudeis* is at least as viable and familiar in classical Greek as the corresponding uses of "nothing" and "nobody" are in English. But an even stronger conclusion is warranted. Doubtless, in terms of frequency, this use cannot fail but appear minor compared to the existential use. But this comparison belies the importance of the characterizing use in the development of Greek concepts. In non-philosophical sources the use is documented in contexts of major dramatic or rhetorical impact. So its literary conspicuousness is high. Given this conspicuousness, we should hardly presume—as has generally been the case—that when "nothing" becomes thematic for a philosophical author focus will necessarily be on the existential sense. A good case can be made, I believe, for the thesis that even in Parmenides *mēden,* where it appears in significant contrast to *eon,* has characterizing sense.[14]

With reference to Plato the characterizing use of *mēden/ouden* must have played a significant role in the development of the doctrine of degrees of reality. The latter, as Vlastos has shown, cannot be coherently understood as a doctrine of degrees of existence, but as one that involves the characterizing F-ness and non-F-ness of sensible particulars.[15] The connection with our theme ought to be obvious: the negative pole in a doctrine of degrees of reality corresponds to the characterizing sense of "nothing," not-F_1 and not-F_2 and . . . not-F_n. If there are to be degrees of reality, there must be degrees of *un*reality; the characterizing use both allows this and projects the relevant extreme.

The connection can be rendered more faithfully and its significance better appreciated if we remind ourselves of other respects in which Plato's doctrine draws on the resources of ordinary speech and on the literary tradition. Plato himself called our attention to one such respect. In *Republic* 479B the notion that there are "ambivalent" or "equivocal" (cf. ἐπαμφοτερίζουσιν) entities is introduced through humorous allusion to the folk riddle:

> A man who was not a man (a eunuch), saw (looked at) but did not see (recognize) a bird that was not a bird (a bat) perched on a tree that was not a tree (a rafter or beam), hit it (hit at it) and did not hit it (actually hit it) with a stone that was not a stone (a draughtboard piece).[16]

Obviously related to this type of folk riddle is one of the most striking forms of the oxymoron figure in Greek literature: "an *F*-person (or thing) that is not an *F*-person (or thing)." A good example can be drawn from that same scene of Sophocles' Electra discussed above: μήτηρ ἀμήτωρ, "unmotherly mother," or "mother hardly a mother" (1154).[17] As in the example cited, this type of oxymoron involves juxtaposition of a noun against a compound consisting of the same noun prefixed by α-negative. A quite distinct, yet significantly related figure, is that of alliteration through α-negative compounds. Here too we have a good example from Sophocles' *Electra*, though not from the same scene discussed earlier: ἄτεκνος . . . ἀνύμφευτος . . . ἀνήνυτον οἶτον ἔχουσα κακῶν, "child*less* . . . *un*married . . . suffering an *un*ending doom of ills" (164–67).[18] An impure variant of this device produces the same effect of pathos through accumulation of α-negative compounds, negative predications, *apo-* compounds and similar expressions. We saw such a figure in the description of the supposed ashes of Orestes.[19] Both α-negative alliteration and its impure variant of accumulating negatives are among the most favored devices of Greek authors, from Homer through the dramatists, the orators, and beyond. What is more, predilection for these devices reflects tendencies characteristic of the Greek language itself. For Greek not only has a richer variety of morphological variants of the negative prefix than any other Indo-European language,[20] it also is by far more productive of negative compounds than the two other ancient languages for which we have a comparable body of literature, Sanskrit and Latin.[21] The conception of a person, thing, action, or event that is characterized in negative terms through and through is no invention of philosophical ontologists; it is one of the commonplaces of Greek literature.

It is thus no idle historical exercise to point out antecedents or prototypes in literature and in forms of speech for Plato's doctrine of degrees of reality. Sources for the intermediate degree lie not only in the type of folk riddle Plato alluded to; they also lie in the oxymoron of the type μήτηρ ἀμήτωρ. Correspondingly, the Platonic μηδαμῇ ὄν, "in no way being," or πάντως μὴ ὄν, "altogether not being," that is equated to *mēden*, "noth-ing," is prefigured and made familiar in the characterizing use of *mēden/mēdeis* etc., especially by the great tragedians, in the figure of α-negative alliteration, and in the figure of accumulating negatives. All of these devices facilitate, reinforce, and promote one another. So it is properly the whole complex that constitutes an important pre-philosophical back-ground for the Platonic doctrine of degrees of reality.

Observations made in this paper can be read as providing support, in yet a different way, for a thesis advanced by Charles H. Kahn[22] and others. In a formulation I prefer, the thesis is that the dialectic of Being in classical Greek speculation focuses not on "What there *is*" but on "*What* it is" or "*How* it is"; not on existence but on *physis*, constitution, or form.[23]

NOTES

[1] See Parmenides B 6.2, cf. B 7.1, B 8.7–13, B 9.4; Plato *Rep.* 478 B 12–C 1, *Tht.* 189 A 10, *Soph.* 237 C7–E 2. Cf. G. E. L. Owen, "Plato on Not-Being," in *Plato, I, Metaphysics and Epistemology*, ed. G. Vlastos (Garden City, N.Y., 1971), pp. 225–27.

[2] Owen, "Plato on Not-Being," pp. 241–48 and passim. For use of this as-sumption in interpreting Parmenides, see D. J. Furley, "Notes on Parmenides," in *Exegesis and Argument: Studies in Greek Philosophy Presented to Gregory Vlastos, Phronesis*, suppl. vol. 1 (Assen and New York, 1973):12.

[3] Owen, "Plato on Not-Being," p. 247.

[4] "A Use of οὐδείς and μηδείς," *Class. Quart.*, n.s. 15 (1965):31–40.

[5] This is my terminology, not Moorhouses's.

[6] It is fascinating to notice how deftly Homer exploits the semantic distinctness of *outis* and *outidanos* in the episode of the blinding of Polyphemus, the Cyclops, in *Od.* 9.364ff. The Cyclops naively believes that Odysseus' name is *Outis*. So his screams, when Odysseus is blinding him, bring no help from the other cyclopes. For they assume he is complaining of a natural illness, hearing him, as they do, cry: "No one (*outis*) is killing me" (9.403–414). Homer's finishing touch to this dramatic pun is at 460. The powerful monster, now reduced to ineffectual groping, yet still confi-dent he will capture Odysseus and take revenge, speaks to his favorite sheep about the ills wrought on him by that "οὐτιδανὸς Οὖτις." In putting the two words to-gether has Polyphemus now finally understood the fateful ambiguity of the sound "*outis*"? Or does he now understand *Outis*—wrongly—merely as a variant of *outidanos*? Or had he foolishly lulled himself from the start with the belief that Odys-seus had called himself *Outis* (= *outidanos*) in abject humility and self-de-precation? Homer leaves us to wonder. In the end, Polyphemus' favorite animal car-ries Odysseus safely out of the cave and beyond the Cyclopes' reach. The crucial point, however, is clear: Odysseus not only is not, as Polyphemus' fellow Cyclopes thought, "no one," he also is not, as Polyphemus himself—at one time or another—thought, "a man of no account."

⁷ R. Lattimore, trans, *The Odes of Pindar* (Chicago, 1947), p. 111, with my own fuller translation of line 2.

⁸ W. Sale, *Electra, by Sophocles: A Translation with Commentary* (Englewood Cliffs, N.J., 1973), pp. 139 and 834.

⁹ There is, of course, a "vital" use or nuance of "to be," "to exist," and correspondingly of *einai*. But the fact that the paraphrases or translations "to live" or "to be alive" and "to die" or "to be dead" are available for positive and negative predications, respectively, in this type of use does not warrant saying that "to be," "to exist" or *einai* in such cases simply *means* "to live" or "to be alive." At the vary least, the vital use of these verbs carries greater rhetorical force, greater pathos, than corresponding use of the predicates "lives" or "dies." This is especially clear in literary examples that might otherwise be taken as pleonastic: ἤ που ζώει τε καὶ ἔστιν (Homer *Od.* 24.262); ζώντων καὶ ὄντων 'Αθηναίων (Demonsthenes 18. 72); ὄλωλεν οὐδ' ἔτ' ἔστι Τροία (Euripides *Troad.* 1292). See J. Klowski, "Zum Entstehen der Begriffe Sein und Nichts und der Weltentstehungs- und Weltschöpfungstheorien im strengen Sinne" (I. Teil), *AGP* 49 (1967):139; C. H. Kahn, *The Verb 'Be' in Ancient Greek,* Foundations of Language, suppl. ser., 16 (Dordrecht and Boston, 1973): 240–45, 378–79.

¹⁰ Cf. G. Vlastos, "Degrees of Reality in Plato," in *New Essays on Plato and Aristotle,* ed. Renford Bambrough (London, 1965), pp. 8–9.

¹¹ The characterizing sense for *ouden* here is guaranteed by the immediate context: "I did not receive you back in the form in which (*hōsper*) I sent you off" (1128); "I sent you off resplendent (λαμπρὸν ἐξέπεμψα)" (1130).

¹² See below, at n. 17.

¹³ See 164–67 ἄτεκνος . . . ἀνύμφευτος . . . ἀνήνυτον οἶτον ἔχουσα κακῶν. 186–92 βίοτος (scil. Electra's) ἀνέλπιστος, οὐδ' ἔτ' ἀρκῶ· ἄτις ἄνευ τεκέων . . . ἇς φίλος οὔτις ἀνὴρ ὑπερίσταται . . . ἀναξία . . . ἀεικεῖ σὺν στολᾷ, κεναῖς (cf. *"not* full") δ' ἀμφίσταμαι τραπέζαις. 230–32 τάδε γὰρ [Electra's woes] ἄλυτα κεκλήσεται· οὐδέ ποτ' ἐκ καμάτων ἀποπαύσομαι ἀνάριθμος ὧδε θρήνων. 813–22 ἀπεστερημένη . . . ἄφιλος . . . (in Electra's life) οὐδεὶς πόθος. Cf. Orestes' remarks: σῶμ' ἀτίμως κάθέως ἐφθαρμένον (1181); φεῦ τῆς ἀνύμφου δυσμόρου τε σῆς τροφῆς (1183).

¹⁴ See "Determinacy and Indeterminacy, Being and Non-Being in the Fragments of Parmenides," in R. A. Shiner and J. King Farlow, *New Essays on Plato and the Pre-Socratics, Canadian Journal of Philosophy,* suppl. vol. 2 (Guelph, Ontario, 1976):45–60.

¹⁵ Vlastos, "Degrees of Reality in Plato," pp. 10–11.

¹⁶ See J. Adam, *The* Republic *of Plato,* edited with Critical Notes, Commentary and Appendices, 2nd ed., 2 vols. (Cambridge, 1963); vol. 1, pp. 342–43 *ad loc.* I have altered slightly the usual interpretation.

¹⁷ For a discussion of the figure, see H. A. Hamilton, *The Negative Compounds in Greek* (Baltimore, 1899), pp. 48–49; cf. A. C. Moorhouse, *Studies in the Greek Negatives* (Cardiff, 1959), pp. 66–68.

¹⁸ Other examples: Homer *Il.* 9.63–64 ἀφρήτωρ ἀθέμιστος ἀνέστιός ἐστιν ἐκεῖνος / ὃς πολέμου ἔραται, Soph, *Ant.* 876 ἄκλαυτος, ἄφιλος,

ἀνυμέναιος ἔρχομαι τὰν πυμάταν ὁδόν. Cf. above, n. 13, and Hamilton, *The Negative Compounds*, pp. 44–45.

[19] Above, at n. 11–12. Cf. description of Electra's predicament, n. 13.

[20] Moorhouse, *Studies*, p. 47.

[21] Hamilton, *The Negative Compound*, p. 58.

[22] See "Why Existence Does Not Emerge as a Distinct Concept in Greek Philosophy," *Arch. f. Gesch. d. Philos.* 58 (1976):323–34; cf. Kahn, *Verb 'Be,'* pp. 394–419.

[23] I thank Friedrich Solmsen and Michael Gagarin for criticism of an early draft of this paper. I have also profited from discussions of the paper at the Society for Ancient Greek Philosophy 1977 meeting at Atlanta, and at classics seminars at The University of Auckland and The University of Sydney.

DAVID J. FURLEY

Anaxagoras in Response to Parmenides

Introduction

66 **W** hat reason is there to suppose that those who did know Parmenides'
poem necessarily thought that he had raised a real problem which
they must try to deal with? Empedocles, perhaps also Anaxagoras, knew
the poem, but they pursue a very different kind of philosophy from Zeno
and Melissus: why, then, must we suppose that they are seeking an alternative answer to the problem posed by Parmenides, and that their ultimate
material elements are to be seen as modifications of the Eleatic ἓν
ἐόν?"

These rhetorical questions, taken from M. L. West's recent book, *Early
Greek Philosophy and the Orient,*[1] make a useful starting point for this inquiry. They are, of course, what the grammar books call "repudiating questions": the answer hoped for is "no reason." The argument with which Mr.
West goes on to support his negative implication is not likely to convince
many students of the Presocratics. He determinedly makes light of Parmenides' chains of argument, apparently on the ground that "these were not the
actual stages of Parmenides' thinking"—as if Parmenides ought to have
been writing his intellectual autobiography instead of a philosophical argument. Misunderstanding Parmenides, he makes it harder for himself to understand the post-Parmenideans. No long discussion, therefore, is needed
just to defend the conventional account of this stretch of history against Mr.
West.

Although the conventional views which Mr. West attacks[2] seem to me
to be right on the whole, nevertheless it is worth pressing some questions
about the nature of the pluralists' response to Parmenides. Which of Parmenides' positions did they accept and which did they reject? Do their surviving fragments show that they argued against the rejected positions, or that

This paper was presented at the 1975 Washington meeting of the Society for Ancient
Greek Philosophy and published in the *Canadian Journal of Philosophy*, supplementary volume
II (1976):61–85; we thank the editors for permission to reprint.

David Furley is Charles Ewing Professor of Greek Language and Literature at Princeton
University.

they merely ignored Parmenides' arguments? Did Anaxagoras and Empedocles take the same course in this respect or did they differ? If so, how, and why? This paper is a result of taking another look at Anaxagoras and Empedocles with these questions in mind. Its conclusion is that Anaxagoras, like Empedocles, certainly thought that Parmenides had raised a real problem which he must try to deal with, but that his method of dealing with it was perhaps more radically different from that of Empedocles than is usually supposed.[3] Not all of these questions can be dealt with here; the focus of the present essay is Anaxagoras.

Simplicius says: "In the first book of his *Physics,* Anaxagoras plainly declares that coming-to-be and perishing are coming together and separating. This is what he writes: 'Coming-to-be (*ginesthai*) and perishing (*apollysthai*) are customarily believed in incorrectly by the Greeks, since nothing comes-to-be or perishes, but rather it is mingled together out of the things that are, and is separated again. Thus they would be correct to call coming-to-be "being mingled together (*symmisgesthai*)" and perishing "being separated (*diakrinesthai*)."' "[4]

A very similar statement is preserved among the fragments of Empedocles:

> When they [*sc.* the four roots—earth, water, air and fire] are mingled together to form a man. . . . then men speak of coming-to-be, and when they are separated, then they speak of ill-fated death. They are right to call them so, and I follow the custom in so speaking.[5]

The text of this fragment is very uncertain; but editors are in general agreement about the sense of the quoted portion, except for the last line. As the manuscripts have it, it is metrically deficient; and one way of remedying this is to put in a negative, thus making Empedocles say the same as Anaxagoras: ordinary men are *not* right to speak of coming-to-be and perishing.

Did they say the same thing or not? It is impossible to be sure, but it is striking that in the preserved fragments of Anaxagoras there are no occurrences of these censured terms, whereas Empedocles has no scruple in using them.[6] It seems likely, therefore, that Empedocles held it to be *right* to speak of coming-to-be and perishing, even though they are to be *explained* as "mingling together" and "separating." The argument of this paper does not at all hang on the interpretation of this line, but it turns out that there is some aptness about this result.

Other fragments confirm that Empedocles wants to approach the concepts of coming-to-be and perishing with much caution:

> Something else I will tell you: there is growth (*physis*)
> of *no one*
> of all mortal things, nor end in baneful death;

but only mingling, and separation of things mingled,
is the case; and "growth" is men's name for these. (B8)

Childish fools—they have no deep-minded thoughts—
who claim that there is a
   coming-to-be of what formerly was not,
or that something dies and perishes utterly. (B11)

From what in no way *is,* no coming-to-be is possible
and that what *is* should perish is unmanageable, unheard of;
it will always be *there*—wherever you may shove it! (B12)

What caused such suspicion of the concepts of coming-to-be and perishing? The only argument against them surviving from an earlier time is that of Parmenides B 8.1–21, which reaches the conclusion: "Hence coming-to-be (*genesis*) is extinguished, and perishing (*olethros*) is unintelligible." There is no trace in the fragments of Anaxagoras and Empedocles of an original argument to this effect. But there is confirmation that it was a conceptual difficulty about coming-to-be *out of what is not* that persuaded all three of them. About Parmenides, there can be no doubt.[7] Anaxagoras B 3 makes the same sharp contrast between what *is* and what *is not*; Empedocles B 11 and 12 appear to be manipulating the same point.

But what are the two of them making of this point?

One of the fragments of Anaxagoras, on which most interpretations are built, is B 10, from a scholium to the text of Gregory of Nazianzus: "How, he says, could hair come-to-be out of not hair, and flesh out of not flesh?" Another "repudiating question": he means that it could not. But if this is rightly taken to be a key to his thought, it surely means that he was taking the Parmenidean conclusion, "nothing comes-to-be out of what is not," in a very strong sense—"nothing comes-to-be out of what *it* is not."

We can see the point simply enough when we compare Anaxagoras with Empedocles on the growth of bones. Empedocles says:

Earth, glad to do it, in its broad-breasted melting-pots
received two parts of bright Nestis [*sc.* water] out of eight,
and four of Hephaistus [*sc.* fire]; and they *came-to-be*
   white bones,
marvellously fitted together by the adhesives of Harmonia. (B 96)

Anaxagoras' view as reported by Lucretius is in line with the question about hair and flesh just quoted: "Bones are born from diminutive, tiny *bones* . . ." (I 835–36). Empedocles accounted for the growth of bone by maintaining that it comes-to-be out of certain quantities of the four elements. There is no coming-to-be in an absolute sense—out of nothing, or out of what in no way is—because the portions of these elements that make up our bone have always been what they are. Anaxagoras, much more rigorous, said that bone does not come-to-be at all: what is now bone has always been *bone*; all change is a matter of redistribution.

We must now explore the lengths to which he carried this idea.

A Difficulty in the Conventional Account of Anaxagoras

That there is a big difference between Anaxagoras and Empedocles has of course been a commonplace of history since the time of Aristotle. "There is a clear opposition between the followers of Anaxagoras and those of Empedocles: Empedocles says that earth, water, air, and fire are four elements and are *simple*, rather than flesh, bone, and similar homoiomerous bodies; the Anaxagoreans say that these [*sc.* the homoiomerous bodies like flesh and bone] are simple, and are elements. . . ."[8] The conventional account of the difference between them is quantitative: Empedocles held that the elements are four, Anaxagoras that they are very numerous—flesh, bone, blood, hair, skin, etc., perhaps bark, leaf, etc., and iron, stone, silver. . . . For Anaxagoras, as Guthrie puts it, "all the infinite number of natural substances . . . must be equally real."[9] Or as Vlastos puts it: "No Ionian had ever said that earth had been 'in' the original matrix. Empedocles had said just that, precisely because he had endowed earth with Parmenidean being. Anaxagoras takes a long step *in the same direction* [my italics]. He holds that earth, air, aether, as well as hair, flesh, and every other substance are 'in' the primitive mixture, for they all have Parmenidean being."[10] Or Cherniss: "To Empedocles, . . . [Anaxagoras] objected that there is no reason for singling out earth, air, fire and water as the only bodies of which the Eleatic law of identity need be asserted. Hair and flesh have characteristics of their own and, if nothing comes into being, hair and flesh must preserve their identity eternally. To paraphrase Anaxagoras' objection, he saw that Empedocles was coming perilously close to a derivation of new characteristics from quantitative differences, and this to his mind was inadmissible on the basis of Eleatic logic."[11]

Thus Empedocles erred in thinking he could comply with Eleatic logic, as set out in Parmenides B 8, by positing four "beings" which are eternally, uninterruptedly, unchangeably and perfectly what they are. Anaxagoras proposed to correct the error by claiming that not just four but *all* the "natural substances" satisfy this description.

But there is a major defect in this hypothesis which appears to have gone unnoticed in the literature. The expression "all the natural substances" has an all-embracing look; but in fact it is being used in a highly selective sense, in which blood, bone, leaf, and silver are natural substances, but men, horses, and trees are not. *Empedocles'* physical theory was certainly concerned with explaining the birth and death of *organisms*—"bushes, and water-housed fishes, and mountain-laired beasts, and wing-borne sea-birds."[12] How are we to suppose that Anaxagoras thought he had done better than Empedocles? In Empedocles' theory, given quantities of earth, water, air, and fire come-to-be a "water-housed fish." In the strict sense, nothing comes-to-be, because the earth, water, air, and fire in the fish remain what they are. But we may say that the fish comes-to-be, so long as we remember the correct analysis. We are asked to suppose that Anaxagoras criticized this theory on the ground that new characters have emerged, in the skin, bones, and flesh of the fish, that *were not* in the four elements. He proposed to correct this by giving eternal being to the skin, bone, and flesh. But what can he say about the *fish*?[13] Presumably he must say just what Empedocles would say about the skin, bones, and flesh—that they do not strictly come-to-be, since they are reducible to given quantities of eternal elements. Unless we can find a reason why Anaxagoras should be content to allow *organisms* to lack "Parmenidean being," while at the same time carefully elevating their *tissues* to that status, he appears merely to have postponed his problem, not to have solved it.

Nutrition and the Homoiomerous Bodies

No one doubts that Anaxagoras did make the tissues such as bone, hair, or flesh into "elementary" substances in some sense; so it may be useful to look carefully at the role played by this proposition in his physical theory.

There is no mention of any of the tissues in those fragments of Anaxagoras that are usually claimed as his own words (the B fragments in Diels-Kranz), except in the sentence (B 10, quoted on p. 72) taken from the scholium to Gregory.[14] This in itself is striking enough: it suggests that Simplicius, the main source for our fragments, although he knew that Anaxagoras was said to have made elements of the tissues, could not find verbatim evidence to illustrate it. Perhaps the emphasis on the tissues—an emphasis that goes back as far as Aristotle—is overdone.

In fact, this emphasis is mainly due to the contrast which was drawn by Aristotle, as we have seen, between Empedocles and Anaxagoras. He looks at their theories through the frame of his own four-tiered analysis of physical bodies. At the base are the four "simple bodies," earth, water, air, and fire, which happen to be the same as the four Empedoclean "Roots"; they are "simple" in that they are not correctly described as being "made of" anything else as components. Next come what Aristotle calls "the homoiomerous bodies" (so I translate the neuter plural adjective—τὰ ὁμοιομερῆ), which are made of the simple bodies as components, although they have characters of their own that are not in the components. They are called "homoiomerous"—"made of like parts"—to distinguish them from the third tier, parts such as a face or a hand. Artistotle explains the meaning of his term "the homoiomerous bodies" in one of the passages in which he talks about Anaxagoras (*GC* I 1, 314 a 17): "He makes the homoiomerous bodies elements—I mean bone, flesh, marrow, and those others whose parts *have the same name as the whole.*" A part of bone is still called "bone," but a part of a face is not called "face." (We must remember this criterion because in some of the secondary evidence about Anaxagoras a different criterion is used.[15]) The fourth tier, to complete the list, is of course the whole organic compound, such as a bird or a bush or a man.

The point that Aristotle makes is simply that Empedocles agrees with him in distinguishing the first two tiers, whereas Anaxagoras puts the homoiomerous bodies into the first tier, making them into noncomposite bodies, and at the same time, so Aristotle claims, denies the status of simple, elementary bodies to earth, water, air, and fire.[16]

It is easy enough to understand, in the case of Empedocles, how his "elements" were supposed to function in a theory of perceptible change. Just as the painter mixes together four colours and produces with them the forms of "trees, men, women, beasts, birds, and water-nurtured fish," so earth, water, air, and fire are mixed together to produce the "mortal things" of the visible world (B 23). The compounds are mortal, but the elements are immortal: they remain through the birth, life, and death of the mortal things that are made of them.

We must now discuss the question, how Anaxagoras, having made the homoiomerous tissues into "elements," put them to use in his theory of change.[17]

Nothing comes-to-be from what it is not.[18] If something new appears, it has merely been "separated out" from an environment that formerly concealed it; if it grows, it is by the addition of similar material that likewise was formerly concealed.[19] The key concepts are what we may call the Principle of Latency, borrowing the term from a phrase Lucretius used in describing Anaxagoras' theory (*quaedam latitandi copia*), and the Principle of Predominance.[20] The whole cosmos, and every part of the cosmos, however small, is a mixture; there is no region of the cosmos where *any* identifiable substance is isolated—indeed (the strongest possible assertion) there is no region of the cosmos from which any substance is *absent*: "everything has a share of everything."[21] But different regions of the cosmos, at least in its present state, differ from each other in the proportions of their ingredients, and only the predominant ingredients are perceptible.[22]

There is good evidence that these ideas were applied to the explanation of nutrition and growth. Here is part of the report of Aëtius, probably reproducing in the main what was written by Theophrastus:

[Anaxagoras] thought it was quite unintelligible how a thing could come into being out of what it is not or perish into what it is not.[23] Now, we take food that is simple and of one form—bread, water—and out of it grow hair, vein, artery, flesh, nerves, bone, etc. Since that is what happens, we have to agree that in the food we take are all the things that there are, and everything grows from things that are. In that food there are parts productive of blood, nerves, bones, etc.[24]—theoretical parts, because we must not refer everything to sense perception, just saying that bread and water produce these things, but there are in them parts that are to be distinguished in theory.[25]

The same text of Aëtius continues with a statement that has caused much trouble: "So, from the fact that in the food the parts (*merê*) are like (*homoia*) the substances generated, he called them "homoiomeries" (feminine plural noun, *homoiomereiai*) and declared that they are the principles of the things that *are*."

The term "homoiomeries" here apparently means the parts, latent in a substance, which may go to build up an apparently different substance—for example, the parts of *hair* in a piece of *meat* which nourish the *hair* of the eater.[26] Lucretius uses the same word "homoiomery" in a slightly different way, to refer to the abstract principle according to which a substance is produced by the addition of like parts.[27]

It has long ago, and often, been pointed out that the fragments of Anaxagoras contain no instance of the word *homoiomerê* or its relatives, that the concept is explained in Plato's *Protagoras* 329 d–e in a way that suggests that it is new there, and that although Aristotle uses the adjective *homoiomeres* as a technical term in his own philosophy, as we have said, the abstract noun *homoiomereia* first occurs in Epicurus. I am convinced[28] that it was Aristotle's statement, often repeated, that Anaxagoras made "the homoiomerous bodies" (in Aristotle's sense) into elements that gave rise to the widespread but mistaken later tradition that Anaxagoras himself used the term *homoiomerê* or *homoiomereia* for his elements, thus claiming that a thing is an element if and only if it is homoiomerous, in some sense. Since this position is already well set out in the literature, there is no point in defending it again here; but it may be useful to pause to ask whether there is any sense in which Anaxagoras *could* have accepted a "principle of homoiomereity" into his physical theory.

A recent article attributes this thesis to Anaxagoras: "Things are made of parts which are like one another and are also like the whole. These parts are the elements out of which all things are made, and are what Aristotle

76

calls *homoiomerê*. . . . This may be called the principle of Homo-iomereity."[29] But Anaxagoras cannot possibly have held a principle of just this form. In the first place, he must (everyone must) recognize some intuitive difference between homoiomerous and nonhomoiomerous things: neither a man nor a tree is made of parts that are like each other and like the whole. Secondly, the expression "made of" is ambiguous. The passage from Aetius, and other evidence, shows that in Anaxagoras' theory flesh is *made of* parts of flesh, in the sense that it is *increased* or *replenished* only by the addition of parts of flesh. But the same text shows that flesh is *not* made of parts of flesh in the sense that if you divide it up you inevitably get *only* parts of flesh. For the same flesh may be eaten, and then it adds not only to the *flesh* of the eater, but also to his hair, bones, skin, etc.—and all these, we know, were parts of the flesh that was eaten. Of course, flesh *may* be divided up into parts that are flesh (as ground beef—*Anglice*, mince): but whereas that is not essential to Anaxagoras' theory of change, it *is* essential that the flesh contains latent parts of all the other substances, which may in some circumstances cease to be latent. Everything is a mixture with the same ingredients; so everything is homoiomerous in a trivial sense. But that does not help to pick out the elements in Anaxagoras' theory.

Genesis and the Seeds

It was convenient to discuss nutrition first, because the role of the homoiomerous tissues in nutrition is described fairly fully by our sources. But the actual surviving fragments of Anaxagoras are more concerned with the origin of the cosmos and its parts.

"All things were together," he begins (B 1); and the question at once arises: what does he mean by "things" (*chremata*)? We have a sort of list in B 4b:[30] "Before these things were separated off,[31] when all things were together,[32] no colour was evident; for the mingling together of all things (*chremata*) prevented it—of the wet and the dry and the hot and the cold and the bright and the dark, much earth being in there also, and seeds infinite in number, in no way like each other, for of the others no one is at all like the other. These things being so, we must believe that all things were there in the whole."

We have three kinds of thing mentioned here as ingredients of the original mixture: the traditional "opposites,"[33] earth,[34] and seeds. There is no mention of the homoiomerous tissues, but we need not doubt that they were included. Apart from Aristotle's testimony that they were "elements," their inclusion follows from other theses attested in the fragments: "in everything there is a portion of everything" (B 6), and "[a thing] could not be separated, nor come to be in isolation; but as in the beginning, so now, all things to-

77

gether" (B 6). Since all things *now* include the tissues as ingredients, they must have been included "in the beginning."

What did Anaxagoras mean by "seeds," and what role did they play in his theory? *Quot homines, tot sententiae*:[35] there are some very elaborate theories. I think he meant it, not as a technical term of his theory for some kind of particle, but in its normal sense. The same word *sperma* does duty in Greek for the seed of both vegetables and animals. I believe that in B 4b Anaxagoras claims that the primitive mixture contained not only all the opposites, and earth, but also the seeds of all plants and animals. Where else, indeed, could they have come from, if nothing comes-to-be? We must look again at the evidence to test this idea.

First, the reasoning in B 4b: ". . . seeds infinite in number, in no way like each other, for of the other [things] no one is at all like the other." He means that all the differences there are must be *original*: if the no-coming-to-be rule is applied strictly, there are no emergent characteristics; all the present differences—between species, sub-species, varieties, perhaps even individuals—must have been latent in the original mixture. "The other things" in the text of the fragment means the things other than the seeds: namely, everything that grows from the seeds. We can see that *they* are infinitely different: therefore, there were infinitely different seeds in the original mixture.[36]

There is only one other mention of the seeds in the fragments:

> These things being so, it is right to think that there are, in all the things that are being put together, many things, of all kinds, and seeds of all things—[seeds] having forms and colours and savours of every kind. And [*sc.* these things being so, it is right to think that] men were compounded and the other living creatures that have soul; and that by the men cities were settled, and farms established, as is the case with us, and that they have a sun and moon and the rest, as is the case with us, and that the earth grows much of every variety for them, of which they collect what is useful into their dwelling and make use of it. This, then, is my doctrine about the separation: that the separation would take place not only with us, but anywhere else. (B 4a)

I take it that the general sense of the fragment is this. Given that there was an original mixture containing all the substances of the natural world and seeds of all things, and given that Mind started a process of "separating out" as described in B 12, then "these things being so" it is only reasonable to expect the formation of a cosmos such as we see around us ("as is the case with us").[37] So far as the seeds are concerned, the fragment suggests that, since they were present in the original mixture, they will be present in "the things being put together" (perhaps the cosmic masses—the earth, sea, air—that are separated out of the mixture in the early stages): and since the

78

mixture also contains everything needed to make them grow, they will accumulate the necessary bone, blood, flesh, etc., to grow into "men and the other living creatures that have soul."[38]

We have the testimony of Theophrastus[39] that Anaxagoras asserted that the air contains the seeds (*spermata*) of all things and that they are brought down by rainwater and so generate plants. Another witness[40] extends the same theory to "animals" (perhaps maggots?). These presumably would be the examples cited by Anaxagoras to make more plausible his theory of seeds lying latent where they might not be suspected.[41]

But what of his view of regular reproduction? There is a passage of Aristotle's De generatione animalium which attributes to people whom he does not name a theory that is entirely in tune with Anaxagoras' thinking as I understand it. It comes from a passage where he gives the view of "some of the *physiologoi*" (among whom he often classes Anaxagoras) on the causes of resemblances between parents and offspring.[42] "There are some who say that the semen (*gonê*), though a unity, is a sort of 'seed-aggregate' (*panspermia*) of many things—as if someone were to blend many juices into one liquid, and then take some of it, and could not take always an equal amount of each one [*sc.* of the juices], but sometimes took more of one, sometimes more of another, and sometimes took some of one, and none of another[43]—and this happens with the semen, which is a multiple mixture. The offspring is like in appearance to that one of its parents from whom most enters into its composition."[44]

The scholium on Gregory of Nazianzus, which we will now quote in full (B 10), fills in some details in a plausible way, although he is not a friendly witness:

Anaxagoras discovered the ancient dogma that nothing comes-to-be out of nothing and abolished coming-to-be, introducing separation (*diakrisis*) instead of coming-to-be. He put forward the nonsensical idea that all things are separated out as they grow. For in the same seed (*gonê*) there are hairs, nails, veins, arteries, nerves, and bones; they are imperceptible because of their fineness, but as they grow, they are gradually separated out. "For how," he says, "could hair come-to-be out of not hair, and flesh out of not flesh?" He said the same about colours, as well as bodies—that there is black in white and white in black. He laid down the same doctrine about weights, declaring that the light is mixed with the heavy and vice versa. All of which is false. How *can* opposites co-exist with their opposites?[45]

Anaxagoras' theory of reproduction is treated at length by Erna Lesky, *Die Zeugungs-und Vererbungslehren der Antike und ihr Nachwirken* (Mainz, 1950) (esp. pp. 51–56). She puts him in the chapter "Die Rechts-Links Theorie" [*sc.* of sex-determination]. This is a little misleading because it suggests that he is *not* relevant to the next chapter, "Die Pangenesislehre" [*sc.* the doctrine that the seed is drawn from all the tissues of the body], a doctrine that she attributes to the Atomists. But there is no inconsistency between the two theories, and the evidence suggests that Anaxagoras held both.

How does the intake of food and drink build tissues that appear to have a different character from what is eaten and drunk? They contain small quantities of the tissues, latent in them, and these are "separated out" in digestion. How does the seed grow into an adult that appears different from itself? It contains, latent within it, small quantities of all the parts of the adult body, and these are "separated out" as nutrition adds to them. How do any of the differentiated stuffs and creatures grow from the primitive mixture, which was apparently homogeneous? It contained, in latent form, everything that would later be separated out in the course of the "whirl" imparted by Mind.

This is a theory which tries, in the most literal-minded way, to show how Parmenides' premise that "what is not" is not to be spoken of, and his argument against coming-to-be, can be accepted, without making the variety and change of the perceptible world mere illusion. The theory depends entirely on the principles of Latency and Predominance: that in anything in the world there are things too small, relatively to other things, to be perceived, and that a thing is perceived just as those things which predominate in it.

Anaxagoras and Zeno

It is very commonly said by those who write about Anaxagoras that his theory was influenced by Zeno. I think this is wrong, and propose to present three arguments against it.

The first point is purely chronological: there is no good external evidence for thinking that Anaxagoras wrote later than Zeno. The second point is that there is nothing in the wording or the content of Anaxagoras' philosophy that cannot be reasonably explained without the hypothesis that he was answering Zeno. The third is that what is often said to be a response to Zeno would be nothing but an *ignoratio elenchi.*

There is no need to do more than sketch the chronological arguments.[46] The best evidence for Zeno's date comes from Plato, who says he was about 25 years younger than Parmenides; and the dramatic setting of the *Parmenides* has Parmenides about sixty-five, Zeno nearly forty, and Socrates very young—perhaps about 450 B.C.[47] Others mention a *floruit* between 468 and 453.[48] Plato mentions that Zeno wrote his book when he was very young. So it seems likely that the book was written between about 470 and 450.

According to the famous "autobiography" of Socrates in the *Phaedo,* when he was young he was very much interested in natural philosophy but was disappointed with its result until he heard someone reading from a book by Anaxagoras which said that Mind organized everything in the world. The implication is that Socrates did not hear Anaxagoras in person. Anaxagoras is said to have come from Clazomenae to Athens at the time of Xerxes' invasion (480) when he was twenty—but he is also said to have begun to philosophize in Athens under the archonship of Kallias (456). These dates can be brought into harmony, as many editors do, by the device of emending "Kallias" to "Kalliades." The latter was archon in 480.

Guthrie[49] includes among the things that "may be said with confidence" that Anaxagoras' book was finished later than 467, the year of the fall of the meteorite at Aegospotami. There is a long tradition associating Anaxagoras with this event, it is true—but the tradition says that he *predicted* it. The likeliest interpretation of that legend is that it arose from Anaxagoras' famous theory that the sun, moon, and stars are all stones: if there are heavy stones in the sky, perhaps they will fall one day. Guthrie says "the theory was suggested or appeared to be confirmed by the fall of a stone apparently from heaven."[50] It hardly needs arguing that empirical evidence is not a necessary precondition for Presocratic theories. And the story of the prediction is explained much better if Anaxagoras' book preceded the meteorite.[51]

The later chronology of Anaxagoras' life is extremely confused.[52] I do not think there is any firm evidence that would tend to force us to abandon the thesis that his book was written before 467. If so, then the chronological arguments suggest that Zeno probably wrote *after* Anaxagoras.

There are two fragments of Anaxagoras that are said to constitute a reply to Zeno:[53]

> For of the small there is no least but always a lesser (for what *is* cannot not be)—but also of the large there is also a larger. And it is equal to the small in πλῆθος, but with respect to itself each thing is both great and small" (B 3).

> These things having been thus separated out, it is right to understand that all things are neither less nor more (since it is not possible that there be more than *all*), but all things are equal always (B 5).

To take the second first: the allegation is that it is a deliberate echo of Zeno B 3: "If there are many, it must be that they are as many as they are and neither more nor less than themselves." Zeno's proposition, in its context, is one half of an antinomy which aims to prove, from the premiss "there are many," *both* "they are finite" *and* "they are infinite." From this contradiction, Zeno wants to deduce that the premiss "there are many" is false. Anaxagoras has no argument against this: the most he could be doing is contradicting Zeno by saying that "being neither more nor less than themselves" does not entail being finite. But the word "always" shows that he is making quite a different point, that the total of things does not change *in time*.⁵⁴ As I have shown earlier in this paper, this proposition is needed as part of Anaxagoras' answer to Parmenides, and there is no need whatever to erect a Zenonian target for him to fire at.

On the contrary, Zeno's argument in B 3 might well be aimed at Anaxagoras. The latter shows no sign of noticing that if things are as many as they are (which is entailed by "all things are equal always") then they are finite. So he asserts both "all things are equal" and "all things are infinite." Zeno could be looking for a contradiction in this.⁵⁵

The first of Anaxagoras' fragments quoted above, B 3, is said to be connected with the Zenonian argument against plurality contained in B 1–2.⁵⁶ The conclusion of the antinomy in this argument is: "Thus if there are many, they must be both large and small—small so as to have no size, large so as to be infinite."

To take the second arm first: Zeno argues that anything having size must be divisible into parts having size, "to say this once is to say it always," therefore anything having size must have an infinite number of parts having size, and therefore it must be infinitely large. So far as I can see, there is nothing in Anaxagoras that answers this argument.

As to the first arm: Zeno argues that each of the alleged "many" must have no size because otherwise it will be divisible and so not be a "one." Again, there appears to be nothing in Anaxagoras that takes note of this.

What Anaxagoras says can be wholly explained as part of his defence of his principles of latency and predominance. A change from A to B is possible, in his view, only if B is latent in A. So if A is so small that it contains nothing latent in it; it cannot change. Since he apparently wanted to set no limits to change,⁵⁷ he had to maintain that there is nothing so small that it can contain nothing latent in it—that is, "there is no least, but always a lesser." Without this assumption, the "portions" of everything that are in everything could be eliminated simply by taking smaller and smaller pieces, so that "what is" would vanish into not-being.

The theory of change depends on the proportions of the ingredients of a thing: the possibility of change depends on there being a relatively large and a relatively small. Any limits on the large and the small would limit the possibility of change. Hence for any given size, there must be a "larger," if latent things can be of any size and can cease to be latent.

When he says the large is "equal to the small in πλῆθος," he probably means that both the large and the small contain an equal number of ingredients—namely, all that there are. The same is said in B 6: "There are equal portions, in number, of the large and the small."

The last clause of B 3, "with respect to itself, each thing is both great and small" is a little puzzling. He has just been talking about *comparative* sizes—small and smaller, large and larger. One might expect him to say that with respect to itself each thing is neither large nor small. I suspect that what he means is that without comparisons a thing is whatever you like to call it—large or small. Large and small are entirely relative terms.[58]

Anaxagoras' theory of infinite divisibility—"of the small there is no least but always a lesser" (B 3)—is then a deduction from three propositions in his response to Parmenides:

1. There is no coming-to-be or perishing.
2. Nevertheless, a thing perceived as A can change into a thing perceived as B.
3. This is possible only if B is latent in A.

There is no reason to think that he was unable to work this out without a nudge from Zeno. On the contrary, if he did work it out after reading Zeno, then he either stupidly misunderstood or shamelessly ignored Zeno's point. For Zeno introduced the infinite divisibility of "what is" *only* to show that it leads to ridiculous and unacceptable consequences. If it is infinitely divisible into an infinite number of ultimate units, then it is impossible to give a non-contradictory account of these units (B 1–2). If it is infinitely divisible without any ultimate units, then you can never traverse it or give any non-contradictory accounts of its limits (the Dichotomy and the Achilles).[59] The Atomists and Aristotle tried to deal with this powerful attack on divisibility; not Anaxagoras. If Zeno had argued *only* that infinite divisibility entails infinitely numerous parts with finite size, then we might believe that Anaxagoras' "of the small there is no least but always a lesser" was a reply to him. But Zeno had already forestalled this alleged reply.

Anaxagoras Compared with Plato

Arthur Peck called his 1931 article "Anaxagoras: Predication as a Problem in Physics." In fact, one can read his article without realising why he chose that title, because he did not make the point explicitly. But it is a penetrating title, in that it starts us on the right road to understanding Anaxagoras. It may also point the way to a strange and little noticed correlation in the history of Greek philosophy: that between Anaxagoras' theory of matter and Plato's theory of Forms, at least in its early appearances.[60]

"Predication" is no doubt too precise a term; it belongs to a later period in the history of grammar. Anaxagoras was concerned simply to show how the things of the perceptible world could reasonably be described as having different characters at different times or in different circumstances, without supposing that any "things that are" (ἐόντα χρήματα) have come-to-be or perished. He aimed to do it by showing how an eternally static quantity ("all things are nothing less nor more . . . but all equal for ever," B 5) of things that *are* can alter the appearances by changing their predominance in different regions. We may observe now that this theory entails that the words we use to describe the physical world are systematically ambiguous. When we say of a portion of the perceptible world (a) "this is a piece of gold," we mean (b) "this is a piece of matter in which gold is the predominant ingredient." In (a), the gold is the perceptible matter; in (b), "gold" means just what gold is.[61]

Of course, a thing may have different characters at the same time: it may be, for example, dark, red, hot, and meat; that is to say, it has a predominant share in all these items. To make this work at all, there must be some intuitive notion of the *sorting* of properties—into pairs of opposites, for example. Dark predominates over *light,* not over sweet, and so on. But there seems to be no trace in Anaxagoras of any theory of categories: the "opposites" such as hot and cold are apparently treated as "things that are" in the original mixture, along with earth and seeds (B 4b).[62] I believe that he meant to be equally indifferent to categorial priorities in dealing with what Aristotle called substances. If my argument is right, man and horse and oak were present in the original mixture in the form of seeds, imperceptibly small; we say "a man has come-to-be" when the seed grows, by addition of like parts, so that the ingredient "man" comes to be predominant; but no man has come-to-be out of what is not man (out of flesh and bone, for instance). The mechanism creaks here a little. The homoiomerous bodies grow by the addition of parts that have the same name—bone by the addition of bone. Man grows not by the addition of *man,* but by the addition of flesh, bone, blood, etc. Anaxagoras does not explain the relation between man and flesh, bone, blood, etc., any more than he explains the relation between any of these and bright, dark, hot, cold, etc.

The analogies with the Platonic theory of Forms are sufficiently obvious, and need not be set out at great length. Both theories explain change in the physical world by introducing entities that are themselves eternally unchanging—with the crucial difference that the early theory makes these entities material, the later immaterial. In both, these entities can be described as "just what [x] is"—"the hot itself," "gold itself," "man himself"; physical objects merely "have a share" of these entities. Again, there is the difference: the "share" in Anaxagoras' theory is a physical quantity (the word he uses is μοῖρα) which is present in the object as an ingredient; Plato uses the same language of "sharing," "participating," "presence in," but whatever this relation is in his theory, it is not physical mixture.

Both theories have the feature that the objects of the physical world are called after whatever Forms (if we may make Anaxagoras a present of this term for convenience) they partake in. Thus they both function as explanations of predication. Anaxagoras' explanation is a very simple *causal* one: X is *F*, because of the predominant quantity of *F* in X. This may help to explain a feature of Plato's theory that has often been found puzzling: the insistence that Forms are αἰτίαι (*Phaedo* 100 b ff.)—the word notoriously has a wider meaning than "cause" in English. "It seems to me that if anything is beautiful besides the beautiful itself, it is beautiful because of nothing at all other than that it participates in that beautiful; and the same goes for all of them. Do you assent to an αἰτία of that kind?" Anaxagoras' theory could not cope with predicates like "beautiful," and that is one reason why Plato transformed the simple physical theory into something quite different;[63] but the new theory must still explain the αἰτία of objects in the physical world having the properties that are predicated of them.

In both theories, the beings that are "just what [X] is" are inaccessible to sense-perception. In Anaxagorean theory, they are inaccessible because no one of them can ever be found in isolation: in the physical world, everything is a mixture. Plato made the Forms imperceptible in principle, in that they have a different mode of being from perceptible things. In both theories, it is held that these beings are accessible to Mind. Νοητά commonly designates the Forms in Plato: Anaxagoras says "[Mind] has all judgement about every thing . . . and the things that were being mingled together and separated out and sorted from each other, Mind knew them all" (B 12).

It is the difference between the two theories that is particularly striking when we consider the actual mechanism of growth and development. What we may call the forms in Anaxagoras attain perceptible status by being partially "separated out"[64] from each other. The transcendent Forms of Plato's theory, as well as being qualitatively invariable, undergo no movement of any kind: they are the models or paradigms which somehow (the vague term cannot be avoided) guide change.

Neither of the two theories (to speak only of Plato's earlier dialogues) arranges the Forms in which particulars may partake into categorial hierarchies. If something is hot; it has a share of the hot itself; if it is fire, it has a share of fire itself. Plato begins to move away from such simplicities in *Phaedo* 103c ff., when he laboriously points out that the predicate "fire" is always accompanied by the predicate "hot," and "snow" always by "cold." His stress on this point may well be due to consciousness that his theory was better able to handle it than Anaxagoras'.

To Plato, the problem did eventually present itself clearly as a problem about predication: if we predicate the same thing of a number of particulars, what is that thing that they all have in common? It does not seem to me that this "one over many" question was one that concerned Anaxagoras much, although his account of matter and its properties could account for it, within limits.

ESSAYS IN ANCIENT GREEK PHILOSOPHY

But this is not the place to pursue this topic further. What I have been concerned to stress is this. Anaxagoras lies on a path in the field of natural philosophy that leads from Parmenides to Plato—especially the Plato of the *Phaedo* and *Republic*. It is a path lined with a vast population of "things that are" (ἐόντα χρήματα, ὄντως ὄντα), showing a huge range of real differentiae. Empedocles took a different path—the one also taken later by the Atomists—through metaphysical territory populated sparsely with just a few primary beings—the four "Roots" and their irreducible properties, or the shape, size, weight, and motion of the atoms. It is perhaps pointless to ask whether Anaxagoras or Empedocles was the more "advanced," since they chose different routes. But my picture of Anaxagoras is of a kind of Ajax among the Presocratics, unable to appreciate the advantages of modern, more flexible ways, and heroically[65] adhering to the strictest interpretation of the Parmenidean code.

NOTES

[1] M. L. West, *Early Greek Philosophy and the Orient* (Oxford: Clarendon, 1971), p. 219.

[2] West singles out W. K. C. Guthrie, *A History of Greek Philosophy*, vol. 2 (Cambridge: Cambridge University Press, 1965), p.1, and G. S. Kirk and J. E. Raven, *The Presocratic Philosophers* (Cambridge: Cambridge University Press, 1957), p. 368 f.

[3] Which wrote first, Anaxagoras or Empedocles? This paper remains neutral on the question. For an extensive discussion of the arguments, see D. O'Brien's article, which concludes that Empedocles wrote later than Anaxagoras, and was influenced by him. D. O'Brien, "The Relation of Anaxagoras and Empedocles," *Journal of Hellenic Studies* 88 (1968):93–113.

[4] Simplicius, *Physics* 163.18 = Anaxagoras B 17. I do not think there is any need to defend the testimony of Simplicius against the attack on it in Daniel E. Gershenson and Daniel A. Greenberg, *Anaxagoras and the Birth of Physics* (New York, 1964). See for example G. B. Kerferd, "Anaxagoras and the Concept of Matter before Aristotle," *Bulletin of the John Rylands Library* 52 (1969):129–43; reprinted in A. P. D. Mourelatos, ed., *The Presocratics* (New York: Doubleday, 1974), pp. 489–503, to which references are given. For this reference, see p. 490, n. 3. The fact that Simplicius' quotations from Anaxagoras' book take different forms in different places does not entail that he did not know the book at first hand. This can be proved by looking at his quotations from the *Timaeus*, which he certainly knew; compare the quotations from *Tm* 51e6–52d1 in his *Physics* 224.30 *ff.*, 539.14 *ff.*, and 43.15 *ff.* A few details vary, but he gets the sense right.

[5] Plutarch *adv. Coloten* 1113 A–B = DK 31B9.

[6] Empedocles B 17.3–4, 11, 35; 21.14; 26.4 and 10 all use some form of γίνεσθαι in a positive exposition of his own theory. Anaxagoras uses them only to reject them, as in B 17.

86

⁷ I have attempted to set out my ideas on Parmenides' argument in an article, "Notes on Parmenides," *Exegesis and Argument*, Studies presented to Gregory Vlastos, *Phronesis*, Suppl. Vol. I (1973):1–15, and will not repeat that discussion here. There may be doubt about what Parmenides meant by "what is not," but not that this was the crucial difficulty for him.

⁸ Aristotle, *GC* I 1, 314 a 24–29. The following portion of this text is discussed below, n. 16.

⁹ Guthrie, *A History of Greek Philosophy*, vol. 2, p. 272.

¹⁰ Gregory Vlastos, "The Physical Theory of Anaxagoras" *Philosophical Review* 59 (1950):31–57; reprinted in R. E. Allen and David J. Furley, *Studies in Presocratic Philosophy*, vol. 2 (London: Routledge and Kegan Paul, 1975) to which references are given. For this reference, see p. 327.

¹¹ Harold F. Cherniss, *Aristotle's Criticism of Presocratic Philosophy* (Baltimore: Johns Hopkins, 1935); reprinted, New York, Octagon, 1964, p. 400.

¹² B 20. Empedocles rather revels in ornately described examples of the "myriad tribes of mortal things, made in every kind of form, a wonder to behold" (B 35.16–17), and there are several others in the fragments.

¹³ Brentlinger writes (p. 65): "Mixtures are not fundamental, since they may come-to-be and cease-to-be. A cat, for instance, is a mixture, hence not an entity the coming-to-be of which is the coming-to-be of any *thing*. Similarly for all perceptible things." But what justification is there for saying that a cat is not a thing? John Brentlinger, "Incomplete Predicates and the Two-World Theory of the *Phaedo*," *Phronesis* 17 (1972):61–79.

¹⁴ Moreover, the use of the word "φησι" by no means guarantees that these are Anaxagoras' own words. See Malcolm Schofield's article for a cautious analysis of this fragment. Malcolm Schofield, "Doxographia Anaxagoras," *Hermes* 103, (1975):1–24.

¹⁵ There is a sort of catalogue of homoiomerous bodies in *Meteor*. IV 10, 388 a 13–20. It may not be by Aristotle, but there is no reason to think Aristotle would dissent. "By homoiomerous bodies I mean, for example, metallic bodies—bronze, gold, silver, tin, iron, stone, etc., and whatever comes from these by being separated out from them—and animal and vegetable tissues, such as flesh, bone, sinew, skin, intestine, hair, fibre, blood-vessels, from which in turn the anhomoiomerous parts are composed, such as face, hand, foot, etc.; and in plants wood, bark, leaf, root, and the like."

¹⁶ It is misleading of Aristotle to *contrast* the homoiomerous tissues with earth, water, air, and fire in Anaxagoras' theory (*De Caelo* 302 b 1, *GC* 314 a 28). Certainly anything that we *perceive* as earth, water, air, or fire contains a portion of everything and so is a mixture; but the same is true of anything we *perceive* as bone, blood, or flesh. Unless I have misunderstood Anaxagoras' theory fundamentally, the four Empedoclean "Roots" must be ingredients in the original mixture and have the same status as the homoiomerous tissues. See Vlastos, "The Physical Theory of Anaxagoras," pp. 329 *ff.*, for more on this.

¹⁷ In general I am in agreement with the account given by Guthrie, *A History of Greek Philosophy*, vol. 2, pp. 279–94. In some respects, I differ with G. B. Kerferd's version, and since that is more recent, and reprinted in an influential collection, I shall offer some arguments against some portions of it.

[18] Aristotle, *Ph.* I 4, 187 a 28 (DK 59 A 52), etc. For the translation of ἐκ τοῦ μὴ ὄντος, see above, p. 72.

[19] "Separating out" (ἀποκρίνεσθαι) in B 2, 4a, 4b, 6, 7, 9, 12, 13, 16; for more on this, see below, n. 64. For growth, see Aetius I 3 5 (DK 59 A 46) or Lucretius I 834–42 (DK 59 A 44).

[20] Lucretius I 875. For the principle of Predominance, see Anaxagoras B 12 *ad fin.*: "Each thing is and was, most evidently, those things of which there is most in it." See n. 61, below.

[21] B 1, B 6, B 8. Aristotle *Ph.* 203 a 23–24.

[22] No doubt the proportions should not be thought of as measured by weight or volume or any such precise parameters, but rather by some vague, intuitive measure such as "strength," as in "strong coffee."

[23] Again, it is necessary to translate τὸ μὴ ὄν as "what *it* is not," rather than as "what is not" or "the non-existent." There is no question, in the case of nutrition, of something coming into existence out of *nothing,* since food is obviously an existent thing.

[24] "Parts productive of" (μόρια γεννητικά) is ambiguous, in that it might mean "parts of character *a, b, c,* etc., capable of changing into things of character *x, y, z,* etc." It certainly does not mean that. This is clear both from a sentence later in Aetius, "the parts in the food are like what is produced," and also from a similar account in Simplicius *Ph.* 460.17–19: "hence he supposed that in food—in water, if trees feed on water—there is wood, bark, leaves, and fruit."

[25] A46 I.e., the tissues nourished by the food are *latent* in the food. The expression λόγῳ θεωρητὰ μόρια may indicate an Epicurean source for this part of Aetius' report; so Diego Lanza, *Anassagora* (Florence: Nuova Italia, 1966), p. 78, and Schofield, "Doxographia."

[26] Simplicius *Ph.* 167.12 uses the word with the same reference, but he takes it to mean that each of these latent "parts" is itself divisible into parts like itself—i.e. he uses the Aristotelian criterion for *Homoiomere* described above.

[27] Lucretius I 834–42: ossa videlicet e pauxillis atque minutis / ossibus . . . gigni.

[28] The arguments are compiled by C. Bailey, *The Greek Atomists and Epicurus* (Oxford: Clarendon, 1928), reprinted, New York, Russell, 1964, pp. 551–56; A. L. Peck, "Predication as a Problem in Physics," *Classical Quarterly* 25 (1931):27–37 and 112–20; I. R. D. Mathewson, "Aristotle and Anaxagoras," *Classical Quarterly* 8(1958):67–81; and Guthrie, *A History of Greek Philosophy,* pp. 282–83.

[29] Kerferd, "Anaxagoras and the Concept of Matter," p. 491.

[30] For this division of what DK prints as one fragment, see Fränkel, *Wege und Formen,* 284 *ff.*

[31] If 4b is separated from 4a, we have no clear reference for ταῦτα. In one of his citations (*Ph.* 156.4) Simplicius leaves the pronoun out; so its reference may well be quite vague, the whole content of the phrase being repeated in the next phrase, "when all things were together."

[32] Notice that "all things" is the neuter plural adjective πάντα here, instead of

πάντα χρήματα in B 1: an indication that the word χρήματα is not a technical term that picks out one class of things from others in Anaxagoras' theory.

[33] For which see Anaximander, DK 12 A 9–10.

[34] See note 16.

[35] A sampling of views, all somewhat different: F. M. Cornford, "Anaxagoras' Theory of Matter," *Classical Quarterly* 24 (1930):14–30, and 83–95; references are to the pagination in the reprinted version in Allen and Furley, vol. II (see above). For this reference, see p. 286. Vlastos, "The Physical Theory of Anaxagoras," pp. 323–29; J. E. Raven, "The Basis of Anaxagoras' Cosmology," *Classical Quarterly* 4 (1954):130–31; Guthrie, *A History of Greek Philosophy*, pp. 298–300. For the right view, but a rather peculiar reason for it ("nothing important is involved"), see Peck, "Predication as a Problem," pp. 114–18.

[36] Compare Hippocrates *De victu* I 4: "These things being so, they [*sc.* the opposites, mixed together] separate off from each other many and various forms of seeds and living creatures in no way like each other in appearance or power." The verbal echoes of 4b are strong enough to make it certain that the author knew Anaxagoras; and he links seeds at once with living creatures. For a commentary on the passage, see R. Joly, *Recherches sur le traité pseudo-hippocratique Du Régime* (Paris: Les Belles Lettres, 1960), pp. 21–24.

[37] For the interpretation of this fragment, see Fränkel, *Wege und Formen*, pp. 284 ff. I think Fränkel's interpretation survives the objection reportedly (see Allen and Furley, vol. II, p. 379 n. 28) raised by G. E. L. Owen, that the indicative χρῶνται in DK II 34.14 rules it out. This indicative, according to the objection, makes it impossible to understand the infinitives as potential. But Fränkel's interpretation, as he himself seems to suggest (p. 281), does not depend on the infinitives being potential. The whole construction is dependent on the opening phrase: τούτων οὕτως ἐχόντων, χρὴ δοκεῖν. The general sense is this: granted that the initial conditions are as we have described them, it is right to suppose (i.e., it is only what one would have expected) that ". . . men were composed . . . and there are cities built by the men . . . just as we see around us (ὥσπερ παρ᾽ ἡμῖν." The potential optative in the last sentence follows quite naturally: given the initial conditions, the same *would happen* anywhere. There is no commitment to "other worlds" here.

[38] Curiously, there is no coherent information on Anaxagoras' idea of soul.

[39] *H. plant.* III 1 4, and *De caus. plant.* I 5 2, cited in DK 59 A 117.

[40] Irenaeus II 14 2 (DK 59 A 113).

[41] Contrast this analysis with one that takes a different view of the seeds. F. M. Cornford wrote as follows: "Whence came the first composite germs, before there were existing plants and animals to reproduce their kind? The germs of plants were washed down with the rainwater out of the air, which contains "Seeds" of all kinds—that is to say, particles of every homoiomerous substance. The germs of animals came from the higher and warmer region of the aether. . . . So much we are told; but not how the first germs were originally formed. We may conjecture that in the Air or Aether (each of which contains Seeds of all kinds) some particles of plant or animal tissue cohered in a sort of molecule" ("Anaxagoras' Theory," p. 281). He

mentions in n. 2 (p. 315) that he will use the word "germ" to avoid confusion with Anaxagoras' use of *"sperma,"* but does not mention that his "germ" translates Theophrastus' *"sperma."* The notion that Anaxagoras used the word *"spermata"* to mean particles of elementary substance comes originally from Aristotle *De caelo* 302 b 1: "Anaxagoras says that the homoiomerous bodies are elements . . . , whereas air and fire are mixtures of these and all other seeds. For each of these two is an aggregate of all the homoiomerous bodies in invisible form." In *GC* 314 a 18 *ff.*, he says that earth, air, fire, fire, and water are composite, "for they are a seed-aggregate *(panspermia)* of these [*sc.* of the homoiomerous bodies]." I do not think these two texts are a good enough foundation for a theory that the seeds in Anaxagoras' theory were particles of elementary substances. (See also n. 16, above.)

Although I think Anaxagoras wanted to include whole organisms among the "things that are," I do not imagine that he would promote artifacts, like the cities and farms mentioned in B 4a, to the same status, or feel any difficulty about leaving them out.

[42] *GA* IV 3,769 a 7 *ff.* The quoted passage begins at line 28.

[43] Anaxagoras' theory would deny this last possibility: everything is in everything.

[44] This passage was said, rather tentatively, to be about the theory of Plato *Timaeus* 73 b–c by H. Cherniss, *Aristotle's Criticism,* p. 284 n. 243, on the ground that Plato there calls the marrow a *panspermia.* This seems quite unlikely. It is claimed for Anaxagoras by Owen Kember "Anaxagoras' Theory of Sex Differentiation and Heredity," *Phronesis* 18 (1973):11–12. See also next note.

[45] This evidence gets a little confirmation, on the subject of seeds, from a passage in Censorinus (5.2 *ff.* = A 107 in Lanza, *Anassagora,* but not in DK), which lists Anaxagoras among those who hold that "non medullis modo, verum etiam et adipe multaque carne mares exhauriri" (that males [*sc.* through the emission of seed] are depleted not only in marrow, but also in fat and much flesh).

About the rest of Anaxagoras' theory of reproduction there is no certainty, because the evidence is confused. There is a contradiction between Aristotle *GA* 763 b 30 *ff.*, where Anaxagoras is included among those who believe that only males emit seed, and Censorinus 5.4 and 6.8. On this problem, see Owen Kember's article, cited in note 44.

[46] Because the evidence is such that however meticulously one examines it, it will never yield a conclusive case.

[47] *Parmenides* 127 a–c.

[48] DK A 1–3.

[49] Guthrie, *A History of Greek Philosophy,* p. 266.

[50] Guthrie, *A History of Greek Philosophy,* p. 303.

[51] He wrote only one: Diogenes Laertius I 16.

[52] See J. A. Davison, "Protagoras, Democritus, and Anaxagoras," *Classical Quarterly* 3 (1953):33–45. See now J. Mansfeld, "The Chronology of Anaxagoras' Athenian Period and the Date of his Trial," *Mnemosyne* 32 (1979):39–69, and 33 (1980):17–95.

[53] See especially Raven, "The Basis of Anaxagoras' Cosmology"; and Kirk and Raven, *The Presocratic Philosophers,* pp. 370–71; Guthrie, *A History of Greek Phi-*

losophy, pp. 289 ff.; Guido Calogero, *Storia della Logica Antica* (Bari: Laterza, 1967), pp. 256 ff. For some excellent critical comments on this position see O. Joehrens, *Die Fragmente des Anaxagoras* (Bochum, 1939), pp. 78–80; and Colin Strang, "The Physical Theory of Anaxagoras," *Archiv für Geschichte der Philosophie* 45 (1963), pp. 101–18; reprinted in Allen and Furley, *Studies in Presocratic Philosophy*, to which references are given. See pp. 366–67, for this reference.

[54] This was pointed out by Strang, "The Physical Theory," p. 377 n. 13.

[55] But it is not necessary to think that Zeno had Anaxagoras in mind as a specific target. He was systematically looking for contradictions to be derived from "there are many," and it is not necessary to think that all the types of pluralism that he attacked were actually asserted by anyone.

[56] On this, see Strang, "The Physical Theory," pp. 366–67.

[57] Simplicus *Ph.* 460.12: Anaxagoras saw "that everything comes into being out of everything, if not immediately, then serially (air from fire, water from air, earth from water, stone from earth, fire from stone again). . . ."

[58] This conclusion is the same as Calogero's (*Storia della Logica*, pp. 261 *ff.*), but I differ from him about many details.

[59] For this interpretation of Zeno, see G. E. L. Owen, "Zeno and the Mathematicians," *Proceedings of the Aristotelian Society* (1957–58):199–222; reprinted in Allen and Furley, *Studies in Presocratic Philosophy*; and see David J. Furley, *Two Studies in the Greek Atomists* (Princeton University Press, 1967), pp. 69–70; reprinted in A. P. D. Mourelatos, ed., *The Presocratics* (New York: Doubleday, 1974), pp. 360–61. Joehrens (*Die Fragmente*, p. 79) adds that Anaxagoras' thesis of infinitely many parts in finite things is contradicted by Zeno's argument (B 1) that infinitely many parts entail infinite size.

[60] John Brentlinger is one who does examine it, in his very interesting and important article "Incomplete Predicates and the Two-World Theory of the *Phaedo*, see note 13, above.

[61] It is an important element in Colin Strang's article to bring out clearly this necessary implication of Anaxagoras' theory. Anaxagoras himself may not have been conscious of the ambiguity, since it does not obtrude itself in particular contexts. In the fragments he says only that the preponderant ingredients of a thing determine what that thing is "most evidently." The Derveni papyrus, which recalls many Anaxagorean ideas, says "each thing *is called* (κέκληται) from what predominates" (see W. Burkert, "La genèse des choses et des mots: le papyrus de Dervéni entre Anaxagore et Cratyle," *Les Études Philosophiques* 4 [1970]:445). Theophrastus *ap.* Simplicius *Ph.* 27.7 uses the phrase "each thing is characterized according to what predominates."

[62] There has been much discussion about the status of the opposites, but there is no need to repeat it. I agree with Guthrie, *A History of Greek Philosophy* (p. 285): "there was no difference in the mode of their being between the opposites . . . and other substances like flesh and gold."

[63] See Brentlinger's article for an account of some of the deficiencies that Plato found in Anaxagoras' theory.

[64] Anaxagoras' word for this separating, ἀποκρίνεσθαι, is a medical

term, used of the *secretion* of substances by the organs of the body. It is used of the secretion of semen, which may well be a significant paradigm for Anaxagoras. The "separation" in his theory is never complete, as we have seen: there is always "a share of everything in everything."

[65] I owe the word to an incredulous comment by Montgomery Furth, on the occasion when I presented an earlier version of this paper to a "Workshop on the Eleatics" at the University of Alberta in 1974. I am grateful to other participants in that meeting also. A second version of the paper was discussed at a meeting of the Society for Ancient Greek Philosophy in Washington in 1975, where it received some useful criticism from Nicholas White, Richard McKirahan, and others. I am particularly grateful to Malcolm Schofield, David Sider, and George Kerferd for written comments on one or other version of the paper.

Anaxagoras and Epicurus

6 6 "Ｏ F the ancients Epicurus received most favorably Anaxagoras, although he opposed him on certain points, and Archelaus, the teacher of Socrates." This astonishing statement made by Diogenes Laertius deserves serious consideration (D.L. 10.12). It is, of course, impossible to prove that Anaxagoras' philosophy directly influenced Epicurus. The most that I can hope to show is that Epicurus in his interpretation of particular philosophic problems departed from Democritus and adopted a point of view similar to that of Anaxagoras.[1]

For Anaxagoras' methodology perhaps the most interesting fragments are those that deal with the color of snow. Sextus Empiricus writes: "We compare that which is perceived by the mind with the phenomena, just as Anaxagoras compared the proposition: 'Snow is congealed water, water is black, and, therefore, snow is black' with 'Snow is white'" (59 A 97). According to Cicero, Anaxagoras said that snow did not even seem white to him because he knew that the water from which it was congealed was black (59 A 97). This interpretation, however, is doubtful, since a scholiast states specifically that Anaxagoras said that black was in the white and the white in the black (59 B 10). Anaxagoras was contrasting the evidence from sense perception with contradictory evidence from deduction.

If Anaxagoras intended to demonstrate that snow was both black and white, he could have done so by using the following arguments:

(1) Snow is congealed water.
   Water is black.
   Therefore, snow is black.

(2) If snow is black, sight is false.
   But sight is not false.
   Therefore, snow is not black.

This paper was presented at the 1975 Washington meeting of the Society for Ancient Greek Philosophy; it has not been published previously but has been extensively revised for this volume.

Margaret Reesor is Professor of Classics at Queen's University, Kingston, Ontario in Canada.

(3) If snow is either black or white, either sight or logos is false.
Neither sight nor logos is false.
Therefore, snow is not either black or white.

(4) If snow is both black and white, both sight and logos are true.
Both sight and logos are true.
Therefore, snow is both black and white.

Anaxagoras' use of an argument of the first type is attested by the passage in Sextus Empiricus quoted above. An argument of the second type is found in fragment B 5 of Anaxagoras: "If all things are more, there would be more than all; it is not possible that there should be more than all; therefore, all things are always equal (i.e., not more)." The third argument is a modified form of the type used by Zeno and by Gorgias in his *Concerning Non-being*. Zeno's scheme reads as follows: "If *S* exists, it must be either *P* or Not-*P*, but if it can be neither P nor Not-*P*, *S* does not exist."[2]

If Anaxagoras had started with the postulate "Snow is both black and white," he would have been faced with the necessity of providing confirmatory evidence or at least of showing that the postulate is not inconceivable. By pouring white and black drop by drop into the other, he could have shown that both black and white were in the mixture and that that which is present in a mixture is not always distinguishable by the senses. We know that Anaxagoras actually performed this experiment. Sextus Empiricus writes: "'Because of our feebleness,' he (*sc.* Anaxagoras) says, 'we cannot discern the true,' and he uses as proof of their unreliability the gradual change of colors. For if we should take two colors, black and white, and then we should pour them drop by drop from one to the other, sight would not be able to distinguish the gradual alterations, although they subsist naturally" (59 B 21). That which we cannot discern is in the mixture; but also that which we can discern is in the mixture. We may, I believe, go one step farther and assume that that which is present in the sense perception is in the mixture.

The experiment itself might be the basis of an inference in an entirely different context. From an experiment similar to the one that I have described, Anaxagoras drew the conclusion that prior to the separation, when all things were together, there was no color visible at all, "for the mixture of all things prevented it" (59 B 4).

When Anaxagoras said that we cannot discern the true, he meant that we cannot discern something that is a part or portion of the mixture. We cannot discern the black or the white in a mixture of black and white. It would seem to follow, therefore, that we can discern visible objects and that these are true. This assumption is supported by a fragment from Melissus, which may, in fact, be an attack on Anaxagoras.[3] The passage reads as follows: "For, if there are many, it is necessary for them to be such as I say the one is. For, if there are earth and water and air and fire and iron and gold, and the living and the dead, and black and white, and the other things which people say are true, if, indeed, this is the case, and we rightly see and hear, it is necessary for each thing to be such as seemed good to me at first" (30 B 8). The word ἀληθές (true) in this passage seems to mean real or actual.[4]

What kind of evidence led Anaxagoras to postulate νοῦς (mind)? Anaxagoras describes the νοῦς as follows:

> Other things have a portion of everything, but νοῦς is infinite and self-ruled, and is mixed with nothing, but it is alone by itself. For if it were not by itself, but were mixed with anything else, it would have a share of all things, if it were mixed with anything. . . . It has all judgment about everything and the greatest strength. All those things which have life both the greater and the less νοῦς controls. And the whole revolution νοῦς controls so that it revolved in the beginning. . . . And all those things which were mingled together and separated off and separated out νοῦς knows. And whatever was going to be and whatever was, whatever is not now, and whatever is now and whatever will be, all these νοῦς organizes, and this revolution in which are now revolving the stars, the sun, the moon, the air and the fire that are being separated off. And the revolution itself caused this separating off. And the dense is separated off from the rare, the hot from the cold, the bright from the dark, and the dry from the moist" (59 B 12).

To support his statement "νοῦς is mixed with nothing" Anaxagoras argued: "But if νοῦς were mixed with anything else, it would be mixed with all things; but νοῦς is not mixed with all things; therefore νοῦς is not mixed with anything else."[5] If Anaxagoras held that the regularity in the movement of the heavenly bodies was a proof (τεκμήριον) of the existence of νοῦς, his argument might have read: "If there is order, there is νοῦς; there is order; therefore, there is νοῦς." The orderly movement of the stars was a phenomenon that provided a vision of the non-evident. From the nature of the phenomenon we can draw conclusions about the nature of the non-evident. This is the meaning of Anaxagoras' famous statement: ὄψις γὰρ τῶν ἀδήλων τὰ φαινόμενα (59 B 21a).[6] Anaxagoras undoubtedly made use of analogy. The νοῦς of man knows, organizes, and controls; accordingly, the νοῦς of the cosmos knows, organizes, and controls. In man the reasoning process is separate from the physical act. So too in the cosmos the νοῦς organizes the revolution, but the revolution itself brings about the separation of the physical components.[7]

In Anaxagoras' philosophy, however, a man's σοφία was based not only on his ability to discern the non-evident through the phenomena, but on his understanding of logic and mathematics. This is made abundantly clear by the following passages: "It is not possible for Being not to be" (59 B 3); "It is not possible that there should be more than all" (59 B 5); "Since the portions of the large and small are equal in number, in this way all things would be in all" (59 B 6); and "Since it is not possible that there should be a smallest, it could not be separated" (59 B 6). Complementing man's powers of reasoning was his ability to make conjectures. Anaxagoras assumes that if "a mixture of all things" similar to that which existed prior to the formation of our cosmos existed elsewhere, it would be followed by a separating off similar to that in our cosmos, and the emergence of a world that would have the same physical structure as our world and the same type of society that we have now (59 B 4). Anaxagoras introduces this passage with the words: "It is necessary to suppose that" (χρὴ δοκεῖν). A δόξα, if we base our interpretation on this passage, is not confirmed and is not contradicted by evidence to the contrary. In a passage in the *Metaphysics* in which he argued that Democritus, Empedocles, Parmenides, and Anaxagoras identified perception and knowledge, regarded perception as alteration, and consequently said that the phenomena that are according to perception are true, Aristotle attributes to Anaxagoras the saying "The things-that-are (τὰ ὄντα) will be such as men assume them to be" (1009b25–8 = 59 A 28). The saying attributed to Anaxagoras, however, may very well be, as Cherniss observed, of a moralistic nature with no significance for Anaxagoras' theory of sense perception at all.[8]

In his interpretation of many particular points Epicurus seems to have parted company with Democritus and adopted a point of view similar to that of Anaxagoras. The most common type of argument used by Epicurus had its own distinctive characteristic: P; if not P, then not Q: but Q; therefore, P. As a specification of this type we may use Epicurus' argument: "Nothing comes into being from that which is non-existent, for everything would come from everything and there would be no need of seeds" (*Ep.* 1.38). This would appear to be a refinement on the less sophisticated type of argument that we found in Anaxagoras, which would read: "If something should come into being from that which is non-existent, everything would come from everything, and there would be no need of seeds; everything does not come from everything, and there is need of seeds; therefore, nothing comes into being from that which is non-existent."

In my discussion of Anaxagoras I pointed out that in the experiment in which he poured white and black drop by drop from one into the other he was demonstrating that it was not inconceivable that black and white were in the mixture, although they were not distinguishable by the senses. Epicurus argued that it was not impossible that there were emanations, and Lucretius that it was not inconceivable that bodies that cannot be seen exist.[9] Epicurus wrote: "What is more, there are impressions similar in shape to the solids, surpassing the phenomena by far in their fineness. For it is not impossible that such emanations should arise in that which surrounds them" (*Ep.* 1.46). Lucretius, trying to show that bodies that cannot be seen exist in things, used the analogy of wet clothes spread out in the sun to dry. The moisture, which eyes cannot see at all, is broken up into small particles (1.266–67 and 305–10).

There is evidence that Epicurus used Anaxagoras' famous phrase ὄψις τῶν ἀδήλων τὰ φαινόμενα (59 B 21a), which may be interpreted to mean that from the nature of the phenomena we can draw conclusions about the non-evident. Plutarch refers to those who say that the phenomena hold evidence for the non-evident (fr. 263). A passage from Philodemus refers to the account that Epicurus gave about men who are not able to observe the relation that exists between the phenomena and the unseen (fr. 212). And finally, Diogenes Laertius, quoting Epicurus, writes: "The fact that we see and hear subsists, just as feeling bodily pain subsists. Accordingly, it is necessary to infer from the phenomena about the non-evident" (10.32). Lucretius uses this principle in his attack on Anaxagoras himself in the first book of the *De Rerum Natura*. If Anaxagoras were correct in his interpretation, he argues, grain, when it is crushed by a grindstone, would give out some sign of blood and blades of grass and pools of water would give out drops with the same flavor as the milk of fleecy ewes (1.881–92).

In our consideration of Epicurus' sense perception we have to distinguish between Epicurus' concept of the true and his belief that the properties of the impression (φαντασία) were the same as the properties of the solid body.[10] Two crucial passages read as follows: (1) Since all that is observed or grasped by apprehension of the mind is true (*Ep.* 1.62)[11]; and (2) "Whatever impression of shape or of properties[12] we get by apprehension of the mind or the senses, this is the shape of the solid object, if it comes about because of the successive repetition of the εἴδωλον (κατὰ τὸ ἑξῆς πύκνωμα) or because of the remaining effect of the εἴδωλον (ἐγκατάλειμμα τοῦ εἰδώλου, *Ep.* 1.50).[13]

When a man views a tower from a distance, his impression reveals the tower as small and round, but when he sees the same tower from a closer range, his impression reveals the tower as large and square. Both impressions are true. When the impression reveals the tower as small and round, the εἴδωλον, that is, the film of atoms in the air that have broken away from the solid object, is small and round. The limits belonging to the εἴδωλα have been broken off by their movements through the air (fr. 247 (209)).[14] He does not assume, however, that the properties of the first impression, which shows the tower as small and round, are the properties of the solid object because he does not experience a successive repetition of the εἴδωλον and his memory image (i.e., the remaining effect of the εἴδωλον) contradicts the impression. His memory image, whether of the tower or of similar towers, tells him that a tower is large and probably square. He does not regard the impression of the small and round tower as accurately reproducing the properties of the tower, but he accepts the impression of the large and rectangular tower as doing so.

Falsehood and error are to be found in the *doxa*. Epicurus writes: "Falsehood and error always lie in the addition made by the *doxa* [regarding what is waiting] to be confirmed or not contradicted, and which is subsequently not confirmed [or is contradicted]"; and "If it is not confirmed or contradicted, falsehood arises; if it is confirmed or not contradicted, the true" (*Ep.* 1.50 and 51).[15] Confirmatory evidence is defined and illustrated in the following passage in Sextus Empiricus: "Confirmatory evidence is apprehension through a clear view (ἐνάργεια) that that which is conjectured is such as it was conjectured to be, as, for example, when Plato is approaching from a distance, I suppose and conjecture (δοξάζω) with reference to the distance that it is Plato, and when he has come nearer with the distance reduced, there is further evidence that it is Plato, and this is confirmed by the clear view itself (fr. 247(212)).[16] The clear view in this example meets the two conditions laid down by Epicurus for an impression whose properties were the properties of the object; it is based on a successive repetition of the εἴδωλον and is consistent with the remaining effect of the εἴδωλον. Contradictory evidence is also evidence from the phenomena. Epicurus writes in his first *Epistle*: "What is more, we must not believe that every magnitude exists in the atoms in order that the phenomena may not contradict us" (1.55).

Although in some cases the properties of the impression were similar to the properties of the εἴδωλον rather than to those of the sense object, in all cases the property of the affection or feeling (πάθος) is the same as the property of that which produces the πάθος. Sextus Empiricus writes:

> For just as the primary affections (πάθη) that is, pleasure and pain, come about from some things which produce them and according to those very things which produce them, as, for example, pleasure from those things which are pleasant, and pain from those things which are painful, and it is not possible that that which is productive of pleasure should not be pleasant or that that which is productive of pain should not be painful, but it is necessary for that which causes pleasure to be pleasant and that which causes pain to be painful in nature (fr. 247(203)).[17]

So far as I have been able to discover there is nothing in the fragments of Democritus which would indicate that he believed that the properties of the impression were the properties of the object. The evidence leads to a very different conclusion. According to Democritus, the names of the sense impressions are according to common usage: "By customary usage, color, by customary usage, sweet, by customary usage, bitter; in truth, atoms and void" (68 B 125 cf. 9). Democritus wrote also: "In reality we understand nothing exactly, but only as it changes according to the disposition of our body, and of those things that come in upon it and of those that resist" (68 B 9). On the other hand, the sense perceptions provide the evidence on the basis of which inferences can be drawn: "There are two forms of knowledge, one genuine, one obscure. To the obscure belong all these, sight, hearing, smell, taste and touch. But the genuine is separated from this. . . . When the obscure can no longer see more minutely or hear or smell or taste or perceive in touch, but ⟨it is necessary to carry out our investigations⟩ to something finer" (68 B 11).[18]

The term *homoeomery* does not appear in any of the fragments of Anaxagoras. Aristotle, however, referred to the elements of Anaxagoras as homoeomeries[19] and defined the term as meaning that the part was the same as the whole.[20] The term homoeomery was probably applied to Anaxagoras' philosophy by Aristotle, if indeed Anaxagoras did not use the term himself, because Anaxagoras argued that that from which an entity emerges has predominant parts that are the same as the predominant parts of the entity. Anaxagoras wrote: "For how could hair come from that which is not hair and flesh from that which is not flesh?" (59 B 10). Epicurus seems to have used the term homoeomery to indicate the likeness that exists between that which emerges and that from which it emerges. For instance, he argued that the current that moves away from that which is speaking or making a noise was broken up into homoeomerous particles (ὁμοιομερεῖς ὄγκους), which preserved an affinity with one another and a distinctive unity that stretched back to that which sent them forth (*Ep.* 1.52). These homoeomerous particles, we may assume, have the same characteristics as the whole from which they emerged. The essential similarity between the εἴδωλον and the solid body is denoted by the term homoeomereity. A fragment from Epicurus' *Concerning Nature* has the lines: "Preserving the same homoeomereity with the solid object" (24.33.2–4).[21] Arrighetti connects this fragment with an earlier fragment from *Concerning Nature*: "In the same position and order" (24.11.3–4)[22] and with lines in Lucretius, which read as follows: "Because the image has an appearance and shape similar to the body from which it is said to have poured forth" (4.52–3). In his discussion of the shapes that Plato attributed to the four elements in the *Timaeus* (55D–56C), Epicurus wrote in *Concerning Nature*: "The shapes which he (Plato) attributes to them are not (sc. incompatible) with the affections which arise because of these four elements, especially the first two (i.e., fire and earth, cf. 29.22), or more precisely, that which has already acquired homoeomereity with the phenomenon (i.e., fire)" (29.27.1–9).[23] Here the term homoeomereity denotes the correspondence between the shape and the affection.

The homoeomereity is not between an atom in a body that has emerged and an atom in the body from which it has emerged, but rather between a body that has emerged and a body from which it has emerged. For instance, in sound homoeomerous particles are "a group of particles which have an affinity with one another" (*Ep.* 1.52). The shape, size, position, and arrangement of the atoms in that which has emerged are similar to the shape, size, position, and arrangement of the atoms in the body from which it has emerged.

In his refutation of Anaxagoras, Lucretius argues that when the tops of trees are rubbed together and flames burst forth it is not necessary to suppose that fire is in the wood, but rather that there are many seeds of fire in the wood (1.897–903). In a passage in book 11, Lucretius writes that nature changes all foods into living bodies, just as she makes dry wood blossom out into flames and turns everything into fire (2.879–82). If there are seeds of fire in the wood, it is reasonable to suppose that there are seeds of flesh in the food. The four parts of the soul, fire, air, *pneuma*, and a fourth nameless part were molecules capable of producing such qualities as anger, fear, and composure (3.287–306).[24] These molecules were not merely anger-producing atoms or fear-producing atoms but they were complexes specified by such terms as fire and air. We are told that there are seeds of wind (*ventus*) and burning heat (*calidus vapor*, 3.126–27).

There is no doubt that Epicurus recognized the existence of molecules—a group of atoms in an entity that are such that they can produce a particular attribute in the entity.[25] Diogenes Laertius in a passage based on Epicurus refers to atoms that are productive of fire (D.L. 10.115 = *Ep.* 2.115). Several passages in Plutarch mention heat-producing atoms in wine. The first passage, which is from the *Adversus Coloten*, reads as follows:

> Therefore, in general, we should not say that wine is productive of heat, but that such a kind of wine is productive of heat in such a nature and in a nature disposed in such a way, or that such a kind of wine is productive of cold in this nature. For there are such natures in such an ἄθροισμα (aggregate, fr. 59).

In a second passage from his *Quaestiones Conviviales* Plutarch writes:

> Epicurus in his *Symposium* spoke at length, and the gist of his remarks, I believe, is something like this. He says that wine is not absolutely hot but that it has some atoms in it productive of heat, and others are productive of cold (fr. 60).

What is the ἄθροισμα to which Plutarch is referring in the first passage quoted above (fr. 59)? The word is used several times in the first *Epistle* of Epicurus to denote the body with which the soul forms a unity,[26] and in another passage to refer to the bodies in which the movement of atoms takes place (1.62.3). Shorey ably defined the ἄθροισμα as a "body, viewed not merely as a material aggregate of atoms, but as a metaphysical complex of qualities."[27] This concept is Platonic in origin (*Theaet.* 157B), but attested for Epicurus in the following passage in Sextus Empiricus: "This (sc. that intelligible bodies are composed of incorporeals) Epicurus acknowledged, for he said that body was conceived according to the ἄθροισμα (aggregate) of shape, magnitude, resistance and weight" (*Math.* 10.257).

We are now in a position to understand the relation between the molecule and the aggregate. The molecule was a group of quality-producing atoms in the aggregate. A particular group of atoms, as, for example, heat-producing atoms, produced a particular quality, such as heat, in the aggregate.

Spontaneity and chance may have been significant features in Anaxagoras' work. Simplicius writes: "Anaxagoras, leaving νοῦς (mind) on one side, as Eudemus says, and introducing spontaneity (αὐτοματίζων), proves many things" (59 A 47). We know also that Anaxagoras argued that none of the things that happen, happen according to fate and that fate is an empty word (59 A 66). A scholiast reports that according to Anaxagoras all human affairs are directed by chance (59 A 66).

Epicurus diverged from the views of Democritus in his interpretation of chance (τύχη) and necessity (ἀνάγκη). Democritus rejected chance altogether, arguing that it was a cause non-evident to human reasoning (68 A 70 cf. A 68). According to Aristotle, Democritus referred all those things that nature uses to necessity; Aetius states that Democritus termed the resistance, movement, and impact of matter (i.e., the atoms) *necessity* (68 A 66). Pseudo-Plutarch in his *Stromateis* attributes to Democritus the statement that the causes of those things that are coming into being now have no beginning, and that all that has come into being and is and will be, without qualification, is "bound by necessity from infinite time in the past" (68 A 39). Here the term *necessity* may mean no more than the movement of the atoms. With these passages we might compare the statement of Diogenes of Oenoanda to the effect that Democritus said that there was no free movement for the atoms because of their collision, and that from this it appeared that all things were moved according to necessity (68 A 50). A passage from Diogenes Laertius tells us that the δίνη (vortex) was by necessity (68 A 1(45)).[28] In these examples, the term ἀνάγκη (necessity) seems to indicate something that has come to pass as the result of causes that are not determined. It did not denote regularity or order. In the area of human activity, Democritus used a system of antecedent causes. Digging, for instance, was the cause of both finding the treasure and planting the olive tree (68 A 68).

Several passages indicate that Epicurus was critical of Democritus' use of ἀνάγκη (necessity). Epicurus wrote: "We must not suppose that the κόσμοι have one shape according to necessity";[29] and again, "For it is not necessary for a gathering of atoms or a vortex to come into being . . . as is supposed, by necessity" (*Ep.* 2.90). He does, however, offer as a possible explanation for the fact that some stars wander from their course but others do not the conjecture that the stars were so constrained by necessity that some moved along a regular orbit and others along one that was irregular (*Ep.* 2.113). A movement that Democritus would have attributed to necessity was usually explained by Epicurus in terms of the physical phenomena. For example, Epicurus offers several explanations that are in accordance with the physical phenomena for the rising and setting of the sun, moon, and the other heavenly bodies (*Ep.* 2.92).

Some early thinker, if not Democritus himself, seems to have argued that human volition was restricted by the agglomeration of atoms. To this Epicurus was strongly opposed. A passage from his writings reads as follows: "Since the cause is to be found in men themselves and not in the primeval agglomeration or in the necessity of that which surrounds us and comes in upon us in accordance with spontaneity" (Arrighetti, 32. 27.1–9).[30] Epicurus distinguished between "that which is in our power" (τὸ παρ' ἡμᾶς) and chance (τύχη, *Ep.* 3.133–4). Τύχη is not a god or an unreal cause (*Ep.* 3.134).[31] It is that which makes possible opportunities for good or evil. As Epicurus wrote: "Opportunities for great good or evil are provided by this" (*Ep.* 3.134–35). Epicurus' "that which is in our power" denotes those particular events that are subject to man's decision.

Although we know that Anaxagoras used spontaneity (αὐτόματον) and τύχη, there are not sufficient grounds for us to assume that Epicurus' τύχη was influenced by Anaxagoras. It may have been drawn from Democritus' use of observed phenomena as the basis of inference. Cole has argued convincingly that five accounts of technology and society found in Diodorus Siculus, Vitruvius, Lucretius, the 90th *Epistle* of Seneca, and Tzetzes' *Commentary on Hesiod* have a common source in Democritus.[32] For instance, as Lucretius relates, when fire scorched the forests with heat, there flowed from the veins of the earth a convergent stream of silver and gold. Then it occurred to men that these when liquefied by heat could flow into any shape and appearance that they might wish (5.1255–63). Democritus' use of the *eventus fortuitus* would seem to be substantiated by a passage in Aelian in which Democritus is said to have referred to the mating of a jackass and a mare by chance (κατὰ τύχην), and to have argued that men learned from this the custom of raising mules (68 A 151). The whole concept of *eventus fortuitus* seems to be inconsistent with Democritus' interpretation of τύχη. The inconsistency, however, lies in the term *eventus fortuitus* itself. For

Democritus the convergent stream of silver and gold was an observed phenomenon on the basis of which an inference could be drawn. Only in Epicurus' system was it a τύχη or *eventus fortuitus*.[33]

In an important passage in which he was discussing the nature of the heavenly bodies, Epicurus referred to that which cannot be otherwise. He wrote as follows: "We must realize that that which may happen in several ways and is capable of being otherwise does not belong here" (*Ep.* 1.78, cf. Arist. *Met.* 1015b12–5). These lines and passages in Lucretius suggest that Epicurus attached considerable importance to the regularity of nature. In the first book of Lucretius, we find such sentences as: "If things should come from nothing . . . the same fruits would not be constant on the trees" (156 and 165); "But now because the several things are born from specific seeds" (169); "Whatever is born is revealed while favorable seasons are present and the life-giving earth sends forth safely her delicate offspring to the shores of light" (177–79). This pattern of regularity that Epicurus recognized in the heavens and in nature itself has strong affinities to the order established by Anaxagoras' νοῦς.

It is, I believe, clear that Epicurus adopted an interpretation of the impression that was alien to Democritus' atomic theory and closer to that of Anaxagoras. Anaxagoras may have believed that the qualities of the impression accurately reproduced the attributes of the objects; and he certainly regarded the objects of sense perception as true. He held that that from which an entity emerges had predominant parts that were the same as the predominant parts of the entity. Anaxagoras' experiments suggest that he was aware in some degree of the principle of confirmatory evidence and evidence to the contrary. His form of argumentation was similar to that of Epicurus to some extent at least. What is more, Anaxagoras used the term *doxa* to denote an opinion for which there is no confirmatory evidence or evidence to the contrary. Anaxagoras made extensive use of material causes but attached particular significance to the regularity of the movement of the heavenly bodies. When Epicurus read the writings of Anaxagoras, he must have found himself in agreement with many of his basic assumptions.

NOTES

[1] An earlier version of this paper was read at the Society for Ancient Greek Philosophy, which met in conjunction with the American Philological Association, in Washington, D. C. on December 29th, 1975.

The fragments of Anaxagoras are cited from H. Diels, ed., *Die Fragmente der Vorsokratiker,* revised by W. Kranz (Zurich, 1966). The fragments of Epicurus were published by H. Usener, *Epicurea* (Leipzig, 1887). For Lucretius, I have used the text of C. Bailey, *Titi Lucreti Cari De Rerum Natura* (Oxford, 1947) I.

[2] See W. Bröcker, "Gorgias contra Parmenides," *Hermes* 86 (1958):435–36,

and H. J. Newiger, *Untersuchungen zu Gorgias' Schrift Über das Nichtseiende* (Berlin, 1973), p. 109.

³ On this passage see H. Diller, "Die philosophiegeschichtliche Stellung des Diogenes von Apollonia," *Hermes* 76 (1941):363–64.

⁴ For the meaning of ἀλήθεια (truth), see A. P. D. Mourelatos, *The Route of Parmenides* (New Haven, 1970), pp. 63–67.

⁵ Furley argued that this type of argument was probably Eleatic in origin and used by Leucippus and Democritus. See D. J. Furley, "Knowledge of Atoms and Void in Epicureanism," *Essays in Ancient Greek Philosophy,* vol. 1, eds. J. P. Anton and G. L. Kustas (Albany, 1971), pp. 612–13.

⁶ See H. Diller, "Opsis adelon ta phaenomena," *Hermes* 67 (1932):14–42. For the meaning of ἄδηλον see J. Mejer, "The Alleged New Fragment of Protagoras," *Hermes* 100 (1972):175–78.

⁷ For a discussion of νοῦς (mind) in Anaxagoras see J. Ferguson, "Dinos," *Phronesis* 16 (1971):104–06, reprinted in this volume.

⁸ H. Cherniss, *Aristotle's Criticism of Presocratic Philosophy* (The Johns Hopkins University Press, 1935), p. 81 and n. 333. Compare W. D. Ross, *Aristotle's Metaphysics,* vol. 1 (Oxford, 1924), p. 275, line 25.

⁹ For the argument "it is not inconceivable that" see P. H. De Lacy and E. A. De Lacy, *Philodemus: On Methods of Inference* (Philadelphia, 1941), pp. 154, 167.

¹⁰ For a discussion of sensation and knowledge in Epicurus' philosophy see M. L. Bourgey, "La doctrine épicurienne sur le rôle de la sensation dans la connaissance et la tradition grecque," *Association Guillaume Budé, Actes du VIII Congrès* (Paris, 1969), pp. 252–58.

¹¹ On this passage see Furley, "Knowledge of Atoms," pp. 615–56.

¹² The properties (συμβεβηκότα) of the solid body are described in the following passage of Epicurus: "But surely, in regard to the shapes, colors, sizes, weights and all other things which are predicated of body as properties . . . we must suppose . . . that the whole body generally has its own everlasting nature from all of these" (*Ep.* 1.68–69 cf. Luc. 1.451–52). On this passage see also G. Arrighetti, *Epicuro* (Turin, 1973), p. 516.

¹³ On this passage see D. J. Furley, *Two Studies in the Greek Atomists* (Princeton University Press, 1967), pp. 200–02; Furley, "Knowledge of Atoms," pp. 610–11; and G. Vlastos, "On the Pre-History of Diodorus," *A.J.P.* 67 (1946):52, n. 12.

¹⁴ Furley, "Knowledge of Atoms," p. 616 writes: "The point of the contrast is that when we experience a mental image, it always pictures accurately the εἴδωλον or set of εἴδωλα which cause it. Error never arises because of a lack of correspondence between the mental picture and the atomic configuration which caused it." See also A. A. Long, "Aisthesis, Prolepsis and Linguistic Theory in Epicurus," *Bulletin Institute of Classical Studies* 18 (1971):117; and J. M. Rist, *Epicurus* (Cambridge University Press, 1972), pp. 17–25.

¹⁵ See Long, "Aisthesis," pp. 117–18.

¹⁶ Rist, *Epicurus,* p. 37 cf. 33, translates ἐνάργεια as "self-evident truth"; Long, "Aisthesis," p. 22 as "clear and distinct impression."

[17] For a discussion of πάθος in Epicurus' philosophy see F. Solmsen, "Aisthesis in Aristotelian and Epicurean Thought," *Med. der Kon. Ned. Akad. von Wetenschappen, Afd. Letterkunde* 24 (1961):241–62, reprinted in F. Solmsen, *Kleine Schriften*, vol. 1, pp. 612–33; H. Steckel, *Epikurs Prinzip der Einheit von Schmerzlosigkeit und Lust* (Göttingen, 1960).

[18] The words that I have bracketed are based on the emendation of Diels. On these fragments of Democritus, see G. Vlastos, "Ethics and Physics in Democritus," *Studies in Presocratic Philosophy*, eds. R. E. Allen and D. J. Furley (London, 1975), pp. 403–04, n. 60–63. For a discussion of Aristotle, *De Anima* 404a27 and *Metaph.* 1009b12, passages in which Aristotle states that Democritus found truth in appearance, see Cherniss, *Aristotle's Criticism*, pp. 79–83 and 313, note 87; and H. Weiss, "Democritus' Theory of Cognition," *C. Q.* 32 (1938):47–56.

[19] *Phys.* 203a20–21, *De Caelo* 302a28, *De Gen. et Corr.* 314a19 and 27–28, *Metaph.* 984a14, 988a28.

[20] *Phys.* 203a23–25 and *De Gen. et Corr.* 314a17–20. On the homoeomeries see G. B. Kerferd, "Anaxagoras and the Concept of Matter Before Aristotle," *Bulletin of the John Rylands Library* 52 (1969):129–43. D. J. Furley, "Anaxagoras in Response to Parmenides," *Canadian Journal of Philosophy*, suppl. vol. 2 (1976):61–85; M. Schofield, *An Essay on Anaxagoras* (Cambridge University Press, 1980), pp. 47–50, 117–8 and 128–32.

[21] The fragments of Epicurus' *Concerning Nature* have been published by Arrighetti, *Epicuro*.

[22] On this line see Arrighetti, *Epicuro*, p. 581, n. on 24.33.

[23] See Arrighetti, *Epicuro*, p. 609, n. 27.

[24] Compare Epicurus, *Ep.* 1.63, in which Epicurus speaks of *pneuma*, heat, and something finer than these. On this passage see Arrighetti, *Epicuro*, pp. 514–5, and G. B. Kerferd, "Epicurus' Doctrine of the Soul," *Phronesis* 16 (1971): 80–96.

[25] For molecules in Epicurus' philosophy see the excellent discussion of Kerferd, "Epicurus' Doctrine," pp. 88–91; and A. A. Long, *Hellenistic Philosophy* (London, 1974), p. 39.

[26] *Ep.* 1.63,4 and 8; 1.64,2 and 3; 1.65,5 and 8; 1.69,6.

[27] P. Shorey, "Plato, Lucretius and Epicurus," *H.S.C.P.* 11 (1901):203.

[28] On these passages see Furley, *Two Studies*, p. 175. For causation in Democritus see Cherniss, *Aristotle's Criticism*, pp. 246–49.

[29] *Ep.* 1.74, cf. Usener, p. 127, fr. 82.

[30] On necessity and the swerve see Arrighetti, *Epicuro*, pp. 513, 631; and Furley, *Two Studies*, pp. 169–95.

[31] Arrighetti, *Epicuro*, p. 544, argued that ἀβέβαιος has the meaning "irreale, non esistente." It is unnecessary, I believe, to accept Bailey's emendation ⟨πάντων⟩ ἀβέβαιον αἰτίαν. See C. Bailey, *Epicurus* (Oxford, 1926), pp. 90, 342. The point that Epicurus is making is that the Epicureans should not regard τύχη as a cause at all.

[32] Diodorus Siculus 1.13.3, Vitruvius, 33.16–23, Lucretius, 5.932, 937–38, 953–54, 1007–08, 1241–57. On these passages see T. Cole, *Democritus and the*

Sources of Greek Anthropology (Western Reserve University, 1967). For the *eventus fortuitus*, see Cole 47 and 119.

[33] A. H. Armstrong, "The Gods in Plato, Plotinus and Epicurus," *C.Q.* 32 (1938):191, writes that chance as a separate force in Epicurus is reminiscent of the "errant cause" in the *Timaeus* (47E–48A). See also A. A. Long, "Chance and Natural Law in Epicureanism," *Phronesis* 22 (1977):63–88.

ARTHUR W. H. ADKINS

Form and Content in Gorgias' *Helen* and *Palamedes*: Rhetoric, Philosophy, Inconsistency and Invalid Argument in Some Greek Thinkers

ORGIAS' *Helen* (B 11) and *Palamedes* (B 11a)[1] are among the longest pieces of continuous prose included in Diels-Kranz, *Fragmente der Vorsokratiker*. We have here a rare opportunity of considering how a writer who merits inclusion in Diels-Kranz develops an argument over a number of pages. Gorgias, it is true, is a rhetorician; and though he has some claim to be regarded as a sophist or Presocratic philosopher also,[2] rhetoric[3] has evidently much to contribute to the *Helen* and *Palamedes*. The extent of the contribution is indeed the primary subject of the first part of my paper. I shall inquire whether Gorgias in the *Helen* indulges in rhetorical flourishes in which form takes precedence over content; whether on the other hand Gorgias' general philosophical position supplies the content of this work and furnishes premises from which conclusions are drawn for Helen's benefit, the rhetoric furnishing no more than a pleasing mode of presentation; or whether a case is being argued, and language manipulated, ad hoc, the rhetoric substituting for logic and valid argument. Gorgias himself terms the *Helen* a παίγνιον (21): I shall briefly consider the meaning of the word in the light of my discussion. I shall discuss the *Palamedes* in less detail and consider whether the presuppositions of the *Helen* and *Palamedes* are inconsistent with one another. Subsequently, I shall raise the question whether inconsistency is per se a mark of a rhetorician at this period, or whether similar inconsistencies may be found in other writers who are philosophically more respectable. I shall also consider to what extent Gorgias' presuppositions, and inconsistencies, are shared with nonphilosophical Greeks in early Greece; and very briefly indicate some

This paper was presented to the 1977 Atlanta meeting of the Society for Ancient Greek Philosophy; not previously published, it has been extensively revised for this volume.

A. W. H. Adkins is Edward Olson Professor of Greek and Professor of Philosophy at the University of Chicago.

long-standing worries of my own about the study of Presocratic philosophers.

Let me first state at greater length the distinction, drawn above, between rhetoric and logical argument based on philosophical premises. Gorgias is wont to use groups of words as if acceptance of the appropriateness of one entailed acceptance of the remainder: for example, in (10) he thus uses θέλγειν (enchant), πείθειν (persuade) and μεθιστάναι (bring about a—here psychological—change in), arguing in effect that anyone who grants that Helen was persuaded to abscond with Paris must also grant that she was in the grip of enchantment and subject to irresistible psychological causation. Now if Gorgias held a philosophical theory that entailed that θέλγειν, πείθειν and μεθιστάναι were synonymous, or that all πείθειν was θέλγειν and all θέλγειν was μεθιστάναι (or if θέλγειν is more strongly causal than μεθιστάναι, that all πείθειν was μεθιστάναι and all μεθιστάναι was θέλγειν), then his conclusions would be justified in terms of his theory, for acceptance of his premises would necessitate acceptance of his conclusions. But if Gorgias held no such theory and was using θέλγειν, πείθειν, and μεθιστάναι in their customary Greek sense, his use was a mere rhetorical trick, since the customary sense of the words does not justify such conclusions.

Gorgias' arguments in the *Helen* begin at (6), where he sets out four possible reasons or causes for Helen's going to Troy with Paris: she did what she did either (a) as a result of the wishes of Chance or the plans of the gods or the decrees of Necessity or (b) because she was carried off by force or (c) because she was persuaded by words (λόγοι) or (d) because she was smitten with love. We might perhaps provisionally grant that Gorgias had furnished a full list of possible reasons or causes,[4] and expect him to demonstrate that Helen was influenced by (b), or possibly (a), since (b) is certainly, and (a) possibly, a valid defense. Gorgias, however, undertakes to show that, no matter which of the four was the reason, Helen should be exonerated from blame. He offers four arguments or groups of arguments, one for each reason or cause.

Argument 1. Suppose Chance, Necessity, or the gods desired, planned, or decreed Helen's journey. By nature (πέφυκε) the stronger (κρεῖσσον) is not prevented by the weaker. No, the weaker is ruled and led (ἄγεσθαι) by the stronger. God (a term that evidently includes Chance and Necessity) is κρεῖσσον than a human being in might, wisdom, and their other characteristics. If then one should ascribe the causation (or the guilt, αἰτία) to Chance and God, one should absolve Helen from her bad reputation.

I shall discuss later whether these pleas are novel.[5] For the moment I note that the argument seems to rest primarily on causality, with the will of the divine powers mentioned acting as a cause. The stronger can compel the actions of the weaker. The argument is logically presented: its acceptability is likely to vary from culture to culture. However, not only logic is employed, nor is causality alone invoked. κρείσσων does not simply mean "stronger": it serves as one of the comparatives of ἀγαθός, "good," so that one may be κρείσσων also in wisdom or cleverness (σοφία), and other characteristics. The wiser or cleverer can circumvent the less wise or clever. Furthermore, it was widely held to be appropriate for the more ἀγαθός to rule the less ἀγαθός:[6] Greek values have a role to play here. Lastly, ἄγεσθαι is the *mot juste* for carrying off prisoners or booty.[7] There is rhetorical skill in choice of words here, not merely skill in argument.

Argument 2. The second argument (7) examines the possibility that Helen was carried off by force. There are rhetorical flourishes: note the tricolon "was carried off . . . suffered violence . . . endured outrage" (ἡρπάσθη . . . ἐβιάσθη . . . ὑβρίσθη), of which the third carries the strongest emotive charge; the manner in which "having perpetrated an outrage" (ὑβρίσας) is used to increase the enormity of "having carried off" (ἁρπάσας); the chiasmus ἐπιχειρήσας βάρβαρος βάρβαρον ἐπιχείρημα; and the other tricola λόγῳ . . . νόμῳ . . . ἔργῳ (repeated) and βιασθεῖσα . . . στερηθεῖσα . . . ὀρφανισθεῖσα. But the flourishes neither impede the logic nor substitute for it. The argument turns on the valid distinction between agent and patient: Paris acted, Helen suffered, Paris committed a crime, Helen suffered a misfortune. The argument from *force majeure* in such circumstances is acceptable in most societies, certainly in ancient Greece.[8] However, in the course of the discussion we shall observe Gorgias several times introducing a distinction that is valid in one context and subsequently applying it more widely.

Argument 3. Gorgias allots much more space (8–14) to the third argument. He writes "it is not hard to make a defence *even* in answer to this"; from which we may infer that the case is more difficult to argue. Gorgias proceeds: "Speech (λόγος) is a mighty potentate (δυνάστης) who accomplishes very wonderful (θειότατα) effects with a tiny invisible body; for he is able (δύναται) to cause fear to cease, to take away grief, to impart (ἐνεργάζεσθαι) joy and to increase pity." The sentence is very skilful rhetorically. Etymologically speaking, a δυνάστης is simply "one who can"; and what Gorgias says λόγος can (δύναται) do is uncontroversial and based on empirical observation. But since the "for" clause is an explanation of δυνάστης, and follows it, the incautious reader may suppose that Gorgias has justified his use of δυνάστης in the full sense of "potentate"; as the reader will certainly have interpreted it, since δυνάστης never occurs in its etymological sense. To think of λόγος as a powerful ruler allies the persuasion-argument with Argument 2, and points forward to "compels" in (12). Again, though θεῖος in Greek of this date may sometimes be translated "wonderful" (e.g., θεῖα πρήγματα, Herodotus 2.66), the associations with the divine cannot be entirely excluded, so that assistance may be sought from Argument 1: if λόγος can accomplish θειότατα, one might infer that λόγος is itself divine, with consequences already argued in 1. Further, all the verbs that follow δύναται are transitive, but ἐνεργάζεσθαι goes further, emphasizing the entry of a cause from without: a point that Gorgias will use again, particularly in the argument about love (15 ff.), but also almost at once (9).

There is skillful rhetoric here; but I see no sign of philosophical theory as yet. Indeed, Gorgias concedes as much, and engages to prove "these things," which I take to be the effects of λόγος characterized in the previous clause. (To do so will not, of course, justify the strong sense of δυνάστης.) He produces a series of examples of the effects of λόγος. He defines poetry as "λόγος with meter," and says that a terrified shudder, tearful pity, and grieved longing enter (εἰσελθεῖν) those who hear poetry. (The language is vivid; but I cannot agree that the combination of emotional adjectives with nouns of physical description, or vice versa, commits Gorgias to any particular philosophical or psychological theory.[9] Homer does the same, as in πολύστονα κήδε' ἐφῆκεν: *Iliad* 1.445.) The rest of the sentence, literally translated and in Greek order, runs: "with respect to the good and ill fortunes of other people's πράγματα and bodies / a πάθημα of its own / through the agency of λόγοι/the ψυχή experiences." Word-order and syntax are very important here. In (8) Gorgias undertakes to exonerate Helen if λόγος persuaded her (or her ψυχή). The rest of (8) elaborates. Now in (9–11) λόγος does not stand as the subject of a transitive verb; and when it does so again in (12) Gorgias feels himself able to interpret "persuaded" as "compelled." The word-order and syntax of the sentence translated above are a step on the way. λόγοι are the agency of persuasion; but they appear merely in a prepositional phrase. To perceive the λόγοι is essential; but there is no word for perception. "Other people's πράγματα and bodies" is closely paralleled with "its own πάθημα," as if the πράγματα and bodies directly caused the πάθημα.[10] The causality of λόγος is the theme of Gorgias' paragraph; but he is moving cautiously, step by step, to the point where he feels able to assert it; and initially that a πρᾶγμα should cause a πάθημα, in the relevant sense of πάθημα (which I shall discuss in a moment) seems *prima facie* more likely—without argument; and none is forthcoming—than that a λόγος should. (I shall argue that there is a similar device in (12).)

Rhetorical sleight of hand is most apparent here; but is philosophy also present? Is Gorgias, by using πάσχειν in (7) of physical suffering, here of the ψυχή, giving "to this subjective emotion an objective, physical reality"?[11] I have no doubt that Gorgias did not clearly distinguish the material from the nonmaterial: I suspect Plato to have been the first to do so. That being so, the objective physical reality is likely to have been assumed unchallenged. What is more important for Gorgias' case is to represent the events as a causal sequence. For this purpose he employs the range of usage of πάσχειν and πάθημα. πάσχειν may mean simply "happen to," as when used of the Nile in Herodotus 2.20; and at least in slightly later Greek πάθημα may mean "emotion, affection" when used with ψυχή (Xenophon, *Education of Cyrus* 3.1.17) or even of the experience of the ψυχή in exercising φρόνησις (Plato, *Phaedo* 79d), which is not an emotion and not passive. In the Plato and Xenophon cited, πάθημα makes no philosophical point; but of course Gorgias chooses πάσχειν and πάθημα for the passivity implied. But the argument seems to be based not on a coherent philosophical position but on a rhetorical transference of πάσχειν from one context to another. I shall argue in favor of my view by pointing out that such transferences are characteristic of the design of the *Helen*.

Gorgias then (10) turns to another type of λόγος. Inspired (ἔνθεοι) incantations through the medium of λόγοι induce pleasure, banish pain; for the power (δύναμις cf. δυνάστης and δύναται) of the incantation (ἐπῳδή) consorting with the opinion of the mind (ψυχή) charms (θέλγειν) it, persuades (πείθειν) it and changes (μεθιστάναι) it by witchcraft (γοητεία). Once again the presence of deity is alluded to (ἔνθεοι, "with gods in them": cf. Argument 1), and power is set in the foreground. But is the "for" clause a philosophical explanation of what precedes? Surely not, in the sense of an explanation drawing on a coherent theory: "the δύναμις of the incantation consorting . . ." can really be read only as a metaphor. It explains nothing; but it does make "power" the subject of the three transitive verbs. This is a stronger expression than πάθημα . . . ἔπαθεν in (9). What Gorgias really offers is a verbal "slide," in which one word is replaced by an alleged synonym that in fact has different implications. θέλγειν, "charm," is the appropriate term with incantations and other magic acts (ἐπῳδή, γοητεία). It has associations of binding with spells against the will: Circe in *Odyssey* 10 (291, 318, 326) could have θέλγειν Odysseus with her magic arts and turned him into an animal had he not had a protective herb. Gorgias then writes πείθειν, implying—without proof—that θέλγειν, when used to instill pleasure and banish pain, is persuasion. He evidently hopes that "persuasion" will be endowed with *all* the associations of θέλγειν, though the examples of θέλγειν given are solely of imparting pleasure and removing pain. Gorgias needs to show not merely that persuasion can impart emotions willy-nilly, but that the emotions will issue in action willy-nilly; and he has really demonstrated neither, even for θέλγειν, and certainly not for πείθειν. Gorgias then uses μεθιστάναι, "change." In a weak sense of "change" the move is harmless, since presumably all data, if they are to be perceived by the mind, must produce some changes therein; but Gorgias needs a strong sense of "change"—"producing necessary changes in the ψυχή which necessarily issue in action." He has offered no *proof* that such a sense of "change" is appropriate; he has merely contrived by skillful use of language to *suggest* that it is. Once again we have a tricolon, θέλγειν, πείθειν, μεθιστάναι: a rhetorical device frequently resorted to for emphasis, rhetorical fullness or other stylistic reasons. Its stylistic function might well help to conceal that it is here used also for sleight of hand in the content of the argument.

In (11) Gorgias makes the point that if everyone had knowledge of past, present, and future, the effect of λόγος would not be the same. But as it is, most people in most circumstances have to resort to opinion as counsellor. "And opinion, which is hazardous and unreliable, involves those who employ it in successes which are hazardous and unreliable." Is there here allusion to a doctrine, like the Socratic, that no one goes against *knowledge*? It seems not. Gorgias is making the common-sense point that if all the facts, including the future, were known, people would act differently: presumably Helen would have acted differently had she known the outcome of the Trojan War. The argument is a digression, and it does not help Gorgias' case. Not all opinions result from persuasion; to "make a mistake" that is a moral error is not normally regarded as excusable in Greek; and Gorgias offers no reasons for a different evaluation. Furthermore, (11) implies that there are actions that are not the effects of external causes; which reveals other flaws in the alleged comprehensiveness of his defense. I shall return to this point later.[12]

The opening words of (12), which are hopelessly corrupt, might have contained some attempt to show the relevance of (11); but none of the proposed emendations has this effect, or even uses the term "opinion." Gorgias returns to the argument of (10), according to the emendations, at the beginning of (12); and visibly does so in the transmitted text at the end of (12): "for λόγος which persuaded her ψυχή compelled (ἀναγκάζειν) the ψυχή which it persuaded to agree with (πείθεσθαι) what was said and to acquiesce in what was done. The one who persuaded committed an injustice in using compulsion, whereas the one who was persuaded, inasmuch as she was compelled by λόγος, is wrongly blamed." Gorgias now finds himself able to say that λόγος persuaded the ψυχή and to slide immediately to "compelled." The form of words is more explicit than in (9): Gorgias advances one step at a time. Gorgias' hearers may find it easier to accept that λόγος compelled Helen's ψυχή than that λόγος compelled Helen, since both λόγος and ψυχή are "psychic"; though he has of course justified neither. He now uses the fact that λόγος is masculine, ψυχή feminine. He writes ὁ μὲν οὖν πείσας, "the one who persuaded," which might refer either to Paris or to the λόγος, while ἡ πεισθεῖσα "the one who was persuaded," might refer either to Helen or to her ψυχή. Since it is not Helen's ψυχή, but Helen, that is being blamed, the hearer is likely to interpret the second participle as referring to Helen, the first to Paris, with the result that it is suggested that Helen was compelled by Paris using λόγος as an instrument: a proposition *prima facie* even less easy to accept than that her ψυχή was compelled by λόγος. There is verbal dexterity also in πείθεσθαι. Since it is the passive of πείθειν, if *A* πείθει *B*, *B* πείθεται; but the range of usage of πείθεσθαι with the dative spans "be persuaded, obey, trust in": the word may suggest that λόγος compelled Helen not merely to the persuaded but to trust in and obey what was said. Once again, I see rhetoric here, but little philosophical theory.

In (13) Gorgias speaks of persuasion added to λόγος "moulding (τυποῦσθαι) the mind as it wishes": the strongest statement yet, and one totally unproved as yet. He adduces as evidence here the arguments of the cosmologists that can take away one opinion and implant (ἐνεργάζεσθαι) another; forensic arguments,[13] in which one argument delights and persuades a crowd not because its statements are true but because it is composed with skill; and philosophical debates, in which quickness of wit can be seen readily making (ποιεῖν) opinion easily changed (εὐμετάβολον). I see no philosophical theory here; and the evidence falls far short of proving Gorgias' point. He adduces examples of persuasion: he needs to argue that all instances of persuasion are instances of necessary, compulsory persuasion, that "you were persuaded by that argument, but you need not have been; the argument is not persuasive" is nonsense. (Compare Aristotle's remarks in *EN* 1110 a 29, which are relevant to Arguments 3 and 4 of the *Helen*.) There is less rhetorical skill here: ἐνεργάζεσθαι (also in (8)) and ποιεῖν to not compare with some of Gorgias' earlier rhetorical effects. Possibly, however, the statement that the cosmologists "cause (ποιεῖν) what is incredible and obscure to appear before the eyes of δόξα" points forward to the fourth argument. "The eyes of δόξα" is a much more unusual expression in Greek than is "the mind's eye" in English, and presumably was chosen with some purpose. In the light of the fourth argument Gorgias could have elaborated the phrase into an assertion that speech presents to the mind images over which we have no more control than over the manner in which what we see presents itself to us. There is no more than a hint here, but it may prepare for (15 ff.). As we have seen, Gorgias is advancing step by step.

In (14) an analogy is drawn between the effects of λόγος and those of φάρμακα, "drugs." Different φάρμακα drive out different humors from the body; some cure, some kill. Similarly, some λόγοι cause grief, some joy, some fear, some boldness, while others "through some harmful persuasion 'drug' (φαρμακεύειν) and bewitch (γοητεύειν) the mind." Once again, Gorgias is trying to equate πείθειν with a causal sequence, for the effect of a drug does not depend on the patient's choice: cure or death follows irrespective of the patient's wish. Is there a philosophical theory here? I see none. Gorgias draws an analogy between the effects of λόγοι on the ψυχή and drugs on the body, and in justification simply says "for drugs have effects a, b, c, etc., while λόγοι have effects k, l, m, etc." No proof is offered that the effects are produced in any analogous way: this is a mere *petitio principii*. Any conviction must be produced by rhetoric, by skilled choice of words. Gorgias' word-order in discussing the effects of λόγος may be intended to help his case. The first two examples, grief and joy, do not suggest specific types of action; the second pair, however, fear and boldness, dispose the mind towards types of action: retreat and advance. (Gorgias has not attempted to prove that the emotions *cause* the relevant actions. He might have used the arguments of 15 ff.: once again he may be advancing step by step.) He concludes with the example of persuasion (after using pleasure and pain as earlier examples, as in 10), and reintroduces a word (10), "bewitched" (ἐκγοητεύειν), where he has already argued for a causal sequence. The use of φαρμακεύειν together with "bewitched" is rhetorically skillful. The word takes up φάρμακα earlier in (14). Now φάρμακα may denote both what we should distinguish as medicinal drugs and magical means of affecting others.[14] (Being unaware how either worked, the Greeks did not distinguish clearly at this period between natural and supernatural causation.) (φάρμακα in (14), closely associated with "humors" (χυμοί), a scientific term,[15] predominantly suggests scientific medicine; but φαρμακεύειν, which has the same range as φάρμακα, when brought into association with both γοητεύειν and the earlier use of φάρμακα readily calls to mind the full range of usage, and binds together the argument of (14) with that of (10), where, Gorgias hopes, a causal sequence has already been conceded. The rhetoric is skillful; of philosophical theory, or of valid philosophical argument from demonstrated premises, there is none. We may note once again the use of a term (γοντεύειν) to cross-refer to an earlier part of the speech in order to suggest the existence of an argument; it seems to be a Gorgianic device. Gorgias sums up his third argument by claiming to have proved that if Helen was persuaded by λόγος, she did not do wrong but was unfortunate (ἀτυχεῖν). She was not the agent but the patient.

Argument 4. The fourth argument, designed to exonerate Helen if it were love that "did" all this, takes a similar line. (Note the immediate ascription of agency, πράττειν, to love: Gorgias' confidence is increasing.) What we see does not have the nature we wish it to have, but whatever it chances to have; and through sight the ψυχή is moulded (τυποῦσθαι again, cf. (13)) in its behavior. For example, if sight perceives a terrifying foe, it is thrown into confusion and confuses (ταράττειν) the ψυχή, so that often men flee in terror from a danger that is still distant. The powerful habit induced by custom (νόμος) is driven out on account of fear induced by sight, and causes one to forget the καλόν of not running away and the ἀγαθόν (benefit) to be gained from victory. Some people (17) have been driven out of their minds by seeing terrifying sights, "so powerful are the images of things seen that sight engraves on the mind. And the things which terrify are many of them left behind, and those which are left behind are like things said."

Gorgias claims a causal sequence: visible object → visual image → emotion in the ψυχή → action. To excuse Helen, he must make one of two further claims: either (a) that the causal sequence is *always* necessary and inevitable or (b) that when the resultant action is (apparently) reprehensible, the causal sequence is always of this nature. (He must argue a general case under which the case of Helen may be subsumed.) When explicitly stated, (b) is a difficult position to take; and Gorgias does not state it explicitly, though the *Helen* read in conjunction with the *Palamedes* might be thought to imply it. (Aristotle was aware of such a doctrine and attacks it, *EN* 1110 b 9 ff.) Gorgias proves neither (a) nor (b). He takes extreme cases, whose existence few would deny: there *are* terrors that only superhuman courage could resist, and one might be driven mad by overmastering fear. The proof is valid (for (a)) if we are prepared to infer that the extreme cases are typical of all actions, or (for (b)) if we are prepared to infer that they are typical of all reprehensible actions. Gorgias wishes the inference to be drawn; but even he can say no more than "often" "some people" "many people." Gorgias needs to argue both that what we see is not under our control and that the visual image of what we see produces an emotional effect that is necessary and overmastering, and inevitably—always or in reprehensible cases—issues in a specific kind of behavior. "Through sight the ψυχή is moulded in its behavior" is in form an open generalization; but "often," "some people," etc., concedes that armies do not always run away in time of terror. The language does not suggest a scale of terror above a certain point on which terror *causes* flight: Gorgias' language suggests merely "sometimes they do, sometimes they don't." Nothing in his argument, moreover, entitles him to claim that whenever they do run away, it was causally determined that they could not do otherwise. The point is not proved, but the argument is designed to suggest this conclusion; and the closing lines (from "so powerful") claim the point, and also liken visual (memory?) images to things said, in their effect on the mind, once again cross-referring, this time to λόγος and persuasion; and Gorgias claims to have successfully defended Helen on this charge already.

Gorgias next (18) observes that painters delight the sight, while sculptors' works furnish a pleasant sight to the eyes. Many objects produce (ἐνεργάζεσθαι again, cf. (8) and (13)) in many people a love and longing for many things and bodies. Gorgias presumably discusses the effects of painting and sculpture, and visible objects in general, to emphasize the status of Paris as a physical object in space, Paris as a speaking human being having been discussed already; but painting and sculpture hardly help his case, since an aesthetic response is not characteristically, and certainly not necessarily, accompanied by action. (Perhaps Gorgias is asserting that one always desires to possess any beautiful painting or sculpture that one sees, but it would be difficult to argue that one is inevitably constrained to steal it.) "If Helen's eye (19), pleased by the body of Paris, handed on an eagerness and a struggle of love to her ψυχή, what is surprising about that?" This sentence again claims a causal sequence, but without explicitly taking the step of translating emotion into action. Gorgias ends with a series of different points drawn from his earlier arguments. Taking up "love" from the previous sentence, he says that if love is a god with divine powers, a mere mortal, being weaker, could not resist (Argument 1); whereas if love is a human disease and ignorance in the ψυχή, one should not blame it as an error but reckon it as misfortune (not explicitly discussed, but possibly hinted at in Argument 3, (11)); it came by the snares of Chance (Argument 1), not the plans of the mind and by the necessities of love, not the devices of art. "Necessities" once again introduces the idea of compulsion by a stronger.

Is there philosophy here? What is said about sight is evidently *compatible* with the view ascribed to Gorgias by Plato (*Meno* 76 a ff.) that color is an effluence from objects, fitting the passages of the eyes, since it asserts a flow from objects *into* the perceiver; but the argument of (15) ff. rests on observable human behavior and would be compatible with many theories of perception and would be rendered no more valid by any theory that stopped short, as Gorgias' does, of claiming more than that certain results "often" follow. There is curious Greek here: it seems strange to say that "sight is thrown into confusion and confuses," that it "engraves images in the mind" and that Helen's eye was pleased and then caused effects in her ψυχή. There may be a philosophical theory; but it is worth observing that similar phrases occur in tragedy. ὄψις, here translated "sight," is a word whose range spans "sight, appearance, face, eyes." The connotation of the word perhaps renders it easier to write that ὄψις is thrown into confusion, disturbed, by terror. Similarly, Electra says to Orestes that his ὄμμα ("eye, face, etc.") is thrown into confusion (ταράττειν), when Orestes' experiences have driven him mad (Euripides, *Orestes* 253). Hades in Aeschylus, *Eumenides* 275 is said to watch over everything δελτογράφῳ φρενί, "with a mind that records on tablets." Again, the Guard in Sophocles, *Antigone* 317, asks "Are you pained in your ears or in your ψυχή?" The idea is used somewhat differently; but the distinction drawn between effects in ears and ψυχή is comprehensible in the absence of any philosophical theory.[16] (The date of *Antigone* makes it impossible to suppose the line affected by Gorgias' famous visit to Athens.) There might be a philosophical theory here nonetheless; after all, metaphor is sometimes a source for philosophical theory, and I shall argue below that there are precedents for some of Gorgias' causal expressions in earlier Greek. It remains true, however, that the theory does not materially assist the argument, which rests shakily on empirical observation—extrapolated—and rhetorical sleight of hand.

It is worth noting that Gorgias' four arguments do not exclude all possibility of condemning Helen. In (11) the possibility of moral error arising out of mistake about one's best interests was mentioned, though not very clearly; and now in (19) we have mention of "the plans of intellect" and "the devices of art" as possible sources of action that are not relevant to Helen's case. (Gorgias does not explain why they are not relevant; and this is a serious flaw in his argument.)

If my analysis is correct, Gorgias is throughout manipulating language with great rhetorical skill to prove a case ad hoc. He is not setting out a philosophical theory held on other grounds, and drawing from it conclusions that serve to acquit Helen. (Nor is he indulging in rhetorical flourishes for their own sake: language is manipulated in a very purposeful manner.) Gorgias' concern is to acquit Helen, and he draws on all his resources of ingenuity to construct a case for so doing. In (8) ff. and (15) ff. he begins from empirical observation, drawing from it conclusions that go far beyond what is justified, but demand no coherent theory and invoke none. The motive power of the arguments is verbal dexterity sustained over the whole work: I have noted the manner in which Gorgias uses words and phrases to allude and cross-refer from one argument to another in order to support one point—not by argument, but by verbal association—with a point he claims to have proved, or is going to "prove" later. (Note how he carefully sets the two less controversial defenses first, and reverses the order (20) when all are "proved," so that the more difficult proofs may be thrust into the foreground.) The arguments of the *Helen* can be *understood* without reference to a philosophical theory. That the conclusions would be acceptable only if a particular type of philosophical theory were held does not prove that Gorgias held such a theory. The structure and method of the *Helen* point in the opposite direction; and the kind of theory needed would have further consequences, which, I shall argue, Gorgias seems not to have accepted.

   (Another philosophical explanation of the structure and method of the *Helen* represents it as a consequence of Gorgias' doctrine (B 3) "Nothing exists; if it existed it could not be known; and if known it could not be communicated."[17] Knowledge is assured in the *Helen*, it is argued, because Gorgias takes *all* the possible reasons why Helen might have gone to Troy, and proves her innocence in each case. The method employed, the logic, guarantees certainty. But Gorgias, as we have seen, acknowledges (11, 19) that he has *not* exhausted all the possibilities in his four arguments; and the reasons I have offered for supposing that Gorgias is not drawing on a philosophy of any kind apply to this theory also.)

I now turn briefly to the *Palamedes*, to discuss the compatibility of the presuppositions of Gorgias 11 and 11a. In the latter, Odysseus has accused Palamedes of treachery; and Palamedes argues that he has committed no treasonable act (5): "for I could not have done it even had I wanted to; and I should not have wanted to even if I could have done it." He works out this contention in detail. In (6) ff. he adduces evidence of impossibility on practical grounds. In (13) ff. he argues that he could have had no adequate motive: he could not have hoped for absolute rule over either the Greeks or the Trojans (13, 14); mere possessions would not have attracted him (15); and honor is not to be gained by treachery, so that even a moderately φρόνιμος person would not attempt treachery for honor's sake (17 ff.). Palamedes turns to Odysseus and says that Odysseus is relying on mere opinion (δόξα), whereas he, Palamedes, has knowledge of his own innocence (24). He accuses Odysseus of inconsistency in imputing to him at one and the same time cleverness (σοφία) and madness (μανία); for the details of what Palamedes is alleged to have done would require σοφία whereas the attempt as a whole is a clear indication of μανία.

The situations of Palamedes and of Helen are quite different. *Pace* Stesichorus and Euripides, that Helen went to Troy is undeniable, and it is this fact that requires excuse; whereas Palamedes is denying that he has done anything wrong. The arguments supplied to him are arguments ἐκ τοῦ εἰκότος, a form of reasoning apparently invented by Gorgias' Sicilian predecessors Corax and Teisias (Plato, *Phaedrus* 273 a-c, Aristotle, *Rhet-*

oric 1402 a 18). εἰκός spans the probable and the reasonable. It is here better rendered "on the basis of what is reasonable," since Palamedes' arguments, where they do not rest upon a claim that a course of action is impossible to carry out (6–12), rest upon an estimate of what a reasonable person might be expected to do in the circumstances described. Palamedes claims to be a reasonable person of moderate desires (15). He does not claim that all are such, but contrasts himself with "those who are slaves of pleasure. . . ." He offers evidence of his past life as guarantee that he is speaking the truth.

The emphases of the *Palamedes* differ from those of the *Helen*. We have seen that the *Helen* does not equate all action, even all reprehensible action, with action externally caused: something is left for "the plans of intellect," "the devices of art," and mistakes about one's own best interests.[18] (I shall have more to say on this topic later.) But in the *Helen* externally caused action is in the foreground; in the *Palamedes* the reasonable person occupies that position. Indeed, one may go further: Palamedes' offering of character evidence (15) conflicts with the use that Gorgias seems to wish to make of the argument in *Helen* (16). Granted, even well-trained armies of brave men do sometimes run away under extreme conditions, and there is no conflict with character evidence offered by Palamedes in very different circumstances. But Gorgias' argument, which emphasizes the loss of "the powerful habit induced by custom," and attempts to extrapolate from extreme cases to all cases, would, if taken seriously, render it impossible to offer any character evidence at all. It would never be possible to forecast how anyone is likely to act on the basis of previous behavior, since what is presented to the mind (15)—and the effects are similar to those of what is said (17)—has whatever nature it chances to have, and the effects follow, whatever they may be, with the reason of the reasonable person playing no role whatever. On the basis of the arguments of the *Helen* one could draw from the fact that the army did not run away on a particular occasion the conclusion that the visual (or in different circumstances, verbal or aural generally) stimulus was insufficient to cause flight, and one might add "to an army of persons so disciplined and with such a character"; but one could only argue thus after the event, for one could not forecast the effects of a visual/aural presentation that in *all* its individual details could never have occurred before. Accordingly, the arguments of *Helen* (16) would render it impossible for Palamedes to argue, as he does, "because I have such and such a character, I did not behave in such and such a manner." If the arguments of the *Helen* are pressed as Gorgias needs to press them to achieve the goal of his reasoning in that speech, the position of the *Helen* is seen to be incompatible with that of the *Palamedes*.

We may be tempted to conclude that such discrepancies are a mark of the παίγνιον, interpreted as a work lacking in seriousness; Gorgias, we may suppose, simply makes whatever assumptions he needs for the argument in hand. The meaning of παίγνιον has been much discussed: it has been compared with *lusus* in Catullus and παίγνια in Philetas, to indicate that works so termed may have been seriously and carefully composed.[19] There is of course a difference between poetry and philosophical argument: one might work long and seriously at a poem on a frivolous topic and produce an excellent poem, but serious work on the production of clever but invalid arguments will be differently evaluated. Gorgias' seriousness about his skill as a rhetorician cannot be doubted, but, as indeed continuing scholarly debate on the subject would suggest, I doubt whether it can be conclusively demonstrated whether or not Gorgias believed his arguments in the *Helen* to be valid. He may have done so, for these are the early days of logic and philosophy; or if he knew that there was something wrong with the arguments, he may not have known what it was. He is certainly not the only Presocratic to argue for extreme conclusions.[20] What can be demonstrated, however, is that similar discrepancies occur in different kinds of work in which there is no question of deliberate rhetorical trickery; and to this I now turn my attention.

For even if the *Helen* and *Palamedes* are rhetorical and contain discrepancies, it does not necessarily follow that their being rhetorical is a *sufficient* explanation for the discrepancies. A rhetorician cannot take any presuppositions he chooses: they must appear plausible to those whom he is trying to convince. Now though his arguments about λόγος and visual data may be novel, Gorgias was not the first Greek to trace action back to causes outside the agent. Action is frequently so characterized in Homer; and similar language appears in fifth-century writers. In a famous and much discussed passage, *Iliad* 19.85 ff.,[21] Agamemnon, having discovered the disastrous effects of offending Achilles, says: "Often indeed did the Greeks tell me this, and abused me. But I am not αἴτιος of this. No; Zeus and μοῖρα and the Fury who walks in darkness are the cause; for they put fierce blindness, ἄτη, into my mind in the assembly when I myself deprived Achilles of his prize. But what could I do? The god brings all things to pass." Again, one may yield to one's θυμός; in *Iliad* 9.109 Agamemnon's behavior in slighting Achilles is thus explained. Here—and numerous examples could be cited—we have ascriptions of cause very similar to those of Gorgias' *Helen*; and Agamemnon even says that he is not αἴτιος. If Gorgias' Helen can be so characterized, she is freed from blame (6). Occasionally, similar moves are made in Homer. In *Iliad* 3.164 f. Priam excuses Helen from responsibility for the war, saying "You are not αἰτίη; in my eyes the gods are αἴτιοι, who have stirred up against me the woeful war with the Greeks." But this attitude toward divine causation is unusual, in

Homer and later. Indeed, Zeus' complaint, *Odyssey* 1.32 ff. (which is not really required by the situation in the poem at this point), that the accusations men bring against the gods are unjustified since mankind bring woes upon themselves ὑπὲρ μόρον seems designed as a rejection of the kind of view expressed by Priam;[22] and set where it is at the beginning of the first book, it is given great prominence and seems programmatic. In *Iliad* 19 Agamemnon does not expect to be excused for what he has done: he offers recompense to Achilles, and indeed follows his statement that three deities were αἴτιοι with "I myself (αὐτός) deprived Achilles . . . ." αὐτός is very emphatic, and expresses Agamemnon's agency very strongly.

In the fifth century it remains unusual to excuse behavior on the grounds that it was caused by deity. There are two recorded instances of Delphi excusing human agents (the priestess Timo and Evenius, in Herodotus 6.135 and 9.93) for actions that, the oracle reveals, the gods have caused themselves; but the conclusion that, if a god caused the action, the human being is not responsible for it, is not usually drawn. Aeschylus in *Agamemnon* 1468 ff. displays a sensitivity to problems of divine causation and human responsibility that is not apparent in his earlier plays.[23] In the *Agamemnon* the chorus speaks of the δαίμων that has fallen on the accursed house. The form of expression is common enough, but Clytemnestra unusually tries to employ it to disclaim responsibility. Later the chorus speaks of Agamemnon as "smitten . . . by a two-edged weapon wielded by the hand of a wife." Clytemnestra realizes that such language ascribes responsibility to her as agent. She denies responsibility, claiming that the Alastor, the avenging spirit of the accursed house, took her shape and killed Agamemnon. The chorus rejects the defense: "Who will bear witness that you are ἀναίτιος of this murder? Yet the avenging spirit sprung from a father's crime might be a sharer in the deed."

Even in the extreme case of the accursed house of Greek tragedy, the accursed may not appeal to the language of divine causation in order to plead that they are not to be held responsible for their actions. The Alastor may be a contributory cause; but, to quote what I have written elsewhere, "while some may be predisposed to do evil by supernatural agency, none are so predestined."[24] Clytemnestra had a choice.

The gods caused Agamemnon to slight Achilles by sending ἄτη upon him (*Iliad* 9.115 f., 19.136 f., etc.); and ἄτη is frequently cited in later Greek as influencing action for the worse. Usually, the ascription to ἄτη furnishes no excuse; and Dodds seems to be correct in supposing that it serves primarily to distance the agent psychologically from the act.[25] Agamemnon feels that had not "something" prevented it, he would have acted sensibly, with a proper calculation of advantages. Clytemnestra, in a psychological revulsion from what she has done (for the scene is psychologically sound; it is not merely a philosophical debate), feels that she would not "herself" have done what has been done.

In earlier Greek, accordingly, it was not uncommon to ascribe the source of actions, particularly—but not solely—actions whose consequences had been, or might be, disastrous, to causes outside the agent, or external to the agent's ego, usually identified with the practical intelligence. That the agent would otherwise have behaved "sensibly" is a tacit assumption of this belief: there is no implied general determinism of action. Now Gorgias' Palamedes is denying that he has done anything wrong; he claims to have acted with the prudence and common sense that would ensure that he would not commit treachery in the circumstances. Helen has performed, or been involved in, an important action with disastrous consequences; and Gorgias has furnished her with a choice of chains of causation beginning outside the agent. In this respect the difference between the analysis of Helen's situation and that of Palamedes is traditional.

I have noted that even in the *Helen* it is conceded (or seems to be conceded; but see below) that not all actions are externally caused, that there is no assertion of a universal determinism of action; and this too is traditional. Gorgias departs from the mainstream of Greek tradition partly by the rhetorical ingenuity with which he argues for and elaborates his causal chains, but more importantly by his insistence that the causal chains furnish grounds for exonerating Helen from blame. It is at this point that the contradictions between the *Helen* and the *Palamedes* become apparent. So long as the causal explanation furnished psychological relief, but not an excuse, it was not important to determine criteria for the class of actions to which the causal explanation was relevant: as we have seen, Agamemnon in the *Iliad* can cite three deities as external causes, and say emphatically that he himself did the deed, all within the space of a few lines. In these circumstances it is comparatively unimportant whether or not the causal explanation is invoked in any particular case. Gorgias, however, in the *Helen* has furnished causal explanations that are intended to excuse, and which could be applied, so far as I can see, *to any misdeed whatever*. Gorgias may allude to miscalculations of interest, to the plans of intellect and the devices of art; but one can always say of any action "I did this because . . ."; and if the agent wished to obtain or avoid something (as presumably he did) then at least Argument 4 will be available to excuse him. Furthermore, good actions have motives too: Argument 4 could furnish a causal explanation for all actions that do not fall under Arguments 1, 2, or 3. A universal determinism of action could easily be generated from what is said in the *Helen*; and such a determinism is not consistent with the *Palamedes*.

Gorgias may have failed to realise all the implications of his arguments in the *Helen*: he is arguing a case for one important action of one important person, and does not overtly generalize his findings. He does not say explicitly—and it would have been shocking to Greek sentiment—that armies that run away are not to be held responsible for their actions. Further, since Paris was presumably under the influence of ἔρως in his behavior towards Helen he should, under the terms of Argument 4, be absolved from blame; but Gorgias does not wish to draw this conclusion (7, 12).

I conclude that Gorgias' *Helen* and *Palamedes* owe much more to rhetoric than to philosophy, but also that each draws on certain assumptions about behavior and causation that date back at least as far as Homer. Gorgias was not taking up different positions in different speeches with conscious sophistry, but in each case elaborating positions that would have been familiar to the Greeks of his day.

Nor is it impossible for an acknowledged philosopher to hold that wrongdoing is involuntary, rightdoing voluntary. Aristotle argues against the position (*EN* 1110 b 9 ff.), defining action done under compulsion as action whose first cause lies outside the agent (οὗ ἔξωθεν ἡ ἀρχή). The definition seems unexceptionable; but Aristotle is aware that it might be argued that actions performed to obtain what is pleasant or καλόν are involuntary, since these objects are outside the agent and exert force to compel him (ἀναγκάζειν, cf. *Helen* (17) with cross-reference to (12)). Aristotle replies that such a theory renders *all* action involuntary, since the desire for what is pleasant or καλόν actuates all men in all their actions; and no one, Aristotle is confident, would accept any theory that had such consequences. (Gorgias, as I said above, seems not to have realized all the possible consequences of his arguments in the *Helen*; and I see no reason to suppose that he would have welcomed them.) Aristotle adds a further point: actions done in pursuit of the pleasant or καλόν are pleasant, and so cannot be done under compulsion; and he observes that it would be absurd to take the credit for noble actions performed in pursuit of the καλόν or pleasant while disclaiming responsibility for bad actions performed for the same motives. Aristotle's own view is that actions done under compulsion are not simply those whose first cause lies outside the agent; the person compelled must have contributed nothing at all; and he holds that being persuaded, or moved to action by desire for the καλόν or pleasant, are elements of action over which the agent exercises some control. Argument 2 of the *Helen* (*force majeure*) remains valid, as possibly does Argument 1 in some circumstances;[26] but the practical wisdom of the *Palamedes* is restored to Arguments 3 and 4 of the *Helen*, thereby breaking the chain of causation.

A little later (*EN* 1111 a 24 ff.) Aristotle considers the internal, nonrational springs of action: θυμός and ἐπιθυμία. If actions performed under their constraint are involuntary, then no child or animal will ever act voluntarily. Once again, Aristotle is confident that no one would accept a theory with such consequences. He then points out that both good and bad actions may be prompted by θυμός or ἐπιθυμία; and it would be absurd to claim credit for good actions, but excuse oneself for bad ones, when the ascribed cause of each group of actions is the same. He concludes (*EN* 1111 b 1 ff.): "It seems that the irrational passions are not less human than reason is. Accordingly, actions which result from θυμός or ἐπιθυμία are the man's actions too. . . . It is absurd, then, to suppose that these are involuntary."

The arguments, particularly those of 1110 b 9 ff., could have Gorgias for their target: they are especially relevant to Argument 4. However, Gorgias cannot be the sole target. Aristotle was aware of more prominent thinkers than Gorgias who had held that no one is voluntarily κα- κός without also maintaining that no one is voluntarily ἀγα- θός, notably Socrates and Plato.[27] The Socratic position could be regarded as a more enlightened version of *Helen* (11): if we were not ignorant of our best interests in the full sense of the phrase, we should act differently. My concern here is not to discuss the Socratic position as such, merely to show that discrepancies of the kind found in Gorgias 11 and 11a are not confined to rhetors and sophists; and for that purpose a brief discussion of the rather different account of "no one is voluntarily κακός," which appears in the *Timaeus*, will be suitable. Timaeus treats the basic stuff of the cosmos as being triangles, a shape from which may be constructed every plane figure and thence every solid. Earth, air, fire, and water differ because they are constituted of different geometric shapes. God made human marrow from primary triangles of the highest quality, and bound human ψυχή into it. He divided the marrow between the head and the spinal column, the head receiving the divine seed of reason, the other parts of the ψυχή being bound into the spinal column. A ψυχή so bound to its body may be affected by it, and some of Timaeus' words (e.g., 86 b) would suggest that ψυχή is under the control of body. There exist diseases of the ψυχή, which result from the condition of the body. Madness in the familiar sense of the term is included; and this is uncontroversially involuntary. But the greatest diseases of the ψυχή are pleasures and pains in excess. The abundant flow of one substance, resulting from the open texture of the bones, is the cause of sexual excess; while bad temper, rashness, cowardice, forgetfulness, and stupidity—all "diseases" of the ψυχή—are ascribed to the presence of acid and salty phlegms and bitter and bilious humors, which wander through the body (86 e) and "find no exit but are pent within the body and blend their vapor with the movement of the ψυχή and cause all manner of diseases to the ψυχή." It is wrong, says Timaeus, to reproach anyone in any of these conditions as if he were voluntarily bad: no one is voluntarily κα-κός (86 d-e). The κακός is so as a result of the unskilled nurture of his body, and the condition is universally detested by its possessors and occurs against their will.

Nowhere else in Plato do we find an explanation of human behavior in such mechanistic terms. One might expect to find an explanation of ἀρετή in similar terms, for the ψυχή seems entangled in a nexus of causes over which it has no control. But consider the following (87 b):

> Furthermore, when men are in such an evil condition (κακός), and the political constitutions are κακαί and speech in the cities, both in private and in public, is κακός, and when lessons which would cure these conditions are nowhere learnt from childhood, as a result of this those of us who are κακοί become κακοί on account of two altogether involuntary causes. We must always regard the parents as responsible for the situation rather than the children and the nurses rather than those in their care; yet each of us must endeavor, so far as in him lies, to flee κακία and pursue the opposite by means of his motive, practices and studies.

The *Timaeus* is a work of philosophy, not composed by a sophist or a rhetor. The speech of Timaeus is presumably to be taken seriously, even if the account is only "probable" (44d, etc.). Yet the speaker does not consider the possibility—indeed, the necessity, in terms of the account of κακία given above—that the bad parents and nurses are involuntarily bad, but is prepared to find fault with them;[28] just as Gorgias does not consider that his causal explanations for Helen's behavior, particularly in Argument 4, could be used to excuse Paris, too. Again, despite the far-reaching explanation of temperaments and behavior in mechanistic terms, Plato adjures adults to flee κακία by their own endeavors. It may be argued that this position need not be self-contradictory; but it requires more defense than it receives in the *Timaeus*. There is no close analogy with curing one's own physical ailments, for any cause, such as apathy, that prevents one from fleeing κακία must surely be itself a disease of the ψυχή. Again, the only sense of "involuntary" which would exculpate is "completely involuntary," the result of a cause or nexus of causes over which one has no control.

One might expect to find in the *Timaeus* an explanation of ἀρετή too in mechanistic terms; but none is offered. It is assumed that once κακία is by some means removed, one is ἀγαθός of one's own free will. The analogy with physical health and illness may—not altogether logically—help Plato here. No one would ask whether another person was voluntarily or involuntarily healthy, for health is a desirable. Yet whether one has a healthy or a sickly constitution may well be determined at birth, and be out of one's control: it is not easy to see why the same may not be true of the ψυχή. Again, illness characteristically restricts action, whereas health does not; but the question whether the actions of a healthy ψυχή or body are free or determined must present itself to a modern thinker. Plato, however, like Gorgias and indeed like all Greeks, philosophers or not, prior to the Epicureans and Stoics,[29] does not find it necessary to discuss the problem of free will, which arises from a universal determinism, however clearly the *Timaeus* seems to pose the problem.

The lesson that I wish to draw from the *Timaeus* is that in Greece at this time not only rhetors and sophists held not completely consistent positions on the kind of topics discussed in the *Helen* and *Palamedes*; and one might add that the account of "no one is voluntarily κακός" differs from that given elsewhere in Plato. It follows that if Gorgias' account of truth and knowledge reported by Sextus Empiricus (Gorgias B 3) does not harmonize with the view of truth, knowledge, and communicability expressed in or implied by the *Helen*, *Palamedes*, or any other Gorgianic work, if the view of human action in the *Helen* fails to agree with that in the *Palamedes*, or if Gorgias overlooks some of the implications of the position he is holding, these features of his work need not be imputed to the fact that Gorgias is a sophistical rhetorician. Gorgias *is* a sophistical rhetorician, and his arguments in the *Helen* depend on rhetoric and linguistic sleight of hand; but if the work of a Plato can display inconsistencies or discrepancies when discussing matters of this kind, it follows that the inconsistencies and discrepancies—as opposed to the rhetorical arguments—in Gorgias, too, may not be the mark of a sophistical rhetorician but characteristic of thinkers of the period.

I conclude with some general reflections. I have argued that some of the content of Gorgias' *Helen*, and its discrepancies with the *Palamedes*, result from presuppositions about human behavior shared with many earlier Greeks; and that some of it is rhetorical, and takes the form it does because of Gorgias' need to argue a case. (Very few, if any, of the words in the *arguments* of the *Helen* and *Palamedes* are there merely to furnish rhetorical flourishes: the rhetorical figures and the language in general subserve the interests of the argument.) Finally, some of the discrepancies in the account of human behavior can be paralleled not merely in nonphilosophical presuppositions but also in Plato.

If the arguments are accepted, they suggest the need for a very careful analysis of Presocratic philosophy; for if some of the presuppositions of Gorgias are shared both by nonphilosophical Greeks and by Plato, similar phenomena might appear in any Presocratic: we cannot suppose other Presocratics to be necessarily more immune to influence from the presuppositions of their culture than was Gorgias, nor more coherent in their arguments than was Plato. And here, surely, we encounter a serious difficulty. I elected to discuss Gorgias because his fragments are quite long. The fragments of most Presocratics are much shorter. Doctrines have to be reconstructed; presuppositions are rarely apparent. In our endeavors to reconstruct doctrines we inevitably argue on the assumption that the doctrines are coherent and the presuppositions fully ascertainable: "but Presocratic philosopher A could not have held doctrine X together with doctrine Y, for they are not logically consistent; so this report of his views is wrong, and he must have held doctrine Z instead." For many years I have been uneasy about this type of argument; and in this paper I have tried to set out my reasons. I hope that some other student of the Presocratics may be able to reassure me.

NOTES

[1] I assume that both are genuine Gorgianic works. See e.g., the discussions cited by Diels-Kranz ad loc.

[2] See especially Gorgias B 3.

[3] I use "rhetoric" to denote not merely textbook devices (e.g., the "Gorgianic figures"), but also the skillful use of words whether merely to give pleasure (or cause amazement) or to suggest the presence of valid argument where none exists. For a discussion of Gorgias' style, see e.g., G. Kennedy, *The Art of Persuasion in Ancient Greece* (Princeton, 1963), pp. 62 ff., 156 ff., and 168 ff.

[4] See below, pp. 112, 117.

[5] Pp. 120 ff.

[6] See e.g., Isocrates, *To Nicocles* 14, Plato, *Meno* 73c9.

[7] See *LSJ* s.v. I.3.

[8] *Force majeure* can be pleaded as a defense (by a nonwarrior) already in Homer, *Odyssey* 22.351. For divine compulsion and influence, see below p. 120 ff.

[9] As C. P. Segal argues in "Gorgias and the Psychology of the Logos," *HSCP* 66 (1962):99–155, and especially 106. It seems to me that in his very valuable and illuminating paper Segal is in fact demonstrating what would have to be the case in order to validate Gorgias' arguments, and claiming that Gorgias held the appropriate tenets. I argue that the structure of the *Helen* indicates that Gorgias is not deriving his defense of Helen from a theory of action held on other grounds, but is ingeniously trying to convince his hearers ad hoc that empirical observation and ordinary language justify his startling conclusions.

[10] "πράγματα and bodies" appears in a prepositional phrase too; but ἀλλοτρίων with πραγμάτων, ἴδιον with πάθημα point the parallelism (and contrast) of thought.

[11] Segal "Gorgias and the Psychology," p. 105.

[12] Pp. 117, 118.

[13] This seems to me to be the most likely rendering of "τοὺς ἀναγκαίους . . . ἀγῶνας."

[14] For example, Hdt. 3.85, Plato *Rep.* 406d.

[15] See e.g., Hippocrates, *De Vet. Med.* 18. For φάρμακα, e.g., Hdt. 7.114, Plato *Rep.* 459c.

[16] It seems apparent from the context in the *Antigone* that Sophocles expected the distinction to be immediately comprehensible.

[17] So G. Bona, "Λόγος e 'Αλήθεια nell' l'"Encomio di *Elena*' di Gorgia," *RFIC* 102 (1974):5–33, especially 31 ff.

[18] See above, p. 112.

[19] See E. Mass, "Untersuchungen zur Geschichte der griechischen Prosa, 1: Über die erhaltenen Reden des Gorgias," *Hermes* 22 (1857); 566 ff., especially 575 ff., and other discussions cited in M. Untersteiner, *The Sophists*, trans. K. Freeman (New York, 1954), p. 131, n. 106.

[20] To go no further, neither Heraclitus nor Parmenides seems to have been worried by the *prima facie* implausibility of their conclusions.

[21] See E. R. Dodds, *The Greeks and the Irrational* (Berkeley, 1951), pp. 1 ff., and my own discussion in *Merit and Responsibility: a Study in Greek Values* (Oxford, 1960; Chicago 1975), pp. 50 ff.

[22] There is usually a common-sense contrast between results and events, for which the gods may be believed to be responsible, and the actions of the agent; see e.g., *Iliad* 9.254 ff. and Sophocles, *Philoct.* 1316 ff.

[23] The oracles given on behalf of Timo and Evenius antedate the *Oresteia* (produced 458 B.C.) and may be symptomatic of a new attitude from which Aeschylus is dissenting.

[24] See Adkins, *Merit and Responsibility*, p. 124.

[25] Dodds, *Greeks*, p. 17 f.

[26] At least in those circumstances in which the gods were believed to have interfered in human affairs in actual presence, in the manner of very powerful human agents, it would seem not unreasonable to allow the plea.

[27] Plato maintains even in the *Laws* (861 d 2 ff.) that no one is voluntarily κακός, long after his psychological analysis of action would have enabled him to offer a less misleading analysis.

[28] Such illogicality is perennial. See e.g., the strictures of Edmund Bergler, *The Superego* (New York, 1952), p. 320, quoted by John Hospers, "What Means This Freedom?" in *Free Will and Determinism*, ed. Bernard Berofsky (New York, 1966), pp. 26–45, 35–36 (reprinted from Sidney Hook, ed., *Determinism and Freedom in the Age of Modern Science* (New York, 1961), pp. 126–42).

[29] It is interesting to compare Gorgias' account of the constraint of external impressions with the Stoic account. The Stoics, while agreeing that we have no control over the nature of the external impressions that reach us, argue for human freedom on the grounds that the human agent is free to take what attitude he will toward those impressions. The defensibility of this position is too large a question to discuss here.

Z. PHILIP AMBROSE

Socrates and Prodicus
in the *Clouds*

HE search for the relationship between the historical and aristo-
phanic Socrates continues. The general view is that Aristophanes'
Socrates is a composite of contemporary thinkers, dressed in comic
conventions.[1] While names like Diogenes of Apollonia, Antiphon, Democritus, Hippias, and especially Protagoras are mentioned in this mélange,
the following study directs attention to the contribution to it of Prodicus of
Ceos.[2]

The burden of the study is to gather and weigh evidence for the hypothesis that Aristophanes in naming Prodicus at *Clouds* 361 nods to a significant influence of Prodicus on the play. General support for this is sought in
the possible role of Prodicus in other comedies in the period from about
424/3 to 422/1 B.C. One critical assumption, for which there is ample evidence, is that it was possible for competitors to allude to one another's plays
in the same festival, just as the individual poet will review and preview his
other works. Although there will be few certain conclusions in this speculation, there will be an opportunity to consider problems in the method of
treating chronology, the relationship between comedy and Plato, and the
conventions of comic allusion. It is hoped that this material will help in the
search for a more comprehensive view of Prodicus' image in comedy.

The evidence will be presented in the following order: (1) the teaching
of Prodicus; (2) *Meteora* in the *Clouds*; (3) correspondences among the
plays of the Dionysia of 423 B.C.; (4) allusions to comedy in Plato's
Protagoras; (5) Prodicus in other plays of the period; (6) Prodicus in the
Clouds.

This paper was presented at the 1970 New York meeting of the Society for Ancient Greek
Philosophy; it has been extensively revised for this volume and has not been otherwise published.

Z. P. Ambrose is Chairman of the Classics Department at the University of Vermont.

1. The Teaching of Prodicus

That too little is known about Prodicus, one of the most famous of the sophists, to make this study easy must be stated at the outset.[3] Besides the mostly Platonic testimony, the longest fragment, the parable of the Choice of Heracles, is related by Socrates in Xenophon's *Memorabilia* as only a summary of what Prodicus actually wrote in the book entitled *The Seasons* (Ὧραι). But from the limited evidence there are at least three clear aspects of Prodicus' teaching: (1) the correct use of words, acriby or orthoepy (esp. evident in Plat. *Cratyl.* and *Protag.*, cf. Diels A 11 and 13); (2) natural science, including the rationalistic view that the veneration of useful things gave rise to the gods (Diels B 3 and 4, from Galen); (3) ethics (Diels B 1 and 2, the Choice of Heracles, from Schol. ad *Clouds* 361 and Xen. *Mem.* II. 1. 21 ff.[4]). In Plato and Xenophon it is especially emphasized that Prodicus was concerned with earning money by teaching. An important motif in the scholiastic tradition is the conflation of Prodicus and Socrates. Aristophanes' presentation of Socrates as concerned with acriby, rationalistic natural theology, ethics, and lucrative teaching may have made an early contribution to this conflation.

2. *Meteora* in the *Clouds*

At *Apol.* 18c Plato cites the comic portrait as a blatant example of the old misunderstanding of Socrates:

ὡς ἔστιν τις Σωκράτης σοφὸς ἀνήρ, τὰ τε μετέωρα φροντιστὴς καὶ τὰ ὑπὸ γῆς πάντα ἀνεζητικὼς καὶ τὸν ἥττω λόγον κρείττω ποιῶν.

In this passage the "things aloft" and "the things under the earth" are physical philosophy, and "making the worse argument the better" is the activity of the sophists. Here Plato appears to be deliberately simplistic for elsewhere he frequently uses μετέωρα in a metaphorical sense for "objects of higher learning."[5] The names, Plato continues, of the long-standing accusers are unknown to Socrates πλὴν εἴ τις κωμῳδοποιὸς τυγχάνει ὤν (18d). The only comic poet actually mentioned is Aristophanes (19c), and ἀεροβατεῖν and μετέωρα φροντιστής (18c) allude specifically to the *Clouds*.

Only the ambiguity of the term *meteorosophist* (*Clouds* 360) would have allowed Plato to claim that Aristophanes had presented Socrates as a physical philosopher. In fact the *meteora* of the play have the same breadth as those in Plato's general usage, encompassing all objects of study.[6] While the entrance of Socrates in a gondola draws attention to physical matters, the sun (225) and the air (230), and τὰ μετέωρα πράγματα (228), the demonstration of Socrates' teaching methods in 476–509 shows that the master's wisdom περὶ τῶν μετεώρων (490) has nothing to do with astronomy or physical science but rather with oratory and legal procedure.[7] If anyone in Socrates' jury of 399 B.C. actually heard Socrates blame Aristophanes' caricature[8] and had a good recollection of what actually happened in the Theater of Dionysus in 423 B.C., he would probably have been aware that Socrates had reduced the facts in the case.

3. Correspondences Among the Plays of the Dionysia of 423 B.C.

The comic victors of 423 B.C. were Cratinas with the *Wine-Flask*, Ameipsias with the *Connus*, and Aristophanes with the *Clouds*. The fragments and testimonia of the lost plays suggest amazing parallels to the *Clouds*. Cratinus' wife Comoedia has been displaced in the old man's affections by the bottle, probably personified as "Mistress Wine-Flask," just as Aristophanes' *Dinos* "Whorl" or "pot" has displaced Zeus. In Fr. 188 the speaker, probably Comoedia herself, vows to break the jugs of her bibulous husband while Strepsiades deprecates the *Dinos* at 1472–74 as a mere pot, perhaps, as some think,[9] smashing a *dinos* in disgust. The tension between the married couple of Cratinus' play corresponds to that between Strepsiades and his citifed wife (41–55), and the personification of Comoedia as the abandoned wife/art is parallel to Aristophanes' personification of *comoedia* in a revised section of his play (534) as his abandoned child/play.

While there is no apparent emphasis on philosophy in the *Wine-Flask*, the mere fact of the correspondences to the *Clouds* is important when one considers even closer proximity to the *Clouds* in the themes of Ameipsias' *Connus*. The title character is the singer to the lyre who taught Socrates.[10] Fr. 9 (Diog. Laert.) not only shows that Socrates is present in the play but that a chorus address him in tones very similar to the chorus' greeting at *Clouds* 358–63. Diogenes Laertius, 2. 27, contrasting the well-washed and shod Socrates of Plato's *Symposium*, 174a, quotes both passages to show that Aristophanes agreed with Ameipsias' image of the frugal Socrates, barefoot and clad in *tribon*:

Σώκρατες ἀνδρῶν βέλτιστ᾽ ὀλίγων, πολλῷ δὲ ματαιόταθ᾽,
ἥκεις
καὶ σὺ πρὸς ἡμᾶς. καρτερικὸς γ᾽ εἶ. πόθεν ἄν σοι
χλαῖνα γένοιτο;
Β. τουτὶ τὸ κακὸν κατ᾽ ἐπήρειαν τῶν σκυτοτόμων γεγένηται.
Α. οὗτος μέντοι πεινῶν οὕτως οὐπώποτ᾽ ἔτλη κολακεῦσαι.

Socrates, shoeless as in the *Clouds*, is either joining or meeting the Thinkers (Φροντισταί) who formed the chorus of the play. Whereas the only members of Aristophanes' *Phrontisterion* actually named are Socrates and Chaerephon, it can be inferred from Athenaeus, *Deipn.* 5. 218c, that the individual members of Ameipsias' chorus were known:

ἐν τούτῳ τῷ δράματι (Κόλαξιν) Εὔπολις τὸν Πρωταγόραν ὡς ἐπιδη-
μοῦντα εἰσάγει, 'Αμειψίας δ' ἐν τῷ Κόννῳ δύο πρότερον ἔτε-
σιν διδαχθέντι οὐ καταριθμεῖ αὐτὸν ἐν τῷ τῶν φροντισ-
τῶν χορῷ

The absence of Protagoras must have been noted either because it was pointed out or because there was some kind of catalogue (with individual costuming?) of the chorus members.[11] In the absence of Protagoras, one might expect that the play included at least one sophist especially noted for orthoepy. Besides Protagoras there was none more eminent than Prodicus, whose presence in the *Connus* would have given an uncanny resonance to his actual name at *Clouds* 361. The "present meteorosophists" (τῶν νῦν μετεωροσοφιστῶν) at 360 would be not merely contemporary thinkers, but those present in the current competition.[12] The existence of a catalogue of Thinkers would have made an interesting contrast with *Clouds* 94–104 where Strepsiades describes the *Phrontisterion* but does not know ἀκριβῶς τοὔνομα of its members except for Chaerephon and Socrates. 'Ακριβῶς is a well-chosen word, alluding to the linguistic activity of the *Phrontisterion*. If Ameipsias' play followed Aristophanes', his catalogue would have filled in the latter's preterition, but if Ameipsias' play preceded the *Clouds*, the audience would have been deftly spared another catalogue of similar content.

Clouds 177–79 suggests an answer to *Connus* Fr. 9, "From where are you to get a cloak?" Using one of the tools of his trade, the geometer's compass, Socrates filches a cloak from the neighboring palaestra and has it sold to pay for the evening meal. Depending on the tone of the *Connus* fragment, a contrast in the treatment of Socrates in the two plays may be discernible, for it goes on to say that Socrates never stoops to flattery or chicanery (cf. Eupolis' title) even though hungry. In the *Clouds*, however, Socrates does satisfy his hunger by trickery, a point very essential to the dramatic unity of the play. The worn condition of Strepsiades' own garment is used to demonstrate the old man's financial distress. Socrates' ruse with the cloak thus serves to assure Strepsiades that he has come to the right address to deal with his problem. Eupolis' *Flatterers* Fr. 159 shows the sophists as parasites, bragging that they have two cloaks to choose from when going to the agora. It may be that in Ameipsias' play Socrates in his wonted worn cloak was contrasted with the conventional sophists of the chorus.[13] But it is impossible to tell how Ameipsias developed his plot and characters.[14] Nor is it more than conjecture that Prodicus had some kind of part in the play. But there is a strong likelihood that there was a chorus of named sophists, a mustering of intellectuals that enlarges the context in which to consider the oldest question about Aristophanes' play: How does it fit the position of the historical Socrates towards the sophists?[15]

4. Allusions to Comedy in Plato's *Protagoras*

It is generally thought that the *Protagoras* of Plato presents a scene similar to that of Eupolis' *Flatterers*, produced in 421 B.C., and that the dialogue was inspired by that play.[16] The following annotations to the *Protagoras* are offered to suggest that Plato is drawing not solely upon Eupolis' lampoon of the symposia in the house of Callias, son of Hipponicus, but also upon other plays, probably from the same period, dealing with the sophists. While Plato seems to have simplified his references to comedy in the *Apology*, the *Protagoras*, itself constructed as a drama, presents a more subtle reminiscence and understanding of the comic art. The material in it on Prodicus should be examined closely.

(a) There are twenty named participants in the *Protagoras*. Many others are present but unnamed. All are grouped around three attractions when Socrates arrives with Hippocrates: Hippias of Elis, Prodicus of Ceos, and Protagoras of Abdera. More than ample enough to have formed a comic chorus, this crowd is in fact seen in this light by Socrates at 315b: "I especially delighted in seeing this chorus, how careful they were not to stand in front of Protagoras, but if he turned about, those with him did also, and indeed well did these auditors divide themselves orderly on this side and that, and, wheeling about in a circle, always stood to his rear in finest fashion."

(b) At 315c Hippias is seated on a throne while his auditors sit at his feet about him on benches (ἐπὶ βάθρων). "They *appeared* [note that the schema suggests the content of the discussion] to be asking Hippias some astronomical questions." Like Socrates in the *Clouds*, Hippias is elevated to his lofty thought. As in the *Apology*, Socrates is made to exclude a metaphorical sense from *meteora*.

(c) At 315d Prodicus has been billeted in a storeroom of Callias' house because of the overflow of guests. Like the effete son of Strepsiades, wrapped in five blankets at *Clouds* 10, "Prodicus still lay abed, covered up in some fleeces and spreads, very many in number, it appeared." The blanket is an important prop in the *Clouds*. Strepsiades, the "Twister," first lies in his blanket, plagued by his debt-bugs (12–13, 37), and later (633–803) receives his instruction on and sometimes under a pallet. Compare (315d) ἐγκεκαλυμμένος to Socrates' οὐκ ἐγκαλυψάμενος ταχέως τι φροντιεῖς; at *Clouds* 735. Is this merely a comical conception of the sophists conceived independently by Plato and Aristophanes? Or could it be that the habit of remaining late in bed and (like a Baroque monarch) discoursing from his quilts was the particular cachet of the historical Prodicus? In the latter case one might suggest that Aristophanes first alludes to Prodicus through the blanket motif and Plato later, without loss of humor, reveals the object of the allusion in the *Protagoras*.

(d) At 316a Socrates says that he could not discern the nature of Prodicus' discourse—although the man seemed thoroughly wise and quite divine—because of the deepness of his voice, which filled the room with a drone (βόμβος). That Prodicus' words should have impressed Socrates so profoundly even though he could not hear them is fine humor, but Plato may also be alluding to a *terminus technicus* in the treatment of the sophists in comedy: in Eupolis, *Flatterers*, Fr. 166 (Suidas) the drone is characteristic of all the parasites of Callias.[17]

(e) At 316e Protagoras, citing Homer, Hesiod, Simonides, Orpheus, and Musaeus, asserts that lyre-playing was often practised by such men as a screen against public disapproval of their sophistic activity. By Protagoras' definition of "sophist" Connus, the lyre-teacher, would have found a natural place beside Ameipsias' chorus of Thinkers.

(f) At 320e–322d Protagoras offers a myth for the rise of civilization, demonstrating that from Prometheus' gift of fire came both religion and the arts, including "clothing, shoes, bedding, and nurture of things from the earth" (322a).[18] If, as Nestle has argued well,[19] Prodicus had expressed his views on the priority of agriculture in the growth of civilization in the *Seasons* (which also included the Choice of Heracles, alluded to pointedly by Socrates at 340d), Plato has here juxtaposed two emphatically contrary views: Protagoras' view that all *technai* derive from fire and Prodicus' that the arts are learned through tilling the earth. But Protagoras avers before the face of Prodicus that agriculture stands last in the series of inventions owed to fire—after shoes and bedding.

(g) At 327d Protagoras refers to the *Wild Men* (Ἄγριοι) of Pherecrates, produced (according to Athen. 5. 218d) in the Lenaea of 420 B.C. Plato seems unperturbed about the anachronism of this reference in a dialogue having characters (the two sons of Pericles) who had died in 429 B.C. The reference is, however, not at all out of harmony with the hypothesis that Plato's attention had been fixed on the dramatic productions of the late 420's in composing this work.

(h) At 335d Socrates refers in passing to his customary garment, the *tribon*. This is a touch of realism characteristic of Plato's art, for it continues Socrates' habit of narrating not only what was said but various aspects of the setting of the dialogue, such as the quilts of Prodicus. Further, the *tribon* serves to remind that Socrates was probably barefoot as well, presenting a most comical costume for one receiving instruction on the rise of civilization, two features of which, he had learned, were ἐσθῆτας καὶ ὑποδέσεις (322a).

(i) At 337 and 340a Prodicus' art of definition (διαίρεσις) forms an important part of Socrates' discourse on the distinction between γίγνεσθαι and εἶναι in Simonides of Ceos (emphasized as a country-man of Prodicus). After professing to have been a student of Prodicus in this art,[20] Socrates at 341ab refers to Prodicus' habit of criticizing him whenever he used δεινός in such expressions of praise as

σοφὸς καὶ δεινός...τὸ γὰρ δεινόν, φησί, κακόν ἐστιν· οὐδεὶς γοῦν λέγει ἑκάστοτε 'δεινοῦ πλούτου' οὐδε 'δεινῆς εἰρήνης' οὐδὲ 'δεινῆς ὑγιείας,' ἀλλὰ 'δεινῆς νόσου' καὶ 'δεινοῦ πολέμου' καὶ 'δεινῆς πενίας,' ὡς τοῦ δεινοῦ κακοῦ ὄντος.

Does the *Protagoras* allude here to the paronomasia on the *Dinos* in the *Clouds*? And perhaps to Prodicus' latent role in that play?

(j) Just as in the early part of the work Socrates compares the setting to a drama consisting of a chorus of admirers charmed by Protagoras/Orpheus, so in the end the dialogue has a dramatic reversal (peripety): the Socrates who had maintained that virtue was not teachable has now demonstrated that since all virtue is knowledge, it is therefore teachable, while the Protagoras who had viewed virtue as teachable has now, in arguing that ignorant people could be courageous, even though courage is virtue, been shown to deny that virtue can be taught.

5. Prodicus in Other Plays of the Period

In addition to *Clouds* 361 Prodicus is referred to by name in only two other passages in Greek comedy: Aristophanes, *Birds* 692 and *Tagenistae* (*Broilers*) Fr. 490 (Schol. *Clouds* 361).

At 690ff. the Birds invite the audience to give ear to their teaching:

ἵν' ἀκούσαντες πάντα παρ' ἡμῶν ὀρθῶς περὶ τῶν μετεώρων
φύσιν οἰονῶν, γένεσίν τε θεῶν, ποταμῶν τ', Ἐρέβους τε
Χάους τε,
εἰδότες ὀρθῶς, παρ' ἐμοῦ Προδίκῳ κλάειν εἴπητε τὸ λοιπόν.

The Birds recognize that in explaining the *meteora* and the origin of the gods they cover topics treated by Prodicus. At 708 ff. they go on to refer to the seasons:

πάντα δὲ θνητοῖς ἐστιν ἀφ' ἡμῶν τῶν ὀρνίθων τὰ μέγιστα.
πρῶτα μὲν ὥρας φαίνομεν ἡμεῖς ἦρος, χειμῶνος, ὀπώρας.

By referring to the ὧραι and the list of their own gifts to civilization—all the great activities, sowing, weaving, shearing, selling, prophesying—the Birds assert their priority to the Seasons of Prodicus and their superiority in usefulness. But they also usurp a principal argument of the Seasons: they have brought farming and from farming come commerce and religion. They are used as the mantic-muses of every season (723 ff.):

> ἢν οὖν ἡμᾶς νομίσητε θεούς
> ἕξετε χρῆσθαι μάντησιμούσαις
> ἦρος ἐν ὥραις, χειμῶνι, θέρει,
> μητρίῳ πνίγει.

They will not remain aloof in the clouds like Zeus, but will bless men with children, plenty, life, peace, youth, laughter, dancing, feasting, even bird's milk. As Nestle has said, "Was hier Aristophanes den Vögeln zuschreibt, das war bei Prodikos das Werk der Horen."[21]

Bergk (FCG II 2. 1146), taking the title to refer to parasites like the *Flatterers*, argued that the teaching of Prodicus came into the plot of the *Tagenistae*.[22] Edmonds, accordingly, takes Frs. 488, 512, 513, and 514 as "take-offs" on Prodicus. Fr. 490 names the sophist:

> τοῦτον τὸν ἄνδρ᾽ ἢ βιβλίον διέφθαρεν
> ἢ Πρόδικος ἢ τῶν ἀδολεσχῶν εἷς γέ τις.

Frs. 513 and 514 (Poll. 10. 47) 'βάθρα,' 'βάθρίδια', ὡς ἐν Ταγηνισταῖς are thought by Edmonds to refer perhaps to the benches of Prodicus' pupils like the *bathra* of Hippias' admirers in *Protagoras* 315c, 317d, and 325e. Suevern thought the plot similar to the *Flatterers* of Eupolis in the treatment of Callias and his parasites, the sophists.[23] Schmid and Lesky[24] think the element of carousal assures a place for Alcibiades in the play and date it accordingly in the last decade of the century, while Edmonds suggests a tentative date of 422 B.C. on the conjecture that Fr. 505 is a possible allusion to the flight from Delium in 424/3 B.C. Gelzer sensibly rejects the certainty of any association with Alcibiades but sees little to go on for dating the play. He does, however, agree that the title refers to parasites, on the basis of Eupolis, *Flatterers*, (?) Fr. 346 (Plutarch, *Quom Adul.* 54b, describing a parasite):[25]

> τῶν περὶ τάγηνον καὶ κατ᾽ ἄριστον φίλων.

The morning setting for this symposium indeed calls to mind the *Protagoras*.

Of the allusions to orthoepy seen by Edmonds, e.g., that Fr. 512 (Galen, *Hipp. Aph.* 18. 147. 8K) 'ἀμφαρίστερον' is the properly coined word for a man with two left hands, one may say that it is not uncommon for modern scholars to compare such comic stuff with the prominence of Prodicus' interest in words.[26] Common sense, however, warns us from too precisely identifying the sources of acriby in Aristophanes. Acriby was a principal interest, surely, of Protagoras (who was especially interested in correct gender) and Prodicus. But it is a universal source of comic delight. The value of citing parallels between Greek comedy and the sophists in this sphere lies in reconstructing the general context of Athenian cultural life, in which the nuances of language struck the fancy of intellectuals, burghers, and farmers alike. Only if the *Tagenistae* in fact gave a prominent role to Prodicus or dealt explicitly with his teaching, would it be necessary to see comic acriby as a deliberate allusion to the sophist.[27] Of the *Tagenistae*, in sum, it may be said that the play seems likely to have treated intellectual parasites (for which the debate between the worlds of the living and the dead in Fr. 488 is perhaps the strongest evidence), but the evidence for dating is very slight.

Apparently it has not been suggested that the *Seasons* (Ὧραι) of Aristophanes in any way alluded to the *Seasons* of Prodicus. Moreau thinks the play dealt with the irregularity in the Athenian calendar.[28] Gelzer[29] considers somewhat probable a production of the play at the Dionysia of 422 B.C. with the *Wasps* or at the Lenaea of 421 B.C. With Moreau's interpretation the play would have thematic affinity with the *Clouds*. There need be, however, no incompatibility between the calendar theme and a specific allusion to the *Seasons* of Prodicus. According to Nestle's reconstruction of Prodicus' work the argument for the priority of the *Seasons* is the *chresimon*, their usefulness to mankind (see below, p. 138). *Seasons*, Fr. 569 is a fifteen-line debate between two speakers in which the first (Edmonds makes it Athena) argues for its usefulness in supplying Athens with the most exotic diet in any season of the year.[30] That the play gave some emphasis to the intellectual salon life of Athens may be tentatively inferred from references to Chaerephon, the Child of Night, in Fr. 573 (Schol. Plat. *Apol.* 20a), to Cephisophon and Euripides in Fr. 580, Sophocles, Frs. 580A, 581, and Callias, Fr. 572 (Schol. Luc. 83R):[31]

ὁ μὲν 'Καλλίας' οὗτος, ὡς Κρατῖνος 'Αρχιλόχοις φησίν,
'Ιππονίκου υἱὸς ἦν, τὸν δῆμον Μελιτεύς, ὡς 'Αριστοφάνης
"Ωραις, πλούσιος καὶ πασχητιῶν καὶ ὑπὸ πορνιδίων δια-
φορούμενος καὶ Κόλακας τρέφων.

If the *Seasons* was chronologically contiguous with the *Clouds* and the *Wasps*, Aristophanes sustained in three plays the theme of conflict between a young man and his father, Callias/Hipponicus, Pheidippides/Strepsiades, and Bdelycleon/Philocleon. Moreover, there would have been at least four plays in the period from 423 to 421 B.C. that treated the sophists: *Connus*,

Clouds, Seasons, and *Flatterers.* With the *Tagenistae* there would have been five. There should be no surprise that Plato's *Protagoras* draws upon certain images from such a concentration in the theater upon philosophy and conflict between generations.

6. Prodicus in the *Clouds*

The interest in words, the theological rationalism, and the ethics of Prodicus have a resonance in several important elements of the *Clouds.* One of the most memorable inventions of the play is the *Dinos.* The advantage of the device is that it allows Aristophanes to beckon in several directions at once, to Diogenes, Antiphon, or Democritus, to the *Wine-Flask* of Cratinus, and to the interest in words that commanded the constant attention of sophists and comic audience alike. The treatment of the *Dinos* also touches upon the teaching of Prodicus, particularly his doctrine of the *chresimon* and his orthoepy. This meteorological force displaces Zeus precisely because it is responsible for the useful works attributed to Zeus by myth. Not anthropomorphic gods but things are shown to be responsible for the weather (cf. Diels B 3 and 4). Strepsiades sees the point of Socrates' comparison (392–93) of thunder to gastric disturbances in the very name of thunder: βροντή sounds so much like its true substance πορδή (393).[32] Like thunder the substance of the *Dinos* is also revealed in its name, for whatever the importance of the *dine* of philosophy, Aristophanes' *Dinos,* masculine like the god Socrates declares that it displaces, is a pun on the word for a kind of pot (cf. Schol. *ad* 381). There is perhaps also a play on the two genitives of Zeus, Ζηνός and Διός.[33] Moreover, the divinity of the *Dinos* is suggested in the play on δεινός "awesome," a term Prodicus is said to have permitted only in a pejorative sense.[34]

Nestle reconstructs the content of the *Seasons* of Prodicus from Themistius, *Oratio* 30, Xenophon's *Oeconomicus,* and the pseudo-Platonic *Axiochus* and *Eryxias.*[35] He argues that Prodicus used the concept of the *chresimon* to affirm the importance of farming in the rise of civilization. At first human life was only nomadic (cf. Protagoras' myth, 322a), but with the development of agricultural societies and their milder manners people began to worship as gods all things that made their life more comfortable: stars, sun, moon, water, rivers, springs, lakes, and the sea (Diels B 5). Thereupon, having discovered that the *artes agriculturae* were invented by great men, people transferred their reverence to these inventors, among whom Heracles many have been included (if not as an example of how labors like those of farming lead to virtue). Heracles in turn was revered then as a god of civilization, just like Aristaeus, the bringer of civilization (cf. Pind. *Pyth.*

9. 59 ff.; Fr. 251), who played a central role in the cult of the Horae in Prodicus' native Ceos, the fertility goddesses of the treatise's title. The arguments (see above, p. 136) for taking the chorus of the *Birds* as a parody of Prodicus' *Seasons* may be applied to the chorus of the *Clouds*. The Clouds at 337 are in fact related to birds and like the bird-chorus credited with the patronage of poetry and language. In both the first and second parabases the Clouds develop at length the argument for their usefulness, primarily as regulators of celestial phenomena and bodies. At the beginning of the first epirrheme (577) the Clouds claim to be of all the gods the most beneficial to the city (cf. *Seasons*, Fr. 569, above, p. 137):

πλεῖστα γὰρ θεῶν ἁπάντων ὠφελούσαις τὴν πόλιν.

There follow examples of their moral influence upon the city (recalling the argument of 346 ff. on the moral effect of the ability of the Clouds to take different shapes). They control the thunder and split the heavens in disapproval of the election of Cleon as general, while the moon threatens to leave her course and the sun never to shine again. The antepirheme develops the usefulness of their companion meteor, the moon, who benefits all (611):

ὠφελοῦσ' ὑμᾶς ἅπαντας οὐ λόγοις ἀλλ' ἐμφανῶς.

The list of the moon's benefits occupies the entire antepirheme (607–26). Similarly, the second parabasis (which should belong to the first version of the play if the present form represents a partial revision) also pleads for the usefulness of the Clouds. But in this parabasis their control of morals is explicitly linked to their control of meteorological phenomena. If in due season (ἐν ὥρᾳ, 1117), the jurors of the comic contest are just (by virtue of giving the prize to their chorus) and wish to reap a rich harvest, the Clouds will rain on their land before their neighbors'. They will guard their crops against drought and downpour (1120), while the man who dishonors them will produce nothing at all. They will destroy his crops with hail (1125, 1127).[36] Immediately following this self-accolade of the chorus, Strepsiades reenters, terrified by the approach of the "old and new day," the last day of the month, when he must pay his debts or be indicted. He is literally threatened by the season. But Pheidippides returns from his new schooling and, greeted as Soter of his house, offers his father rescue in a redefinition of the "old and new day." Dividing τὴν ἕνην τε καὶ τὴν νέαν (cf. Prodicus' διαίρεσις) into two days (1178–1200), he makes the νέα equivalent to the νουμηνία, the first day of the month. The plaintiffs who have deposited suit money against Strepsiades will have lost it (1181) through the strict application of the etymology of a calendar term. The season that once threatened Strepsiades will now serve him in his defense against the creditors. Hence Strepsiades rejects Pasias' citation to appear in court on the "old and the new" with the quibble that the summons is for two different days (1222–23).

Since in the age of the *Dissoi Logoi* there were many essays like the contest between Better and Worse Argument, it is wrong to seek exclusive dependence upon Prodicus' Choice of Heracles or any other *epideixis*. It may be that this *agon* is one of the major revisions in the play. The Heracles fable would not be in this case part of any Prodicean element in the production of 423 B.C.[37] With this caveat but in the assumption that any revision would have been made no more than a few years after 423 B.C. it is only fair to note with others the general similarity of this contest to the Choice of Heracles. Lucian's account of his own choice of vocation, containing elements drawn from both Prodicus' parable and Aristophanes' *agon*, suggests that the similarity was noted in antiquity.[38] Cataudella has suggested that the references to Heracles at 1050–51 allude to Prodicus' work.[39] It may be added that the line of argument also contains an important strain of the parable. Prodicus apparently based his story on Hesiod, *Erga* 287 ff. (cf. Plat. *Protag.* 340d), where the easy and rough roads lead to opposite goals, to virtue and vice. Prodicus' *Kakia*, however, asserts that she will lead Heracles to the same goal offered by *Arete* (*Mem.* II. 1. 29):

Ἐννοεῖς, ὦ Ἡράκλεις, ὡς χαλεπὴν καὶ μακρὰν ὁδὸν ἐπὶ τὰς εὐφροσύνας ἡ γυνή σοι αὕτη διηγεῖται; ἐγὼ δὲ ῥᾳδίαν καὶ βραχεῖαν ὁδὸν ἐπὶ τὴν εὐδαιμονίαν ἄξω σε.

It is suggestive of Prodicus' influence upon the debate of the *Clouds* that in the very beginning of Worse Argument's rebuttal Heracles is cited as an example of how the easy road leads to virtue (1045 ff.):

WA: By what reasoning do you object to warm baths?
BA: Because it makes a man base and cowardly.
WA: Hold on! I've got you now. Tell me; which mortal child of Zeus do you think has the noblest soul? And did the most labors?
BA: In my opinion none other than Heracles.
WA: Well, did you ever know the baths of Heracles to be cold? And who is braver than he?

Worse Argument has assumed for the moment that the debate turns not upon the goal of education but upon the method. A traditional virtue, Heraclean bravery, is shown by his example to be attainable through the new *paideusis* associated with the easy living of the new gymnasia (cf. 1059).[40]

As one ear may hear a cross-relationship in polyphonic music where another may not, so the ancient spectators and readers of comedy must have drawn different lines of allusion in the vast array of themes, characters, and plot-patterns, presented not only across the years, but even in the same festival. The pieces of evidence offered above suggest that some would have seen enough of Prodicus in Aristophanes' drama of sophistic venality and possibly in other plays of the same period to turn their glance toward the fifty-drachma professor.

NOTES

[1] For a survey of the literature see T. Gelzer, *RE* Supplementband XII (1970), cols. 1441–45. Gelzer himself, "Aristophanes und sein Sokrates," *MH* 13 (1956):65–93, sees Socrates as basically a comic type while H. Erbse, "Sokrates im Schatten der Aristophanischen Wolken," *Hermes* 82 (1954):385–420, argues that Socrates is carefully distinguished in the play from the sophists in general. For Socrates as a composite of sophists see C. H. Whitman, *Aristophanes and the Comic Hero* (Cambridge, 1964), pp. 141 ff. In this article citations of lost comedies and fragments will be from J. M. Edmonds, *The Fragments of Attic Comedy* (Leiden, 1957), henceforth "Edmonds." Reference to the text will follow *Aristophanes Clouds, edited with Introduction and Commentary* by K. J. Dover (Oxford, 1968), henceforth "Dover." Other editions with commentaries cited below are J. Van Leeuwen, *Aristophanis Nubes*, 2nd ed. (Leiden, 1898) and W. J. M. Starkie, *The Clouds of Aristophanes* (Amsterdam, 1966), henceforth "Van Leeuwen" and "Starkie."

[2] W. Nestle, *Vom Mythos zum Logos*, 2nd ed. (Stuttgart, 1941, reprint ed. Aalen, 1966), pp. 465–468, lists Diogenes of Apollonia as important for the title of the play, Antiphon and Democritus for the *Dinos* [but see J. Ferguson, "Dinos," Part One of this volume.], Hippon of Rhegium, Meton, Gorgias, Hippias (meter and rhythm), and for orthoepy and the new education especially Protagoras. Beyond the name he allots no part in the play to Prodicus' teaching. Erbse, however, "Sokrates im Schatten," p. 408, n. 5, approves the view of Starkie and Van Leeuwen (*ad* 361) that the naming of Prodicus prepares for the *agon* of Better and Worse Argument. Q. Cataudella, "Intorno a Prodico di Ceo," *Studi di antichita in onore di E. Ciaceri* (Naples, 1940):41–62, extends the latter view, assigning many details of the play specifically to Prodicus. The present study favors a more general adumbration of Prodicus in the *Clouds* and other comedies.

[3] For general treatment of Prodicus see W. Schmid, *Geschichte der griechischen Literatur*, I. Teil, 3. Band (Munich, 1940), pp. 40–49. He thinks, p. 43, that the legend that Prodicus was required to drink hemlock for corrupting the youth (reported in Suidas) was perhaps spun from Ar. *Tagenistae* Fr. 490. See also K. Freeman, *Companion to the Pre-Socratic Philosophers*, 2nd ed. (Cambridge, Mass., 1959), pp. 370–374; E. Zeller, *Die Philosophie der Griechen*, I. Teil, 2. Hälfte, 6th ed. by W. Nestle (Leipzig, 1920), pp. 1311–15; K. v. Fritz, "Prodikos 3," *RE* Band XXIII, 1, cols. 85–89; and W. K. C. Guthrie, *A History of Greek Philosophy*, Vol. III (Cambridge, 1969), pp. 238–42 and 274–80.

[4] That Plato knew this fable as part of a book is probable from *Symp.* 177b. Nestle's reconstruction is given above, p. 138.

[5] *Rep.* 529b; *Phaedr.* 269e–70a; *Theat.* 173e, appealing to Pindar as precedent

for the metaphor of the mind raised aloft from the earth. See W. Capelle, "Μετέωρος-μετεωρολογία," *Philologus* 71 (1912):414–56; L. Edelstein, "*Peri Aerōn* und die Sammlung der *Hippokratischen Schriften*," *Problemeta* IV (Berlin, 1932):129–35, and *Ancient Medicine* (Baltimore, 1967):118–19, and H. Erbse, "Sokrates im Schatten," pp. 405–08 (cited above, note 1).

[6] See Erbse, "Sokrates im Schatten," p. 408. H.-J. Newiger, *Metapher und Allegorie. Zetemanta* 16 (Munich, 1957), pp. 55–57, takes μετέωρα πράγματα (228) metaphorically but seems to take meteorosophistry (360) as referring to astronomy: "Spekulation über die Natur und Redefertigkeit, die alles erreichen kann, hängen also aufs engste zusammen. Für diesen Zusammenhang ist das Wort und seine Ableitungen wesentlich, denn in ihm treffen sich die beiden Sphären."

[7] In spite of Erbse's arguments ("Sokrates im Schatten"), it is difficult to see a serious difference between Socrates and any teacher of rhetoric. W. S. Teuffel, *Die Wolken des Aristophanes*, 2nd ed. revised by O. Kaehler (Leipzig, 1887), *ad* 488, 490, misunderstanding the metaphorical use of meteora, took this passage as evidence that in the second edition of the play questions concerning purely physical matters had been discarded. What older commentators have missed (cf. M. W. Humphreys, *Aristophanes Clouds, edited on the basis of Koch's edition* (Boston, 1913), *Introduction*, p. 39) is that all the teaching of the play, whether about things or words, is meteoric.

[8] There is no reference to it in Xenophon's *Apology* or *Memorabilia* although the latter (IV. 7. 6) offers a perfect opportunity to reject Aristophanes' portrait: Ὅλως δὲ τῶν οὐρανίων, ἧ ἕκαστα ὁ θεὸς μηχανᾶται, φροντιστὴν γίγνεσθαι ἀπέτρεπεν.

[9] See Starkie, ad loc., and S. R. Winans, "Notes on Aristophanes' *Clouds*," *AJP* 16 (1895):73–77.

[10] Plat. *Euthyd.* 272c, *Menex.* 235a. The Metrobius of Cratinus' *Archilochuses* Fr. 1 may have been Connus' father. That play contained a catalogue of poets, Fr. 2 (Clem. Alex. *Str.* i. 23), a σοφιστῶν σμῆνος which perhaps formed a chorus something like that of Ameipsias' *Connus*.

[11] Aristophanes knows the technique: he names the twenty-four individuals of the chorus at *Birds* 297–304.

[12] N. Demand, "The Identity of the *Frogs*," *CPh* (1970):83–87, points to such an allusion to a competitive chorus in arguing that the frog-chorus is meant as a parody of Phrynichus, whose name means "frog-like."

[13] The distinction Erbse sees between the sophists and Socrates in the *Clouds* would in this case suit the play of Ameipsias.

[14] There is no convincing evidence yet to take the play as identical with the *Connus* of Phrynichus, who as an innovator in music might well have found his own way to exploit the figure of Connus.

[15] A fine reconciliation between the two images is given by Victor Cousin, *Fragments philosophiques*, vol. 1 (Paris, 1847), pp. 115–21.

[16] So Edmonds, vol. 1, p. 370.

[17] βομβοῦσι· "Ὀρέστης,' 'Μαρψίας,' Καλλίου τοῦ 'Αθηναίου κόλακες σὺν ἑτέροις.

[18] See above, p. 134, h.

[19] W. Nestle, "Die Horen des Prodikos," *Hermes* 71 (1936):151–170, taking

Xen. *Oec.*, esp. 5. 17, as referring to the teaching of Prodicus: καλῶς δὲ κἀκεῖνος εἶπεν, ὃς ἔφη τὴν γεωργίαν τῶν ἄλλων τεχνῶν μητέρα καὶ τρόφον εἶναι.

[20] Plat. *Cratyl.* 348b, *Meno* 96d, *Charm.* 163d.

[21] Nestle, "Die Horen," (see n. 19, above).

[22] Edmonds, vol. I, pp. 708–09.

[23] G. Dindorf, *Aristophanis Comoedia* (Oxford, 1835), vol. 2, p. 646.

[24] W. Schmid, *Geschichte der griechischen Literatur*, I. Teil, 4. Band (Munich, 1946), p. 197; A. Lesky, *Geschichte der griechischen Literatur*, 2nd ed. (Bern, 1957–58), p. 483.

[25] *RE* Supplementband XII, col. 1411.

[26] See L. Rademacher, "Prodicos bei Aristophanes," *RhM* 69 (1914):87–94, who suggests cautiously that Euripides' attack upon Aeschylus' use of words reflects the teaching of Prodicus.

[27] It is on this basis that H. Rosenstrauch, "Quomodo Aristophanes lusu verborum sophistas ludibrio habuerit," *Eos* 51 (1961):45–54, sees special reference to Prodicus in the linguistic humor of the play.

[28] J. Moreau, "Sur les *Saisons* d'Aristophane," *NCl* 6 (1954):327–44, referring esp. to *Peace* 414–15 and *Clouds* 575 ff.

[29] *RE* Supplementband XII, cols. 1411 and 1414.

[30] W. Schmid, *Geschichte der griechischen Literatur*, I. Teil, 4. Band, p. 196 and n. 4, thinks the play was a contest between native and foreign gods in which Sabazius is finally banished from Athens. But Cic. *Leg.* 2. 15 and Strabo 10. 471. 18 do not name the play for which they give this plot. Fr. 566 does name Sabazius, but it could be in passing as at *Birds* 873, *Wasps* 9, and *Lysistrata* 388.

[31] Edmonds, vol. 1, p. 27, thinks the Callias referred to is the brother-in-law of Cimon, not the Callias of Plato's *Protagoras*, and that the two are confused here. Nestle, *Vom Mythos*, p. 458, however, takes him as the "Sophistengönner." Edmonds' date, vol. 1, p. 995, of 449 B.C. for Cratinus' *Archilochuses* would be impossible with this identification. But if the play was in the early 420s and prior to 423 B.C. (Cratinus' last known production), this testimony implies that Callias was lampooned for squandering his father's wealth well before Hipponicus' death and that Eupolis' *Flatterers* of 421 B.C. was not the first comedy to treat the topic.

A 422 B.C. date for the *Seasons* would rule out Fr. 578A (Hesychius) as a reference to Plato the philosopher, who would have been only five years old: ''Αρίστυλλος'·'Αρίστωνος.

Cratinus had earlier produced a *Seasons*, himself, but there is in the fragments no hint of philosophy.

[32] Cf. Strepsiades' retort to the divine thunder of the approaching Clouds at 293–94. For anagram in Aristophanes see Z. P. Ambrose, "The Lekythion and the Anagram of *Frogs* 1203," *AJP* 89 (1968):342–346.

[33] Perhaps it is only of incidental interest that Socrates, *Cratyl.* 396a, discourses on the meaning of the two forms: Zeus is lord of all, through whom (διά) all things have life (ζῆν).

[34] Plat. *Protag.* 341ab, see above, p. 135. The *Dinos-Dios*-pot joke is repeated at *Wasps* 618, where Aristophanes reminds his audience of his recent achievement.

[35] See n. 19 above.

[36] These are the specific meteorological dangers to farming in Xen. *Oec*. 5. 19 and pseud-Plat. *Axiochus* 368c, passages Nestle, "Die Horen," p. 157 (see above, n. 19), thinks are based on Prodicus' *Seasons*.

[37] See Dover's careful analysis of the evidence for revision, *Clouds, Introduction*, p. xc.

[38] Lucian, *Somn*. 6 and 9.

[39] See n. 2 above.

[40] Contrast Heracles' choice with that of Achilles: glory or mediocrity, the former through a short and difficult life, the latter through a long and easy one. Heracles must ask, "Shall I attain glory by following the way of Vice or the way of Virtue?" Cf. Sallust, *Cat*. 11. 1: Nam gloriam, honorem, imperium bonus et ignavus quoque sibi exoptant; sed ille vera via nititur, huic quia bonae artes desunt, dolis atque fallaciis contendit.

PART II

PLATO

ERIC A. HAVELOCK

The Socratic Problem:
Some Second Thoughts

T HE Socratic problem has had a long history traceable as far back as 1768, when Lessing published a short essay of interpretation devoted to that portrait of Socrates found in Aristophanes' *Clouds*. During nearly two supervening centuries the problem has been investigated and reinvestigated without achieving any agreed solution. It exists and always will. In the words of Guthrie's magisterial treatment: "This is inevitable since he wrote nothing and all we know about him and his thoughts comes from the writings of men of the most varied character, from philosophers to comic poets, some of whom were passionately devoted to him, while others thought his influence pernicious." The search for the historical Socrates can in fact be compared in this respect to the quest for the historical Jesus, and for similar reasons, but with one difference. The latter, whether or not it has established that a "Jesus of History" can exist in identifiable form, has at least succeeded in illuminating the thought world, both Jewish and eschatological, in which Jesus grew up, and which immediately preceded his birth.[1] The search for Socrates, so largely concentrated on documentation that post-dated his death, has not succeeded in performing a like service for its own subject.

In the three decades following the conclusion of the Second World War, scholarship surrounding the Socratic problem has ended in a dilemma of contradiction, recalling in spirit those aporetic dialogues of Plato to which investigators of the problem make such frequent appeal. On the one hand, the skepticism of Gigon and Chroust[2] has argued that it is inherently insoluble because of the nature of our sources. For Chroust these are of a fictional character, for Gigon they are "poetic" creations.[3] As an alternative to skepticism, Vlastos (1971, as author and editor), Irwin (1977), and Santas (1979),[4] have more recently offered in variant versions a reconstruction of

This paper was presented to the 1979 Boston meeting of the Society for Ancient Greek Philosophy; it has not been published elsewhere but has been extensively revised for this volume. The author retains copyright.

Eric Havelock is Sterling Professor of Classics Emeritus at Yale University.

Socraticism that seeks to isolate and identify the master's own teaching from that of his disciples by drawing heavily on what is put into his mouth and said about him in the so-called "early" or "Socratic" dialogues of Plato. For Dover, who gives the problem succinct coverage in the introduction to his edition to the *Clouds* (1968) and for Guthrie, who gives the problem extended treatment in the third volume of his *History of Greek Philosophy* (1969),[5] "early Plato" is still central, but not quite enough. Their reconstructions require the partial use of Xenophon, and for Guthrie the Aristotelian testimonies are also a vital supplement. As for Aristophanes, his rejection as a serviceable source is unanimous, on the part of both believers and skeptics.

It is to that criterion of evidence which is implied in the formula "early" or "Socratic" dialogues of Plato that the present paper is addressed. One feels its dominance in all that has been written about Socrates in the period under review. "Early Plato" becomes a Socratic orthodoxy to be defended or repudiated. For the skeptics, to establish the fictional or at least mythical character of these dialogues becomes a prime objective; for the believers, these same works taken as a whole contain a body of teaching specifically Socratic, either shared by Plato or later to be amended by him, but separable in tone and content from the body of "Platonism," which is expounded in the dialogues classified as "middle" or "late." The opening sentence of the Vlastos volume states the case unequivocally: "The Socrates of this book is the Platonic Socrates, or to be more precise the Socrates of Plato's early dialogues. That this figure is a faithful and imaginative recreation of the historical Socrates is the conclusion of some very responsible scholars though not of all." The preface to the Santas volume is equally explicit:

> This is a philosophical study of Plato's Socrates—the man and his talks, his philosophical method, his questions, his arguments and his belief about what is good and right. . . . Though my concern is with Plato's Socrates, I do not of course discuss all the dialogues in which Socrates is the protagonist—I take as a starting point the accepted division of Plato's dialogues into early, middle and late and I deal almost exclusively with the first third appropriately called the Socratic dialogues.

For Irwin, whose professed intention is "to understand and evaluate Plato's views on ethical questions" (*Preface*, p. vii), the Socratic problem as such is necessarily incidental, but his reiterated description of given dialogues as both "early" and "Socratic" reveals what in essence his solution to the problem would be. His methodology of separation, however, between Socraticism and Platonism is considerably more sophisticated than that employed in the Vlastos and Santas volumes: even within the "early" dialogues can be discerned two strands of doctrine, an original Socratic one, together with comment and correction by Plato. Consequently Irwin feels free to repeat the formula "Socrates and Plato" in some contexts and "Plato" alone in others, sometimes with a very blurred boundary between the two.

To the question "What, at least in outline, did the Socraticism isolated by these critical methods amount to?" answers are given varying in emphasis and sometimes in substance. For Vlastos, author of the first article in the edited volume, there is a "gospel" of Socrates to be preached, and a mission to be fulfilled (pp. 4–5). Plato's *Apology* is drawn on to support as Socratic the principle: What shall it profit a man if he gain the whole world and lose his own soul? (p. 5). The *Crito*, treated as a document with equal evidential authority, reveals the kernel of Socrates' ethical teaching, at once a revelation and a revolution in moral philosophy: render to no man evil for evil. This is the historical Socrates speaking: he argues the principle dialectically and uses it to defend his own equanimity and passivity when confronted with death at the hands of the laws of Athens. Later in the same volume, this posture, described as a rejection of civil disobedience, is elaborately examined with a view to removing its apparent contradiction with other stated views of Socrates. Five chapters[6] seek to isolate in the early dialogues a specifically Socratic elenchus exercised on behalf of achieving ethical definitions. The Socrates of Santas, while still identified with the convictions expressed by the morally heroic figure of the *Crito*, is primarily that kind of thinker whose interests and methodology are congenial to the analytic school of modern philosophy. "It is only Plato's Socrates that is of major interest to the contemporary philosopher. . . . I have concentrated on the topics in which I thought I could make some progress using contemporary techniques of analysis and scholarship."[7] Irwin would begin by insisting on a distinction between a Socratic view of virtue (arete) as a craft (techne) and a Platonic critique of this position producing a metamorphosis into the doctrine that virtue must be good in and for itself, and that in its "real" form it requires a knowledge of transcendent forms. The first book of the *Republic* offers an unsuccessful defense of the Socratic view; apparently the book is both Socratic (in what is defended) and non-Socratic (in the refutations offered).[8] The Socratic craft analogy rationally leads to the denial of the possibility of incontinence, and also to the unrestricted hedonism of the *Protagoras*; "there is no reason to doubt that the hedonism is Socrates' own doctrine."[9] This does not prevent Irwin from designating as "Socrates' view" the startlingly different doctrine of the *Crito*, that justice must be pursued "at any cost to oneself." The *Gorgias*, on the other hand, pursuing the same otherworldly thesis, "is unlike the Socratic dialogues" in that it begins to face awkward questions, raised by Plato[10] (presumably for Socrates).

In the common use of a criterion of evidence identified as "early Plato" or "early Socratic dialogues" it becomes pertinent to point to some difficulties raised by the ambiguity of the criterion itself. What is meant by "early"? An accepted canon of chronology, dividing the dialogues into three groups, assigns *Meno, Republic, Symposium, Euthydemus* to the "middle" group, and *Theaetetus* to the late group.[11] Yet in seeking evidential sources for Socraticism, in addition to the dialogues of the "early" group, the Vlastos volume draws on *Meno, Republic, Symposium, Euthydemus, Theaetetus*; the Santas volume on the *Meno*, and Irwin on *Phaedo, Republic, Meno, Euthydemus*. One may excuse this variety of departures from the chronological canon by arguing that only partial use is made of them, but what is the use of arguing that in certain selected texts Plato writes out of a close and recent memory of Socrates' teaching and a desire to preserve it, while in others he has moved away from this memory in order to develop his own system, when some of the more personalized representations (I avoid calling them reports) occur in these "later" works. The *Theaetetus*, the latest source to be drawn on, offers a crucial instance of this dilemma. In the Vlastos volume we read that this dialogue "despite its late date—still has much of" the spirit of the Socratic dialogue "containing as it does the comparison of Socrates to a midwife—so apt for what seems to emerge as one general picture of Socrates."[12] Dover, using more stringent logic to exclude *Theaetetus* from the "early" and "middle" groups, appears to regard the midwife comparison as a commonplace "neglected by Plato in his earlier representations of Socrates . . . and exploited at a comparatively late date, in one dialogue alone." This judgment allows him to dismiss the apparent parallel in *Clouds* line 137 (with 139, which he does not discuss) as also non-Socratic.[13]

As for the "early" group itself, order of composition within it is unsettled, and the margins that separate it from the "middle" group are blurred. Is the *Gorgias*, for example, written out of a recent experience of Socrates' "martyrdom" and the teaching that led to it, or was it written only after Plato's return from his first visit to Sicily? Does the *Protagoras* follow it, in order to correct its naivete, or precede it in order to be corrected?[14] Does the *Apology* represent a composition issued "hot from the press" immediately following Plato's experience of the trial (and perhaps of the execution) or was it an answer to the *Kategoria* of Polycrates, composed as an item in the polemical Socratic literature that grew up in the years succeeding the trial?[15]

This cursory and incomplete review of some of the ways in which the dialogues, considered as sources for Socraticism, lend themselves to manipulation, is sufficient to illuminate a few conclusions:

1. Discrepancies of choice: both the Vlastos and Santas volumes ignore the *Ion* as also does Guthrie, an interesting omission that perhaps indicates the presence of a blind spot in the conduct of the search for the Socrates of history.[16] Irwin (p. 74) notices its Socratic critique of poetry as a pseudo-

craft. The Vlastos volume ignores the *Lysis*: Santas would add *Hippias Minor* to *Hippias Major* but unlike the Vlastos volume avoids drawing on any dialogues of the "middle" group except the *Meno*.

2. More importantly, how can a criterion of Socraticism founded on a use of "early Plato" conceivably draw so heavily upon the *Meno*, *Phaedo*, *Symposium*, *Republic*, and even *Theaetetus*? A glance at the *index locorum* to Guthrie's *Socrates*, a comprehensive work written in a cautionary and conservative spirit, reveals the dilemma. Citations from these five works are used with some freedom to illuminate not merely the Socratic personality but also Socratic teaching. The fact seems to be that these five, composed at any time between fifteen and thirty years after the death of their subject and presumably devoted to the formulation of a Platonism growing to maturity, contain expositions of doctrine that as one reads become hard to dissever from the personality to whom they are ascribed—a personality that critics for varying reasons find attractive.

A hypothesis put forward seventy years ago under the joint names of John Burnet and A. E. Taylor argued that the doctrines (including the Theory of Forms), and not just the personality, of the "middle" dialogues were a faithful report of the beliefs and arguments of the historical Socrates. This cut the knot of the Socratic problem, but at the price of reducing Plato to the status of a reporter, even if an intelligent and sympathetic one who in his later years was allowed by the hypothesis to develop some second thoughts about this body of doctrine. One philosophic identity was thus created—that of the older man—but on condition of destroying another—that of his presumed pupil. Since it was the latter who alone undertook the task of formulating the doctrine in writing, this heroic solution did not seem very plausible. But it did have a kind of desperate honesty, which much that has been written about the problem has lacked. It confronted squarely an awkward fact that so many critics have shied away from facing, namely that their own reconstructions of Socraticism have to draw so freely upon these same middle dialogues. Burnet and Taylor merely asked for consistency in the application of the criterion.

3. I have noted, above, the uneasy place occupied by the *Protagoras* and *Gorgias* in the canon of "early Plato." Their chronological order, philosophical interrelationships, and dates of composition, relative to the events in Plato's life that occurred years after the trial, have all been matters of speculation and dispute. Yet one notices how heavily these two works seem to count in those reconstructions of Socraticism that are supposedly guided by the criterion of "early Plato." The readiness with which they are exploited raises a larger critical question. When one reads and reads again the accounts of Socraticism composed by what I may call the "Platonist" school of historians, one receives an impression of the use of three favorite sources:

the *Apology*, *Crito*, and *Gorgias*, all of which dramatize in different ways the heroic role of the true philosopher in a hostile world. The trouble with this group is that, to a greater extent than is characteristic of Plato's corpus otherwise, they are protreptic in tone and rely for their argumentative effect on a considerable degree of rhetoric. This is obviously true of the *Apology*, containing as it does only a brief though possibly significant passage of cross-examination. What the reader of the *Crito* is made to feel as he reads is that the dialectical portion is placed at the service of the climactic speech spoken by the laws of Athens; the whole purpose of the previous argument is to lead up to and support the admonition to avoid civil disobedience. And one forms the same impression as one reads the *Gorgias*. Roughly one quarter of this work is made up of passages of eloquence lasting between one and four pages of the Stephanus text, spoken by Gorgias or by an impassioned Callicles or by a Socrates sometimes equally impassioned. It is precisely this quality in all three that makes them favorite sources for the style and substance of Socratic teaching. But what one may ask has happened to the style of the elenchus, the irony, the aporia, the suspension of judgment, otherwise attributed to the master? May these works not be exercises in Platonic rhetoric rather than Socratic argument?

It is perhaps in sympathy with the effect of their use that the critics themselves, seeking to identify Socraticism, can themselves occasionally succumb to the temptation of a style that substitutes rhetoric for critical analysis. Santas, professedly devoted to tracing the cool analytic disciplines of a Socratically employed logic, offers a supportive preface consisting of a series of no less than nine rhetorical questions, headed by "Did not Socrates show in the *Charmides*" etc., and continuing with a series of similar "Did nots" occupying a page of his text. Vlastos, as proof of authority, asks "How could Plato be saying to his fellow citizens: 'This is the man you murdered—look at him, listen to him' and point to a figment of his own imagining?" Such a style lends itself to settling complex problems by dogmatic pronouncement: "The one thing certain is this . . . ," "It is impossible to believe that . . ."; or else to exaggeration and inflation of what is purportedly discovered: "Plato's Socrates is in fact the only Socrates worth talking about." Even Guthrie, in his determination to uphold the reliability of Aristotle as an authority independent of Plato, can dismiss the contrary view put forward with close reasoning and careful scrutiny nearly seventy years ago,[17] as "a mass of tedious and frequently perverse argument"; while what Aristotle himself has to say is characterized as "a few crisp sentences"— surely a remarkable verdict on two asides in the *Metaphysics*[18] notable not less for their discursive style than for their ambiguous reference, the interpretation of which is crucial to Guthrie's own reconstruction.

Investigation of the Socratic problem has been beset by uneasiness: that is the unavoidable impression created for anyone who studies the record of inconsistencies, contradictions, and fervent generalizations. The sources examined seem incapable of yielding any other results. It becomes possible to argue that one should begin to look in a different direction altogether. Before considering what this may be, there is one further point to make about the general character of the investigation, or rather, one pertinent question to ask. Why have so many sober scholars found it so easy to ignore these difficulties, or at least gloss over their existence? Two books recently published,[19] though not addressed to the Socratic problem as such, throw indirect light on the answer; they describe that image of Greek antiquity formed for themselves by the Victorians (and, one should add, the Edwardians), at a time when the classics dominated higher education in Britain; an image that they also imposed upon themselves. A central component in its formation was a desire to provide in classical Greek culture either a reinforcement for Christianity or, in an age of declining faith, a substitute for it. The management of the Socratic problem at that time reflected this theological and moral conservatism, and still does, manifesting itself in two ways: on the one hand, in the "martyrdom dialogues" (*Apology, Crito, Phaedo*, and to a large extent the *Gorgias*) there is the temptation to discern an anticipation of a later "Passion," and to assume that the reasons for both were comparable; on the other, in the contention portrayed in other dialogues with philosophical opponents, usually labeled "sophists," there is eagerness to discern a Socrates fighting the good fight on behalf of absolute moral values, considered as objectively real, in line with the teaching of the Judaeo-Christian tradition; as against the corruption of moral relativism, materialism, and empiricism of the "sophists," the difference being only that this Socrates offers logic as an alternative resource to religious revelation. The eagerness, of course, is confined to a rather restricted circle of scholarship, something of a backwater in the tides of modern thought, but it is sympathetic with a trend in classical studies in general, which inclines the discipline toward an emphasis on the role of religion and ritual in Greek antiquity, on Pythagorean or Orphic mysticism and Dionysiac inspiration, rather than on rationalism and naturalism; and toward a political conservatism that would stress the supposed failure of Greek democracy at the time of Socrates' trial, rather than its achievements at the time when he grew up. In very altered circumstances, the effects of this late Victorian reaction against that kind of solution to the Socratic problem adumbrated by George Grote[20] are still being felt.

A main motive for the skeptical treatment of the Socratic problem has always been found in the obvious disparities and sometimes downright contradictions that are visible between all our documented authorities. Rather than choose between them or eclectically try to put together a harmony of some or all of them, the skeptics ask us to conclude from the entire character of the corpus that no authority can be treating its subject historically in our sense of historical, else there could not be such wide disagreement; therefore no historical reconstruction is possible. With the major premise—that none of these accounts is historical or was intended to be—the argument of this paper is in agreement, though not necessarily with the conclusion that no solution is possible.

There has been a mistake of critical judgment concerning the precise character that is shared by these documents. In a familiar passage early in his *Poetics*,[21] Aristotle refers to the "Socratic discourses" (*logoi*), as a species of *mimesis* within the genus of mimetic "*poiesis*." The other members of this species are the mimes of Sophron and Xenarchus, and metrical composition in general—"poetry" in our sense. There are two other species comprehended within the genus; these respectively are music and dance. In contrast to these the one under consideration is marked off by employing not music or dance but only prose (the Socratic logoi and the mimes) or meter; that is (though Aristotle does not explicitly say so), it is a mimetic art that employs language alone; and it is "anonymous." Aristotle is seeking to identify a species hitherto not recognized and so not properly "named" (responding to the methodology laid down in Plato's *Politicus*). I myself would argue that his little essay in classification is explicable on the basis of a dawning recognition of one effect of the transition in classical Greece from nonliteracy to literacy—namely, that verbal composition was being designed in Aristotle's day to be read and has been so designed for some time, thus lacking the musical and/or choreographic accompaniment that had previously enabled it to survive and become transmissible under oral conditions of publication.

However that may be, Guthrie's attempt (*Socrates*, pp. 332–33) to evade the implications of this classification does not seem to me to be successful; the point Aristotle is making is not that the Socratic works are *logoi*, but that they are mimetic, in the sense in which the mimes and all poetry are mimetic. It did not occur to Aristotle to include "history" or historical writing, let alone biographical writing, in this category. For him the "Socrates" of all the logoi, Platonic or otherwise, should from our modern point of view appear within quotation marks. The name speaks as a "character," a creation of his creator, as would a speaker in a mime or drama. This, of course, does not exclude "realism"; on the contrary, realism is required, but it is a realism of art not historical reproduction. It is amazing how many readers of Plato can get hung up on a confusion between the two, as though dramatic realism were a sign of historical fidelity.

What is referred to by "the Socratic logoi"? Aristotle is viewing an accepted genre of Greek literature known in his day by that title. No one doubts that it covers among other things Plato's "Socratic" dialogues. But *logos* is not restricted to the sense "dialogue"; as can be seen in the present passage, "bare logoi" (*psiloi*) are contrasted with "meters," signifying the contrast between prose and poetry. A "Socratic logos" therefore need not confine itself to conversation: what does the word "Socratic" mean? Clearly it cannot designate authorship, whether written or oral, for that would require the formula "the logoi of Socrates." It designates logoi "of a Socratic kind," whatever that means. Remembering the comparison with the mimes and the general overriding category of mimesis in which Aristotle is placing these works, one draws the natural conclusion that "Socrates" is the name of a leading "character" in these compositions, in the same sense in which Oedipus, say, is a leading character and speaker in the play named after him, a character who can as in any drama utter speeches or engage in dialogue.

Oedipus was the name of a mythic character; "Socrates" was identifiable as an historical one personally known. Does this invalidate the comparison? The outline of an answer begins to emerge as the known proportions of the genre are gradually enlarged. The existence of the genre is confirmed by its known remains: first, Xenophon's *Memorabilia* (the bulk of which consists of Socratic conversations) and his three other Socratic logoi, an *Apology*, a *Symposium*, and an *Oeconomicus*; second, the fragments of seven Socratic logoi by Aeschines of Sphettus; third, the titles of three logoi attributed to Antisthenes the Socratic, namely *Aspasia*, *Alcibiades* and *Menexenus*, together with a *Heracles* and two surviving orations spoken in the names of *Odysseus* and *Ajax*; fourth, the Socratic logoi (unnamed) attributed to Aristippus of Cyrene and to Phaedo of Elis, both Socratics; fifth, the recorded titles of logoi attributed to the Socratic Eucleides of Megara, namely *Crito*, *Eroticus*, *Alcibiades*, *Aeschines*.

This outline of the remains is not exhaustive, but it is sufficient to demonstrate the following facts:

1. The genre included the exploitation of discourse supposedly spoken by mythical figures
2. and also discourse supposedly held by historical figures other than Socrates (probably in converse with Socrates).
3. There is an overlap between titles of Plato's logoi and those of other Socratics, his contemporaries. In other words, just as a "Socrates" was used as common property by these authors, so also was an "Alcibiades," an "Aspasia," a "Crito" or a "Callias," or a "Menexenus." The significance of this custom or convention has been obscured by the habit, almost universal among students of the Socratic problem, to assume that the works of Plato that carry these names (or else, as in the case of Callias, include the name as

a speaker) are authentic reports of the historical Socrates, which their counterparts were not. This kind of judgment is a tribute to the spell effectively cast by Plato's genius as a writer, but it is no tribute to critical acumen on the part of classical scholarship. The vital fact remains that Plato is writing within a genre which for whatever reason is "Socratic," but within which the rules of composition, whatever they are, must in general be identical, and which in fact must be "mimetic" in Aristotle's sense, that is, artistic and manipulative.

4. The composition of logoi also included rhetorical addresses, some "Socratic," others mythical; we have already observed the presence of the same form in Plato. One particular sub-type of address is when a speaker delivers an *Apologia pro vita sua*; this convention is applied to Socrates by both Plato and Xenophon.

Persons beyond the Socratic circle, as usually defined, engaged in this particular type of authorship. Socratic *Apologies* are recorded as among the works of the orator Lysias early in the fourth century and of Theodectes and Demetrius of Phalerum in the latter half. This form had a counterpart in the *Accusations of Socrates* (*Kategoriai*), one of which, by the orator Polycrates early in the fourth century, can in outline be partially reconstructed. Serious scholarship has seen a possible interconnection, in terms of an exchange of polemics, between the *Apology* and *Gorgias* of Plato, the *Memorabilia* and *Apology* of Xenophon, and the *Kategoria* of Polycrates, without reaching agreement as to the chronological order in which these works were written.

The presence of all these *Apologies* in the literature of the fourth century B.C. points towards a further enlargement of the literary context within which they were composed. The *Apology* of Socrates by Plato, the most familiar and congenial of all the "Socratic" documents, has a design that reproduces, to the extent of verbal reminiscence, an *Apology of Palamedes* composed by the "sophist" Gorgias perhaps twenty years earlier.[21a] Within the genre of logoi, we have already seen the conjunction of mythical and historical names. The literary connection between the sophistic and Platonic compositions is a striking fact. Once it is recognized, it gives reasonable support to the hypothesis that Plato wrote his *Apologia of Socrates* as a genre piece designed to expound Platonic doctrines or purposes, using a convention that his readers would immediately recognize, just as Gorgias had used the figure of Palamedes to expound Gorgian ideas.

It is to be observed that the choice of Palamedes was not arbitrary; he is defended for his role as an inventor of the arts of civilized man—an *euergetes* or benefactor, as also is his Socratic counterpart. Gorgias' intentions are, we might say, anthropological; his Palamedes is already established in Greek tradition as a name suitable for his didactic purpose. So also is Socrates chosen and treated not arbitrarily but as a figure in a philosophical tradition already authenticated in memory, and perhaps (remembering the Palamedes analogy) invented by him. But such a use of him effectively destroys the historicity of the speech put into his mouth, using the term *historicity* in the sense in which a historical scholar would use it.

Before dismissing this conclusion as incredible, or at least intolerable (which for many true believers is the same thing), one should remember that Isocrates toward the close of a long active career as publicist and educator composed in his turn an *Apologia pro vita sua*—his *Antidosis*—modelled closely on Plato's Socratic *Apologia*. That is to say, Isocrates speaks (or rather writes) as though he were a "Socrates" placed in the same legal position as that portrayed in Plato's *Apology* and responding to it in the same way—we might even say, with the same ploy. Is such a literary choice explicable, except on the assumption that Isocrates was working within a Socratic convention already created by previous authors, and in particular knew that Plato had employed a similar convention, knew that his readers knew this too, and saw no reason why he should not employ it himself; but now in a first person, which discards the name "Socrates" and substitutes his own personality?

What the modern scholar, whether philosopher, historian, or literary critic, faces here is a convention—a mode of composition—unfamiliar to him. More than two millennia of written record since Socrates' day have accustomed us to a basic distinction between fact and fiction. The formal separation between them has emerged as an effect of the growing practice of historical scholarship and natural science. In the period of authorship under consideration, such a distinction, or more correctly the necessity of enforcing it, still remained below the level of conscious recognition or at least conscious acceptance. The ambiguous practice of these writers is for us dishonest but was for them a creative and congenial activity appropriate to its purpose.

The reasons for this situation at the time lay in a transition that was taking place, or had just taken place, in the technology of communication. During the years from Socrates' birth to the latter part of the fourth century, during which the Socratic problem was created for us, Greek society was passing from a condition of oral to one of literate communication. I have offered elsewhere[22] some conclusions about the character of the Greek cultural experience in the fifth century that may prove to have a direct bearing upon the Socratic problem. The Athenians, so I have argued, did not become fully literate until the closing years of the century. This achievement, which coincided with the arrival of what we would call a reading public, depended upon the introduction of letters (*grammata*) at the primary level of schooling, not at the secondary; the issue turned on the availability of in-

struction not in writing as such but in fluent reading; the two are not synonymous. This is unlikely to have taken place until approximately the time
when the *Clouds* was produced, or maybe ten years earlier. In Greece overseas, on the other hand, both in Ionia and the West, various evidences point
to an achievement of literacy at an earlier date. The mainland in this one respect lagged behind, possibly with advantage to certain creative energies
that had an oral component. A period that in Athens extends from the age of
Pisistratus to the aftermath of Salamis could be described as either proto-
literate or craft-literate, depending on one's point of view, with corresponding effect upon the styles of its art forms, particularly the verbal ones. Further back, in the eighth and seventh centuries, Greek culture was essentially
an oral one, and in a general sense Homeric. The alphabet was practiced as
a craft, and of course used in this way to transcribe the poetry of the period,
but not as a medium of general communication. One common-sense way of
putting it is to say that there was not enough writing around to make it worth
while for most people to learn to read as a habit. These views have proved
controversial, but I detect some movement in the direction of their acceptance as representing something at least not far from the truth.

In an orally conditioned culture, verbal memory of actual fact, let alone
detail, is short. Mnemonic reasons required that preservable communication
be rhythmic. The personalities recorded in it, as they were rerecorded, came
to inhabit a no man's land between fact and fiction. They became mythic
and were interpreted and manipulated mythically; the original is not totally
forgotten or obliterated but turned into an archetype. In Athens this process
occurred preeminently upon the stage, both tragic and comic. In the years of
Socrates' youth, aside from Homer, lyric poetry recited at symposia, proces-
sional hymns and choric dances and eulogistic odes commissioned by important personages—and of course the drama—what other "literature" was
there and how many people read it? It is sometimes necessary to state the
obvious in order to restore historical perspective.

The tragic drama did not confine itself to figures of legend; the populace
of a Persian court or an Ionian city could be brought forward to speak and
describe its own destruction and defeat. But the manipulation of historical
and even contemporary personages was a particular feature of the comic
stage, and by no means confined to burlesque. The plot of the *Demes* of
Eupolis, produced when the historic Socrates was about fifty, resurrected
from the dead Solon, Miltiades, Aristides, and (most recently) Pericles to
preside over or reform an Athens represented as distressed by war and mis-
governed by contemporary politicians. Aristides even delivered an oration
beginning "I issue a proclamation to all the entire city, that men should be
just. For whoever is just. . . ."[23] The rest of the definition is lost. That is to
say, the traditional name "Aristides" is employed for contemporary didactic

purposes: he has become an archetype of which the original oral memory is simultaneously partially preserved and partially manipulated. A possible parallel between "Aristides" and the "Socrates" posthumously resurrected by the Socratics will not escape the alert critic.

There happens in fact to be an overlap between the names in the *Demes* and those that are either spoken of (Pericles, Solon) or given speaking parts (Miltiades) in the Socratic logoi. Are we to judge the *Demes* as fact or fiction, as history or myth?

The sophistic logoi, to sum up, constituted a genus of which the Socratic logoi were a species. Both were composed within conventions derived from the age-old practice of composing speech in orally preservable form. For the Athenians of the sixth and fifth centuries, that form found itself in inherited epic and contemporary drama, both tragic and comic. Publication occurred through performance, which called for a degree of empathy on the part of the audience, and even of participation. The language used remained governed by rhythm, and the personalities described tended to recede into myth or semi-myth. But as speech came to be written down in increasing quantities, it became preservable as an artifact, replacing the living memory. The aid of rhythm is no longer needed; the logoi can become prosaic, taking the form of treatises (*technae*). But traditional conventions cannot be discarded overnight; much of the oral genius of epic and stage play is retained, in the forms of dialogue and rhetoric. The personalities who speak still tend to recede into myth and semi-myth, a myth not inherited but created by the process of composition. Personalities are still created with that creative freedom characteristic of oral composition.

This does not answer the question: What purpose did these logoi serve? What precisely was the motive of their authors in writing them at this time? Communication preserved orally performed for its society a didactic function. It at once preserved, transmitted, and recommended the social mores, the law and ethics of the community. This had been done implicitly within the framework of narrative and drama. In the sophistic and Socratic logoi, this function for the first time becomes explicit. Previously, the performance of the didactic function had clothed itself in the garment of entertainment pursuing seduction through aesthetic pleasure, necessarily so, in order to enlist popular attention and beguile the social memory. From such practice the composers drew their reward in the form of popular esteem, prizes, and emoluments. But the logoi now appearing were no longer epic poems or stage plays; though still sometimes recited,[24] they were essentially addressed to a reading audience and, one would have thought, not a popular one.

The motive for their composition was created by one of the technological effects of the transition to literacy. If the written word could now survive without benefit of memorization, the way was open to separate out the didactic content of epic and drama, which meant its "moral" content, and relegate the description of it to written prose, leaving to poetic composition the more modest role of becoming an aesthetic instrument, designed to please, and relieved of the burden of edification. The production of the logoi signalled this act of separation. Accordingly, as their content becomes more identifiably didactic, they also become specialized as instruments of education, with the result that education itself—*paideusis* or *paideia*—became a recognizable and separate faculty, a social enterprise requiring the adoption of fresh institutional forms, of which Plato's Academy furnished the prototype.

This theoretic analysis of the character of the logoi, viewed as a byproduct of the literate revolution, is supported by a review of the actual objective which these documents state it is their purpose to achieve. They are all in their different ways educational textbooks, and indeed have been used as such ever since their production. "Early Plato" is in this sense typical of them all, even though unique in its compositional genius. The dialogues in succession endeavor to supply systematic definitions to the "virtues"—*aretai*—required of the citizen of the Greek polis. These had hitherto been communicated by indirection, intuitively and from a later written standpoint unsystematically, in the traditional poetic authors. The *Republic* endeavors to draw this whole body of moral didacticism together into a system of state education.

To return to the problem of the historical Socrates: if in Plato the name represents a figure hovering all the time between fiction and fact, and exploited to furnish mouthpiece and example for this paideutic purpose: if the means used for this purpose are sought in the models furnished by previous oral *paideia*, as found in epic recitation and stage performance; if these forms are imitated "mimetically," to furnish suitable settings for the model and chief speaker to act in as the carrier of the educational programme—if all this is true, a great many of the formal elements in the composition of these works begin to fall into place.

There is, for example, the conventional exordium to Plato's *Apology*—elaborate and self-deprecatory, as contrived and formal a piece of rhetoric as anything in the sophists or orators. There is the literary device of allowing the speaker the improbable opportunity of delivering two extra speeches, rising in eloquence to a climax of impassioned reflection; including an apparent prophecy after the event, to the effect that his death will be followed by a polemical defense of his memory. Or again, there is the projection of the speaker as a public benefactor, in the role of Palamedes, or as a performer of labors, in the role of Hercules, or as a hero accepting death, in the role of Achilles. Then there is the climax of the *Crito*, in which dia-

logue is so contrived as to give way to rhetoric, delivered in the person of a
stage chorus of laws who address the lead character. The scene is borrowed
from the *Laws* of Cratinus,[25] and the didactic motive of such a personification of traditional mores is also derived from the same source. The author of
this Socratic logos could cast an effective spell upon the contemporary
reader by exploiting his memory of such a famous play. We can similarly
follow both motive and method in the staging of the *Protagoras*, at a dramatic date four years before the writer was born, but drawing on another famous play by Eupolis, the third of the "Big Three" comedians,[26] who in
421 B.C. (when Plato was eight) had staged his *Flatterers* as a gathering of
Protagoras and other sophists at the house of Callias.[27] The scene we may
say is both recalled and rewritten to allow the presence of the Platonic hero,
who will take over control of the discourse that is held. Or again, there is
the prison scene on the hero's last day narrated in the *Phaedo*. It takes place
not in a cell but a domestic apartment in which at one time or another no
less than eighteen persons are present. The lead character is able to retire for
an interval to the interior of the house to take a ritual bath and receive wife
and children for the last time before dismissing them to rejoin the philosophical company. Toward sunset a state official calls, explaining that the last
hour has come and he wishes to pay his respects and say goodbye. He retires
overcome by emotion, which prompts the protagonist to comment as a guest
upon the courtesy his host has shown him during these past days.

He next announces he is ready for his evening draught. Will someone
please have it brought in? A domestic slave is sent out of the room to fetch
the actual cup bearer, who after entry and in response to request gives brief
instructions about the proper things to do after drinking it. The protagonist
drains it with apparent ease and satisfaction. The assembled company burst
into tears. They do have this one function, but it is reserved for the conclusion, where they perform briefly as a kind of chorus offering that lamenta-
tion over the dead or dying which could be an expected feature of Greek theater.

The protagonist has been allowed to discard his fetters for the whole
day, which allows him in the decorous conclusion to walk about preparatory
to lying down to await the end. The medical effects of hemlock are in reality
convulsive, catastrophic, and repulsive. The effect invented by the author allows that soul whose immortality has recently been eloquently defended to
retreat upwards from feet to heart, its traditional seat. Then, as it leaves in-
tact, its bodily mansion feels a slight tremor as the door, so to speak, is shut
behind it. A little drama has been contrived to form part and parcel of previous demonstration of doctrine.[28] It is theater again, recalling and reproducing that Hellenic tragic convention that allowed corpses on stage only in
poses of composure, under conditions formally suitable for obsequies,

though doctrine in this case forbids that expression of these should take on funereal meaning.

This review has only sampled a few of the compositional devices employed in "early" and "middle" Plato. Properly speaking, they are not devices but thematic forms drawn from traditional sources and in the fourth century still understood and accepted as such. They are placed at the service of a didactic programme designed in a variety of modes to identify and rationalize the nomos and ethos of Hellenism—a body of traditional directives previously stated implicitly in the poetic tradition but now reducible to written prosaic formulation by authors who by genius or temperament were inclined to this enterprise.

These conditions surrounding the production of all paideutic logoi, Socratic or otherwise, make it clear why any attempt to solve the Socratic problem by the use of "early Plato" must always remain futile. All of Plato is essentially Plato; the name Socrates in his writings is a mask for his own thinking, as applied to the task in hand. Possessed of a uniquely powerful philosophic mind, he was also an astonishingly effective literary artist—an unusual combination, which since his day has not been matched. Neither of these roles is compatible with the notion that he was also a historian in the modern sense, or interested in the task of historical reconstruction as we conceive it. As a thinker his role was to manipulate, arrange, interpret, correct, and deduce. As an artist his aim was to produce agreement with his own thinking by any means available; the main means employed being powerfully dramatic. If he employs a historical figure for this purpose, it will be because some things about the man's career made him appropriate for this purpose, as, for example, Xenophon employed the figure of Cyrus the Great. In Plato's particular case, he had known the man, had found his mind sympathetic to his own, had in some respects felt close to him, as he grew up—for there was a great difference in age between them and it was only in the closing years of the older man's life that the two became acquainted. Even Isocrates, chronologically speaking, had had a better chance to know Socrates than did Plato or Xenophon. The corpus we know as Plato's works was written by Plato, all of it, after the historical figure who supplied his dramatis persona was already dead, and much of it long after. It is sometimes necessary to restate the obvious, in the face of much popular writing that beguiles the reader into thinking he has been allowed to listen to a historical Socrates speaking. The corpus in fact *is* Plato. He would not exist in the history of philosophy, except as a shadowed mentality, if the corpus did not exist. The mask as borrowed converts a historical figure into a hero placed in heroic situations, for reasons closely connected with what was current literary convention. In doing so, it is inherently likely that by accident or design the corpus includes reminiscences of the historical figure, particularly because in this case the writer had known him personally. Since the writer is a philosopher, his interest in the historical figure is likely to be philosophical. But since everything he writes is his own, addressed to his own philosophical purposes, such reminiscences as there are will not be amenable to mechanical segregation, as though every now and then he took time off from his own enterprise in order to indulge in biography. If there is a mind of Socrates discoverable in the writings of Plato, it is intermingled with them chemically and is as likely or unlikely to appear in one place as in another, in an early or a later dialogue, in the *Republic* or *Theaetetus*, just as much or as little as in the *Apology* or *Crito*.

A Socratic "biography" therefore in the modern sense does not exist. Is there any means by which a Socratic "mind" can be reconstructed, distinct from the mind of a Plato, a Xenophon, or any other writer of logoi? It is this after all, and not the biography, that would be of interest to philosophers, and historians of philosophy, if recoverable. That mind we recall came to maturity during the middle of the fifth century, not the fourth. Remembering this, an initial clue to the possible character of the original "Socraticism" may lie in what seems the initial obstacle to any clue—namely, the curious character of these texts of education using an ambivalent blend of fact and fiction to propagate their message. In the history of literary production, they point forward but also backward to those oral conditions of communication mentioned above that were beginning to be terminated somewhere around 430 B.C. The Socratic "mind," whatever it was, must have matured before this happened. The mask or persona borrowed by the logoi writers in the fourth century must have represented a character already established in tradition as appropriate for this role. He must at the least have been an educator of some rank, and the methodologies in the logoi must have recalled something of his style. But the original style was not that of a writer but an oralist, and between the two a gulf exists, difficult to estimate, but still a gulf.

Style in this instance was (and still is) a matter of language. The language of orally preserved speech is governed by certain rules that are subject to gradual change as such speech is rendered visible and readable. Simplifying a complex process, we can say that the difference is exposed by comparing Homer's vocabulary and syntax with Plato's. In my *Greek Concept of Justice*,[29] I have sought to expound an example of this change as it occurs in the linguistic management of the two Greek terms *dike* and *dikaiosune*, illustrating a movement away from *dike* symbolizing a procedure between parties, which is externalized, towards *dikaiosune* identifying a conceptual principle, which can be internalized. An alteration in the name used, which occurs in this case, is not essential. For example, *soma*, which refers to a dead body in orally framed speech, becomes "body" in general, i.e., tangible matter, in documented speech. The pressure for changes of this sort begins building up in the so-called physical philosophers who preceded Socrates. Indeed their entire enterprise can from one point of view be described as an attempt to replace an oral, i.e. Homeric and Hesiodic, language of description with one that is conceptual and abstract, rather than applying a ready-made, abstract language to the formulation of cosmological systems.[30]

The names of things alter their reference only as they are connected to each other in syntactical systems, which also alter. Memorized speech tends to be "narrativized." It is the story form that is memorizable, not the thesis form. Subjects and objects are preferred that act on each other rather than stay in fixed relationships to each other. In documented speech, as the pressure to memorize is reduced, they can take up static postures, in which a definition replaces an activity, that is, an event. If I may cite a somewhat simple-minded illustration: orally preserved speech is likely to be unfriendly to such a statement as "The angles of a triangle are equal to two right angles." To say, however, that "The triangle stood firm in battle, poised with its two legs on the ground, fighting resolutely to protect its enclosed two right angles against the attacks of the enemy" you would be casting Euclid backwards into Homeric dress, giving him a preliterate form.

Grammatically, the change becomes most evident, as this example indirectly may indicate, in the usage of that verb one translates in English as *is* and *are*, the so-called verb *to be*. Orally preserved speech is not friendly to the "is" statement when it performs a logical, i.e., conceptual, function. This means that Greek literature before Plato is not friendly to it either. A large part of Plato's writings can be considered as devoted to the task of establishing the status and importance of "is" statements, particularly as they can be used to define common norms of human conduct.

The encouragement that a growing literacy gave to the formation of abstract statements was indirect, the result of lifting the pressure to memorize, which meant to phrase language in memorizable form. It produced also a more direct result, and a rather simple one. In a culture of oral communication, what is spoken exists only as it is uttered by a speaker and absorbed by a listener. This situation discourages the members of the culture from conceptualizing language itself as a thing, an object with an identity separate from the persons who use it. But with progressive alphabetization, as more and more of the Greek tongue assumed visible, i.e., inscribed, form, it became possible to identify the existence of language as such in separation from the user of it, and to think about it and make it an object of discourse. Language begins to be exploited in such a way that it can talk about itself, and analyze its own elements, identify its own "grammar"; etymologically speaking, "grammar" recognizes words only as they become written *gram-*

mata. One is compelled to say that an intellectual advance, a new discipline, is brought to birth by a shift in the use of the physical senses, as the vision of the reader is called on to supplement or replace the hearing of the listener. It is precisely in the fifth century and in Athens that we encounter the first appearance of this new discipline, introduced by the intellectuals who preceded Plato, and who were foreigners. Their leading representatives included not only Protagoras, Prodicus, and Gorgias, classified as "sophists," but also Democritus, usually classified as a "scientist." The thing they were talking about fascinated them; it was so new; it seemed to open up endless possibilities of exploitation. What were they to call it? *Glotta*, the "tongue," *phone*, the "voice," *phatis* and *epos*, the "utterance"—these were the traditional terms, the Homeric ones, by which the act of speech and its sounds were recognized. But their genius was oral, and moreover they symbolized precisely that style and substance of speech that the new movement towards abstraction was trying to get away from. There was a better candidate to fill the required role, namely logos, which for Plato's predecessors became not only an instrument but a disembodied force, the language of argument, analysis, and persuasion combined, a new power in the land.

Separation of language from the speaker had a second effect of making the speaker separately recognizable as the source of the language. As source, he seemed to be more than lips, tongue, and larynx. Was there not something else in him that devised the language and purposively utilized it? Did not the recognition of language as a separate object call for the recognition of the human consciousness as a separate subject? What name, in this period of new names and new applications of old names, should we give to this thing in man in general, or in "me" and "you" personally? Homeric usage offered several possibilities, the most comprehensive of which was *psyche* because it embraced the sense of a man's "life." Homerically, this psyche was denied the use of language, at least in its disembodied state in Hades, though even in this regard, its status was ambiguous. Could it be revived, reinvigorated, as the symbol of that total consciousness that expresses itself in language? The fifth century intellectuals were not sure of this. They saw psyche as something that responded to the persuasion of logos, as being acted upon, but could it act, plan, decide, think? Democritus might perhaps say "yes" and Gorgias "no"[31] and Protagoras and Prodicus maybe were not interested.

What, however, they all seem to have realized is that changes of linguistic usage of the sort they were experimenting with were symptoms of changes in the way they were thinking or, more accurately, of a new way of using the mind which we can identify with sheer "intellection"; a new level of consciousness. All terms for psychic activity are slippery, never more so than in the fifth century. One can say in general that as the century advances, the Homeric terminology covering aspects of the human consciousness becomes more specialized, in particular through a growing need to identify those particular powers that were being mobilized to produce the logos of abstraction. This movement in vocabulary had begun with the pre-Socratics and became intensified in the activities of the sophists. The verbs *noein* and *phrontizein* and their corresponding nouns take on new levels of emphasis and significance. The age of the "thinker" is dawning, ushered in by the age of literacy.

Hegel and Nietzsche in the last century perceived the change in consciousness and connected it with the Socratic problem. Julius Stenzel in this century perceived that the Socratic problem was intimately connected with the powers of the logos.[32] It is due to the genius of Plato to say that he uniquely grasped what had happened in the realm of language and mind, grasping it as a dynamic process rather than formulating it in the rigidities of an achieved system, and set it down on paper. In so doing, he laid the foundations of modernity, creating the first model of literate European man, ready to seek and search, formulate and understand, by the light of concepts and categories systematically arranged in fixed relations. Whether such an understanding is inferior to the Homeric one is a question lying beyond the confines of my text. In this enterprise his writings associate the name Socrates with himself. But the historic Socrates belongs to a preceding generation, the period of the crisis, not its resolution. Are there means to determine what role if any he played in it? That role to have significance must have been primarily linguistic; it is likely also to have been psychological, in the sense of recognizing the mental habits that were being called into play and identifying their source. But what criteria can separate his contribution from (a) the philosophical processes and positions either dramatized or described in Plato's writings? (b) the intellectual or linguistic activities attributed to the intellectuals who were his contemporaries?

The initial one, I suggest, is also the simplest, hitherto regarded not as a clue but as an obstacle to finding any clues. The historical Socrates by common consent left no written account of his ideas or teaching. There is no hint of the existence of so much as a paragraph or memorandum, let alone essay or monograph. This fact, taken in the context of an assumed literacy for most Athenians throughout the fifth century, has inevitably been put down as an eccentricity or as a deliberate choice to refrain from doing what he might normally have done. Gigon, for example, (*Sokrates* pp. 17–18), correctly discerning the importance of the fact, calls it something "which in itself need mean anything or nothing. What is required is to determine the philosophical-poetic motive which elevates the mere fact to the level of a significant decision. Here we have the *deliberate renunciation* of the written

word as an inadequate means for expressing the special essence of philosophical thought" [my italics].

This pronouncement it is fair to say reflects an assumption shared by all
scholars of the Socratic problem: in Socrates' day, to write was normal, to
teach orally was abnormal, and also regressive, a "renunciation." But suppose the reverse is true. The case then alters. Suppose his abstention from
the written word was a function of his nonliteracy. If Socrates was an
"oralist," at least the latter part of his life and teaching was conducted within
the context of a literate revolution that came to be consummated not by himself but in the writings of his pupil. The contemporary thinkers whom he
may be supposed to have known, and whose association with him is portrayed in comedy and the later Socratic logoi, were writers, all of them. But
the older ones were Greeks from overseas, where, as I have proposed, they
had had a head start.[33] They had all been schooled in letters at the elementary level before puberty. When it came to Plato's turn, Athens was
equipped to teach him on the same lines, but that was forty years later, and
Plato records the experience in a dialogue written perhaps eighty years later.

The initial step to take in any attempt to reconstruct the original "Socraticism" is to treat it as a historical phenomenon rooted in the pre-Platonic era
of language and thought, and to treat its author as a partner with his intellectual peers, foreigners from overseas, in the attempt to fashion a vocabulary
and syntax for conceptual discourse. But he himself must be treated as a
very unusual partner. What could his oralism contribute when placed in partnership with their literacy?

I would propose that the answer is supplied in the need for what may be
called the "interrupting question," one might even say the "disruptive" question requiring a repetition and rewording of what has just been said. This is
an oral technique attributed to him in all our sources, contemporary and
posthumous. The abstract nouns forming the subjects of conceptual statements had to be initially wrested so to speak out of their subordinate roles in
orally preserved communication, in particular out of the epic. These new abstractions were intended to be non-agents, non-persons, but they continued
stubbornly to behave in language as though they were still persons acting
and acting upon. The incipient process of wresting, half-imagist and half-
conceptual, can be seen at work in Hesiod's treatment of "justice" (*dike*).[34]
But even in post-Hesiodic Greek poetry, strictly conceptual discourse lies
beyond the range of composition. To compel these names, of virtue and
courage and justice and wealth and love and war and peace and the like, to
stop behaving and start "existing," in a veridical sense, not necessarily a
metaphysical one, required the administration of shock tactics, applied to the
actual syntax of all poetized speech. It was difficult to do this in the fifth

century in writing because writing tended to reproduce the narrative format already familiar, that is, Homeric myth and rhetoric. This tended to happen when the sophists wrote anything. The process needed the help of cross comparison and contradiction, i.e., the collaboration of two personalities, and this could only be readily supplied by an oralist, who, listening (in accordance with custom) to a pronouncement or a quotation from a poet, could say, "What does "it" (or "you") say?" (i.e., *mean*; the same Greek word in both senses); "Say that again." The alternative version would never reproduce the original. The two could then be matched, contrasts drawn, producing doubt or hesitancy, leading to the further question "What *is* it we are talking about?" And with the intrusion of the verb *to be* there is insinuated the pressure to resort to "is" statements in what has become a dialectical situation. Such statements are elicited by the *erotesis* out of the existing "Homeric" discourse—there is nowhere else to get it from—which has not hitherto been using the "is" syntax as a method of connecting one abstraction to another. It is difficult to see how in the circumstances an analytic discourse could have been forced out of an oral-poetic one and fully realized by any other method; but equally, it would still have been impossible if the intellectualism of the pre-Socratics and sophists had not already begun to wrestle with the problem. One can form the paradoxical hypothesis that a cultural collaboration between sophistic literacy and Socratic nonliteracy was brought to its completion in the written dialectic of Plato. In saying this, however, it is a mistake to exclude the possibility that the sophists also resorted to oral exchange as a teaching method, but without pushing it to the extremes practised by the Socratic discipline.

One thing more must be said. The construction of such discourse, whether of the sophistic or Socratic type, could not possibly be conducted as a casual affair. It involved some procedure, some shared language, whether as one listened as audience to a disquisition or partook in an *erotesis-apokrisis*, a question-and-answer session. The process had to have some continuity to get anywhere; the persons involved had to share some time together, for which the current term was *diatribe*, in a kind of linguistic partnership, for which the term was *sunousia*. Consequently it was unavoidable that the procedure should take on the appearance and the actuality of an educational experiment—a *paideusis*. The type of instruction in Socrates' case may have been novel; it might be claimed for him later that it was not really instruction, in the sense in which sophistic exposition was. But instruction it certainly was, and it is difficult to see how it could have avoided a relationship we would define as that between teacher and pupils or at least associates. What in fact the literate revolution created was a felt need for what might be called the conceptual management of affairs, political, commercial and personal, an ability to analyze and arrange, using language for this purpose—a design that achieves its extreme form in Plato's *Republic*. The need could be met only by a new type of educational curriculum, and if we are to take seriously the possibility that a meaningful relationship existed between Plato and Socrates, we cannot avoid the conclusion that Plato's preoccupation with education, the single most powerful motive behind his writings, was anticipated in the activities of the man whose mask he borrowed.

One therefore is tempted to visualize a historical Socrates as an orally minded man who knew his poets, having had the normal education in "music," and was deeply entrenched in previous and traditional habits of speech and thought; but who had become aware of the vocabulary of new names or of old names exploited in a new way, as they were occurring in new types of discourse thrown about by his literate contemporaries; and aware also of their awareness that some new psychological effort was needed in these procedures, an effort let us say of intellection; and aware also that the entire procedure involved a new type of language, which he, like them, preferred to call *logos*. Where could the seat or source of this novel activity reside except inside "you" and "me," that is, in our "psyche," as we engage in an interchange of *erotesis* and *apokrisis* and discover in the process our capability for this kind of conceptual effort? And again, aside from the new names or old names now spoken in a new way, what new phenomenon is being thrown off by this dynamo within you and me that can use this language if not pure "thought" (*phrontis, phrontisma*) and "thoughts," a precious commodity indeed. Because of his traditional upbringing, he reconverted the fruits of literacy back into oral form, making himself his own discourse, thus producing a new living word devoted to the dispossession of the previous living word, a paradox indeed, one that might give deep offense just because of its deceptive closeness to traditional habits. Lastly, since he had committed himself to a method that only worked in partnership with other persons, he found himself compelled to organize their participation on some kind of formal basis, thus turning himself into something more than a private citizen, becoming in fact a recognized educator like his professional contemporaries, though on novel lines.

The above tentative reconstruction of Socraticism is speculative, drawn from a theoretic consideration of the likely effects of the Greek literate revolution upon the Greek consciousness. But it has not been reached without assistance from a contemporary document. The *Clouds* of Aristophanes was a comedy (to once more state the necessary obvious) designed among other things to amuse. It would do this by the use of burlesque, but not travesty. If the representation of Socrates in this play had been unfaithful to his known interests and associations, by suggesting a partnership between him and the contemporary sophists and scientists, the audience would have been confused, and the comedy would not have worked. An audience will respond gleefully to satire at the expense of known tastes, ideas, and attitudes of a known member or members of a movement or coterie, but they will be puzzled and put off by confusion of these with quite different ideas and attitudes known by them to be different. Gilbert and Sullivan's *Patience* exploits a disguised version of Oscar Wilde to satirize the aesthetic movement of which he was the acknowledged leader. To have combined this in the same opera with satire upon the movement to promote higher education for women (*Princess Ida*) or the reform of the House of Peers (*Iolanthe*) would have ruined the comic effect.

Moreover, despite the judgment of scholars who prefer to jest through clenched teeth rather than laugh with their bellies, the play is not a hostile attack. If it were, it would not have been funny. As its author himself ruefully admits (speaking of the original acted version) it had proved too sophisticated for its audience.[35] If it exploited an intellectualist movement for humorous purposes, choosing a known protagonist of the movement, this artistic purpose called for a measure of sympathy for and understanding of what the movement was all about. To describe Aristophanes, in connection with his authorship of the *Clouds*, as one to whom "all philosophical and scientific speculation, all disinterested intellectual curiosity, is boring and silly"[36] may reveal something of the tastes of the author of such a statement but is a travesty of the interests of the author who produced not only the *Clouds*, but the *Birds*, *Lysistrata*, *Ecclesiazusae*, and *Plutus*.

Lying buried in the *Clouds* and made the constant victims of linguistic burlesque are precisely those features of Socraticism that I have endeavored to extrapolate from the cultural context of the fifth century. The play is an essay in intellectual history, offered by indirection. There is the new fascination with names and their definitions, the employment of question and answer to break through the common consciousness and extract these from a man's own self;[37] there is the new fangled notion, still laughable to a contemporary audience, that a man indeed has a "self," a *psyche*, which is the seat of a novel process of abstract thinking; there is even the "think tank" (*phrontisterion*), apparently a private house utilized for the purpose of maintaining sustained association between a group of "thinkers." There are above all the clouds themselves, a choric dramatization of the new realm of the intellect inhabited by those abstract ideas whose existence is now being clearly revealed for the first time by Socraticism. Can Strepsiades, wearing the mask of the common traditional sensibility, with its preconceptual language, begin to grasp what is going on?

The play calls for a detailed examination on these lines for which there is no space in this article. Its nuances are too remote from our day to make sense, until we place them in the context of the Greek literate revolution.

When we do so place them, we begin to see, in outline at least, the mind of a man in the mind of an age.

NOTES

[1] Lessing's short essay is printed in G. E. Lessing, *Collected Works*, ed. Lachmann, vol. 10 (Stuttgart, 1886–1924), pp. 168–71. R. Pfeiffer, *History of New Testament Times* (New York, 1949) describes Judaic literature and thought produced before and during the inception of the Christian era. For the eschatological and linguistic background, see Albert Schweitzer, *Quest of the Historical Jesus* (New York, 1968; reprint, Eng. trans. of *Von Reimarus zu Wrede,* 1906), Chapters 15, 17; in particular, pp. 234, n. 2; and 235, n. 1.

[2] O. Gigon, *Sokrates* (Bern, 1947); A-H. Chroust, *Socrates, Man and Myth* (London, 1957). For some further bibliography, see E. A. Havelock, "The Socratic Self," *YCS* XXII (1970):1–18.

[3] He concludes discussion of the testimonies on the *daimonion* with (p. 178): "Da gebietet es uns die Methode, lieber den Anteil der Dichtung vielleicht noch Grösser einzuschätzen, als er letzen Endes gewesen sein mag, anstatt dass wir uns über die geschichtliche Wirklichkeit in Spekulationen ergehen, für die uns jede Basis fehlt."

[4] G. Vlastos, ed., *The Philosophy of Socrates: A Collection of Critical Essays* (New York, 1971); Terence Irwin, *Plato's Moral Theory: The Early and Middle Dialogues* (Oxford, 1971); G. X. Santas, *Socrates' Philosophy in Plato's Early Dialogues* (London and Boston, 1979).

[5] Excerpted and issued separately as *Socrates* (Cambridge, 1971). N. Gulley, *The Philosophy of Socrates* (London, 1958) reflects similar critical assumptions.

[6] Caps. 4 and 5 on "Elenchus" and 6 on "Definition," by R. Robinson; cap. 7 on "Elenchtic Definitions" by George Nakhnikian; cap. 8 on "Definition of Piety" by S. M. Cohen.

[7] Santas, *Socrates' Philosophy*, preface, p. x.

[8] Irwin, *Plato's Moral Theory*, pp. 178–84.

[9] Irwin, *Plato's Moral Theory*, p. 114.

[10] Irwin, *Plato's Moral Theory*, pp. 58–61, 125–31.

[11] W. K. C. Guthrie, *History of Greek Philosophy*, vol. 4, *Plato: Early Period* (Cambridge, 1975), p. 50.

[12] From cap. 2 "Our Knowledge of Socrates" by A. R. Lacey.

[13] K. J. Dover, *Aristophanes' Clouds* (Oxford, 1968), intro. p. XLII; cf. also Guthrie, *Socrates* (Cambridge, 1971), p. 124, n. 3.

[14] Guthrie, *History of Greek Philosophy*, vol. 4, pp. 213–14 (on the *Protagoras*) and pp. 284–85 (on the *Gorgias*) reviews some of the relevant scholarly literature and its contradictory conclusions.

[15] Guthrie, *History of Greek Philosophy*, vol. 4, pp. 71–72.

[16] See p. 167 on the application of Socratic *erōtēsis* to epic.

[17] By Heinrich Maier: see Havelock, "The Socratic Self," p. 1, n. 1.

[18] *Met.* A 6 987 a29–b7; *Met.* M 4 1078 b17–32. Both contexts are polemical: a Socratic nonseparation of the Forms is mentioned incidental to a statement of Plato's different and incorrect position on this philosophical issue of the fourth century.

[19] Richard Jenkyns, *The Victorians and Ancient Greece* (Cambridge, Mass, 1980); Frank M. Turner, *The Greek Heritage in Victorian Britain* (New Haven, 1981); see the review of both books by Bernard Knox, "The Greek Conquest of Britain," *NYR* (June 11, 1981):24–28. The sanctified status accorded to Plato can still be felt in Guthrie's words (*History of Greek Philosophy*, vol. 4, p. 154, echoing Wilamowitz) "The privilege of watching the gradual growth to maturity of the ideas of a man like Plato is no small one."

[20] See Knox, "The Greek Conquest," p. 26: "Not content with this rehabilitation of figures (sc. the Sophists) who were blamed by the great German historians of philosophy . . . as the cause of Athens' decay, Grote included Socrates in their number, on the grounds that he had 'awakened the analytical consciousness of his fellow citizens to encourage effective social and political action and he had carried that skill into the study of ethics in the manner normally associated with Bentham.'"

[21] *Poet.* 1. 1447 a21–b16; the adjective "anonymous" supplied by editors has dropped from the manuscript but is required by the syntactical context.

[21a] J. A. Coulter, "The Relation of the *Apology of Socrates* to Gorgias' *Defense of Palamedes* and Plato's Critique of Gorgianic Rhetoric," *HSCP* 68 (1964): 269–303.

[22] E. A. Havelock, *Preface to Plato* (Cambridge, Mass. and Oxford, 1963), cap. 3. *The Literate Revolution in Greece and its Cultural Consequences* (Princeton, 1982).

[23] Gilbert Norwood, *Greek Comedy* (London, 1931; reprint, 1964), pp. 184–88.

[24] Gilbert Ryle, *Plato's Progress* (Cambridge, 1966).

[25] For a summary of what little is known of this comedy see Norwood, *Greek Comedy*, p. 136; the chorus were (probably) portrayed as "old men sorely stricken in years," a role appropriate to their portrayal as parents at *Crito* 50D. Thematically, the play anticipated the *Demes* (above n. 23); compare the subversion of "the established laws" by Pheidippides at *Clouds* 1400. All three plays could be interpreted as exploiting for comic but also didactic purposes the cultural strains created by the Greek Enlightenment.

[26] Horace *Sat.* 1.4.1.

[27] Norwood, *Greek Comedy*, pp. 190, 192; cf. Guthrie, *History of Greek Philosophy*, vol. 4, p. 215, n. 2 where the play's title *Kolakes* is translated as "Parasites."

[28] Christopher Gill, "The Death of Socrates," *C.Q.* 23, no. 1 (1973):25–28; W. B. Ober, M.D., "Did Socrates Die of Hemlock Poisoning?" *New York State Journal of Medicine* 77 no. 2 (Feb. 1977):254–58. The "theater" of the "Socratic" dialogues is compatible with the not unreasonable thesis that Plato became a writer at the time of the founding of the Academy, when lapse of time would have lent artistic "distance" to the last half of the fifth century. The thesis has been argued by B.

Witte, *Die Wissenschaft vom Guten und Bösen: Interpretationen zu Platon's 'Charmides'* (Berlin, 1970); cf. Guthrie, *History of Greek Philosophy*, p. 67, n. 2.

[29] E. A. Havelock, *Greek Concept of Justice* (Cambridge, Mass., 1978).

[30] E. A. Havelock, "Linguisitic Task of the Presocratics," in Kevin Robb (ed.) *Language and Thought in Early Greek Philosophy* (Monist Library of Philosophy, vol. 4, 1983).

[31] D. B. Claus, *Toward the Soul*, Yale Classical Monographs 3 (New Haven and London, 1981), pp. 142–48, on Democritus; pp. 149–50, on Gorgias.

[32] J. Stenzel, "Sokrates," RE 2 Reihe v. Halbb (1927) who observes that Socrates' concern was with "der Logos der Sprache, der gemeinsame Besitz sinnvoller Vorstellungen einer Sprach-gemeinschaft."

[33] E. A. Havelock, *Literate Revolution*, cap. I with note 34.

[34] E. A. Havelock, *Greek Concept*, caps. II and I2.

[35] E. A. Havelock, "The Socratic Self," pp. 16–17.

[36] Dover, *Aristophanes' Clouds*, intro. lii.

[37] E. A. Havelock, "The Socratic Self," pp. 10–13.

ROBERT S. BRUMBAUGH

Doctrine and Dramatic Dates of Plato's Dialogues

M Y purpose in this discussion is to raise—without expecting to finally resolve—the question of the doctrinal significance of the several internal cross-references in Plato's dialogues, and particularly his indications of a proper sequence for the reader. In the background, I will assume an order of *dates of composition* that, at least by groups of dialogues, is generally accepted. And part of my discussion will aim to establish a match between this chronology and the author's several strategic purposes, as the works reflect them.

There are two reasons for this exploration, one metaphysical, one largely technical. The *technical* reason is that those of us who insist on the inseparability of "literary" and "argument" dimensions of Plato's work have not done very well in articulating the *larger* literary questions of sequence as functions of the central drama of ideas. The *metaphysical* reason is that there is a necessary problem of perspective inherent in the Platonic theory of forms, anticipated in Plato's own statements and destined to haunt and divide the Platonic tradition into a neo-Platonic "formalist" view and a "process" view.

Platonic metaphysics does not lend itself to literal, didactic presentation. Part, at least, of the reason is that the metaphysician must address us from a definite standpoint in his reporting. If that standpoint looks to the forms as future alternative goals or values, its prospective report will differ from the purely descriptive accounts of the forms as classes or universals that look to them in a nontemporal eternal present.

In short, the different functions of the forms involve different refractions through becoming, and no one account can do justice to the theory.

But there are other problems of perspective. One of these is the relation of the knower to what is known. Here we are confronted with the simultaneous ideas of philosophy as final vision and philosophy as unending inquiry.

This paper was presented at the 1979 New York meeting of the Society for Ancient Greek Philosophy; it has not previously been published.
Robert Brumbaugh is Professor of Philosophy at Yale University.

This may, again, be a question of temporal stance: $7 + 5 = x$ is a problem, a theme for inquiry, until x is "seen"; but then, retrospectively, $7 + 5 = 12$ is an analytic insight.

Another is the puzzling problem of participation. Whitehead suggested that this relation is different from the standard relations of mathematics and technology in that it is asymmetrical in respect to its "internal" or "external" character.[1] That is, if A is a form, and a is an instance, the participation relation $P(A,a)$ is *external* from the standpoint of A, but *internal* from the standpoint of a. Whether $a = A$ or $A = a$ depends on whether we stand with the form (by itself, just what it is) or the participant (owing its name and its identity to the form it grasps). It is disquieting to have to accept such pairs of alternative accounts that seem at first glance exclusive. For example, in the *Parmenides* we find Parmenides saying that if, indeed, the forms are independent of our world, they will be unknowable by us; but if they enter into relations with us so that they interact with our knowing, they will become partly mind-dependent. The difficulty is not eased by the fact that between the "forms" taken in their immanent qualitative presentation, there are intermediate stages of formal determination—paradigms, types, roles, type specimens—each of which presents the same asymmetry of internal-external relatedness to the entities above it and below it in the formal hierarchy.

Very early in his career, as soon as he tried to develop his defense of Socrates into a systematic philosophic vision, Plato discovered this difficulty. Having written the *Phaedo*, in which Socrates has attained "blessedness" by realization of the form of justice, Plato felt compelled to complete the picture with the contrasting *Symposium*. Where the *Phaedo* gives forms that are perfect, pure, and attainable, the *Symposium* gives forms that lie at the end of an impossible quest, a demonic pursuit of creativity.[2] If for an instant the *Symposium* allows a glimpse of the Beautiful, that glimpse is followed by a return to time in which the philosopher again functions as a *daimon*. The two dialogues, by every test of style, structure, and historical reference, were written almost at the same date. They are internally linked by parallel detail that relate them as a comedy to a tragedy—as an initial point of relatedness in contrast here, we note that the patron of the *Symposium* is Dionysus, the patron of the *Phaedo* is Apollo.

This attempt to get the portrait of Socrates and his thought properly done, by doing it in two contrasting lights and styles, addresses a problem that is reflected throughout the Platonic tradition. Within that tradition, there tends to be a polarization between interpretations that follow the *Phaedo* in a stress on the purity and remoteness of the real world—this is the orientation of neo-Platonism—and interpretations more appreciative of the role of Eros, of the forms as creative powers—this is the orientation, today, of process philosophy; earlier, Renaissance admirers of the *Symposium* shared the view. The neo-Platonic tradition tends to take the mythology of the *Phaedo* literally and to treat the forms as remote and separate and as completely determinate particulars; this rules out any rational account of participation. The process view, reducing the forms to relevant possibilities, makes their actuality dependent on choices and minds, and loses the objectivity of ethical value standards that was the most important original impetus to the theory.

The theme of my present discussion is that Plato's indications of the inter-relations of various dialogues represent his attempt to indicate relatively complete perspectival accounts of his philosophy. How optimistic he was about the final success of a great projected sequence of eight successive Socratic discourses to provide a complete, perspective-including picture we are not sure. But the final judgment of *Letter VII*, Plato's or not (and I am certain that it *is* his own), is surely right: Platonic philosophy does not lend itself, as other topics do, to literal, textbook forms of statement.[3]

It is generally assumed by twentieth-century readers that the doctrines of the "later dialogues" and of the middle ones, particularly the *Phaedo*, are incompatible. The explanation usually given is that Plato discovered that the "middle dialogue" theory of forms had two defects: first, it was not needed to explain the phenomena of knowledge and communication that it had been invoked to account for; second, it was not coherent in the face of rigorous logical analysis. It is also generally assumed in the twentieth century that a satisfactory but metaphysically far more modest theory is found in the "logical" later dialogues. A further assumption—and this is one that goes back to the earliest neo-Platonists—is that the theory of forms in the middle-dialogue version is given a *literal* statement by Plato's Socrates in the final section of the *Phaedo*.

What I propose to do is, first, to organize the dialogues in groups related by common internal cross-reference or common strategy; second, to show how this illuminates the inter-relation of the "logical" later series; third, to reconstruct the location and method of *The Philosopher* as part of this projected set; fourth, to show that if the *Phaedo* is correctly read, it can appropriately come *after The Philosopher* in a dialectical order. If this is convincing, I will have shown that the open alternatives for understanding Plato remain, as they have always been, a neo-Platonic stress on transcendence or a process philosophy stress on immanence and emergence; and that the contemporary attempts to read Plato as an analytic or linguistic philosopher completely miss the intended strategy of the texts usually taken as central in this Megarian enterprise.

Literary form, internal indications of rhetorical intention, and (with increasing relevance for the later work) stylometric data, fit together consistently in a grouping of dialogues that approximately matches their supposed dates of composition.[4]

After the death of Socrates, young Plato—presumably in Megara—began writing dialogues in defense of his older friend and hero. The *Euthyphro, Apology*, and *Crito* certainly belong here. Of these, the first defends Socrates against the charge of impiety by contrasting his attitude toward religion and the gods with that of the fundamentalist, Euthyphro. The second, a recreation of Socrates' speech at his trial, at once makes it clear what the real basis of the charges against him were (namely, his persistent inquiry), and brings out his seriousness. (Xenophon's *Apology* is evidence that many Athenians saw Socrates as a kind of eccentric crank.) The third defends Socrates against the charge of bad citizenship, implied in the phrasing of both counts of the indictment. The form is highly dramatic, brief, and without much metaphysics or positive doctrine. A next set of dialogues is the *Lysis—Laches—Charmides*, which defend Socrates against the charge of corrupting the youth, by showing him in action. The case studies are designed to show his concern and the good effect of his method on young audiences—if not on elderly generals. Again, the form is highly dramatic, the conversations brief (an Aristotelian critic would say that Plato deliberately uses a form that has a beginning and middle, but no end), the emphasis ethical, metaphysics relatively lacking. Another, though implicit, charge that Plato felt a need to answer was the notion—central to Aristophanes' *Clouds*, and persisting in the public mind—that Socrates was just another sophist. In fact, as Plato saw it, the whole project of Socratic inquiry presupposed a nonrelativistic possibility for rational treatment of value questions that was at the opposite pole from the sophisticated intellectuals of the "sophist" persuasion. In presenting this second line of defense, Plato has Socrates encounter the leading intellectuals of the day. These dialogues are longer; the casts are larger, the action more dramatically complex. An element of contest enters, more strongly than before, with Socrates the winner. Plato's Socrates, in these discussions, now introduces myths to illustrate his points and begins to use mathematical examples. The theory that knowledge is recollection becomes explicit in the *Meno*, one of the later dialogues in this set.

In his middle dialogues, Plato tries to carry out the project of systematizing the philosophic vision of Socrates and of offering a final justification for Socrates' behavior. M. Fox drew attention some years ago to the way in which Socrates describes his final conversation as a "trial" in which he defends his way of life before a jury of philosophers: if Ionian naturalism were the final philosophic answer, Socrates' idealism would indeed have been unrealistic.[5] The *Phaedo* is a presentation of Socrates' thoughts on the subject of immortality; it is a continuation of the *Euthyphro-Apology-Crito*, but both form and content indicate a later date of writing, with the Socrates-versus-sophists set, ending with the *Meno*, in between. But at about the same time, the *Symposium* gives an alternative portrait of an engaged Socrates, a *daimon*, in pursuit of immortality by his creativity. These two dialogues fit closely together by every criterion—style, relative length, explicit systematic extension of Socrates' insights—and parallel details stress their intended complementary character. But "the" Platonic philosophy they present offers a strong temptation to take one *or* the other. It is important to notice Plato's careful parallel construction, designed to force his reader to accept both accounts, rather than to reject one in favor of the other.

The middle dialogues continue with the great philosophic vision of the *Republic*, developed by dialectic; and the account of philosophic rhetoric in the *Phaedrus*, where Phaedrus' character forces Socrates to persuade him by myth and cosmological argument of doctrines Plato proves by something more like ontological or teleological arguments elsewhere. In these dialogues, we are dealing with a full-scale philosophic vision; myth and mathematics alternate in importance; the method depends heavily on analogy and metaphor. The outcome is a picture of the sort of world in which Socrates' conduct is justified, his vision confirmed, and systematic metaphysics established. In particular, the "divided line" of the *Republic* summarizes a new epistemology and projects a new plan of education, consistent with a Socratic inquiry that hopes to find constructive solutions.

These middle dialogues have interesting structural properties. The drama instantiates the argument—that is, the characters with their problems and notions offer concrete examples of what the discussion is about. (Thus the cast of *Republic* II–X has a spokesman for each of the three "parts of the soul.") At the same time, when a method is an important topic of discussion, that method is illustrated by the contextual dialogue (so "dialectic" is illustrated by the *Republic*, "philosophical rhetoric" by the *Phaedrus*).

So far, except for readers who wonder about the compatibility of the types of immortality offered by the *Symposium* and *Phaedo*, or about the compatibility of the method of division of the *Phaedrus* and the speculative dialectic of the *Republic*, this is a classification with which there is pretty general agreement. But note that in the conclusion of the *Phaedo* Socrates presents his project for a philosophic-scientific system as just that: a vision, a hope, a project. And in describing Plato's middle dialogues as "vision," we try to do justice to an evident emphasis on speculative coherence that sets aside precision and sharp refutation.

This leaves Plato, after the middle dialogues, with three lines of investigation to follow. The first is *logical*: can the four-level theory of knowledge of the *Republic* establish itself against critics who argue that the forms are

(a) not intelligible, or (b) not necessary, or (c) not as extended a domain as the *Republic* makes them? The second line of investigation is *cosmological* or *physical*: does the mythical faith that nature and history are ordered with regard for value find confirmation in empirical science and in historical plausibility? The third line is *ethical*: if this philosophy is true, it should be possible to take it back to the marketplace from the Academy, and to show that, indeed, far from being "idle talking" (Isocrates' description of Plato's work in the Academy) it is a practical tool for human betterment.

Quite clearly, the second of these purposes motivated the projected *Republic-Timaeus-Critias-Hermocrates* tetralogy. Bracketing the more metaphysical portions of Socrates' account of his city in the skies, Timaeus concentrates on the empirical details of natural science,[6] ending with medicine. In the next dialogue, Critias, in turn, moves from cosmology to mythical history, with his "true" story of a small but virtuous state (ancient Athens) triumphing over Atlantis, a large but bad one. Hermocrates, in turn, could be expected to give an account of the fate of a later Athens that had lost the excellence of the ancient city in Critias' story. (This theme of Greek history, from mythical to contemporary, was transferred by Plato to the *Laws*, leaving the *Hermocrates* unwritten [and the *Critias* unfinished, though perhaps for another reason.]) The thrust of the *Timaeus* throughout is that natural phenomena can be explained by models and laws that embody aesthetic properties of beauty, simplicity, and precision. The implications of this were stated earlier in the myths that conclude the *Republic* and the *Phaedo*.

The third strategic target of Plato's later writings is clearly the motivation of the *Philebus* and the *Laws*. The *Philebus* both by theme ("not the good itself, but the good for human life") and the cast (young men who are not very philosophical) centers on the practical application of philosophy; the *Laws* offers a concrete sample demonstration of the philosophic legislator in action, establishing "right measure."

The *first* of the strategic sequels to the middle dialogues is a more complex affair. It opens with the *Parmenides*, a dialogue with a double strategic purpose. The first point this dialogue aims to establish is that neither the Megarian nor the Eudoxian interpretation of the Socratic theory of forms is tenable. Both are consistent, but the former has no room for sensible things, and the latter makes its forms immanent in process, and so, in effect, sensibles. If we take these two positions—Megarian formalism and Eudoxian process—as exclusive and exhaustive world-hypotheses, we have a real antinomy. But are the forms necessary at all? Yes, Plato argues that they are. But it follows from the *Parmenides* deductions that a theory of forms must do more than explore *hypotheses*: on the level of *dianoia*, there are many logically consistent alternatives that are nonetheless philosophically incomplete. Thus, when Parmenides decides to demonstrate what happens to the theory of forms on the level of *dianoia*, the result is an indirect proof that forms on the *noetic* level are necessary. (We were prepared for this when these forms—the beautiful, the right, and the good—came early into the discussion with Parmenides before the dazzling hypotheses.)[7]

We have thus a model of a *reductio* proof that the forms are necessary; that this must include the noetic "value" forms is shown by the incoherence of an account of "unity" that tries to do without them. The divided line cannot be simplified, then, simply by dismissing the top level. Monsignor Diès caught this point clearly in his remark that "the word *nous* and its derivatives are absent in this dialogue, with the exception of the rejection of conceptualism. . . ."[8]

What would happen, however, if someone with a pragmatic temperament suggested that "forms" are philosophically redundant, whether we treat them as *dianoetic* classes or as *noetic* systematic patterns? The answer is that it would be impossible to explain the possibility of knowledge that nevertheless we actually have. For mere memory and experience can never give us the necessity or universality of mathematics and ethics. The *Theaetetus* is an indirect proof of this. Note that the cast has a spokesman for each of the four kinds of knowledge distinguished on the divided line.[9] It turns out that Theaetetus' adventures with physical-physiological models—models that become the standard paradigms of later Western psychology and epistemology—cannot explain mathematics or Socratic ethics. (And we are given examples in context—Theodorus' and Theaetetus' incommensurability theorems, and Socrates' "digression" on the life of the philosopher—which show that mathematical and philosophical knowledge must indeed be possible, since both are actual.) The intention on Plato's part to have this strategic line of inquiry intersect the ethical-biographical earlier dialogues is shown, not simply in the explicit reference to the indictment at the end of the discussion, but throughout in the attention to trials, law, legal imagery (which would, without this explanation, seem puzzling intrusions, needing the sort of external explanation that Gilbert Ryle proposed).[10]

Cornford catches the point tersely, as Diès had for the *Parmenides*. "The forms do not appear," he writes, for the reason that Plato wants to show the futility of an attempt to do without them.[11] If we claim to have other entities, such as "concepts," "dispositions," or "ideas in our minds," serve as alternative to the "forms," this is not because Plato endorses the substitution!

The *Theaetetus* still recognizes the existence of arts and crafts. These depend on some sort of paradigms for construction, enumeration, operation. If there are no forms of a systematic, *noetic* sort, there is no philosophy; if there are none of a universal, *dianoetic* type, no mathematics or philosophy; but what if a critic of the theory rejects even the common-sense world of paradigms and copies of the *Theaetetus*, and insists on a total identification of *epistēmē* with *eikasia*? Would anyone try this? Yes, a thoroughgoing sophist well might. But the price he must pay for this is to give up the art of communication—of refutation, or persuasion, or deception—and this deprives him of his income and function. The forms are still presupposed here, but only in the very weakened role that they play as public "meanings" that make discourse possible, and as the "syntactical relational frames," connecting isolated meanings into assertions. A demonstration is given of a "method of division" that at first seems able to handle the relations of "forms" without reference to systems, wholes, and so on; it does not turn out until the end of the next dialogue in the series that the method in fact presupposes more elaborate logical and metaphysical distinctions. But with the final capture of the Sophist, at the end of the hunt, this most radical proposal for dispensing with "forms" seems to be laid to rest.

What one would now expect is a rehabilitation of the theory, arguing from the existence of arts and crafts to the fact that these presuppose forms as types and measures, then from the existence of formal systems of measures and types to the fact that these connections presuppose normative forms of system, the value forms.

This return is begun in the *Statesman*, where the forms are presupposed by the arts of statesmanship as the criterion for "right amount" that separates the "too great" from the "too small"; and since there are arts, there "must be such measures." We are tentatively promised a "later" discussion of the nature of "normative measure."

As the project is set up, the Eleatic Stranger has served his turn: he has handled the levels of *eikasia* and *doxa* admirably with his critical logic, but now Socrates and his namesake, Young Socrates, should carry on the conversation in *The Philosopher*. That conversation should, in terms of the symmetry of the dialogue set, argue to a systematic logical order among the forms—not necessarily to the total normative system of the middle dialogues, but to the sort of coherence that is presupposed by the deductions of the *Parmenides*, the definitions of the *Sophist*, the operational accounts of the *Statesman* and the *Theaetetus*. The result would be something like the theory of forms that Socrates describes himself as devising in the *Phaedo*, before his encounter with the book of Anaxagoras set him off on a further line of speculation.[12] In effect, this stage of the theory rests on the axiom that logic is relevant to physics and ethics because the systematic relations of the forms are causally projected and binding on their participants. But this does not yet tell us *why* the formal system is organized as it is, nor whether there are normative functions for the forms that require that they be more than simple "classes," "types," or "universals."

Why Plato never wrote the *Philosopher* admits no final answer. But our discussion of the grouping of casts and topics does suggest what it was destined to say had it been written. We can show this in a tabular form.

NOESIS	*(Republic)*			(????????)
DIANOIA	PARMENIDES			[PHILOSOPHER]
PISTIS		THEAETETUS	STATESMAN	
EIKASIA			SOPHIST	

Should one go back, from the *Statesman* to the *Parmenides*, where Young Socrates is the respondent, and imagine Old Socrates now speaking the lines of the great Parmenides, as *The Philosopher*? Should one assume that this part of the project inspired the Lecture on the Good, which "was highly mathematical," and aimed at a proof of the unity of the system of forms? Might we go off in another direction, and say, as Klein suggested (but only half-seriously), that perhaps the *Apology* is really also *The Philosopher*?[13]

In any case, the sequence of these logical later dialogues has an announced theme and a proposed structure of questioners and respondents that is related symmetrically to the metaphysics of the *Republic* via a symmetrical descent and ascent of the levels of the divided line. We are clearly entitled to locate the *Republic* where we have: Adeimantus and Glaucon are put into the cast of the *Parmenides* for that cross-reference, and the four-person cast of the *Theaetetus* is clearly meant to be a projection of the four levels of cognition.

Notice also that the theme of justice and law that is built into the *Theaetetus*—partly via "digression"—is also central in the *Sophist* and, as an art of justice, central to the *Statesman*. (An earlier political overtone was the selection of young Aristoteles, "who later became one of the Thirty," as the second respondent in the *Parmenides*.)

The crucial point is that the last word of Plato's Socrates is still the *Phaedo*, going beyond the technical, projected *Philosopher*. There have been intervening discoveries in cosmology, logic, and law incorporated by way of qualifying remarks in dramatically earlier conversations, anticipating changes and objections chronologically later, but Plato refers us back to the *Phaedo* to bring the story to its close. Once more, he offers us side-by-side presentations of positions that later readers prefer to think of as exclusive. The Megarian type of analysis of the *reductio* defense of forms contrasts to the visionary Myth of the True Earth as precise analytic philosophy does to exuberant mysticism.

There are, however, two comments in order here. The *Phaedo* must be correctly read. In particular, one must not miss the point of the final myth. Socrates, having given up natural science, recounts his next adventures in two stages. First, he develops a new and powerful, logical method, hypothetical-deductive, but from constantly strengthened "hypotheses"; and this leads to the proof that soul is indestructible.[14] (It does not prove personal immortality, however, which is the main interest of the audience.) Then, inspired by Anaxagoras, he forms a notion of a still better method of explanation: this would be to relate the order of all things, forms and cosmos alike, to the Good as a first principle.[15] If this can be done, philosophy will be able, perhaps, to establish the existence of Cosmic Justice, written in the stars. In a world ordered in that way, the fact that Socrates *ought* to have personal immortality would lead to the conclusion that he does have it. But this is only a story, a hope; it is a project bequeathed by Socrates and pursued throughout his career by Plato.

The Myth of the True Earth has two important properties. First, it expresses Socrates' faith that the insight into the Good as ordering principle is sound. It is a myth inspired by Apollo. And in the story, something a modern reader may not immediately recognize, the findings of scientific geology—the work of the impious atheists who "pry into things beneath the earth"—exactly match and confirm the Orphic stories of a subterranean purgatory.[16] The problem of the shape and stability of the earth is solved by an appeal to what is best, and the mix of eschatology and geology proceeds on the same line. When Aristotle cites two causal explanations of thunder, fire quenched by cloud and a noise to frighten prisoners in Tartarus, the notion that both may apply, exactly echoes this mythical application of the search for what is best.

The second property of the story is that, as myth should, the account transforms abstractions into personifications and reifications. Thus the True Earth has showcases of precious stones and living gods who greet visitors to their temples face to face. The invariability of an atemporal logical domain is represented by the beauty of the museum of perfect instantiation. Such projections are as philosophically misleading, when their proper status is not recognized, as they are aesthetically and religiously effective. One can hardly resist comparing this great Myth to Kant's account, in his Third Critique, of religious vision as an aesthetically coherent presentation of "what we may hope." Like Socrates, Kant had his own conjectures—of the way in which the various planets are used for education of our souls and their purification. (But a number of editors and translators have omitted this unscientific final section from their editions of the *Universal Natural History of the Heavens*.)[17]

By the time of his farewell to Socrates, before the *Laws*, Plato had developed his philosophy systematically. As he wrote successive conversations, he managed to correct—by anticipations if one follows the dramatic dates, by newer findings if we follow the topical and chronological grouping—misinterpretations and to take account of new findings. In the end, he saw that Socrates' faith in a total moral and aesthetic order, and in philosophy as contemplation of that ideal, remained not only a central hope, but one of the central insights of Platonism. But Socrates' last word was a message of purification and escape; and it did not do justice to the Socrates who challenged his fellow Athenians, bringing philosophy into the everyday arguments of the Agora. For that, a further extension was in order; an extension that would once more find its expression in a pair of aspects that modern readers at first glance find antithetical.

The second part of that contrapuntal final portrait is the "process-oriented" doctrine of the Athenian Stranger in the *Laws*. The Athenian Stranger is, like Socrates in the *Phaedo*, an old man. He has had wide political experience, but has only lately encountered higher mathematics and cosmology. His arguments are empirical and cosmological. Nevertheless, those arguments carry him to certainties strong enough to be the basis of law, proofs of the rightness of Anaxagoras' conjecture well beyond the knowledge available to Socrates at the time of the *Phaedo*.[18] And the two traditions of Platonism—the ascetic moment of the *Phaedo*, where we see the whole earth from remote space, and the engaged creativity of the *Laws*, where we regulate and survey all of the fields and rivers in our own section of the earth—are once more presented together in the final strategy of Plato's philosophic presentation.

An appendix to the *Laws* seems also to have been drafted by Plato, though it is doubtful how far our extant text represents his own execution or if it is his, how completely it carries through his intention. But the *Epinomis*, a sequel to the *Laws*, is an astronomical myth parallel in location, similar in theme, and probably intended to be similar in its moral, to the Myth of Er at the conclusion of the *Republic*. And both of these myths seem to draw their inspiration, ultimately, from the Myth of the True Earth at the end of the *Phaedo*.

NOTES

[1] A. N. Whitehead, *Science and the Modern World* (New York, 1925), chap. 10, "Abstraction."

[2] A contrast frequently noted, but not very adequately reconciled; see, for example, R. S. Brumbaugh, *Plato for the Modern Age* (reprint, Westport, 1979), pp. 83–115.

[3] *Epistle VII*, 342A ff.

[4] For a discussion of the evidence for dramatic and chronological dates, see the discussions in W. K. C. Guthrie, *A History of Greek Philosophy*, vols. 4, 5 (Cambridge, 1971, 1975). Various other orderings are not relevant here, for example, Thrasyllus' organization by philosophic theme, or the several arrangements for maximum pedagogical value reported by Albinus.

[5] Marvin Fox, "The Trials of Socrates," *Archiv. für Gesch. d. Philosophie*, 6 (1956):226–61.

[6] In the summary of the *Republic* that opens the *Timaeus*, the metaphysical section (Books VI and VII) is omitted. Since Proclus, commentators have suggested a connection between this fact and the cryptic "One, two, three, but where is the fourth . . . ," with which the dialogue opens.

[7] *Parmenides* 130B6–C1.

[8] A. Diès, "Notice," *Platon Parménide*, ed. A. Diès (Paris, 1950), pp. 47–48.

[9] The correlation is as follows: *Noesis* : Socrates :: *Dianoia* : Theodorus :: *Pistis* : Theaetetus :: *Eikasia* : Ghost of Protagoras.

[10] Gilbert Ryle, *Plato's Progress* (Cambridge, 1966), pp. 275–80, esp. p. 278. On this general approach to Plato's treatments of lawyers and litigation, see my review of Ryle, *Journal of Value Inquiry* (1967):271–74.

[11] F. M. Cornford, *Plato's Theory of Knowledge* (reprint, Indianapolis, 1957), esp. pp. 12–13.

[12] *Phaedo* 95A–97C; 99D–107C.

[13] Jacob Klein, *Plato's Trilogy* (Chicago, 1977), p. 5.

[14] *Phaedo* 99D–107C.

[15] *Phaedo* 95A–97C.

[16] Aristotle takes the geology seriously—something he does not do for such other Platonic myths as the Myth of Er, the Myth of Metals, the *Gorgias* Myth of Last Judgment; Aristotle, *Meteorology*, II.1, 355b32–356b2.

[17] Kant, *Critique of Judgment*; *Universal Natural History of the Heavens*.

[18] *Laws* X.

The Tragic and Comic Poet of the *Symposium*

P LATO'S *Symposium* breaks up only at dawn. For some, his celebration of Eros lasts longer than it should. At its end not only have Phaedrus, Eryximachus, and still others escaped into the night, but Plato's commentators have fallen asleep—like all but three or four of those still present in Agathon's banquet room. Ficino composed no *Oratio octava* to represent or comment upon Socrates' conversation with Agathon and Aristophanes. As for Louis Le Roi, whose *Le Sympose de Platon* (1558) was the first French translation of the *Symposium* and at the same time a sort of marriage manual for the newly married dauphin (pp. 71–72), not only does he fail to translate and comment upon the last scene of the dialogue, but he ends his *Sympose* with Diotima's last words.[1] Of modern commentaries, only one treats the last scene of the *Symposium* as an integral and essential part of the dialogue rather than an "epilogue."[2]

Plato's *Symposium* does not conclude with the last speech in praise of Eros—Alcibiades' praise of Socrates. Rather his celebration continues a discussion which survives the epiphany of new revellers just at the end of Alcibiades' Dionysian speech. *Thorybos* invades the banquet room. Vast quantities of wine are consumed. And Phaedrus escapes into the night. He had been the "father" of the argument of the *Symposium:* the praise of Eros. That praise seems to have been fittingly offered with Alcibiades' encomium of Socrates. But a very different conversation continues the action of the dialogue to daybreak.

Just at the point where Agathon's victory celebration begins to break up, our knowledge of what was said and done hangs on a slender thread. Aristodemus is our only link to what went on when both the character and theme of the banquet radically change their course. And he fell asleep. And so there remain dark edges surrounding the most brilliant portrait Plato ever

This paper was presented at the 1974 Chicago meeting of the Society for Ancient Greek Philosophy and was published in *Arion* NS 2 (1975):238–61; we thank the editors and Boston University for permission to reprint.

Diskin Clay is Professor of Classics at the Johns Hopkins University.

drew of Socrates. When Aristodemus awakens he opens his eyes upon a scene that has been transformed:

> He said that he woke up near daybreak, when the cocks were already crowing, and he saw that the others were asleep or had departed. Agathon, Aristophanes, and Socrates were the only ones still awake, and they were drinking from a large cup which they were passing from left to right. And Socrates was having a discussion with them. Aristodemus said that he could not remember all of what was said for he hadn't been on hand to hear the beginning and was drowsing off. But the main point was that Socrates was forcing them to agree that it is possible for one and the same man to know how to create comedy and tragedy, and that the man who has the skill of a tragic poet is also a comic poet. Compelled to these conclusions and not entirely following the line of argument, they began to nod off. Aristophanes was the first to fall asleep, and then, when it was already daylight, Agathon followed suit. And once he had seen them asleep, Socrates got up, and went away. (223 CD)

And after Socrates had spent his day as usual and returned home at nightfall to get some sleep, the dialogue between Plato and his reader begins. For we are brought to ask what comedy and tragedy have to do with one another; and what the last argument of the *Symposium* has to do with its central argument: the praise of Eros.

I

The answer to the Platonic riddle propounded at the end of the *Symposium* does not lie in the history of Greek literature. In the early spring of 416 there was no Greek or Athenian dramatist who wrote both comedy and tragedy. Only in Hellenistic times do we discover a poet who wrote both tragedies and comedies: sixty of one and thirty of the other.[3] Shakespeare arrived on the scene of the Globe twenty centuries after Socrates argued his paradox. If it is to be found anywhere, the answer to our riddle lies submerged in the dialogue itself.

The *Symposium* is a drama narrated within the frame of a dramatic dialogue. It begins with the dramatic recital which leads to the narrative of what was said and done at Agathon's victory celebration. It confuses the ancient categories invented to describe the Platonic dialogues, or rather it belongs to that category which mixes both narrative and speech, for it is both narrative and dramatic.[4] Within the frame dialogue supported by the syntactical reminders of accusatives and infinitives and the string of "he saids," the heart of Plato's *Symposium* is made up of direct discourse. Some of the most telling indications we have for the staging of the drama of the banquet hall come from the narrative links which Aristodemus carefully provided Apollodorus as he moved from speech to speech. The dramatic action of the *Symposium* requires a cast of seven speakers. There are others present who do not speak in Plato's dialogue, but who did speak in praise of Eros (180 C). By this detail we come to realize that there is a difference between Plato's *Symposium* and Agathon's banquet. There are also a number of drunken intruders who say nothing, but are anything but κωφὰ πρόσωπα.

When Socrates finally appears in the middle of the feast, he discovers Phaedrus reclining on the first of the banqueting benches. Between Phaedrus and Pausanias he could see some other guests, but we never learn who they were or what they said (180 C). Then came Aristophanes, and next to him Eryximachus (185 C). Aristodemus came next, but he is forgotten from the moment Agathon invited him to take his place (175 A). Our momentary expectation that Aristodemus will speak in turn after Eryximachus is disappointed. The effect of this gap is to throw into the sharpest focus the final arrangement which brings Aristophanes and Agathon together. The same technique brings into contact the *logoi* of Phaedrus and Pausanias. At Agathon's banquet they were spoken at an interval. In Plato's *Symposium* they come one after another.[5]

It is *by chance* that Socrates found Agathon alone (175 C). Taking the place next to his host, Socrates becomes ἔσχατος and least honored. It is an accident too that Aristophanes is prevented from speaking after Pausanias by a sudden and severe bout of hiccoughs (185 CD). He should have spoken after Pausanias and *before* Eryximachus. But Aristophanes' hiccough is no more an accident than Socrates' position in the banquet. Aristophanes might have had too much to eat, but Aristodemus can imagine "some other cause" for his hiccough (185 C). Unable to carry on, or indeed to speak coherently, Aristophanes asks Eryximachus to either cure him or to speak in his place. Unwisely, the learned Eryximachus offers to do both. As it turns out, Aristophanes is suffering from an acute attack of hiccoughs and requires all of the therapeutic measures the doctor prescribes. He holds his breath—but must gasp when he comes up for air. He gargles, and when this remedy too proves ineffective, he teases his nose to produce a sneeze.

What all this means is that as Eryximachus is delivering himself of his pompous and profound description of Eros, his unfortunate neighbor is hiccoughing, gasping, gargling, wheezing, snorting, and sneezing. If Aristophanes has any cue for these eruptions it must be Eryximachus' repetition of the word *kosmion* (cf. 189 C). This is rare comedy. But Aristophanes' hiccough must also have a more serious and philosophical explanation. Ancient and late references to it have a simple explanation for the hiccough: Plato is making fun of the comic Aristophanes.[6] Why they do not say. Victor Brochard discovered an explanation only seventy years ago: in inflicting a seizure of hiccoughs on Aristophanes, Plato is taking his revenge for

Aristophanes' comic treatment of Socrates in two versions of the *Clouds*.[7]
Yet if it is revenge Plato wanted, he chose an odd way to take it, for he gave
Aristophanes one of the most important speeches in the *Symposium*—a
speech so important that Diotima refers to it (205 D) and Aristophanes recognizes himself in what Diotima says (212 C).

Φθόνος is not a philosophical emotion and it is not Plato's reason for inflicting a hiccough on Aristophanes. Opinions are many on the
cause of hiccoughs,[8] but why Plato made Aristophanes hiccough begins to
become visible in the larger plan of the dialogue. Karl Reinhardt noticed the
obvious when he saw that Plato could only play with a plan once he had
one.[9] On the most serious plane of the dialogue, what is effected by the accident of Aristophanes' hiccough is that unexpectedly a comic and a tragic
poet are brought together. Plato planned his party with great care. His apparent arrangement is to separate Aristophanes and Agathon by Eryximachus
and Aristodemus. But when the sequence of praise that moves toward
Socrates from left to right is dislocated by Aristophanes' hiccough, the underlying plan of the dialogue is revealed. Comic and tragic poet are brought
together.

There are other disruptions in what might have been an orderly and
unusually sober banquet, and they point to the riddle of the end of the
Symposium. Once Socrates has reported to the company his conversations
with Diotima, Alcibiades breaks into the scene σφόδρα μεθύ-
οντος (212 D). He is so drunk that he has to be led to his host. His head
is festooned with a garland of violets, ivy, and ribbons (a perfect crown for
the author of the *Antheus*) which he proposes to transfer to the head of
Agathon. As he puts it—to the head of the most skillful and fairest (τοῦ
σοφωτάτου καὶ καλλίστου, 212 E). The ribbons of the garland he
holds out before him prevent him from catching sight of Socrates as he
takes a place next to Agathon. When he sees that his neighbor is Socrates,
he springs up and asks him why he is not sitting next to Aristophanes or
someone else who thinks he's a clown (οὐ παρὰ Ἀριστοφάνει
οὐδὲ εἴ τις ἄλλος γελοῖος, ἔστι, 213 C). By implication, his name
for Aristophanes is *geloios*. His name for Agathon was *kallistos*. And Socrates is caught between these poles. If Socrates is *geloios*, he belongs next
to the comic Aristophanes. But Plato carefully arranged for the accident
that places him last and next to Agathon. He has created a tension between
the comic and the tragic, as he understood comic and tragic, and Socrates
is caught between the levels suggested by the words *geloios* and *kallistos*.
By a dramatic detail that will become philosophical, Plato has reminded
us that Socrates seems to belong in the company of the clownish characters
he resembles. But Socrates also belongs next to the fair, or contrives to
get next to them.[10] This was the philosophical motivation of Socrates' ele-

gance that memorable evening. The fact that he was bathed and shod reminds us that he seldom washed and usually went barefoot.[11]

In Plato ἄτοπος and γελοῖος are *the* Socratic epithets.[12] The word, laughable, ridiculous, is first used in the *Symposium* to describe the awkward situation of Aristodemus who had arrived at Agathon's party at Socrates' invitation, but without Socrates.[13] It then describes the kind of talk Eryximachus fears Aristophanes will produce (189 B) and is accompanied by the laughter of the comic poet and Aristophanes' protests that Eryximachus will make fun of what he has said.[14] With the eruption of Alcibiades on the scene, laughter returns to the dialogue. *Geloios* describes both Aristophanes and Socrates. Alcibiades repeats the word when he launches into his Dionysian praise of Socrates by means of "likenesses": "Possibly this character will think that I am trying to make sport of him, but my purpose will be truth, not comedy" (215 A). The grotesque similes of Socrates as Marsyas, a silene, and satyr, also convey an image of what his *logoi* are like. These are utterly ridiculous (παγγέλοιοι): "He is forever talking of pack asses, and tinkers, and cobblers, and tanners" (221 E).

Paradoxically, Alcibiades asks Agathon to surrender some strands from the victory garland he has just placed on his wise and fair head and give them over to their companion—to "this amazing head" (213 D). Agathon won his victory only yesterday, but Socrates triumphs in words over all men every day (213 E). Alcibiades has done what Plato set out to do.[15] Under the influence of Dionysos he has placed a crown on the head of the κάλλιστος and σοφώτατος—σοφώτατος not in the sense of poetic skill, but in another sense of this word which describes the wisest and most eloquent of all men.[16]

Inevitably, we are brought back to the beginning of the banquet and the exchange of compliments between a poet and philosopher. Agathon embellishes his invitation to Socrates to join him on his couch. He wants to enjoy the piece of wisdom which came to Socrates as he stood in the neighboring doorway. Agathon's choice of the word *sophon* brings Socrates to contrast his *sophia* with that of Agathon: "Mine is a thing of little significance, dubious and disputable, like a dream. But yours is brilliant and holds great promise" (175 E).

When Alcibiades had finished his speech in praise of Socrates, and Plato had paid a great part of his tribute to a Socratic Eros and erotic Socrates, Agathon gets up to put himself "below" Socrates. For just a moment it seems that Socrates will praise Agathon. But what Socrates would have said in praise of Agathon is left unspoken as Agathon gets up to cope with a new band of intruders. For a moment, the needle veers from the center of all that has been said and done in the dialogue in order to return to it. At the end of the dialogue Socrates remains on center stage, with a comic and a tragic poet. As Aristophanes and then Agathon fall asleep, we are subtly brought back to the contest proposed by Agathon at the very beginning of the dialogue. And we realize that Agathon's theatrical language was not a fugitive metaphor: "A little later we will settle our claims to *sophia* with Dionysos as our arbitrator" (175 E). As Agathon falls asleep at daybreak we have the final judgment of the same god who had inspired Alcibiades to crown Socrates. No one had ever seen Socrates drunk (220 A).

II

Socrates who was "last" in Agathon's banquet is at the center of Plato's *Symposium*. Around him center the major themes of the dialogue. He is at the center of the tensions and antitheses of the seven speeches, and he mediates the final paradox at the end of the dialogue. To state this much is to open the door to the distant unity underlying the diversity and multiplicity of what was said and done at Agathon's gathering, and to watch the project of a proper praise of Eros recede into the distance. But from even a resumé which is no more than a cartoon of the dialogue, it can be seen that the Socratic paradox of a tragic and comic poet continues and deepens the major themes of the dialogue.

Growing out of the dialectic of what is said and done in the *Symposium*, there is a tension between apparent antitheses: high and low, divine and human, noble and base, wisdom and ignorance, fair and ugly. These seemingly contrary themes are part and parcel of the paradox that arises so unexpectedly at the end of the dialogue. In the tacit exchange between the *logoi* of the *Symposium*, the terms which underlie the diverse conceptions of *Eros* and *eros* develop and take on a range greater than that of any single contribution to the banquet. As *Eros* and *eros* grow in significance and complexity, so do the conceptions of *poiesis* and *sophia*. To follow these themes is to arrive at the end of the dialogue.

The dialogue begins with Apollodorus setting Socrates above all men and a first statement of the profound effect and profit of hearing what Socrates has to say (173 CD; cf. 172 A–173 B; 215 D). But paradoxically this Socrates is not fair; he has *become* fair to join the company at Agathon's (174 A). His follower Aristodemus speaks Homerically of the lesser sort of men going to feast with their betters: with the noble and wise (174 BC). Then something funny happens to both Socrates and Aristodemus: Socrates stops dead in his tracks, lost in thought, and Aristodemus appears at Agathon's uninvited (174 E). In these seemingly insignificant details begins the philosophical and poetic project of the *Symposium:* the approach to the fair, the wise, and superior. In Aristodemus we have the first mention of an *erastes*. And he is Socrates' lover (173 B).

191

It is Phaedrus, with the prompting of Eryximachus, who begins the celebration of Eros—a god no man had *dared* to praise before that evening (177 C; cf. 214 D; 222 C), even though lesser things had been taken seriously. For Phaedrus, to praise Eros is to say that he is the most ancient of the gods—and as a consequence the most honored and responsible for the greatest goods to men. Here already we have the fundamentals of a divine hymn: to say adequately what a god is, and to enumerate his gifts to men (cf. 195 A; 201 D). And here appears the distinction between the fair and the base or shameful which carries throughout the dialogue. So too the ambiguity of the relation between the lover and beloved and the power of Eros to make a man *entheos* (178 D; cf. 197 B). The relation between Achilles and his lover Patroclus prepares for the more complex relation between Socrates and Alcibiades, who was, like Achilles, younger and fairer than the man who seemed his lover. In the one case the *eromenos* defended his *erastes* (180 AB); in the other the *erastes* who becomes the *eromenos* defends the *eromenos* become *erastes* (220 D–221 C).

For Pausanias, Eros is not a single god; there are two Erotes. One centers on the soul, the other on the body. The heavenly love has an object that is steady; the common or "pandemic," an object that is not abiding. Their objects define their lovers: the low, the low and the better, the high. A lover of decent character is made better by his love (185 AB). Pausanias' speech is full of antithetical notions. In its initial distinction, a separation appears. In reserving his praise for the "Ouranian" Eros, *arete, sophia,* and *philosophia,* Pausanias has created a gap. There is nothing but a name to connect the high and the low.

Eryximachus' speech, in extending the range of Eros to *eros* and *epithymia* (186 B), and the association of gods and men (188 A), has as its project the reconciliation of the separate and opposing Erotes of Pausanias. He agrees with Pausanias that Eros is double, but his art of medicine allows him to observe that Eros is a wonderful god whose influence extends over everything (186 C; cf. 202 E; 222 A)—both things human and divine. But in this antithesis, which he thinks comprehensive, Eryximachus forgets that there are such things as demons (cf. 202 DE). The most important and problematic thing Eryximachus has to say is that like does not like like, but rather that love and desire are for an object that is dissimilar (*anomoion*). This promise of reconciliation is not fulfilled. Eryximachus' quotation from Heraclitus to the effect that "the one while disagreeing with itself yet agrees with itself, like the 'harmony' of a lyre or bow" brings into view the possible reconciliation or "healing" of the opposites involved in the speech of Aristophanes and the demonology of Diotima. All that Eryximachus' art can do is to encourage the love of the fair and deny the love or lust for what is base and ugly. As it extends to poetry, the encouragement of the fair Eros

PLATO

makes men better. And although both Erotes need to be watched after (187 E), only the base needs restraint (187 E). The doctor is true to his precept when he threatens to stand guard over what Aristophanes might say (189 A). We already know that Aristophanes' entire life as a comic poet centers on Aphrodite (the "pandemic") and Dionysos (177 E).

Comic and tragic poet then speak. In what he says Aristophanes names many things both low and laughable. But to say what is laughable (*geloia*) is the province and reward of Aristophanes' Muse (189 B). Eryximachus is worried that his neighbor will try to provoke laughter and he is prepared to "stand guard" over what he said (189 AB). He proposes to restrain Aristophanes' αἰσχρὸς ἔρως. True to his Muse, Aristophanes goes on to mention eggs, sorb-apples, cobblers, tumblers, limping, purses, a last, cicadas, sandal fish,[17] navels, and genitals. But remarkably, the company does not laugh at the end of Aristophanes' speech. In this speech the essential project of the *Symposium* first comes clearly into sight. A middle term appears in the race of "men-women" (*androgynon*, 189 C); ancient amputations are *healed* (189 D); and love (*eros*) is called by its right name: the desire for and pursuit of the whole (192 E).

The tragic poet's praise of Eros is on all points contrary to what Diotima says of him. Even when their words are the same, what they mean by them is not. The god Agathon praises is young—the youngest of all the gods. He is blessed, tender, and languid. He dwells in flowers, and is attracted by what he resembles (195 A). His "aretalogy" comprehends *dikaiosyne, sophrosyne, andreia,* and *sophia*. He is a poet and makes others poets (196 E). Here "poetry" becomes a comprehensive term for most of human action—like eros itself (cf. 205 B–D). Agathon ends his encomium by saying that he has offered it to Eros as a mixture of play (*paidia*) and some seriousness (*spoude*). Play and seriousness dominate the speeches of the comic and tragic poets just as they characterize the *logoi* of Socrates (216 E). It is tempting to say that Aristophanes was playfully serious. But of Agathon all that can be said is that he spoke playfully, beautifully, with solemnity, but falsely (198 B, D; 199 A).

Like Eryximachus, Agathon finishes with an illusion of completeness (188 E; 198 B). This is shattered by what follows. The project of the *Symposium* reveals itself in Diotima's instruction of Socrates and in Alcibiades' words and deeds. In departing from the "law" of Agathon's banquet, Alcibiades reveals the intention of the *Symposium*. He crowns Socrates and praises not Eros but Socrates. The Socrates of Alcibiades' Dionysian speech resembles the Eros of Diotima's.[18] As Diotima describes him, Eros is neither a god nor a mortal, but a great *daimon* who binds the realms and mediates the oppositions that none of the earlier speeches had succeeded in bringing together (202 E). He is the demonic man who is *sophos* in how

193

gods and men communicate. By contrast, any other skill, poetic or manual, is that of a mechanic (*banausos,* 203 A). Here the contrast between the *sophia* of Agathon and Socrates becomes more clearly defined and the gap between the two meanings of the word wider. In a human and poetic sense, Eros is *sophos,* but on a more than human level, he is *philosophos* (204 AB).

Eros' nature is not as Agathon had described it. He is the son of Poros and Penia. The son of Poverty, he is always poor and lacking in what he is in need of. And far from being fair (*kalos*), as most people (including Agathon) think, he is tough, goes barefoot, has no fixed abode, keeps low to the ground, and sleeps without bedding in doorways and on the road; or under the open sky (203 D). The son of his father, he is constantly scheming after the fair and noble. He is brave, impetuous, a fierce and clever hunter. He is ardent for wisdom and can find his way wherever he is. Throughout his entire life he philosophizes, is an awesome wizard, and spell-binder, and sophist. He is also a poet. He can produce in the souls of those he loves and those who become his lovers, wisdom (*phronesis*) and all of the rest of virtue (209 A, D). And his best piece of poetry is not his three sons, but that piece of poetry in which his memory has become immortal (208 B). This he created in the soul of Plato.

III

Alcibiades' praise of Socrates provokes laughter for a second time in the banquet room (222 B). It also provokes Socrates' characterization of Alcibiades' Dionysian speech as "a satyr and silene drama" (222 C). Socrates' language preserves the conception of Agathon's banquet as a drama (cf. 175 E; 194 B) and points to the paradox with which it ends. But more than this, it also suggests that the speeches in praise of love which preceded Alcibiades' praise of Socrates were "tragic." They were followed by the final satyr play. And so Wilamowitz was mistaken, but not wildly wrong, when he called the *Symposium* a comedy and the *Phaedo* a tragedy.[19] The only proper description of the *Symposium* is that it is a tragi-comedy. Or a new form of philosophical drama which, in the object of its imitation, comprehends and transcends both tragedy and comedy.

What is "tragic" for us was not tragic to Plato. For Plato, tragedy centered on the high and serious, comedy on the low and laughable. Tragedy produced in the theater of Dionysos fear, grief, pity; and comedy produced laughter through arousing the ignorant emotion of *phthonos.* Both are defined by the high or what is considered high in human experience, and the low or what is considered low. The two genres take on their character from the objects of their imitation. Both imitate men in action (πράττοντας, *Rep.* 603 C), but the character of the action of tragedy and comedy differs radically. Tragedy is serious, solemn, awe-inspiring.[20] Comedy is low and laughable. Its essential, *to geloion,* and the emotion that underlies the laughter of the audience, *phthonos,* are grouped under the banner of base ignorance.[21] Within the *Symposium,* laughter and the ridiculous center on Aristophanes and Socrates. And Agathon, who spoke with a mixture of playfulness and seriousness, yet solemnly (199 A), provoked in Socrates confusion (*ekplexis*) and fear (198 B).

Outside of the *Symposium,* there are abundant passages which illustrate Plato's conception of tragedy and comedy and have a bearing on the Socratic paradox of a tragic and comic poet. Three stand out. The first comes from the book of the *Laws* (VII) which prolongs Socrates' discussion of the place of poetry in his *politeia* (*Republic* II, III, X). The second comes from the *Cratylus.* And the third comes from the *Philebus* where the metaphor of the tragedy and comedy of life makes its appearance in Socrates' discussion of the mixed class of pleasures and pains that affect the soul. Indeed, the entire discussion of how pleasure can be mixed with pain involves an analysis of the emotions proper to tragedy and comedy.

According to Socrates' analysis, the comic (τὸ γελοῖον) arises in the incongruity between the weak who fancy themselves powerful and their inability to get even if they are injured or abused (*Philebus* 49 B).[22] The peculiar pleasure we feel at the misfortunes of "friends" who fancy themselves superior involves a mixture of pleasure and pain. Pain because Protarchus has agreed that *phthonos* is a kind of pleasure and pain that has no justification (49 D). So Socrates concludes: "and so surely what our argument shows is a mixture of pleasure and pain, not only in dirges and tragedies, but in the entire tragedy and comedy of life." This is the life of the *polis* in which pleasure and pain are kings (*Rep.* 607 A).

Tragodia, solemn, serious, awesome, is also goatish. An etymological understanding of tragedy as goatish begins with Plato and continues into the Middle Ages.[23] But the connection between tragedy and *tragos* is extremely rare in Greek for the simple reason that the canon of the separation of genres and levels of style could not easily admit an understanding of tragedy which connected and confused the high and the low. Only Socrates is capable of making the obvious and repugnant connection between the character of tragedy and goats. At the end of his disquisition on divine names in the *Cratylus,* Hermogenes and Hermes bring him naturally to Pan. Pan gets his name because language (*logos*) "signifies all, revolves, and is always in motion." It has a double nature in being true and false:

> Now isn't the true part of Pan smooth and divine, and does it not dwell among the gods above; but down below, the false half dwells among the

common run of mankind and is rough (τραχύς) and goatlike—or tragic (τραγοειδής)? For there dwell the greatest abundance of myths and lies concerning the "tragic" life. (408 C)

Here the perspective on things human shifts radically. What seems serious or "tragic" on this lower level here on earth becomes, when seen from another vantage, false, rough, and goatish.

Last, there is another kind of tragedy: the truest kind of tragedy which is not the tragedy of the Attic stage, but *poiesis* of quite a different sort. Only late in his literary career does Plato, who began as a tragic poet and whose dialogues are filled with the language of the stage,[24] invent the metaphor which extends the serious imitations of the festivals of Dionysos to the greater stage of the life of the *polis*. In the *Laws*, the unnamed Athenian had spoken of men as the puppets of the gods (I 644 DE). At a much later stage in the conversation, he concedes to Megillos that mankind is not something altogether insignificant (*phaulon*), but worthy of some serious consideration (*spoudes*, VII 804 B). But when he confronts an itinerant company of tragedians who have arrived at the walls of his city with all their gear in tow, he has this to say:

> Best of strangers, we ourselves are creators of tragedy, to the best of our ability—a tragedy which is the fairest and best. For all of our city has been founded as an imitation of the fairest and best life, and this we call what is in reality the truest tragedy. (VII 817 AB)

In such a *polis* there existed neither tragedy nor comedy as it was known in Greece (cf. *Laws* VII 811 C–E), but an imitation and praise of what was best and fairest in life.

IV

The answer to the Socratic paradox propounded at the end of the *Symposium* is to be found in the *Symposium*; and also in Plato. One and the same man can be both a tragic and a comic poet. The tragic and comic poet of the *Symposium* is Plato and the object of his imitation, Socrates. This poet of both tragedy and comedy began his literary career as a poet of dithyrambs and a single tragic tetralogy, but when he encountered in Socrates the only object worthy of serious imitation, he became a tragic and comic poet.[25] In his older friend Socrates, Plato discovered a force that drove him to destroy the tragedy he was about to stage in the theater of Dionysos. But this force was protreptic, not apotropaic.[26] Like Pico della Mirandola and Botticelli, and Ficino himself, Plato destroyed his early work. Unlike them he was driven to develop a new form of expression—the Socratic dialogue, and to combine in a new form of imitation the arts and objects of the tragic and comic poet. To become this, the tragic poet had to become a comic poet.

The poetics of the *Symposium* are fundamentally the poetics of the *Republic* and *Laws*. In the *Republic* and *Laws* a new form of poetry is envisaged, as is a new function for truly political poetry. This poetry involved production (*poiesis*) as well as *praxis*. Its aim is to implant into the soul the image and example of human character which are good and noble (*Rep.* 401 B). Although Plato never says as much in any of his dialogues, the object of the imitation of this new poetry is Socrates. Because of this silence, the *Republic* is as indirect and as puzzling as the *Symposium*.

In his discussion of *mimesis* in the *Republic* (III 392 C ff.), Socrates is caught up in one of Plato's most ironic utterances; for Socrates speaks in a context in which he does not recognize the full significance of what he says. Socrates' problem is that of imitation and its object. And Adeimantus has some difficulties in understanding the point he is making. The point is this: style (*lexis*) can be divided into dramatic, narrative, and a combination of the two. This last is the style of the *Symposium* which both imitates what was said and narrates what was done (cf. *Rep.* 392 A ff.). Socrates' ethical and political problem centers mainly on *imitation*. In order to imitate Chryses, Homer had to shift from a style in which he spoke as himself to a style in which he spoke not as a narrator but as Chryses (393 BC). And so, he comes to resemble the object of his imitation. If the poet never *concealed himself* in the dramatic speeches of his characters, his style would be simply narrative (*Rep.* 393 CD). But this *concealment,* which is at the heart of Platonic style, has its dangers. To use the language of another tragic and comic poet, the imitator's nature "is subdued to what it works in, like the Dyers hand."

For Socrates, there is only one solution to the problem of dramatic poetry: it is that of a moderate man imitating, and by his imitation becoming, a good man acting surely and intelligently (396 C). This precisely is the style of imitation Plato adopted from Homer—the greatest of the tragic poets.[27] He spoke as Socrates; and he added the narrative links between the speeches not as Plato, but as still another *persona*.

The difficulties of this new enterprise Plato only hints at (*Rep.* 604 E). But Alcibiades' praise of Socrates brings before us the argument required by the poetics of the *Republic:* a character "intelligent, and easy, and always resembling himself." In part, this is the complex character of Socrates as he seemed to many—including the comic poets (*Sym.* 221 B; *Clouds* 362). But like Eros and Pan, Socrates is caught between two worlds. He was not what he seemed. The apparent duplicity of his simple character finds its best expression in one of Alcibiades' *ikons* of Socrates:

His words too are very much like those figures of Silenus which open up and come apart. If a person were willing to listen to Socrates' conversation, he would have a perfectly ridiculous impression at first. On the outside, what he says seems to wrap itself up in queer words and phrases— just like the hide of an outrageous satyr. He is forever talking of pack asses, and tinkers, and cobblers, and tanners, and he seems to be always saying the same things, using the same illustrations. As a result a person who is foolish and had never heard him speak before would simply laugh. But once Socrates' words are opened up, one can get inside them and have a look. He will discover first that Socrates' talk is the only kind of talk which makes sense; then that his discourse is most godlike and contains within itself the greatest number of images of virtue; and that it has the greatest significance. He will discover still more: that it has as its object all that matters for the man who means to become brave and virtuous. (221 D–222 A)

But what of the comic poet? It is no accident that the laughter of the *Symposium* centers on Socrates.[28] In Socrates, Plato had discovered an object of imitation that was both comic and tragic. It is a mistake to see in Socrates a tragic and serious figure and in Aristophanes, or Alcibiades, or the sophists, comic and low characters.[29] Socrates himself was both comic and tragic. It is not hard to understand what made Socrates' seem comic. Alcibiades *ikons* of Socrates and his peculiar *logoi* make the point clearly enough. Socrates resembles a satyr, a silene, a Marsyas—precisely those perverse creatures the Athenian stranger wanted expelled from his city (*Laws* 815 C).[30] And undeniably there was something about Socrates that destined him for the comic stage. We know this comic figure from the second production of Aristophanes' *Clouds.* He was often seen on stage in the 20s of the fifth century—among other things barefoot and a bane to shoemakers.[31] K. J. Dover asked pertinently if Socrates needed a special portrait mask to appear in the *Clouds,* and his conclusions were: "The mask maker who wanted to produce a good caricature of Socrates for *Clouds* was faced with a difficulty of an unusual kind, and I do not know how, or whether, he surmounted it: the result of his attempt to portray a real person would resemble what he had often done before in portraying fictitious characters."[32] That is, Socrates resembled one of the conventional comic types.

In his comic and tragic imitation of Socrates, Plato comprehended the realms of appearance and reality: what seemed low and laughable and what was serious and high. From the point of view of the audience in the theater of Dionysos, Socrates was a comic character. From the point of view of the Ionians who at Potidaea came out with their bedding to see the strange sight of Socrates seized with some problem and immobile from dawn to dusk, Socrates was a curiosity. They wanted to discover if he would keep standing the entire night. He did—until daybreak. Then he went away, after making a prayer to the sun (220 CD). What he was thinking about we do not learn. But it was something that made human affairs seem like so much nonsense (cf. 211 E). From this point of view all of the seemingly serious affairs of this life seem "tragic" or comic.

V

Thanks to Aristodemus' drowsiness and Plato's reticence, we shall never learn how Socrates compelled Agathon and Aristophanes to agree to his paradox that a single poet could compose both tragedies and comedies. All we know is that the paradox was so bizarre that tragic and comic poet were forced to agree to it and even under compulsion did not quite follow its argument. But the scene is unforgettable. At the end of the celebration of Agathon's tragic victory, and at the conclusion of Plato's celebration of Socrates, there remain on center stage a tragic poet, a comic poet, and Socrates. Perhaps we shall never know just how Socrates managed his argument, but the character of his paradox is clear in its outlines.

Bernard Knox has stated the nature of the paradox simply and decisively: "For the fifth-century Athenian, tragedy was tragedy, and comedy comedy, and never the twain should meet."[33] Comedy was what Aristophanes wrote, tragedy what Agathon wrote. In the fifth century, no poet did both. Much earlier in the century a philosopher depended on the clear separation of these genres to give point to the explanation of how the addition or shifting of elements in a compound can radically change its appearance: "for *tragoidia* and *komoidia* are made up of the same letters."[34] From the point of view of the early atomists, there was a unity underlying apparent contraries. Like Eryximachus before the paradox of Heraclitus (185 AB), Aristophanes and Agathon cannot understand how there can be a harmony and common *logos* between the high and the low. The paradox is a violent one. Socrates must force out of a tragic poet who is *kalos* and a comic poet who is *geloios* assent to his proposition that a single poet, by virtue of his skill (τέχνη) and understanding (ἐπιστήμη), can imitate both the high and the low. That Agathon, if he truly had understanding and art, could produce a play centering on a low character named Trygaios and mounted on a dung beetle; and that Aristophanes could produce an *Antheus*.[35]

The words Aristodemus remembered, τέχνη and ἐπίστασθαι ποιεῖν, point in the direction of other Socratic conversations: especially three conversations between Socrates and Diotima, Ion of Ephesus, and Adeimantus.[36] With Adeimantus, Socrates argues that a single individual can do only one thing well (*Rep.* III 394 E; cf. II 374 A; X 598 D). In weighing the question whether they should allow tragedy and comedy into their city and its education, Socrates outlines two fundamental objections (III 394 D–396 E): one involves the fragmentation of human nature which allows an individual to do only one thing well; the other the effect of imitation on the imitator—the argument of the dyer's hand. Because of our fragmentation, one and the same man cannot create both comedy and tragedy; not even the actors of tragedy and comedy are the same (395 A). And the danger of the city's guardians coming to resemble (ἀφομοιοῦσθαι) what they imitate is too great to permit tragedy and comedy into the newly founded *polis* (395 B–396 E). Yet Plato says nothing of the philosopher king.

In Socrates' encounter with the triumphant Ion, it becomes clear that the rhapsode's character is a shard of the broken whole of our nature. He understands Homer (ἐπίσταται) because he knows him by heart. But his more ambitious claim is that he also understands and can explain Homer's meaning.[37] Yet he has no interest in other poets and begins to doze off when conversation turns to them (532 C). Because of this limitation, Socrates argues that Ion has neither the art nor understanding to speak about Homer (532 C; cf. 536 C; 541 D); ποιητικὴ γάρ πού ἐστιν τὸ ὅλον.

What this understanding of the whole art of poetry is, is suggested in another Socratic conversation: that he had with Diotima. Developing the concept of *eros* which had already appeared in Eryximachus' speech (186 D), Diotima asserts that our love or will for (*boulesis*) happiness is something common to all men (205 A). In this case Greek is deceptive, for *eros* describes a whole (ὅλον), but men restrict the word to one form of love. They do the same with the term *poiesis*. *Poiesis* is properly the name for a whole which is production or creation. *Eros* and *poiesis* are connected in the fact that our desire to have and continue to enjoy the good makes us poets: of our children and "immortal memory" (208 DE). Poets are makers in the fact that they are the "begetters" of *phronesis* and the other virtues (209 A).

Finally one is brought to ask if the whole glimpsed at the end of the *Symposium,* and made visible throughout the dialogue, is not the object of Plato's poetry, and if its object in Socrates does not explain the Socratic paradox. For it is Socrates, or Eros, or whatever name it is right to call this *daimon,* who fills the gap between the high and the low, gods and men, and makes a whole of tragedy and comedy, binding this whole to himself: συμπληροῖ ὥστε τὸ πᾶν αὐτὸ αὐτῶι ξυνδεδέσθαι (202E).

NOTES

[1] "J'ay esté conseillé par mes amis d'omettre le reste que Platon a adiousté seulement pour plaisir, servant au temps et à la licencieuse vie de son pays," 180.

[2] This is Krüger's *Einsicht und Leidenschaft* (Frankfurt am Maine, 1936), pp. 292–308.

[3] Timon of Phlius, Diogenes Laertius IX 109 (= Snell, *Tragicorum Graecorum Fragmenta* I [1971] no. 112).

[4] Diogenes Laertius III 49, which originates in *Rep.* III 394 C ff.

[5] The speeches are linked by Pausanias' reference to Phaedrus' encomium, 180 C.

[6] ἐκωμῳδῆσε: Olympiodorus, *Vita Platonis* 3; Athenaeus, 187 C; Aristeides *Or.* 46, II p. 287 (Dindorf).

For what little can be said about these explanations, see Bury, *The Symposium of Plato* (Cambridge, 1932), p. xxii.

[7] "Sur le Banquet de Platon," in *Études de philosophie ancienne et de philosophie moderne* (Paris, 1926), 74:89–90.

[8] For the ancient lore, see the *Scholia Platonica* ad loc., and Le Roi, *Le Sympose de Platon* (Paris, 1558), pp. 26–27. Plochmann, "Hiccoughs and Hangovers in the Symposium," *Bucknell Review* vol. 9, no. 3 (1963):10, attempts to connect Aristophanes' hiccough with a "disharmony of the diaphragm" which divides the two lower parts of the soul in *Tim.* 70 A. But we do not know that Plato connected hiccoughs with the diaphragm.

[9] "Man spielt mit einem Plan, nur wenn man ihn erst hat," *Vermächtnis der Antike* (Göttingen, 1960):245.

[10] Cf. 174 A; 203 D; 213 C; and Diogenes Laertius II 28.

[11] Something easily turned to comedy: cf. *Birds* 1354; *Clouds* 835. But the ridicule of the comic poets can also be turned to praise: cf. Maximus of Tyre, *Philosophoumena* XVIII (Hobein) 221.12; Diogenes Laertius II 27.

[12] In the *Symposium* alone: 175 A; 221 C for Socrates' ἀτοπία; 199 D (cf. 214 E); 215 E; 221 E; 222 B for the epithet *geloios*.

[13] The same word describes the awkward situation of Philippos in Xenophon's *Symposium*, I.12.

[14] 193 BE. Aristophanes, Alcibiades, and especially Socrates are at the center of the comic or what can be made comic in the *Symposium*. See note 28.

[15] For appreciations of the significance of this gesture, see Helen Bacon, "Socrates Crowned," *The Virginia Quarterly Review* 35 (1959):415–30, and John Anton in *CJ* 58 (1962/1963):51.

[16] 213 DE. The ambiguity of the terms σοφός and σοφία develops in a dialectic between Agathon and Socrates: 174 C; 175 DE; 194 A; 196 DE; 197 D; 203 A; 204 AB.

[17] Plato quotes from Aristophanes not once (as Vicaire claims in his *Platon critique littéraire* [Paris 1960], p. 187), but twice. For the germ of Aristophanes' speech, see *Lysistrata* 115.

[18] The points of resemblance have long been recognized: by Maximus of Tyre, *Philosophoumena* XVIII 84 B (Hobein); and Ficino, *Commentaire sur le Banquet de Platon*, ed. Marcel (Paris, 1956), p. 242.

[19] *Platon* I (Berlin, 1920), p. 356.

[20] *Gorgias* 502 B; *Laws* 838 C; *Meno* 76 E (and Bluck in *Mnemosyne*, 4 ser. 14 [1961]:289–95); *Rep.* 413 B; The hegemony of Homer over tragedy also lends it a certain grandeur; *Rep.* 595 B; cf. *Theaet.* 152 E; *Rep.* 599 D; 605 C. Yet ultimately, it is not a serious form of imitation; *Rep.* 603 B, and the judgment of Solon in Plutarch, *Vita Sol.* 29.3.

[21] *Philebus* 48 B; 50 BC; *Rep.* 606 C; *Laws* 816E; 935 DE; 936C. The connection between *phthonos* and *poneria* is also drawn by Aristotle in *EN* 1107a9; cf. *Rhetoric* 1386b16–1388a30.

[22] The question provoked by this distinction is: What of those who have the strength and power to avenge themselves? Is this the beginning of a discussion of tragedy?

[23] Dante, *Epistle* X.10. Earlier, the connections between *tragos* and *tragoidia* are more aetiological than etymological: they can be studied as a whole in Brink's commentary to Horace, *Ars Poetica* 220, *Horace on Poetry* II (Cambridge, 1971), pp. 277–78.

[24] A repertory of this language has been put together by Dorothy Tarrant, "Plato as Dramatist," *JHS* 75 (1955):82–89.

[25] Diogenes Laertius III 56 and Snell *Tragicorum Graecorum Fragmenta*, I (1971), no. 46.

[26] So Proclus in his commentary to the *Republic*, I.204.4 (Kroll).

[27] For Homer as a tragic poet, see note 20. Also Vicaire, *Platon critique*, pp. 243–49.

[28] 202 E; 212 E; 214 E; 221 E (cf. 198 C); 222 B.

[29] This is the form in which Helen Bacon, "Socrates Crowned," pp. 428–30, and Kuhn, "The True Tragedy, I" *HSCP* (1941):32, attempt to resolve the tensions of the Socratic paradox of a tragic and comic poet by making of Socrates only one half of the object of his imitation.

[30] Other witnesses to Socrates' appearance: Xenophon, *Symposium* II 19; V 5; 7; *Theaet.* 143 E–144 B; *Clouds* 361–63.

[31] As he is styled by Ameipsias in the *Cloak* (DL II 28). The fragmentary details of Σωκράτης κωμωιδοποιούμενος come mainly from Diogenes Laertius II 18–19; 27–28.

[32] "Portrait Masks in Aristophanes," in KOMOIDOTRAGEMATA: *Studia Viri Aristophanei W. J. W. Koster in honorem*, ed. Boerma (Amsterdam, 1967):28.

[33] "Euripidean Comedy," in *The Rarer Action: Essays in Honor of Francis Fergusson* (New Brunswick, 1970), p. 69.

[34] Aristotle, *De Gen. et Corr.* A 1.315b6 (DK 67 A 9).

[35] The potential sublimity of Trygaios is seen by Leo Strauss: "No better emblem of the Aristophanean comedy could be imagined than a flight to heaven of the thinly disguised poet on the back of a dung beetle," *Socrates and Aristophanes* (New York, 1966), p. 139.

[36] The possible relevance of the *Ion* for an understanding of the paradox of the *Symposium* is well stated by Friedländer, *Plato* II, trans. Meyerhoff (New York, 1964), p. 133; that of the *Republic*, by Adams in his comments on *Rep.* III 395 A.

[37] 530 B. ἐπίστασθαι is ambiguous in Greek. It can mean to know by heart and so to be able to recite: *Gorg.* 484 B; *Prot.* 339 B; *Rep.* 393 E. It can also mean to understand: cf. Xenophon, *Symposium* III 6 for the "understanding" of the rhapsodes.

An earlier version of this paper is known to Richard Hamilton and Bernd Seidensticker, and I owe them thanks that it is not known to others.

L. A. KOSMAN

Charmides' First Definition: Sophrosyne as Quietness

I

The *Charmides*, like other early Platonic dialogues, conducts the reader gently and almost imperceptibly into the arena of dialectic. One moment we are witness to the graceful and elegant love play of a middle-aged man and a young beauty of his day; their conversation is philosophically fraught, but courtly and deferent. The next moment we are in the midst of a search for the definition of a frustratingly complex and elusive virtue, a search in which reputations are at stake, technique is heard everywhere, and sophistic banners fly.

Socrates' request of Charmides for an account of sophrosyne, like the discussion with Cephalus at the beginning of the *Republic*, straddles both moments of the dialogue, and Charmides is uncertain how to deal with it. How could he have known that love-talk would lead so easily into philosophy? Modest and reticent, he is at first reluctant to answer. But then he says (159B) that sophrosyne seems to him "doing everything in an orderly and quiet way—κοσμίως καὶ ἡσυχῇ—and that what Socrates asks for is, in a word, "a certain quietness—ἡσυχιότης τις." The argument is under way.

Socrates' response (159C–160D) is swift and decisive; it consists of showing (1) that sophrosyne is καλόν, an admirable thing, (2) that in a narrow but exhaustive range of activities, it is action that is quick and sharp—ταχὺς καὶ ὀξύς—that is called for and is admirable, not action that is quiet, and (3) that sophrosyne is consequently *not* a certain quietness nor the σώφρων life a quiet one.

II

How good is Socrates' argument? Here is one answer: "It is characteristic of the stage of logical advance which Plato had reached when he wrote

This paper was presented at the 1973 Atlanta meeting of the Society for Ancient Greek Philosophy; it has been revised for publication in this volume.

L. A. Kosman is Professor of Philosophy at Haverford College.

this small work, that his Socrates commits a paralogism, inferring from the beauty of both temperance and quickness that quickness is temperate."[1]

Not every Socratic fallacy, however, is a Socratic paralogism. Socrates may commit sophisms for other than sophistic reasons, interested, for example, in carrying a particular interlocutor through a piece of fallacious reasoning for the sake of his enlightenment, or that of someone else in the company. More importantly, no Socratic fallacy is *eo ipso* a Platonic fallacy, just because it is, as we read, "his Socrates," that is, just because our Socrates is a fictional character in a Platonic dialogue, whose words are created by, but are not the words of, Plato. Plato was a philosophical poet, which means that the arguments we encounter in his works are mimetic; they are, so to speak, imitation arguments: not Plato's, but Socrates', Theatetus', Critias', and so on. The errors of these *disputationis personae* are not the errors of Plato. They may of course *result* from errors of Plato, but then again they need not; they may serve important philosophical purposes of which Plato is aware. Just such a purpose, I shall suggest, is at work in the more outrageous and blatant fallacy by which the dialogue later moves from discussion of a person's knowledge of himself to knowledge that is of itself.

What of Socrates' argument here? Suppose we understand the argument, particularly in its summary form at 160C7–D3, to take the following form: all sophrosyne is admirable, some quietness is not admirable, and therefore some quietness is not sophrosyne. It therefore follows that sophrosyne is badly defined as a kind of quietness. The first part of this argument is a staunch and unassailable Baroco syllogism, and its major premise is clearly a central element in Socrates' argument (mentioned no fewer than five times, at 159C1, D8, D11, 160B8, D11). But can we find the minor premise in the somewhat more baroque version that Socrates gives, and does the conclusion of the syllogism in fact justify the conclusion of the larger argument that sophrosyne is not a kind of quietness?

The answer to the first question involves first an observation concerning the precise meaning of the word that I have been translating as "quietness." For it might seem patently illicit on Socrates' part to prove anything concerning *quietness* by arguments about *quickness* and *sharpness*. But the kind of quietness that is central to Greek ἥσυχος / ἡσυχιότης is of that which is calm, gentle, tranquil, and still, and it is this calm quietness that is contrasted (as part of a general, topical, and important dialectical relation between sophrosyne and courage; e.g., *Statesman* 307) to sharp, swift, and vigorous action. Given this fact, we can see Socrates' argument as showing that in those cases when it is swift and vigorous action that is admirable and called for, calm and tranquil behavior is, just in that respect, not what is admirable. Whether in fact this can be sustained is a question to which I shall return, but it is at least plausible to see the considerations that take up the major part of the argument as an attempt on Socrates' part to establish the minor premise of a valid argument. We will, of course, need a suppressed premise to the effect that insofar as the vigorous is admirable and insofar as the vigorous is, in the way I've suggested, opposite to the quiet, just so far is the quiet not admirable. But given that, showing the swift and vigorous to be admirable can be seen as a legitimate part of a larger argument, in the context of which the remark at 159D10 might appear more innocuous.

If quietness is offered as an essential definition of sophrosyne, if, that is, being quiet is what it is to be σώφρων, then surely any instance of the required sort of quietness would be an instance of sophrosyne, so that showing that there are some instances of quietness that are not instances of sophrosyne would in some important sense impugn the definition. That could not be *what it was to be* sophrosyne, for how else could there be instances of just that sort of thing that are *not* instances of sophrosyne? Socrates' argument can then be restated in its entirety: suppose that the quietness of which you speak were what it was to be σώφρων. Then any instance of being quiet in this way would be to be σώφρων. But to be σώφρων is clearly something that is admirable, and therefore being quiet in this way would be admirable. But there are in fact many instances in which it is not being quiet in this way that is admirable, but just its opposite. Therefore our initial supposition was a bad one, and that sort of quietness is not what sophrosyne is. So it appears that Socrates' argument may be a good one after all.

III

Read this way, the opening argument of the *Charmides* reminds us of other arguments that Socrates uses in the early dialogues, arguments in which two concepts are shown to be dissimilar because important things that can be said about one cannot be said about the other. In the brief and spare argument by which Socrates dismisses Charmides' second account of sophrosyne, a simple proof text from the *Odyssey* establishes the fact that whereas sophrosyne is an admirable thing, modesty is sometimes an admirable thing, sometimes not so admirable, and therefore sophrosyne could not be modesty.

Perhaps the closest parallel to our argument is the early argument of the *Laches*, in which Socrates persuades Laches that his account of courage as a certain steadfast endurance, καρτερία τις, is in need of further refinement. Here both the language and structure of argument seem to be closely allied to that of ours. Courage, Laches says, seems to him to be a certain endurance of a soul (192B9). But surely courage is τῶν καλῶν πραγμάτων, one of the things that is admirable (C6), and while wise endurance, καρτερία μετὰ φρονήσεως, *is* admirable (C8), foolish endurance, μετ' ἀφροσύνης, is as clearly not (D1–6). Therefore endurance cannot be said to be what courage is, since some forms of it are not admirable, whereas courage is admirable (D7–8). In both cases we seem to have an argument of the form: some virtue is (always) admirable (courage, sophrosyne), whereas some quality that is suggested as a definition of the virtue is not always (endurance, quietness); therefore the definition will not work.

But there are at least two differences between the arguments. (1) In the argument of the *Laches*, there is said to be *a kind of* endurance that is not admirable and whose existence consequently impugns the definition, whereas in the argument of the *Charmides*, it is rather that there are certain *circumstances in which* the quality in question appears not to be admirable that causes trouble for the proposed definition. (2) In the *Charmides*, the argument is apparently taken by the parties of the discussion to constitute a ground for discarding altogether the suggestion that sophrosyne might be a kind of quietness (160E). Socrates does not encourage the young Charmides to look more closely at what he has said and attempt to reformulate his account in the light of Socrates' criticism; he rather urges him to start all over again, look away from what they have been talking about into himself, and come up with a new definition, which Charmides does. But the move of the *Laches* is quite different. For here Socrates does not (yet) discard endurance as an element in the definition of courage; his argument pretends only to show that not *every* form of endurance constitutes courage (192C3–4), and explicitly concludes that some particular kind of endurance (foolish) is not courage. But then Laches never said that every form of endurance constituted courage, but only that courage was καρτερία τις, a certain *kind* of endurance. The conclusion at 192D10, "Then wise endurance according to your view would be courage" need not therefore be seen as a *refutation* of Laches' first view, but as an *elaboration*, or filling in of the specific *kind* of endurance that constitutes courage.

Why couldn't Charmides have made a similar move to that depicted in the *Laches*? Given that Socrates' argument shows that not all quietness is σώφρων and that quietness per se is consequently an inadequate characteristic in terms of which to define sophrosyne, what follows concerning sophrosyne as ἡσυχιότης τις, a certain quietness? Why can't Charmides answer: of course not *all* quietness is σώφρων; it is, as I said from the beginning, only a certain *kind* of quietness that constitutes sophrosyne. Surely it is the possibility of exactly some such rejoinder that, on a more charitable reading than that which I gave, lies behind the criticism of Socrates' argument that I earlier quoted.

One response might refer us back to the first difference I noted, and point out the distinction between qualifying a definition by some internal modification (wise endurance as against endurance neat) and qualifying a definition by specifying circumstances in which the definition is not appropriate. It may be licit to qualify a definition in the former way but not in the latter; perhaps that does not count in any important sense as a qualification in the *definition*, but merely as a recognition that there are certain circumstances in which the definition does not work.

This answer suggests that the job may not be able to be done in any simple way such as is accomplished in the *Laches*. It remains true, however, that the argument that shows quietness not to constitute a defining characteristic of sophrosyne allows the possibility that some modification might have made sense of the definition, and that Socrates' conclusion at 160B7, "so then sophrosyne can't be a certain kind of quietness," is too strong.

It is, however, Socrates' conclusion, and it shows that we cannot facilely suppose, without saying something more, that Plato might have allowed even a certain kind of quietness to serve as an element in our understanding of sophrosyne.

I have sketched the different directions taken by the arguments of the *Charmides* and *Laches* because they seem to me to represent two dialectically contrasting attitudes which Plato invites us to enjoy with respect to the "unsatisfactory" definitions of these aporetic dialogues and which I shall say more about in the next section. It is the dialogue itself, I shall suggest, which is meant to resolve this opposition, which performs the office of making acceptable the unacceptable, of "saving the phenomena," so to speak, of our common definitional understanding.

Many commentators, in spite of the apparent strength of Socrates' conclusion at 160B7, have tried to steer a double course, wishing to see quietness as an element in a vulgar or prereflective understanding of sophrosyne, but not as a satisfactory element in the refined, philosophical account that Socrates demands. This attempt may take several forms; sometimes quietness is said to constitute the outer manifestation of an inner determinative character that is being sought, sometimes the style rather than content of a virtuous disposition, sometimes merely a traditional behavioral as against refined Platonic (where this often means intellectual) account.

All these attempts, it seems to me, are founded upon the proper recognition that the account of sophrosyne as quietness must in *some* sense be correct, if only in specifying the external symptoms or recognitional criteria of the virtue. Plato, I think, wants something stronger than that; the account of sophrosyne as quietness, like definitions generally in the early Socratic dialogues, must ultimately be made legitimate and be taken up (must, as other philosophers might say, be *aufgehoben*) into the *final* understanding meant to emerge from the dialogue. Our task as readers, like that of the dialogue's characters, is to understand exactly in what sense quietness is to be included in the proper understanding of sophrosyne.

My undertaking in the remainder of this paper will be twofold. I will first sketch a general account of what I take to be for Plato important features of the relationship between the definitions within a dialogue and the ultimate understanding that is meant to emerge from that dialogue. Then I shall suggest in what specific sense quietness may be thought to be a constituent element in the proper understanding of the virtue of sophrosyne.

IV

A form for Plato, the form, say, of beauty, is a principle of integrity and unity for the particular entities that are instances of that form, for example, particular beautiful things, insofar as they are just that: insofar, that is, as they are *beautiful*. How we are to understand this, how it is accomplished, what sorts of being forms are: these of course remain vexed questions, both for Plato and for us; but the description nonetheless seems to me in some sense importantly true. In the same way, a form is a principle of integrity and unity for the various *accounts* of what it is to be an instance of the form in question, that is, for the various definitions of the being that the form fixes. Thus, for example, the competing and potentially disintegrative accounts of justice in the *Republic* are mediated and brought into the unity that constitutes them as (better or worse) *accounts of justice* by The Just Itself, in the same way that the various and different instances of being just are brought into that unity that constitutes them all as *instances of being just* by The Just Itself. Forms, that is to say, have sovereignty over *logos* as well as *ergon*; they determine the structure of our theoretical talk about the world, what we say about what counts as F and what it is to be F, as much as they determine the ontic structure of the entities themselves which are F. This is merely to recognize, after all, as is recognized throughout the dialogues, that language is itself an image of the real. The objective necessity of the intelligible world is thus mirrored in the necessary structure of our logos about that world; it is for this reason that dialogues, responsible to the *truth*, cannot go just any old way.

An account of what it is to be F, then, is ontologically similar to an instance of F in that neither in itself constitues, but each is only an image (of a very different sort) of the principle of being F, the form of F, which form transcends both account and instance. Since a logos specifying what it is to be F, an account of F, is an image of but does not embody or constitute the form of F, any such logos may succeed or fail as a vehicle for the noetic understanding of the form. That understanding has as its object an entity transcending both logoi and the entities whose being logoi present an account of;

it consequently transcends both *dianoia*, the understanding that is of logoi, and the minimal grounded trust of *pistis*, the understanding of instantial entities. This transcendent understanding is achieved by dialectic. For it is in dialectic, in the discursive activity that is mimetically shown us in the dialogues themselves, that understanding may arise out of the confrontation between differing logoi. The process mirrors that in which "the form flashes forth" when different instances of justice, like firesticks, are rubbed against one another (*Republic*, 435A).

The understanding which emerges dialectically from this process must not be thought of as embodied uniquely in another specific logos, an account which captures specifically the form, just as the form must not, as we know from the beginning of the *Parmenides* and elsewhere, be thought of as another individual entity in the manifold governed by it. This fact is at the heart of dialectic: the fact that the truth cannot simply be said, but must be made to speak forth from what is said.

It is part of this fact that preliminary definitions and accounts are not merely provisional and propaedeutic, but are in some important sense correct. For the process of elenchus central to the dialogues is not a process of rejection relative to a preferred logos, but a process of *catharsis*, of purifying the elements of traditional orthodox wisdom and of the common understanding as embodied in logos.

Dialectic itself is "cathartic" in this sense; it transforms language that is opaque into a transparent medium for the noetic presentation of Being. I mean to use the word "transparent" here in a very special sense: the transparent is that which is the necessary medium for the appearance of some entity and which does not prove, through its own opacity, inhibitory to that appearance. We are accustomed to think of transparency, following a certain visual model, as second-best to the existence of no intervening entity at all. The ideal situation, we suppose, is that there be nothing between subject and object; failing that, we settle for the intervention of a transparent being through which, with greater or lesser degrees of difficulty, the object may appear. This model proposes a scale of desirability ranging from the existence of an intervening opaque entity to the intervention of no entity at all, with transparency somewhere in the middle. It may be an appropriate model in terms of which to talk about vision. (Aristotle thought that even there it was incorrect [*On the Soul*, 419a15–20], but that was because he thought light was the activity of a transparent substance.) In other cases, however, opacity of a medium and the existence of no medium present the same difficulty. In both situations, though in different ways, appearance is prevented, in the one because an opaque entity gets in the way, in the other because there is no medium through which the object can appear. The model that we need in such cases is one that makes transparency the ideal, and the opacity and nonexistence of the medium two modes of falling short of that ideal. On this model, the transparent, the diaphanous, does not allow appearance negatively and incidentally; it is the medium, the necessary agent of appearance.

It is not only cases of imaging and appearing that demand the existence of beings transparent in this sense. There are also contexts that require "transparent" principles of coherence and relationship. Aristotle's discussion of form at *Metaphysics* Z, 17, for example (to which the argument in the opening of the *Parmenides* is avuncular), makes just this point. Form is indispensible to the being of an entity; it is the principle of that entity's elements being brought together in such a way as to constitute *that* entity. Consequently the entity cannot do without form and still be that entity; but neither, as Aristotle argues, can the form be another element in the composition of that entity. Failure to appreciate this leads to the mistake in supposing that for Aristotle substance consists of matter and form; substance consists only of matter, but of matter in a certain form. Form cannot therefore disappear, but must become, as it were, ontologically diaphanous, must not itself become another concrete element in the composition of the entity.

These two modes of transparency, which we might think of as that of image and that of form, are both at work in Plato's thought. Depending on our point of view, what is higher in the spatial metaphor of *Republic* VI is transparent relative to what is lower, or vice versa. Forms as principles of unity and being are transparent in one sense, and thus what is higher is transparent to what is lower; images, that is, appearances, are (ideally) transparent in the other sense, and thus what is lower is transparent to what is higher. To understand one mode of transparency, that of forms, is to understand, among other things, the nexus of problems surrounding the first part of the *Parmenides*, the problems connected with the ways in which forms are and are not entities in the world (or for that matter, the ways in which a "material object" does and does not transcend its appearances). To understand the other mode is to understand why Plato and the tradition to which he is heir choose to speak of the relation between the "noetic" and the "empirical" worlds as a relation of imaging, of appearance and seeming. This relationship, itself imaged in the relationship at the lower sections of the line between the objects of *eikasia* and *pistis*, demands that the empirical world not be forsaken, but be made pure and transparent, made the medium of the appearance of that higher world that is in turn its own principle of intelligibility. That "this" world is the *image* or *appearance* of "that" means that entities are seen correctly when they become transparent to their forms; it is this seeing that the philosopher, who unlike the sophist, recognizes the world as image, strives to accomplish. To see both modes of transparency together is to see the sense in which the (one) world is only its own appearance.

But all this is another story about Plato's ontology. Here I wish only to specify the sense in which dialectic is "cathartic" in its transforming language into the transparent medium of understanding. The transformation that is the result of philosophical catharsis and that allows such a transparent presentation of a form may entail no substantial change in an account itself, but only a change in an individual's understanding, whether that individual be a character in the dialogue or the reader, who is after all only a participant in the outer invisible ring of concentric frames that make up most of the early dialogues. The critical difference, for example, between the earliest account of justice at 331E of the *Republic*, so easily and devastatingly dismissed by Socrates, and the final account of Book IV, 433, upon which the company agrees, is not so much a difference in formulation as a sense of the discourse having provided the relevant import of "rendering" (ἀποδιδόναι) and of "what is due" (ὀφειλόμενα); it is not, in other words, the formulation that has changed, but how the formula is understood by those present. Theoretical accounts do not fail or succeed as accounts merely by virtue of their formulaic character. For any account in the particular circumstances dramatically presented in a dialogue may be ill or well understood; typically, we encounter throughout the dialogues characters who have the right thing to say, but say it wrongly, or without the proper understanding, or at the wrong time, or in the wrong context. This is merely to say that we encounter in the dialogues people who are able to speak a wisdom not fully theirs. The dialogues are in this sense a kind of cultural anamnesis, the recollection, as it were, of a wisdom present but forgotten.

None of this, which I claim follows from Plato's understanding of logos and form, means that one definition cannot be better than another. It means only that no definition, no matter how good, can be guaranteed to provide the understanding of that being which it attempts to articulate, and specifically, that no account can be judged adequate by virtue of its verbal form alone. Furthermore, it means that the likelihood of any given account being capable of transparency without the supporting structure of dialectic is slight; only as the form itself comes to be understood in the process of dialectical exploration does the sense in which the form can be expressed in this or that account become clear. Just as learning means learning how to experience particulars, how to see things for what they are so that their being shines through them, so it means learning how to read theory, how to hear a logos, from what perspective to listen, how, in short, to *understand*. Insofar as definitions still lack that richer background of meaning and perspective that dialectic gives them, they must be "rejected." But insofar as they need only be correctly read by experienced eyes and an understanding mind, they need not be rejected, but only redeemed by coming to be understood, redeemed, that is, by the proper appropriative reading. This is the opposition of which I spoke earlier, an opposition, I think, the resolution of which lies at least implicit in the early dialogues.

Ultimately the dialogues are exercises in the redemptive appropriation of a common wisdom. Often this appropriation is ironic and witty, as when in the *Phaedo* Socrates assures his young friends that those who think of philosophers as a half-dead lot deserving of death are right but do not understand the sense in which they are right, and then proceeds through a series of arguments to reveal this sense and to reveal it as philosophically significant. At most times it is more straightforward, as in the inquiries into the meaning of "know yourself" or "give to each his due." At all times it is serious: the deep philosophical task of making manifest and understood a latent and (merely) formulaic wisdom.

It is this quality that makes Plato's dialogues so continually relevant. At their best, they teach us what kind of a task appropriation is, what it means to attempt to salvage orthodoxy from the shambles of forgetfulness and of the tradition's infidelity to itself in which we so often find it.

It would be more correct to say, "in which we characteristically find it." For surely it is part of the nature of culture and thus of the tradition that it defines, that it is continuously forgetting itself and continuously engaged in the task of its own recovery. This dialectic of self-loss and self-recovery (which we know equally well from its ontological analogue in Plato) is what I meant earlier to refer to by the phrase "cultural anamnesis": the tradition's recollection of itself. In ascribing such a task to the Platonic dialogue, I have meant to claim that the process that I have described is seen by Plato as the deepest task of philosophical hermeneutics; for according to Plato, understanding *is* recollection, and human self-interpretation—the project of reclaiming human self-understanding—is therefore fundamentally a project of self-recollection.

An examination of the method by which the dialogues undertake this project and attempt to perform the maieutic task of bringing forth the understanding implicit in our knowledge, or, to shift metaphors, the catharsis that allows our talk and thinking about the world to reveal it, would constitute an examination of Plato's theory of dialectic. It would need to consider the complex nexus of relations between tradition, formula, example, and speaker, the effect of elenchus, the role of the mimetic character of the arguments, the place of the constantly oblique point of view, the reciprocal structure of rhetoric and hermeneutics, in short the whole art of that dialectical poetry of Plato that we call (correctly) his philosophy. I have tried here to settle for the small claim that definitions must be properly understood, and that when properly understood are often "right."

V

There is an intermediate or "journeyman" stage in the cultivation of arts and skills in which an artisan achieves control and mastery as the immediate result of successful effort. Such control signals the superior strength or craft that the agent has achieved relative to the forces with which she is working; she has gained victory over them. But there is also a mastery that is beyond effort and beyond restraint, a skill in which technique and control disappear, become, in another version of the sense I have tried to explore, *transparent*. For such skill, work is not at odds with its object; mastery does not assert itself over a recalcitrant and alien other, but leads, as the ruler leads the happy city, or reason the happy person.

In this skill, the control is a noncontrol, without compulsion or restraint. The master does not *will* to work smoothly (how could she?). Like the sage, she is quiet because she is not moved; she has acquired the high art of relinquishing control and will. Consider, for instance, the apprentice and master potter. The apprentice becomes frustrated as the clay proves more and more refractory. His muscles tense, he struggles, holds tight, tries to force the clay back to center, works to keep control. "Relax," the master admonishes him, "you're trying too hard: too much effort, too much *control*; you must learn to let go, to allow the pot to make itself. Watch me." The master brings the clay up effortlessly, without trying, with quiet speed and total mastery (perfect control!). The apprentice tries to follow her advice, lets go; but the pot collapses. "You are not yet ready to give up control," the master says; "keep working at it till you learn."

In a more general context of moral life and action, that skill that is the unrestrained mastery beyond control has for its object the agent himself. Sophrosyne is the paradigm mode of that reflexive self-directed skill; this is only to say that to be σώφρων is to be a person who is *master of oneself.*

But this is not to be in control of or master of oneself in the *intermediate* manner I have sketched; that virtue is what Plato and Aristotle called ἐγκράτεια. The distinction between the virtue of the σώφρων and that of the ἐγκρατής, which was to become central to Aristotle's moral vision, is the distinction between self-mastery in the sense of a bonded self-restraint and self-control, and self-mastery in the sense of the free and effortless guiding of the self.

It is inviting to think of the distinction between these two modes of self-mastery in moral terms as the difference between, on the one hand, experiencing temptation and overcoming it through strength and effort of the will, and, on the other, experiencing no temptation at all. While the vision of sophrosyne as granting a life free of temptation seems to me both true to the Hellenic moral vision (particularly in Aristotle) and a proper goal of the moral life, it is important to distinguish the freedom from temptation that characterizes the saint and moral hero, and that which characterizes the innocent, even the holy innocent. It is a difference as important as that between the loss of and the transcendence of control. The hero has acquired a virtue with respect to that which tempts the rest of us: an aptitude of serene disdain. It is perhaps in one sense indistinguishable from the innocent unconcern of the naive, but that is only because his mastery has become transparent, the control wholly infixed and diaphanous. Self-mastery is not less a skill because in its final stages it becomes transparent, any more than the skill of the master artisan is less a skill because it has become transparent. It is possible, as a consequence, that a philosopher should agree with Antiphon (B59) that sophrosyne must be won with struggle and the conquering of temptation, and still see it as a virtue in which, achieved, there is no longer any struggle: a noncontrol achieved by disciplined control. (Is this in the background of Simonides' poem in the *Protagoras*?)

There is a more critical difference between a theory that sees self-mastery as a kind of self-control and a theory that sees it as a virtue ideally transcendent of such control. For on one view self-mastery is the virtue of a person in conflict with her desires, divided against herself, one part of her, however, stronger than the other; on the other view, it may be rare that sophrosyne is fully exemplified, but its highest form is the virtue of a person harmonious, at one with herself.

It is tempting to see Plato and Aristotle ranged against one another in just this way; Plato shares with others in the tradition the identification or near-identification of ἐγκράτεια and sophrosyne, whereas Aristotle first introduces the distinction so important to his ethical thought. Such a view of Plato is perhaps understandable; it is part of an interpretation according to which Plato views bodily desires and passions as things mean and needing to be held in check. It would seem to be this view that lies behind the imagery of the *Phaedrus* (237) and the explicit account of sophrosyne at *Republic* 430E as "the control of pleasures and desires—ἡδονῶν καὶ ἐπιθυμιῶν ἐγκράτεια," and as characterized by a person's higher elements being in control (ἐγκρατής) of the lower.

But it should be of considerable interest that in our dialogue, devoted to the topic of sophrosyne and covering a broad range of the traditional understanding, the concept of ἐγκράτεια plays no part in the attempt at definition. For sophrosyne understood as self-control is the virtue in its common or vulgar sense; but there is a higher sophrosyne that transcends this mode of strong-willed containment and is equivalent to the wisdom by virtue of which the sage is freed from the need for restraint (*Laws*, 710A; *Phaedo*, 69A). It is this wisdom that, ruling the city, allows for that *political* virtue of sophrosyne that is in marked contrast to the forceful control of the citizenry characteristic of tyranny. And when in the *Republic*, the fully virtuous person is described, he is revealed as a person in total harmony, one rather than many, at peace with himself (443D). It is, I think, in reference to such a person that the virtues are said, as in the *Protagoras*, to be one. In such a person, where justice determines that each of his parts acts according to its proper virtue, wisdom that he know what he's doing, and so on, how could there be a need for the restrained, bonded self-control of ἐγκράτεια? (A discussion of the *Laches* might ask the same question with regard to courage and endurance.)

In the *Phaedo* (69C), this refined and harmonious virtue, "whether sophrosyne or justice or courage or wisdom itself," is described as a kind of purification, a catharsis from pleasure and pain. I take this to mean that true virtue consists not in the exchanging of one pleasure for another, or in the acceptance of one pain to avoid another, but in the cathartic wisdom that detaches the philosopher from pleasure and pain, allows him to transcend and accept his pleasure and pain, and thus to exhibit the serene tranquility by virtue of which, as in the *Republic* (443F), he is able to go virtuously about whatever business of life he sets for himself.

In "enkratic" self-control, the self becomes its own object and thus alienated and divided from itself. This is the force, to turn to a later part of the *Charmides*, of the confusion concerning self-knowledge into which Socrates leads Critias as he conducts him through the cunningly falacious argument that moves from ἐπιστήμη ἑαυτοῦ as one's knowledge of one-self to ἐπιστήμη ἑαυτῆς, that is, ἐπιστήμη ἐπιστήμης, knowledge of knowledge.

Here, as so often in the dialogues, an outrageous fallacy sheds light, and things somehow work out in that typically mad and witty Platonic fashion: people make all the wrong moves, but the argument, like a God's oracle, relentlessly finds its way to its proper conclusion. For what else would work for the elaboration of sophrosyne than the concept of a transparent, pure, objectless knowledge. Sophrosyne is precisely the virtue of a general and un-self-conscious self-mastery and self-possession, of a universal grace and effortless command neither specified by particular action, which would transform it from sophrosyne to some particular virtue, nor checked by any opacity, which would translate it into a mode of self-control. The σώφρων, in contrast to the ἐγκρατής, is the person whose "self-control" is not really *control*, is invisible and totally translucent, the easy effortless control of the master, not the tight and strained control of the novice.

Sophrosyne is thus in a sense a virtue of self without self, the virtue of the empty and mindless peace that belongs to the fully mindful and enlightened sage. It is the wisdom of self-mastery in which wisdom, self, and mastery vanish, and what remains is the quiet, orderly, effortless grace of skilled living.

VI

Imagine now a somewhat different Charmides. He is asked to give an account of sophrosyne; he hesitates, then suggests a traditional and aristocratic mode of behavior: a kind of elegant quietness in walking, talking, and other such activities. That won't do, says Socrates; in cases where it is swift and vigorous action that is called for, calm and quiet behavior is not what is admirable. But sophrosyne is always admirable, so it cannot be what you say.

You have not understood the quietness I am speaking of, our Charmides replies. I mean the quiet mastery that may characterize any action, fast or slow, energetic or leisurely, loud or soft; I mean the quiet, smooth rightness of the master artisan or statesman or warrior, which alone makes possible their acting swiftly and vigorously. You think I mean not moving fast; I mean not speeding. I mean the calm quietness that is knowing who you are, what you want, how to do it; that is always admirable. And that is why the quietness of which I speak, rightly understood by my aristocratic friends and teachers to be associated with modest reverence and the self-knowing of which the god speaks, is the sophrosyne after which you ask.

One can perhaps imagine such a fanciful Charmides, who tries, as I have suggested Plato tries, to save the traditional knowing, to redeem an old and common maxim. But the dialogue does not go this way. For the speech I have imagined comes too early and too easily; much more conceptual development must take place for the proverb to become wisdom. We have to follow sophrosyne through its complex logos: to talk about modesty, about knowing your place, about knowing your mind, about self-understanding in general, about knowing what to do, about the empty wisdom that knows itself. When the dialectical structure of that logos has been followed through, then *perhaps* we can see *how* sophrosyne is quietness, and then like Charmides and Socrates, we can forget sophrosyne, and forget the resisting of temptation, and return (quietly) to love, which was the business at hand.

NOTE

¹ Wincenty Łutoslawski, *The Origin and Growth of Plato's Logic* (New York, 1897), p. 203.

C. C. W. TAYLOR

The Arguments in the *Phaedo* Concerning the Thesis That the Soul Is a *Harmonia*[1]

A T *Phaedo* 85e–86d Simmias puts forward an argument to show that the soul cannot be immortal. The premises of the argument are firstly that the soul is a *harmonia* of the elements that compose the body, the hot, cold, wet, dry and so on (86b6–c2), and secondly that no *harmonia* can exist unless the elements of which it is a *harmonia* maintain the proper interrelation. (This point is made in 85e3–86b5 with reference only to a particular case, the *harmonia* of a lyre, but is clearly to be taken generally.) It follows that when the interrelation of the bodily elements has been dissolved by death, the soul-*harmonia* cannot exist apart. This argument is presented in the dialogue as posing a major objection to the thesis of the immortality of the soul; those who had been convinced by Socrates' previous arguments are now thoroughly dismayed (88c). It is, therefore, worth some consideration, particularly since the premise that the soul is a *harmonia* expresses a philosophical doctrine whose sense is far from clear. Furthermore, the counter-arguments by which Socrates claims to refute Simmias have provoked considerable disagreement among commentators as to their interpretation, while questions may be raised as to their validity. I propose, then, first to ask what is the meaning of the thesis that the soul is a *harmonia* and second to examine Socrates' arguments against Simmias.

The ambiguity of the thesis that the soul is a *harmonia* emerges from consideration of the different shades of meaning that the word *harmonia* may have. Formed from the verb *harmozein* ("fit together") it expresses the idea of things being fitted together in an exact arrangement to make an integrated whole, but particular uses express various aspects of the basic sense. Thus the word sometimes means "proportion," particularly in contexts where elements are mingled in proportion, as where Empedocles describes

This paper was presented to the 1970 Philadelphia meeting of the Society for Ancient Greek Philosophy. It has been revised for publication in this volume.
C. C. W. Taylor is a Fellow of Corpus Christi College, Oxford.

painters mixing their colors "mixing them in proportion, some more and some less" (DK 31 B 23, line 4), and sometimes "arrangement" or "organization" (conveying the idea of the proper relation of parts), as when Heraclitus refers to the *harmonia* of opposite forces in a bow or a lyre (DK 22 B 51). Or again a *harmonia* may be identical with a complex of parts in a certain order or arrangement; this is the sense in which the word can mean "joint" or "framework" (see Liddell and Scott). Aristotle's discussion of the soul-*harmonia* thesis at *De Anima* I.4 deals certainly with the first two senses, and perhaps also with the third. In one sense a *harmonia* is the *logos* of a mixture, i.e., the ratio of the elements, which may be expressed mathematically. In another it is a combination (*synthesis*) of physical objects, probably in the sense of the arrangement of a number of physical parts but perhaps also as the complex of those parts in that arrangement. There appears also to be a fourth sense of *harmonia* that Aristotle ignores, in which a *harmonia* is something causally dependent on a certain disposition of materials; e.g., a melody is distinct from the strings that produce it, and equally from the tuning of the strings, though without strings there could be no tuning, and without tuning no melody. The word has this sense especially in musical contexts, meaning variously "scale," "mode," or generally "music" (see Liddell and Scott). Given, then, that the elements in question are those that compose the human body, the hot, the cold, etc., (which are presumably thought of as different kinds of stuff), there appear to be four possible interpretations of the thesis that the soul is a *harmonia* of those elements:

1. the soul is identical with the ratio or formula according to which the elements are combined to form the living man;

2. the soul is identical with the mixture or combination of those elements according to that formula;

3. the soul is some entity produced by the combination of those elements according to that formula, but distinct alike from them and from the formula itself;

4. the soul is identical with a state of the bodily elements, viz., the state of being combined according to that formula.

It might be objected at this point that the third alternative is illusory, since even when the *harmonia* is a scale or melody it must be considered identical with a mixture of elements. This seems implausible on the assumption that the elements in question are strings or other physical objects composing the instrument that produces the music, but that assumption is mistaken. Just as the elements of a physical organism such as a living human body are the hot, the cold, etc., so the elements of a piece of music are the high and the low, which are conceived of as being mixed together in the proper proportions to give the right notes, either in the sense that each note is thought of as consisting of so much of the high mixed with so much of the low, or in the sense that each mode or scale is produced by combining so many high notes in fixed ratios with so many low notes. The elements, therefore, of a musical *harmonia* are themselves musical entities, the high and the low, not the physical objects that produce the sounds. This theory is clearly expressed for instance in the pseudo-Aristotelian treatise *De Mundo* 396b7 ff. (DK 22 B 10): "Music makes a single *harmonia* out of different sounds by mixing together high and low, long and short notes." On this view of musical *harmonia*, then, the *harmonia* cannot be separated from its elements, and so this view does not admit interpretation 3 as an alternative to the others.

But while this view of the nature of musical *harmonia* appears to have been the standard view of musical theory and gives the most exact parallel to other kinds of *harmonia* (e.g., the formation of physical substances out of the elements), it is emphatically not the view of musical *harmonia* that Simmias uses to illustrate his thesis. For his presentation of that thesis involves positing a parallelism between two relations, of each of which the terms are (a) a physical object and (b) a nonphysical entity causally dependent on that object. Thus corresponding to the incorporeal soul we have the musical *harmonia*, which is "invisible and incorporeal and all-beautiful and divine" (85e5–6), while corresponding to the physical body we have not the high and the low but the physical strings and pegs of the lyre, which can be broken apart and left lying around after the *harmonia* has vanished. It is true that Simmias slightly distorts the parallel when he says (85b5–c1) that the soul is a *harmonia* of the hot, cold, etc. in the body, since a more exact parallel to the strings, etc., of the lyre would be provided by the limbs and organs of the body than by their microscopic elements. But the essential point is the contrast of the incorporeal product with its physical cause, and for that contrast it is unnecessary for Simmias to distinguish the macroscopic parts of the body from their own elements, which are no doubt conceived of as minute but equally corporeal parts. The relation of musical *harmonia* to its elements, which Simmias is using, cannot therefore be that between a scale or tune and the musical elements of high and low, etc., but must be that between a musical instrument and some nonphysical entity produced by a certain state of the instrument.

This enables us immediately to eliminate interpretation 2 above. For it would clearly be absurd to make a sharp contrast between the physical elements and the nonphysical *harmonia*, if the latter were just the elements themselves in a certain arrangement. One might as sensibly contrast the invisible, incorporeal plum pudding with the gross, earthy suet, raisins, flour, etc., that compose it. This still leaves three of the original four alternatives, that the relation of the soul to the body is (using the original numbering) (1) that of the ratio of the tuned strings to the strings themselves, or (3) that of the music produced by the instrument to the instrument itself, or (4) that of the state of being in tune to the strings.

There is no conclusive evidence from the text which alternative Plato had in mind, or indeed whether he had distinguished the three. Various phrases give some hints, but these are conflicting and inconclusive. Thus the description of musical *harmonia* as "all-beautiful and divine" might seem most readily applicable to the music produced by the instrument; but when we reflect that the speaker is a pupil of the Pythagorean Philolaos, who might therefore be expected to have a lively reverence for numbers as the source of all things, this argument seems to have little force as between alternatives 1 and 3. Rather stronger is the argument from Simmias' statement at 92d2 that the soul-*harmonia* doctrine is accepted by most people; surely, it may be argued, this indicates that the soul is something distinct from a mathematical ratio, since such an obscure theory can never have been held by the majority. On the other hand, the view that the soul is something nonphysical, which is yet dependent on a certain state of the body, so that when that state is disrupted the soul is dissipated, might seem to be quite congenial to common sense. But against this we have the comparison of the soul at 86c6–7 to "*harmoniai* in sounds and in all the works of the craftsmen." "All the works of the craftsmen" must include statuary and painting, and probably carpentry and house-building as well. Where, in the products of these arts, are we to look for the nonphysical product of the physical elements? Surely in the harmony or proportion of the constituent parts, as exemplified by the proportions between different amounts of different pigments, or by the relations between the dimensions of the various parts of a statue or a piece of furniture. It would be too fantastic to suggest that to every well-made table there corresponds a nonphysical entity that is related to the disposition of its parts as the nonphysical soul is to the disposition of the bodily elements, or as the nonphysical music is to the disposition of the strings. This comparison, then, tends to support alternatives 1 and 4, rather than 3, which was suggested by the claim of popular acceptance for the *harmonia* thesis. Further difficulty is created by the description of the soul at 86b9 as a mixture (*krasis*) of the bodily elements. The word *krasis*, which is regularly used as a synonym for *harmonia* (e. g., Aristotle, *De Anima* 408a30–1), commonly occurs, like the English "mixture" in contexts that leave it open whether the word refers to the compound of elements that are mixed, or to the state of those elements of being mixed. We have seen that the former alternative is unacceptable, but what about the latter? Can Plato mean that the soul is identical neither with a ratio nor with any nonphysical product of a ratio, but rather with a certain state of the body, viz., the state in which the elements of the body are in a certain ratio? While on the one hand this would give a fair account of the comparison of the soul with *harmoniai* in works of art, on the other hand it fits rather ill with the sharp contrast between the invisible, divine musical *harmonia* and the physical instrument, while again it might well seem very dubious that most people believe that the soul is nothing other than a bodily state. There appear, then, to be hints of support in the dialogue for all three possible interpretations of the soul-*harmonia* thesis, which might suggest that Plato has failed to distinguish these alternatives. Before leaving this question, however, we should look at some evidence from other sources, to see whether these throw any light on Plato's meaning.

First, there is the fact already mentioned that in *De Anima* I.4 Aristotle ignores the possibility that on the *harmonia* theory the soul might be a nonphysical entity causally dependent on the ratio of bodily elements, while explicitly mentioning the possibilities of its being identical with that ratio and of its being identical with an arrangement of parts, which is itself ambiguous between "identical with the parts as arranged" and "identical with the state of being arranged which characterises the parts." Not only does he not give the first-mentioned possibility as a possible interpretation of the thesis, but he appears to introduce it as an alternative view of the soul, which would be unacceptable to an adherent of the *harmonia* theory. After producing objections first to the suggestion that the soul is a combination of limbs and then to the suggestion that it is the ratio of the mixture of elements he adds (408a20–1) "Is it the ratio which is the soul, or is it rather something separate which comes to be in the parts of the body?" The implication is that he is here suggesting a more plausible alternative theory, not giving an interpretation that a supporter of the theory would accept as expressing his meaning. Yet in order to take this as a basis for the interpretation of the thesis of the *Phaedo* we should have to have some reason to believe that Aristotle's target in the *De Anima* is specifically the thesis proposed in that dialogue, rather than any other version. Such reason is lacking. Aristotle describes the theory as widely current (407b27–8), but does not ascribe it to anyone in particular, and does not mention the *Phaedo* in his discussion. We know that a version of the theory was held by Aristotle's follower Aristoxenus (for the evidence see H. B. Gottschalk, "Soul as Harmonia," *Phronesis* xvi (1971):179–98), and it is possible that a version different from that of the *Phaedo* was maintained by Philolaos (see below). The *harmonia* theory was, then, a current theory of the soul,[2] and we are safest to suppose Aristotle to be attempting to expose the fundamental errors of the theory as such, rather than give an exact exposition of any version of it.

One might hope to throw some light on the precise sense of the theory by considering its origins, but here too it is impossible to reach any positive conclusions. None of the speakers in the dialogue attributes it to any named philosopher, but since Simmias says that "we" hold the soul to be a *harmonia* (88b6–7) and Echecrates that he has always been very impressed by that thesis (88d3–4), it would be natural to assume that it was current in the Pythagorean circle to which they belonged. Though they are described as pupils of Philolaos (61d–e, cf. Diogenes Laertius VIII.46), the theory itself is not ascribed to Philolaos by any writer earlier than Macrobius (fourth to fifth centuries A.D.), who says that Pythagoras and Philolaos held that the soul is a *harmonia* (DK 44 A 23). It is not clear how much reliance can be put on this testimony, since there is obviously a possibility that it may derive ultimately from this very passage of the *Phaedo*. But whatever the truth about that, Philolaos' view of the soul cannot be reconciled with the *harmonia* theory as expounded by Simmias. For at 61a–62b it is implied that Philolaos taught that suicide is wrong on the ground that the soul is put by the gods in the body as a prison for a set time, and must not seek to escape before the time of its release, though a philosopher will welcome death, presumably because his soul will have a better existence in separation from the body. This is supported by a quotation from Philolaos given by Clement of Alexandria (DK 44 B 14): "The soul is yoked to the body and as it were buried in this tomb as a punishment." The conclusion is plain that unlike his pupils who take part in the dialogue Philolaos believed that the soul exists independently of the body. It is not impossible that he may have held some version of the theory, in which the soul was a nonphysical entity whose association with the body depended on the maintainance of the proper bodily ratio, but the divergence from the view expressed by Simmias is so great that it is obviously fruitless to attempt to interpret the latter in such a way as to assimilate it to some conjectural reconstruction of Philolaos' views.[3]

I conclude, then, that not only is there no evidence that the soul-*harmonia* thesis definitely identifies the soul either with a ratio of bodily elements or with the state of being in that ratio or with some entity dependent on the possession of that ratio, but that we can best account for what is said on the assumption that Plato did not clearly distinguish the three possibilities. In considering the arguments against the thesis we shall therefore regard them as concerned with a thesis containing those three alternatives in undifferentiated form.

Socrates' first counter-argument requires little comment. He points out that the thesis is inconsistent with the doctrine accepted earlier that all knowledge is in fact recollection of what the soul had learned in a previous, disembodied existence. No *harmonia* can exist unless the elements of which it is a *harmonia* are already in existence, and hence if the soul is a *harmonia* of the bodily elements it cannot have had a previous nonbodily existence (91e–92e). This argument is cogent against any interpretation of the thesis; obviously a bodily state cannot exist unless some body exists of which it is a state, and equally obviously a nonphysical entity causally dependent on a ratio of bodily elements cannot exist before those elements have been combined in that ratio. A defender of the thesis might, however, argue that it is not cogent against the identification of the soul with the mathematical ratio itself. For a ratio, being a timeless mathematical entity, cannot itself be said to come into existence whenever it is embodied in some particular material. Since it exists equally at all times, it may truly be said to have existed before a certain body came into being, and hence the argument from recollection does not refute this version of the thesis. This defense is not, indeed, adopted by Simmias, who agrees that his thesis is inconsistent with the doctrine that knowledge is recollection. Nor is it difficult to see why. For it is possible to use this defense only at the cost of making the soul-*harmonia* a universal; if a pair of elements combines in the ratio ¾, then indeed that ratio existed before the combination of those elements, but what existed was *the* ratio ¾, i.e., the very same ratio that is exemplified whenever three units are related to four units. Thus anyone holding this theory would have to admit that many things must have the same soul, including things generally reckoned inanimate, e.g., geometrical diagrams, since the same ratio that is embodied in a human being and is his soul may also hold between certain lines and angles. It is not, of course, impossible that anyone might have believed something like this; it might, for instance, provide a theory to account for transmigration. Empedocles would on this view have been a bush, a fish, etc. (DK 31 B 117) because one and the same ratio would have been embodied in bush, fish, and Empedocles; i.e., they all had the same soul. Simmias, however, will have none of this; if his version of the theory is interpreted as making the soul a mathematical entity, it must be such an entity individuated by being embodied in these bodily elements. As such it cannot exist independently of the elements by reference to which it is individuated, any more than Socrates' height can exist independently of Socrates, though in the sense in which Socrates' height is a universal, say 5 feet 6 inches, that length may be said always to have existed whether or not Socrates exists. This way of looking at the thesis has the advantage of preserving as a necessary truth the thesis that different persons have numerically different souls, whereas on the other interpretation it might be discovered as the result of physiological investigation that two different people had the same soul. It leaves the thesis open, however, to attack on the grounds of inconsistency with the doctrine that knowledge is recollection; whether one considers it refuted on that ground will naturally depend on the strength of one's conviction of the truth of that doctrine.

The remaining arguments are more problematical, in that commentators have disagreed not merely on their conclusiveness but also on how many arguments are employed, and precisely what these arguments are. Like

Hicken, Bluck (R. S. Bluck, *Plato's Phaedo* [London, 1955]), and Gallop, I discern two arguments, as opposed to the four specified by Philoponus in his commentary on *De Anima* I.4.[4] These arguments are not, however, presented consecutively; at 92e4–93a10 Socrates gives a set of propositions A1–A4 that are not immediately used in the argument.[5] Instead at 93a11–12 he begins a new argument by formulating a principle B1 that is to some extent independent of A1–A4. This argument (argument *B*) continues to its conclusion at 94a12–b3. Then at 94b4 Socrates returns to A1–A4, which he uses to construct the second argument (argument *A*), whose conclusion is reached at 95a2. While I shall deal first with argument *B*, it is necessary first to look at A1–A4 in order to determine their relation to B1.

Socrates begins by securing Simmias' acceptance of the proposition that the properties of a *harmonia* are determined by those of its elements (92e4–93a2; A1). We then have three successive applications of this principle, first to all activities and passivities of the *harmonia* (a4–5; A2) and then to some particular activities and passivities that are excluded by the principle. It is impossible for a *harmonia* to lead or control its elements, but it must rather be controlled by them (a6–7; A3), and it is impossible for it to be affected or behave in any way contrary to that which its elements determine (93a8–9; A4). At 93a11–12 we have the principle that marks the beginning of argument *B*: "Well now, doesn't every *harmonia* have to be the kind of *harmonia* that corresponds to the way that it is ordered?" (B1).[6] It is not easy to find a translation that is both exact and comprehensible but the next sentence, giving an application of the principle, makes the meaning fairly clear; if a *harmonia* is more ordered it is more (of) a *harmonia*, and if it is less ordered it is less (of) a *harmonia* (93a14–b2; B2). The sense of B1 itself can then best be expressed formally, as follows, that where *F* stands for an adjective that can apply to a *harmonia*, and where *F*-ly stands for the adverb formed from the adjective for which *F* stands, then for all *X*, if *X* is a *harmonia*, if *X* is ordered *F*-ly, *X* is an *F harmonia*. While this certainly goes beyond anything that is said in A1–A4, this "formal" account of the dependence of a *harmonia* on what gives rise to it may nonetheless be seen as continuing the line of thought begun there. The crucial difference, emphasized by Gallop, *Plato, Phaedo*, p. 158, is that whereas in A1–A4 we are concerned with the dependence of the *harmonia* on its elements, B1 states the dependence of the *harmonia* on the order or arrangement of the elements.

Argument *B* proceeds by way of three further premises, B3 that a soul is no more or less (of) a soul than any other (b4–6), B4 that there are some good souls and some bad (b8–c2) and B5 that a good soul is in order and a bad soul out of order (c3–10). None of these premises is felt to require any justification or explanation; the sense of the third is clearly that the good man is not a prey to the conflicting desires and impulses that are the mark of the bad man, but has all his wants properly under control with a view to the attainment of the right ends. We now come to one of the most problematical passages in the argument: at d1–5 Socrates says that premise B3 is the same as the proposition (B7) that no *harmonia* is more or less (of) a *harmonia* than any other, and Simmias agrees. Of course B3 is not as it stands equivalent to B7, and the question is what additional assumptions Plato must have used in order to produce what he regarded as a valid equivalence. Clearly we cannot derive such an equivalence simply by making the most obvious assumption, viz., the assumption under examination in this argument, that the soul is a *harmonia* (B6), since taken together with B3 that would still allow that some *harmoniai* might be more or less *harmoniai* than others. But did Plato see that? I am inclined to think that he did not, but rather, assuming the soul to be a *harmonia*, took this to imply that whatever is true of soul is also true of *harmonia* (using the terms in the unquantified style familiar from Aristotle). In effect this is to confuse implication with equivalence, which seems a possible error for Plato to commit at this stage in his philosophical development. (See Gallop, *Plato, Phaedo*, pp. 162–63.)

The standard modern interpretation of this sentence, adopted by Archer-Hind, Bluck, Hackforth and Hicken (but not by John Burnet, *Plato's Phaedo* [Oxford, 1925] or Gallop) differs from the above in taking Socrates to be asserting not a general proposition about all *harmoniai* but a specific proposition about the sort of *harmonia* that souls are, viz., that no soul-*harmonia* is more or less a *harmonia* than any other. As this requires an admittedly unnatural reading of the text as it stands, many scholars (see Hackforth's note, *Plato's Phaedo*, p. 116) have suggested deleting the word *harmonias* from d4, thus making the sentence read "And this (namely, the admission that no soul is more or less a soul than any other) is the admission that no (soul) is more or less a *harmonia* than any other." But since this emendation lacks any manuscript authority and destroys what looks like a very emphatic and deliberate parallelism of sentence construction, it is worth asking whether there are cogent grounds for emending the text or for reading the received text in a sense other than its natural one. The strongest ground appears to be that urged by Hicken, that since the argument is to depend on the assumption that some *harmoniai* (in particular, goodness) admit of degrees, it would be flatly inconsistent if Plato also relied on the assumption that no *harmonia* admits of degrees. I doubt the cogency of this argument, which seems to depend on a confusion in the notion of "degrees of *harmonia*." For the thesis that some *harmoniai* (e.g., goodness) admit of degrees comes to this, that some things, e.g., the parts of the soul, may be so arranged as to approximate more or less closely to some norm that represents the perfect arrangement of those things. But that is in no way incompatible with the thesis that I take Plato to be asserting at 93d1–5, viz., that if what a thing is is a *harmonia*, it cannot be more or less a *harmonia* than anything else that is a *harmonia*. This amounts to to an extension of the truism "Everything is what it is," and applies alike to perfect and to imperfect orderings. Every ordering of parts of the soul, at whatever remove from the norm, is equally an ordering of parts of the soul. There is, then, no general inconsistency between the theses "No *harmonia* is more or less a *harmonia* than any other" and "Some things are more ordered (in Platonic terms 'partake more of order') than others." Plato, however, thinks that contradiction is generated if one says that one *harmonia* is more ordered than another; that he is wrong even in this restricted thesis will be seen once the argument is viewed as a whole.

The next step (93d6–8; B8) is that something that is neither more nor less a *harmonia* is neither more nor less ordered; this follows directly by contraposition from B2. Another problematic sentence follows (d9–11; B9): "And does that which is neither more nor less ordered partake more or less of order, or to just the same extent? To the same extent." At first sight it might appear that this is the converse of B8. But, firstly, in contrast to the previous sentence, where the subject is "that which *is* neither more nor less a *harmonia*" the predicate of B9 is "*partakes of* (i.e., is characterized by) *harmonia* more or less." While one might indeed see here a confusion between predication and identity, it is more charitable to take the shift in terminology as indicating that a new point is being made by the introduction of a further premise. Secondly, if B9 is read as the converse of B8, it has no subsequent role in the argument; whereas if it is read as "Something which is neither more nor less ordered has neither more nor less order," we have a straightforward argument, as will be seen immediately.

Socrates next concludes (d12–e2; B10) that no soul is more or less ordered than any other, giving as premise B3. In fact B10 follows, not from B3, but from B6, 7, and 8 (see appendix). Socrates' derivation of B10 from B3 presumably indicates that he is relying on the fallacious derivation of B7 from B3 (together with B6). From this point the argument is straightforward. From B9 and B10 it follows that no soul is more or less ordered than any other (e4–5; B11), and hence by B5 and B11 that no soul is better or worse than any other (e7–94a10; B12). It is agreed (94a12–b3) that this conclusion is absurd, and hence one of the premises from which it is derived must be false; obviously, the premise to be rejected is the assumption that the soul is a *harmonia*.

It appears, therefore, that we have in argument *B* a single argument that is, despite some obscurities, clear in its main lines and (perhaps not so clearly) fallacious. The flaw is not simply the fallacious equivalence of B3 and B7, since one might patch this up by introducing B7 as a premise; it is perfectly plausible to suggest that, where F is a predicate saying what kind of thing its subject is, if A and B are both Fs, A can't be more (of) an F than B. That emendation still leaves a fallacious argument, though the text leaves room for more than one account of the fallacy.

One possibility is the following. The argument is invalid through Plato's failure to recognize that ". . . is a *harmonia* (ordering)" and ". . . is ordered" are incomplete predicates, requiring to be completed as ". . . is an ordering of elements of type E" (hereafter ". . . is an E-ordering") and ". . . is ordered with respect to elements of type E" (hereafter ". . . is E-ordered"). The distinction is crucial, since one and the same thing may consist of elements of two types E and E', such that that thing is an ordering of elements of type E, while it neither is an ordering of elements of type E' nor is characterized by order in respect of elements of that type. Imagine a university composed of independent multi-disciplinary colleges, which also has a faculty structure crossing collegiate boundaries. Imagine further that, while the relations of the faculties to one another and to the university are fully organized, intercollegiate relations and relations between the university and the colleges are anarchic. (Readers familiar with the Universities of Oxford and Cambridge will note elements both of verisimilitude and of exaggeration.) The questions "Is the university an organization?" (I treat the term *organization* as interchangeable for the purpose of this illustration with *ordering*) and "Is the university organized?" (= "ordered") have no determinate answers. It is an organization of faculties, but (despite being composed of colleges) it is not an organization of colleges, nor is it organized in respect of the colleges. The situation of the soul, on the assumptions of the *harmonia* theory, is parallel. It is *ex hypothesi* an ordering of the bodily elements (allowing for the ambiguity of that thesis as discussed above). In virtue of that relation of bodily elements the soul consists of psychic elements, desires, intellect, etc., which may themselves be organized in a coherent way (the state of a good soul), or may lack organization (the state of a bad soul). No soul, good or bad, is more an ordering of bodily elements than any other, for an ordering of bodily elements is just what a soul is. But orderings of bodily elements may be more or less ordered in respect of psychic components.

The various steps of the argument have now to be rephrased in terms of the complete predicates ". . . is an E-ordering" etc. The crucial changes are as follows:

for B2 substitute B2'—Any E-ordering that is more E-ordered is more of

an E-ordering, and any that is less E-ordered is less of an E-ordering;
for B5 substitute B5′—A good soul is ps-ordered (possesses psychic order), a bad soul is ps-disordered (lacks psychic order);
for B6 substitute B6′—The soul is a ph-ordering (i.e., an ordering of physical elements);
for B7 substitute B7′—No E-ordering is more an E-ordering than any other;
for B8 substitute B8′—That which is neither more nor less an E-ordering is neither more nor less E-ordered;
for B9 substitute B9′—That which is neither more or less E-ordered has neither more nor less E-order.

It is now clear that the argument fails to lead to a *reductio*. From B6′, 7′, and 8′ we derive B10′: "No soul is more or less ph-ordered than any other". And from B9′ and B10′ we derive B11′: "No soul has more or less ph-order than any other". But from B5′ and B11′ it is impossible to derive B12. For by B5′ bad souls possess less ps-order than good souls, while by B11′ all souls have equal amounts of ph-order. B12 does not follow, and hence there is no contradiction with B4 and no *reductio*. It is, then, not inconsistent to maintain that an entity that arises from the organization of bodily elements may itself contain parts or elements of another sort that lack organization, or alternatively that a certain organizational state of bodily elements (i.e., the state of being ensouled) may be in a particular case further characterizable as a state of psychic disorganization.

An alternative diagnosis of the fallacy is provided by Gallop, *Plato, Phaedo*, pp. 163–66. On this view the flaw is not the failure to supply different completions for an incomplete predicate at different stages of the argument but rather a failure to observe an ambiguity in the term *harmonia* between "tuning" or "order" ("attunement$_1$" in Gallop's terminology) and "correct tuning" or "good order" ("attunement$_2$"). While every attunement$_1$ is equally an attunement$_1$ different attunements$_1$ may be characterized by attunement$_2$ to different extents. (Essentially the same point is made by pointing out that the sentence "A is more ordered than B" is ambiguous between "A is more of an ordering than B" and "A is better ordered than B.") Hence B12, "No soul is better or worse than any other," does not follow from B11: "No soul has more or less order than any other". For the predicate in B12 is an instance of ". . . is characterized by attunement$_2$" whereas that in B11 is ". . . is characterized by attunement$_1$." As far as I can see, this suggestion fits the text as closely as that given above. Since Plato is arguing from the premise that all souls share equally in the ordering of physical elements to the (absurd) conclusion that all share equally in the good ordering of psychic elements, it is not surprising that the text should leave it open whether the failure of the argument turns on the slip from "ph-order" to "*ps*-order" (my suggestion) or on that from "order" to "correct order" (Gallop's suggestion). Either is sufficient to generate a fallacy, while the text allows for both.

Argument *A* is resumed immediately. It is agreed that in a sensible man the soul controls and opposes bodily inclinations such as hunger and thirst (94b4–c1; A5). Socrates now (c3–e6) recalls steps A3 and A4, to the effect that a *harmonia* can never control or be opposed to its elements. Hence (94e8–95a2) the soul cannot be a *harmonia*. This concludes the discussion of the thesis.

In this case it is clear that the crucial slip is that from *ph*-order to *ps*-order. (This may be some small reason for preferring that account of the fallacy in argument *B*.) If the *harmonia* thesis is to be refuted by this argument, the soul's control of bodily inclinations must be a case of what is denied by A3, viz., the soul's controlling its elements. But according to the thesis, the elements of which the soul is a *harmonia* are not any sort of inclinations but bodily elements, the hot, the cold, the wet, the dry, etc. On Simmias' statement of the thesis the activity of the soul is determined by the interrelations of those elements, so that, for instance, a certain mixture of hot and cold will produce anger in the soul, or a certain proportion of dry to wet the desire for a drink. But in argument *A* Socrates treats such events as being angry or wanting a drink as themselves impulses of the physical elements of which the soul is *ex hypothesi* a *harmonia,* and insists on the incompatibility of A3 and A4 with the view that *the soul* opposes these impulses, in the sense that *the reason* often opposes such desires. Clearly, there is no inconsistency. All that a defender of the *harmonia* thesis need say is that in the case of such a conflict of reason and desire we see, not the soul-*harmonia* opposing and controlling its elements, but rather one part of the soul-*harmonia* opposing and controlling another. And he might add that of course the controlling part is as determined as the controlled part by some disposition of bodily elements. In effect this would be to replace the soul-body dualism of the *Phaedo* with an account akin to that of the divided soul in the *Republic* and *Phaedrus*, with the addition of a thesis of physicalistic determinism of the functioning of all parts of the soul.

Plato's intention in arguing against the *harmonia* thesis is no doubt partly to resist this determinism, in support for the insistence on the autonomy of the rational soul that pervades the *Phaedo*. Yet our discussion of argument *B* has shown that it is hard to disentangle arguments against the thesis that the soul is a *harmonia* of physical elements from the thesis that it is a *harmonia* of elements of any kind. (Gallop's analysis of the fallacy is independent of the nature of the elements.) Yet the development of Plato's thought requires that he should at some stage have made that distinction, since there seems to be a perfectly good sense in which the tripartite soul of the *Republic* and *Phaedrus* may be called a *harmonia*, in that it is a composite entity composed of parts whose relations affect its functioning as a whole. Perhaps argument *B* of the *Phaedo* discussion was directed specifically against the account of the soul as a *physical harmonia*, and was not intended to apply to any other sort. (This would count against Gallop's interpretation.) Alternatively, assuming Gallop to be right, Plato had spotted the fallacy by the time he developed the theory of the tripartite soul and saw that that theory was safe against the arguments of the *Phaedo*. It is, however, necessary to attribute extraordinary obtuseness to Plato if one accepts, with Hicken and others, that the arguments of the *Phaedo are* conclusive against the thesis. For if those arguments are sound, they refute the theory of the tripartite soul, in which case the whole political organization of the *Republic* is based on a psychological theory that Plato had already (assuming the priority of the *Phaedo*) refuted.

APPENDIX

Analysis of the arguments

92e4–93a2	A1	The properties of an ordering are determined by those of its elements.	P(remiss)
a4–5	A2	The activities and passivities of an ordering are determined by those of its elements.	from A1
a6–7	A3	An ordering cannot control its elements but must be controlled by them.	from A2
a8–9	A4	An ordering cannot be affected or behave in any way opposed to (the behavior of) its elements.	from A2
a11–12	B1	Any ordering that is ordered *F*-ly is an *F* ordering.	P
a14–b2	B2	Any ordering that is more ordered is more of an ordering, and any that is less ordered is less of an ordering.	from B1
b4–6	B3	No soul is more or less of a soul than any other.	P
b8–c2	B4	There are some good souls and some bad.	P
c3–10	B5	A good soul is ordered (possesses order); a bad soul is disordered (lacks order).	P
(understood)	B6	The soul is an ordering.	P
d1–5	B7	No ordering is more of an ordering than any other	from B3, B6 (invalid)
d6–8	B8	That which is neither more nor less an ordering is neither more nor less ordered.	from B2
d9–11	B9	That which is neither more nor less ordered has neither more nor less order.	P
d12–e2	B10	No soul is more nor less ordered than any other.	from B6, B7, B8

e4–5	B11	No soul has more nor less order than any other.	from B9, B10
e7–94a10	B12	No soul is better or worse than any other.	from B5, B11
a12–b3	Concl.	Since B12 contradicts B4, B6 is false.	from B4, B6, B12 (RAA)
b4–c1	A5	The soul controls and opposes bodily desires.	P
(understood)	A6	An ordering opposes and controls its elements.	from B6, A5
c3–e6	A7	A6 contradicts A3 and A4	from A4, A4, A6
e8–95a2	Concl.	B6 is false.	From B6, A7 (RAA)

NOTES

[1] An earlier version of this paper was written in 1970 and delivered (in the author's absence) at the meeting of the eastern division of the American Philosophical Association in December of that year (see *Journal of Philosophy* lxvii (1970):724). It is that version which is mentioned by David Gallop, *Plato, Phaedo* (Oxford, 1975), p. 157. In preparing this revision I have profited not only from Gallop's valuable discussion but also from the comments of Gareth Matthews on the 1970 version of the paper.

[2] Lucretius discusses the thesis that the "sensus animi" is a *harmonia* at III.98–135, attributing it merely to "(the) Greeks."

[3] For a fuller discussion (leading to similar conclusions) see Gottschalk, "Soul as Harmonia."

[4] The grounds for rejecting Philoponus' analysis, which is followed, not without incoherence, by R. D. Archer-Hind, *The Phaedo of Plato* (London, 1883); and R. Hackforth, *Plato's Phaedo* (Cambridge, England, 1955), are cogently stated by W. F. Hicken, "*Phaedo* 93a11–94b3," *Classical Quarterly* xlviii (1954):17–18, and by D. Gallop, *Plato, Phaedo*, pp. 160–61.

[5] See appendix.

[6] The verb translated "order" (*harmozein*) may equally properly be rendered "attune," "arrange" or "organize." I shall adhere to "order" throughout.

GERASIMOS SANTAS

The Form of the Good
in Plato's *Republic*[1]

"Looking into the orb of light he [Plato] sees nothing, but he is warmed and elevated."

JOWETT

No writer has made loftier claims for the concept of goodness than Plato makes for the Form of the Good in the middle books of the *Republic*. We are told that without knowledge of the Form of the Good we cannot know that anything else is good, and that without knowledge of this Form all other knowledge would be of no benefit to us (505–06). Further, the Form of the Good is "the cause" of truth and knowledge. Further yet, the objects of knowledge receive "their being and essence" from the Form of the Good, though it is not essence "but still transcends essence in dignity and surpassing power" (509 AB). As if these intriguing views were not paradoxical enough, Plato has Socrates suggest that even the foundations of mathematics are insecure unless we have knowledge of the Good: the beginnings of geometry and arithmetic are "hypotheses," not known until the soul can "ascend" from them to the Form of the Good and "descend" back from it to them (509B–511V).

These dark sayings are not incidental to Plato's philosophy. On the contrary they are the centerpiece of canonical Platonism, Plato's ethics, epistemology, and metaphysics of the middle period. The Form of the Good is given the privileged position: it is prior, ethically, epistemologically, and ontologically to everything else in Plato's universe. In the *Republic* the theory of the Form of the Good represents Plato's attempt to base his ethics and politics on the theory of Forms. Probably a case can also be made that the theory is presupposed in the teleological explanation of the *Phaedo* (97–99),

This paper was presented to the 1977 Washington meeting of the Society for Ancient Greek Philosophy and published in *Philosophical Inquiry* (winter 1980):374–403; we thank the editor for permission to reprint.

Gerasimos Santas is Professor of Philosophy at the University of California at Irvine.

the "creation" of the physical universe in the *Timaeus* (29–33), and even the theory of love in the *Symposium*.

Why did Plato assign such a supreme position to the Form of the Good? What conception of goodness did he have, which allowed him to think of the Form of the Good not only as the final cause of everything that we do, but also as "the cause" of the knowability and even of the very being of his favorite entities, the Forms? And what connection did he see between the Form of the Good and mathematics?

As might well be expected, a considerable body of literature has been built around the relevant passages.[2] Yet, it is no hyperbole to say that we have no satisfactory or widely accepted answers to our questions.[3] In this paper I propose to re-examine closely what Plato actually says with the hope of making some progress. I think it can be shown that what Plato says about the Form of the Good is intelligible and coherent and coheres well with what is now known about his metaphysics, epistemology, and ethics of the middle period. So far as I know, the interpretation I propose has never been put forward by anyone, but it relies heavily on some of the excellent discussions about Plato's metaphysics, which have appeared in the last quarter century, especially the discussions on self-predication and the distinction between the ideal and proper attributes of Forms.[4]

I divide Plato's discussion about the Good into three rounds, or (as they may well be called) three waves of paradox, and discuss each in turn. My first object is to state, on the basis of the texts, the main propositions that constitute Plato's theory of the Form of the Good. This is completed by the middle of the second round. I then discuss the distinction between proper and ideal attributes of the Forms, which the theory seems to presuppose, the assumption of self-predication that goes with it, and some of the difficulties and implications of the theory.

I   The First Round: Ethics, Politics, and the Form of the Good

Plato's discussion of the Form of the Good occurs in a section of Book VI which is concerned with the education of the rulers (500 ff.). We are told that it is not sufficient for the rulers to learn what justice, temperance, courage, and wisdom are, according to the definitions established in Book IV. These definitions do not provide a sufficient and exact understanding of these virtues. There is something greater than these virtues, and there is a "longer way" to understanding these things, a way that culminates in "the greatest study":

G1   The greatest study is the study of the Form of the Good, by participation in which just things and all the rest become useful and beneficial. (505A)

G2   If we do not know the Form of the Good, then even if without such
     knowledge we know everything else, it (the knowledge of everything
     else) would be of no benefit to us, just as no possession would be (of
     benefit) without possession of the Good. (505AB)

G3   If we know all things without knowing the Good, (this would be of
     no benefit because) we would not know (that) anything (is) beautiful
     and good. (505B)

Next, Plato rejects two hypotheses concerning the nature of the Good: (a)
The Good is knowledge, and (b) the Good is pleasure. The first hypothesis
is rejected on the ground that those who hold it are unable to answer the
question "Knowledge of what?" except by saying "Knowledge of the
Good," thus ending up with the circular and uninformative definition that
the Good is knowledge of the Good. The second hypothesis is rejected on
the ground that those who hold it admit that there are bad pleasures, and are
thus compelled to admit that the same things (bad pleasures) are both good
and bad (presumably a contradiction). Thus:

G4   The Good is not (identical with) knowledge or pleasure. (505BCD)

Plato concludes this round by asserting two propositions about good things
and the Good and by emphasizing the importance of knowledge of the Good
for the rulers:

G5   Many people prefer what appears to be just and honorable but is not,
     but no one prefers to pursue or possess what appears good but is not.
     (505DE)[5]

G6   The Good every soul pursues and does everything for its sake, divin-
     ing what it is and yet baffled and not having an adequate apprehen-
     sion of its nature nor a stable opinion about it as it has about other
     things, and because of this failing to have any benefit from other
     things. (505E)

G7   Our constitution will not be perfectly ordered unless the rulers know
     how just and honorable things are good and they will not know this
     unless they know the Good. (506AB)

This round is the least paradoxical of the three and the easiest to understand in the general setting of Plato's theory of Forms and his ethics. The
main metaphysical and epistemological assertions that Plato makes here
about the Form of the Good are simply instances of his general metaphysics
and epistemology. Thus the second part of G1 is simply an instance of a
general proposition that Plato holds, namely:

F1   It is by virtue of participation in the Form F-ness or the F that any-
     thing which is F is F.[6]

And G3 is an instance of the general epistemological proposition that goes together with the theory of Forms, namely:

F2 If we do not know F-ness or the F, we do not know that anything is F.[7]

Thus G3 and the second part of G1 do not assign to the Form of the Good any privileged position over other Forms. On the other hand, the first part of G1 (and perhaps G2 and G7) does assign to the *study* of the Good a privileged position over all other studies and to the knowledge of the Good over all other knowledge. But this privileged position, so far, can be accounted for and understood by reference to G6, another standard Socratic and Platonic ethical view. If all our actions, pursuits, and undertaking are for the sake of the Good, then knowledge of the Good would indeed seem to be the most important knowledge we can have: for without it we would never know that anything for the sake of which we did anything else was good (by G3). We would be like archers who lived for the sake of hitting their targets but could never see them clearly and, what is worse, could never know whether what they hit were their targets! Can we imagine anything more frustrating or less satisfying? Had Plato's assertions about the Good stopped here, his position would have been only mildly paradoxical and not all that different from Aristotle's; and the paradox and the difference would derive from his application of F1 and F2 to the case of goodness. We might say that the conjunction of G1, G3, and G6 assigns an ethical or practical priority to the study of the Good, and this priority might well have been thought sufficient for the paradox of the Philosopher-King.

II The Second Round: the Epistemological and Ontological Priority of the Good

The second round is a wave of paradox indeed: Plato seems to assign to the Form of the Good an ontological and epistemological priority over all other Forms. The round (506B–509C) begins when Socrates is challenged to say what the Form of the Good is, if it is not knowledge or pleasure. Socrates implies that he does not know what the Form of the Good is, and when asked to give at least his opinion he proposes to let go for the moment the question about the nature of the Good and to speak of "the offspring of the Good which is most like it." He now prepares the ground for the simile of the Sun by first making the usual Platonic distinction between good things, and beautiful things, objects of vision but not thought, on the one hand, and the Good itself and the Beautiful itself, objects of thought but not vision, on the other. In the case of vision and visible things a man may have the power of vision and a thing may be visible but there may be no actual vision (seeing) if a third element is not present, namely, light which is provided by the chief of the heavenly divinities, the Sun, "whose light makes the faculty of sight see best and visible things to be seen." (508A) Socrates now states and elaborates the simile as follows:

G8 As the Good is in the intelligible region to reason and to the objects of reason, so is the Sun in the visible world to vision and the objects of vision. (508C)

G9 The Sun (by its light) gives the objects of sight their visibility and the faculty of sight its vision; similarly, the Form of the Good gives the objects of reason their truth and to reason its knowledge of them. (508B, 508DE)

G10 The Sun is the cause of light and vision, and light and vision are sunlike but not identical with the Sun; similarly, the Form of the Good is the cause of truth and knowledge, and truth and knowledge are like the Form of the Good but they are not identical with it. (509A)

G11 The Sun not only furnishes the visibles the power of visibility but also provides for their generation and growth and nurture, though it is not itself generation; similarly, the objects of knowledge receive not only their being known from the presence of the Good, but also their being and essence (reality) comes from it, though the Good is not essence but still transcends essence in dignity and surpassing power. (509B, Shorey trans.)

In Shorey's translation, Plato's next two lines read: "And Glaucon very ludicrously said, 'Heaven save us, hyperbole can no further go.'"

As Socrates' reluctance and Glaucon's response indicate, the second round is far more difficult to understand and interpret than the first. Let us start by distinguishing sharply between the two rounds. The first round deals with relations between the Form of the Good and anything that is good, whether a Form or a sensible thing. But the second round deals with relations between the Form of the Good and Forms *only*: between the Form of the Good and objects of knowledge or thought, i.e., Forms. Thus it is reasonable to suppose that it is the attributes of the Forms *qua* Forms or their *ideal* attributes that is being explained or accounted for by reference to the Form of the Good; not their *proper* attributes, i.e., the attributes that each Form has by virtue of being the particular Form it is.[8] This is an important clue in understanding the second round and we shall return to it shortly. The second difference is that while the first round assigns an ethical and practical priority to the study of the Form of the Good over every other study, the second round assigns ontological and epistemological priorities to the Form of the Good over every other Form. And it is precisely these latter priorities that have to be understood.

Essentially, the second round contains three distinct but related assertions: (1) the Form of the Good is "the cause" of the knowability of the Forms; (2) the Form of the Good is "the cause" of reason's actually knowing the Forms; and (3) the Form of the Good is "the cause" of "the being and essence [reality]" of the Forms.[9] Let us consider (1) and (3) together. We have a chance, I think, to understand these two assertions if we can answer the following three questions: Q1—What constitutes the being and essence of the Forms? Q2—What is the relation between the being and essence of the Forms and their knowability? Q3—Given an answer to Q1, how can we understand the Form of the Good so as to make sense of Plato's view that it is "the cause," in some appropriate Platonic sense of "cause," of the being and essence of the Forms?

The context of the second round, the distinction between ideal and proper attributes, and Professor Vlastos' recent studies of Plato's doctrine of degrees of reality[10] make it possible, I think, to give a fairly confident answer to our first question (Q1). In a series of passages in the middle dialogues Plato contrasts Forms with the sensibles that participate in them; in these contrasts, systematically studied by Vlastos, Plato brings into relief a number of attributes which Forms have but which the sensibles that participate in them do not have. These attributes—which we may provisionally call ideal attributes of the Forms—constitute the being and essence of the Forms. Moreover—to skip for a moment to our second question (Q2)—it is precisely these attributes that make possible the knowability of the Forms or the Forms' being "cognitively reliable," in Vlastos' phrase; so that if we can understand how the Form of the Good is "the cause" of the ideal attributes, we will also be able to understand how it is "the cause" of the Forms' knowability. Let us look briefly at these contrasts.

In the *Symposium* 211AB Plato says that unlike the many beautiful sensible things that participate in it, Beauty itself always exists, it is neither generated nor destroyed, it does not increase or decrease, and it exists by itself. This is one set of Ideal attributes—"I1" for short. In addition, he says that in contrast to sensible beautiful things, Beauty itself is not beautiful in one respect and ugly in another, nor beautiful at one time and not at another nor beautiful in comparison to one thing and ugly in comparison to another nor beautiful here and ugly there being beautiful for some and ugly for others. Let us call the set of attributes of Beauty implied by this statement "I2".[11] Now in the *Republic* Plato tells us several times (477A, 478D, 478E, 479A–C) that the objects of knowledge, the Forms, "are" whereas the objects of belief, the sensibles that participate in Forms, "both are and

237

are not." Professor Vlastos has argued convincingly, I think, that it is not existence that is here being asserted of the Forms and both asserted and denied of sensibles, but rather perfection or complete reality; and this in turn is to be interpreted in terms of the Ideal attributes (I1 and I2) listed in the *Symposium*.[12] On this view, to say, e.g., that the Form Circle "is" whereas a sensible circle "is and is not," is to say that the Form Circle is circular in all respects, is always circular, is circular no matter compared to what, and is circular to all who apprehend it no matter from where; whereas a sensible circle is not circular in all respects, not always circular, and so on. As Vlastos points out, Plato himself expands the "is and is not" formula in some of these ways at 479AC for the case of beautiful things, just things, and so on. In all these contrasts Plato surely intends to bring into relief "the being and reality" of the Forms, and he does this in terms of I1 and I2. Moreover, in *Republic* Bk. V, sensibles are said to be unknowable and only objects of belief precisely because they lack the ideal attributes of the Forms;[13] and this supports our answer to the second question, Q2, that it is the ideal attributes of the Forms that make possible the knowability of the Forms. In sum, and in answers to Q1 and Q2, the being and essence of the Forms consists in their ideal attributes (I1 and I2), and an object must have these to be knowable.

Let us now go to our third and more difficult question (Q3), assuming the answers we gave to Q1 and Q2. Let us first tackle part of Q3: in what sense of "cause" can we plausibly suppose that the Form of the Good is the cause of the ideal attributes (being and essence) of the Forms? In the case of the Sun and sensible things, the Sun is presumably the (an) efficient cause of their generation and growth as well as their visibility. But there is no generation and growth and nurture in the case of the Forms, nor are the Forms probably ever conceived by Plato as efficient causes.[14] In all probability formal causation is meant via the relation of participation.[15] If so, then the Form of the Good is the cause of the ideal attributes of the other Forms in the sense that: G11.1 It is by virtue of participating in the Form of the Good that all the other Forms have ideal attributes. This is our interpretation of the relevant part of G11.

We are now within sight of an answer to the more difficult part of Q3, the part concerning the nature of the Form of the Good. For it seems to follow[16] from G11.1 and the distinction between ideal and proper attributes that:

G12 The ideal attributes of all the Forms other than the Form of the Good are proper attributes of the Form of the Good.

A host of questions now faces us. I will list and discuss them in an order that might help us answer them. Q4—Why should Plato think that the Form of the Good, rather than some other Form or no Form at all, is the formal cause of the ideal attributes of all the other Forms? Q5—Did Plato conflate reality and goodness, as the joining of the present interpretation with Vlastos' interpretation of the doctrine of degrees of reality would seem to imply? Q6—What is the distinction between ideal and proper attributes, and did Plato make it or at least observe it so that we are justified in attributing G12 to him partly on the basis of it? Q7—How is the goodness of sensible things to be accounted for on the present interpretation? These are large and difficult questions and I can only hope to indicate in outline what I think are the right answers.

We can begin to see a connection between goodness and the ideal attributes of the Forms if we assume *one* of Plato's standard ways of conceiving the Forms in the middle dialogues, that is, not as properties but as ideal exemplars complete with non-Pauline self-predication.[17] On this assumption, each Form is the best object of its kind there is or can be. The Form Circle, for example, is the best circle there is or can be, the Form Justice the best (most) just thing there is or can be. Now Plato thinks, I believe, that it is by virtue of its ideal attributes that each Form (other than the Form of the Good) is the best object of its kind. Let us take the examples of Circle and Justice, a mathematical and an ethical Form, and try to see this connection with each of the four ideal attributes I2. It is the ideal attribute of being circular in every respect or part of itself that makes the Form Circle a perfect circle or the best circle there is or can be; it is precisely the lack of this attribute that makes sensible circles imperfect circles, "in contact with the straight everywhere."[18] Again, the ideal attribute of being circular no matter compared to what assures us that there is no circle relative to which the Form Circle is not or is less circular. On the other hand, it is more difficult, as Keyt has noted,[19] to see a connection between being always circular and the superlative goodness of kind of the Form Circle. Actually, there are connections here and there from which Plato may have over-generalized: for example, we count durability or high degree of resistance to change as a good-making characteristic in the case of such artifacts as knives, shields, and cars. Plato himself makes a similar connection in *Republic* 380D–381B, where he argues that the better a state or condition a thing is in the less liable it is to change. And in the case of some ethical concepts such as justice the connection seems very plausible: a man who is always just is more of a just man than one who is just in some temporal stretches and not others, other things being equal. But probably, given Plato's assumption that only what is invariable can be known, the best connection we can make between the ideal attribute of, say, being always circular and the superlative goodness of kind of the Form Circle is between the attributes and the epistemic value of the Form: this attribute contributes to the Form Circle's being the epistemic paradigm of its kind, the best object of its kind to know. And the same seems to be true of the fourth ideal attribute, being circular to all who apprehend it no matter from where. It seems then that the first two ideal attributes of the Form Circle contribute to its being the best circle there is or can be, and the remaining two attributes contribute to its being the best circle to know. And presumably similarly for the other Forms other than the Form of the Good. If so, we can add another proposition to Plato's theory of the Form of the Good:

> G13 It is by virtue of their ideal attributes that the Forms (other than the Form of the Good) are the best objects of their kind (or, have superlative goodness of kind.)

And from G11.1 and G13, it seems that we can derive the proposition:

> G14 It is by virtue of participating in the Form of the Good that all the other Forms are the best objects of their kind and the best objects of their kind to know.

Thus the Form of the Good is, as it should be, the formal cause of the superlative goodness of kind of all the other Forms. We can see, perhaps in a short-circuit way, that this proposition is on the right track, from a Platonic point of view, on the assumption that the Forms (other than the Good) are ideal exemplars: for on this assumption the Forms have something in common, namely, their being the best objects of their kind; so it is natural that there should be a Form in virtue of which they have this in common, and in view of what this common feature is, it is natural that the Form would be the Good.

But now, having seen how it is appropriate for the Good to be the formal cause of the superlative goodness of kind of the Forms, we are faced with the question of how it is that it is also appropriate for the Good to be the formal cause of the superlative reality of kind of the Forms. For on Vlastos' interpretation of the doctrine of degrees of reality it is by virtue of (what we have called) their ideal attributes that the Forms are the most real objects of their kind. And from this and G11.1 it seems that we can derive the proposition:

> G15 It is by virtue of participation in the Form of the Good that all the other Forms are the most real objects of their kind.

The answer to our question is, I believe, that here we do have a conflation of superlative reality and superlative goodness of kind. For it is by virtue of the very same ideal attributes, it seems, that a Form is both the best object of its kind and the most real object of the same kind. Thus the superlative goodness of a given kind and the superlative reality of the same kind coincide, not only in the sense that the best and most real object of a given kind are one and the same, i.e., the Form of that kind, but also in the stronger sense that it is the very same ideal attributes of a Form that constitute both its superlative reality and its superlative goodness of kind. But here we must be careful when we speak of "conflation": Vlastos has argued successfully, I believe, that Plato distinguishes between reality and existence, and thus the above conflation does not by itself imply a confusion of existence and goodness. It is by means of this distinction, between reality and goodness on the one hand and existence on the other, that the theory would attempt to escape a Humean objection that one cannot validly derive "ought" (value) from "is" (fact) alone.[20]

III   Ideal and Proper Attributes

To make further progress we need to go to Q6, the question concerning the distinction between ideal and proper attributes. This distinction is crucial to our interpretation for a number of reasons, two of which are as follows: first, we answered the question concerning "the being and essence" of the Forms in terms of the ideal attributes of the Forms, which of course presupposes the distinction; second, we attributed to Plato G12 partly on the basis of this distinction, and G12 itself is slated in terms of the distinction, so that we can hardly understand what G12 tells us about the Form of the Good unless we understand the distinction. Moreover, one would think that, as Keyt has pointed out,[21] the distinction seems a necessary one for a logical realist like Plato to draw or observe; or at any rate a useful one to draw or observe, if he could,[22] since e.g., it would enable him to disarm the two-level paradoxes often hurled by Aristotle against the theory of Forms.[23]

The distinction has been recently discussed by Owen, Keyt, and Vlastos, though the terms "ideal" and "proper" are used only by Keyt.[24] All three writers find the source of the distinction in Aristotle, especially *Topics* 137b3–13, but it is not clear that they conceive the distinction exactly in the same way, and they disagree whether Plato or the Academy ever drew or observed or could have drawn the distinction (as well as to whether Aristotle ever concedes it to the Platonists). Let us first take a brief look at the ways they draw it. Owen writes:

> Given any Platonic Idea, at least two and possibly three very different sorts
> of things can be said about it. (A) Certain things will be true of it in virtue
> of its status as an Idea, e.g., that it is immutable. These predicates (call
> them 'A-predicates') will be true of any Idea whatever. (B) Certain things
> will be true of it in virtue of the particular, concept it represents; these (call
> them 'B-predicates') are sometimes held to fall into two radically different
> groups. (B1) . . . (B2) Other predicates belong to the idea because . . .

they are simply accepted as serving to define the particular concept in question. Man, for instance is two-footed and an animal. ("Dialectic and Eristic," p. 108; cf. also pp. 119–20).

We are not interested here in B1-predicates, but only in the distinction between A-predicates, corresponding to Keyt's ideal attributes, and B2-predicates, Keyt's proper attributes. Vlastos introduces the distinction in Aristotle's terms:

> . . . sentences of the form "the Idea of F is P" . . . are analyzed by Aristotle as true if P is predicated of "the Idea *qua* Idea" and false if predicated of it "*qua* F" as, e.g., "The Idea of Man is resting," whose ambiguity is resolved by the observation that "resting belongs to Man-himself not *qua* man, but *qua* Idea. (Here Vlastos quotes *Topics* 137b6–7. *Platonic Studies*, p. 323).

Presumably, the predicates that belong to the Idea Man *qua* Idea correspond to Owen's A-predicates and Keyt's ideal attributes; those that belong to the Idea Man *qua* man to their B-2 predicates and proper attributes. Finally, Keyt discusses the same *Topics* text, introduces and defines "ideal" and "proper" as follows:

> Aristotle here distinguishes two respects in which a Form may possess an attribute. The attribute of rest belongs to the Idea of man as Idea; on the other hand, the attribute of being composed of soul and body belongs to the Idea of living creature as living creature. An attribute that belongs to an Idea as Idea I shall call an "ideal" attribute. An ideal attribute is one whose absence from a thing entails that the thing is not a Platonic Idea. This is my definition, not Aristotle's; but I hope it marks out the class of attributes he has in mind. . . .

> The second respect in which a Form may possess an attribute enters into Aristotle's characterization of a proprium; what is allegedly a proprium of such and such is really a proprium if and only if (1) it is an attribute of the Form of such and such, and (2) it belongs to the Form because the Form is such and such. Thus being composed of soul and body is a proprium of living creature since it is an attribute of the Form of living creature and an attribute because the Form is a living creature (b11–13); but rest is not a proprium of man since, although an attribute of the Form of man, it is not an attribute because the Form is a man.

Noting that Aristotle here has characterized a proprium in a broader fashion than usual, Keyt introduces his notion of a proper attribute:

> Taking my lead from Aristotle's temporary, broad characterization of a propium, I shall call an attribute that belongs to a Form in this second respect a "proper" attribute. I use 'proper' here in the sense in which it

means 'peculiar' and is opposed to 'common'. Again, I suggest a definition that I hope captures the class of attributes Aristotle has in mind: a *proper* attribute of a given Form is one whose absence from a thing entails that the thing is not an instance of the given Form. Thus animal is a proper attribute of the Form of man; for if a thing is not an animal it cannot be a man. ("Plato's Paradox," pp. 12, 13).

The first question that arises is whether the distinction between proper and ideal attributes of Forms is compatible with the ontology of Plato's theory of Forms. Vlastos seems to argue that it is not. If he is right, it can hardly be a good idea to expound Plato's theory of the Form of the Good using this distinction, as I have done. We can use a distinction an author does not explicitly make to expound and illuminate his theory, provided the distinction is compatible with the theory; Vlastos himself did so in his illuminating paper, "An Ambiguity in the *Sophist*." But if the distinction is not compatible, we will probably end up distorting the theory. Is Vlastos then right? Well, I think he is and he isn't. The issue turns on two points: (1) whether we conceive of the Forms as ideal exemplars complete with non-Pauline self-predication, or as properties that are not self-predicational; and, perhaps, (2) on how we construe sentences of the form "*P* belongs to the Form *F qua F*." Vlastos is right, I think, if we conceive of the Forms as (transcendent) properties that are not non-Pauline self-predicational; and he is right in the sense that, under this conception, the distinction would not apply to the Forms at all. For, so far as I can see, if the Forms are not non-Pauline self-predicational, they would have no proper attributes at all and the distinction would be at the very least idle as applied to the Forms; and Vlastos would be right in arguing, as he does (*Platonic Studies*, p. 332), that while the expression "the Idea of Animal *qua* Idea" would have a referent, namely the Form Animal, the expression "the Idea of Animal *qua* Animal" could or would have none (for indeed the latter expression implies that the Idea of Animal is an animal). On the other hand, if the Forms are conceived as ideal exemplars with non-Pauline self-predication, the distinction is perfectly compatible with the theory of Forms and applies to Forms; under this conception, the referent of the above two expressions would be one and the same, the Form Animal. To go to point (2), the function of the word translated "*qua*" in the present context is, I think, simply to indicate the inferential basis on which the attribute is asserted of the subject. Though we need a systematic study of Aristotle's uses of this important little word (he puts it to many important uses, and the notion is crucial to some later philosophers, such as Spinoza), I believe that in its present use it is the descendant, so to speak, of Plato's "in virtue of" and can plausibly be rendered by "because," as Owen and Keyt often take it. Thus to say, e.g., that rest belongs to Living Creature *qua* From is to indicate the inferential basis on which the attribute of rest is asserted of Living Creature itself. The complete inference is: Living Creature itself is a Form; all Forms are at rest; therefore, Living Creature itself is at rest. Similarly, to say that being composed of body and soul belongs to Living Creature itself *qua* living creature is to indicate the inferential basis on which the attribute is asserted of the subject. The complete inference is: Living creature itself is a living creature; all living creatures are composed of body and soul; therefore, Living Creature itself is composed of body and soul. Here non-Pauline self-predication is explicitly stated on the complete inference, and is implicit in the expression "*qua* living creature." This construction of "*qua*," essentially as "because," begins to disarm, I think, the other objection that Vlastos has to applying the distinction to Forms. He cites *Symposium* 211A, where Plato denies that the Form Beauty "is beautiful in one way, ugly in another," and says that "the Aristotelian formula establishes the P-distinction at the price of losing this very feature of the Idea, allowing it to be P and not-P but in different respects, P ῇ F, not-P ῇ ἰδέα τοῦ F." (*Platonic Studies*, p. 331). But on the present interpretation of "*qua*" as "because" I do not think that the objection is sound: to allow that the attribute P belongs to the Form *F qua F* but not to the Form *F qua* Form is not necessarily to allow that the Form *F* is *P* in one respect and not-*P* in another; for on the present interpretation of "*qua*" as "because" the negation sign goes in front of the whole "because" clause, not in front of the attribute sign *P*. What is denied is not that *P* belongs to the Form of *F*, but only that *P* belongs to the Form *F* because it is a Form; and the latter denial is perfectly compatible with *P* belonging to the Form *F*. Thus, Plato can deny that the attribute of being composed of body and soul belongs to the Form Living Creature because it is a Form, without denying that this attribute belongs to this Form. And the *Euthyphro* shows that Plato is capable of making such a point, since there he denies that anything, including Holiness, is holy because it is loved by all the gods while allowing that Holiness is loved by all the gods. In any case, in the *Symposium* passage what Plato is denying is that the Form Beauty can be qualified in any way relative to its proper, self-predicational attributes; i.e., he wants to say that the Form Beauty is beautiful in all respects, always, etc. This point would not be compromised by his allowing that the Form Beauty is beautiful because of the particular Form it is and also that it is at rest (invariant) because it is a Form.

I conclude, then, that the distinction between ideal and proper attributes is perfectly compatible with the ontology of Plato's theory of Forms, provided that we conceive of the Forms as ideal exemplars with self-predication, and provided that we interpret "qua" as "because." Here I must make it explicit that I am not maintaining that Plato always and consistently conceived of the Forms as ideal exemplars with self-predication. I am only maintaining that sometimes he so conceived them, and in particular that he so conceived them in the middle dialogues and in conjunction with his theory of goodness in the *Republic*. We shall presently see that this conception seems indeed essential to his theory of the Form of the Good.

We are now free to take up the question whether Plato ever made explicitly the distinction between proper and ideal attributes—which he never did—or the more interesting question whether he observed the distinction in practice. This question is related to our question Q7, how the goodness of sensible things is to be accounted for on the theory of the Form of the Good as we have interpreted it. Now Keyt has produced striking evidence that Plato actually confused ideal and proper attributes of Forms:

> Although Aristotle, in commenting on the theory of Forms, draws this very distinction, there is striking evidence that Plato himself overlooked it. The evidence, apart from his silence on the matter, consists of some bad mistakes that he would have been unlikely to make if he had seen it. ("The Mad Craftsman of the *Timaeus*," p. 230).

The "bad mistakes" consist of certain inferences that Plato makes in the *Timaeus* from certain Forms, used as models, having certain features to their sensible copies having these features. The general context is familiar. The divine craftsman (the Demiurge), being good and unenvious, wishes to make the sensible world as good as possible; to do this he takes the Forms as his models and fashions the sensible world after the Forms as much as possible. In particular the Demiurge copies the Form of living creature. This Form, Keyt says, "has only one feature that a sane craftsman would copy, having a soul and a body" (a proper attribute of the Form); but "the Demiurge is not content to stop here. He notices that his model is unique, timeless, and generic, and proceeds to copy these attributes" (presumably ideal attributes, p. 232). For the argument from uniqueness, Keyt quotes *Timaeus* 31A2–5 and interprets:

> Plato's argument is this: the cosmos was made according to its model; its model is unique; therefore, the cosmos is unique. If Plato accepts this argument, he should also accept the following one, which in his system has true premises and a false conclusion: the planet Mercury was made according to its model (the Form of heavenly god); its model is unique; therefore, Mercury is the only heavenly god (that is the only celestial body)." (pp. 232–33)

Concerning the inference from the second ideal attribute, Keyt cites 37c6–38c3 and interprets:

> Plato's argument is this: the cosmos resembles its model as closely as it can; its model is timeless, which it cannot be; so the cosmos has a feature

that resembles, although it falls short of, the timelessness of its model (namely, eternal temporal duration). By the same reasoning a circle that is drawn on paper and preserved for a year would resemble the Form of circle more closely than one that is drawn with the same accuracy but immediately erased.

Keyt makes a similar point regarding a similar inference from the attribute of being generic. He also cites *Parmenides* 132c9–11 as containing a similar argument, the argument "that since Forms are thoughts (a hypothesis momentarily proposed by Socrates) and things share in the Forms, each of these things is itself composed of thoughts," and says that this argument is "a paradigm of the fallacy of division." (pp. 234–35). It is because he copies these ideal attributes of the Forms that the Demiurge is "mad." And Vlastos, in his *Plato's Universe*, understandably refers to one of these inferences of Plato's as "a curious error" (p. 29).

We are now in the happy or unhappy position to show that, given our interpretation of the Form of the Good in the *Republic*, Plato "had" to make these "curious errors" and his divine craftsman had to be "mad." For we can show that copying the ideal attributes of the Forms, if one wishes to make sensible things as good as possible, is a direct consequence of the views that the Form of the Good is the formal cause of the being and essence of the Forms and that the being and essence of the Forms consist in their ideal attributes. We are assuming that in the *Timaeus*, when Plato was making these errors, the Forms are still conceived as ideal exemplars—the best objects of their kind—for why else would the Demiurge copy *them* if he wished to make sensible things as good as possible? And the position is happy for our interpretation since it provides evidence for it, but unhappy for Plato if the inferences are the "bad mistakes" Keyt seems to show them to be.

To see why it is that Plato had to make the "curious mistakes" and why his Demiurge had to be "mad," on the interpretation we have given of the Form of the Good, let us go to our question Q7: on this interpretation how is the goodness of sensible things to be accounted for? Let us work with three kinds of examples, a mathematical Form, Circle, a "natural kind" Form, Living Creature, and an ethical Form, Justice. To be a circle or circular a sensible must participate in the Form Circle, and this is participation in the proper attributes of the Form, namely being circular (and perhaps to all those attributes being entailed by this proper attribute, e.g. being a figure). But to be a good circle (to some degree) a sensible, on the interpretation we have given, must participate (to some degree) in the *ideal* attributes of the Form Circle: for, on that interpretation, it is the ideal attributes of the Form Circle that constitute its superlative goodness and it is by virtue of having these ideal attributes that the Form Circle participates in the Form of the Good. Participation only in the proper attributes of the Form Circle (to some degree, if degrees of participation in proper attributes is allowed) would have no tendency to show that the sensible is a good circle (to some degree), for there is not necessarily any connection between the proper attributes of this Form (or the Form Triangle, or Square, or Chiliagon, or Four or Five) and the Form of the Good. But participation (to some degree, and here degrees are appropriate) in the ideal attributes of being circular in every respect, always, no matter compared to what, and to all who apprehend it no matter from where, would show that the participant is a good circle (to some degree, or comparatively), for it is these attributes that make the Form Circle the best circle there is or can be and it is by virtue of having these that it participates in the Form of the Good. And similarly with the goodness of sensible living creatures. Thus, if the Demiurge wished merely to create or fashion a sensible living creature it would be sufficient for him to copy the proper attributes of the Form of living creature, such as being composed of body and soul. But if he wishes to create a sensible living creature that is as good as possible he can *only* do so, given the present interpretation of the Form of the Good of the *Republic*, by copying as much as possible the ideal attributes of the Form. Thus, far from being "mad" for doing so, he would be "mad"—or rather futile—if he didn't! Correspondingly, "the curious mistakes" and the "bad arguments" of Plato should begin to appear less curious and not as bad: for we are now to understand the theory of the Form of the Good in the *Republic* as an implicit premise(s) in these arguments. For example, the argument "from eternity" would be more complicated, roughly perhaps as follows: the Form of Living Creature is the best living creature there is or can be: it is by virtue of being eternal (among other things, or "eternal" standing for a summary of its ideal attributes) that it is the best object of its kind and it is by virtue of this that it participates in the Form of the Good; therefore, if one wishes to fashion a sensible living creature as good as possible one must copy the "eternity" of the Form as much as possible.[25] Of course I am speaking here to the validity of Plato's argument, not its soundness—but this is the point to which Keyt is speaking and certainly part of Vlastos' "curious." The soundness of the argument is quite another matter, for this depends on the truth of the theory that according to me is the theoretical backbone of the argument.[26]

Even a casual glance at the theory reveals several faults or unclarities. One fault lies in the combination of the conception of Forms as self-predicational with the theory of goodness, the theory that the Form of the Good is the formal cause of the ideal attributes of the Forms and that it is by virtue of these that the Forms are the best objects of their kind. Without self-predication this theory of goodness would collapse; for without it the Forms would not be ideal examplars—the best objects of their kind—and so there would be no motivation at all for supposing that the Form of the Good is the

247

formal cause of the being and essence of the Forms.[27] But why is this combination faulty? One fault is that the theory seems to imply all the absurdities of non-Pauline self-predication. To be the best possible shield—the best object of its kind—a thing would have to be both a Form and a shield, an immaterial shield that cannot protect![28] Another difficulty is that it is not clear how this theory of goodness coheres with the *other* theory of goodness we find in *Republic* I, the theory of function and virtue. According to the latter theory, a thing of a given kind is a good thing of that kind in so far as and to the degree to which it performs well the function proper to things of that kind. So we seem to have two criteria of kind or attributive goodness of sensible things: the degree to which a sensible of a kind resembles the ideal attributes of the Form of that kind, and the degree to which that sensible does well the function proper to its kind. How are the two criteria related? Plato uses both, and no doubt he holds that the theory of the Form of the Good is the more fundamental one. If so, the view he probably holds of the relation of the two criteria is that the more a thing of a given kind resembles the ideal attributes of the Form of that kind the better it performs the function proper to things of that kind. (Or, if we like slogans, we might say that for Plato "function always follows form.") So far as I am aware Plato does not give us adequate reasons for believing that this proposition is always true. There is little doubt though that he holds the theory of the Form of the Good to be more fundamental than the functional theory of goodness. His holding this explains well enough his remark in the first round that the definitions of the virtues in Book IV have not been sufficiently established; for these definitions have been constructed on the basis of the functional criterion, and for them to be "sufficiently" established Plato would have to show that they are at least consistent with, or perhaps that they are confirmed by, the theory of the Form of the Good. So far as I am aware, Plato never tries to do this either, though he tells us that the philosophers who have come to know the Good "shall use it as a pattern for the right ordering of the state and the citizens and themselves . . ." (540A).[29] A third unclarity in the theory is that there seems to be a stronger connection between certain ethical Forms and the Form of the Good than Plato's theory allows. For Plato, being a just man (or a just city) entails being a good man (or a good city). But being just is certainly a proper attribute in the Form Justice. So, in addition to the connection between the ideality of the Form Justice and the Form of the Good (a connection which is the same as that between the ideality of any Form and the Form of the Good), there is a strong entailment connection between the proper attribute of the Form, being just, and the Form of the Good. This, it appears, is as it should be—I mean there ought to be such a connection. But if so, it seems to contradict the theory of the Form of the Good we have been expounding; or, at any rate, if this is so,

PLATO

the Form of the Good cannot consist just in the ideality common to all the Forms. And in the latter case why should we suppose that the goodness entailed by being just is the same as the goodness by virtue of which all the Forms are the best objects of their kind, or that there is even any connection between the two?[30]

Have we succeeded in showing that the distinction between ideal and proper attributes, though not explicitly drawn by Plato, is consistent with his expressed views and arguments? Perhaps not entirely, though it is illuminating to expound his theory of the Form of the Good in terms of it. Let us look again at our data and indulge in some hopefully educated speculation. In the passages in the *Symposium* and the *Republic*, where Plato contrasts the Forms with the sensibles that participate in them, we found the following situation: unlike the sensibles that participate in it, the Form Beauty (I1) always exists, is neither generated or destroyed, does not increase or decrease, exists by itself; further it (I2) is beautiful in all respects, is always beautiful no matter compared to what, and is beautiful to all who apprehend it no matter from where. Now Plato in these passages was clear, I think, that the Form Beauty "has" these two sets of attributes whereas its sensible participants do not; and presumably similarly with the other Forms listed in these passages. Further, it is clear that the Form Beauty could have the first set of attributes (I1) whether it were conceived as a property without non-Pauline self-predication or as an ideal exemplar with such self-predication. But the Form Beauty could not have the second set of attributes (I2) unless it were non-Pauline self-predicational; for it obviously could not be always beautiful or beautiful in all respects unless it were beautiful to begin with. And similarly with the other Forms. This much is not speculation. But now when we bring in the distinction between ideal and proper attributes a curious situation develops. The attributes I1 are ideal attributes of the Forms no matter whether we draw the distinction according to Aristotle, Owen, Keyt, or Vlastos. And being beautiful, being circular, being just (and all the attributes entailed by them) are proper attributes of the corresponding Forms, at least according to Keyt's definition (and, I think, Owen's and Aristotle's). But the attributes of set I2—e.g., being always beautiful, being beautiful in all respects, etc., "straddle the fence": these attributes, which I "provisionally" called ideal attributes above, are neither ideal attributes nor proper attributes according to Keyt's definitions, yet they have connections with both. Unlike the attribute of being circular, being always circular is not a proper attribute of the Form Circle according to Keyt's definition since *its* absence from a thing would not entail that the thing is not an instance of the Form Circle; according to Plato sensible circles are instances of the Form Circle and yet none of them is always circular. Again, the attribute of always being circular is not an ideal attribute of the Form Circle according to

249

Keyt's definition since the absence of it from a thing would not entail that the thing is not a Platonic Idea; for Plato there are lots of Forms, e.g., the Form Square, that are not circular at all and hence not always circular. At the same time, attributes I2 have connections to both proper attributes and ideal attributes I1. The connection with proper attributes is that attributes I2 entail the corresponding proper attributes; being always beautiful entails being beautiful, being beautiful in all respects entails being beautiful. In this respect attributes I2 are unlike attributes I1. But there is an important respect in which I1 and I2 are alike: just as without being a Form a thing could not have attributes I1, so without being a Form a thing could not have attributes I2. Nothing could be always such and such or such and such in all respects, etc., without being a Form. And this is my justification for calling these "provisionally" ideal attributes. We can put the "straddling of the fence" feature of I2 attributes in a nutshell as follows: The Form Circle is circular (proper attribute) not because it is a Form, but because of the particular Form it is; it is indestructible (I1) not because of the particular Form it is but because it is a Form; but it is always circular (I2) both because it is a Form and because of the particular form it is.[31] Now we can speculate that it is pretty unlikely that somebody would see this point unless he drew the distinction between proper and ideal attributes explicitly and asked himself to which genus the three types of attributes (I2, I2, and proper) belong. And since Plato never explicitly drew the distinction it is pretty unlikely that he did this. But Plato does work with the three types of attributes in the various contexts. And the theory of the Form of the Good in the *Republic*, in which the form of the Good is the formal cause of the being and essence of the Forms, requires him to include attributes of type I2, as well as type I1, in the being and essence of the Forms. For, as we have argued, without I2 the Forms would not be ideal exemplars, the best objects of their kind. Nor would they be the best objects of their kind to *know*, since in his epistemology the best objects to know must be undeceptive, and this is assured by some I2 attributes such as the attribute of not appearing such and such from one point of view and not such from another. So in the context of the theory of the Form of the Good and the epistemology of the *Republic* Plato was probably lumping together I1 and I2 as belonging to the same genus, the ideality of the Forms. And Plato uses general summary phrases that could cover both.[32] At the same time, when Plato is thinking in general of participation in the Forms he is probably thinking of participation in the proper attributes of the Forms. But when he is thinking of the goodness of sensible things, in the context of the theory of the Form of the Good in the *Republic*, he is required to think, as we argued, of participation in the I2 attributes of the Forms if such participation is going to be a ground for the sensibles being good of a kind to some degree—and this is the context probably of the

Timaeus arguments. Now since I2 attributes entail the corresponding proper attributes, such participation would entail participation also in the proper attributes.[33] Here in a sense I2 and proper attributes are lumped together. But this lumping together is perhaps harmless so long as participation in I2 attributes admits of degrees, which assures degrees of goodness, and so long as such participation always "falls short" of complete participation, which blocks the disastrous result that such participation would entail that the sensibles are Forms (a parallel result to the result of the *Parmenides* 132c9–11 argument mentioned by Keyt).

It must also be noted that since the I2 attributes of a Form entail its proper attributes (e.g., being always beautiful entails being beautiful), there is room here for a confusion that would be vast indeed. If the Form of the Good is thought of as containing or consisting in the I2 attributes of the Forms in a concrete rather than an abstract sense, then the Form of the Good would indeed entail all the proper attributes of all the other Forms. But I seriously doubt that Plato ever thought of the matter in this way. On such an interpretation, the Form of the Good would be a vast conjunction, a wild motley indeed, of all the I2 attributes, concretely conceived, of all the other Forms. I think that Plato thinks of the I2 attributes in an abstract way insofar as they are contained in the Form of the Good: it is in virtue of participating in the Form of the Good that the other Forms are "always the same," "the same in all respects," "the same no matter compared to what," and "the same to all who apprehend them no matter from where." These abstract phrases, the first of which he uses quite often, are supposed to catch the idea that, e.g., it is not in virtue of participating in the Form of the Good that Square itself contains four right angles, but it is in virtue of participating in the Form of the Good that it *always* contains four right angles, contains four right angles *to all who apprehend it no matter from where*, and so on. We have to think here of I2 attributes in abstraction from the proper attributes contained in them. Plato, lacking the device of variables, tries to catch this abstraction, I believe, with the above abstract phrases ("always the same," "the same in all respects," and so on). It is important to see how very Platonic this abstraction is: these phrases attempt to catch precisely what is common to I2 attributes.

We can finally end this long discussion of the second round by some hopefully educated speculation on what the Form of the Good would be given our interpretation of the theory. G12 tells us that the ideal attributes of all the other Forms are proper attributes of the Form of the Good, and G11.1 tells us that the Form of the Good is the formal cause of the other Forms having their ideal attributes. So it would seem that the Form of the Good consists in or is constituted by the very ideality common to all the other Forms by virtue of which they are the best objects of their kind and the best objects of their kind to know. Such ideality, it would seem, would have to be conceived pretty abstractly, supergenerally as it were. For one thing, it is not ideality, superlative goodness and superlative reality, of kind, as is the case with the other Forms. The Form of the Good is not a superlatively "good something or other," as Cooper points out; it is presumably superlatively good, period. The goodness of the other Forms is indeed superlative but also partial, the goodness of kind. Moreover, the other Forms are not in a sense self-sufficient: they are the best objects of their kind of virtue of participating in the Form of the Good, and they are the most real objects of their kind for the same reason. But the Good itself is what it is presumably by virtue of itself.[34]

IV   The Third Round: the Divided Line

The third wave of paradox is the simile of the divided line, especially the upper two sections (509C–511E). Though the Form of the Good is not explicitly mentioned in these passages (perhaps implicitly at 509D), there is almost universal agreement that the Form of the Good is at the top of the ontological division and knowledge of it at the top of the epistemological division. Fortunately, we are not concerned here with all of the line or a general interpretation of it, but only with the relations, ontological and epistemological, between the upper two sections. The chief passages are 509B, 510C–E, 511BCD. An immense amount has been written about these passages. Here I wish only to dispute two widely accepted points of interpretation and suggest an alternative interpretation which is the natural outcome of our discussion of the second round.

The first thing I wish to dispute is that Plato's point in calling the beginning of mathematics "hypotheses" is that they are underived, unproved, or undemonstrated. Concerning what hypotheses Plato was referring to there is much dispute; just about everything has been suggested, including the odd itself and figures themselves, propositions asserting the existence of these, axioms attributing properties to these, or definitions of the odd, figures, and angles. In this dispute I do not enter. I assume that Plato was referring to whatever the mathematicians of his day used as Euclid uses definitions, axioms, and postulates. My concern is with his point in calling these "hypotheses." The majority of commentators (Adam, Cornford, Ross, to mention only a few)[35] suppose that his point is that these things are unproved, underived, or undemonstrated; and of course if they were used as Euclid uses definitions and axioms, they are. But I do not believe that this is Plato's point in calling them "hypotheses" in the present context. For one thing, while Plato calls the beginnings of arithmetic and geometry "hypotheses" and "hypothetical" (he uses the noun, the verb, and the adjective), he twice in these passages calls the beginning point of dialectic, that is, the Good or knowledge of it, "unhypothetical." Now if this is meant to be a contrast, as it seems to be, it would suggest, given the point we are disputing, that Plato meant that the Form of the Good or knowledge of it is derived or proved. But there is no evidence in our passages that Plato thought this of the Form of the Good; on the contrary, by placing it at the top of the Line he implies that it is not proved or derived from anything. Indeed from what could it be derived in the present context? Adam, making the assumption we are disputing, says that it (the Good) is "itself proved by an exhaustive scrutiny of all noeta" (intelligibles). Just what this means—and how this would make the Good "unhypothetical"—he does not tell us. In the second place, and aside from evidence, if one of Plato's complaints about mathematics were that its beginnings are underived or unproved, a defect that dialectic does not have and can remedy, he would be holding an obviously untenable position: for dialectic too has to start somewhere and no matter where it started its beginning would have the same defect. But if the interpretation of "hypotheses" we are disputing is not correct, what is? I think Plato's point in calling the beginning of mathematics "hypotheses" is simply that they are not known, they do not constitute knowledge. As to whether the mathematicians realize this, Plato's text is somewhat ambiguous; he says that they regard them "as known," "give no account of them," supposing "they are obvious to everybody." (510C) But he seems clear that dialectic "does not consider the hypotheses beginnings but really hypotheses." (511B) As to why the hypotheses do not constitute knowledge—and how dialectic can be of service to mathematics—we shall take up shortly.

The second major point of interpretation I wish to dispute is that Plato holds that once we (doing dialectic) have reached the Form of the Good and have knowledge of it, we can deduce or derive from this knowledge the hypotheses of the mathematicians. This idea goes naturally with the first point we disputed, since such a deduction would remedy the alleged defect of the hypotheses of the mathematicians. The idea that Plato had such a deduction in view is also widely held, from Adam to Cornford to Ross and beyond.[36] Indeed Cornford tried to suggest how such a deduction might possibly go by introducing another Form at the top, alongside the Good, namely Unity, presumably a mathematical Form. Ross correctly pointed out that there is no evidence whatsoever for this in our texts, but nevertheless continued to hold on to the idea of such a deduction. Now this idea seems to be the height of paradox indeed. To aim at deducing all of mathematics from a few principles is an ambitious but not paradoxical ideal, one that perhaps began to be approached in this century. To suppose that all of mathematics can be deduced from a single Platonic Form may begin to sound incredible. But to suppose further that this is the Form of the Good is paradoxical indeed; for there does not seem to be even a *prima facie* connection between goodness and numbers and figures; for this role the Form of the Good seems to be the wrong Form altogether. Do we really have good evidence to suppose that in our passages Plato had such a deduction in mind? The passages in which Plato briefly describes the "descent" from the Form of the Good to other Forms are obscure and ambiguous and the meaning of his words and phrases much in dispute. Moreover, such a view would seem to involve a vast confusion of ideal and proper attributes. For the hypotheses of the mathematicians are about the proper attributes of the Forms the hypotheses are about; they are about the proper attributes of the Forms Odd, Even, Square, Acute Angle, and so on. But the Form of the Good is the formal cause of the ideal attributes of these and all the other Forms. How then are we going to get entailment relations between the attributes of the Form of the Good and the proper attributes of these mathematical Forms? Further, the Form of the Good is the formal cause of the ideal attributes of all the other Forms. Why then should the proper attributes of (some) mathematical Forms be singled out for such a deduction? And if they are not singled out, we would have similar deductions and entailment relations between the attributes of the Form of the Good and the proper attributes of other kinds of Forms, Forms such as Living Creature, Artifact, Planet, and what have you. And in that case what would the Form of the Good be? Instead of or in addition to being the very ideality of the Forms, it would also have to be, it seems, a conjunction of several diverse kinds of Forms, mathematical, natural, artificial, and so on. I see no evidence whatsoever that Plato thought of the Form of the Good in this way in our passages. It must be admitted of course that the idea of such a deduction is a powerful one and is probably modeled on the deduction of theorems from hypotheses by the mathematicians; if the hypotheses are known, valid derivations from them of the theorems will yield knowledge of the theorems; similarly, valid derivations of the hypotheses from known things will yield knowledge of the hypotheses. Moreover, the influence of the Pythagoreans, the high esteem in which Plato held mathematics, the high place of mathematical studies in the education of the rulers, all these render general plausibility to the idea that Plato held that there is some intrinsic connection between some mathematical Forms and the Form of the Good. All the same I doubt that this interpretation is correct.

But if it isn't, what is? It seems to me that the epistemology of the upper portions of the divided line should be interpreted on the basis of the second round. An obvious clue and a solid handle is provided by the idea of the second round that the Form of the Good is "the cause" of the knowability of the Forms. The sense we have given to this idea is that it is by virtue of their ideal attributes (I1 & I2) that the Forms are knowable entities and that the Form of the Good is the formal cause of the other Forms' ideal attributes.

We have here clearly a theory as to what a knowable object is: to be knowable an object must be ungenerated, indestructible, not subject to increase and decrease, must exist by itself (I1 attributes), it must always be the same, the same in every respect, the same no matter compared to what, and the same to all who apprehend it no matter from where (I2 attributes). This theory has at least one virtue: it is difficult to see how anyone who was acquainted (with "the mind's eye") with such entities could make a mistake about them; at any rate a whole set of mistakes due to variability and spatial location have been summarily excluded, (though it is difficult to see how purely logical errors have also been excluded). And this coheres well with the very strong distinction drawn at the end of Book V between knowledge and belief in terms of their powers and their objects. Now this puts the dialectician in an epistemologically superior position to the mathematician. For unlike the latter, the former deals only with Forms: both in the ascent and descent to and from the Form of the Good the dialectician begins, deals with, and ends with nothing but Forms. Because of this and the nature of his objects, he is assured freedom from error; at any rate freedom from error as to what his objects are, the attributes that a Form can be "seen" to have without recourse to inference. The mathematicians, on the other hand, are at best in an ambiguous epistemological position; they deal with Forms and with visible figures as images of Forms; they talk about the visible figures but they are thinking about their models and making their hypotheses about them. Their hypotheses could be interpreted, by others perhaps, as being either about the visible figures or about their models. Insofar as their thought, their mathematical intuitions, derive from the visible figures, they are not assured freedom from error (even though they may not be making any actual error). Plato says that they regard their hypotheses as known and obvious to everybody and give no account of them. What sort of being "known" and "obviousness" is he talking about? I think the "obviousness" of the visible figures; it is the visible illustrations that would make the hypotheses "obvious to everyone," precisely the things that, in Plato's theory, could not make the hypotheses knowledge. And what sort of "account" is it that the mathematicians do not give of their hypotheses? I have argued that he does not mean that they are underived; and I think he does not mean that they give no definitions of the concepts they use, for surely they did construct definitions, and Euclid's *Elements* (much later of course) begins with definitions. I think Plato means that the mathematicians give no epistemological account of the sorts of objects they want their hypotheses to be about, not the visible figures but their models. They do not, for example ask themselves and seek to answer the question, what sorts of objects must the objects of our hypotheses be if our hypotheses are to be always true? They have no theory of the objects their hypotheses must (according to Plato anyway) be about if the hypotheses are to be true and to constitute knowledge. Because of their practice of using sensible figures they are liable to error or at least are not assured freedom from error. Because of this practice they are also not in a position to "see" the objects of their hypotheses "in splendid isolation" from sensible figures and thus begin to appreciate their nature. And also because, as mathematicians at least, they do not raise the above type of questions, they lack a theory of objects proper to mathematics. The dialectician, dealing only with Forms, has a chance to appreciate their common nature, their nature as ideal objects possessing ideal attributes I1 and I2. And if he asks the perfectly Platonic question, "By virtue of what do the Forms have these attributes in common?" presumably he will arrive at the conception of the Good. Looking downward from the Form of the Good the dialectician would see clearly what are Forms and what are not Forms; he would never make the mistake of confusing Forms with sensible instances, for he has now grasped the nature of the Forms, the notion of what it is to be a Form. And if at any rate he has Plato's conception of knowledge, the dialectician would see that only the Forms are possible objects of knowledge, that mathematics must be only about Forms if it is to be knowledge, and that the visible figures are irrelevant to the truth or knowability of the hypotheses. It is in this sense that the Form of the Good is the "cause" of reason's knowing the Forms, mathematical or otherwise. What the super science of dialectic would do for mathematics is not to provide a supergeneral known basis from which mathematical hypotheses can be deduced, but rather provide a theory of objects that mathematical hypotheses must be about if mathematics is to be knowledge. Such a theory would "free" mathematics from sensible figures in the sense that according to it sensible figures are never evidence that the hypotheses are true or known.

V   Summary

What is the moral of our story? I think it is that the theory of the Form of the Good in the *Republic* is truly the centerpiece of the canonical Platonism of the middle dialogues, the centerpiece of Plato's metaphysics, epistemology, ethics and politics, and even his theory of love and art. The Form of the Good serves his metaphysics by bringing into relief the very ideality of the Forms, the eternal order and stability of the entities that must exist if this world is not to be a "vast sea of dissimilarity." It serves his epistemology by bringing into relief the knowability of the Forms, the attributes some objects must have if there is to be knowledge. The Form of the Good serves his ethics and politics, and his theory of love and art, by bringing into relief the superlative goodness of the Forms, the features that must be imitated if the imitations are to have any value. In his theory of the Form of the Good

Plato was truly the first grand philosophical synthesizer. If to achieve such a grand synthesis he had to employ a few unholy combinations, such as the combination of reality, goodness, and self-predication, he may perhaps be forgiven—at least if he is understood.

A minor moral, I hope, is that when Plato looked into "the orb of light" he really did see something. It is perhaps an ironic tribute to his artistry, so evident in the three great similies, that when many others looked into the same orb of light through Plato's telescope they were warmed and elevated even though, apparently, they saw nothing.

NOTES

[1] An earlier draft of this paper was read at the Claremont Graduate School and at the December 1977 meeting of the Society for Ancient Greek Philosophy. I am indebted to several members of the audience for helpful comments, especially to Professors Charles Young, Mike Ferejohn, Charles Kahn, and Bill Jacobs.

[2] Among the older, extensive and useful discussions of the relevant texts are the following: Paul Shorey, "The Idea of the Good in Plato's *Republic*," *University of Chicago Studies in Classical Philology*, vol. 1 (1894); F. M. Cornford, "Mathematics and Dialectic in the *Republic* VI–VII," in *Studies in Plato's Metaphysics*, ed. R. E. Allen (1965), and the relevant commentary in his translation of the *Republic*, 1941; W. D. Ross, *Plato's Theory of Ideas* (1951), pp. 39–69; R. Robinson, *Plato's Earlier Dialectic*, 2nd ed. (1953), chs. X & XI. More recent discussions include: R. C. Cross and A. D. Woozley, *Plato's Republic* (1964), chs. 8–10; I. M. Crombie, *Plato's Doctrines*, vol. 1 (1962), pp. 103–33; J. C. B. Gosling, *Plato* (1975), chs. IV & VII. I regret that there is no space to discuss these and others in any detail; as a poor substitute, as I go along I try to indicate some of the discussions with which I disagree as well as those on which I rely for support. A dominant theme in these discussions is that what Plato says about the Form of the Good is not very intelligible or coherent. At the beginning of his paper Shorey gives a delightful review of this theme in the older literature. Aside from the Jowett quote, he cites Grote's view that in the relevant passages Plato, unable to solve difficulties, "makes his escape in a cloud of metaphor." Writing a century later, Crombie asks some good questions, makes a suggestion (that goodness in Plato is to be understood in terms of "conformability to reason"), and then he gives up with the remark that "it is legitimate to suspect that we be dealing more with a vision than with a clear idea, and that it may well be because the vision faded as he attempted to clarify it that Plato nowhere repeats this theme," p. 124. I hope to have shown in this paper that Plato had a coherent and clear idea and that the theory was given up in so far as self-predication was given up in later dialogues.

[3] Perhaps a fairly reliable index of the present state of affairs is afforded by Nicholas White's list of puzzling questions about the Form of the Good, which remain unanswered: *Plato on Knowledge and Reality* (1976), pp. 99–103.

[4] I am especially indebted to the following: G. Vlastos, "Degrees of Reality in Plato," "A Metaphysical Paradox," "The 'Two-Level Paradoxes' in Aristotle," "Rea-

sons and Causes in the *Phaedo*," "The Unity of Virtues in the *Protagoras*," all in *Platonic Studies* (1973); D. Keyt, "Plato's Paradox that the Immutable is Unknowable," *Philosophical Quarterly* (1969), and "The Mad Craftsman of the *Timaeus*," *Philosophical Review* (1971); G. E. L. Owen, "Dialectic and Eristic in the Treatment of Forms," in *Aristotle on Dialectic*, ed. G. E. L. Owen (1968).

⁵ For the first part of G5 see the speeches of Glaucon and Adeimantus in *Republic* Book II.

⁶ The attribution of this proposition to Plato has been widely discussed in connection with the TMA; see, e.g., *Platonic Studies*, p. 348. Charles Young has pointed out that, as I myself say later, the application of F1 to goodness is different for the case of the goodness of Forms and the goodness of sensible. A Form has goodness of kind by virtue of participating in the Form of the Good; a sensible has goodness of kind (attributive goodness) by participating in the Form of that kind and that Form in turn participating in the Form of the Good. The goodness of sensibles is attributive and involves participation in at least two Forms one of which is the Form of the Good.

⁷ A Socratic version of this has been discussed by P. Geach and myself; see "The Socratic Fallacy," *JHP* (April 1972). In *Socrates*, Keagan Paul, 1979, I find that the evidence heavily favors Geach's attribution of this proposition in Plato. In the *Republic* G3 itself is such evidence. For a more recent discussion see M. F. Burnyeat, "Examples in Epistemology: Socrates, Theaetetus and G. E. Moore," *Philosophy* 52 (1977), especially p. 390.

⁸ This point has been emphasized by Ross, *Plato's Theory*, pp. 40–41.

⁹ In our passage Plato does not explicitly refer to the Form of the Good as a "cause" but later on he does, for example at 517C.

¹⁰ "Degrees of Reality in Plato" and "A Metaphysical Paradox."

¹¹ The implied attributes are that Beauty itself is beautiful in all respects, always, no matter compared to what, or apprehended from what point of view. These attributes clearly presuppose that Beauty itself is self-predicational or self-exemplifying. For a discussion of this assumption see Vlastos, *Platonic Studies*, pp. 262–63, and J. M. E. Moravscik, "Reason and Eros in the 'Ascent' Passage of the *Symposium*," in *Essays in Ancient Greek Philosophy*, ed. John P. Anton and G. L. Kustas (1971), pp. 296–300.

¹² Vlastos, *Platonic Studies*, particularly pp. 62–63, 66–67, and note 21. For discussions that disagree with Vlastos on this point, see e.g., Cross and Woozley, *Plato's Republic* (1964), p. 145, and perhaps J. Gosling, "*Rep.* V: *ta polla kala*, etc.," *Phronesis* 5 (1960).

¹³ See the relevant parts of J. Hintikka, "Knowledge and its Objects in Plato," and my comments in J. M. E. Moravcsik, ed. *Patterns in Plato's Thought* (1973).

¹⁴ See Vlastos, "Reasons and Causes in the *Phaedo*," especially pp. 88–91.

¹⁵ T. Irwin, in some very brief remarks about the Form of the Good, says, among other things, that "The Good is the formal and final cause of the Forms' being what they are," *Plato's Moral Theory* (1977). I am in agreement with the first part of this statement, but I find it difficult to see how the Good is the final cause of the Forms' being what they are since I would have thought that final causes are invoked to explain actions, activities, and movements, whereas the Forms are "at rest." My

discussion of the first round clearly allows, though, that the Form of the Good can be the final cause of sensible things, for example, men's activities and actions. Professor Charles Kahn expressed doubts that in his middle period Plato had the notion of the Forms participating in Forms, though he did of course in his later dialogues. Perhaps so, but I see no hope of making sense of his theory of the Form of the Good unless we allow formal causation and participation here.

[16] Professor Mike Ferejohn wrote that we need at least self-participation applied to the Form of the Good for this derivation. In the last paragraph of this round I indeed allow for such self-participation or at any rate for self-predication (and in this use "good" is not used attributively).

[17] The conception of the Forms as paradigms or ideal exemplars, self-predicational or self-exemplifying has been brought out by a number of authors: P. Geach, "The Third Man Again," *Philosophical Review* (1956); G. Vlastos, "A Metaphysical Paradox"; M. M. E. Moravscik, "Recollecting the Theory of Forms," in *Facets of Plato's Philosophy*, ed. W. H. Werkmeister (1976); R. Smith, "Mass Terms, Generic Expressions, and Plato's Theory of Forms," *Journal of the History of Philosophy* (April, 1978); and many others. The self-predication assumption is of course extremely controversial. Since Vlastos' influential paper on the Third Man, authors have disagreed whether Plato ever made this assumption, on what the meaning of the assumption is, and on its scope. Though I cannot enter this controversy here, the theory of the Form of the Good I am presenting presupposes that the Forms are self-predicational or self-exemplifying during Plato's middle period—at least in the *Republic*, the *Symposium*, the *Timaeus*, and the *Phaedo*. I shall have something to say on the meaning of the assumption when I discuss the distinction between proper and ideal attributes. Suffice it to say here that by "self-predication" I do not mean the weak version that Vlastos calls "Pauline self-predication" but something stronger. Vlastos disambiguates the sentence

(1) Justice is just

into

(2) The Form Justice is itself just

and

(3) Justice is such that anyone who has this property is (necessarily) just.

and calls (3) "Pauline self-predication." "A Note on 'Pauline Predications' in Plato," *Phronesis*, XIX, 2 (1974). How strong a non-Pauline self-predication assumption is needed for the theory of the Form of the Good will be discussed below.

[18] See Wedberg's discussion, especially pp. 49–50 and notes in his *Plato's Philosophy of Mathematics* (Stockholm, 1955).

[19] "The Mad Craftsman of the *Timaeus*," e.g., p. 233.

[20] On the present theory, to say that a sensible exists, say, a drawn circle, is to say that it participates in the proper attributes of some Form, the Form Circle. On the other hand, to say that a sensible circle is a good circle is to say that it participates to some significant degree in the ideal attributes of the Form Circle; or, to take a simpler, comparative case, to say that some sensible circle is better than another is to say that it participates to a greater degree in the ideal attributes of the Form Circle. On this interpretation existence does not admit of degrees, whereas goodness and reality do, and the former does not imply the later. Thus, so far as the existence and good-

ness of sensibles is concerned, the theory does not violate the Humean dictum; whether it fares equally well for the case of the existence and goodness of Forms is unclear.

[21] "The Mad Craftsman of the *Timaeus*," p. 230.

[22] In "The 'Two-Level Paradoxes' in Aristotle" Vlastos argues that the distinction is incompatible with the Platonic ontology. We take up this point shortly.

[23] Vlastos, "The 'Two-Level Paradoxes' in Aristotle," and G. E. L. Owen, "Dialectic and Eristic." I wish to note briefly here that within the assumption of non-Pauline self-predication there will be certain two-level paradoxes against which the distinction between ideal and proper attributes of Forms is totally helpless. The Form Change provides an extreme example; if it is conceived with non-Pauline self-predication, some of its proper attributes will contradict flatly some of its ideal attributes, and the distinction fails to disarm the contradiction. In his discussion of such paradoxes Aristotle has nothing to be ashamed about in not bringing in this distinction.

[24] Owen, "Dialectic and Eristic"; Keyt, "Plato's Paradox"; and Vlastos, "The 'Two-Level Paradoxes.'"

[25] The other two "bad arguments" would be more difficult to reconstruct along the lines we reconstructed the "eternity argument." I am not satisfied that a confusion of ideal proper attributes is involved here. Let us look briefly at the "bad argument" about uniqueness. The first question we have to ask ourselves is what sort of uniqueness is involved here. It seems to me that it is not the uniqueness that is true of every Form: every Form in Plato is unique in the sense that for every kind (or, for every, at any rate unambiguous, predicate) there is exactly one Form (whereas every Form can have, and usually does, many sensible participants). Now if this uniqueness were involved in the argument as Keyt reconstructs it, the argument would be not only fallacious but disastrous: for parallel arguments in the case of each Form would show that each Form can have only one sensible participant. To avoid this result, we would have to suppose either that it is not just this uniqueness that is involved in the case of Living Creature, or perhaps that the mode of imitation in this case is somehow different. The way I read the text it is not this uniqueness that is at issue, but rather the uniqueness of "embracing all intelligible Living Creatures" (31a4)—the special completeness of this Form, which its parts do not have (31a4–b2). Now what would it be for the Demiurge to fashion two worlds resembled this model as completely as possible, i.e., contained in it sensible living creatures of all the kinds included in the Intelligible Living Creature? The two worlds would be indistinguishable, except possibly in the numbers of individual sensibles they contained for each species, a difference not in question since this difference can obtain in our world from, say, year to year. The only way the Demiurge could create relevantly distinguishable worlds is by imitating first a subordinate Form (a "part" of Living Creature) and then another— but in that case he would not be imitating the right Form (this reasoning is I think implicit in 31a5–8). Keyt recognizes that "The Form of living creature, the model for the cosmos, *is* a rather special Form, and the creation of the cosmos a rather special event," and says that one perhaps should not conclude from such a special case that Plato draws no line between the proper and ideal attributes of a Form. To counter this he cites the *Parmenides* argument. But while this argument seems clearly enough

to confuse the two sets of attributes, the only evidence here that Plato made such a confusion is his silence about the argument. This is very weak evidence, I think, in view of the fact that it is Parmenides who gives the argument and Plato has no real interest in defending the view that Forms are thoughts. What is more essential, do we have any evidence that Plato ever made the mistake of supposing that since sensibles participate in the Forms, the sensibles have the ideal attributes of the Forms (a species of which is Keyt's "since Forms are intelligible entities and things share in Forms, each thing is an intelligible entity")? I think none; his whole ontology counts against making such a mistake. The closest he comes is the "eternity argument" discussed above; and here his ontology—of which the sharp contrasts between Forms and sensibles is a part—saves him by forcing a distinction between eternity and everlastingness (and this again in the special case of the cosmos).

²⁶ We may note, in addition, that Plato or his craftsman would never make the mad mistakes of some of Keyt's illustrations, for example the mistake of making a paper shield and justifying himself on the ground that his pattern (model) was of paper (p. 231). Far from sanctioning such mistakes the theory excludes them wholesale: for no sensible object is a reliable model, certainly never the best model, for making a good object of a kind; only the best objects of a kind are, the ideal exemplars, the Forms; sensible objects are copies or copies of copies. The "paperness" of the "model" paper shield, far from making it the best shield there is or can be, makes it one of the worst—a point we can accept. Of course Keyt was only illustrating in this passage the type of mistake he is attributing to Plato—he was not saying that Plato or his Demiurge would make this mistake. But now we can see why they wouldn't. If we construct a parallel argument, to the one we have reconstructed above about "eternity," but with the sensible object as the model, the theoretical premises of this argument would be false for Plato: for him no sensible object is the best object of its kind; and far from the ideal attributes of material objects—their materiality, their variable nature—being what makes them the best objects of their kind, they are precisely what makes them irremediably defective.

²⁷ A similar point is brought out by Vlastos in "A Metaphysical Paradox": "Only when Forms assume their other role, as objects of value, and the kind of value Plato claimed for them, would the self-characterization of Forms like Beauty have any point whatever." (p. 56). The notions of Forms as ideal exemplars, self-predication, and the Form of the Good as the formal cause of the being and essence of the Forms—all these go hand in hand. In so far as Plato gave up non-Pauline self-predication in later dialogues such as the *Sophist*—and the prominence of such a Form as Change may have forced him to do it—he would also be giving up, I think, the theory of the Form of the Good of the *Republic*. This would begin to account for his silence on the matter in later dialogues. Whether the theory is held in the *Philebus* seems more difficult to make out.

²⁸ It is not within the scope of this paper to detail all the varieties and absurdities of self-predication. For a recent account see Vlastos, *Platonic Studies*, pp. 259–65; for an earlier account, R. E. Allen, *Studies in Plato's Metaphysics*, pp. 43–45. In correspondence Professor Charles Young raised the interesting question whether something less than full blown non-Pauline self-predication may not be sufficient for the theory of the Form of the Good, sufficient, that is, for the Forms being

the best objects of their kind. In particular, we might draw a distinction between the *formal* attributes of sensible things and their *material* attributes; the formal attributes of, say, sensible knives (e.g., sharpness) are those mentioned in the definition of knifehood, which sensible knives have by virtue of participating in the Form knife; material attributes (e.g., being made of iron) are those they have by being the particular knives they are. We can then say that it is only those attributes that knives have as formal attributes that the Form knife has as proper attributes (and only these would be included in self-predications). This suggestion has two virtues: first, it avoids the absurdities of attributing materiality to Forms, and second, it still allows Forms to be the best objects of their kind since materiality detracts rather than contributes to goodness. We are still left, though, with sharpness as a proper attribute of the Form, and in any case some material attributes, e.g., being made of rust resistant metal, appear to be good-making attributes of knives.

²⁹ The fact that Plato does not directly derive from knowledge of the Form of the Good any propositions as to what is good or right is the basis of Popper's referring to the theory of the Form of the Good as "this empty formalism." (*The Open Society and its Enemies*, vol. 1, p. 146). In a sense Popper is right: the Form of the Good is a "formal" property since it is the formal cause of the ideal or formal attributes of the Forms and not of their proper attributes. But the charge that this formalism is "empty" is probably misguided. One might as well complain that one cannot directly derive information as to what things are good from Rawls' definition of "attributive goodness," (*A Theory of Justice*, p. 399). We have seen that the goodness of sensible things (and of Forms) is attributive goodness or goodness of kind. It is part of the notion of attributive goodness that one cannot derive from knowledge alone of what goodness is the proposition that something is a good K; one must also know the kind K. In Plato's theory one could not derive from knowledge of the Form of the Good alone the proposition that, say, Socrates is a good man; one would also need to know the Form Man (as well as information about Socrates). It is presumably the task of the sciences and/or dialectic to know the various Forms; and from that and knowledge of the Good knowledge or at least true belief about the goodness of particular things could be derived. The Form of the Good would be used as a "pattern" in this indirect way. It is perhaps also worth noting here that Plato's theory of goodness is probably the background notion of goodness underlying theories of rightness Rawls calls "perfectionist," since on Plato's view goodness of kind is essentially perfection of kind; each Form is the perfect specimen of its kind.

³⁰ To this we may add the related and unresolved difficulty of accounting for the negative ethical forms (the unjust, the bad) mentioned by Socrates at *Rep*.476a. This difficulty was brought to my attenion by Bill Jacobs. For a brief recent discussion, see N. White, *A Companion to Plato's Republic* (1979), p. 41.

³¹ Consistent with this characterization, Mike Ferejohn suggests that I2 attributes can be derived from proper attributes and I1 attributes. Thus, for example, from being beautiful (a proper attribute of Beauty) and from being eternal (an I1 attribute of Beauty) we can derive being always beautiful.

³² See, e.g., *Republic* 479A, 479E, 485B, 484B, 500C, 585BD. In "An Ambiguity in the Sophist" Vlastos finds the same and similar phrases in the *Philebus* and the *Timaeus* (pp. 276–77).

[33] It may seem puzzling to speak, as I have, of things participating in attributes. Ferejohn notes that where I speak of a thing participating in an attribute of a Form I can instead speak of a thing having a property which resembles the attribute of the Form. As he also notes, the resemblance notion goes well with the conception of Forms as ideal exemplars and with the fact that Plato's theory of the Form of the Good requires degrees of participation.

[34] "The Psychology of Justice in Plato," *APQ* (April 1977):154. I am indebted to Cooper not only for his illuminating remarks about the Form of the Good (pp. 154–55), but also for giving me the courage to try to think seriously about this difficult topic. Aside from the mathematical interpretation of the Form of the Good, some of Cooper's characterizations do not appear consistent with the superlative goodness of *kind* of the Forms (other than the Form of the Good); for example the statement, "Every other good, being good only is some or relation or from some point of view, is also not so good, or even quite bad, in some other way" (p. 154). This I think holds only of sensible goods, not the Forms.

[35] See, e.g., J. Adam, *The Republic of Plato*, 2nd ed.; D. A. Rees (1963), vol. II, pp. 66–67; Cornford, "Mathematics and Dialectic," pp. 65–66; Ross, *Plato's Theory*, pp. 54–55.

[36] Adam, *The Republic of Plato*, p. 67, Cornford, "Mathematics and Dialectic," pp. 82–83, Ross, *Plato's Theory*, pp. 54–56.

EDWARD M. GALLIGAN

Logos in the *Theaetetus* and the *Sophist*[1]

I N this paper I am concerned with the *Theaetetus'* dreamed theory and its refutation in that dialogue. From the vantage point of the *Sophist*, I ask (1) whether and how Plato changed the theory's view of *logos* and (2) whether and how he might have been able to loosen the dilemma that refutes the theory.

A Way of Looking at the Dreamed Theory and Its Refutation

In the *Protagoras*[2] Socrates poses two *paradeigmata*, in terms of which the great sophist and he may articulate opposing positions on the question: How do the virtues stand in relation to one another? The *paradeigmata* are those of a face and a lump of gold. In keeping with the leading question about the relation of the virtues, Socrates develops the part-part aspect of his examples. According to him, eye and ear are not alike nor is their function (*dynamis*) the same, but the parts of a lump of gold do not differ at all, except quantitatively.[3] In their discussions, Protagoras maintains that the virtues stand to one another like the parts of a face while Socrates tries to show that they are more like the parts of a lump of gold. Naturally enough, the whole-part aspect of these *paradeigmata* remains comparatively undeveloped. Socrates does say that there are only quantitative differences between a whole lump of gold and its parts. Still, he makes no contrasting remarks for the case of a face and its parts. As a reason for his silence, one need only remind oneself that the main question concerns the relation of the virtues to one another and not to the whole of virtue. Further, in contrast to "organic" parts of a face like eye or an ear, a face does not have a similarly obvious *dynamis*.[4] Still, there are interesting predicate differences between faces and

This is an abridgment of a paper presented at the 1968 Washington meeting of the Society for Ancient Greek Philosophy; it has not been published previously.

Edward M. Galligan is Associate Professor of Philosophy at the University of North Carolina at Chapel Hill.

their parts. For example, faces look astonished or perplexed; mouths drop or eyebrows curl. Thus supplemented, the lump of gold and the face examples provide us with two radically contrasting sorts of wholes: wholes that have character symmetry with their parts and whose parts have character symmetry with one another versus wholes that do not have character symmetry with their parts and whose parts do not have character symmetry with one another.

The *paradeigmata* of the *Protagoras* are interesting for an understanding of the discussion of the dreamed theory in the *Theaetetus*. The relevant data about the dreamed theory that form the basis of comparison with the *Protagoras'* examples are: (1) that the dreamed theory has its own model example of a whole-part type—syllables and letters, (2) that the part of the theory that is subjected to criticism is its claim that complexes and their elemental constituents lack a certain symmetry of character, and (3) that the criticism of the theory is cast in a generalized treatment of different kinds of wholes.

According to the theory of Socrates' dream, complexes are knowable and statable, but the parts of such complexes that are elements are neither knowable nor statable; such elements can only be perceived and named. A complex is stated when we weave together the names of the elements of such a complex—this being just what a logos is.[5] A complex has a logos but its elemental parts do not. In terms of the theory's own *paradeigma*, which Socrates will interrogate,[6] letters are namables but not knowables;[7] syllables are knowables and have an account or logos. Thus, according to the theory, syllables and letters are wholes and parts that lack a certain character symmetry. In this much they are similar to the face example.

What of the part-part aspect of syllables and letters? In contrast to the *Protagoras*, part-part contrasts remain comparatively undeveloped in the dreamed theory. Theaetetus, however, does classify the letters into vowels, consonants, and mutes.[8] And Socrates talks about the letters in such a way that opens the possibility that not all the letters do combine with one another.[9] Though these remarks are suggestive, the distinction of the letters is made by Theaetetus, not Socrates, when the latter explains the theory and Socrates' possibility of the limitations on the combinations of the letters appears to be something to which he is alluding *en passant*.

But the passage that ought to be given more weight as pointing to a part-part contrast occurs in Socrates' explanation of why it is that an element cannot be stated.[10] Stating an element, and it alone, cannot be done because one must add to it something other than the element itself. Even to say of an element that it is, or that it is not, one must add being or nonbeing to the element.[11] The example recalls Socrates' criticism of the thesis that perception is knowledge, earlier in the dialogue.[12] The point was there made that to know anything of a perceptible required the mind's thinking of things that were not proper to any sense organ but common to everything. Being and nonbeing, as well as sameness and difference, likeness and unlikeness, and unity and the numbers, were mentioned as such common things.[13] The dreamed theory makes no such sharp distinction. Rather, for its rationale of the view that elements cannot be stated, the dreamed theory seems to have need only of saying that an element is numerically distinct from its being or nonbeing. Whether being or nonbeing is another element, perceptible, namable and nonstatable, is left indeterminate. However, if complexes can be stated by combining names of the elements of such complexes and the theory of Socrates' dream is supposed to be understood as being consistent on its face, then being and nonbeing ought to be on a par with other elements. If E is the name of an element, then to state that E is, would be to state a complex by combining the names of the perceptible elements E and being.[14] Admittedly, this suppression of a part-part contrast in the dreamed theory is rather forced. The alternative is indefiniteness on the status of being and nonbeing. In either case, however, the dreamed theory does not incorporate in a clear manner any part-part contrasts. The consequences for a logos are that the parts of a logos are not distinguished as to kind or function. (It is worth noting that the dreamed theory does not even allude to, much less make anything of, the contrast of *onoma* and *rhēma*.[15]) The mention and hints of part-part contrasts concerning the dreamed theory's *paradeigma*, letters and syllables, are thus not clearly reflected in the dreamed theory itself.

In general, then, the dreamed theory presents an example of a whole with parts that is intermediate between the lump of gold and the face. Like the face, but unlike the lump of gold, complexes and their parts lack character symmetry; like the lump of gold, but unlike the face, the parts of a complex seem not to have interesting character asymmetry.

The striking feature of the dreamed theory is its lack of symmetry of character between whole and part, i.e., that wholes are knowable and statable but that their elemental parts are not knowable but only namable.[16] On this point Socrates constructs a dilemma. Put in briefest form: either syllables and their parts are both knowable or both are unknowable. Syllables and letters are both knowable if a syllable is a whole or a sum of its parts. Syllables and letters are both unknowable if a syllable is other than a whole or a sum of its parts. But whichever horn one opts for, the theory is wrong—wrong in what it says about parts in the first case, wrong in what it says about wholes in the second case. In this way, Socrates' dilemma against the dreamed theory tries to restore symmetry of character to complexes and their parts and reduce the syllable-letter example to one having the structural features of the *Protagoras'* lump of gold.[17]

II.   A Few Critical Remarks Concerning the
Dreamed Theory and Its Refutation

Simple theories have a perennial fascination among philosophers that is not difficult to explain. For, if a theory is simple, its inadequacies, if any, ought to be very clear to us. In many cases, to state a shortcoming will readily suggest how to construct a more complicated theory that will be more adequate. Such may be the case with the *Theaetetus'* dreamed theory.

The theory of Socrates' dream is not powerful enough to distinguish a statement from a collection of words or names.[18] The former states something or makes a claim; the latter need not state anything or make any claim. Further, since a collection of names need not say anything, *a fortiori* it need not say anything that is true or false. So the dreamed theory's account of logos, far from being *the* addition that might turn true opinion into knowledge, does not even require that any statement of what one knows about anything be a statement of an opinion that is true.

A statement is a collection of names or words. But when is such a collection a statement? What further must be said about collections of names or words so as to demark those that are statements from those that are not? To this question, I discern two types of answers: a part-whole one and a part-part one. The part-whole answer extends the contrast of name and statement a bit further than the dreamed theory. Statements are not merely collections of names but collections of names in a certain order. The order may be understood to picture a way that things stand, a way in which elements denoted by the names hang together. If a statement is true, then a state of affairs holds and is a fact. If a statement is false, then a state of affairs does not hold and is not a fact. The chief ingredients in such an extension of the dreamed theory are the order of names in a statement to distinguish statements from nonstatements and nonexisting states of affairs to account for a false statement's having sense.[19] Such a view loosely characterizes Wittgenstein's *Tractatus*.[20] On the other hand, the part-part answer involves laying down necessary conditions on the parts of a statement, describing their relevant and crucial differences in terms of syntax, semantics, or pragmatics. Roughly again, this is the subject-predicate approach to the analysis of a statement. As we shall see, it is this view that has its beginning in Plato's *Sophist*. And it is to such beginnings, we shall be claiming, that the inadequacies of the dreamed theory point.

I turn now to the dilemma brought against the dreamed theory. If syllables are sums of their letters, then if syllables are known, then so are their letters, despite what the dreamed theory claims. Allowing that syllables are the sums of their letters, it might be urged that one could know syllables though not their letters. An example might be of one who could recognize and distinguish different syllables but did not know the names of the letters. Similarities and differences among *rabbit, robbery,* and *robin* might easily be detected and indicated by one who did not know the names of the relevant letters. To this objection Socrates might reply that probably a dreamed theory proponent would argue that such a man would have true opinion but not knowledge. He could know syllables only when he possessed knowledge of their letter parts and could name the letter parts of given syllables. It then becomes not only a necessary condition but a defining condition of a man's having knowledge of syllables that he know the letters that make them up. So understood, Socrates' point is entirely telling against the dreamed theory.

The second horn of Socrates' dilemma seems the more interesting of the two. But the argument is not without a rather pervasive difficulty.

Socrates suggests that ". . . perhaps we ought to have posited that the syllable is not the letters but some one kind of thing that has come into being from them, having its own character and different from the elements.[21] There could be at least two distinct claims involved here: (1) that a syllable is not materially identical with the letters that make it up, or even the sum of such letters, and (2) as a character asymmetry claim, that a syllable has a character of its own that its parts do not have. The one is a denial of a material identity of a whole with its parts; the other is a denial of a predication regarding parts, which predication holds in the case of the whole. It is the former that is examined by Socrates. He proceeds to argue that if a syllable is not the same as all the parts or the sum of the parts, then it has no parts and is not a whole having parts. He concludes that such a syllable should have the same status accorded to the dreamed theory's elements, viz. unknowability and unstatability. Moreover, if this argument were satisfactory, it could not be that a syllable would have a special character of its own, at least in the sense that such a character could be expressed or known. It seems then that the two options for construing Socrates' suggestion are incompatible.

But is a whole or sum that is not the same as all its parts something that has no parts? It is difficult to answer this question straightaway because Socrates provides no clue as to how he wishes his point to be understood in the case of syllables. Still, an example adapted from Aristotle may be instructive.[22] Two different syllables, say *ba* and *ab* may have letter parts that are the same in each case but differ only in order. So the two syllables, because they differ from one another, are not materially identical with the sums of their parts, where the sums do not specify a necessary order of letters. Now it simply does not follow that the syllables *ba* and *ab* do not have letter parts at all, if, in one sense, they are not identical with the sums of their parts. Moreover, we might think of several ways of expressing the character of a syllable like *ab*, e.g., *a* before *b*, the first syllable of the verb *abjure*, pronouncing the syllable itself, etc.—none of which is something true of the letter parts. Disarming Socrates' refutation in this manner, we may see that the two constructions put upon his suggestion need not lead to any incompatibility. And it is well that this is so not only for specific cases of syllables but also for a syllable as a general kind of thing. For we may suppose that a syllable is a combination of written letters in some acceptable order, that together form something that is at least a minimum pronounceable and that within the pronounced syllable there are distinguishable phonetic elements.[23] Then, say, when we put together suitably the letters *b*, *o*, *x*, something comes to be, a syllable, with a character of its own, pronounceability, which none of its letter parts has. Here we deny material identity and character symmetry for the syllable as a kind of thing in relation to its elemental parts but are not pressed at all to deny that the syllable has parts.

III. The *Sophist* and Logos

In the *Sophist*, the Stranger from Elea has just dismissed the possibilities that none of the forms combine and that all do. Then he says,

> Because some will do this and others not, they are in quite the same condition as letters. For some of these also do not fit together with one another, others fit together. . . . And the vowels, more so than the others, are like a bond running through them all, so that without any of them, it is not possible to fit together any of the others with anything.[24]

Though the word for syllable does not occur in these passages, it is hard to think that the letters that fit together because of a vowel can be anything other than a syllable. Some letters do not fit together, e.g., *b* and *g*; others do fit together, e.g., *ba* and *ba*; the vowels are particularly good at fitting the others together, e.g., *bag* and *beg*. The fittings here are all syllabic. Again, though what is special about letters that do fit together, as opposed to those that do not, is not explicitly explained, it is hard to think otherwise than that such fittings are pronounceable and nonfittings are not.[25]

If we read the passage as indicated and ignore the point that vowels are themselves syllabic on occasion, then two ideas about syllables are presented: (1) that a syllable must contain vowel and nonvowel parts, and (2) that it is due to the presence of a vowel that the other letters are fitted together into a syllable, something pronounceable. The first suggests an important character asymmetry among syllable parts; the second suggests an asymmetry of character between the syllable as a whole and its letter parts. A syllable is pronounceable but its letter parts are not. A syllable's pronounceability is explained in terms of a vowel's fitting nonvowels together.[26] The special character of the whole is thus explained in terms of differences among parts.

At 261d, the Stranger invites us to consider words in the same way that he has considered letters. Corresponding to differences among letters, among words (*onomata*) he distinguishes those that are names (*onomata*) and those that are verbs (*rhēmata*). A name applies to what performs an action; a verb applies to an action. He then claims that a string of names alone, or a string of verbs alone, do not make a statement. Rather only the weaving together of verb and name constitutes statement. In contrast to a word, which merely names something, a statement determines something. A statement states things of something.

Statements then have part-part asymmetry and part-whole asymmetry. Statement parts must be of different kinds and statements have characters that their parts do not have. Statements and syllables have the structural features of the face *paradeigma*.

The dreamed theory and the *Sophist* differ about *logos* in rather much the way they differ about syllables. Though the *Theaetetus* contains a distinction of letters into kinds, not much was made of these distinctions. But according to the *Sophist*, vowels make nonvowels pronounceable. The latter dialogue claims part-part asymmetry for syllables. As for logos, the dreamed theory does not clearly have any part-part asymmetry, whereas the *Sophist* articulates just such a distinction. On the other hand, concerning the whole-part aspect of logoi, the dreamed theory and the *Sophist* are closer. According to the dreamed theory, by means of a statement we can express our knowledge of complexes, but what we can only name, elements, we can neither know nor state. According to the *Sophist*, we can name beings by means of a name or a verb, but in doing so we do not state anything of anything.

The *Sophist*'s view of both statement and syllable seems to be that they are wholes that come to be when their parts are put together and that the wholes have a character that their parts do not have. This suggests that syllables and statements are open to whatever force there is in the second horn of the dilemma brought against the dreamed theory.

Let us concentrate on statements and ignore syllables. It might be objected that the dilemma against the dreamed theory is concerned more with ontological wholes than with linguistic ones. So much is true but the second horn of the dilemma is much more general than such an admission would lead one to believe. Put generally, the second horn would read: if any whole comes to be from its elemental parts, is not identical with the sum of such parts and has character asymmetry with them, then such a whole has no parts and is itself an element with the characters originally ascribed to elemental parts. So put, the soundness of the second horn of the dilemma in no

PLATO

way depends on the argument's content being ontological rather than linguistic wholes. Then, one who puts credence in this dilemma, as Socrates did in the *Theaetetus*, might see it as applying to the *Sophist*'s view of logos. To what extent is this so?

Suppose that the elemental parts of the statement are *onomata*,[27] and that these do not state anything of anything. Putting together *onomata* suitably, i.e., name with verb, will bring about a statement that states things of something.[28] Stating things of something will be a character that a logos has as a whole, but one that none of the elemental parts has.

But is a logos a whole that is not identical with the sum of its elemental parts? The typical case in which a whole is not identical with the sum of its parts occurs when such a whole must be specified in terms of an order of parts, as was the case with our earlier example of the syllables *ab* and *ba*. "The cat is on the mat" and "The mat is on the cat" furnish hackneyed examples of different logoi having the same constituents. Neither of these logoi is identical with the sum of its parts. We might easily extend our point by noting that languages do not countenance merely any possible ordering of words as something statemental. "On the the is mat cat" is not a statement in English.

In his requirements for a logos, the Stranger does not mention order. Rather, his only interest in successions of words that are significant, as opposed to those that are not, begins and ends in the recognition that a logos must contain a name and a verb.[29] (Apparently, "Weeps the number seven" would pass as a sequence meeting this requirement. The Stranger's account of the necessary features of a logos are not sufficient ones.)

A logos is not identical with the sum of its parts. Thus it meets one of the conditions of the second horn of the dilemma brought against the dreamed theory. But admittedly this is not a comfortable fit. Nothing said explicitly in the *Sophist* about logos or its parts brings about such a result.

Let us then turn to the other conditions of the second horn of the dilemma. From what has been said, it is plain that a logos is a whole constituted from suitably selected parts and that it has a character of its own different from those of any of its parts. On this point, the Stranger's requirements for a logos, and his description of what a logos is, definitely commit him to the fulfillment of the remaining conditions that brought about the conclusion of the second horn of the dilemma.

Why is it then not the case that a logos is a kind of element that is inexplicable because it does not have any parts? Why is it then that a statement is not an *onoma*?[30]

One answer might be our earlier one that the argument does not have bite in any case. Such a whole put together from names and verbs, having characteristics different from them and not identical with the sum of them,

271

still has parts despite what a proponent of the dilemma may think that he has proved. All the same, some account ought to be forthcoming of just how the different parts of the logos are related to the special characteristics of a logos, in order that name and verb be understood not merely as necessary parts of a logos but as being necessary parts of what a logos is and does.

A modern philosopher looking at the texts in the *Sophist* concerning statement will be rather disappointed. For example, consider something like the Fregean distinction between the sense and the reference of expressions. In place of any distinction between a referent and a sense, we have *being* as what expressions in speech are about.[31] Expressions in speech are divided into name and verb—the former applying to agents; the latter to actions. These are the only kinds of being mentioned that expressions might be about. As statement parts, the Stranger's distinction is excessively narrow, even for what can go into places in statements of the simplest kind.[32] For instance, adjectives and state verbs are ignored. Generalizing sufficiently on name and verb in order to encompass such types of cases leads in the direction of the subject-predicate distinction and not toward sense versus reference.

Nor would a Fregean be consoled by any distinction among the speech act verbs occurring in the texts corresponding to *denotes* (or *refers*) versus *expresses* (or *means*) for expressions. The verbs σημαίνω and δηλόω do not appear to bear any such hard distinction. They are in fact used interchangeably for what a name does and for what a verb does.[33] More importantly, these same verbs are used to describe what a logos does. Words that fit together, where the fit will be a logos, are described as δηλοῦντο τι. Words that do not fit together, nonstatements, are described as μηδὲν σημαίνοντα.[34]

The moral here is clear: Plato's language in the *Sophist* does not exhibit anything like the degree or kind of regimentation that one can find common among modern semanticists.

Plato does distinguish naming and stating. In the process of doing so, he admits that words are about actions and agents but points out that in no case do they, or strings of each kind, state anything.[35] He also makes the point that there must be things about which statements are. And a statement's being about something looks similar to a word's being about something. However, these are kept somewhat distinct through a certain amount of regimentation in the use of prepositions and cases. For a word in relation to its object, whether agent or action, Plato most frequently has *epi* plus the dative; for a statement in relation to its object, he has most often the possessive genitive or *peri* plus the genitive.[36] These distinctions are not easy to English by means of verbs or nouns, especially in light of the fact that terms in this area tend to have technical associations or none at all. Despite this, let us say that *onomata* "apply" to things but that logoi state things "about" things.

Consider now the sample statements that the Stranger introduces: "Theaetetus sits" and "Theaetetus flies." Both the Stranger and Theaetetus agree that each statement is about Theaetetus. If we are meant to take these examples seriously, the answer to the questions περὶ οὗ καὶ ὅτου are given in the name part of the examples themselves. What a statement is about is just that to which the names in it apply. So one special feature of a logos is a function of what one part of a logos *does*.

A statement, whether true or false, states things. "Theaetetus sits" states things as they are (λέγει . . . τὰ ὄντα ὡς ἔστιν). "Theaetetus flies" states things different than the things that are (ἕτερα τῶν ὄντων), i.e., it states things that are not as being (τὰ μὴ ὄντ' ἄρα ὡς ὄντα λέγει). But still our example of a false statement states things, though these things are different than the things that are concerning Theaetetus (ὄντων δέ γε ὄντα ἕτερα περὶ σοῦ).[37]

What sorts of things are the *onta* and *hetera* in this account of truth and falsity? Let us consider briefly some possibilities.

Though many writers have commented on the beginnings of a propositional view of knowledge in Plato's later dialogues, a proposition is not quite the object of stating in the *Sophist*. The Stranger could have written of each of his sample statements that λέγει ὅτι. . . . But he did not. Rather he has the formula that each λέγει ὄντα (ἕτερα) περί τινος. Nor will it do to say that the *onta* that are stated really amount only to the logos itself. A logos is a complex, not of *onta*, but of *onomata*, viz. *onoma* and *rhēma*. Further, if *onta* and *hetera* had propositional or sentential complexity, then *peri tinos* would always be redundant. The example of a true statement would then state that Theaeatetus is sitting of Theaetetus, or it would state: "Theaetetus is sitting" of Theaetetus. Yet the Stranger takes great pain to emphasize *peri tinos* and has it as a special requirement that a statement be about something.

In the case of the examples, perhaps *onta* are a complex not of *onomata* but of Theaetetus and what he is doing. After all, the Stranger does say: "I shall state a logos for you, putting together a thing with an action through a name and a verb.[38] It is hard to know quite what to make of this remark. It occurs just before the examples of truth and falsity and the accounts that the Stranger gives to each. I should like to think that "putting together a thing with an action" is meant to give way to the more technical "saying things of something." But there is a supporting argument for not pressing the Stranger's remark too hard. For it seems to be a description not of what a statement does but of what a true statement does. If by succeeding to put together a name and a verb, one succeeds in putting together agent and action, it would appear that the agent is doing just what the logos states that he is doing. But whether an agent is put together with an action ought not to depend on what one does with words. It might then have been more felicitous for the Stranger to have said that what he was *trying* to do was to put together an agent and an action through a name and a verb. Success or failure would attach to his endeavor just inasmuch as truth or falsity would attach to his logos.

A final argument that what is stated does not have the complexity of a proposition, logos or agent-plus-action: by contrasting *onta* and *hetera* as what is said, the Stranger distinguishes what is said in the case of a true statement from what is said in the case of a false statement. But the distinction of *onta* and *hetera* becomes somewhat blurred and in need of qualification, if Theaetetus or his name is a partner to both *onta* and *hetera*. Different complexes would then have the same individual part.

What then are *onta* and *hetera*? Not without misgivings, I suggest that flying is what is other than what is concerning Theaetetus and sitting is what is concerning him. Since flying and sitting are taken as examples of actions or doings, then what is stated, whether the statement be true or false, is an action, that to which a verb applies.

A statement states things about something. For a sequence of words to be a statement it must state things and be about something. Neither of the necessary parts of a statement manages to state anything or be about anything. Yet each necessary part makes its own contribution to what a statement is. A statement is about those things to which the names in it apply. A statement states those things to which the verbs in the statement apply. The characters of a statement whole are explicable in terms of its parts. A logos is not a *stoicheion*.

The dreamed theory was an ontological theory that set conditions on knowledge and logos. According to it, the world consisted of complexes, which in turn consisted of perceptible elements. The latter could only be named but the former could be known. We know complexes when we have a logos that enumerates the perceptible elements of the complex. Thus the dreamed theory makes *a* distinction between naming and stating. So did the *Sophist*. But what was satisfactory for the dreamed theory is not good enough for the *Sophist*. A collection of *onomata*, otherwise unspecified, need not be a logos. The *Sophist* makes a needed distinction between the parts of statement. We have tried to see how this distinction might be viewed in order to disarm as much as possible the dilemma that brought down the theory of Socrates' dream.

NOTES

[1] Much work on these topics has been done since the original paper was presented; I hope that at least the general perspective will still be found interesting.

[2] At 329c–330b and again at 349d.

[3] Πότερον, ἔφην, ὥσπερ προσώπου τὰ μόρια μόριά ἐστιν, στόμα τε καὶ ῥὶς καὶ ὀφθαλμοὶ καὶ ὦτα, ἢ ὥσπερ τὰ τοῦ χρυσοῦ μόρια οὐδὲν διαφέρει τὰ ἕτερα τῶν ἑτέρων, ἀλλήλων καὶ τοῦ ὅλου, ἀλλ' ἢ μεγέθει καὶ σμικρότητι; (Protagoras 329d4–8). On dynamis and part in connection with the lump of gold example, see Gregory Vlastos, "The Physical Theory of Anaxagoras," Philosophical Review, vol. 59 (1950):31–57.

[4] But compare Aristotle's line of reasoning in the Nicomachean Ethics, 1097b31–34: ἢ καθάπερ ὀφθαλμοῦ καὶ χειρὸς καὶ ποδὸς καὶ ὅλως ἑκάσ του τῶν μορίων φαίνεταί τι ἔργον, οὕτω καὶ ἀνθρώπου παρὰ πάντα ταῦτα θείη τις ἂν ἔργον τι;

[5] ὀνομάτων γὰρ συμπλοκὴν εἶναι λόγου οὐσίαν (202b5).

[6] . . . ὥσπερ γὰρ ὁμήρους ἔχομεν τοῦ λόγου τὰ παραδείγ ματα οἷς χρώμενος εἶπε πάντα ταῦτα.
Ποῖα δή;
Τὰ τῶν γραμμάτων στοιχεῖά τε καὶ συλλαβάς (202e2–6).

[7] Theaetetus asks: Καὶ πῶς τοῦ στοιχείου τις ἐρεῖ στοιχεῖα; (203b2). (203b2).

[8] 202b3–7. See also Philebus 18b6–d2.

[9] Ἐχέτω δὴ ὡς νῦν φαμεν, μία ἰδέα ἐξ ἑκάστων τῶν συναρ μοττόντων στοιχείων γιγνομένη ἡ συλλαβή, ὁμοίως ἕν τε γράμμασι καὶ ἐν τοῖς ἄλλοις ἅπασι (204a1–3) italics mine.

[10] 201e2–202b2.

[11] According to Wittgenstein of the Tractatus also, one could not state an element; i.e., one could not state that it exists. But Wittgenstein's reason seems to have been that such a statement would not have a denial that presented a possible state of affairs. Such a reason would not have been that of the dream theorist.

[12] 184b4–186e12.

[13] 185c4–d3.

[14] That the existent E is not a complex of the order of persons and other things (201a1–2) should not be surprising. To know a complex and state what we know would involve listing in a logos all the elements of such a complex. Falling far short of such thoroughness, "E exists" would perhaps be only a true opinion. Cf. the treatment given to the example of the hundred pieces of Hesiod's wagon at 207b8–c3.

[15] Cratylus, 431a7–c2 and the Seventh Epistle, 343a9–b6, both mention but do not make much of this contrast.

[16] So Socrates, ". . . ἓν μέντοι τί με τῶν ῥηθέντων ἀπαρέσκει. . . . Ὃ καὶ δοκεῖ λέγεσθαι κομψότατα, ὡς τὰ μὲν στοιχεῖα ἄγνωστα, τὸ δὲ τῶν συλλαβῶν γένος γνωστόν" (202d8, d10–e1). It is to be noted that the perceptibility of the elements is mostly ignored in the critical discussion of the theory. 206a1–8 is an exception.

[17] There is one important exception to this reduction of the syllable-letter *paradeigma*. The first horn of the dilemma holds that if a syllable is known, then so are its letters. The logos of the syllable *So* is given through the enumeration of its constituent letters by name. But nothing analogous can be done for the letters themselves. So a letter can be known though it has no logos. Nothing further said in the *Theaetetus* quite upsets this part of the dreamed theory. Independently of the dilemma brought against the dreamed theory, then, the theory manages to retain a certain character asymmetry for wholes and parts. Simples cannot be stated though the complexes of which they are parts can. However, that an element cannot be stated depends on the view that a statement concatenates names of the *elemental parts of a thing*. If this is not what a statement does, it becomes an open question whether, in some sense, an element can be stated. On these matters, see Gilbert Ryle, "Letters and Syllables in Plato," *Philosophical Review*, vol. 69 (1960):431–51. Ryle's distinction of phonetics and graphology is overdrawn and his thesis that "gramma" for Plato had the sense of "phonetic element" is just wrong for several passages. On these points, see D. Gallop, "Plato and the Alphabet," *Philosophical Review*, vol. 72 (1963):364–76. It might be added that Ryle's view that for Plato a syllable has distinguishable but not separable parts, and that this has implications for the *Sophist* on logos and brings about certain analogies between Plato and Frege, seems not to be very securely based. For the possibility of a syllable's being something radically different from its parts is entertained in the *Theaetetus* at 203e2–5 and the syllable is there described as "ἐξ ἐκείνων ἕν τι γεγονὸς εἶδος." (Italics mine) Such a genetic whole, whose parts would seem to have a prior existence, just does not fit Ryle's phonetic model of a syllable. Analogously, the Stranger in the *Sophist* is committed to holding that *onomata* outside of a statemental context have application to things. See 216e4–262a8.

[18] I say *collection* and not *list*. These need not to be the same. Usually lists are constructed *for* some purpose and *of* things of some sort. One who enters items on a list supposes but need not state that things on the list do so stand, e.g., that So-and-So was archon at Athens. One may list correctly or incorrectly but not truly or falsely. But a collection of names or words need not even be a list.

[19] Clearly the dreamed theory has no mention of possible but not actual complexes and an enumeration of elements that is less than complete is described as true opinion and not false logos. Can then the dreamed theory give an account of the distinction of truth or falsity? If we state only complexes and the only complexes are actual, then it seems not—at least not in any way that would evade the sophistic paradox of stating what is not. Some (e.g., Cornford) have thought that the proponent of the dreamed theory would not have acknowledged falsity. And this seems natural enough inasmuch as logos is brought into the discussion as what would, in addition to true opinion, define knowledge.

[20] I mean to be understood as subscribing to the line of interpretation on the *Tractatus*, which holds that objects include neither properties nor relations. See Irving M. Copi, "Objects, Properties, and Relations in the *Tractatus*," in *Essays on Wittgenstein's Tractatus*, ed. Irving M. Copi and Robert W. Beard (Macmillan, 1966), pp. 167–87.

[21] χρῆν γὰρ ἴσως τὴν συλλαβὴν τίθεσθαι μὴ τὰ στοιχεῖα ἀλλ' ἐξ ἐκεί-

νων ἕν τι γεγονὸς εἶδος, ἰδέαν μίαν αὐτὸ αὑτοῦ ἔχον, ἕτερον δὲ τῶν στοιχείων (203e2-5).

[22] See *Metaphysics*, Z, 17, 1041b9-33 and also the report in A, 4, 985b14-17 on the differences among the atoms according to Democritus and Leucippus. For the discussion of the relevant passages from the *Metaphysics*, see Winifred Hicken, "The Character and Provenance of Socrates' dream in the *Theaetetus*," *Phronesis*, vol. 3 (1958):126-45.

[23] Since vowels can sometimes be syllabic, our assumption is contrary to fact. But neither Plato nor Aristotle seems to have been bothered about this point. They seem to have assumed that a syllable must have a degree of complexity greater than that of *any* letter.

[24] Ὅτε δὴ τὰ μὲν ἐθέλει τοῦτο δρᾶν, τὰ δ' οὔ, σχεδὸν οἷον τὰ γράμματα πεπονθότ' ἂν εἴη. καὶ γὰρ ἐκείνων τὰ μὲν ἀναρμοστεῖ που πρὸς ἄλληλα, τὰ δὲ συναρμόττει. . . . Τὰ δέ γε φωνήεντα διαφερόντως τῶν ἄλλων οἷον δεσμὸς διὰ πάντων κεχώρηκεν, ὥστε ἄνευ τινὸς αὐτῶν ἀδύνατον ἁρμόττειν καὶ τῶν ἄλλων ἕτερον ἑτέρῳ (252e9-253a2, 253a4-6).

[25] Other possibilities, such as mere sequences of written characters or phonetic elements, words, etc., will plainly not do.

[26] Or, adapting the language of *Theaetetus* 203b and *Philebus* 18b, a vowel gives voice to mutes and consonants. A syllable is something voiced and has phonetic complexity greater than that of any vowel.

[27] Hermogenes answers "no" to Socrates' question: Ἔστιν οὖν ὅτι λέγεις λόγου σμικρότερον μόριον ἄλλο ἢ ὄνομα; (*Cratylus* 385c7).

[28] In addition, a statement is true or false. Can a name be true or false? Despite the *Cratylus'* preference for the view that *onomata* have truth values (385bc), the account given in the *Sophist* of truth and falsity could hardly hold of *onomata*. Logoi are true or false on the condition that they state things. But a word does not state anything. Truth or falsity as characters of logoi, and not *onomata*, contribute further to asymmetry of such wholes and parts.

[29] 261d8 -262c5.

[30] That a statement is quite like a statement part was Frege's view. According to him, a statement, like a proper name, has a reference and a sense. It denotes the true or the false and expresses a thought. For him naming and stating were not so distinct. (See "On Sense and Reference," in *Translations from the Philosophical Writings of Gottlob Frege*, ed. Max Black and Peter Geach, [Oxford, 1952], pp. 56-78.)

[31] ἔστι γὰρ ἡμῖν που τῶν τῇ φωνῇ περὶ τὴν οὐσίαν δηλωμάτων διττὸν γένος (261e4-6).

[32] 262c9-10 .

[33] σημαίνει in connection with actions, 262b6; δηλοῖ for either, 262c4 Cf. τὰ τῇ φωνῇ δηλώματα as a genus for ὄνομα and ῥῆμα, 261e5; a ῥῆμα is a δήλωμα, 262a3; an ὄνομα is a σημεῖον τῆς φωνῆς, 262a6-7; τὰ τῆς φωνῆς σημεῖα include ὀνόματα and ῥήματα, 262d9.

[34] 261e1 and 261e1-2, respectively. But 'δηλοῦντα τι' seems to be a preliminary way of speaking that will give way to "state things," once naming and stating have been distinguished.

[35] ὀνομάζειν includes what may be done with either ὄνομα or ῥῆμα alone.

[36] For ἐπί plus the dative, see 262a3–262a7. For περί plus the genitive, and the possessive genitive, see 262e12–263a10, 263b4–5, b11 (but b12 has περὶ ἕκαστον, recalling 261d4–6), c1, c5, c7, c9–11, d1.

[37] This explanation is given: πολλὰ μὲν γὰρ ἔφαμεν ὄντα περὶ ἕκαστον εἶναί που, πολλὰ δὲ οὐκ ὄντα (263b11). And this recalls 255–59, especially 256e4–6: Περὶ ἕκαστον ἄρα τῶν εἰδῶν πολὺ μέν ἐστι τὸ ὄν, ἄπειρον δὲ πλήθει τὸ μὴ ὄν. The reference here is to εἴδη but at 263b11–12 the reference is to Theaetetus.

[38] Λέξω τοίνυν σοι λόγον συνθεὶς πρᾶγμα πράξει δι᾿ ὀνόματος καὶ ῥήματος . . . (262e12–14). This troublesome little passage tends to be overlooked. For example, it is not mentioned by A. L. Peck in "Plato's *Sophist*: the συμπλοκὴ τῶν εἰδῶν," *Phronesis*, vol. 7:46–66. It might or might not have led him to qualify the sharp distinction between συμπλοκὴ τῶν εἰδῶν and συμπλοκὴ τῶν ὀνομάτων that he sees as beginning at 261d1.

ROBERT G. TURNBULL

Episteme and *Doxa*: Some Reflections on Eleatic and Heraclitean Themes in Plato

I

IT is a truism of Plato interpretation that Plato wants at once a "world" that *is* and a "world" that *is* and *is not*. It is equally truistic that, if he is to have both "worlds," he must engage in some rather complex philosophical footwork. Or, to shift the metaphor, Plato must build a philosophical house in which both Parmenides and Heracleitus can be comfortably accommodated. Since Plato thinks that the satisfaction of his wants requires of him plausible accounts both of our knowledge of principles and also of our perceptual experience (and a relating of them), it will help us in understanding both the desire for two "worlds" and Plato's philosophical footwork to attend at the same time to his accounts of *episteme* and *doxa*. It is obviously impossible to attempt anything like exhaustive or definitive accounts of either of these in the brief compass of a single paper. What can be done in that compass is to point up some unnoticed features of the interrelationships of *episteme* and *doxa* that help to explain some difficult texts and that I take to be *archai* of their definitive accounts. I shall assume that Plato's wants are genuine philosophical *desiderata*, and it is part of my purpose to show that he has means of securing them that are both ingenious and of a piece with his general patterns of thinking. Obviously, much will turn on how *is* is to be understood and whether or not it can be said to have different senses. To give the general orientation that I think necessary for serious discussion of this matter I turn immediately to summarizing some interpretation and argument that I published in 1978.[1]

This paper was presented at the 1978 Washington meeting of the Society for Ancient Greek Philosophy; it has not previously been published but has been extensively revised for inclusion in this volume.
Robert Turnbull is Professor of Philosophy at The Ohio State University.

II

Despite the existence of a number of translations to the contrary, Plato does not have in Attic Greek any linguistic distinction corresponding to the English one made by *is* and *exists*. He is thus spared some of the tortures of late medieval and modern philosophy. He does, however, have a distinction between *is* (*eimi*) and *comes to be* (*gignomai*). Though there is some temptation to tarry on the parallels between that distinction and the one between *is* and *exists*, I should like for the time being to ignore *comes to be* and attend to *is*. That the mature Plato (at least) links *is* to the doctrine of forms is beyond question. What is not so universally recognized is that it is less illuminating to say, for Plato, that the forms *are* than it is to say that *to be is to be a form* and, for nonforms, to say that *to be is to be informed*. This remark obviously needs explanation and expansion. Providing them will enable me to make a number of relevant distinctions and clarifications.

Though I shall not offer detailed argument here for the interpretation, I wish to claim that, for the mature Plato (at least), forms are principles of structure. By the use of *principles* I wish to convey the idea of *structure itself* as contrasted with something (or things) structur*ed*. Thus The Triangle Itself is contrasted with this golden triangle (a structured piece of gold). The House Itself is contrasted with this wooden house. The Courageous Itself contrasts with courage in Achilles. Perhaps the primary reason for so considering forms is that, only by considering them in this way can Plato maintain that each form is one or single—and thus fend off attacks that are put in the mouth of Parmenides in the dialogue of that name, attacks on the uniqueness or singleness of each form.[2] Any number of things may have the same structure. But structure itself, just by itself, is, in any given case, single. With forms so understood, the much-discussed issue of the "separation" (*chorismos*) of the forms is simply the issue of the intelligibility of holding that there are principles of structure just by themselves, in "separation" from anything structur*ed*.

Plato's standard way of referring to a form is by means of expressions like "The *F* Itself" (*auto to F*). And this contrasts with "This *F*," "A certain *F*," and so on. There is, I think, a striking similarity between this contrast and that between abstract singular terms (as in "The triangle has three sides") and individualized singular terms (as in "This triangle has three sides" or "This triangle is made of gold").[3] Major interest lies in the fact that sentences with abstract singulars as their subjects entail universal sentences (as in "Every triangle has three sides").[4]

With proper development of what I take to be the mature Plato's doctrine of participation (*methexis*), Plato has machinery for explaining how it is that, granted that The *F* Itself is *G*, if anything can be referred to by "This

F," that thing will necessarily be *G*. There are problems, of course, in interpreting sentences like "The *F* Itself is *G*." Alexander Nehamas[5] has suggested a way of handling sentences about forms, which promises to free Plato from the morass of self-predication problems. He would read "The *F* itself is *F*" as "The *F* Itself is what it is to be *F*." Values for "what it is to be *F*" will, of course, look like definitions as, for example, "(to be *or* being) *G* which is *H*" (or "which *H*'s"). Or "what it is to be *G* which is *H*." On the view I am pressing, these would be ways of getting at or talking about principles of structure. And, obviously, principles of structure so considered may be internally related in a manner that is perspicuously displayed by genera/species orderings.[6] Thus, in a hackneyed example, the relatedness of The Plane Figure Itself (or, if you please, *being plane figurate*) and The Triangle Itself (or, if you please, *being triangular*) and the identity of The Triangle Itself and The Three-Sided Plane Figure.

There are two important consequences of all this for the present purposes. First, if what it is to be *F* includes *G* (or *being G*), then, if anything has a share of The *F* Itself, *necessarily* (*kath auto*) it is or has a share of The *G* Itself. In such necessities lies, I believe, the serious applicability of Platonic science (*episteme*) to the world of structured things or, if you please, the world of becoming. Second, it is possible that one may have linguistic or conceptual means of referring to The *F* Itself without, simply by virtue of having that conceptual means, being able to articulate or express what it is to be *F*, though he or she may have the means of somehow doing so "within" himself or herself. If we can explain this last clause, we shall have a clear sense in which one may find out or discover, by dint of effort, method, and perhaps native intelligence, what it is to be *F*. If one who has knowledge (*episteme*) is one who is able to express or articulate what it is to be *F* (or whatever), then his or her knowledge, however "definitional" it may be, is a dearly won achievement. And it is *of* the forms, not as some sort of peek, glimpse, or ineffable vision of them, but as what, for the moment, I shall call an "articulate awareness" of them.

III

Suppose forms to be principles of structure and articulate awareness of them to be definitional in character. Whatever it is that one is aware of in having an articulate awareness of The *F* Itself (i.e., an awareness of what it is to be *F*), it must be something to which spatial and temporal predicates cannot intelligibly be applied. *F*'s may lurk in corners, have learned geometry, be about to start a race, be ten feet tall, come to be, pass away, and so on. But what it is to be *F* can hardly be subject to any of these vicissitudes. Indeed, what it is to lurk in a corner, what it is to learn geometry, and so on are equally immune. Since it is absurd to think that The *F* Itself or what it is to be *F* could "become" *G* (or what it is to be *G*) or even "have become" The *F* Itself (or what it is to be *F*), there is reasonable ground for thinking of the forms as "eternal." If, as I have claimed, to be is to be a form or, if you please, principles of structure are principles of *being*, the "world" that *is* must be the (interrelated) forms. And it is that "world" of which we are aware in what I have called "articulate awareness."

IV

We shall return to this matter of definitions and articulate awareness, but I should like now rather abruptly to look at how "participation" comes out on this general way of construing Plato. On that way, it seems obvious that, if anything were to have a share of (*metechein*) of a form (principle of structure), (a) it would not itself be a principle of structure, but rather, *qua* "having a share," structur*ed* and (b) it would not have the form as a part (either numerically or specifically).

(a) is based, of course, on the work that *having a share* does for Plato. And that work is to provide an intelligible frame for various things' being *F*, *G*, or whatever—as contrasted with being what it is to be *F*, *G*, or whatever. On this view, to be *F* is to be structured in a certain way—the *F* way. Thus "has a share" (*metechei*) becomes a technical Platonic term for exhibiting one of the meanings of *is* in standard usage, viz., that in such sentences as "This man is tall," "This triangle is made of gold," and the like. This meaning of *is*, unlike that in sentences about forms, admits of tensed usage. It makes good sense to say that something *had* a share of The *F* Itself or that it *will have* a share of it. (We have noted, however, that no sense can be attached to saying that The *F* Itself was or will be what it is to be *F*.) I hasten to add that, on the interpretation I am pressing for, *having a share* is not limited to what is expressed by predicates or verbs, as the difference between The *F* Itself and This *F* requires. In the predicational use of *is*, a structur*ed* thing is said to have (had, have had, be about to have) some other or some contained or subordinate structure. And Plato, in *Parmenides*, makes a point of the need for having a share of The *This* (as *this man, this beautiful*, and the like), where The *This* is, as it were, a syncategorematic form.[7] More will be said in a later section on this score in commenting briefly on some passages in the *Parmenides* and *Sophist*. Though it is not strictly germane to the present project, I may note that, with the conception of forms as principles of structure, one may think of forms in a genera*l*/species hierarchy as containing (or being contained by) others. Those contained may be said to "have shares" of the containing. But this is only a hint, in want of lengthy development, especially in the light of the *Parmenides*.[8]

With regard to (b), it is worth underlining the point that things that have a common structure do not have a common part either numerically (as adjacent rooms have a common wall) or specifically (as bronze contains tin). Yet it is perfectly sensible to say that certain houses, automobiles, statues, triangles, or whatever all have the *same* structure. Indeed, we commonly say that they are the *same* house, *same* automobile, and so on. To add a bit to (b), we may note that Plato is an atomist, with tetrahedral, cubical, octahedral, and icosahedral atoms (omitting, for the present purpose, *their* construction from triangles). The basic materials of Plato's world thus share structures, and mixtures of them share (mathematical) structures.[9] Indeed, without straining the use of *mathematical*, one may claim that Plato's material world, just insofar as it *is* at all, is through and through mathematically structured. Thus anything that *is* at all *is* by virtue of some structure or other, i.e., by having a share of a form. This simply fleshes out a bit what I claimed early in the paper, viz., that, for nonforms, *to be is to be informed*.

V

All of this requires obviously that the "world" of structur*ed* things have (at bottom, as it were) non-something which, in itself, cannot be said to "be" at all. As Plato puts it, since proper inquiry can get at only things that *are* either in the (articulation of) principles sense or in the participational sense, non-something can be apprehended only by a kind of "bastard reasoning."[10] By such "bastard reasoning" one may say that "it" (non-something) takes, accepts, or admits structure but in "itself" neither is nor has structure (and thus no *being*). In this respect "it," as has been often noted, is like the so-called *prime matter* of Aristotle.

Neither Plato's "receptacle" nor Aristotle's prime matter *is* (or is ever found to be) in its "natural" condition. Whatever *is* and is found *to be* (participationally) is something or other, i.e., something structur*ed*. In Plato's case, bedrock seems to be the structuring given the receptacle by the demiurge as the elementary atoms of tetrahedra, cubes, octahedra, and icosahedra (or, if you please, the elementary triangles[11]). The reasoning (*logismos*) that gets us to the receptacle, the non-something, is *bastard* (*nothos*) because, as Timaeus puts it, it is without the aid of sensation (*anaisthesis*) and "scarcely to be trusted."[12] In context Plato suggests that the requirement of the receptacle is all one with the requirement of space (*chora*) or place.

So much for the arena of participation or having shares and of multiplicity and change. I am very aware that proper discussion of this difficult portion of *Timaeus* would require the sort of treatment given it by, say, Vlastos,[13] wherein proper attention is given to random movements, the so-called "errant cause," the images of nurse and mother, and so on.

VI

It seems clear enough that, with the conception of forms as principles of structure, "something" may have a certain structure, *F*, at one time and have, instead, a different structure, *G*, at a later time (where *F* and *G* are contraries). Given the notion of contrariety, which is in Plato as early as *Phaedo*,[14] we may then say that it is *F* at a certain time and, later, *is not F*. Though the *Sophist* reading of "is not *F*" as "has a share of the Different from *F*" (one of the "parts" of Different) does not as such build in contrariety,[15] it obviously accommodates contrariety.

I have intentionally left out any definite subject term in the above paragraph, but now I wish to return to an idea developed a little in Part IV above, namely, that of having a share of *The This*, an idea that is obviously linked with the usage, "This *F*," to refer to something, as contrasted with saying something about an object or thing referred to. In order to refer successfully, there must *be* something referred to—by which I mean not simply that there must be some structur*ed* thing, but also that the *F* be capable of joining with *The* and *Itself* to refer to a principle of structure or a form. With *The This* there enters into the picture the idea of a *subject* that is itself structur*ed*. Though Socrates, early in the *Parmenides*, is made to express doubt about how to treat "substance" forms like *man*, *ox*, and *fire*[16] and how there might be shares of them, Plato fairly obviously treats sortals as having forms in the later dialogues.[17]

It is noteworthy as well that the *Parmenides* suggests the idea of something's remaining the same while going through a process of change. Put in the terms of this paper, something could be structur*ed* in a certain way through a stretch of time during which another sort or sorts of structuring of it were changing. The obvious illustrations of this are of the "sortal" kind, as a man's remaining the same while getting larger or smaller, changing location, and so on. In the *Parmenides'* terms, remaining in one respect "in the same" while, in another, being (in the stretch of time involved) "always in a different."[18] Thus there does seem to be a case to be made for saying that certain structured things, normally gotten at by subject terms, both *are* and *are not* in the sense of now having a share of a form and later having a share of a different (and contrary) form.

In his reply to Zeno in the early part of the *Parmenides*,[19] Socrates calls attention to a nontemporal sense in which he, Socrates, both is and is not, when he points out that he may have shares both of The One Itself (in being one man) and The Many Itself (as having many parts). There is yet another nontemporal sense in which structured things may be and not be, which many have pointed out[20] and which involves correlatives, as large/small, beautiful/ugly, and the like. Thus something that is large relative to X may be small relative to Y and therefore be both large and not large, small and not small, beautiful relative to X and ugly relative to Y and therefore be both beautiful and not beautiful, ugly and not ugly. Though the status of such relative forms for mature Plato at least is somewhat unclear (What does the paradox of the *Republic* finger, which is both large and small, lead one to?[21]), it is clear enough that Plato uses relatives in exhibiting how things in the "world of becoming" both are and are not.

Some other relatives do not present the grounds for saying that something is and is not, in particular, master/slave and knowledge/known (or knowable) of the *Parmenides*.[22] Though a master is always *of* a slave and vice versa, there is nothing in these relatives that supports a claim that something both is and is not a master (or a slave). So too in the knowledge/knowable case. In the *Theaetetus*, Plato speaks of the correlatives, *aisthesis/aistheton* (if you please, sensing/sensed),[23] where these do not *as such* seem to require that something be and not be, but where there is an *is* and *is not* in the neighborhood. This comes in, of course, with the idea that one and the same wind may be both hot and cold (to different perceivers at the same time or to a single one at different times), and the like. Generally, since according to the "secret doctrine" of the *Theaetetus* what is present as an *aistheton*, though paired with an *aisthesis*, is a function both of something "outside" and of a sense organ, sensory presentations (*aistheta*) vary between persons and for the same person at different times. And so, insofar as such sensory presentations are taken as indicative of things, one must say of those things that they present themselves to sense as both white and not white, both sweet and not sweet, both loud and not loud, and so on.

VII

As everyone who has had an introductory Plato course knows, in *Republic V*,[24] Plato links *doxa* (opinion) with *is* and *is not* and links *episteme* with *is* (and he links *agnoia* with *is not*). *Doxa* as used here and elsewhere (though not uniformly) is some sort of propensity or settled disposition, indeed, a many-track disposition or propensity, including (as we shall note at length in VIII, below) importantly linguistic disposition(s). I may have *doxa* in regard to many different parts of what *is* and *is not*. Given what we have been saying about *is* and *is not*, it would seem that there could be *doxa* in regard to a horse, the sun, an action—anything generally thought to be "perceptible." In *Republic V*, *doxa* is linked with sights and sounds, and the doxastic person is characterized as typically a "lover of sights and sounds." The doxastic person is contrasted sharply with the *epistemic* person, the latter being given the name *philosopher* or *lover of wisdom*.[25] In contrast with the doxastic lover of sights and sounds, who is characterized as "asleep and dreaming," the epistemic person is characterized as wide awake. Since the awareness of sights and sounds, i.e., sensation or *aisthesis*, was taken by the Greeks (as it is by us) as the critical indication of being awake, Plato's contrast is (deliberately) paradoxical in the extreme.

At many other points in various dialogues, Plato associates *doxa* with persuasion. The doxastic person is fair game for the orator or sophist. *Doxa*, as something believed or opined, is something that one can be persuaded into, be persuaded to deny, or be persuaded to amend or change. As such, it contrasts sharply with what one has learned or knowledge, the possession of which is secure from persuasion. Plato associates persuasion with pleasure and pain and, in *Theaetetus* at least,[26] treats the latter as kinds of *aisthesis*. I think that what he has in mind is that, for a number of commonplace pleasures and pains at least, more or less intense sensory presentations (experiences, *aistheseis*?) are themselves pleasures or pains. Thus a very loud sound, a very sour and bitter taste, intense heat, etc., are in themselves pains. Similarly, visual, olfactory, tactual, etc., sensory presentations are in themselves pleasures. This idea together with the association of *doxa* and *aisthesis* seems to underlie the major theme of *Gorgias*,[27] namely, that, even as a cook panders to people's palates and not to their constitutions, so the rhetorician panders to the association of opinion with pleasure and pain and fails to inculcate true opinions (and thus surely not knowledge) that are associated with people's good(s).

Doxai are linked with sensation (*aisthesis*). Sensation, in turn, is linked with the external and material world (the world of Plato's atoms) via our senses. The doxastic person, thus, is typically attached to and takes as "real" the material world as mediated by his or her sensations or sense presentations. Since sights and sounds make up a large part of the latter, Plato speaks of the doxastic person as "the lover of sights and sounds." In the celebrated analogy of the line in *Republic VI*,[28] *doxa* is taken to encompass both *eikasia* and *pistis*. The *eikastic* person appears to be a victim of very naive perceptual acceptance, suggesting the state of mind of someone taken in by "shadow paintings,"[29] i.e., paintings involving both perspective and the use of shadows to suggest three-dimensionality. He or she seems to be the prime candidate to be the "lover of sights and sounds" whose attachment to the sights and sounds of naive perceptual consciousness is rather like the dreamer's attachment to his or her dreams. And, given our account of the various ways in which things may be said both *to be* and also *not to be*, the *eikastic* form of *doxa* seems inevitably to be of what *is* and *is not*. *Pistis* improves on the naive perceptual acceptance of *eikasia* in its recognition that adjustments must be made in our awareness of things around us to compensate for perspective, near and distant objects, different lighting conditions, and the like. Even so, *pistic doxa* is still awareness of the "world of becoming" (in the terms used earlier, "structured things") and that by way of sense presentations. And, as we saw in section VI, it must be an awareness of what *is* and *is not*.

VIII

I should like now to shift the scene rather abruptly in the interest of getting before us some not-often-noticed features of the *doxastic* story, features that I think important as well to the *epistemic* story and to that of the "world" that *is*. However we are to characterize *doxa* exactly, it is quite clear that *doxa* is expressed linguistically. I hope, starting with this truism, to get a rather sweeping claim concerning Plato's theory of and reliance upon language on the table. In doing so, I shall make rather liberal use of a published paper of my former student, Jeffrey Gold,[30] and shall be articulating some features of some conversations I have had with him concerning Plato's *Cratylus*.

Cratylus makes a great deal of a mythical name-giver who provides us (strictly, speakers of Attic Greek, but the inheritors of any perspicuous language will do for "us") with "conventional" linguistic resources that are tailored to a remarkable set of Platonic forms, namely, *name* forms. And *Cratylus* suggests that quite different conventional linguistic resources could be and are tailored to that same set of forms, so that there could be and are the same names in quite different conventional languages. Since the name forms that the name-giver looks to are linked with the remaining forms (in the *pros ti* or "of" sense discussed in VI.), we may presumably be sure that the conventional names provided by the name-giver are or can be linked with those remaining forms and/or shares of them (in the earlier terms of this paper, with the principles of structure and structur*ed* things). Name forms are thus principles of structure, and shares of them (the structur*eds*) would be structur*ed* patterns of speech (dispositions) manifested in overt and covert[31] utterances of conventional names (and name-strings) given by the name-giver. On this view and in communities blessed with appropriate conventional languages, toddlers, in learning to speak their native tongue, are being provided with their chief means of apprehending Platonic forms. I hasten to add, however, that the articulate apprehension of the forms will be a dearly won achievement, and, statistically speaking, they are not likely to achieve it.

Those same toddlers are also being provided with the linguistic means of expressing *doxa*, indeed with their chief means of apprehension of the many structur*ed* things around them. The linkage of this use of language with *aisthesis* seems obvious enough. When in the presence of an *F*-thing (or what comes to the same, when the language teacher believes the child is so affected as to have a certain *aisthesis/aistheton*[32]), the child is conditioned to say or utter *F*. And there are, of course, any number of values of *F* that can be similarly linked with sensation or *aisthesis* situations. If one were to speak of developmental stages, this appears to be an ideal candidate for the stage of primitive *eikasia* and the initial cathexis on sights and sounds. But, of course, the name-giver has provided us with a rich enough vocabulary to express the learning, so to speak, that things have other sides than the facing side, that receding things look smaller, that the same thing can be touched and seen, and so on. Even so, that vocabulary is acquired and expressed in linkage with *aisthesis*. And, even though one by its acquisition and employment reaches the stage of *pistis*, the familiar objects of *doxastic* man are the structured things of the "world" that, on Plato's view, *is* and *is not*.

IX

The moral of the tale for Plato's doctrine of *doxa* is the idea that, in acquiring a native language, one acquires it virtually entirely in a *use* (or, if you please, object language) context *and*, given the associations with *aisthesis*, inevitably comes to the "acceptance" of the aisthesis-associated things as "real." A consequence of this sort of "acceptance" is that, unreflectively, one looks for "causes" and interconnections between such things *in* or among those things. Put crudely, one—at least at first—becomes or is naturally an empiric. Add pleasure and pain to this as obvious features of the linkage with *aisthesis*, and one can discern pretty clearly the association of *doxa* with persuasion. Though the name-giver may have been a great benefactor, his unreflective beneficiaries, conscious of a "world" of things only by the associative tie of names with things *via aisthesis* contexts, are rather easily moved by orators, especially under the associative influence of pleasure or pain, to loosen linguistic ties and be led into associations not intended by the name-giver. The touching speech of Socrates in the *Phaedo*,[33] urging his followers not to become misologists, even if he fails to produce a certain argument, assumes a new significance when seen against this kind of background. As I shall try to show shortly, the search for genuine knowledge (*episteme*), as Plato sees it, is in a tough sense *logistic*. Plato thinks of its alternative as a return to knacks, routines, and loose association, the sort of thing dealt with so scathingly in the *Gorgias*.[34]

Let me pause a moment before starting the next section for a couple of remarks about the name-giver and his work. Whatever Plato's view may have been concerning the existence of some linguistic benefactor of the remote past, *we* can demythologize talk about such a figure by thinking about the development of (Attic) Greek through hundreds of years of cultural change and interchange with other Mediterranean cultures. Without attempting to state or trace the causes, I think it simply factual that a rich and complex culture developed in and among the Greek-speaking people(s) of the eastern Mediterranean. Agriculture, husbandry, building arts, metal-working crafts, ship-building, navigation, warfare arts, measuring arts, medicine, arts of government, household management, trade and commerce, and the like were developed to a high level indeed. What tends to go unnoticed is that, along with this much admired development, went appropriate linguistic change and development. What I mean is, of course, the development of an appropriate vocabulary (and the linguistic dispositions) for materials, tools, procedures, social and political activities, artifacts, measuring and counting, explaining, assessing, evaluating, approving and disapproving, exchange, and so on. Indeed, one is tempted to find increased "naturalism" in vocabulary and usage as one moves from earlier to later Greek pieces of literature, one that accompanies the improving state of Greek "arts."[35]

The second comment has to do with Plato's deploring the activities of sophists and rhetoricians. Insofar as they are seen to be artificers of persuasion and instillers of *doxa*, they can be seen as perverters of the language, that is, as taking a language that is suited to (and grew out of) craft performance and (reasonably) successful coping with nature and society and loosening its connections with such performance and coping. Plato can then be seen as finding such loosening as linking the older vocabulary of "objective" craft performance with "subjective" rigamaroles for gratification and pleasure.

X

Let me now put our issues a bit differently and bring back the forms-as-being theme. Plato clearly thinks that all of the being and, as well, the interconnections of things in the world of becoming consist in their being or having shares of the world of forms, i.e., in the terms of this paper, things having structure for which the forms are the principles. *Cratylus* claims that there are name-forms, these, in the present view, being principles of structure that parallel the other forms (being *of* them) and that are properly embodied in, or enstructured in, linguistic habits and dispositions. The *Cratylus* fiction of the name-giver is that of an omniscient ancestor who has provided us with a sufficiently articulated set of sounds (and marks) to be the material tokens for linguistic dispositions that are or can embody the structures that name-forms are. Young children, as we have noted, acquire the linguistic dispositions of the name-giver in contexts involving *aisthesis* (at least the first ones). Enamored by the sights and sounds and suffering from the illusion that truth is to be found in the objects of perception, they fix their attention on what they are aware of by way of sights and sounds.

If they are fortunate, they will encounter a Socrates who will invite them to turn away from sights and sounds, from the *F*'s and *G*'s, and try to say what it is to be *F*, what it is to be *G* , and so on. For these purposes the sights and sounds are hindrances; what is needed is attention to the linguistic dispositions by means of which (with *aisthesis*) they see things. From what has been said in the foregoing, it should be clear that, on the view here being outlined, the inquiry is in a sense linguistic and in another sense *not*. Interestingly, if one were to collect texts of Plato in which he is talking about the forms and the investigation of them, one would collect a very large number of uses of linguistic or linguistic-associated terms. Typically: *logos* (especially in uses commonly translated by 'reason'), *dialektike*, and *dialegesthai*. Illustrative and typical of several texts is Parmenides' remark to the young Socrates: "When you were just now speaking to him [Zeno], I was impressed that you did not stay simply with visibles nor let your review wander about concerning them, but rather concerning those which one grasps simply by *logos* and must be thought of as forms (*eide*)."[36]

In the above paragraph I said something about "attention to the linguistic dispositions. . . ." This is, of course, misleading. Explaining how it is misleading will help unpack my remark about the inquiry's being both linguistic and nonlinguistic and will, I think, be best done by making some comments first about object languages and metalanguages.

XI

American philosophers of the mid-twentieth century have all grown up on the distinction between object language and metalanguage. And most of us have discovered that it is deceptively simple. In particular it does not help us to understand how any sort of language manages to be *about* anything, and it does not help (and may hinder) our ability to make distinctions that are crucial for sophisticated talk about language. The *Cratylus'* name-giver would have played a poor joke indeed if all he had bequeathed future language-users were the conditioning of them to utter some sounds and sound-sequences. But, of course, it is difficult to imagine the acquisition of such conditioning without linkage with *aisthesis* as a (passive) source of stimuli. And, of course, Plato supposed that *aisthesis* to be produced by motion in or from various things in the environment (and thus to link with those things via their motions). Were there no such linkage to the "world," the dispositions produced in the heirs of the name-giver would be a poor gift and lead to a great deal of practical difficulty. And Plato assumes, I think, that the vocabulary provided us by the name-giver *also* links with the forms, since its most important terms are vehicles for the embodiment of name-forms in linguistic dispositions.

Before proceeding with the development of the last paragraph, I think it is worth noting that, in stressing the linkage of terms with *aisthesis* in language learning, I have not stressed the linkage of terms with one another that would, of course, have to be part of the name-giver's patrimony. If he has done his job well, his conventional sounds (and marks) will include the panoply of particles, nouns, verbs, inflections, conjugations, singulars, plurals, and so on, necessary to get the job done. This consideration gives an added dimension to the analogy, in *Cratylus*,[37] of the shuttle-maker to the name-giver. Plato is at some pains to require that the shuttle used in any given case be the proper sort of shuttle to get a particular job with a particular sort of fiber done properly.

So we are supplied with appropriate conventional tokens (marks and noises) and dispositions for an object language, i.e., one suited for speaking about the "world" in connection with *aisthesis*. And it has been often noted that both in *Theaetetus* and in *Sophist*[38] Plato tells us that "thought" is *inner speech*. If for the moment we think of such thought as "object language" inner speech (which is certainly intended by Plato in *Sophist*), it is fairly clear that such thought (as well as overt linguistic expression) is *doxastic* in the *Republic* sense, i.e., it is of what *is* and *is not*. And it is clear enough in *Sophist* that Plato thinks *doxa* to be sometimes true, at least in the sense of being able to articulate what *is* or what *is not* the case.[39]

It is also clear enough that Plato was well aware of the possibility of speaking about language both in the sense of speaking about particular words and strings of words[40] and in the sense of speaking about articulate sounds and strings of sounds.[41] The former task belongs to the grammarian; the latter, perhaps, is part of the task of the name-giver. Plato obviously attaches great importance to the "discovery" of Theuth of the means of classifying vowels and consonants.[42] What that discovery, as recounted in *Philebus*, comes to is, I think, the discovery of the means necessary for a usable alphabet. But we are here in the presence of the means for inventing, systematizing, and describing the conventional words of spoken and written language—in this sense a metalanguage or metalanguages. And though those means may be necessary for there to be spoken and written language, they are surely not sufficient for a language that "carves nature at its joints" and can be used to get at *being*.

If one supposes, as I think Plato did, that the language really does (or, at any rate, can) enable its users to express or get at the world, though through the associations with *aisthesis* it can be *mis*used, he or she will attempt to find and use such resources as may be available for describing or articulating the "joints" at which nature is to be cut. And, of course, Plato finds those resources in the language. Where a number of contemporary philosophers find *rules* of language statable in a metalanguage and then turn to difficult questions concerning the "objectivity" of human knowledge,[43] Plato finds in what I shall call the "reflective" use of language the means of referring to and articulating the principles of *being*.

XII

In an earlier section of this paper I spoke of the possibility of someone's being able to use expressions of the form, The *F* Itself, significantly without, by that very fact, being able to say what it is to be *F*. I think that we are now in a position to say how that might be possible and also how one might, by a reflective use of language, find out what it is to be *F*. Any number of early and middle Platonic dialogues are instructive in this regard, involving, as they do, much discussed "What is *X*?" questions. "What is justice?" "What is the pious?" "What is *arete* (virtue)?"—the list is well known to thousands of college sophomores. Still staying with the myth of the name-giver, we may suppose that he has provided the linguistic resources for asking such questions, in particular, in Greek, the ability to link the definite article to a substantive (say, "justice") or an adjective (say, "pious") both in questions and in sentences expressing generality with abstract singular terms as subjects (as in "The triangle has three sides"). Of course, Socrates' interlocutors regularly profess ability to answer a "What is *X*?" question and with equal regularity start off by giving or alluding to examples of *X* or listing some kinds of *X*. Socrates, commonly with ironic reference to their pretensions to knowledge, manages usually to get them to grasp what sort of answer to the question might be relevant, however incorrect it may be.

In *Euthyphro*, Socrates even says to Euthyphro that what he wants, in asking "What is the pious?" is the *eidos* or the *idea*,[44] using the very terms that Plato, in later dialogues, uses for his separated forms. Whether this is good evidence for Plato's holding the separated-forms doctrine at the time of writing *Euthyphro* does not concern me here. What is relevant for my purpose is Socrates' use of the terms in the effort to jar Euthyphro out of standard object language use of terms (e.g., "Prosecuting my father is pious") and into what I have been calling *reflective* use of language. I am also interested in the assumption, often stated, that Socrates' interlocutors, properly questioned, will be able to answer "What is *X*?" questions and the related profession of Socrates that he needs only the sufferance of one person in reaching agreement on an answer. At bottom, I think, that assumption is based on the sound idea that someone who has learned the language and can use it properly can be brought round to formulating (some of) its rules. In the Socratic-Platonic case, however, since what is asked is a question, viz., "What is (it to be) *X*?" what is called for is a definition that states the *eidos*. But, though it could be said that, if Euthyphro knew the rule(s) for the proper use of *pious*, he would know whether prosecuting his father is a pious act, it could also be said that, if he knew what it is to be pious, he would know as much. And it is plausible enough that reflection on the language he knows will be as likely to give him the latter (the definition) as the former.

But, of course, Plato is no conventionalist (except for the sounds or marks of language). What he—and, presumably, Socrates—is looking for is the *ground* of object language usage. Since he has expressions of the form, The *F* Itself, as well as substantives with the Greek equivalent of -*ness* or -*hood* endings, and these are obvious candidates for definition and plausibly referential, it is perfectly plausible that he uses the techniques of what I have been calling reflection to arrive at articulated knowledge of the principles of *being*. Such reflection obviously contrasts sharply with any sort of hunting or searching that makes use of *aisthesis*. Indeed, sights and sounds are a positive hindrance to such reflective inquiry (though one may point out counter-examples to a proposed definition by reference to goings-on in the "world of becoming" and the use of object language vocabulary). Such reflective inquiry is, in a tough etymological sense, *logistic* and fully justifies Plato's insistence upon *dialektike*, *logos*, and kindred terms for describing the mode of inquiry. Whether, as Aristotle testifies, the historical Socrates limited the scope of his inquiries and did not think of what he defined as "separated," whereas Plato did, makes no difference to the point that the inquiry proceeds by *logistic* means and involves the "reflective" use of language. Though extremely important for other purposes, it also makes no difference for the present purpose that Plato himself manifestly moves from inquiry by dialogue between two persons to inquiry by collection and division (which, presumably, can be carried on alone). The same resources are being tapped, namely, those provided by *Cratylus'* mythical name-giver. And we have earlier noted that the name-giver can be construed as simply a picturesque way of claiming that a language, developed and refined through many centuries of varied and complex experience, will, when used reflectively, yield to us the order and interconnection of the principles of *being*.

XIII. Some Concluding Comments

First, the conceit of the person who has *episteme* as wide awake and the *doxastic* person as asleep and dreaming joins a number of predominantly visual metaphors that Plato is fond of in describing the acquisition and possession of *episteme*. Though these may have some association with the mysteries and have continued to be used to express the enthusiasm of insight, Plato uses any number of opportunities to make it quite clear *aisthesis*, visual or otherwise, does not as such play any role for the *epistemic* person.

Second, I distinguished at the outset between forms as principles of structure and structur*ed* things. Except for some discomfort in fitting them into adjectival usage, I could as well have used the distinction between natures and natur*ed* things. In either case the important point is Plato's insistence upon there being natures or principles of structure quite independent of anything natur*ed* or structur*ed*. These *are*; natur*ed* or structur*ed* things *are* and *are not*. The only place in Plato's dialogues where the so-called "separation" (*chorismos*) of the forms is emphasized by Plato is in the *Parmenides* where the issue is really, I believe, one of the clarification of *having a share* of the forms.[45] And the critic, Parmenides, is quite explicit in his insistence that the forms must *be*. It will hardly do to insist that the forms themselves be natur*ed* or structur*ed* and then to find their "separation" strange.

Third, I am aware, of course, that the Plato I have herein depicted, manner of expression aside, has a resemblance to W. V. O. Quine and Wilfrid Sellars in, at the least, the account of language and its connection(s) with *aisthesis* and the physical world around us. I have also pointed out, conventional *symbols* aside, that Plato is no conventionalist. What is important here is that, in fact, Plato is closer to them on the relevant matters than to the tradition that Richard Rorty castigates as modern epistemology[46] and in whose terms Plato has been so often understood. What I have been calling "articulate awareness" of the forms is, of course, an achievement, not a glimpse or a peek, nor even a Russellian "act of acquaintance".[47] To have such an awareness of a form or forms is, I think, rather more like knowing Newton's laws of motion or the Pythagorean theorem than like knowing one's neighbors or glimpsing a prothonotary warbler. On the interpretation here being defended knowing is rather more the condition of one who, having learned, knows than of one who, having seen, remembers or recognizes. It is not enough obviously merely to be able to use phrases of the form, The *F* Itself; what is required is the ability to say what it is to be *F*. Plato's insistence is that, in exhibiting conceptual necessities *via* dialectic, one gets at the ordering principles of the world. The Platonic tradition, with the idea that the same principles that order the world inform the human soul in its encounter with the world, has been rich, varied, and attractive.

Fourth, this paper has drawn upon the resources of dialogues that, by almost anyone's reckoning, belong to different periods. Though I should certainly argue that Plato's philosophy developed and changed, the general picture limned in this paper is either background or foreground for dialogues from the "later early" period. Showing that is obviously a longer task than an article, but I can hope that the idea of such a general picture has at least some initial plausibility.

Fifth and last, does this reading make Plato a "linguistic philosopher"? Yes and no. Yes, in that it contends that Plato was more respectful of language and what it can make known than is commonly recognized. No, in that Plato is emphatically interested in what the use of the language makes known and would be shocked by any sort of conventionalism or instrumentalism. And the reading leaves room for Plato's doctrine of active soul, for the soul's erotic attachment to the forms, and even for his poetical flights. What it does attempt to nail down is the distinction between *doxa* and *episteme* and the sort of disciplined inquiry that leads to the latter and makes it worth having.

NOTES

[1] Robert G. Turnbull, "Knowledge and the Forms in the Later Platonic Dialogues," *Proceedings and Addresses of the American Philosophical Association* 52 (1978):735–58.

[2] *Parmenides* 130E4–133A10. How can the form be one or unique if (a) those having shares of it have the whole form as shares, (b) those having shares of it have parts as shares, (c) the form is taken to be the "look" or *idea* of those having shares, or (d) the form is taken as pattern and the shares as copies or likenesses? I list (a) through (d) merely as reminders, not as serious interpretations. The present point is simply that, taking the form as a principle of structure (or a nature) and as in no way structur*ed* (or natur*ed*), the very idea of a form's being many is simply unintelligible. (I am, of course, prepared to argue that the so-called "second part" of *Parmenides* does take forms as, in effect, principles of structure, but this is not the place to present that argument. It will appear before long in a book on *Parmenides*.)

[3] I am, of course, suggesting that, reflecting on standard English usage of abstract singular terms, we could easily wonder about the status of the flag (the one mentioned in "The flag is flown on state occasions") or the whale (the one mentioned in "The whale is herbivorous"), and that worry would be appropriately similar to the worry about the beautiful mentioned in the phrase, "The Beautiful Itself." Indeed, we should have a similar worry concerning what is being mentioned in lecture or paper topics like "The Beautiful" (which aesthetician Jones lectured on last night) or "The Forward Pass" (which coach Smith wrote an article about).

[4] "The triangle has three sides" clearly entails "Every triangle has three sides." If one takes "The Triangle" in the first as making reference to a nature or principle of structure, one will need some of the apparatus of participation of exemplification to explain the entailment. If one takes the first sentence as material mode of speech for a metalinguistic sentence used to state a rule, the entailment can also be explained. As Wilfrid Sellars has shown, the latter course is open even to a nominalist who will not admit *abstracta*. Part of the thrust of the present paper is to show that, by sternly denying that his principles of structure are structur*ed*, Plato can make the former course very plausible indeed.

[5] Alexander Nehamas, "Self-Predication and Plato's Theory of Forms," *American Philosophical Quarterly* 16 (1979):93–103. In my handling of definitional expressions, I have gone considerably farther than Nehamas goes in the use of the phrase "what it is to be *F*" in self-predications.

[6] I have attempted detailed explanation of such genera/species orderings in "The Later Platonic Concept of Scientific Explanation" in *Plato and the Sciences*, ed. John P. Anton (Albany, 1980), pp. 75–101. The attempt occurs in commenting on Socrates' Promethean discovery at *Philebus* 16C–17A.

[7] *Parmenides* 160E, 3–7: "And, furthermore, the one which is not has a share of the *that*, the *a certain*, the *this*, the *to, in, or by means of this*, and of all other such. For the one could not be said, nor could the differents from the one, nor could anything to it or in it or of it be said, if there were not a share for it of the *a certain* or of those others." The context is one in which, in order to say that something is not *F*, it must be assumed that the thing said not to be *F* exists. (In this respect it is like the requirement of *Sophist* 262 that a sentence be *of* something, as "Theaetetus is not flying" is *of* Theaetetus.) For schematic example, "A certain *G* is not *F*" would not be true or false unless something could be truly characterized as *a certain G*.

[8] In *Parmenides* 142B–155E, the so-called "second hypothesis," Parmenides, after stating that "to say that the one has a share of being expresses nothing other than what is expressed briefly when one says that one is" (142C, 6–7), proceeds to use "has(ve) a share of" (*metechein*) fairly liberally. And he uses it in contexts that, though I admit the difficulty of the *Parmenides*, seem to require the sense of forms having shares of forms. Though he also uses alternative vocabulary, the Eleatic Stranger of *Sophist* occasionally (e.g., 255B, in speaking of motion and rest as "having shares of" Same and Different) speaks of forms as having shares of forms.

[9] As I read the *Timaeus*, Plato's atomism has a profoundly different motivation from that attributed to Leucippus and Democritus and exploited in later Epicureanism. The aim of the demiurge is to bring about a compromise with *ananke* that leaves as much intelligibility as possible for the world of becoming. He produces material atoms in the geometrically tidy form of the regular solids, thus making the material constituents of the world mathematically intelligible, despite their being many and occupying and moving about in "space." Compounds "made" from them can, as well, be thought of as having shares of (mathematically intelligible) structure, and so on. Plato in effect is giving credibility to the Pythagorean distinction between sensible and intelligible "numbers." As capable of transmutation into one another (excepting the cubes), grouping and regrouping as larger and smaller, as joining in compounds and separating, and as moving about, Plato's atoms obviously *are* and *are not*.

[10] *Timaeus* 52B, 2–3: ". . . itself to be apprehended by a sort of bastard reasoning along with non-aisthesis. . . ." A line or two earlier Timaeus has (as this paper does) linked *doxa* with *aisthesis*—thus there is no *doxa* of the receptacle. And it is improper to say of it that it *is* and *is not*. Nor, to use the terms of the latter part of this paper (especially sections XI and XII), is it properly apprehended (as the forms are) by the "reflective" use of language or concepts.

[11] I leave the vexing question of the regrouping triangles (which make up the faces of the regular solids) to another occasion. But let me note that one is really not

required by the *Timaeus* text or its sense to picture two-dimensional triangles flying about in the receptacle. Suffice it to say that it would serve Plato's mathematical purposes to require that, in the transmutation of the elements or in their increase or diminution, the areas and shapes of the sides of the regular solids be maintained. The possibility of giving an appropriate mathematical description of the sides of the solids by triangles (albeit different sorts for tetrahedra, octahedra, and icosahedra from those for cubes) could satisfy the condition without the curiosity of two-dimensional occupiers of space.

¹² As noted in n. 10, *doxa* occurs with *aisthesis*. *Pistis,* in the *Republic* analogy of the line, is a form of *doxa*. To describe the apprehension of place (*chora*) or the receptacle as "hardly even *pistis*" hints at the difficulty. Properly parented *logismos* would presumably at least have sensation on its side and would have the warrant of some sort of *being* term. Even the *not* of *Sophist* turns out to have a *being* warrant, namely, the *Different* or one of its parts.

¹³ G. Vlastos, "The Disorderly Motion in the *Timaeus*," *Classical Quarterly* 33 (1939):71–83. Also R. D. Mohr, "Image, Flux, and Space in Plato's *Timaeus*," *Phoenix* 34 (1980):138–52 and "The Gold Analogy in Plato's *Timaeus*," *Phronesis* 23 (1978):243–52.

¹⁴ *Phaedo* 70D and ff.

¹⁵ That is, the claim that "*A* is not *F*" is to be understood as "*A* has a share of The Different-from-F" does not require that *A* have a share of a contrary of *F* nor even that *F* have a contrary.

¹⁶ *Parmenides* 130C.

¹⁷ For example, the animal(s) of *Timaeus*, Theuth's sounds in *Philebus*, others from the divisions of *Sophist* and *Statesman*.

¹⁸ *Parmenides* 145E 9–146A 5: "It is at rest somewhere since it is in itself. For, being in the one and not going out from it, it would be in the same, in itself. . . . That which is always in the same must, of course, always be at rest. . . . What of this? Must not the opposite, always being in a different, never being in the same and, never being in the same not being at rest and, not being at rest, be in motion?"

¹⁹ *Parmenides* 129C 4–D 7.

²⁰ See, e.g., Alexander Nehamas, "Predication and Forms of Opposites in the *Phaedo*," *Review of Metaphysics* (March 1973):461–91; also Gregory Vlastos, "Degrees of Reality in Plato," in *New Essays on Plato and Aristotle*, ed. R. Bambrough (New York, 1965), pp. 1–20.

²¹ The finger's being both large (relative to a smaller finger) and small (relative to a larger finger) is supposed to arouse one from his or her *doxastic* slumbers and invite attention to the world of forms (which *is*). The passage in *Republic* (523B–525B) where the example is given is difficult and highly provocative. Since Socrates extends the contrariety to all of the sense modalities (thick/thin, soft/hard, light/heavy, etc.) and goes on to the general claim that it is the *doxastic* (with sensation) experience of such *is*'s and *is not*'s (contraries) which invites entry to the forms, the suggestion (at 524C) is that one is to be moved to attend to each of the contraries individually and not (as in perception) confused together. This is followed, however, by the suggestion that one may be moved to contemplate the *one* as such and thus be led to the intelligible numbers. In *Parmenides* 142B ff., the so-called

"second hypothesis," starting from the *one which is*, Parmenides "generates" the numbers. It is tempting indeed to connect this passage with the move out of *doxastic* experience to thought or knowledge where real arithmetic (not simple calculation) is the first serious study. But the serious attempt to do so forms no part of this paper.

²² *Parmenides* 133D 7–134E 6.

²³ *Theaetetus* 156A ff. The *aistheseis* are, e.g., seeing, hearing, etc. The *aistheta* are, e.g., the colors, sounds, etc. These are the "twins" to which the physical process described in the passage gives birth. The emphasis is here on their being correlatives and, as such, tailored to each other. Colors, as such *aistheta*, are, I believe, colors as seen or "presented." Such colors are, as both the passage and the context suggests, relative to the conditions of the eye and things in the environment. Thus two different eyes meeting with the same thing in the environment may join in the production of quite different *aistheta*.

²⁴ *Republic* 473D–480A 7 (the end of the Book). The whole matter comes up in the context of Socrates' claim that the rulers of his *polis* should be philosophers.

²⁵ *Republic* 476B.

²⁶ *Theaetetus* 156B 1–C2. See n. 23. The list of *aistheseis* includes, in addition to seeing, hearing, etc., pleasures and pains, desires and fears.

²⁷ Noteworthy is Socrates' insistence to Polus that rhetoric is simply not a craft (*techne*) at all but rather a knack or "routine" for producing pleasure or invoking pleasurable associations in hearers (*Gorgias* 462 C ff.). By invoking pleasurable (or painful) associations with certain beliefs or courses of action, the rhetorician can induce belief or desired activity. Knacks are, of course, sharply contrasted with genuine crafts (*technai*), where the latter have standards and are productive of goods.

²⁸ *Republic* 509D–511E.

²⁹ The objects of *doxa* are "the visible kind" (*to horomenon genos*). These are divided into "shadows" (*skiai*) and "appearances" (*phantasmata*) in water and in smooth and shiny surfaces"—the objects of *eikasia*—and "the inanimate kind"—the objects of *pistis*. And the latter are taken to be "causes" of the former. My linkage of *skiagraphia* (defined by Liddell and Scott as "painting with shadows so as to produce an illusion of solidity at a distance") with the use of *skiai* here is based on Plato's use of *skiagraphia* elsewhere. He uses it in *Republic* (365C) in connection with cultivating the appearance of virtue while devoting oneself to the pursuit of profit, in *Critias* (107D) in connection with our lack of toleration of inexactness in the painting of our own bodies, and in *Phaedo* (69B) in connection with creating the illusion of virtue. The use of *skiai* for objects of *eikasia* as shadows produced by the (comparatively) *real* objects of *pistis* is straightforward. Shadows and images (in water or mirrors) are, of course, *of* real physical things. But Plato's point can hardly be that the victims of *eikasia* are quite so simple as to be taken in by shadows and mirror images. This obvious distinction is, I believe, an analogy for that between our sensations and the (external) causes of them. To be taken in by the sensations is, of course, to take the obvious deliverances of sense as real. For an extended discussion of this and related matters see my paper, "The Role of the 'Special Sensibles' in the Perception Theories of Plato and Aristotle," in *Studies in Perception* ed. P. K. Machamer and R. G. Turnbull (Columbus, 1978), pp. 3–26.

PLATO

³⁰ Jeffrey B. Gold, "The Ambiguity of 'Name' in Plato's *Cratylus*," *Philosophical Studies* 34 (1978):223–51.

³¹ I.e., inner speech.

³² This is, of course, the by now standard Quinean or Sellarsian situation where the "teacher" has reason to believe that appropriate sensory stimulation is occurring in the child.

³³ *Phaedo* 89D–91B. Socrates compares naive trust and subsequent disappointment in people with naive trust and subsequent disappointment in arguments.

³⁴ See n. 27. *Gorgias* is a model of the technique of showing an interlocutor that he does not himself "really" believe claims he makes. For example, Polus is shown that he cannot really believe that it is better to do than to suffer injustice by his own understanding (when pressed) of *kalon* and *agathon*. Callicles, by similar means, that he does not really believe his own claims concerning "natural justice." The technique requires, if not the recognition, at least the falling into standard usage of terms.

³⁵ The matter is complex, and demonstration of it would be lengthy. Vlastos' masterful first chapter in *Plato's Universe* (Seattle, 1975) in its treatment of *ate* is a good illustration. The move is, generally speaking, from explanation of odd behavior by reference to *ate* (and also from blaming the victim of *ate* for actions really produced by a god or gods) to explanation by reference to character, circumstance, etc. (and more appropriate assignation of blame).

³⁶ *Parmenides* 135D 7–E 4.

³⁷ *Cratylus* 388E 5–390E 3.

³⁸ *Theaetetus* 189E 5–190A 4; *Sophist* 263E 3–5.

³⁹ *Sophist* 263B–C.

⁴⁰ See, e.g., *Cratylus* 431E 6–432A 3 for the work of the grammarian.

⁴¹ *Cratylus* 431.

⁴² *Philebus* 18B–D.

⁴³ If " 'P' is true" is taken as *authorizing* disquotation, i.e., as authorizing the removal of quotation marks around 'P' and such authorizations as expressing linguistic rules, questions arise concerning the "objectivity" or warrant for such rules. This is hardly the place for serious discussion of the exact nature of those questions, *a fortiori*, of attempts to answer them.

⁴⁴ *Euthyphro* 6D–E.

⁴⁵ *Parmenides* 130A 6–B 5. Parmenides says, after Socrates has responded to Zeno: "How admirably carried away you are by your zest for arguments, Socrates! Tell me, have you yourself made this division you describe, separating, on the one side, the forms themselves, on the other, those having shares of them? And does it seem to you that there is Likeness Itself quite separated from the likeness we have in us, and also One, Many, and all the others of which you just now heard Zeno speak?"

Later, after several unsuccessful attempts to understand how individuals may have shares of forms and drawing some unacceptable conclusions (the gods cannot know us or be our masters) from the failure, Parmenides says, "On the other hand, Socrates, if anyone will not allow the forms to be, transfixed by all the present and

299

yet other objections, and does not make off a form of each one, he will have nowhere to turn and to fix his thought, since he does not acknowledge a form of each of the beings which is always the same. And in this way he will completely destroy the power of discourse" (*Parmenides* 135B 5–C 2).

[46] Richard Rorty, *Philosophy and the Mirror of Nature* (Princeton, 1980; second printing, with corrections).

[47] Bertrand Russell, *The Problems of Philosophy* (Oxford, 1912; paperback issue, 1959), chapter X, p. 101. "Let us consider first the knowledge of universals by acquaintance. It is obvious, to begin with, that we are acquainted with such universals as white, red, black, sweet, sour, loud, hard, etc., i.e., with qualities which are exemplified in sense-data. When we see a white patch, we are acquainted, in the first instance, with the particular patch; but by seeing many white patches, we easily learn to abstract the whiteness which they all have in common, and in learning to do this we are learning to be acquainted with whiteness." Needless to say, I think that this sort of *acquaintance*, this bare mental act, is a piece of mythology (and the account of "abstraction" at least as mythological). What is disturbing for the present paper is temptation that Russell (and G. E. Moore) has given to Plato scholars to think that Plato thought of our awareness of forms as some sort of Russellian acquaintance.

Part III

ARISTOTLE

WILLIAM W. FORTENBAUGH

On the Antecedents of Aristotle's Bipartite Psychology

THIS essay is concerned with the antecedents of Aristotle's bipartite or moral psychology.[1] It considers two common theses: (1) Aristotle's bipartite psychology is in origin a popular psychology already present (though not clearly formulated) in Euripides' *Medea* and *Hippolytus*; (2) Aristotle's bipartite psychology developed out of tripartition by collapsing together the two lower elements of tripartition. Roughly, I shall be qualifying the first and rejecting the second thesis. In both cases I hope to develop and make more precise the origins of Aristotle's bipartite psychology.

I

It is generally recognized that Euripides' depiction of Medea in the tragedy bearing her name and of Phaedra in the *Hippolytus* involves some sort of distinction between passion and reasoned deliberation, and that this distinction is important for understanding the development of Greek psychology and ethics.[2] In particular the famous monologues of Medea (*Med.* 1021–80) and Phaedra (*Hipp.* 373–430) are said to present a kind of psychic dichotomy that anticipates in some way the dichotomy of Aristotle's bipartite or moral psychology. In this section I want to clarify this thesis. First I shall try to make more precise the way in which Euripides' *Medea* may be said to anticipate and elucidate Aristotle's moral psychology. Then I shall point out that Euripides' characterization of Phaedra differs significantly from his characterization of Medea and that this characterization of Phaedra cannot be used without considerable qualification to illustrate Aristotle's bipartite psychology.

It is true, I think, that the *Medea* as a whole and the famous monologue in particular are especially useful for illustrating and understanding Aris-

This paper was presented at the 1969 San Francisco meeting of the Society for Ancient Greek Philosophy and published in *Greek, Roman, and Byzantine Studies*, vol. 2. no. 3 (Autumn 1970); we thank the editors for permission to reprint.
William Fortenbaugh is Professor of Classics at Rutgers University.

totle's moral psychology, because they distinguish implicitly spirit or emotion from *both* deliberation about means *and* also reasoned reflection about emotional response. Medea's monologue implies two distinctions that have been present earlier in the play and that are essential for an understanding of Aristotle's bipartite psychology. Bipartition is not a simple dichotomy between emotional response and means-end deliberation alone. Rather it is a dichotomy between emotional response on the one hand and means-end deliberation *together with* reasoned reflection about emotional response on the other.[3] Let me develop this point by considering relevant portions of the *Medea*.

At the beginning of the play we learn from the nurse that Medea is filled with hate and grief (16, 24–35), because she thinks herself dishonored by Jason (20, 26). Medea's emotional state is not in doubt. What is in doubt, and what especially troubles the nurse, is Medea's plans or deliberations (βουλεύειν 37). Here we have a partial expression of the dichotomy of bipartition. Medea's anger and grief, or more generally her emotions, are distinguished from the deliberations that follow upon and are given direction by her emotions. Considering herself outraged and so desiring revenge, Medea must deliberate about how to achieve revenge. Some way or means must be discovered (260) before her emotion and desire for revenge can be translated effectively into action.

The same distinction between emotional response and means-end deliberation is implied later when Creon confronts Medea and orders her to leave Corinth. Creon acknowledges being frightened of Medea and explains his fear by pointing out that Medea is clever (σοφή 285) and pained at the loss of Jason's love (286). In other words, Medea is not only angered by Jason's behavior but is capable of following up her anger with successful deliberations about means to achieve revenge. This same distinction between emotion and cleverness occurs again when Creon says that he fears lest Medea be planning something (317) and then adds that a sharp-tempered (ὀξύθυμος 319) person is easier to guard against than a silent but clever (σοφός 320) person. A sharp-tempered person responds emotionally straightway and without deliberation. The silent and clever person does not act without deliberation. In his case anger is the occasion for deliberation about means.

Emotion is distinct from means-end deliberation, and this distinction is part of the dichotomy of bipartition. Emotion is also distinguished from reasoned reflection about emotional response, and this distinction, too, is part of the dichotomy of bipartition. We can gain a clearer understanding of this latter distinction if we consider Medea's first meeting with Jason. During this meeting Medea criticizes herself for having followed and aided Jason, describing herself as eager (πρόθυμος 485) rather than wise (σοφοτερα 485). Medea does not, of course, mean that her actions on behalf of Jason were lacking in cleverness. On the contrary she makes clear that without her skills Jason would never have escaped danger. (She begins and ends her opening statement with the claim to have saved Jason [476, 515].) Her point is simply that reason was not controlling emotion when she aided Jason. Her actions were motivated by the particular emotion of love.⁴ With this piece of self-analysis Jason is in full agreement. He credits Medea with a subtle mind (529) but restricts her clever deliberations to means-end reasoning. Love was dominant and determined the course of her deliberations (527–31). Medea's cleverness at finding the means to effect a desired goal is never in doubt. All Greece knows that Medea is clever (σοφήν 539). But if she is skilled in means-end deliberations following upon emotional response, she is not similarly effective in reflecting upon and altering her emotional response in accordance with reasoned consideration (cf. 600). In contrast Jason's actions—or so Jason claims—are guided by reasoned reflection. He is not motivated by desire (556). He has considered (βε-βούλευμαι 567) his actions and their consequences and so can claim to be wise (σοφός 548).⁵

A similar distinction between emotion and reasoned reflection appears during the second meeting of Medea and Jason (866–93). In the course of this meeting, the emotion of Medea is alleged to be under the control of reasoned reflection. Medea begins by asking Jason to pardon her anger (ὀργάς 870) and by saying that she has engaged in discussion (λόγων 872) with herself. Then she subjects her angry emotion to criticism (873–81) and indicates that she will give up her anger (θυμοῦ 879). Claiming to have considered (ἐννοήσασ' 882) her children and the impending exile without friends, Medea states that she has exhibited a lack of good sense (ἀβουλίαν 882, ἄφρων 885) and that her anger has been foolish (883). She admits that her previous conduct was unreasonable but claims now to have considered (βεβούλευμαι 893) the matter and come to a better understanding. Jason is fooled by Medea's speech and replies sympathetically. He allows that Medea's anger (ὀργάς 909) was after all quite natural and that now at last Medea has come to better reasoning (βουλήν 913). He credits Medea with having reflected reasonably and having altered her emotions in accordance with reason.

Emotion, then, may be distinguished from reasoned reflection as well as from means-end deliberation. It is now time to look at Medea's monologue which, as I have suggested, implies both distinctions and so may be said to illustrate fully the dichotomy of bipartition. Medea begins the monologue by reflecting upon the evil consequences of her actions, by considering the personal loss involved in killing her children (1021–39). This reflection, together with the pathetic sight of her children,⁶ causes her to alter briefly her intentions. She abandons her plans (βουλεύματα) and states that she will take her children away with her (1040–48). But her desire for full revenge returns swiftly. She chides herself for having listened to soft arguments (μαλθακοὺς λόγους) and sends the children indoors to await death (1049–55). Then for a second time she falters, addressing her spirit (θυμός) and pointing out the joy that the children can bring in exile (1056–58). This time her hesitation is of even shorter duration. Once again she determines to kill the children. She is quite conscious of the terrible path that she has chosen for herself and the even more terrible path that she has chosen for the children (1067–68). But now she does not falter. She understands (μανθάνω) that her forthcoming deed is evil (1078), but she also realizes that her reasoned reflections are unable to alter her angry desire for full revenge. As she puts, it, θυμός is stronger than βουλεύματα (1079).

By means of this monologue Euripides has depicted a mother torn between an angry desire for total revenge and the realization that total revenge is in the long run an evil for herself and her children. From a dramatic point of view, the monologue does not set forth explicitly the dichotomy of bipartition. For reasoned reflection and means-end deliberation are on different sides of Medea's dilemma. Her reflections enable her to see the horror of her planned revenge and so argue for abandoning the plans that bring total revenge. But if the dichotomy of bipartition is not dramatically set forth in this monologue, it is, I think, clearly implicit in the monologue. Medea's emotions are distinguished from her βουλεύματα. And these βουλεύματα include both the deliberate plans (1044, 1048) which follow upon and are given direction by emotion and also the reflections (1079) which consider the reasonableness of emotion and on occasion alter emotion. It would be, of course, overstatement to say that by using βουλεύματα in an inclusive sense, Euripedes has captured (consciously) the dichotomy of bipartition: deliberation and reflection in contrast with emotional response. But it can be said that this double usage of βουλεύματα encourages the dichotomy of bipartition, that the dichotomy is implicit or latent in Medea's monologue, so that the monologue can be used with caution to illustrate the dichotomy of bipartition.[7]

It is this dichotomy with which Aristotle works and which enables him at one time to treat reason as something that follows emotion and at another time to treat reason as something that controls emotion. When Aristotle says that the alogical soul is obedient to reason (EN 1098a4, 1102b31), he is thinking primarily of reasoned reflection and its ability to control and alter emotion. A virtuous man subjects his emotional responses to reasoned reflection.[8] He contrasts with Medea in that he heeds reason, altering or abandoning his emotional responses according to the dictates of reasoned reflection.[9] Still, the virtuous man is like Medea in regard to means-end deliberation. In this respect his reason may be said to follow his emotion. When Aristotle says that moral virtue makes correct the goal and practical wisdom the means (*EN* 1144a7–9, 1145a5–6), he is thinking primarily of means-end deliberation in relation to emotional response. Means-end deliberation follows upon and is given direction by emotional response.[10] Since the latter is the province of moral virtue, and the former of practical wisdom, Aristotle can say that moral virtue makes correct the goal and practical wisdom the means without implying that practical wisdom is altogether restricted to means-end deliberations.[11] The distinction between moral virtue and practical wisdom is founded upon the dichotomy of bipartition, and this dichotomy is in a way complex. Reason is related to emotion not only as deliberation that follows emotion but also as reflection that can control emotion.

The *Medea* can also help us to understand Aristotle's assertion in the *Politics* (1260a13) that women possess the deliberative faculty (τὸ βουλευτικόν), lacking in authority (ἄκυρον). Aristotle does not mean that women cannot think straight. He is well aware that many women are like Medea in being able to deliberate and reflect. Aristotle's point is that their reasoning does not control their emotion. Just as Medea engaged in reflections concerning her response to Jason's betrayal but was not able to control her response, so for Aristotle women are able to reflect and in general to deliberate (they possess τὸ βουλευτικόν) but are unable to guide their emotions by reasoned reflection. In the case of women, reasoning is effective or authoritative only in the sphere of means-end deliberation. Within this area the deliberations of women can be most effective, and indeed disastrous. Women can be most clever contrivers of every kind of evil (409). But in the area of reasoned reflection about emotional response, a woman's reasoning is not authoritative. It cannot effectively guide or alter emotional response.

We may be tempted to go on and illustrate further Aristotle's view of women by reference to Euripides' *Hippolytus*. For in this play Phaedra is presented as a woman who knows that she is behaving improperly but is unable to control her behavior. Like Medea, Phaedra reflects upon her dilemma in an impressive monologue and describes her weakness as a common failing: "We know and apprehend the good but do not bring it to fulfillment" (380–81). Phaedra recognizes that women are generally despised (406, cf. *Med.* 407–09, 889–90), and may be thought to illustrate together with Medea Aristotle's view of women. Here caution is necessary, for the characterization of Phaedra differs considerably from the characterization of Medea. Phaedra's behavior is not a clear case of uncontrolled emotional response. Unlike Medea, who perceives herself outraged,[12] and so responds angrily, Phaedra is said to be afflicted by a disease (νόσος and cognates, 40, 131, 176, 186, 205, 269, 279, 283, 293, 294, 393, 405, 463, 477). Diseases are not open to reasoned reflection in the way that anger and other emotions are. Anger invites reasoned criticism and is frequently abandoned, if shown to be unreasonable. A disease, however, is not an emotion and is not given up, if shown to be unreasonable. Indeed, diseases are neither reasonable nor unreasonable. They are afflictions that must be cured. While an emotion like anger is grounded upon evaluation or assessment (e.g., "Jason has treated me unjustly," *Med.* 26), a disease is not. It is caused by bodily disorder. So long as Phaedra is viewed as a victim of disease, her behavior is significantly different from that of Medea and cannot be used without considerable qualification to illustrate Aristotle's view of women and bipartite psychology in general. A disease may be the occasion for means-end deliberation (how to restore health), but it does not invite reasoned reflection in the way that an emotion like anger does. Anger or fear or any similar emotion is not only the occasion for means-end deliberation; it also admits reflection concerning the reasonableness of the emotion itself.

Reasoning, then, is related to emotion in two distinguishable ways. This twofold relationship between reason and emotion is fundamental to Aristotle's moral psychology. It determines his account of moral virtue and practical wisdom and also his view of women. Still, this twofold relationship is not an Aristotelian discovery. It was ready at hand in popular thought and more or less clearly implied in a tragedy like Euripides' *Medea*. Aristotle along with other members of the Academy gave the dichotomy formal recognition, but they did not invent it.

II

If Aristotle's bipartite psychology developed out of a popular distinction between reason and emotion as explained in the preceding section, can it also be said to have developed out of Plato's tripartite psychology? More precisely, did Aristotle's own moral psychology develop through bringing together the θυμοειδές and ἐπιθυμητικόν of tripartition? Here I think we must say not only that Aristotle's bipartite psychology is significantly different from such a bipartite version of tripartition[13] but also that Aristotle himself was aware of the difference and prepared to criticize bipartition whenever it took the form of a simplified tripartition. Perhaps I can support this claim, and at the same time clear up a persistent misunderstanding, by focusing upon the criticism of bipartition advanced in the *De Anima*.

Here (432a22–b7) at the beginning of his account of locomotion, Aristotle makes some prefatory remarks about psychic divisions and criticizes cursorily both those persons who offer a tripartite psychology and those who offer a bipartite psychology (432a24–26). It has been widely assumed and sometimes stated that this criticism of persons advancing bipartition is in part at least a self-criticism. Aristotle's remarks, we are told, are directed not only against members of the Academy who may have developed or advanced a bipartite psychology, but also against Aristotle himself, insofar as he employed bipartition both in earlier writings like the *Protrepticus* and *De Justitia* and in more mature treatises like the *Ethics* and *Politics*.[14] This view seems to me unacceptable. I want to suggest that Aristotle's criticism of bipartition is not a self-criticism. His remarks are directed against members of the Academy who had simply altered tripartition by collapsing the spirited and appetitive elements into a single psychic part and thereby created a particular kind of bipartite psychology. Aristotle's own bipartite or moral psychology differs in important ways from this Academic version and so should not be confused with it.

We may begin by considering two passages that create difficulties for anyone who tries to identify the bipartition criticized in the *De Anima* with Aristotle's own moral psychology. One of these passages occurs in Book I of the *Nicomachean Ethics* (1097b33–1098a5). Here Aristotle is trying to pin down the function of man. Toward this end he introduces first the nutritive life of plants, then the sensitive life of animals, and finally the practical life of the rational element. At this point he adds a note to the effect that the rational element is twofold: one part being obedient to reason and the other part possessing it and being deliberative (1098a4–5).[15] This note is important, for it clearly relates Aristotle's bipartite or moral psychology to his scientific psychology. The division between the alogical and logical halves of the moral psychology occurs within the scientific faculty of intellect. The division does not coincide with the scientific division between sensation and intellect. The reason for this is clear enough.[16] Bipartition is a human psychology that is useful for explaining intelligent (human) actions.[17] It is based upon a distinction between emotional response (which is intelligent in that it necessarily involves certain kinds of cognitions[18]) and reasoned deliberation. The alogical soul is primarily the capacity for emotional response, while the logical soul is primarily the capacity for reasoned deliberation. Both acts are intelligent, so that both capacities are cognitive. In contrast, the scientific faculty of sensation is not cognitive and so can be possessed by animals that cannot act intelligently.

It is, of course, possible to extend the alogical soul to include non-cognitive functions like nutrition and sensation. Aristotle does this in respect to nutrition at *EN* 1102a32–b12 (cf. *EE* 1219b31–32). But neither nutrition nor sensation are essential components of the alogical soul.[19] Bipartition is fundamentally a distinction between two kinds of intelligent action. Moreover, there can be no serious question about including either nutrition or sensation in the logical soul of Aristotle's moral psychology. Aristotle cannot seriously suggest that someone might try to house the scientific faculty of sensation within the logical soul of his own moral psychology. Such an attempt would be foolish. In regard to Aristotle's own bipartite psychology the assignment of sensation is clear. It is properly located outside (or "below") the dichotomy, though the alogical soul can be extended ("downward") to include it. And if this is true, difficulties arise for anyone who will refer the criticisms of bipartition advanced in the De Anima to Aristotle's own moral psychology. For in terms of Aristotle's own bipartite psychology, there can be no question concerning the assignation of the αἰσθητικόν. If the De Anima passage (432a30–31) presents a serious puzzle, it must be directed against a different version of bipartition that suggests the possibility of locating sensation in the logical as well as in the alogical part. As we shall see, the Timaeus suggests such a version of bipartition.[20]

The second passage that causes difficulties occurs in the Politics (1334b6–28). Here Aristotle is concerned to point out that habituation is employed in education before λόγος is employed. In the course of his argument, Aristotle introduces his own moral psychology and locates θυμός, βούλησις, and ἐπιθυμία on the alogical side of the dichotomy (1334b22–23). This creates difficulties, if it is assumed that Aristotle's criticism of bipartition in the De Anima is directed in part against his own moral psychology. For in the De Anima Aristotle locates βούλησις on the logical side (432b5). This location may be necessary, if Aristotle is going to charge bipartition with splitting up ὄρεξις. But the location needs considerable explanation if it is assumed that the bipartition in question is Aristotle's own moral psychology. For as the Politics makes clear, Aristotle's own bipartite psychology locates βούλησις on the alogical side.[21]

These difficulties can be removed if we understand that bipartition takes more than one form. The fact that in the De Anima Aristotle does not seem to include himself among the proponents of bipartition and then brings forth arguments largely ineffective against his own moral psychology becomes intelligible when we realize that Aristotle is not criticizing his own bipartite psychology. Rather he is criticizing a particular kind of bipartition that was developed in the Academy out of tripartition by bringing together the spirited and the appetitive faculties. A closer look at 432b5–6 will help to make this point clearer. Here Aristotle is criticizing bipartition, but instead of employing the label τὸ λόγον ἔχον to refer to the logical half, he uses the label λογιστικόν, which belongs to the vocabulary of tripartition (432a25). Is this a confusion? Perhaps, but only a very minor one. For Aristotle is criticizing a variety of bipartition which identifies the logical half of the dichotomy with the λογιστικόν of tripartition. Aristotle has in mind that kind of bipartition which is already suggested in the *Republic*[22] and clearly indicated in the *Timaeus*—a dialogue which groups together the spirited and appetitive elements as the mortal soul and opposes this combination to the λογιστικόν as the immortal soul. Apparently tripartition and this related form of bipartition enjoyed a contemporaneous life within the Academy. At least the *Topics*, which seems frequently to reflect discussion within the Academy, introduces for illustrative purposes not only tripartition but also that version of bipartition which is a variation on tripartition (129a10–16).[23] We may suspect that, just as in the *Topics* Aristotle takes note of two closely related Academic psychologies, so in the *De Anima* he is concerned with members of the Academy, when he criticizes those who advance tripartition and those who advance bipartition (432a24–26).

The *Timaeus* can help us to understand Aristotle's charge that the αἰσθητικόν cannot be comfortably located in either the logical or alogical soul (432a30–31). While the *Timaeus* introduces tripartition and even assigns each of the three psychic parts its own bodily location, the *Timaeus*, as we have already said, presents a bipartite version of tripartition. The λογιστικόν is divine and elevated spatially to a seat in the head. The other two psychic parts are mortal and are located in the trunk of the body. For our purposes the important point is that the *Timaeus* not only employs this bipartite version of tripartition but also attempts to handle sense perception. And this attempt seems to result in just the kind of difficulty which Aristotle asserts does occur when the sensitive faculty is referred to bipartition. For at one time the *Timaeus* seems to treat the λογιστικόν or immortal soul as the center of consciousness to which sensory motions are transmitted (43–44, 64B), and at another time it seems to associate the mortal soul with αἴσθησις (61C, 69D). In this regard certain passages are especially difficult, if not confusing. In explaining pleasure and pain, the *Timaeus* first connects sensation with the φρόνιμον (64B5, apparently the brain, which is the locus of the immortal soul or λογιστικόν)[24] and subsequently refers pleasurable sensations caused by sudden replenishments to the mortal soul (65A5). The sensation of taste is explained by reference to veins that are said to extend to the heart (which is in the region of the θυμοειδές) and that apparently do not continue on to the brain or seat of the λογιστικόν.[25] By contrast, the effect of bad odors is said to extend from the head to the navel (67A4–5) and so would seem to affect the entire soul, both its mortal and immortal portions.[26] Similarly, hearing is described as a process extending not only to the brain and head (67B3–4) but also to the liver (67B5).[27] And finally, discussing the maintenance of mortal creatures, the *Timaeus* first introduces plants, which are said to possess the ἐπιθυμητικόν and αἴσθησις (77B3–6),[28] and then considers

311

veins, which not only water the body but also divide in the region of the head and so seem to serve the brain and λογιστικόν in regard to sense perception (77D6–E6).[29] Whether or not we think that each of these passages presents a difficulty for the location of sensation within a bipartite version of tripartition, we can, I think, agree that collectively these passages do indicate a problem. We can agree[30] that in the *Timaeus* Plato has not altered sufficiently his psychic framework to house the scientific (i.e., biological) faculty of sensation. And we may suspect that when Aristotle criticizes bipartition for its inability to handle sensation, he is thinking of bipartition much as it appears in the *Timaeus*.[31] He is thinking of certain members of the Academy who collapsed the spirited and appetitive faculties into one and so formed a bipartite version of tripartition.

This suspicion seems to be confirmed when we reflect again on Aristotle's charge that bipartition splits up ὄρεξις (432b4–6). Addressed to his own version of bipartition, the charge is very odd. For Aristotle frequently refers to ὄρεξις as a mark of the alogical soul.[32] He never refers it to the logical soul. Further (and this is the important point), βούλησις cannot be located in Aristotle's logical soul.[33] This is not just a matter of textual evidence, though the evidence of the *Politics* (1334b22–23) is important. It is also and primarily a matter of how Aristotle conceives of the dichotomy of bipartition. For Aristotle the dichotomy of bipartition is primarily a dichotomy between reasoned deliberation and emotional response. Practical wisdom, which is the virtue of the logical soul, is a perfection of deliberation. Moral virtue, which is the virtue of the alogical soul, is a perfected disposition is regard to emotion (*EN* 1105b19–1106a13). All emotion is located in the alogical soul. This is not true of tripartition and (we may add) the bipartite version of tripartition. For these Academic psychologies assign βούλησις, αἰσχύνη, and possibly other emotions to the λογιστικόν.[34] Each psychic part including the λογιστικόν has its own peculiar drives and desires.[35] In contrast Aristotle's own moral psychology groups together all desires and emotions in the alogical soul. The logical soul is no longer the seat of desires and emotions like βούλησις and αἰσχύνη. It is the seat of means-end deliberation and reasoned reflection concerning emotional response. Of course, reasoning can direct or alter desires and emotions, but it is distinct. In terms of Aristotle's own bipartite psychology, there can be no question of splitting up ὄρεξις and locating βούλησις in the logical part. That question arises only when bipartition is conceived of as a simple variant of tripartion.

My conclusion, then, is that there are different kinds of bipartition and that a failure to note the differences has misled some commentators into supposing that Aristotle's criticism of bipartition is in part a self-criticism.

Aristotle is not criticizing his own moral psychology but rather an Academic version of bipartition that arose from tripartition by collapsing together the θυμοειδές and ἐπιθυμητικόν. Aristotle did not identify his own moral psychology with this variant on tripartition and would have objected to the (unqualified) suggestion that his own bipartite psychology developed out of tripartition.

NOTES

[1] This article is an expanded and corrected version of a paper distributed to the members of the Society for Ancient Greek Philosophy and subsequently discussed by members of the Society on 30 December 1969 in San Francisco. I wish to thank all those who participated in the discussion and offered criticisms. My thanks go also to Professors Bernard M. W. Knox, Charles P. Segal, and S. Marc Cohen, who communicated to me privately their reactions to an earlier version of this paper, and to Drs. Herwig Görgemanns and Gustav Seeck, who discussed with me ideas presented in this paper. Finally I want to acknowledge the helpful criticisms of an anonymous referee.

[2] See, for example, F. Dirlmeier, "Vom Monolog der Dichtung zum 'inneren' Logos bei Platon und Aristoteles," *Gymnasium* 67 (1960):31–32; M. Pohlenz, *Freedom in Greek Life and Thought* (New York, 1966), p. 67; H. Görgemanns, *Beiträge zur Interpretation von Platons Nomoi* (*Zetemata* 25, München, 1960), p. 159; J. J. Walsh, *Aristotle's Conception of Moral Weakness* (New York, 1963), pp. 16–22. See also my "Aristotle: Emotion and Moral Virtue," *Arethusa* 2 (1969):184, n. 31.

[3] A proper understanding of the dichotomy of bipartition is an essential prerequisite for an adequate understanding of Aristotle's distinction between moral virtue (ἠθικὴ ἀρετή) and practical wisdom (φρόνησις). As the psychic dichotomy does not oppose emotional response to means-end deliberation alone, so the distinction between moral virtue and practical wisdom is not a simple distinction between perfection in regard to emotional response and perfection in regard to means-end deliberation alone. Practical wisdom has as its province both deliberation about means and reflection about emotional response because the dichotomy of bipartition groups together both these performances and distinguishes them from emotional response. See n. 11.

[4] At the opening of the play the chorus made clear that in regard to Medea's emotional side (θυμόν 8), love (ἔρωτι 8) was dominant. Cf. 330 and 530.

[5] Jason would say, of course, that in some sense his actions, too, are guided by emotion. He would say that he is motivated by feelings of friendly affection, by a desire to aid and preserve Medea and her children (595, 620). But he would add that his emotional responses and subsequent plans can stand and have stood the test of reasoned reflection. While Medea's emotions motivate her to act in unreasonable ways, Jason's emotions do not. At least, Jason thinks he can defend and justify his own behavior.

[6] It would be wrong to say that Medea's reasoned reflections alone effected a

momentary change in her emotional response and planned revenge. Certainly the sight of her children contributed to her momentary change. But so did her reflections, and it is these reasoned reflections that are of special interest.

⁷ H. D. Voigtländer, "Spätere Überarbeitungen im grossen Medeamonolog," *Philologus* 101 (1957):228; A. Lesky, in *Euripide, Sept exposés et discussions* (Genève, 1960), p. 83; and E. Schlesinger, "Zu Euripides' Medea," *Hermes* 94 (1966):29–30, point out correctly that βουλεύματα is not restricted to a single, well-defined (technical) usage. Certainly it is wrong to think that Euripides is operating with some clearly formulated psychology (like Plato's tripartite psychology, Schlesinger, p. 29). But we can say that the opposition between θυμός and βουλεύματα reflects an everyday distinction employed by ordinary men in describing human action and subsequently formulated in the dichotomy of bipartition. H. Strohm, *Euripides* (*Zetemata* 15, München, 1957), p. 103 n. 1, seems to go too far when he says that βουλεύματα cannot be selected as a label to designate the opposite of θυμός because in 1079 βουλευμάτων refers only to the preceding μανθάνω, while in 1048 βουλεύματα is used for the murder plans. Instead of ruling out βουλεύματα, this double usage may be thought to qualify βουλεύματα as a technical label for one-half of the dichotomy of bipartition. Taking βουλεύματα inclusively so as to include both deliberations about means (murder plans) and reflections about emotional response (whether this kind of angry response is an over-response), we can see in the usage of βουλεύματα and its opposition to θυμός a striking anticipation of Aristotle's logical soul and its opposition to τὸ ἄλογον.

H. Diller, "Θυμὸς δὲ κρείσσων τῶν ἐμῶν βουλευμάτων," *Hermes* 94 (1966):273–75, followed by H. Rohdich, *Die Euripideische Tragödie* (Heidelberg, 1968), p. 64, does not recognize in Euripides a wide usage of βουλεύματα signifying deliberation and reflection in general. He interprets 1079 so that anger rules or guides (κρείσσων, cf. Walsh, *Aristotle's Conception*, p. 19, who seems to have anticipated Diller) Medea's plans (βουλευμάτων having the same reference as βουλεύματα in 1044 and 1048). This thesis seems to me unacceptable. In the first place it seems more natural to construe βουλευμάτων (1079) closely with μανθάνω (1078). By reasoned reflection Medea has learned that she is about to do evil (1078). But her reflections are powerless to affect her emotion, so that she declares her angry emotion stronger than her reasoned reflections (1079). In the second place and more importantly, Diller's argument seems to focus too closely on the single word βουλεύματα and on the monologue itself. We should, I think, take note of Medea's second meeting with Jason (866–93). For in the course of this meeting the emotion of Medea is said to be controlled by reasoned reflection, and this reflection is twice (893, 913) referred to by words cognate with βουλεύματα. Perhaps similarities in vocabulary should not be pressed. Still, it may be observed that this exchange between Medea and Jason agrees with the monologue in opposing θυμός or a cognate form (879, 883, 1056, 1079) to βουλεύειν or a cognate form (reflections: 882, 893, 913, 1079; plans or deliberations: 874, 1044, 1048) and in using the word λόγος in reference to reasoned reflection about emotional response (872, 1052). More important, however, is an agreement in content. Both passages oppose emotional response to reasoned reflection. Both passages indicate one important respect in which emotion is commonly opposed to reason. Emotional responses are subject to rational criticism and in many cases can be altered by reasoned reflection. Indeed, Medea's words to Jason are able to deceive just because Jason assumes that reasonable consideration will guide emotional response. Of course Jason is deceived in this matter. But as a working hypothesis his assumption is not foolish. Much of the time reflection is able to guide emotional response. But not always. For in Medea's monologue it becomes clear that reason can fail, that emotion may be stronger than reasoned reflection (1079, cf. 447, 590).

[8] A qualification is necessary. A virtuous man subjects his emotional responses to reasoned reflection when time permits. The virtuous man confronted with sudden danger does not have time to reflect. He must respond out of character and without reasoning (*EN* 1117a17–22). To illustrate further emotional response in sudden situations we may take a hint from Plutarch (*Moralia* 475A) and refer to Odysseus' meeting with the dog Argos. When Odysseus and Eumaios reach the palace, they come upon the ancient and all but dead Argos. The dog recognizes his former master and struggles in vain to move off the dung heap where he lies. Odysseus is moved by the pathetic sight of Argos and turns aside to wipe away a tear, unnoticed by Eumaios (*Od.* 17.291–305). As Plutarch comments, Odysseus fell into this situation quite suddenly and unexpectedly (475A). His behavior is not the result of reasoning (whether reflection about how one should respond to the situation or deliberation about how to prepare for the situation). Rather it is an expression of emotion quite in keeping with Odysseus' character. He sheds a tear but also turns away and so escapes the notice of Eumaios. We can contrast this response with Odysseus' behavior a little earlier when reviled by the goatherd Melanthios. The words of Melanthios stir the heart of Odysseus (17.215–16). But after reflection Odysseus restrains himself (17.235–38). On this occasion Odysseus has time to reflect and to permit reason to control his emotional response.

[9] We may add that the virtuous man heeds not only his own reasoned reflections but also those of other men. Unlike the sullen man who hides anger within himself, so that no one can persuade him to give up his anger (*EN* 1126a23–24), the virtuous man pays attention to the reasoned arguments of others.

[10] Cf. *Rhet.* 1383a6–7, where Aristotle says that fear makes men deliberate. In other words, emotional response is often the occasion for means-end deliberation.

[11] I agree with D. J. Allen, *The Philosophy of Aristotle* (London, 1952), pp. 181–82, that Aristotle never wanted to restrict practical wisdom to means-end deliberations. But I cannot agree with Allen insofar as he (following R. Loening, *Die Zurechnungslehre des Aristoteles* [Jena, 1903]) assumes an identity between the alogical soul of bipartition and the sensitive and motive faculties of the scientific psychology. Comparisons with the scientific psychology will not help and may impede an adequate understanding of why the logical soul of bipartition is not restricted to means-end deliberation. To understand Aristotle's dichotomy we should keep in mind that emotional response (which includes cognition as well as sensation and drive) is related to reasoning in two different ways. As the *Medea* illustrates, an enraged person may engage in reasoning either to realize a goal or to reflect upon his emotional state.

[12] See n. 18.

[13] Elsewhere ("Aristotle's *Rhetoric* on Emotions," *Archiv für Geschichte der Philosophie* 52 [1970]:40–70) I have argued that Aristotle's moral psychology is significantly different from tripartition because tripartition did not draw a clear distinction between emotional responses and bodily drives. Aristotle's moral psychology is a dichotomy between reasoning and emotional response—those πάθη that necessarily involve some assessment and so are amenable to reason. In contrast, bodily drives are caused by physiological disturbance and are in general not remedied by reasoned reflection.

[14] That Aristotle's criticism of bipartition applies in some way to his own bipartite psychology either is stated explicitly or seems to be implied in the comments of the following scholars: Simpl. 289.7–19; Philop. 547.1; E. Wallace, *Aristotle's Psychology* (Cambridge, 1882), p. 284; R. Heinze, *Xenokrates* (Leipzig, 1892), p. 142; R. D. Hicks, *Aristotle, De Anima* (Cambridge, 1907), p. 550, cf. 300; D. A. Rees, "Bipartition of the Soul in the Early Academy," *JHS* 77 (1957):118; R. Gauthier and J. Jolif, *L'Éthique à Nicomaque*, vol. 2 (Louvain, 1959), p. 93; W. Theiler, *Aristoteles, Über die Seele* (Berlin, 1959), pp. 149–50; Sir David Ross, *Aristotle, De Anima* (Oxford, 1961), p. 312; A. Jannone and E. Barbotin, *Aristote, De L'Ame* (Paris, 1966), p. 109; D. W. Hamlyn, *Aristotle's De Anima* (Oxford, 1968), p. 150. Cf. H. v. Arnim, "Das Ethische in Aristoteles Topik," *SB Wien* 205.4 (1927):7, 66; P. Moraux, *Le Dialogue "Sur la Justice"* (Louvain, 1957), pp. 43–44; F. Dirlmeier, *Aristoteles, Nikomachische Ethik* (Berlin, 1964), p. 278; *Aristoteles, Magna Moralia* (Berlin, 1958), p. 164.

The comments of F. Trendelenburg, *Aristoteles, De Anima Libri Tres* (Berlin, 1877), p. 441, and of G. Rodier, *Aristote, Traité de L'Ame*, vol. 2 (Paris, 1900), pp. 529–530, suggest that the *De Anima's* criticism does not apply to Aristotle's bipartite psychology because Aristotle does not commit himself to separate soul parts. Trendelenburg and Rodier are correct in ruling out Aristotle's own bipartite psychology as an object of criticism, but their reason does not get to the heart of the matter. The *De Anima* passage is concerned not only with whether or not there are spatially separate psychic parts (432a20), but also and primarily with how many parts or faculties are to be recognized (432a23). The advocates of bipartition are being criticized especially for having failed to distinguish adequately between the several psychic parts or faculties (432a24–26). And in this regard the criticisms developed in the *De Anima* do not seem to attack Aristotle's own brand of bipartition. Even if Aristotle's bipartite psychology did involve a commitment to separable psychic parts (and it did not, *EN* 1102a28–32), this particular bipartite psychology would not seem to be under attack. As we shall see, the attack of the *De Anima* is directed against an Academic version of bipartition that differs in fundamental ways from Aristotle's own bipartite or moral psychology.

[15] On the genuineness of this note see my "Aristotle: Emotion and Moral Virtue," pp. 181–82, n. 22.

[16] See my "Aristotle: Emotion and Moral Virtue," pp. 173–77, in which I have tried to explain why the divisions of the moral and scientific psychologies do not coincide neatly.

[17] Cf. Moraux *Le Dialogue*, pp. 44, 47 and Simplicius *In de An.* 289.15–16.

[18] On the necessary involvement of cognition in emotional response, see my "Aristotle's *Rhetoric*." Here again it may be useful to refer to Euripides' *Medea*. At the outset of the play the nurse tells us that Medea perceives herself dishonored (26, cf. 20) and so is filled with hate and grief (16, 24–35). Her emotional condition is not in doubt. It is Medea's deliberations that are unknown and of especial concern to the nurse (37). We should note that the nurse's remarks do not suggest a dichotomy that locates all cognition on the side of deliberation. Part of being angry is perceiving or thinking oneself outraged (26). This evaluation, together with the desire for revenge, may be distinguished both from the means-end deliberations that follow upon emotional response and also from the reasoned reflections that consider the emotional response—that is, the reasoning that asks whether the evaluation is correct and the desired goal appropriate, so that the emotional response may be deemed reasonable and justifiable.

[19] See Plutarch (*Moralia* 442B), who is correct insofar as he distinguishes the scientific faculties of nutrition and sensation from the alogical soul of bipartition on the grounds that nutrition and sensation are bodily offshoots without any share in λόγος.

[20] It might be suggested that Aristotle is not presenting a "serious" puzzle or difficulty for bipartition. Aristotle says that the αἰσθητικόν cannot be classified easily as either alogical or logical (432a30–31) because he knows full well that his own scientific faculty of sensation is essentially outside the dichotomy of his own moral psychology. This suggestion seems to me unacceptable, not only because it reduces the stated difficulty to a mere quibble, but also because it fails to consider the entire criticism of bipartition advanced in this portion of the *De Anima*. In particular, it ignores the fact that Aristotle goes on to say that bipartition splits up the ὀρεκτικόν (432b3–6). This is not true of Aristotle's own bipartite psychology. When both criticisms of bipartition (432a30–31, 432b3–6) are considered together, it becomes most unlikely that Aristotle is criticizing his own moral psychology.

[21] We cannot construe *De Anima* 432b5 to mean that βούλησις is a logical ὄρεξις only in that it responds to the injunctions of λόγος (see Alexander 74.6–13). The *De Anima* passage is quite clear in its wording. βούλησις is said "to occur in the λογιστικόν." As at *Topics* 126a13, βούλησις is located in the λογιστικόν. W. Newman, *The Politics of Aristotle*, vol. 3 (Oxford, 1902), p. 456, following Eaton, suggests that Aristotle's usage of βούλησις is not uniform, for in the *Politics* βούλησις is connected with the alogical and not with the logical soul as in the *De Anima*. Certainly the word βούλησις is used in different ways. (See the remarks of H. G. Ingenkamp, *Untersuchungen zu den pseudoplatonischen Definitionen* [Wiesbaden, 1967], pp. 64–65.) For at least a partial understanding of the different usages of βούλησις and especially for a fuller understanding of why the *De Anima* and *Politics* differ in locating βούλησις, we should, I think, consider the possibility of two different kinds of bipartition: an Aristotelian version (*Pol.* 1334b6–28), and an Academic version that developed out of tripartition by bringing together the two lower faculties into a single ἄλογον (cf. *De An.* 432b5–6 with *Top.* 126a3–16, and see below).

[22] At 439B5 Glaucon suggests that spirit is not some third psychic element but

rather identical in nature to the appetitive element. At 571C3–572B1 Socrates describes two different kinds of sleep by opposing the λογιστικόν to the two lower elements. See Dirlmeier, *Nikomachische Ethik*, pp. 278–79.

²³ To illustrate that a relative property may be a difference that holds usually and in most cases, the *Topics* distinguishes the λογιστικόν from the ἐπιθυμητικόν and θυμικόν and states that the one commands and the other serves usually but not always (129a10–16). This passage from the *Topics* names the three psychic parts of tripartition. In this respect it agrees with *De Anima* 432a25, which also names the λογιστικόν, θυμικόν and ἐπιθυμητικόν. However, it seems to differ from *De Anima* 432a25 in an important respect. While *De Anima* 432a25 is introducing tripartition in contrast with bipartition, the *Topics* passage appears to be dealing with a bipartite version of tripartition. By growing together the θυμικόν and ἐπιθυμητικόν in opposition to the λογιστικόν, the *Topics* passage creates a particular kind of bipartition— namely, that kind that is under consideration at *De Anima* 432b5–6 and that groups together spirit and appetite to form a single alogical faculty. On 129a10–16 and bipartition, see Dirlmeier, *Magna Moralia*, pp. 164; on tripartition in the *Topics*, see v. Arnim, "Das Ethische."

²⁴ See the note of A. E. Taylor, *A Commentary on Plato's* Timaeus (Oxford, 1928), p. 447.

²⁵ The account of tastes is particularly perplexing. It is not explicitly said that the veins terminate at the heart, and so the possibility is left open that the veins continue on to the brain. Taylor, *A Commentary*, p. 465, assumes some kind of connection between the heart and the brain. F. M. Cornford, *Plato's Cosmology* (London, 1937), p. 270, suggests that the sense messages do not have to pass through the heart to reach the brain. Further, pungent tastes are associated with particles that rise toward the senses (or sense organs) in the head (65E7) and so seem to have little connection with the veins extending to the heart. F. Solmsen, "Antecedents of Aristotle's Psychology and Scale of Beings," *AJP* 76 (1955), p. 156, n. 26, cautions that the heart is not strictly speaking the seat of the θυμοειδές (the heart is in the region of and closely associated with the θυμοειδές [70A7–D6] but is not its seat), and suggests that had Plato wished to indicate a connection between tongue and soul, he would have made the connection explicit. In whatever way we interpret this passage, we can, I think, say that it helps point up the difficulty of handling a scientific or biological faculty of sensation within the framework of a bipartite version of tripartition.

²⁶ For the navel as a boundary of the ἐπιθυμητικόν see 70E1, 77B4. See also Taylor, *A Commentary*, p. 476: "Since at 70E1 the navel is mentioned as the boundary of the tenement devised for the ἐπιθυμητικόν the result is that smells affect the whole 'seat of the soul' from one end to the other."

²⁷ The liver is located in the region of the ἐπιθυμητικόν (71A7–B1).

²⁸ At 77A4–5 Timaios says that plants are endowed with αἰσθήσεις different from those possessed by men. Hence when Timaios subsequently says that plants possess the third kind of soul, which concerns pleasant and painful αἴσθησις in conjunction with ἐπιθυμίαι (77B5–6), he would seem to be connecting

the ἐπιθυμητικόν with αἰσθήσεις different from those possessed by man. This portion of the *Timaeus* would seem to have been partly responsible for Aristotle's insistence that there is no sixth sense (*DeAn.* 424b22–425b11). See Solmsen, "Antecedents," 153.

²⁹ See Taylor, *A Commentary*, pp. 546–47.

³⁰ With Solmsen, "Antecedents," pp. 154–55.

³¹ It is not surprising that the *De Anima*'s criticism of bipartition can be referred for elucidation to a literal interpretation of the *Timaeus*. We may compare how in Book I of the *De Anima* (406b26–407b11) Aristotle construes (too) literally the myth of the *Timaeus* and so can fault Timaios' account of the world soul. (See Ross, *Aristotle, De Anima*, p. 189: "He (Ar.) may well be criticized as having taken the myth as if it were sober prose.") Certainly the objection to spatially separated parts (432a20) is directed most naturally against a version of bipartition (or tripartition) like that advanced in the *Timaeus*. For taken literally, the *Timaeus* has a different bodily seat for each psychic part. Still, it would be a mistake to think that Aristotle's criticism is directed only (or perhaps even primarily) against the *Timaeus*. (We might expect Aristotle to name Timaios as at 406b26.) Most probably Aristotle is criticizing a group (οἱ δέ 432a26) within the Academy who followed the lead of Plato's *Timaeus* and endeavored to handle biological soul functions within a particular bipartite framework. We may compare the ἀπορίαι considered by Aristotle toward the beginning of his discussion of moral weakness in the *Nicomachean Ethics*. First Aristotle introduces some men (τινες *EN* 1145b22) who deny the possibility of doing wrong knowingly. Here Aristotle mentions Socrates and is quite certainly referring to Plato's *Protagoras* (352B). After remarking that this view goes against the phenomena and needs further clarification, Aristotle turns to another group (τινες *EN* 1145b31) that tries to explain moral weakness by making a psychological distinction between knowledge, which is strong, and opinion, which is weak. Here Aristotle seems to have in mind certain members of the Academy who may have been influenced by a passage like *Timaeus* 51DE. See Dirlmeier, *Nikomachische Ethik*, p. 478.

³² See, for example, *EN* 1102b30, 1139a17–b5; *Pol.* 1334b20. I say "a mark of the alogical soul" because I want to avoid the suggestion that the alogical soul is to be identified with the ὀρεκτικόν (together with the αἰσθητικόν and φανταστικόν). I have argued already (n. 16) that the alogical soul is the capacity of emotional response and so includes not only motive force (ὄρεξις) but also cognition. This is clearly implied at *EN* 1098a3–5. Still, for the purposes of refuting the suggestion that Aristotle's criticism of bipartition is a self-criticism, it does not matter whether the alogical soul is restricted to noncognitive functions like ὄρεξις or includes certain cognitive functions. In either case all ὄρεξις belongs on the alogical side, so that Aristotle's charge of splitting up the faculty of locomotion cannot be leveled against his own brand of bipartition.

³³ Cf. Gauthier and Jolif, *L'Éthique*, vol. 2, p. 193.

³⁴ For βούλησις and αἰσχύνη in the λογιστικόν see *Topics* 126a8, 13. v. Arnim, "Das Ethische," pp. 74–76, suggests that φιλία and μίσος should be assigned to the λογιστικόν and that φιλία is a kind of βούλησις. Whether

or not we follow v. Arnim in his interpretation of 126a12–13 (I do not think he adequately explains 112b2), we must agree that φιλία is closely related to βούλησις and that in his account of emotions Aristotle defines φιλεῖν as a particular kind of βούλεσθαι (*Rhet.* 1380b36–37).

[35] The *Republic* states that each of the three psychic parts has its own ἐπιθυμίαι (580D). The λογιστικόν is said not to care about wealth and reputation but to be directed wholly toward knowledge (581A5–7). See, for example, Raphael Demos, *The Philosophy of Plato* (New York, 1939), pp. 317–18, who points out that each of Plato's three psychic parts "is really a complete soul, in the sense that it includes all the characteristic psychical functions" (318). Each enjoys not only a cognitive aspect but also a desiderative and emotional aspect. This is not true for Aristotle's bipartite psychology.

THEODORE TRACY, S. J.

Heart and Soul in Aristotle

U NDER this rather sentimental sounding title I should like to recall a
critical problem in Aristotle's psychology, trace briefly some of the
discussion of that problem, and suggest several considerations that I
hope advance the discussion beyond what has already been proposed by others. The problem is, of course, that which Francois Nuyens raised over
thirty years ago (*L'Évolution de la Psychologie d'Aristote*, Louvain, 1948)
when he declared Aristotle's famous definition of the soul in *De Anima*
(= *DA*)[1] 412b5-6 to be "absolument incompatible" (p. 165) with the notion of the soul present "in the heart" and operating principally through the
heart, a notion he finds prominent in some of the *Parva Naturalia* (= *PN*)
and the majority of the biological works. This incompatibility, assumed
throughout Nuyens' study (pp. 45, 47, 55–58, 119, 159–71, etc.), served as
his chief criterion for dividing Aristotle's works chronologically into those
of an earlier "transitional period" and those of the "terminal period" of
hylomorphism.

Nuyens' use of a single criterion for distributing the works chronologically promised an advantage over the procedure of Jaeger, who depended
upon particular internal criteria established for each treatise. Nuyens' work
was acclaimed and accepted substantially by some very great scholars, notably by Augustin Mansion and Sir David Ross, along with Drossaart Lulofs,
Pierre Louis, Barbotin, Gauthier, D. A. Rees, and others.[2] Ingemar Düring,
in his article on Aristotle published in Pauly-Wissowa (Suppl. XI, 253–54)
in 1968, expressed the judgment that Nuyens' position at that time could
"als die herrschende Meinung betrachtet werden." Yet even while Düring's
article was being written, the most searching critiques of Nuyens' view, especially as adopted by Ross, were already in print.

Objections to details of Nuyens' work had been raised, of course, from
the time of its publication. But the first serious challenge to the validity of
his main criterion seems to have been published by Irving Block in his paper

This paper was presented at the 1974 Chicago meeting of the Society for Ancient Greek
Philosophy and has been revised for inclusion in this volume.

Theodore Tracy taught at the University of Illinois at Chicago Circle when this paper was
presented, and is now at Ignatius House in Chicago.

"The Order of Aristotle's Psychological Writings," in *AJP* 82 (1961):50–77. Block argued first that Aristotle's definition of soul as form or entelechy of the body does not *logically* forbid him to emphasize a particular organ as source of the activities whereby the body lives. Secondly, Block analyzed the passages from the *De Sensu* (= *Sens.*) cited by Ross as illustrating a "two-substance theory of body and soul" and provided alternative interpretations and arguments to show that these statements could be reconciled with the hylomorphic view of soul. Thirdly, Block here first called attention in print to the important passage in *Metaphysics* Zeta (1035b14 ff.) where Aristotle speaks clearly of the soul as "form and essence of the body" and at the same time refers to it as being present primarily in a dominant organ of the body, thereby indicating that these notions, absolutely incompatible for Nuyens, apparently were not so for Aristotle. Block's effort in this part of his paper was largely negative, countering the arguments of Ross especially, yet providing solid evidence that the "entelechy view" and the "heart view" were not incompatible in Aristotle's mind. Two years later Marjorie Grene's *A Portrait of Aristotle* appeared (Chicago, 1963), presenting further evidence against Nuyens' view by pointing out (p. 35) that both the hylomorphic soul and the doctrine of the heart as source of life are found side by side in the *De Generatione Animalium* (= *GA*), a work that Nuyens dates with *DA* in the latest period of Aristotle's development.

This evidence from *GA* and the passage from *Metaphysics* Zeta were both incorporated in W. F. R. Hardie's article "Aristotle's Treatment of the Relation Between the Soul and the Body," published in 1964 (*Philosophical Quarterly* 14:53–72) but written some years earlier. Hardie used them effectively against two propositions assumed by Nuyens, namely, (1) that Aristotle knew or believed there was a contradiction between the "entelechy view" and the "heart view" of the soul, and (2) that he gave up the latter after developing the former. In support of his position Hardie also presented a long analysis of the passage in *De Motu Animalium* (= *MA*) on the origin of movement in animals (699a14–b7, 702a21–b11), showing it consistent with the cryptic description of the same in *DA* III, 433b21–29, a consistency acknowledged by Ross in this commentary on *DA* (p. 317). Hardie found evidence of the hylomorphic view, too, in *DA* I, *Sens.*, and *De Memoria* (= *Mem.*), all regarded by Ross as written before Aristotle adopted the entelechy view. Thus Hardie succeeded in establishing that "Aristotle finds no inconsistency between the hylomorphic doctrine and localization in the heart" (p. 67) and in detecting inconsistencies in the position of Nuyens and Ross. However, his attempt to go beyond this, to show that the two doctrines complement each other (p. 67 ff.), was only partially successful.

While Nuyens' position, in Düring's judgment, could be considered the prevailing view in 1968, these critiques were having their effect. That same year saw the appearance of G. E. R. Lloyd's *Aristotle: The Growth and Structure of His Thought* (Cambridge, England) in which Lloyd remarks of Nuyens' position on the "entelechy view" versus the "heart view" (p. 25): ". . . scholars such as Block and Hardie have shown . . . that whatever we may think of the relationship between the two doctrines in question, Aristotle himself was unaware of any incompatibility between them." Two years later, in 1970, R. A. Gauthier published the revision of his introduction to *Aristote: L'Éthique à Nicomaque* (2nd ed., vol. I, part 1, Louvain), retaining Nuyens' chronology and dealing briefly with these critiques (pp. 46–47, n. 113). His effectiveness, and theirs, was evaluated thus by Jonathan Barnes in his review in *AGP* 55 (1973):80: "The distinction between Instrumentism and Hylemorphism, which forms the core of Nuyens' position, has been demolished by Block . . . and by Hardie. . . . Gauthier discusses Block's and Hardie's criticisms . . . but fails to appreciate their direction and their force."

If we accept Barnes' opinion that the core of Nuyens' position "has been demolished by Block and by Hardie," what more remains to be done? Have their discussions settled the problem, leaving room for nothing but autopsy? Perhaps not. These studies have presented compelling evidence that the "entelechy view" and the "heart view" of the soul, though regarded as incompatible by Nuyens and Ross (see his *PN*, pp. 7–12), apparently presented no incompatibility to Aristotle's mind since they appear together in the same context and the same works. This is enough, of course, to demolish the core of Nuyens' position and the basis for his chronological distribution of Aristotle's writings. But it leaves the problem that troubled Nuyens in the first place, to which he offered his developmental or chronological solution. There does seem to be something incompatible between the notion of the soul as entelechy of the whole body (so that every organ, to be alive, must be "ensouled") and statements that the soul is "in the heart" (e.g., *De Juventute* = *Juv* 469a5–7) and that "there is no need of soul in each part" as long as it "is present in some ruling center of the body" (*MA* 703a36–37). If Aristotle did not regard these as incompatible, how would *he* reconcile them? What relationship would he see between them? How are they compatible in his terms?

Block argued that the notion of the soul present in the whole body is logically compatible with the notion of the soul centered in one part, using as illustration the electric light bulb and its filament (pp. 52–53). Hardie dealt helpfully with the passage from *MA* 702a21 ff., but backed away from the troublesome statement just quoted (703a36–37) with the warning that we should not press it too hard (p. 60). Brief but valuable suggestions on how Aristotle might relate the two doctrines appear in Paul Siwek's introduction to his *De Anima* (Rome, 1965, pp. 18–19) and in H. J. Easterling's "Note on *de Anima* 413a8–9," (*Phronesis* 11 [1966]:161–62). But perhaps the most helpful contribution in this direction was Charles Kahn's study "Sensation and Consciousness in Aristotle's Psychology" published in *AGP*, vol. 48, no. 1 (1966):43–81.

Kahn's study was limited specifically to the relationship of the psychic to the physical aspect of *sensation* in Aristotle, and showed that Aristotle's "sensitive soul" comprises a single psychological system in which the functions of the special senses are integrated by the *sensus communis*, identical under other aspects with the faculty producing time sense, phantasms, memories, sleep, and dreams. But in Aristotle's terms, the "sensitive soul" must inform, and function physiologically through, an appropriate organic system. For Aristotle, this can only be the organs of the special senses in connection with the organ of the *sensus communis*, the heart. Reflecting on the implications of Aristotle's description of the "sensitive soul" and its functions as presented in *DA*, Kahn argued that they *require* the physiological system eventually presented in the *PN*, so that the discussion of sensation and the "sensitive soul" begun in the *DA* is continued, and not contradicted, by that of the *PN* (Kahn, pp. 67–68).

While Kahn's study represents a considerable advance it still leaves a number of critical questions unanswered:

1. If, as Kahn (correctly) maintains, the physiological system of the later *PN* is logically required by the "sensitive soul" and its functions as described in *DA*, why is there so little said of the physiological aspect, and the heart hardly mentioned in *DA*? Kahn suggests (versus Block) that the reason is methodological, not chronological:

> The *De Anima* takes up a somewhat different point of view, since it abstracts from all consideration of physiological detail. But there is really no reason to suppose that the physiological model in Aristotle's mind, which he systematically refrains from introducing into the *De Anima*, is in any way different from that which is actually expounded by him in the other works. (pp. 68–69)

Accepting this suggestion, I propose to show, however, that an examination of even the few references to the heart in *DA* does in fact reveal the same physiological model in that treatise as in the *PN* and the biological works, not only for the "sensitive soul" but for the entire animal soul.

2. Does the entire animal soul described in *DA* *necessarily* inform and activate the body through a single central organ; and does Aristotle *himself* clearly indicate this necessity?

3. Nuyens and Ross consider certain phrases and expressions in the *PN* and biological works incompatible with hylomorphism. How can these be reconciled with a hylomorphic context?

These three problems will be dealt with in turn.

I. The Heart in the *De Anima*

In *DA* the heart is mentioned explicitly four times (403a31, 408b8, 420b25–26, 432b31) and referred to implicitly at least five (408b23–28, 423b23, 426b16, 431a18, 433b19–27). Nuyens ignored all but one of these (420b25–26; see his p. 247, n. 77), while Ross considered Aristotle's relative silence on the heart in *DA* a sign that he had abandoned the psychophysiology of the biological works (*PN* 7–8, 12). We may agree with Ross that in these passages the heart is "mentioned only incidentally and in other connections" (*PN* 12), but disagree that in none of them "is any primary importance attached to it" (*DA* 10). Incidental references may be more revealing for what they assume or imply.

The "heart view" of the biological works, which Ross considers incompatible with hylomorphism, is characterized by him as follows: "In this phase of Aristotle's thought, soul is thought of as closely associated with heat, and with the hottest organ in the body, the heart" (*PN* 6). Ross then cites as typical of the "heart view" selections from *De Partibus Animalium* (= *PA*) where Aristotle asserts that the soul, while not itself fire, uses heat as a most apt instrument in its operations, specifically nutrition and the imparting of motion (652b7–16); that the heart is the center of life and vital heat (653b5–6), the source of motion and sensation (665a10–13) essential to all animals (678b1–4). I submit that these same functions are attributed to vital heat and to the heart in the *DA* also, where the "entelechy view" is proposed in detail.

1. Turning to *DA*, Book II (". . . in all probability the latest of Aristotle's writings on psychology": Ross *PN* 17), we find Aristotle denying that "the nature of fire" is the cause, without qualification, of nutrition and growth, but asserting that "A co-cause, in a sense, it certainly is; but not the cause absolutely; that is rather the soul" (416a13–15). He then explains (416b20 ff.) that in nutrition (1) it is the body that is nourished, (2) the "nutritive soul" that nourishes, while (3) that *by which* the body is nourished includes (a) the food, which must be concocted, and (b) the vital *heat*, which effects concoction. The same passage (416b9 ff.) describes how indispensible an instrument heat is to the soul: For what is ensouled or alive preserves its substance only as long as it is nourished (416b14–15); but "all nourishment must be able to be digested; and what produces digestion is heat; therefore everything that is ensouled possesses heat" (416b28–29). Clearly then, in *DA* as in the biological works, the soul operates through the vital heat, its co-cause or primary instrument in the processes of nutrition and growth.

2. Also in *DA*, Book II, Aristotle indicates that he is not thinking of all parts of the animal body as possessing this heat in equal degree. For while explaining that nature uses breath to regulate the internal heat of the body

(420b20–21) he mentions, incidentally but explicitly, that the area that needs cooling before all others is the one surrounding the heart (420b25–26). This implies clearly that Aristotle here regards the heart as "the hottest organ in the body" and is perfectly consistent with his description of heat distribution at *Juv* 469b6 ff.: "Now in animals all the parts of the body as a whole contain a certain natural innate heat. . . . And the source of this heat in blooded animals must be in the heart . . ." (b6–11).

3. Ross himself admits that three explicit references to the heart in *DA* treat it as the seat of emotions,[3] which implies that it is also the principal organ of the "sensitive soul," i.e., of power of the common sense and of those activities that are functions of or depend upon it—imagination, pleasure and pain reaction, memory, and even "reasoning" (διανοεῖσθαι). Thus, in a context emphasizing the bodily aspect of psychic states (408b1–19), Aristotle specifies: "For example, to be angry or to fear is for the heart to be changed (moved) in this way or that, and to reason (διανοεῖσθαι) involves this organ or some other" (408b7–9; or "that the heart be changed in a similar way or some other": Ox. trans.; Hicks 274 *ad* b9).[4] It is perhaps surprising to find "reasoning" linked to a change in the heart. Yet in a continuation of this passage, Aristotle again links "reasoning" with emotions (love and hate) as dependent upon a certain physical organ that somehow "possesses" the thinking soul (408b27); in which the soul is present (b23); an interior organ (b25) whose disturbance by drunkenness, disease, or old age impairs the rational processes (b22–25); upon which memory too is dependent (b27–28). Ross in his commentary (*DA* 198–99 *ad* 408b25) identifies this internal organ as the heart.

4. Consistent with this is another implicit reference in Book II, 422b17 ff., where Aristotle makes it clear that the common organ of touch and taste is not the outer flesh but some interior organ (423b23). Ross (*DA* 262–63 *ad* 423a15–16, b23) suggests that Aristotle here has the doctrine of *Sens.* 439a1–2 in mind, where the common organ is said to be "near" or "closely related to" the heart. Better, in *Juv.* 469a10–16 Aristotle argues to the location of the common sensorium on the ground that "we see clearly that two senses, touch and taste, extend to the heart, so that the others must also" (a12–14). Accordingly, Aristotle must have the heart in mind when he returns in book III to discussion of the *sensus communis* (426b12 ff.) and the "ultimate" sense organ through which it operates (426b16, 431a18) in producing images (427b12 ff.) necessary for the thought processes (429a10 ff., 431b2–5) and the pleasure-pain reactions that trigger the activities of pursuit and avoidance (431a10–14).

5. In analyzing the origin of motion in man and animals (432a15 ff.) Aristotle explicitly mentions the heart as the physical organ affected by the image of something painful or pleasant (432b29–433a1). And Ross, with

most commentators, agrees that Aristotle refers to the heart when he speaks (433b19–27) of the "bodily part" that the appetitive faculty uses as its organ to move the animal (*DA* 317 *ad* 433b21–27, 25–27). Something of the basic dynamics of emotion and the origin of movement in the heart had already been suggested by Aristotle in Book I (403a3 ff.) where he points to the material and formal aspects of psychic events such as emotions (403a7, 17–18), illustrating them by the opposing reactions of anger and fear (403a19–26, b18, 408b8). In this context the material aspect of anger is explicitly defined as "a boiling of the blood around the heart" (403a31–b1). This links the heart's function as thermal center of the organism (see above) with its function as center of emotional response and movement; for it suggests that if the bodily aspect of anger is an abnormal increase of vital heat in the heart and its blood, the bodily aspect of the opposite, fear, must be a cooling down of the blood in that organ, which ties in precisely with the detailed physiology of fear offered in *De Respiratione* (= *Resp.*) 479b19–26. Contraction and expansion under opposite thermal changes in the heart would account for the "pushing and pulling" communicated from the central organ in Aristotle's description of the origin of movement at *DA* 433b20–31, a passage basic to the more concrete description in *MA*, especially 701b13 ff.

6. Finally, in Book II, 420b27–33, the origin of voice production is explicitly traced to soul operating in the region of the heart. Discussing sound and voice, Aristotle asserts that nature uses breath for two purposes, refrigeration and voice production. Refrigeration is needed most at the heart (b25–26). Voice is a striking of inhaled air against the windpipe "under the influence of soul in these parts" (b28); for it is distinguished from mere mechanical sound (e.g., a cough) in that for voice "the sound-impact must be ensouled, i.e., its production accompanied by an act of the image-making faculty. For voice is the kind of sound that conveys meaning" (b29–33). *Meaning* here is of the most elemental type, a signal of pain or pleasure possible to animals as well as man (who also has the power of speech), since both "have sensations of pain and pleasure and signal these to one another" (*Politics* 1253a11–14). Clearly implied, then, is that the "soul in these parts" functions in sense perception, imagination, emotion or pleasure-pain reaction, and the communication of emotion through production of appropriate sound, implying control of breath and bodily organs. These are obviously activities of the "sensitive soul" integrated in the common sensorium, the heart.[5]

Thus the explicit and implicit references to the heart in *DA*, though relatively few and introduced incidentally, indicate clearly enough that Aristotle is thinking of the heart also in this work as the central organ of the nutritive and sensitive life, a doctrine developed explicitly and in detail in the *PN* and

ESSAYS IN ANCIENT GREEK PHILOSOPHY

the biological works.[6] Even in Book II, where he introduces the definition of soul as entelechy of the body, Aristotle thinks of soul as being present and operating on the nutritive and sensitive levels "in these parts," i.e., in the heart and surrounding organs, notions that Nuyens and Ross considered incompatible. What then was the relationship between the two notions for Aristotle? I propose that he not only thought of them as compatible but even as joined by *necessity*, that his presuppositions about the soul and his conception of soul as described in *DA* II made it necessary, in his eyes, to postulate a single dominant organ in which the soul functions primarily in animals and man. This is the antithesis of Nuyens' position.[7]

II. The Necessity of the Heart as Center in Hylomorphism

First let us recall the characteristics of the hylomorphic soul and the conditions of its existence presented in *DA*. The critique of previous theories in Book I is important since, as Ross remarks (*DA* 12), Aristotle's own views about soul "are largely shaped by his sense of the objections to which earlier views were exposed." A review of these objections indicates certain of Aristotle's presuppositions, namely, that soul is single (411a26–30) with multiple powers (410b16–27), immaterial (403b28 ff.) but existing only in a connatural material body equipped with organs suitable to its functions, and to this particular type of soul, there being many (403a3–b19, 407b1–25, 410b16–27). Soul itself does not move but is the source of movement in the ensouled organism (405b31–407a2, 408a30–b32).

With these presuppositions Aristotle undertakes his own positive definition in Book II. There is no need to rehearse his development of the definition of soul as the substantial form, entelechy or actuality, and first actuality, of a natural body having life potentially (421a1–29). This aspect, especially the notion of soul as entelechy of the *entire* body, receives close attention from Nuyens (pp. 66 ff., 238 ff.) and Ross (*DA* 10 ff.). But there is little to be found in the commentators and, for that matter, in the *DA* itself, about that part of the definition describing the *kind of body* the soul can inform and activate. It is identified first as "a natural body having life potentially" (412a28), which is immediately specified as "a natural body equipped with organs." Aristotle hastens to point out that the definition applies to plants since they also have organs (412b1–4). In contrast to an artifact, it must be "a natural body of a particular kind, viz., one having in itself a principle or source (ἀρχή) of its motion or rest" (412b16–17, cf. *Physics* 192b4–23). Later, after distinguishing the various powers of soul in plants, animals, and man, Aristotle reinforces the point that each kind of soul can exist only in a body proper to it, since "the actuality of any given thing can only be realized . . . in a matter of its own appropriate to it" (414a25–27).

But in the *DA* Aristotle has not much more to say directly about the body beyond these generalizations.[8]

We must turn then to other works that obviously share with *DA* the hylomorphic view of soul. Both Nuyens (e.g., 176–77) and Ross (*DA* 11) regard the *Metaphysics* as closely related to *DA* in this respect. There the now familiar passage at Zeta 1035b14 ff. is instructive. Discussing the relation of parts to the whole, Aristotle describes soul in hylomorphic terms as the "form or essence of a body of a certain kind" (b16) and explains that the soul and its parts, as essential substance, are prior to the animal and to the body and its parts; though in a sense they are not, since they cannot exist apart from the concrete whole, the composite of body and soul. Then, speaking of the relationship of parts of the *composite* to the whole, he goes on to remark without qualification: "Some parts are neither prior nor posterior to the composite, namely, those that are *controlling* (κύρια) and *in which the formula*, i.e., *the essential substance* (ὁ λόγος καὶ ἡ οὐσία) *is primarily present* (ἐν ᾧ πρώτῳ), e.g., the *heart*, or perhaps the brain—for it does not matter which of the two is of such a nature" (b25–28).

Here, as has been remarked, Aristotle speaks of the hylomorphic soul as being "present in" some particular controlling organ (at the moment he is not interested in taking sides on whether this be heart or brain; see below). The soul is present in this controlling organ *primarily*. And the organ is one that is not prior or posterior to the composite but comes into existence simultaneously (ἅμα) with it. The context of Aristotle's thought is clarified by a related passage in *Metaphysics* Delta where, in listing various meanings of the word ἀρχή (source, beginning), he mentions in third place "that thing as a result of whose presence something first comes into being, e.g., as the keel is the beginning of a ship, the foundation the beginning of a house, and in the case of animals some say the heart, others the brain, others something similar . . ." (1013a4–6),

Though these passages do not commit Aristotle to either the heart or the brain, they certainly make it clear that he considers it a *fact* that the hylomorphic soul is present in, forming and informing, some one principal or controlling organ first in the generation of the animal. And the moment that organ is formed marks the beginning of the animal, the composite. For the rest of the animal is formed from this organ and around it as its beginning and source. So much for the fact. What of the *necessity*?

The necessity, as well as the dynamics, of this process is brought out forcefully in *GA*, a work that Nuyens regards as *hylémorphique* (pp. 256–63). The hylomorphic soul of the *DA* cannot exist except as formal cause informing an appropriate organ or system of organs; it is also the efficient cause, the source of change and motion, which forms and functions in the composite; and it is the final cause for the sake of whose functions the complete organism, the End, is developed and maintained. Accordingly, in *GA* 735b34 ff. Aristotle explains that to initiate the independent life of a new animal the soul *must* form a *single primary organ* from the residue of seed, which ensouled organ becomes the source of all other organs subsequently formed (742a33–b3):

> First of all it is necessary (ἀναγκαῖον) that some part exist in which the source of motion is present, since of course this part of the End, being single and all-controlling (ἓν καὶ κυριώτατον); and then after this the whole organism, i.e., the End. . . . So that if there is some such part—which *must* (ἀναγκαῖον) be present in animals, one which possesses the principle (ἀρχή) and the End of the animal's whole nature— it is necessary (ἀναγκαῖον) that this be formed *first* (πρῶτον) *qua* instrument of change (κινητικόν) but *simultaneously* with the whole organism *qua* part of the End.

The implications are no doubt clear. The soul must form, inform, and activate a single controlling organ from the start by means of which it produces the natural growth of the other organs necessary for the functioning of all its powers or faculties. This organ is not only chronologically first in generation but also the dominant or controlling organ in the fully formed animal, since it must continue to do its work as primary control center of the life processes if the organism is to continue to be nourished, refreshed by sleep, etc., so as to maintain itself. Hence the soul is present in this organ primarily and as controlling the other organs through it. This is not to deny that the soul also forms, informs, and activates—and so is present in—the other organs necessary to all its functions. But it can do this only because it is present first in one organ formed to serve as origin and control center (ἀρχή) of the others. Thus soul is present in all the organs of the body, but not in the same way. It must be, and continue to be, present in one organ πρώτως καὶ κυρίως. Yet this organ, like any other, lives and functions only as part of a living whole.[9]

GA leaves no doubt about which organ this is (e.g., 741b16–17): "The first to be formed is the source (ἀρχή), which in blooded animals is the heart. . . ." Aristotle establishes the heart (versus those who favor the brain) as the primary organ on the basis of several considerations: the heart is observed to be the first formed in the embryo; it is the center of the vascular system from which nourishment (blood) is pumped to the other organs; it is the center of vital heat necessary for the nutritive and formative (see 740b30–741a3) processes; it is located in the place of command at the geometrical center of the organism. In lower animals it is an organ analogous to the heart. And even plants grow out symmetrically from some part formed as an ἀρχή (*GA* 762b18–21).

We have been concerned with the processes of formation, nutrition, and growth—all functions of the "nutritive soul," which, as we have seen, *necessarily* informs a primary organ, the heart, as source and control center of these processes in the developing and in the mature animal. But the distinguishing characteristic of an animal is the presence of a "sensitive soul." What necessity connects this with the "nutritive soul" and the heart? *GA* is of little help here.

Returning to *DA*, we recall that for Aristotle the "nutritive soul" and "sensitive soul" are not really distinct, but only rationally distinguishable faculties of the one animal soul (413b13–32, 432a22 ff.). Examination of the incidental references to the heart in *DA* revealed that Aristotle was thinking of this soul as embodied in a unified physiological system centered in that organ. As Kahn has pointed out (p. 59), this first becomes explicit in the *De Somno* (= *Somn.* 455a12–22), where Aristotle's explanation of sleep and waking involves the heart not only as the common sensorium but also as center of the nutritive functions. For what specifies the "incapacity of the sense faculty" in sleep is that it is caused by thermal changes in the heart, center of vital heat and of the vascular system; and these changes are induced by the ingestion of food (456a30 ff.). Thus the functions of the "nutritive soul" closely affect those of the "sensitive soul" because both nutritive and sensory systems are united in their common central organ, the heart.

Though Aristotle identifies the heart as center of both systems in *Somn.* he does not there use the vocabulary of necessity that would reveal his conviction that the animal soul *must* be actualized in a body unified by the heart. This is reserved until he has completed his discussion of the "sensitive soul" and allied subjects in the first five treatises of the *PN* and has returned to consideration of topics related to the "nutritive soul" in the last three.

These are so closely related that they constitute a continuous discussion (Hett, Loeb 388).[10] The first treatise introduces the subject of the length and shortness of life, describing the ultimate physical constituents of various organisms and their role in determining the life-span of each. Following this, Aristotle plans to explore in detail the subjects of youth, old age, death, and the related topic of respiration (467b10–13). In preparation he discusses explicitly the relation of the "parts" of the animal soul to each other and to the body, referring to his treatment of soul in *DA* and connecting the notion of soul developed there with a body unified through a central controlling organ (467b13–16): "Since we have discussed the soul in precise detail in another treatise and it is clear that its essential nature cannot be corporeal, nevertheless it is also evident that soul is present in some particular bodily part, and this one of the parts having control over the rest."

We have seen Aristotle use the language of necessity in *GA* in connecting the operation of the "nutritive soul" to a single primary organ. Here he employs it again to establish the unity of the nutritive and sensitive soul in a controlling organ (467b18–23):

> Regarding things that are said to be "animals" and to be "alive"—in those organisms to which both these terms apply (viz., to be an animal and to be alive) it is *necessary* (ἀνάγκη) that there be a single identical part in virtue of which the organism both "lives" and is called an "animal." For it is impossible for an "animal" *qua* "animal" *not* to be alive. . . .

An organism endowed with an animal ("sensitive") soul must always possess the powers of the "nutritive" soul in virtue of which it *lives* (*DA* 414b28–415a2). And the single soul with both nutritive and sensitive powers *must* operate through a single controlling organ. This organ, to be a suitable instrument for such a soul, "must be numerically one and the same but have multiple and different modes of being, since to be 'animal' and to be 'alive' are not identical" (467b25–27).

Aristotle proceeds next (b27 ff.) to establish that this organ is the *heart*, on the basis that (1) the organ of the *sensus communis* and the source of the nutritive faculty would occupy a central position in the body; (2) the heart is observed to be formed first in the embryo; (3) the heart is the source of the blood vessels that carry nourishment (blood) to the rest of the body. "Therefore it is *necessary* (ἀνάγκη) that in blooded animals the source and control center (ἀρχή) of both the 'sensitive' and 'nutritive' soul be in the heart" (469a5–7). The conclusion is further reinforced by observation that the central sense is located in the heart since the basic senses of touch and taste are traced to that organ (469a10–16); and by deduction from the principle that nature always works to achieve the best, and the central position is the best for control (a28–b1). Aristotle closes the argument with the statement (469b3–6): "Since therefore an animal is defined by the possession of a 'sensitive soul,' in blooded animals it is *necessary* (ἀναγκαῖον) that this have its source and control center (ἀρχή) in the heart."

What is the nature of the "necessity" that Aristotle has in mind in these statements? Probably that which he explains in another context (*Somn.* 455b26–28): "I use the term 'necessity' in its conditional sense, meaning that if an animal is to exist and have its own proper nature, by necessity certain things must belong to it; and if these are to belong to it, certain others must also belong to it." Following this direction, we might suppose his reasoning would proceed somewhat as follows: if the hylomorphic animal soul, being one with several faculties, is to exist, it must be realized in an appropriate body. But this must be a "body equipped with organs" in such a way that the one soul can carry on its complex functions in a unified and coordinated manner. But this can only be done through a complex system of appropriate organs unified under a single central and controlling organ through which the soul can operate as source of motion and rest in the entire organism, integrating and controlling the life functions on both the nutritive and sensitive levels. But in blooded animals this must be the central and controlling organ of the vascular system and the sensory system, the heart.

The best-constructed animals, Aristotle remarks (468b11–13), have a nature that is, as far as possible, one. Paul Siwek has seen that, unlike Plato's tripartite soul, Aristotle's hylomorphic soul can only incorporate its unity by forming, and informing, a body integrated about a single controlling organ (Introduction to De Anima, p. 19): "Tunc solummodo unitas entis vivi potest salvari." The same point was made several centuries ago by Jacopo Zabarella in his commentary on DA II (In Libr. II de Anima, cap. II, 295 D):

Ad unitatem vero animalis servandam unum tantum praecipuum membrum est concedendum, in quo tota sit anima radicata et a quo tamquam principio et fonte ad omnes corporis partes effundatur. . . .

III.   Soul in the Heart and in the Body as a Whole

In the light of these considerations, how are we to deal with Aristotle's statements that the soul "is present in εἶναι ἐν) some particular part of the body" (Juv. 467b15), that some part of the body "possesses" the sensitive soul (ἔχει αὐτήν: Mem. 450a29), that the ἀρχή of the sensitive and nutritive soul is "in the heart" (ἐν τῇ καρδίᾳ: Juv. 469a6–7)? How can Aristotle speak in these terms and at the same time conceive the soul as form or entelechy, the principle of life throughout the body?

This is obviously the problem that led Nuyens to declare the "entelechy view" incompatible with the "heart view" and to propose his chronological solution. Kahn, discussing sensation only, suggests a more promising approach (p. 69): "Since the sensory soul . . . includes not only the general power of sensation but also the special faculties of external sense, it must be thought of as *informing the entire sense apparatus*, although it does so *from its source or foundation* (archê) *in the heart*. Thus there is a derivative psychic power resident in the eye. . . ."

If Kahn's statement were broadened to include the whole nutritive-sensory soul, it could apply to the animal as a whole, thus: The soul must be thought of as informing the entire nutritive and sensory apparatus, i.e., all the organs of the body, but as doing so from its source or foundation in the primary and first-formed organ of the body, the heart. The psychic power informing and maintaining the other organs is derivative in that it originated genetically in the heart, formed the other organs and preserves them in dependence on the heart, imparts change and movement to them from its center in the heart.

To say that the soul has its source in the heart is not to deny its presence in the rest of the body, but only to affirm that it is present in a different way in the heart and in the other organs. For the soul forms and activates the heart as the primary and controlling organ of the body and so is present in the heart in a way *different from* its presence in all secondary and subordinate organs, i.e., it is present in the heart as the control center of all functions carried out through the organic systems that constitute the body. Conceived in this way, some of Aristotle's difficult statements about the presence of the soul "in the heart" are more easily understandable.

Nuyens and Ross find a contradiction between the notion of soul as form or entelechy of the whole body and soul as being present "in the heart" because they evidently understand the latter expression to imply local presence in the strict sense. Thus Nuyens interprets the phrase as equivalent to "localisée à une place definie" (p. 259); and Ross takes it as meaning "being located in" (*PN* 12; *DA* 10). Understood in this way, the soul would "be located in" the heart as wine is in a jar, to use Aristotle's example (*Physics* 210a24 ff.). This, of course, would certainly preclude its being present in the same way at the same time in the rest of the body.

However, as Sorabji points out, "The soul does not meet Aristotle's requirements for 'being in a place.'"[11] (Cf. *DA* 406a12–16 and *Physics* 210b32 ff.). To Aristotle, "being in place" implies matter and extension, as does moving from place to place. The soul, therefore, being incorporeal, can no more "be in place," of itself than it can move locally, of itself (*DA* 405b32 ff.). Aristotle can hardly have intended, then, that the immaterial soul be understood to be "in the heart" *locally*. He must have in mind some other mode of "being in" that organ.

As a preliminary to his discussion of space in the *Physics*, Aristotle enumerates eight different senses in which one thing is said to "be in" another (210a14–24). The last, signifying localization in the strict sense, is inapplicable to soul and heart, as are the first four, which involve the relationship of part to whole and genus to species. The fifth concerns the relationship between form and matter, since the form is said to "be in" the matter of the compound. Perhaps Aristotle speaks of the soul "in the heart" in this sense.

Aristotle certainly affirms that the soul is "in" a *body* as its form or entelechy. He agrees with those who think that the soul cannot exist without a body, though itself not body: "For it is not a body, but something belonging to a body, and for this reason is present *in* a body" (ἐν σώματι ὑπάρχει: *DA* 414a21–23). But then Aristotle goes on to insist that this must be "a body of a particular kind; not at all as our predecessors supposed, who fitted it to any body without specifying in which or what kind of body, though obviously one chance thing does not receive another" (a23–25). The actuality or soul of each organism comes to exist only in what is potentially such by nature, i.e., in its own proper matter.

We have seen that for Aristotle the matter necessary and proper for activation by the soul of a blooded animal (including man) is a body generated from and integrated by one primary and controlling organ, the heart. Clearly the animal and human soul can properly be said to "be in" the *whole* of such a body as form in its proper matter. But could it also be said to "be in" the *heart* in this sense? Certainly not if this is understood in an exclusive sense to mean that the soul is present "in the heart" as form in its proper matter but *not* in the other organs. For they also must be informed and activated by soul to be alive; and a heart is not a heart except as part of a living whole, as Aristotle insists. But is there a sense in which the soul can be said to be in the heart as form in its proper matter without excluding its presence in the other organs?

Discussing the notion of cause in *Metaphysics* Delta 1013a24 ff., Aristotle remarks that "causes are spoken of in many senses, and even of those which are of the same kind some are causes in a *prior* and some in a *posterior* sense" (1013b31–32). Later, discussing the material cause of generable natural substances and events in *Metaphysics* Eta (1044a15 ff.), he maintains that we must state not only all the causes (material, formal, efficient, final) but the most *proximate* (1044b2), i.e., not fire or earth as the material cause of man, but that which is proper or peculiar to his form. Turning to the example of sleep, he asks what is its proper material, what is the *proximate* material affected (b15–20)? The *whole* animal, he agrees, is certainly affected. But with respect to what, and of what *proximately*? His answer is "the heart, or some other part" (b18). (The "other part" can be disregarded, introduced here for pacific reasons.) And what particular affection of that part, and *not* of the whole animal? It is a special kind of immobility, induced in that part (the heart), the *proximate* subject. (Aristotle assumes the psychophysiology of sleep explained in *Somn.* 456a30 ff.).

The distinction introduced here between the *heart* and the *whole* animal as proximate and secondary material cause may be important. While designating the heart as the primary or proximate subject of sleep, Aristotle does not deny, but specifically affirms, that the whole animal is the subject of sleep. But the whole animal sleeps because of a specific affection or immobility in the controlling organ. The proper and proximate material subject of sleep is the heart; the whole animal is the proper but secondary subject of that affection.

It is possible, then, that when Aristotle speaks of the soul "in the heart" he has in mind the heart as primary and proximate material organ of the soul, the controlling organ originally informed and activated by the soul, upon which all other organs depend for their formation and activation by the soul. They too live, i.e., are informed and activated by the soul, but in a way that is *secondary* and more remote. To speak of the soul as existing "in the heart," then, is not to deny its presence in the other organs but only to indicate the primary and proximate subject it informs and activates. A heart would be no heart if not part of a living whole.

Aristotle uses another difficult phrase when he speaks of a certain part of the body that "possesses" the sensitive soul (ἐν . . . τῷ μορίῳ . . . ἔχοντι αὐτήν: *Mem* 450a29). This suggests an exclusive possession incompatible with hylomorphism. And it *is* incompatible if understood in the sense that a part of the body "possesses" or "holds" the sensitive soul "as the container holds the contained." This is the third sense of the verb "to possess, to hold" (ἔχειν) distinguished by Aristotle in *Metaphysics* Delta 1023a8–25 and illustrated by the example "as the jar holds the liquid" (a15–16). Obviously this sense brings us back to that strict localization in space that for Aristotle is inapplicable to the immaterial soul. He must be using the verb in another sense, probably the second, which he explains thus (a12–13): "We say something 'possesses' or 'holds' another when the other is present in it as in receptive material, e.g., as the bronze 'possesses' or 'holds' the shape of the statue." In this sense a certain part of the body (the heart) would "possess" the sensitive soul as the material organ "possesses" its form. As we have seen, this need not imply that other organs do not "possess" the sensitive soul, but only that the one organ, the heart, "possesses" it primarily as proximate material cause.

What of the troublesome passage at the end of *MA* 703a28 ff.? There Aristotle, after describing the psychophysiology of the origin of motion in the heart, compares the animal organism to a well-governed city-state where, once a constitutional order is set up, there is no need for several separate monarchs to preside over various areas of operation, since each individual performs his function as ordered under a single source of command. The same, he says, comes about in the animal organism through natural growth and structure, each part formed by nature to fulfill its proper function, so that—and here is the difficult statement (703a36–b2)—"there is no need for soul to be in each part (ἐν ἑκάστῳ εἶναι), but with the soul being present in some center of control (ἀρχή [or 'central origin of authority,' Forster, Loeb 477][12]) over the body, the other parts live by organic unity with it (προσπεφυκέναι: cf. *Metaphysics* 1014b20–23) and perform their own functions through their natural formation."

It seems clear from the nature of the treatise and the immediate context that Aristotle is thinking here of the soul not as formal but as *efficient* cause and is describing particularly how and where the soul initiates movement or change in the animal body so as to control its functions and locomotion. He is insisting that *under this aspect* the soul occupies and operates from only one control center, the heart. This is a brief echo of a point he makes constantly and at length in *PA*, namely, that one source and center of control is best (657b20–21, 665b14–16, 666a14) and that this is the heart, which occupies the center, the place of leadership and command (665a10–13, 665b18–21). Ultimately, as we have seen, Aristotle links this with the unity of the animal soul. "The sensory soul is, in all animals, one actually; therefore the part which primarily (πρώτως) possesses this soul is also one . . ." (667b23–24). Here Aristotle characterizes the heart as possessing the soul *primarily*, implying that the other organs possess it, but in a secondary mode, i.e., not as control centers but as controlled. The soul *as originating change and controlling the life functions* is present in the heart in a way in which it is not present in other organs.

Aristotle apparently makes this point against other thinkers (Plato?) who postulate more than one control center in the animal. At *PA* 665b27–29 he criticizes certain persons who claim that the source of the blood-vessels is in the head, on the ground that "first of all they set up many control centers (ἀρχαί) scattered about." He may have these in mind in *MA* 703a31–33: there is no more need for separate control centers in different parts of the animal organism than there is for separate monarchs to occupy and oversee different sections of a well-organized city-state. In the animal organism, as in the body politic, one center of control is best.

Among the various ways one thing is said to "be in" another, listed at *Physics* 210a14 ff., Aristotle distinguishes the sixth way thus: "As the affairs of the Hellenes are said to 'be in' the king and, in general, as something is said to 'be in' the primary agent of motion or change" (ἐν τῷ πρώτῳ κινητικῷ: 210a21–22). This may be the meaning Aristotle has in mind with regard to the soul and the heart at *MA* 703a37: as the "affairs of the Hellenes" are in the whole social organism so the animal soul is in the whole animal organism. But as the affairs of the Hellenes are "in the king" in a special way so the animal soul is present "in the heart" alone in the same special way, i.e., as in the primary source of change and control.[13]

NOTES

[1] The following symbols will be used in referring to the works of Aristotle: *DA* = *De Anima*; *GA* = *De Generatione Animalium*; *Juv* = *De Juventute et Senectute*; *MA* = *De Motu Animalium*; *Mem* = *De Memoria*; *PA* = *De Partibus Animalium*; *Resp* = *De Respiratione*; *Sens* = *De Sensu*; *Somn* = *De Somno*; *PN* = *Parva Naturalia*. Ross *PN* and Ross *DA* refer to his edition, with commentary, of those works.

[2] A survey of reactions to Nuyens up to fifteen years ago can be found in William Fortenbaugh, "Recent Scholarship in the Psychology of Aristotle," *CW* 60 (1967):318–20. Contributions and reactions published up to 1973 appear in the early part of this paper, which was composed for presentation in 1974. At that time the comprehensive review and critique of Nuyens' work by Charles Lefèvre (*Sur l'évolution d'Aristote en psychologie* [Louvain, 1972]) was still unknown in this country. Lefèvre examines and tests Nuyens' work in detail, reviews the "instrumentalist" and "hylomorphic" notions of soul in *GA, M, DA*, and other biological writings, and concludes that Nuyens is not justified in postulating a separate period of "instrumentism" in the development of Aristotle's psychology; apparent discrepancies in his treatment of the body-soul relationship are better explained on methodological rather than chronological grounds (see pp. 287–89). After Lefèvre's critique, Nuyens' principal thesis seems no longer tenable. For a recent contribution to the debate on Nuyens, see Martha Nussbaum, *Aristotle's De Motu Animalium* (Princeton, 1978), pp. 143–64.

[3] Ross *DA* 10: ". . . in 403a31, 408b8, and 432b31 it is still treated as the seat of anger and fear." When considering these one should bear in mind a principle upon which Aristotle insists in the *DA*, namely, that the existence of one sense power in part of an animal, even the lowest, implies the coexistence of others in the same part: "If there is sense perception, there is also imagination and appetite; for where sense perception exists there is also pleasure and pain, and where these, desire necessarily exists" (413b22–24; and see 414b1–6, 433b27–434a7). The same principle is restated in *Somn* 454b29–31, which goes on to attribute these conscious activities to the central sense faculty whose organ is the heart.

[4] Nuyens never cites or comments on these lines in which the heart is specified as the organ immediately involved in the movements of anger, fear, and reasoning, though he quite properly cites the following lines (408b11–18) some seventeen times as illustrative of the hylomorphic theory.

[5] The anatomy, physiology, and teleology of this is detailed in *PA* (664a37 ff., esp. 665a7–26), while *GA* states clearly that the heart is the source of voice (776b18) and explains differences in male and female voice quality by relative taughtness or slackness of the heart (787b15–788a16).

[6] Most of these references to the heart in the *DA*, taken *separately*, have of course been pointed out by other commentators, including Ross. Kahn (pp. 64–65, n. 50) grouped some together as indicating that Aristotle regards the heart as common sensorium and seat of the emotions in the *DA* as well as in the *PN*. As far as I know, however, there has been no previous attempt to bring together all the references to the heart in *DA*, to point out their implications, and to make a case for the theory that emerges from them collectively.

[7] Kahn (pp. 67–68) has argued that there is such a necessity for the "sensible soul." I shall show that the necessity holds for the entire animal (and human) soul, both in the earliest developmental stages of the organism and in its maturity.

[8] Nor should we expect him to go beyond this in a work on the soul, though we have seen in his incidental references to the heart in *DA* that he thinks of the heart as the central organ in man and other blooded animals. But Aristotle could not properly discuss the appropriateness of this body or the bodily structure demanded by any

soul, until he had first presented a more comprehensive account of the varieties and functions of soul, the soul as efficient and final as well as formal cause of the organism, the soul's nutritive, sensitive, locomotive, and intellectual faculties and their objects, which is what he does in the remainder of *DA* and continues to do through the early treatises of the *PN*.

⁹ Perhaps it is this that Aristotle has in mind at *DA* II 412b16–17, where he describes the body appropriate for the hylomorphic soul as "a natural body of a particular kind, viz., one having in itself a principle or source (ἀρχή) of its motion and rest." Of course the soul must always be the ultimate source of motion and rest; but it can only exist as incorporated in an appropriate organ.

¹⁰ W. S. Hett, ed. and trans., *Aristotle On the Soul, Parva Naturalia, On Breath*, Loeb Classical Library (Cambridge, Mass., 1936).

¹¹ Richard Sorabji, "Body and Soul in Aristotle," *Philosophy* 49 (1974):85, n. 62.

¹² A. L. Peck and E. S. Forster, ed. and trans., *Aristotle, Parts of Animals, Movement of Animals, Progression of Animals*, Loeb Classical Library (Cambridge, Mass., 1973).

¹³ An earlier version of this paper was presented before the Society for Ancient Greek Philosophy at the kind invitation of the then president, Rosamond Kent Sprague. I am indebted to my colleagues Matthew Dickie and Leo Sweeney for a number of suggestions and corrections, and especially to David Furley for his helpful advice on revision. Any errors or shortcomings remain my own.

Eidos as Norm in Aristotle's Biology

Introduction

IDOS, species or form, is a central concept in many of Aristotle's works, but the peculiarly Aristotelian character of the *eidos* concept was developed in his biological investigations. Some scholars have studied the meaning of "*eidos*" in the biological works, notably Marjorie Grene and David Balme;[1] the present essay begins with an exploration of the same territory, but perhaps not always on the same paths. Once the biological sense of *eidos* has been presented, it will be possible to compare uses of this concept in the normative treatises. Two passages will be examined, *Nicomachean Ethics* X. 4–5, and *Politics* IV, especially IV. 4. In both places Aristotle appeals to the biological concept of *eidos* in order to explain, in the one instance, pleasure and the kinds of pleasures, in the other, the reasons for the variations in the kinds of government.

This essay will not examine the concept of *eidos* as it appears in the *Metaphysics*, although it is clear that an understanding of the biological concept of *eidos* would increase comprehension of many passages in that work, just as the metaphysical uses of *eidos* are often assumed and influential in the biological works. Indeed, Aristotle distinguishes his own philosophy from that of Plato partially in terms of the biological sense of *eidos:*

> It is obvious that the generator is the same in kind as the generated in the case of natural products (for man begets man) . . . so it is quite unnecessary to set up a Form (*eidos*) as a pattern. . . . The begetter is adequate to the making of the product and responsible for the *eidos* being in the matter. (*Metaphysics* Z. 8, 1033b30 ff)

This paper was presented at the 1977 Washington meeting of the Society for Ancient Greek Philosophy and was published in *Nature and System* I (1979):79–101. We thank the editor for permission to reprint.

Anthony Preus is Professor of Philosophy at SUNY-Binghamton and is co-editor of this volume.

Aristotle and Modern Taxonomy

A useful step in explaining Aristotle's biological sense of *eidos* as species or form is an examination of the meaning of "species" for the modern philosopher and scientist. Ontologists and logicians often suppose that biological species are paradigmatic and intuitively obvious cases of natural kinds, from which one might confidently work toward a future ontology.[2] Biologists themselves admit difficulty in distinguishing species, to the extent that many taxonomists believe that species distinctions are essentially and necessarily arbitrary. The living world is seen as *continuous*, in two ways. In the first way, Darwinian evolutionary theory assumes that speciation over time occurs in very small steps; each generation belongs to the same species as its parents, but each individual has ancestors at some number of generations which are *not* the same in species. Thus there are no determinate temporal boundaries of species. Secondly, some parts of the living world present synchronic polytypical continuities, called "clines," in which variations are subspecific from each local population to the next, but types removed at some distance are judged, by any standard, to be of different species.[3] Thus there seem to be no dependable co-temporal boundaries between species. If *a* is the same in species as *b*, and *b* is the same in species as *c*, it seems not necessary but contingent that *a* be the same in species as *c*. Co-specificity is not necessarily a transitive relation, or rather it is a limitedly transitive relation.

Modern biologists approach the problem of distinguishing kinds in several different ways. Some[4] start from the observed similarities and dissimilarities, feeding numerically analyzed data about the phenotype, the apparent form, into a computer; the procedure owes much to Hume and positivism, and claims to be objective and purely empirical. Other biologists believe that genetic relationships are the basis of class membership, and thus attempt to classify according either to genotype (ultimately and perhaps ideally, by the information content of the DNA) or by geneology, by analysis of the evolutionary descent of the individual or population.[5]

Aristotle and Noah's Ark

Diachronic and synchronic continuities are taken to be good evidence against a taxonomic theory which Mayr, for example (1969, p. 66), calls Aristotelian essentialism or "typology": "This philosophy . . . attempts to assign the variability of nature to a fixed number of basic types at various levels. It postulates that all members of a taxon reflect the same essential nature, or in other words that they conform to the same type." Since Aristotle does not seem to have been an essentialist in the sense distinguished by

341

Mayr, I would prefer to call this theory "Noah's Ark Essentialism."[6] The popular understanding of species often does include the idea that it would be possible for a diligent Noah to select appropriate samples of each biological kind for inclusion in some capacious ark (or, for that matter, a museum or zoo); modern taxonomists assert that such a Noah would frequently be faced by non-obvious distinctions to be made, unless some Adam (to continue the Biblical metaphor) had already made them by selecting paradigmatic cases ("holotypes") and setting the boundaries of the kinds.

That Aristotle was not a Noah's Ark Essentialist may be seen from passages like *Parts of Animals* IV. 5, 681a12–15: "Nature proceeds continuously from inanimate things to the animals through living things which are not animals, so that there seems to be an infinitesimal difference from one class to the next."[7] His theory of "dualising," as A. L. Peck[8] calls ἐπαμφοτερίζειν, also counts against any allegiance to Noah's Ark Essentialism. Kinds of animals "dualize" if they have characteristics which are typical of two different, and generally separate, classes. Sea-animals which live attached "dualize" with plants;[9] the *genos* of pigs dualizes because there are both cloven-hooved and solid-hooved subspecies;[10] the hermit crab dualizes between crayfish (in respect of *physis*) and testacea (in manner of life);[11] primates dualize between man and quadruped;[12] cetaceans "are in a way both land and water animals";[13] seals and bats dualize,[14] seals between land and water-animals, bats between land-animals and fliers: "διὰ τοῦτο ἀμφοτέρων τε μετέχουσι καὶ οὐδετέρων, thus they are of both and neither" (697b2). Similarly the ostrich has "some things of a bird, and some of a quadruped" (697b15). A dualizing animal is an example of the difficulty, if not impossibility, of developing hard-line distinctions between kinds of life. Even more clearly, the generation of mules indicates the fuzziness of the edges of the species-concept in Aristotle; the mule forms a *genos*, even if *agonon*.[15] Should Noah include mules in his ark or not?

Aristotle does say some things which sound rather like Noah's Ark Essentialism, for example in *Parts of Animals* I. 4, 644a24 ff.:

. . . it is the ultimate species (*eidē*) that are beings (*ousiai*), while these things [those which differ by the more and the less] (like Socrates and Coriscus) are undifferentiated in respect of species. . . . In so far as being (*ousia*) is that which is indivisible in species, it is best (if possible) to investigate separately those that are particular and specifically indivisible—as of man, so of bird (for this is a genus possessing species) but of every sort of bird among the indivisibles, like sparrow or crane and so on.[16]

But despite statements like these, I believe that Aristotle is not committed to Noah's Ark Essentialism, to "typology," or to put it most paradoxically, he is not committed to the taxonomic theory which is sometimes called Aristotelian Essentialism.

Genetic and Phenetic Species

A comparison of Aristotle's concept of a species with those developed in modern genetic and phenetic approaches to taxonomy can be rather complicated. We may say from the start that Aristotle leaves almost no room for a phylogenetic theory of kinds because evolution is not a part of his biological theory. Aristotle generally assumes that the kinds of animals which exist today have always existed. But that leaves room for a Linnean (Noah's Ark) geneological theory, each *eidos* as a geneological continuity. This is surely close to one aspect of his theory; in fact, as Balme points out (*CQ* 1962), Aristotle tends to use the word *genos* in this connection: a *genos* is formed by those individuals which share a common ancestry, though of course the word *genos* is used in other senses too. The root sense of *genos* (often lost sight of) is derived from γίγνεσθαι and γεννᾶν; we may say that Aristotle tends to have a genetic theory of *genos*, and consequently (to the extent that he uses *eidos* and *genos* as synonyms) a genetic theory of *eidos* as well. Unlike the modern biologist, however, he is not very concerned about inter-sterility (reproductive isolation) as a test of species membership. He thinks that the limitations on hybridization are in terms of the "times," gestation periods, and general body size, not the difference in *eidos* or *genos*.[17] Fox and dog cross, and so do partridge and common chicken; the hawks and probably some fish also cross, and "Libya is always bringing forth something new,"[18] because animals of different species meet at the water hole and copulate. Because he is familiar with the fertility of the hybrid canines and galliform birds, he is at great pains (*GA* IV) to explain the sterility of the mule. Hybrids do not necessarily breed true—after several generations of interbreeding, they eventually revert to the appearance of the female, just as seeds of plants come to vary according to the soil on which they grow.[19]

If Aristotle does not have the idea of a species (or even *genos*) as a reproductively isolated population, then the *genetic* aspect of the modern species definition will not hold for him in that respect, or at least will apply only in a very much weakened form. (Also, his tendency to deny reproductive isolation is a further bit of evidence showing that Aristotelian essentialism is not Noah's Ark Essentialism.)

But there is another form of genetic taxonomy, that which classifies according to the genetic material. It is theoretically, and to some extent practically, possible to classify species in terms of the character of the genetic information carried in the chromosomes. Theoretically a genetic taxonomy of this kind would have a high predictive and explanatory value; DNA is supposed to be (have) the information by which the living being constructs itself, and that information, the genotype, is much less variant, we suppose, than the phenotypes which result after environmentally influenced developments. A genotypic taxonomy of this kind would be comparable to a taxonomy of buildings based on a comparison of their blueprints, rather than on a comparison of the appearances of the completed structures.

There is a sense in which Aristotle was groping for a genotypic taxonomy. In *GA* IV, when explaining why some individuals are generated as male and others as female, and why some individuals resemble one parent more, and the other less, he says: "When the *archē* does not control and is not able to concoct because of lack of heat, and cannot bring the material to its own *eidos*, but is worsted by it, necessarily it changes over to the opposite" (*GA* IV. 1, 766a18, after Peck). He means that the semen, in its attempt to impose its *eidos* on the menstrual fluid or egg, sometimes is not able to do so, and the *eidos* of the mother wins out. The account of form or species in generation has been rather thoroughly explored elsewhere;[20] let me just recall that Aristotle has a theory that the semen and the female contribution to generation, whether mense or egg, has in it complex movements, perhaps movements of *pneuma*, which preserve the form of the parent through the process of generation. Having used this theory to explain why some offspring are male, others female, Aristotle goes on to use it to explain resemblance and lack of resemblance to parents, in *GA* IV. 3. The *logos* of the movement (767b21) preserves the peculiar and individual, above all (767b30); but the *genos* is also present in generation, so if the "powers" (*dynameis*) of the individual are not imposed on the material, the generic movements gain the upper hand, first in expressing the character of an ancestor, but if not that, then "only what is common and what it is to be human. For this follows all the individual traits" (*GA* IV. 3, 768b12). In some cases, the lack of resemblance, or failure of the movements to master the material, goes so far that that which is generated is not even human, but "only an animal," in which case it is a "monster" (*teras*), for animal is the "most general" (μάλιστα καθόλου, 769b13).

Aristotle's difficulty throughout this passage, and elsewhere in *GA* where he relies on this sort of analysis (notably II. 3 and II. 6), is that the *eidos* or *genos* which is present in the generative materials as "movements" and "powers" is not directly observable by him. The movements and powers are theoretical entities, and the evidence for their existence must be taken from what happens on the level of the phenotype. Consequently, although he believes (more or less correctly) that the form of the species, the *logos* of the *ousia*, is present in the generative semen and mense, he cannot use that belief for any *taxonomic* purpose because he cannot test the genotype independently of the phenotype.

However, the theory of sexual generation in *GA* does show one way in which Aristotle's theory of *eidos* is normative: there is a scale of values explicitly employed throughout the account of "mastery" and "changing over," according to which the best result is assumed to be the preservation of the *idion eidos* of the male parent, next best the *idean* of the female (766a28), then general humanity, and finally animality, which is taken to be "monstrous." But although monstrous, it is not completely unnatural (IV. 4, 770b10) because it does not "happen in a random fashion" (770b15); it is not an alteration "to a different nature" (770b24).

Thus there is a sense in which Aristotle has a genotypical concept of species (and he does use the word *eidos* at least once in this connection); this genotypical concept is at the same time normative, since the form which is carried in the generative material is regarded as carrying a potential for an entity with at least as much excellence as its male parent, and variations from the form of the male parent are regarded as *failures*. They are not, however, seen as failures to achieve an *ideal* member of a (Noah's Ark) species; semen is not trying to achieve the perfect man (horse, dog, whatever), but only reproduction of the powers of *this* man, and if not, of *this* woman, and if not, of ancestors, and if not that, hopefully of a human being (at least).

In fact, despite his genotypic instincts, Aristotle is driven to reliance upon phenotypic methods in classifying animals—to the extent that he classifies at all. The word *eidos* rather obviously emphasizes *visible* characteristics, since it is derived from *ειδω, "see"; the word *eidos* originally meant the visible shape or form. Aristotle uses it this way sometimes—the "look" of a bird with variegated coloring (*HA* II. 12, 504a13), the "looks" which attract us through pleasure of vision to another person who may eventually become our friend or lover (*EN* IX. 5, 1167a5). He often talks as though one can distinguish kinds of animals by simple inspection, and of course within one small geographical territory, at a given time, it usually is possible to make unambiguous species distinctions by simple inspection. Aristotle relies strongly on phenomenal characteristics, not only in the sense of the observed phenotype, but also in another sense of "phenomena" nicely distinguished by G. E. L. Owen:[21] as much as possible, Aristotle accepts the traditional distinctions and classifications of animals, at least for the purposes of doing the sorts of analyses of the parts and habits of animals which he carries out in the *History* and *Parts of Animals*.[22] The traditional distinctions have been made, he notes, "mainly by the shapes of the parts and of the whole body, wherever they bear a similarity" (*PA* I. 4, 644a8, Balme). Nature, Aristotle often says, is "that which happens always or for the most part,"[23] and that is a starting point for the distinction of natural kinds.

Parts of Animals I. 2–4 seems to be an essay on classification, containing a good many recommendations about how one ought properly to carry out a zoological taxonomy.[24] These chapters can be quite misleading, for several reasons. Most importantly, the entire passage is *polemical*, directed against some Platonists, called "dichotomists" at 642b22, who proposed classifying animals by always dividing classes in two, and whose practice was always to use just one characteristic as decisive for taxon-creation. Aristotle's polemical passages are notoriously unreliable for his positive theory (how reliable is *Physics* I, for example?). Furthermore, Aristotle's positive practice is only very incompletely consonant with his recommendations here; we might say that *PA* I. 2–4 represents an attempt to lay out the groundwork for a truly scientific classification of animals, but the *HA* and *PA* do not have as part of their purpose the building of that accurate systematic.[25] However, we should look at least briefly at this section, both because it reveals some similarities and differences between his approach and that of modern taxonomists, especially those taxonomists emphasizing phenotypical characteristics, and because we gain a clearer notion of Aristotle's ontological goals.

The "dichotomists" used single-character distinctions and negative characteristics, or "privations," in classification. Privations should not be used, says Aristotle, because "there cannot be *eidē* of the non-existent" (*PA* I. 3, 642b23). He obviously does not follow this recommendation in his own distinctions among animals; the major division of the animal kingdom is into those which have (red) blood and those which do *not* have (red) blood (*enaima/anaima*).[26] Probably more crucial for Aristotle is the question of the number and kinds of characteristics which should be used in classification; Aristotle himself argues that one ought to use several sorts of characteristics at the same time, that species will be distinguished from other, closely related, species in terms of the *degree* to which they express a number of features. He adduces several arguments; most striking is that "the number of differences (which distinguish species) would be equal to the number of individual kinds of animals"[27] according to the dichotomists' system. If that were the case, then one could unambiguously use the "last differences" as proper names of species; obviously that would be absurd. Sometimes students think that Aristotle really meant to do something like that with his definition by genus and differentia—if the difference determines the species, wouldn't it uniquely designate? The example which students mention in this connection is "man is a rational animal"; wouldn't that mean that "rational" uniquely designates man? But even the legendary Platonists would not have fallen into that trap, for in defining "man" as "featherless biped" they surely did not mean to claim that man is the only featherless animal.[28] (Incidentally, that story gives a good example of a privation used to determine a species; Aristotle's argument is philosophically more destructive, if less dramatic, than the action of the person who threw a plucked chicken over the wall into the Academy garden shouting, "Here's another student for you.")

"Rather one should try to take the animals by kinds in the way already shown by the popular distinction between *bird* kind and *fish* kind. Each of these has been marked off by many differentiae, not dichotomously" (*PA* I. 3, 643b10, Balme). "All kinds that differ by degree and by *the more and the less* have been linked under one kind, while all that are analogous have been separated. I mean for example that bird differs from bird by the more or by degree (one is long-feathered, another is short-feathered), but fishes differ from bird by analogy (what is feather in one is scale in the other)" (I. 4, 644a17, Balme; cf. *HA* I. 1, 486a16). Taken by themselves, these positive positions resemble the theory of the modern phenetic taxonomist, except that the modern taxonomist attempts to collapse the distinctions between kinds that are comparable only analogously, by trying to fit feathers and scales (for example) onto one continuum. In practice, Aristotle certainly does appeal to whole sets of characteristics in his definitions of kinds of animals; often these characteristics are somewhat hidden in the generic, or class, word, and not spelled out in the definition, but when necessary, he appeals to the appropriate features. However, despite the implicit appeal to measurement, proportion, and ratio, in *PA* I. 4, Aristotle never gives any mathematical relationships, except in the most general qualitative terms. He obviously envisages the possibility of a "numerical taxonomy," at least among the species of one genus, but he does not seriously begin to carry out the project. He claims, for example, that "the larger the animal, the greater the quantity of corporeal or earthy matter there is in it" and thus horned animals are generally among the larger animals, as they tend to have a surplus of earthy matter which can be used for defensive weapons (*PA* III. 2, 663b22 ff.). It would not have been difficult to weigh carcasses of various animals, then to weigh their bone systems, and to compare ratios, in order to substantiate this claim. But he simply relies on the general observation that large animals have larger bones, even in proportion. In theory, if not in practice, Aristotle does have tendencies which lead eventually to phenetic taxonomy.

But Aristotle's taxonomic theory is markedly different from that of modern phenetic taxonomists in one essential respect: the phenetic taxonomist tends to claim that he is prepared, in theory at least, to take account of *all* characters of living things; from fear of being called an "essentialist" (Platonist, Aristotelian, Typologist, or some other equally frightening thing), the pheneticist claims to compare "the total phenetic manifestations of the genome of an organism or a taxon."[29] But then some features are, after all, ignored because they are "not a reflection of the inherent nature of the organisms themselves" (p. 103). Precisely. Aristotle intends to select all and only those characteristics which are manifestations of functional needs

347

of animals. He does not determine species-membership by abstracting from common characteristics, but rather he picks out as of prime importance those characteristics which are necessary for the existence of the species (at all). Thus large groups of animals are distinguished first by that which maintains their life (blood or some other fluid), and the "blooded" animals are distinguished by their mode of reproduction (vivipara, ovovivipara, ovipara). Other characteristics which Aristotle often uses for distinguishing the larger groups include location of "life" (water or land), means of cooling (i.e., respiration), type of food, method of locomotion.[30] The *major* distinctions between kinds of animals are all made in terms of the ways in which these animals carry out the functions which are necessary for life and for the continued existence of the species. From Aristotle's point of view, features which are conditionally necessary for life are most obviously "inherent in the nature of the species."

Three Normative Determinants of *Eidos*

We may be more precise about Aristotle's account of how conditionally necessary characteristics determine the nature of kinds of animals, by applying three general scales:

1. the scale of degree of necessity,
2. the scale of generality (roughly, a hierarchical scale),
3. the scale of value or "scala naturae."

In proposing the application of these three scales, I recognize that I am imposing a scheme of interpretation on Aristotle's account which he has not himself developed in any precise way; his own theories of what he is doing are more allusive. Still, this hypothesis concerning his presuppositions may well fit the facts.

1. The scale of the "degree of necessity" may be discerned in *PA* I. 1, where Aristotle insists that the sort of necessity operative in biological contexts is conditional necessity; this sort of necessity is also defined in *Metaphysics* Δ 5, where we read:

> We call "necessary" that without which, as a condition, a thing cannot live; e.g. breathing and food are necessary for an animal; for it is incapable of existing without these; the conditions without which good cannot be or come to be, or without which we cannot get rid or be freed of evil; e.g. drinking the medicine is necessary in order that we may be cured of disease, and a man's sailing to Aegina is necessary that he may get his money. (1015a20–27, Ross)

These two degrees, *sine qua non* and "for the better," shade into one another in biological contexts, so we may say in a general way that all "adaptive"

348

features of animals to which Aristotle appeals in defining species are "necessary" along the scale of conditional necessity; that is, species determining characteristics are characteristics which are necessary or valuable for the species (or for the genus to which the species belongs, see 2), or are structural consequences of necessary or valuable characteristics. A great deal depends, for Aristotle, on "where the kind has its life," where it spends its time, feeds, reproduces. An example of this sort of argument may be found in *IA* 15, 713a15 ff., where Aristotle argues that "troglodytic" or hole-dwelling animals tend to have their legs out to the sides, close to the ground, and flexed to the side, "because that way they are useful for crawling easily into the hole and sitting on their eggs to guard them"; when they are out of their holes, they can lift themselves up by drawing the legs underneath.[31]

In *GA* V. 1, Aristotle distinguishes the functional and non-functional features, stating the ways in which these may be related to the definition of the kind:

> Whatever things are not the product of nature working upon the animal kingdom as a whole, nor yet characteristic of each separate kind, none of these is for some end or generated for something. An eye is for something, but blue is not for something, unless this characteristic is peculiar to a particular class. In some cases it doesn't even connect with the definition of the entity (*logos* of the *ousia*), but happens necessarily, leading back the causes to the matter and the moving origin. (778a32 ff.; cf. 778b11 ff.)

His discussion of eye-color leads to the conclusion that he supposes that variability and non-variability of eye-color depends upon other characteristics of the species, some of which might very well be conditionally necessary.[32] We may call this the lower end of the scale of conditional necessity—neither useful nor indicative of class-membership.

2. There are some features of animals which are found in some individuals and species where they are non-functional, yet they have definitive significance because they are features which are functional in the genus (kind, class) to which this individual or species belongs. I have already mentioned the useless eyes of the mole in this connection; in *PA* III. 7, 669b27 ff., Aristotle says that some animals have a spleen which is non-functional (he seems to be wrong about its non-functional character, but never mind), but is present σημείου χάριν, "for the sake of a sign." I think that what he means is that the spleen is a sign or vestige of membership in a larger class of animals, in some of which the spleen *is* useful (it "draws off the residual humors from the stomach and . . . assists in their concoction" (*PA* III. 7, 670b5). Similarly at *PA* IV. 10, 689b1, Aristotle argues that nearly all quadrupeds have a tail, though in some it is only a small one, σημείου γ' ἕνεκεν.

A complex example of this sort of thinking occurs in the explanation of

349

the elephant's nose, *PA* II. 16, 659b22. The elephant is a "polydactylous" animal, with its feet divided into toes; animals of this kind generally use their forefeet for getting food and conveying it to their mouths, but the elephant cannot do this because his feet are spoiled for this function by the necessity of holding up all that weight. Thus, because there is a (conditionally) necessary function which cannot be performed by the usual organ, "nature presses into service" (καταχρῆται) the nose, which was elongated anyway for the purpose of breathing in deep water.

This sort of concomitant variation is sometimes ascribed to the "*logos* of the *ousia*," for example in the case of a certain kind of octopus, which has only one row of suckers on its tentacles, because the tentacles are so long and narrow. Aristotle doesn't tell us why the tentacles are long and narrow, though one supposes that he would think that *that* had a functional purpose; but having one row of suckers only is *per se* "not for the better" (*PA* IV. 9, 685b13 ff.). Aristotle also thinks of consequences of functional structures at *PA* III. 3, 664a30, where the trachea is said to be functionally long, and the oesophagus consequently also long; the phrase "*logos* of the *ousia*" is used again in this sort of connection in comparing the structures of males and females in *GA* II. 1, and in discussion of the segmentation of insects at *PA* IV. 6, 682b28.

The more general class to which a species belongs establishes a norm for the various kinds which belong to it. This is clear from cases in which an entire species is said to be "maimed" (πεπηρωμένον) in some respect, even when that feature of the animal is clearly adaptive for its way of life. The feet of the seal (*IA* 19, *HA* II. 1, 498a32) are thus "maimed" although clearly excellent for swimming; the feet of the bat (*IA* 19) also are maimed for walking, although well adapted to flight. The seal is also "maimed" in comparison with other four-footed animals in that it does not have ear lobes, but only the auditory passages (*PA* II. 12, 657a23), yet this is of advantage to the seal in its aquatic life (*GA* V. 1, 781b22). Similarly the (spiny) lobster is a deformed species in respect of its claws, since it does not use them as claws (as crabs do) but for local movement (*PA* IV. 8, 684a35). Even the whole class of testaceans (e.g., snails) is deformed in respect of their manner of movement, since they do not conform to the model of movement of higher animals (*IA* 19). At this point the idea of "maimed" species shades into the idea of the *scala naturae*.

3. The third sort of continuum which determines characteristics of various kinds of animals is the "scale of nature" to which I alluded earlier in arguing that Aristotle is not a Noah's Ark Essentialist. Aristotle attempts to hold two principles simultaneously: that each kind of animal is best adapted to its particular kind of life, its particular ecological niche as we would say, and that nevertheless we can order the kinds of life, and correlative kinds of

beings, on a scale of value corresponding to the absolute value of the functions performed. How he holds both principles together is best understood, I believe, by comparing the theory of the good in the *Nicomachean Ethics*. There, each of the functions of the soul has its own virtue or excellence, the good performance of what it is best qualified to do, yet the functions (powers, parts) of the soul are ranked in value: health is a summation of the excellences of the physiological powers, the moral virtues are excellences of the powers of the soul to act intentionally, prudence and wisdom are excellences of the mind. We may say that some degree of excellence is necessary conditionally for the possibility of excellence of the next level, and thus good as a means toward the "higher" functions, but Aristotle makes it abundantly clear, particularly in *EN* X, that the activity of the intellect is the best activity possible for man—just as it is the sole activity of God in *Metaphysics* Λ.

When, in *EN* I. 6, Aristotle suggests that the word *good* may be defined ʿἀφ᾽ ἑνός᾽, ʿπρὸς ἕν᾽, or ʿκατ᾽ ἀναλογίαν᾽ he is at the same time allowing for not only an ethical but also a biological (and generally ontological) use of this distinction. "As sight is good in the body, so intelligence is good in the soul, and so other things are good within their respective fields" (1096b27). Similarly, as legs are good for land-locomotion, so wings are good for flight and fins for swimming (cf. *HA* I. 1–6). The goodness of the organs and functions of various species of animals is relative to the life which each has, and is thus analogous, as the parts themselves are said to be analogous (if differing more than by the "more of less"). But as the lower functions of man serve the higher, and ultimately the intellect, and are thus seen as πρὸς ἕν good, so "plants exist to give subsistence to animals, and animals to give it to men. . . . as nature makes nothing purposeless or in vain, all animals must have been made by nature for the sake of men" (*Politics* I. 3, 1256b17 ff.). Aristotle can argue in this (possibly frightening, from an ecological point of view) way because he has a prior concept of a scale of value running throughout creation; in every case, the less *timion* exists for the sake of the more *timion*.

This three-way analysis, in terms of degree of conditional necessity, of conformity (or lack of conformity) to the definition of the larger *genos*, and of comparative value of the species in terms of kind of function, shows how Aristotle's concept of species is normative in three ways: (1) features are selected as definitive of kinds on the ground of their conditional necessity, utility, or value for the life of the kind; thus Aristotle's taxonomy, although based for the most part on phenotype, is not purely descriptive, since there is an evaluative basis for selection of taxonomically significant characteristics. (2) Once a *genos*, of whatever degree of universality or "generality" has been discerned on the basis of a communality of function, the possession of properly functioning organs typical of the *genos* is a kind of standard for all species in the class. Generally, failure to have fully actualized organic function is ascribed to a more pressing need for this particular kind, not typical of the genus as a whole (the feet of the elephant, the forelegs/wings of the bat, the earlessness of seals), or else to the lack of need for the generic function in a particular kind (the blindness of moles, the vestigial spleen or tail in various animals). These so-called "mutilations" seem to be so because it is theoretically, in general, better for the animal to be able to actualize all its potentialities, for all its powers to be functional. In some cases, the power is actualized by a quite different organ than is normally the case for the genus, as the nose of the elephant. This generic normality leads easily to the idea of the scale of nature. (3) In the scale of nature, species and whole genera are compared to each other in terms of their relative value.

A good deal more could be said about Aristotle's biological concept of species (indeed, Grene, Balme, and others have much to add to the present account); however, some of the major features have been distinguished sufficiently to show, at least briefly, how Aristotle applies his concept of a normative *eidos* in some of his non-biological books. We may be sure that both the *Nicomachean Ethics* and the *Politics* date from the latest period of Aristotle's life, when he was teaching in the Lyceum, and that the *History, Parts,* and *Progression of Animals,* if not the *Generation of Animals,* were composed either entirely or for the most part during the middle period, even if completed or partially revised at the Lyceum. Thus, the appeal in *EN* and *Pol* to concepts developed in the biological books is retrospective rather than prospective, and may reveal the consequences of biological thinking for other parts of Aristotle's thought.

The Taxonomy of Pleasures

The taxonomy of pleasures, in *EN* X. 4–5, is a good deal simpler than a taxonomy of animals would be, if only because pleasures do not have an internal structure which can be used in classifying them. A pleasure has a complete *eidos* at any moment; it does not have any unactualized potentialities (*EN* X. 4, 1174a15, b5). Pleasures are classified by the sense of which they are completions (1174b26), since each sense has its own peculiar pleasure; they are also classified by their source (X. 5, 1175a22), since different activities bring about different and possibly contrary pleasures; and finally they are classified by the species of animal or man in which they are typical (1176a3).[33]

Taking *EN* X. 4–5 by itself,[34] we may see that Aristotle gives a classification based partially on the material conditions of pleasures, first in terms of the sensory organ or power which can experience this pleasure, then in terms of the species of animal or type of man which can experience this pleasure; we may say that these are two ways of looking at the necessary conditions of pleasure. The other basis of classification is the moving cause; in this respect the taxonomy proposed is genetic in character. To the extent that Aristotle could possibly give a phenetic account of pleasures, he would be forced to appeal to the common experience of mankind, since nothing could be more difficult than to describe a pleasure objectively, independently of its sense and source!

We may also note that while Aristotle attempts to argue for discrete kinds of pleasures, since they may conflict, and since we make value judgments, finding some of them good and some of them not so good, nevertheless he is quite willing to find continuities and overlappings in pleasures, particularly in those which are experienced by men as distinct from those experienced by animals (1176a10); that is, Aristotle is not a Noah's Ark Essentialist about pleasures, even though he does try to distinguish several kinds.

If we apply our three continua, the degree of conditional necessity, the scale of generality, and the scale of nature, we can see rather quickly that pleasures are distinguished normatively in all three ways. The *scala naturae* is applied directly—"Each animal is thought to have its own proper pleasure, just as each has its own function. . . . As Heracleitus says, an ass would prefer chaff to gold" (1176a3, Ostwald). As everyone knows, there are certain pleasures which are proper to man, most particularly the "theoretical life."[35] The *scala naturae* thus appears in the proof that the life of the mind is the best life, and the pleasure of this life is the best pleasure.[36]

The scale of conditional necessity is not applied by Aristotle in this passage as clearly as it was to be applied by Epicurus (e.g., *Letter to Menoeceus* 127b ff.), but there are indications of degrees of value dependent upon the desirability or "avoidability" of the activity which gives rise to the pleasure (1175b24 ff.). Just as the various species of animals have their proper pleasures, so the individual organs and activities have their pleasures, and these are ranked in terms of the value of the activity. It's interesting to note that Aristotle does not rate the pleasures belonging to the *sine qua non* activities very highly—food, drink, and sex are regarded as rather banal sources of pleasure; they are activities which exist not for their own sake, but for the sake of some higher end; the better or more honorable pleasures are those for the sake of which the physical activities and pleasures exist. I think that we can read this distinction of pleasures back into the distinction between degrees of conditional necessity, and understand that those features of animals which are *very* necessary conditionally differ from those which are "for the better" by an inverse scale of value. So I read 1176a1: "Sight is superior in purity to touch, and hearing and smell are superior to taste. . . . the pleasures of thought in turn are superior to the pleasures of the senses" (Ostwald). As in Plato, this scale of value of the various activities is laid off against the scale of complexity (sensitivity) of the various kinds of living being.

The generic normative concept is applied most clearly in the comparison between virtuous and vicious pleasures, on the one hand, and healthy and sick pleasures on the other (1176a10 ff.). Aristotle appears to suppose that the *spoudaios* is the standard by which the activities and pleasures of other men are judged. Biologically, we may say that the *spoudaios,* if one may be found, would be the "holotype" which determines species membership. Pleasures which do not match this standard are consequently "corrupted and perverted" (1176a21), comparable we may say to the maimed nature of the eyes of the mole or the reproductive organs of the mule. Some whole groups of human beings seem to be less than human: savage tribes near the Black Sea "delight in eating raw meat or human flesh" (VII. 5, 1148b15); "those who are irrational by nature and live only by their senses, as do some distant barbarian tribes, are brutish" (1149a9, Ostwald). We may well be reminded of the notion of "dualizing" and the continuity of the scale of nature; how much higher than the apes would Aristotle think these θηριώ-δεις, animal-species, men who delight in things which are natural for animals but not natural for man? "Some things are pleasant by nature, and of these some are simply pleasant, some according to the *genos* of animals and men; some are not pleasant except through maiming [πηρώσεις, like the feet of the seal] or habit, some because of perverted natures" (1148b15 ff.). Brutishness is taking pleasure in that which is not generically typical of man to enjoy, though it may not be untypical of some beasts. If through bad habituation or mental illness a man has depraved pleasures, he has fallen away from the norm of humanity as the *teras* is born no longer human but only animal.

A good deal more could be said on the biological concept of *eidos* as it is applied in the *Nicomachean Ethics;* these remarks indicate something of the way in which the problem may be approached.[37]

The Taxonomy of Constitutions

A good case could be made out for saying that Aristotle has a philosophically more developed taxonomy of political organizations than he has of animals. Certainly he regards the project of determining the "essence and attributes of the various kinds of governments"[38] as of pre-eminent importance. Influenced by Plato's classification of kinds of government in the *Republic,* Aristotle tries several different sorts of classifications; for example, in *Pol* III. 7, he lists three "true" (ὀρθαί) kinds and three "perversions": kingship/tyranny, aristocracy/oligarch, *politeia*/democracy. He then begins a subdivision of each kind, listing four (or five) kinds of kingship (III. 14), and turning his attention to what we may call a phylogeny of the various forms of government (III. 15, 1286b8). Book IV returns to the contrast between oligarchical and democratic governments, trying to make sense of their many forms. Distinguishing between rich and poor, various sorts of armament which citizens may afford, and the various sorts of economic functions, he argues that "of these elements, sometimes all, sometimes the lesser and sometimes the greater number, have a share in government. It is evident then that there must be many forms of government, differing in kind (*eidē*), since the parts of which they are composed differ from each other in king" (IV. 3, 1290a5, Jowett).

It is at this point in his argument that he appeals to the analogy between the *eidē* of animal and the *eidē* of state:

> If we aimed at a classification of the different kinds of animals, we should begin by enumerating the parts, or organs, which are necessary to every animal. These will include, for example, some of the sensory organs: they will also include the organs for getting and digesting food, such as the mouth and stomach; they will further include the organs of locomotion which are used by the different animals. Now if there are only so many parts, and if there are differences of these, different kinds of mouths, stomachs, sensory organs, and organs of locomotion, we shall conclude that all the possible combinations of these will produce the kinds (*eidē*) of animals. . . . It is the same with the constitutions mentioned. (*Pol* IV. 4, 1290b25 ff., Barker with modifications)

Enumerating eight necessary functions of the state, he argues that the varieties of oligarchies and democracies depend upon the ways that these functions are performed. Democratic governments are related in an evolutionary series, each causally related to the next (IV. 6). Then a scale of value is introduced, with the *politeia* at the top, and completed with the claim that all other forms of government are "perversions" by comparison (IV. 8).

So much for a brief reminder of the taxonomic argument of *Pol* IV. 4; in fact, the analogy of state and animal is one which carries forward much of the argument in the entire work, as a comparable analogy gave shape to Plato's *Republic*.

It would be futile to point out the many passages which cite continuities, *contra* Noah's Ark Essentialism, in the *Politics*. One of many such passages tells us that "in many states the constitution established by law, although not democratic, owing to the education and habits of the people may be administered democratically, and conversely in other states the established constitution may incline to democracy, but may be administered in an oligarchical spirit" (IV. 5, 1292b12, Jowett). Given the manner in which historical continuities between different forms of government occur, one would be rather surprised if clear lines of demarcation could be made (cf. V. 1, 1301b13).

If we apply genetic and phenetic standards to Aristotle's taxonomy of states, we learn very quickly that neither fits precisely, both are suggestive but both inadequate. In fact Aristotle expressly claims that his taxonomy is *functional* in character, and he is quite willing to accept the idea that various forms of states arise according to the conditions, that one kind of state may be more advantageous under one set of conditions, another under another: "Democracy may meet the needs of some better than oligarchy, and conversely" (IV. 2, 1289b19). Similarly, barbarians tend to have rather despotic kings, because of their servile characters (III. 14, 1285a18), while "the people who are suited for constitutional freedom are those among whom there naturally exists a warlike multitude able to rule and to obey in turn by a law which gives offices to the well-to-do according to their desert" (III. 17, 1288a12, Jowett). The functional parameters include not only the character of the people, but also the character of the territory, and the character of surrounding countries (II. 6, 1265a19). In other words, the character of the state is determined at least in part by the proximate matter (citizens) and the ecological niche which it occupies.

In dealing with political realities, Aristotle has much less motivation to suppose that each *eidos* is everlasting than he had in the biological books. Some constitutions seem to be fairly permanent, but others are obviously subject to destruction and revolution (see *Pol* V). We have historical evidence which tends to support some hypotheses concerning *regular* ways in which one sort of system or organization may turn into (or be turned into) another. Socrates in the *Republic* (VIII) had already developed an evolutionary theory of this kind; Aristotle attempts to extend and improve upon that theory. Just because political organizations are unstable, Aristotle is all the less tempted to suppose that a particular *eidos* of state is unified by its geneological history. To be sure, an individual state is unified by its genetic history, at least in part; indeed, the racial unity seems more permanent than the *eidos* of the government: "Shall we say that while the race of inhabitants and their place of abode remain the same, the city is also the same? . . . Since the state is a partnership, of citizens in a constitution, when the form of the government changes, then it may be supposed that the state is no longer the same, just as the tragic differs from the comic chorus, although the members may be identical" (III. 3, 1276a35, Jowett with modifications). This difference between states and individuals points up a limitation on the organic theory of the state, the analogy between individual states and individual persons so strongly presented in III. 4: if the form of government is comparable to the soul, then a revolution would be like a death, but revolutions occur with less damage to the component parts of the state than deaths do to the organs of the body. A state may change its system of government with considerably more ease than the leopard its spots.

A different, and more accurate, form of genetic continuity in the *eidos* of government is that which occurs when a state endeavors to establish its own form of government in its neighbors; Aristotle notes that Athens tried to establish democracies, Sparta oligarchies, during the time of their conflict (IV. 11, 1296a32; V. 7, 1307b21). But although Aristotle notices this formal and efficient cause, working from outside on an appropriate matter, he does not claim analogy with the male principle imposing an *eidos* on the female principle. The failure to do so may well be significant; we tend to think of species as continuities carried in the act of procreation, and passages which we noted in *GA* show that that idea is not foreign to Aristotle either. However, once we accept the idea of the state as an organism, we easily think of the imposition of a form of government by some foreign power as analogous to Aristotle's description of the action of the male on the female; the procreational model must not be very important in Aristotle's own eyes, since he does not appeal to it in his discussion of the forms of the state, even though he is well aware of possible examples.

If we base a decision upon a contrast between genetic and phenetic taxonomies, we will come to the conclusion that Aristotle's taxonomy of systems of government is much more nearly based upon phenotype, upon the apparent structure of the state. As is well known, Aristotle supervised the description of 158 different constitutions, of which the *Athenaion Politeia* is the sole surviving example. These descriptions, or some of them at least, were surely a basis of his mature taxonomy of states.[39] The other basis is the *a priori* schemes of Plato's *Republic* and other utopian theorists, outlined in some detail in *Pol* II. 1–8. His thought-process seems to have been one of starting from a schema of the various types of states, then adjusting it to the observed facts. He clearly believed that the standard accounts of the various types of states were ultimately inadequate to the phenomena, that there are more kinds of states than commonly supposed, "for democracy, like other constitutions, has more than one form" (IV. 13, 1297b29). Clearly too, he considers previous attempts to classify states as inadequate largely because they have emphasized just one criterion (or one criterion at a time). Some have distinguished states simply on the basis of how many people share in its affairs; Aristotle is rather scornful, saying that on that basis, "a government in which the offices were given according to stature, as is said to be the case in Ethiopia, or according to beauty, would be an oligarchy, for the number of tall or good-looking men is small" (IV. 4, 1290a4). Just as he emphasizes the simultaneous application of several criteria in *PA* I. 3, so he appeals to the same principle in *Pol* IV. 4.

Also as in the biological works, Aristotle's principle of selection of classificatory criteria is functional; that is why the selection of rulers by height or beauty is only a curiosity, but the wealth and talent of rulers tend to determine the kind of state in which they rule.

The three scales of normative determination distinguished earlier, the scale of conditional necessity, the scale of class extension, and the scale of nature or relative value, may also be discovered in the *Politics*. There are clear similarities between states and animals in respect of the degrees of conditional necessity and of relative value, and very possibly one might also find an analogy of the genus/species series applicable in the political context.

Governments, like animals, are defined by their organs and functions, the ways in which their conditionally necessary activities are performed. On the basis of the analogy posited in *Pol* IV. 4, Aristotle argues for a scale of value of governmental functions like that which he finds in animals, putting the production of food, a *sine qua non* function, at the bottom of the scale, and those functions which are "for the better" at the top: "As the soul may be said to be more a part of the animal than the body, so the higher parts of states than those ministering to the necessary functions" (IV. 4, 1291a24). The military, judicial, and administrative functions are more important and more definitive of the state than the productive and distributive functions. In other words, we do not classify states by their mode of food production— some states live on agriculture, some herd cattle, some rely on hunting or fishing, but although these occupations have some influence on the kind of state which depends on them for its life, yet Aristotle (and we) do not use them as the critical factor for classification; rather Aristotle concentrates on the deliberative, executive, and judicial powers (IV. 4, 1297b40)—who may exercise them, how much involvement each class of citizen has with each of these functions.

Aristotle's scale of value comes to us in at least two forms; in one, there are three valid forms of government and three perversions; in the other, the best form of government is the *Politeia,* and all other forms are ordered in a series of decreasing worth. The second arrangement more nearly resembles the scale of the animal kingdom in *HA* VIII. 1 and *PA* IV. 5: "They all fall short of the most perfect form of government, and so they are reckoned among perversions, and the really perverted forms are perversions of these" (IV. 8, 1293b25, Jowett). So in VII, Aristotle begins over again, from the top (so to speak), describing the best state, and presuming that the examination of the functional parts of the best state will reveal the model to which *all* states may be compared. Again, Aristotle's normative method seems to us a good deal more plausible when applied to the political context than it does in biology; although everyone will agree that the system of government must be adapted to the education, culture, climate, topography, and international relations of the state, nevertheless most people believe that some forms of government are better than others, for roughly the sort of reason which Aristotle gives in *Pol* VII—the citizens are happier in one sort of state than they are in another, one form of government carries out the superior functions of states more satisfactorily than another. For Aristotle, it was just as obvious that eagles are superior to jellyfish as it was that the rule of law is better than the rule of men. While some social scientists may pretend not to make evaluative judgments of this kind, true objectivity (or relativism) is probably rare; biologists are more likely to take each species for what it is, and if they make any assertions about value, may want to claim that all life is intrinsically valuable. In any case, Aristotle finds a continuum of value in his comparison of the various forms of government which he himself finds analogous to the continuum of value derived from a comparison of the forms of life. This way of thinking unifies Aristotle's theoretical investigations; states and animals are categorized as "defective" in comparison with the best state or animal, and the ordering of degrees of defect defines the nature of each.

The scale of generality would be discerned in the definition of states by discovering cases in which Aristotle claims that some state has some particular feature because it is typical of the *eidos* of this state, although in the given instance this feature is either of no particular advantage, or is actually disadvantageous. We can easily find passages in which Aristotle says that some given state has a disadvantageous feature because that is one of the defects of this kind of state; oligarchies, for example, are composed of men accustomed to command slaves, and they tend to work to their own disadvantage in their treatment of free citizens in a high-handed manner (1280a, 1305b, *et al.*), but that sort of thing can be ascribed to the scale of value. We can also find passages in which certain constitutions are said to share in two different kinds of government, in some cases to some relative disadvantage; the discussion of the Ephorate in Sparta is like that: "It is a defect of this institution that it is so important, and so much in the nature of a dictatorship, that even the kings have been compelled to court the favor of the Ephors. The result has been that . . . the whole constitution has suffered from their overgrown power, and from being an aristocracy, it has tended to turn into a democracy. But it must be admitted that the Ephorate is a force which holds the constitution together" (II. 6, 1270b7 ff., Barker). One might say that Sparta "dualizes" in this respect. The account of the government of Crete is comparable: the Cosmoi have the power and some of the defects of the Spartan Ephors, remedied by a method typical of a "dynastic" state rather than a constitution; confederacies are formed to put bothersome Cosmoi out of office by force. This has the effect of a periodic anarchy; "for

359

a time it is no longer a *polis*, but political society is dissolved" (II. 7, 1272b10–16). These "second best" methods used to remedy defects in some systems of government may remind us of the alternative means which some animals have for remedying theirs, like the elephant's nose. In the biological works, such instances were regarded as indications of the membership in a class, and may be so here too.

No doubt more might be said about the ways in which the normative scales apply to the definitions of states in the *Politics;* my objective here has been only to suggest several parallels which can be illuminated by a consideration of Aristotle's biological method, and to suggest the application of the normative aspects of this method to Aristotle's objectives in the biological books. Clearly he believed in a systematic continuity between biological and social levels of complexity, and also believed that normative parameters are applicable in comparable ways, to the extent that analogies and continuities exist. This is one of the ways in which Aristotle contributed to the mode of investigation which we now call "systems theory."[40]

NOTES

[1] M. Grene, "Aristotle and Modern Biology," *Journal of the History of Ideas* 33 (1972), reprinted in *The Understanding of Nature*, and "Is Genus to Species as Matter to Form? Aristotle and Taxonomy," *The Understanding of Nature*, ch. VI; D. Balme, "*Genos* and *Eidos* in Aristotle's Biology," *Classical Quarterly* 12 (1962):81–98; "Aristotle's Use of Differentiae in Zoology," *Articles on Aristotle* I: *Science*, ed. Barnes, Schofield, and Sorabji; "Form and Species in Aristotle's Biology," paper presented at the 1976 Princeton conference on Aristotle; see also A. C. Lloyd, *Phronesis* 7 (1962):67–90; G. E. R. Lloyd, *Phronesis* 6 (1961):59–81; Montgomery Furth, paper presented to SAGP 1975; Stephen Clark, *Aristotle's Man* (Oxford: Oxford University Press, 1975), ch. II.

[2] Hilary Putnam, "Is Semantics Possible?" and W. V. Quine, "Natural Kinds," in S. P. Schwartz, *Naming, Necessity, and Natural Kinds,* 1977.

[3] Morton Beckner, *The Biological Way of Thought*, ch. 4, citing the work of A. C. Kinsey with wasps; my discussion of contemporary taxonomy follows G. G. Simpson, *Principles of Animal Taxonomy* (New York: Columbia University Press, 1961), Ernst Mayr, *Principles of Systematic Zoology* (New York: McGraw-Hill, 1969), and R. A. Crowson, *Classification and Biology* (New York: Atherton, 1970).

[4] Cf. R. R. Sokal and P. A. Sneath, *Principles of Numerical Taxonomy* (San Francisco, 1963).

[5] Michael Ruse, *The Philosophy of Biology* (London: Hutchinson, 1973), ch. 7 and 8, compares the genetic and phenetic approaches to taxonomy, and I rely partially on his analysis; see also Grene, *Understanding of Nature*, p. 99; G. G. Simpson, *Principles of Animal Taxonomy*, Ernst Mayr, *Principles of Systematic Zoology*, and R. A. Crowson, *Classification*.

[6] A less contentious name would be "museum" essentialism; see Crowson, pp. 281 ff., but not all museum systematists are essentialists in the requisite sense. It

should be noted that I am not attempting to discuss Aristotelian essentialism in the sense distinguished by, for example, Nicholas P. White, "Origins of Aristotle's Essentialism," *Review of Metaphysics* 26 (1972/3):57–85. There is a sense in which the present essay *fills in* many of White's comments, and perhaps makes the difference between Aristotle and formalistic philosophy more obviously clear. Furthermore, I am intentionally avoiding discussion of Aristotle's *Metaphysics* in the present essay. It is possible that his treatment of *eidos* in the *Metaphysics* involves a theory in which *eidē* within the *genos* are discontinuous; some chapters of *Metaphysics* VII, VIII, and X, may well develop a theory which is not consistent with the use of the word *eidos* in the biological works. If that is true, it would take an essay longer than the present one to explain the discrepancy.

[7] *PA* IV. 5, 681a12–15: ἡ γὰρ φύσις μεταβαίνει συνεχῶς ἀπὸ τῶν ἀψύχων εἰς τὰ ζῷα διὰ τῶν ζώντων μὲν οὐκ ὄντων δὲ ζῴων, οὕτως ὥστε δοκεῖν πάμπαν μικρὸν διαφέρειν θατέρου θάτερον τῷ σύνεγγυς ἀλλήλοις CF. *HA* VIII. 1, 588b4–17; in *PA* II. 9, 655a17, the continuum of the skeletal structures of chordata is described, παραλλάτει κατὰ μικρὸν ἡ φύσις; cf. *GA* II. 1, 733a34; 3, 736a32.

[8] Aristotle, *History of Animals*, Loeb ed., Peck introduction to vol. I, p. lxiii.

[9] *PA* IV. 5, 681a36 ff.: ἃς δὲ καλοῦσιν οἱ μὲν κνίδας οἱ δ' ἀκαλήφας ἐστι μὲν οὐκ ὀστρακόδερμα ἀλλ' ἔξω πίπτει τῶν διῃρημένων γενῶν, ἐπαμφοτερίζει δὲ τοῦτο καὶ φυτῷ καὶ ζῴῳ τὴν φύσιν. "The so-called Cnides or Akalephae are not testacea, but fall outside the defined classes; it dualizes in nature both to plant and to animal."

[10] *HA* II. 1, 499b11, b21; cf. *HA* I. 1, 488a1: some animals are gregarious, some solitary, some dualize; of dualizers in this respect, man is mentioned.

[11] *HA* IV. 4, 529b20 ff.

[12] *HA* II. 8, 502a16; cf. *PA* IV. 10, 689b32.

[13] *PA* IV. 13, 697a29.

[14] 697b2; cf. *HA* VI. 12, 566b27.

[15] *GA* II. 8, 747a25, b34; cf. I. 20, 728b10. See also Richard Rorty, "Genus as Matter: A Reading of *Metaphysics* Z-H," in *Exegesis and Argument,* eds. Lee, Mourelatos, and Rorty, *Phronesis* supplement 1 (1973), pp. 393–420. He jokingly calls this paper "Two Concepts of Mules," discussing the use of *genos* as applied to mules at 1033b–1034a2, pp. 412 ff.

[16] Balme's translation in the Clarendon Aristotle series, with minor changes; Peck's reading is idiosyncratic—cf. Düring, *Aristoteles De partibus animalium* (Göteborg, 1943). The passage from which this quotation is taken is discussed below.

[17] *GA* II. 4, 738b27; 7, 746a29.

[18] *GA* II. 7, 746b8; cf. *HA* VIII. 28, 606b17.

[19] *GA* II. 4, 738b32.

[20] See my *Science and Philosophy in Aristotle's Biological Works* (Hildesheim: Olms, 1975), ch. 2, or *Journal of the History of Biology* (1970); Furth's 1975 SAGP essay, *et al.*

[21] G. E. L. Owen, "Τιθέναι τὰ Φαινόμενα." Symposium Aristotelicum, ed. S. Mansion (Louvain, 1961), pp. 83–103.

[22] *PA* I. 3, 643b11, ὡς οἱ πολλοί; cf. I. 4, 644b3; see Peck's introductions to

the Loeb editions of the biological books; G. E. R. Loyd, *Phronesis* 6 (1961): 59 ff.; Balme, *"Genos* and *Eidos," Aristotle's PA I and GA I.* "Aristotle's Use of Differentiae," and "Form and Species."

²³ *Phys* II. 8, 198b35; *GC* II. 6, 333b5; *Juv passim; GA* IV. 8, 777a20; and especially *PA* III. 2, 663b27: "One must investigate nature looking at many cases, for the nature is in the universal or in the majority" (ἐν τῷ παντὶ ἤ ὡς ἐπὶ τὸ πολύ).

²⁴ David Balme, *Aristotle's De Part. An.* I and *De Gen. An.* I (Oxford: Oxford University Press, 1972), pp. 101–22, has the best discussion of this passage.

²⁵ Cf. Balme, *"Genos* and *Eidos."*

²⁶ Balme, *Aristotle's De Part.,* pp. 108–10 makes a good case for claiming that Aristotle's practice does not really contradict his position taken against the dichotomists; *they* made privations into essential characteristics of species, while Aristotle believes that the essence of the bloodless animals includes whatever they have instead of blood, of footless animals whatever they have for locomotion instead of feet. Balme does suggest that blindness is a positive characteristic of the mole, referring to *de An* III. 1, 425a11, but that is a mistake I think; the blindness of the mole is a "deformity" which "happens in the process of generation" (cf. *HA* I. 9, 491b28; IV. 8, 533a2). Aristotle makes a point of arguing that the mole does have eyes, which are an essential characteristic of the "blooded" animals. A mole with unimpaired eyes would still be a mole, on Aristotle's showing and for the modern biologist—for there are sighted moles too.

²⁷ 643a8; a18: ἔσονται δ' αἱ διαφοραὶ ἴσαι τοῖς ἀτόμοις ζῴοις. . . . ἀναγκαῖον ἴσας τὰς ἐσχάτας εἶναι διαφορὰς τοῖς ζῴοις πᾶσι τοῖς ἀτόμοις τῷ εἴδει.

²⁸ Cf. *Metaphysics* Z. 11, where it is suggested that a man could exist made of a different matter. If a machine were capable of doing everything which human beings now do, would that machine be human, on Aristotle's showing? It wouldn't be an *animal,* and thus not a member of the same *genos,* but Z. 11 indicates the possibility of some vacillation on this point. The idea of humanoid automata was not foreign to Aristotle; Homer (*Iliad* XVIII. 368 ff.) writes of "golden maidens" of Haephaestus who "looked like real girls and could not only speak and use their limbs, but were endowed with intelligence and trained in handiwork by the immortal gods." Plato mentions the statues of Daedelus, reputed to be so lifelike that they might run away (*Euthyphro* 11b, *Meno* 97d); Aristotle uses the existent automata of his own day to explain animal movement (*Movement of Animals* 7, 710b2–10) and animal generation (*GA* II. 1, 734b11–13, and my *Science and Philosophy,* p. 291).

²⁹ Sokal and Sneath, *Principles of Numerical Taxonomy,* p. 96.

³⁰ For details, see Peck's introduction in *HA* and *PA.*

³¹ For a discussion of conditional necessity in *PA* I. 1, see my "Aristotle's Natural Necessity," *Studi Internazionali di Filosofia* I (1969):91–100, and *Science and Philosophy,* pp. 183–200. Aristotle's account of conditional necessity and teleological explanation are well-known, particularly his often repeated line, "nature does nothing in vain, but is always the cause of the better of the possibles" (*PA* II. 14, 658a8; *IA* 8, 708a10; *GA* II. 5, 741b4; II. 4, 739b19; *PA* IV. 11, 694a15; III. 1, 661b24; IV. 13, 695b19, etc.; cf. *Science and Philosophy,* pp. 223–48.

[32] See my *Science and Philosophy*, pp. 153 ff.

[33] The two extended discussions of pleasure in *EN* have been examined recently by several scholars: among the more useful articles are G. E. L. Owen, "Aristotelian Pleasures," *Proceedings of the Aristotelian Society* (1971/2):135–52, with reply by J. C. B. Gosling, "More Aristotelian Pleasures," *PAS* (1973):15–34, and Amelia Oksenberg Rorty, "The Place of Pleasure in Aristotle's Ethics," *Mind* 83 (1974): 481–97. Rorty's paper puts most emphasis upon what I call the taxonomy of pleasures.

[34] Given the discrepancies between VII and X, I prefer to stick with the one passage for my present purpose, rather than to try to synthesize theories which seem to have been developed with different goals in mind.

[35] *Bios theoretikos*, see Trond Berg Eriksen, *Bios Theoretikos* (Oslo Universitetsforlaget, 1976), pp. 56 ff. and 96 ff.

[36] John Cooper, *Reason and Human Good in Aristotle* (1975), ch. III, pp. 144 ff., argues that the intellectualism of *EN* is more extreme than the theory of the best life in *EE;* it may also be that Aristotle gives more credit to variations among kinds of men in *EE*, allowing for alternative truly human lives.

[37] Other relevant studies include W. Jaeger, "Aristotle's Use of Medicine as a Model of Method in his Ethics," *Journal of Hellenic Studies* 77 (1957):54–61; T. Tracy, *Physiological Theory and the Doctrine of the Mean in Plato and Aristotle* (Chicago, 1969); G. E. R. Lloyd, "Aspects of the Relations between Medicine, Magic, and Philosophy in Ancient Greece," *Apeiron* (1975):1–16.

[38] *Pol* III. 1, 1274b33: τῷ περὶ πολιτείας ἐπισκοποῦνται, καὶ τίς ἑκάστη κὰι ποία τις, σχεδὸν πρώτη σκέψις περὶ πόλεως ἰδεῖν, τί ποτ' ἐστὶν ἡ πόλις.

[39] See W. Jaeger, *Aristotle,* ch. X and XIII. Jaeger is right in supposing that the extensive empirical investigation of large numbers of constitutions dates from the last period of Aristotle's life; unlike Jaeger, I believe that the *History* and *Parts of Animals* were mainly completed in the middle period, providing a kind of model for the political investigations.

[40] The research upon which this study depends was begun during the tenure of a SUNY Research Foundation summer grant, and was completed with the help of National Science Foundation Grant No. SCC77–00497.

William Jacobs responded to this paper, "Preus on Aristotle's *Eide*," in *Nature and System* III (1981):115–18, and I replied in the same issue, pp. 119–21, "Reply to Jacobs."

Intellectualism in Aristotle

I

WHEN Aristotle returns to the topic of happiness at the end of the *Nicomachean Ethics* (X.6–8) presumably to give us his final and best thoughts on the matter, he says that perfect happiness (ἡ τελεία εὐδαιμονία) is theoretical activity (θεωρητικὴ ἐνέργεια), that happiness and contemplation (θεωρία) are coextensive, and that the life of reason (ὁ κατὰ τὸν νοῦν βίος), also called the philosophical or theoretical life (I.5.1095b19,[1] *E.E.* I.4.1215b1–2, *et passim*), is the happiest life (X.7.1177a12–18, 1178a4–8, 8.1178b7–32). He goes on to say that the life in accordance with the other excellence (ὁ κατὰ τὴν ἄλλην ἀρετὴν βίος)—namely, the life in accordance with practical wisdom and moral virtue, elsewhere called the political or practical life (I.5.1095b18, *Pol.* VII.2.1324a40)—is the second happiest life (X.8.1178a9–22). And he draws a sharp contrast between the activities that characterize the two lives: theoretical activity is leisured, aims at no end beyond itself, and is loved for its own sake whereas practical activity is unleisured, aims at an end (other than itself), and is not chosen for its own sake (X.7.1177b1–26). As for the relation between the two sorts of activity, Aristotle implies that practical activity is merely a means to theoretical activity: ". . . we work in order that we may have leisure and wage war in order that we may have peace" (X.7.1177b4–6).

These remarks raise a major and well-known interpretive problem about Aristotle's ethical ideal and his conception of the best life for a man, for they seem to conflict with things he says earlier in the *Nicomachean Ethics* and elsewhere. They seem to conflict, in particular, with his account of the distinction between making (ποίησις) and doing (πρᾶξις) and with the conclusion of the function argument. In distinguishing making and doing, Aristotle says that "the end of making is something different from the making, but not the end of doing; for *good action* (εὐπραξία) *itself is*

This is a revised version of a paper presented at the 1978 meeting of the Society for Ancient Greek Philosophy in Washington, D.C., and originally published in the Special Aristotle Issue of *Paideia* (1978):138–57. Reprinted by permission.
David Keyt is Professor of Philosophy at the University of Washington in Seattle.

an end" (VI.5.1140b6–7); and in arguing that the goodness of an action is unlike the goodness of a product of one of the arts, he insists that for an act to be good it must be chosen for its own sake. The goodness of a product of one of the arts (a shoe or a statue) is a quality of the work itself; but, Aristotle argues, the goodness of an act is not a quality of the act itself. One must also consider the agent's state of knowledge, his motive, and his character. For an act to be good it must be done with knowledge, it must be chosen and *chosen for its own sake*, and it must issue from a stable character (II.4.1105a26–b9). This account of good action appears to directly contradict Aristotle's statement in the tenth book of the *Nicomachean Ethics* that practical activity, in contrast to theoretical, aims at an end (other than itself) and is not chosen for its own sake.

The conclusion of the function argument is that "the good for man turns out to be activity of soul in accordance with virtue (κατ' ἀρετήν), and if there are several virtues, in accordance with the best and most final" (or "most complete," τελειοτάτην) (I.7.1098a16–18). There are two interpretations of τελειοτάτη ἀρετή. According to the exclusionary interpretation,[2] Aristotle uses the expression to single out the highest excellence, theoretical wisdom, from among the rest; and the conclusion of the argument thus foreshadows the view of the tenth book that perfect happiness (ἡ τελεία εὐδαιμονία) is theoretical activity. According to the inclusive interpretation,[3] Aristotle uses the expression to refer to complete virtue—that is to say, to the combination of all the virtues, both moral and intellectual—and the conclusion of the argument conflicts, at least *prima facie*, with the view of the tenth book. The latter interpretation must be the correct one, for both the conceptual analysis that immediately precedes the function argument and the force of the argument itself require it.

In the passage immediately preceding the function argument Aristotle distinguishes three types of end (τέλος) (I.7.1097a25–b6). First, there are ends such as wealth, flutes, and instruments in general that are chosen only for the sake of other things. Secondly, there are ends such as honor, pleasure, and reason that are chosen both for their own sake and for the sake of other things. And, finally, there are ends such as happiness that are always chosen for their own sake and never for the sake of anything else. I shall call an end of the first type a *subservient* end, of the second type a *subordinate* end, and of the third type an *ultimate* end. An ultimate end is more final (τελειότερον) than a subordinate end, and a subordinate end than a subservient end. Furthermore, an ultimate end cannot be made more worthy of choice by the addition of anything. For if two ends are each chosen for their own sake but both together are more worthy of choice than either separately, then there is a compound end that embraces both to which each is subordinate (see X.2.1172b23–34, and compare *Top.* III.2.117

a16–24 and *Rhet.* I.7.1363b12–21). Happiness is such an inclusive end (I.7.1097b17–20) and as such is the most final (τελειότατον) end (1097 a30). The subordinate ends mentioned by Aristotle—honor, pleasure, and reason (νοῦς)—are the ends of the three lives, the political, the apolaustic, and the philosophic respectively (see I.5, 6.1096b23–24, and *E.E.* 1.4). The thrust of the entire passage is thus that theoretical activity, the activity of νοῦς, is a subordinate end that is included as one component among others of the ultimate end, happiness. It would seem, then, that the activity in accordance with the most final virtue referred to in the conclusion of the function argument must be the activity that constitutes the most final end—namely, activity in accordance with all the virtues, moral and intellectual.[4]

A second reason for favoring an inclusive rather than an exclusionary interpretation of the conclusion of the function argument is that the argument itself entails that the good for man is activity, not only in accordance with philosophical wisdom, but also in accordance with moral virtue and practical wisdom. In interpreting this argument I have attempted, by supplying its implicit premises, to cast it into the form of a valid deductive argument.

Aristotle distinguishes four general functions in the animate world: to reproduce and to use food, to perceive, to move from one place to another, and to think (see *De An.* I.1.402b12–13, II.4.415a26, III.9.432a15–17). These four functions define three general forms of life: the nutritive and reproductive life, which is shared by all (mortal) living things (ζῶντα); the perceptive life, which is shared by all animals (ζῷα); and "the practical life of that which has a rational principle," which is special to man (I.7.1098a1–4, *G.A.* I.23.731a24–b8, *Pol.* VII.13.1332b3–5). In describing this third life as a πρακτικὴ ζωή, a practical life, Aristotle is presumably using the word πρακτική in a generic sense that includes theoretical activity as well as practical activity in the specific sense (see *Pol.* VII.3.1325b14–21). Practical activity in the specific sense must be included since "man alone of animals is capable of deliberation" (*H.A.* I.1.488b24–25), and theoretical activity is implied since that which has a rational principle (ὁ λόγον ἔχων) is part practical and part theoretical (*Pol.* VII.14.1333a25–27). Aristotle does not distinguish a locomotive life since, except for a few immobile marine animals such as the oyster (*P.A.* IV.7.683b4–11, *H.A.* I.1.487b6–15), locomotion and perception are coextensive (*De An.* III.9.432a15–17).

That there are these four general functions in the animate world so distributed is the material premise of the function argument. The conclusion follows when this premise is combined with four general principles. First, one kind of mortal[5] living thing is *lower* than another if, and only if, normal members of the one kind lack a function that normal members of the other possess (*De An.* II.2.413a20–b13, III.12); moreover, mortal living things are *lower* than immortal (*Met.*Θ.8.1050b6–7). Thus plants are lower than animals; animals with fewer sense modalities (say, touch alone) lower than those with more (say, touch and sight); and animals other than man lower than man. Secondly, a form of life or an activity of the soul⁶ is the *distinctive function*⁷ of a kind of living thing if, and only if, every normal member of this kind and no member of a lower kind can perform it (see I.7.1097b33–34). Thus to reproduce and use food is the distinctive function of plants; to perceive, that of the lower animals; and "activity of soul in accordance with rational principle (κατὰ λόγον) or not without rational principle" (I.7.1098a7–8), that of man. It would seem to follow from this second general principle that God has no distinctive function since God's life consists entirely of theoretical activity, an activity in which man can share (X.8.1178b7–23, *Met.* Λ.7.1072b13–30). This is a problem that needs to be addressed, and I will return to it below. Thirdly, a *good member* of a kind is one that performs the distinctive function of its kind well (compared with other members of its kind) (I.7.1098a8–12). Thus a good man (σπουδαῖος ἀνήρ) is one whose rule governed activity accords with excellence (1098a12–15). Finally, *the good for*—that is to say, *the ultimate end of*—a member of a kind is to be a good member of its kind. Thus the good for a particular man, his most choice-worthy end, is to be a good man. This is a consequence about which one might be skeptical⁸ since there are occasions when a good man might be called upon to sacrifice his life (see IX.8.1169a18–26). But the last principle, though problematic, is absolutely crucial to the argument. For the function argument is introduced to give content to the characterization of happiness as "something final and self-sufficient, being the end of action" (I.7.1097b20–25), and without this final principle there will be no connection between the argument and this characterization. The conclusion now follows that the good for man is practical and theoretical activity that accords with excellence. Aristotle's own statement of the conclusion—"the good for man turns out to be activity of soul in accordance with excellence, and if there are several excellences, in accordance with the best and most final" (1098a16–18)—should, if possible, be interpreted as saying this; for Aristotle obviously intended the conclusion of his argument to be entailed by its premises. Since, as we have seen, it is possible to take Aristotle to be referring in the last phrase to the combination of all the virtues or excellences and since Aristotle does intend to assert that there are several virtues, his conclusion must be that the good for man is activity of soul in accordance with the best and most complete (τελειοτάτην) virtue—namely, the combination of all the virtues, moral and intellectual. To return now to the point that led to this lengthy discussion of the function argument, this seems to contradict Aristotle's assertion in the tenth book that perfect happiness (ἡ τελεία εὐδαιμονία) is theoretical activity alone.

II

The issue raised by the apparent conflict of Aristotle's remarks in the tenth book of the *Nicomachean Ethics* with those expressed earlier in the treatise and in other works[9] is that of the relation of the life of practical wisdom and moral virtue to the best life for a man—the relation of moral action to happiness. Does Aristotle abandon in Book X the view of Book I and elsewhere that moral activity is a subordinate end, a component of happiness, in favor of the view that it is merely a subservient end, only a means to happiness?

The difference between a *component* and a *means* may be illustrated by the difference between the activity of an ancient choregus in selecting the members of a chorus, outfitting it with costumes and masks, and providing for its training, which is one of the means to a dramatic performance, and the activity of the chorus in the performance of a play, which is a component, though perhaps a secondary component, of the dramatic performance itself.[10] This distinction is similar to one that Aristotle himself draws between a part (μέρος) and a necessary condition[11] that is not a part (*E.E.* I.2.1214b11–27, *Pol.* VII.8.1328a21–b4, 9.1329a34–39). A citizen, for example, is a part of a polis (*Pol.* III.1.1274b38–41) whereas property is not a part but only a necessary condition (*Pol.* VII.8.1328a33–35). Eating meat and taking a walk after dinner are for some people necessary conditions of health without being themselves parts of health (*E.E.* I.2.1214b14–24).

In Book X Aristotle seems to be espousing the view, which I shall call *strict intellectualism*, that theoretical activity is the sole component of the best life for a man and that practical activity has value only as a means to theoretical activity. Some scholars have attributed this view to him without hesitation: Alexander Grant,[12] for example, in the nineteenth century and John Cooper[13] and Anthony Kenny[14] today. But some hesitation is in order. For strict intellectualism, as is well known,[15] in addition to being inconsistent with the doctrine of Book I, has unpalatable moral consequences, which Aristotle (at least in his more worldly moments) would not accept. According to strict intellectualism it would be right for one person to steal from or to defraud another in order to obtain the wealth required to have the leisure for theoretical activity, for on this view the end justifies the means. But Aristotle says that theft is always wrong: "It is not possible ever to be right with regard to these things [namely, such things as adultery, theft, and murder], but to do them is always to be wrong" (II.6.1107a14–15). Aristotle may be espousing strict intellectualism in Book X without being aware of its unpalatable consequences or in spite of them. Still, it may be worthwhile to try once more to rescue Aristotle's ethical philosophy from inconsistency and immorality.

One possibility is that Aristotle is embracing a moderate rather than a strict intellectualism in Book X. By *moderate intellectualism* I mean the view that theoretical activity is the primary but not the sole component of the best life for a man, moral action being a secondary component. Moderate, unlike strict, intellectualism is consistent with the doctrine of Book I. But there are several versions of moderate intellectualism corresponding to the various ways of combining moral and intellectual activity while preserving the primacy of the latter. And some of these have consequences almost as unpalatable as those of strict intellectualism. So it will be well before turning to Book X to sort and grade the various possibilities.

Suppose that moral action, as moderate intellectualism affirms, has value in itself and not simply as a means to theoretical activity. The value it has independently will then either be commensurable[16] with the value of theoretical activity or not. Suppose it is commensurable. In this case the independent value of moral action can always be weighed against the value of theoretical activity; and when a situation arises in which one must choose between engaging in contemplative activity and performing some moral action, the activity of lesser value can be sacrificed for that of greater value with the aim of maximizing the total value in one's life. I shall call this the *trade-off* view. According to it, the value of theoretical activity, which for Aristotle resembles the activity of God, is related to the independent value of moral activity, activity that is wholly human, as the value of gold is to silver. The details of this view—namely, how to measure the value of moral and theoretical activity and how to balance the value of the one activity against the value of the other—are difficult to envisage, but the view is sufficiently precise for one to see some of its consequences. Since on the trade-off view the value of a moral action can sometimes exceed that of a competing theoretical activity, an adherent of the view will sometimes sacrifice theoretical for moral activity. He might, for example, trade an hour of contemplative activity for an act of liberality or munificence. Similarly, the owner of a silver mine might pay his workers in gold. On the other hand, it would be right according to the trade-off view for a person who is poor but intelligent to steal from or to defraud another person if this were the only means he had to obtain the wealth required to have the leisure for theoretical activity. For the value of an act of honesty (in this case refraining from theft or fraud) can, on this view, be outweighed by the value of a certain amount of theoretical activity. An adherent of the trade-off view will, of course, have scruples in many cases where the strict intellectualist will not since the former, unlike the latter, needs always to consider whether the end of theoretical activity can be achieved without acting contrary to the moral virtues and, if not, whether the theoretical activity sought is worth the moral cost.

Suppose, to take the other alternative, that moral action has value in itself and not simply as a means to theoretical activity but that the value it has independently is incommensurable with (and thus cannot be weighed against) the value of theoretical activity. One will want to consider in this case whether theoretical activity is absolutely prior to moral activity or not. If it is, we have the *absolute priority* view. An adherent of this view will act on the precept: maximize theoretical activity first; then maximize moral activity. Thus he will perform moral actions for their own sake but only when they do not interfere with his theoretical activity. He will never, for example, sacrifice a moment of theoretical activity, however uninspired, for a disinterested moral action, however noble. The consequences of this view are only slightly less unpalatable than those of strict intellectualism. Unlike the strict intellectualist, whose attitude toward any action that neither promotes nor hinders his theoretical activity is indifference, an adherent of the absolute priority view will act in accordance with the moral virtues when unable to contemplate or to do anything that will promote his theoretical activity; but, like the strict intellectualist, he will do anything, however base, that promotes his theoretical activity.

Suppose, to take the final case, that theoretical activity is the primary, and moral action a secondary, component of the best life for a man; that the value that moral action has in itself is incommensurable with the value of theoretical activity; but that theoretical activity is not absolutely prior to moral action. There *is* a view that fits this description. According to it, theoretical activity is more desirable than moral activity—one would spend all of one's time engaged in it if that were humanly possible—and is in this sense the primary component of happiness. But what is more desirable must be pursued within the constraints placed upon a person by his bodily nature, by his family and friends, and by his polis. The idea is that theoretical activity is to be maximized but only within the constraints of the life of practical wisdom and moral virtue. Moral activity is the foundation, and theoretical activity the superstructure, of the best life for a man. Moral action will not, on this view, be absolutely prior to theoretical activity. This view is not simply the converse of the preceding one. The demands of civic and domestic life are so indefinite and potentially so all-consuming that there would be few, if any, opportunities for contemplation if moral activity were given absolute priority over theoretical. Such a priority would violate the primacy of theoretical activity. According to the *superstructure* view, the moral life sets certain minimum requirements that must be satisfied before one is to engage in theoretical activity; but the view does not demand that one should never shirk a duty, however trivial, for an opportunity to contemplate. Where the line is drawn will presumably be determined by the moral intuition of the practically wise man (ὁ φρόνιμος).

The following table displays the various possibilities:

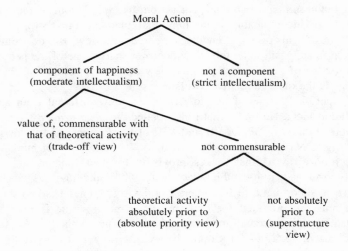

III

Ackrill's and Cooper's acute but divergent discussions of Aristotle's account of εὐδαιμονία exemplify in various ways each of the four specific possibilities.

Ackrill maintains that "the question [how θεωρία and virtuous action would combine in the best human life] is incapable of even an outline answer that Aristotle could accept" ("*Eudaimonia*," p. 32). Ackrill reaches this conclusion because it seems to him that Aristotle's theology and anthropology together yield a consequence that is irreconcilable with his respect for ordinary moral views. Ackrill's argument, as I interpret it, goes like this. According to Aristotle's theology, the divine is incommensurably more valuable than the merely human. And, according to his anthropology, man is "a compound of 'something divine' and much that is not divine" (p. 33). θεωρία is the activity of man's divine component while virtuous action belongs to his earthly nature. Therefore, θεωρία is "incommensurably more valuable" than virtuous action and in the best life for man must be given absolute priority over it (p. 32). Aristotle's anthropology and theology thus lead to what I called the *absolute priority* view. But this view, Ackrill points out, has the consequence "that one should do anything however monstrous if doing it has the slightest tendency to promote *the-*

371

oria . . ."—a consequence that Aristotle must find "paradoxical" since he wishes to adhere "reasonably closely to ordinary moral views" (p. 32).

"The only way to avoid such paradoxical and inhuman consequences," Ackrill believes, "would be to allow a certain amount of compromise and trading between *theoria* and virtuous action, treating the one as more important but not incomparably more important than the other" (pp. 32–33). Ackrill thus for his own part endorses the trade-off view. But he seems to be mistaken in supposing that this view does not share some of the paradoxical consequences of the absolute priority view and in supposing that the trade-off view is the only alternative available.

Cooper, in fact, attributes to Aristotle a view different from any that Ackrill considers. He finds what I have called the *superstructure* view in the *Eudemian Ethics*, in Books VII and VIII of the *Politics*, and in the middle books of the *Nicomachean Ethics*—namely, "a conception of human flourishing [εὐδαιμονία] that makes provision for two fundamental ends— morally virtuous activity and intellectual activity of the highest kind. Neither of these is subordinate to the other; moral virtue comes first, in the sense that it must be provided for first, but once moral virtue is securely entrenched, then intellectual goods are allowed to predominate" (*Reason and Human Good*, pp. 142–43). Cooper believes, however, that Aristotle adopts an intellectualist ideal of the best life in Book X of the *Nicomachean Ethics* and that he paves the way for this ideal in Book I (pp. 100, 147–48, *et passim*). By *intellectualism* Cooper means "the view that human flourishing consists exclusively in pure intellectual activity of the best kind" (p. 90)— the view that I have called *strict intellectualism*. What leads Aristotle to embrace strict intellectualism, according to Cooper, is his doctrine that "one *is* his theoretical mind" (p. 168). Aristotle does not, on Cooper's interpretation, completely abandon the superstructure view; the life described by this view is simply downgraded in the final book of the *Nicomachean Ethics* from best to second-best (pp. 177–80).

Cooper is led to this interpretation of Book X partly by a philological consideration—by what he things Aristotle can and cannot mean by the Greek word βίος ("life"). This matter needs to be examined since it raises a fundamental issue of how Aristotle is to be read.

IV

What does Aristotle mean by a "life," a βίος? The traditional answer is that each of the various "lives" that Aristotle mentions—the apolaustic,[17] the political,[18] the philosophic,[19] the agricultural,[20] the military,[21] and so forth—is a personification of an abstraction.[22] On this interpretation none of these lives need be more than one aspect of the total life led by some particular person. Thus the life of a person like Xenophon might combine the military, the political, the agricultural, and the literary.[23]

Cooper has challenged this idea (*Reason and Human Good*, pp. 159–60). He denies that the word βίος can be used in Greek to refer to an aspect or phase of a person's total life. According to Cooper, the word "means always '(mode of) life,' and in any one period of time one can only have one mode of life." "Hence," he concludes, "when Aristotle contrasts an 'intellectual life (*bios*)' with a 'moral life (*bios*),' he cannot mean . . . the intellectual life and the moral life of a single person. The Greek expression can only mean two different lives led by two different kinds of persons." Cooper here is making two distinct claims. The first and weaker claim denies that one person can live two or more distinct βίοι synchronously but does not rule out the possibility that a person might lead one βίος at one time and another βίος at another time—that a person might, for example, lead an agricultural life during one part of the year and a military life during another. The second and stronger claim denies, or seems to deny, that one person can live two or more distinct βίοι either synchronously or successively.

There are passages in Plato and Aristotle that refute both claims. In his discussion of domestic economy in the first book of the *Politics* Aristotle lists five lives (βίοι) that procure their sustenance through their own work rather than through the exchange of goods—the pastoral, the agricultural, the piratical, the life of fishing, and the life of hunting (I.8.1256a40–b1). Aristotle goes on to say that some people combine one mode of life with another when the one is insufficient for their needs—for example, "some live a pastoral and piratical life at the same time (ἅμα), others an agricultural and hunting life, and similarly with the others" (1256b2–6). This passage shows that the stronger claim about the word βίος, that one person cannot live two or more distinct βίοι either synchronously or successively, is clearly false. But in spite of the occurrence of the word ἅμα, it probably does not refute the weaker claim as well. For Aristotle presumably does not mean to say that some people hunt while they plow but rather that within some interval of time—a year, say—they both hunt and plow.

That the weaker claim is also false is demonstrated by a passage in Plato's *Laws* (V.733D7–734E2). Plato considers four lives (βίοι)—the temperate, the brave, the wise, and the healthy—and their opposites—the profligate, the cowardly, the foolish, and the diseased—and maintains that each of the first four is more pleasant than its opposite. He concludes from this that the life of excellence with respect to the body or the soul—that is to say, the life that combines, and of course combines synchronously, the first four lives—is more pleasant than the life of depravity, which combines the four opposite lives.

Thus it is clear that the Greek word βίος can be used to signify, not only a person's total life, but also one particular phase or aspect of it. Furthermore, there are positive indications that Aristotle intended, at least in *Nicomachean Ethics* X.7–8, to signify two distinct aspects of a total life by "the life of reason" (ὁ κατὰ τὸν νοῦν βίος) (1178a6–7) and "the life in accordance with the other excellence" (ὁ κατὰ τὴν ἄλλην βίος) (1178a9). For he says that a person lives the one life "as possessor of something divine" (ᾗ θεῖόν τι ἐν αὐτῷ ὑπάρχει) 1177 b28)—that is to say, as demigod—whereas he lives the other "as he is man" (ᾗ ἄνθρωπός ἐστιν) (1177b27, 1178b5). And Aristotle uses this ᾗ ("as," "qua") locution as part of his standard terminology to signify one aspect of a thing in abstraction from all others. He says, to take a simple example, that "the infinite *qua* infinite is unknowable (*Phys.* I.4.187b7; see also III.6.207a25–26) meaning by this that an infinite object need not be completely unknowable but only in the respect in which it is infinite: if a surface were infinitely long but only an inch wide, one could know its width but not its length. Or, to consider another example, speaking of natural science Aristotle says that there are many statements about things merely *qua* moving (ᾗ κινούμενα), apart from what each thing is and from their incidental properties" (*Met.* M.3.1077b23–24).

There is now an answer, or a sort of answer, to a puzzle that arose in analyzing the function argument. It seemed that of all living things God alone lacked a distinctive function since his only activity, contemplation, is an activity in which man can share. The answer is that man does not engage in this activity as man but only as possessor of something divine, namely, reason or νοῦς.[24] In so far as man can contemplate he is a god himself.

V

The way is now clear for an interpretation of *Nicomachean Ethics* X.6–8 that minimizes the conflict between it and the rest of the work. Aristotle begins his final and consummative discussion of happiness by considering whether happiness lies in play (X.6). This preliminary discussion raises at least two interpretive questions. First, what exactly is the view that Aristotle is considering? And, secondly, what contribution, if any, does this discussion make to Aristotle's ultimate conclusion that perfect happiness is theoretical activity?

The word παιδιά along with two other words that figure in the discussion in Chapter 6, παιδικός ("childish") (1176b33) and παίζειν ("to play like a child"—then: "to play," "to jest," "to dance," "to sing," "to play at a game") (1176b30, 33), is derived from the word παῖς ("child") (1176 b22, 23). This derivation undoubtedly assists the conclusion of Chapter 6 that happiness does not lie in play (1176b27–28): since a παῖς is ἀτελής (undeveloped) (see *Pol.* I.12.1259b3–4), παιδιά can hardly be the τέλος (end) of a man (see *E.E.* II.1.1219b4–8).

The range of application of the word παιδιά is very wide. In Plato, for example, παιδιά covers among other things children's games (*Polit.* 308d3–4, *Laws* 643b4–d4, 793e3–794a4), war games (*Laws* 829b7–c1), singing and dancing (*Laws* 803e1–2), the mimetic arts from dancing to drama (*Soph.* 234b1 ff., *Rep.* 602b6–10, *Polit.* 288c1–10), religious sacrifices (*Laws* 803e1), puns (*Crat.* 406c3–4), and carousing (*Prot.* 347d6, *Laws* 673e8 ff.). Human life for Plato is divided into just two phases—play (παιδιά) and seriousness (σπουδή) (for the dichotomy see *Rep.* 602b8, *Polit.* 288c9–10, *Laws* 643b6, 647d6–7, 732d6, 797a7 ff., 942a8)—play being a preparation for, a means to, or a relaxation from, serious endeavors (*Laws* 643b4–d4, 796a1–d5, *Phil.* 30e6–7). It is not so clear what activities Aristotle counts as παιδιαί, for he is not as lavish with examples as Plato. But a few examples may be gleaned from the *Nicomachean Ethics* and the *Politics.* He mentions children's games (*Pol.* VII.17.1336a21–31) and urban and witty conversation (εὐτραπελία) (*E.N.* II.7.1108a23–26 and IV.8) and reports the common view that the purpose of sleep, drink, music, and dance is play and relaxation (*Pol.* VIII.5.1339a14–21). Interestingly, in Chapter 6 Aristotle alludes to the things valued among boys (1176b22), to those who are ready-witted (εὐτράπελοι) in the pastimes of tyrants (1176b12–16), and to the bodily pleasures (1176b19–21, 1177a6–7) (under which would fall the pleasures of sleeping, drinking, and dancing).

The association of play with the bodily pleasures connects the discussion in Chapter 6 with that of the apolaustic life in I.5.[25] The two discussions are also connected by one of Aristotle's reasons for considering the view that happiness lies in play—namely, that the pleasures of play seem to be chosen for their own sake (1176b9–11). For it is Aristotle's view that the apolaustic life is the only life besides the political and the philosophic that is chosen for its own sake. Aristotle notes in the *Eudemian Ethics* that there are other modes of life besides these three—for example, that of the laborer, the artisan, and the trader—but he believes that they are always entered into for the sake of the necessities of life (*E.E.* I.4.1215a25–32), not for their own sake (see I.5.1096a5–7). All who happen to have the means, he remarks, choose to live either a political, a philosophic, or an apolaustic life (*E.E.* I.4.1215a35–36). It seems, therefore, that the life of play and the apolaustic life are the same.

Aristotle offers two reasons for supposing that happiness lies in the pleasures of play: the one just mentioned, that they seem to be chosen for their own sake, not for the sake of anything else; and, secondly, that they are pursued by persons deemed happy, such as tyrants and others in positions of power (1176b9–17). Both reasons are rejected: tyrants are not trust-

375

worthy judges any more than (immature) boys (1176b17–27); and in the proper ordering of life play is a relaxation from toil and a means to further exertion, not an end in itself (1176b28–1177a1).²⁶ Aristotle rounds off his discussion of play with the following argument, the major premises of which play a leading role in the discussion in Chapters 7 and 8: "The happy life seems to be a life in accordance with excellence"; the activity of one's higher faculties accords more with excellence and is thus more conducive to happiness than that of one's lower faculties; but play does not engage one's higher faculties; therefore, happiness cannot lie in play (1177a1–11).

The stage is now set for the discussion of Chapters 7 and 8. One of the three nominees for happiest life has been eliminated. Thus if one of the two remaining candidates can be shown to be happier than the other, it will follow that this one is also the happiest life possible.

<h1>VI</h1>

In Chapter 7 Aristotle considers in turn six attributes that *seem* to characterize the activity that constitutes happiness or the happy life. (For the form of the various conjuncts of the major premise of Aristotle's argument, see 1177a1–2, b4.) The six are collected from different sources. The first comes from the conclusion of the function argument and reflects a philosophical thesis; the others reflect various common opinions (ἔνδοξα) about happiness and goodness. Thus the activity that constitutes happiness seems to be:

1. in accordance with excellence (κατ' ἀρετήν) (1177a1–2, 12 compare I.7.1098a16–17),

2. continuous (συνεχής) (1177a21–22; compare I.10.1100b11–22, IX.9.1170a4–8, and *Rhet.* I.7.1364b30–31),

3. pleasurable (ἡδύς) (1177a22–23; compare I.8.1099a7–31, VII. 13.1153b14–15, IX.19.1170a4, and *Rhet.* I.7.1364b23, 1365b11–13),

4. self-sufficient (αὐτάρκης) (1177a27–28; compare I.7.1097 b6–16, IX.9.1169b4–5, and *Rhet.* I.7.1364a5–9),

5. loved for itself (δι' αὐτὴν ἀγαπᾶσθαι) (1176b2–5, 1177b1–2; compare I.7.1097a34–b6 and *Rhet.* I.6.1362a21–22, 7.1364a1–5),

6. leisured (σχολαστικόν) (1177b4, 22).

If the attribute under consideration admits of degrees, Aristotle argues that theoretical activity (θεωρία) possesses it to a higher degree than practical (that is, moral and political) activity (πρᾶξις) 1177a12–b1). If the attribute does not admit of degrees, he argues that it characterizes theoretical but not practical activity (1177b1–15).²⁷ Aristotle then infers (1177b16–26) that perfect (or complete) happiness (ἡ τελεία εὐδαιμονία) is theoretical activity or, alternatively expressed, that the life of reason, the theoretical life, is the happiest life.[28]

As it stands, this is not a valid argument. For one thing it does not rule out the possibility that some third type of activity—making pots, writing dramas, or reveling in the bodily pleasures—is superior to both theoretical and practical activity in respect of the six attributes under consideration. For another it allows the possibility that the list of attributes is incomplete, that the six considered do not include all that are essential to an activity that constitutes happiness. Furthermore, the conclusion is categorical—"The life of reason *is* the happiest life" (1178a7–8)—whereas the conjuncts of the major premise are qualified—"The happy life *seems* to be a life in accordance with excellence" (1177a1–2). The solution of the first weakness is to add the implicit conclusion of Chapter 6, that happiness consists of either theoretical or practical activity, as an additional premise. As for the other two weaknesses, I shall simply assume, in order to raise a more interesting question about the argument, that Aristotle intended his major premise to be read in a strengthened form: (1) that he intended to assert that the attributes he considers actually do characterize, rather than merely seem to characterize, any activity that constitutes happiness, and (2) that the six he considers include all that are essential to an activity that constitutes happiness.

The more interesting question concerns the interpretation of Aristotle's conclusion—that ἡ τελεία εὐδαιμονία is theoretical activity or, alternatively expressed, that the theoretical βίος is the happiest βίος. What exactly is the force of this assertion? Does Aristotle mean to assert, as Cooper claims, "that the best plan of life is to pursue constantly the single end of theoretical contemplation in preference to all else" (*Reason and Human Good*, p. 156)? Does he mean that the best total life for a man is one in which theoretical activity is constantly, exclusively, and (of course) successfully pursued? Or is he making the more modest assertion, as Stewart and Gauthier claim, that the best *element* of the best total life for a man is its theoretical activity?[29] As I have argued in Section IV above, Aristotle's use of the word βίος coupled with ἤ not only permits, but supports, the latter interpretation. The word τελεία in ἡ τελεία εὐδαιμονία, on the other hand, is perfectly ambiguous and allows either interpretation. In *Metaphysics* Δ.16 Aristotle distinguishes three senses of τέλειος:

1. having all of its parts: captured in English by the word *complete*, as the complete time (χρόνος τέλειος) of a thing (1021b12–14).

2. being best of its kind: captured in English by the word *perfect*, as a perfect doctor (τέλειος ἰατρός) perfect thief, or perfect circle (1021b14–23, *Phys.* VII.3.246a13–16).

3. having reached its end (τέλος): captured in English by such expressions as *fully realized* and *fully developed* and predicated, for example, of an adult in contrast to a child (1021b23–30, *Pol.* I.12.1259b3–4).[30]

If τελεία has sense 1 in the expression ἡ τελεία εὐδαιμονία, then Aristotle's conclusion expresses the strict intellectualist view that complete (or total) happiness is theoretical activity. If τελεία has either sense 2 or sense 3, then his conclusion can be given a weaker, moderate intellectualist interpretation—that perfect or fully realized, as distinct from complete, happiness is theoretical activity.

Both formulations of Aristotle's conclusion will thus bear a moderate intellectualist interpretation. Although such an interpretation even seems indicated for one of the two, the perfect ambiguity of the other makes one hesitate to claim on the basis of an analysis of the verbal formulations alone that such an interpretation of Aristotle's conclusion is demanded. One must also consider Aristotle's argument. What sort of intellectualism does it entail— moderate or strict? If Aristotle's argument entails one view but not the other, this is a good reason for attributing the one rather than the other to him.[31]

On one interpretation strict intellectualism is entailed by the part of Aristotle's argument that is based on the philosophical idea that the activity that constitutes happiness is activity in accordance with excellence. This subargument opens (1177a12–21) and closes (1177b26–1178a8) Chapter 7, though its leading ideas are introduced at the end of Aristotle's discussion of play (6.1177a1–11). Most English translations of these passages obscure the simple relations between the key terms of the argument and make it almost unintelligible, so a few elementary comments about its terminology are in order. The argument is based on the noun ἀρετή ("goodness," "excellence," "virtue") (see 1177a2, 10, 12, 17, b29) and three forms of the comparative and superlative of its simple adjective ἀγαθός ("good"):

comparative: "better"	superlative: "best"
βελτίων (1177a3, 4, 6)	βέλτιστος
κρείττων(1177a6, b26)	κράτιστος (1177a13, 19, b34, 1178a5–6)
ἀμείνων (1178a3)	ἄριστος (1177a13)

Rendered literally, the argument of 1177a1–21 runs as follows:

1. Happiness is activity in accordance with goodness (a1–2, 12).

2. And the activity of the better part of a man is better and hence more conducive to happiness (a5–6).

3. So the activity of the best part is best and most conducive to happiness (see a12–13).

4. Reason (νοῦς) is the best thing in us, and its objects are the best of knowable objects (a20–21, see Stewart, *Notes, ad loc.*).

5. Therefore, the activity of reason is the best activity and the one most conducive to happiness. As Aristotle expresses it, ". . . the activity [of reason] in accordance with its proper goodness will be ἡ τελεία εὐδαιμονία" (a16–17).

The premises of this argument entail not that theoretical activity is complete happiness, but only that it is perfect or fully realized happiness.

But when Aristotle returns to this theme at the end of Chapter 7, he seems to advance beyond his earlier claim that reason is the best (but not the only) thing in us and to claim now that a man and his reason are identical: "This [viz., reason] would also seem to be each man, since it is the authoritative and better part. Thus it would be odd if he were to choose not his own life but that of someone else" (1178a2–4). Similar assertions occur in two earlier passages in Book IX (4.1166a10–23, 8.1168b28–1169a18). However, the element or faculty with which a man is (or seems to be) identified is not the same in the two books. In Book IX the thinking or reasoning element (τὸ διανοητικόν, τὸ νοοῦν, νοῦς) with which a man seems to be identified (1166a16–17, 22–23, 1168b35), since it has the ability to guide action and to control the passions, must be either his practical reason[32] or his intellect as a whole[33]—practical, productive, and theoretical. In Book X, on the other hand, the reason in question must be the theoretical reason alone.[34] For its activity is said to be theoretical (1177a17–18 *et passim*), and practical wisdom (φρόνησις) is explicitly distinguished from it (8.1178a16–22).[35] But, in spite of these differences, the passages in Book IX, as we shall see, provide the clue to the proper interpretation of 1178a2–4.

Now, if a man is strictly identical with his theoretical reason and if practical reason is not a part of theoretical reason, then practical reason is not a part of a man. On the strict-identity hypothesis practical reason will be merely something without which a man cannot exist, like food (*Met.* Δ.5.1015b20–22)—not a part of a man but only a necessary condition of his existence.[36] Practical and theoretical reason will be related as the lower and higher order in Aristotle's ideal state (see *Pol.* VI.4.1291a24–28 and VII.8–9). The warriors, officeholders, and priests who compose its higher order are its parts. The farmers, craftsmen, and tradesmen who compose its lower order, though the state cannot exist without them, are not parts of it: their role is to serve the members of the higher order. On the strict-identity hypothesis practical reason will be subservient to theoretical in just the same way; and Aristotle will, as Cooper claims (*Reason and Human Good*, pp. 162–63), be embracing strict intellectualism.

But does Aristotle really mean to claim that a man is strictly identical with his theoretical reason? There is good reason for thinking not since his statement that reason "would also seem *to be* each man" (1178a2) is immediately qualified: ". . . for man, then, the life according to reason is best and pleasantest, since this [viz., reason] *most of all* (μάλιστα) is man" (a6–7). To be most of all man is to be less than, and so nonidentical with, man.[37] That this reservation is seriously intended is indicated by its earlier appearance in the two passages in Book IX where a man is identified with his

thinking faculty. In the first of these Aristotle says that "the reasoning element would seem to be, or to be *most of all* (ἢ μάλιστα), each man"
(4.1166a22–23); and the reservation is repeated in almost the same words in
the second—"That this [*viz.*, reason] is, or is *most of all* (ἢ μάλιστα),
each man is clear" (8.1169a2). But to claim that reason is the most important, but not the sole, part of a man is simply to reiterate a premise—line
4—of the argument of 1177a1–21, an argument that does not entail strict intellectualism.

Another part of the overall argument of Chapter 7 that needs to be examined is that in which Aristotle tries to show that theoretical activity is leisured and alone loved for its own sake whereas military and political activities (the pre-eminent practical activities) are not chosen for their own sakes
and are unleisured (1177b1–24). The claim that theoretical activity alone is
loved for its own sake, in conjunction with Aristotle's earlier requirement
that the activity that constitutes happiness must be chosen for its own sake
(X.6.1176b2–5), entails that theoretical activity is the sole component of
happiness (strict intellectualism). And Aristotle's statement in the course of
this discussion that "we work in order that we may have leisure and wage
war in order that we may have peace" (1177b4–6), given the association of
theoretical activity with leisure and military and political activities with
work, also points toward strict intellectualism; for it seems to imply that
practical activity has value only as a means to theoretical.

Aristotle's argument has a single premise, that military and political activities aim at an external end but theoretical activity does not—a premise
that seems to conflict with his earlier assertion that "good action itself is an
end" (VI.5.1140b7).[38]

In examining this argument the first thing to notice is that the conflict
between Aristotle's various remarks on action is only apparent. Good action
on Aristotle's theory is typically double-barreled, the target of one barrel being different from that of the other. A man may act in accordance with
a particular virtue such as temperance, bravery, or justice for the sake of
the particular temperate, brave, or just act itself; and he may also at the
same time seek an end apart from the action—a τέλος παρὰ τὴν
πρᾶξιν—such as health or victory or the reform of a wrongdoer. Although this distinction between an *internal* and an *external* end is never
drawn explicitly by Aristotle, it underlies his treatment of bravery[39] and
once drawn provides a key to several puzzles in Aristotle's ethics. The brave
man on the field of battle wishes to do two things: to attain the morally
beautiful (τὸ καλόν) while avoiding the morally ugly (τὸ
αἰσχρόν)[40] and to defeat his enemy while avoiding death and wounds.[41]
And like Hector facing Achilles he may attain the one goal but not the
other.[42] (Failure to attain the external goal may mean, as it did to Hector

and his family, the destruction of happiness [see I.10.1100b22–1101a8].) Aristotle's remarks on action appear to conflict because some refer to the internal, some to the external, end.[43]

Unfortunately, Aristotle does not always keep this distinction clearly in mind. Otherwise he would not have inferred that theoretical activity "alone[44] would seem to be loved for its own sake" from the premise that "nothing arises from it apart from the theorizing, whereas from practical activities we gain more or less apart from the action" (1177b1–4). That an action has an external end does not prevent it from being loved for its own sake. What follows from Aristotle's premise, as W.F.R. Hardie points out, is that theoretical activity "alone is loved for its own sake alone."[45] Thus even though the conclusion of this argument, in conjunction with the requirement that the activity that constitutes happiness must be chosen for its own sake, entails strict intellectualism, Aristotle's reason for accepting the conclusion itself is inadequate. To my mind, the invalid conclusion of this argument is the only basis Aristotle provides for a strict intellectualist interpretation of Chapter 7.[46]

The distinction between an internal and an external end of action is also helpful in interpreting Aristotle's remark that "we work in order that we may have leisure and wage war in order that we may have peace" (1177b4–6). If an action can be performed for its own sake as well as for an end apart from the action, then work can have value both in itself and as a means to peace and leisure. The munificent man who uses his wealth to outfit a trireme (IV.2.1122a24, b23), though he wishes to help secure the safety of his polis, acts also for the sake of the morally beautiful (1122b6–7, 1123a24–27).[47] Moreover, Aristotle's distinction between work and leisure does not correspond to his distinction between practical and theoretical activity. The moral virtues have a role to play in both phases of life: "Bravery and endurance are needed for work, philosophy for leisure, temperance and justice at both times, and more especially when men observe peace and have leisure; for war compels men to be just and temperate, whereas the enjoyment of good fortune and the possession of leisure accompanied by peace makes them rather insolent" (Pol. VII.15.1334a22–28). Aristotle's remark that work is for the sake of leisure thus does not imply strict intellectualism.

VII

Chapter 8 contains three additional arguments for the conclusion that perfect happiness is theoretical activity. (1) The gods are paradigms of happiness but their lives consist entirely of theoretical, rather than practical or productive, activity; "so of human activities that which is most akin to this is the most conducive to happiness" (1178b7–23). (2) The whole of the life of the gods, consisting as it does of ceaseless contemplation, is blessed (μακάριος); so too is the life of man insofar as it is spent in such activity; but none of the lower animals are happy since they in no way share in contemplation. "As far, then, as contemplation extends, so also does happiness; and to those to whom contemplation more fully belongs happiness also more fully belongs, not incidentally but in virtue of the contemplation." Therefore happiness is a kind of contemplation (b24–32). (3) He who exercises his (theoretical) reason is most loved by the gods; those most loved by the gods are the happiest; therefore, the wise man is the happiest (1179a22–32).

The second argument requires examination, for the part of it that is directly quoted seems to identify happiness and contemplation straightforwardly and, consequently, to be an unambiguous expression of strict intellectualism. But the argument will, I think, bear another interpretation. The second argument follows directly upon the first and begins with the words "A proof, too, is that . . ." (σημεῖον δὲ καὶ . . .). This indicates that it is intended to establish the same conclusion as the first, that ἡ τελεία εὐδαιμονία is theoretical activity (1178b7–8). Now, if ἡ τελεία εὐδαιμονία means, as it seems to, perfect or fully realized, rather than complete, happiness throughout X.7–8 and if μακάριος and εὐδαιμονία mean τελεία εὐδαιμονία in argument (2), then Aristotle's statement that happiness and contemplation are coextensive will mean simply that perfect or fully realized happiness is coextensive with contemplation. But this assertion is compatible with a moderate intellectualism that allows a place for the secondary happiness of moral and political activity. This interpretation also resolves a small puzzle about the argument—namely, that Aristotle's explanation of the fact that happiness is not attributed to the lower animals seems inadequate. They are incapable of happiness, one would suppose, not simply because they are incapable of contemplating but also because they are incapable of practical thinking.[48] But if Aristotle is thinking only of perfect or fully realized happiness, his explanation is completely adequate.

VIII

Thus with the exception of the one statement that theoretical activity "alone would seem to be loved for its own sake" (1177b1–2) there seems to be nothing in X.6–8 that is inconsistent with a moderate intellectualism and with the rest of the *Nicomachean Ethics*. This is a fairly weak conclusion. Can it be strengthened? Is there anything in these three chapters that can be taken to be an expression of moderate intellectualism? In particular, can anything be taken to be an expression of the only reasonable version of mod-

ARISTOTLE

erate intellectualism—namely, the superstructure view according to which theoretical activity is to be maximized within the constraints of the life of practical wisdom and moral virtue?

Aristotle's famous injunction "as far as possible to immortalize oneself and to do everything with a view to living in accordance with the best thing in oneself [*viz.*, the theoretical reason]" (7.1177b33–34) is an expression of the superstructure view if the restriction signified by the words "as far as possible" includes moral restrictions as well as those of mind, body, and estate. Does it? The answer to this question can be inferred, I think, from a passage in Chapter 8 where Aristotle is discussing the extent to which the theoretical life and the life in accordance with practical wisdom and moral virtue need external equipment and where he seems for once to combine the two lives: "The person who contemplates has no need of such things [*viz.*, external goods] for his activity; but they are so to speak even impediments, at least to contemplation; however, as he is a man and lives with a number of others, he chooses to do those things that are in accordance with [*scil.* moral] virtue; he will therefore need such things with a view to living as a man" (1178b3–7). Here Aristotle states explicitly that the person who contemplates (ὁ θεωρῶν), *qua* man, *chooses* to act in accordance with moral virtue.[49] It has been denied, however, that Aristotle intends by this statement to imply that the person who contemplates will be a morally virtuous person. Cooper in defending his strict intellectualist interpretation of Book X claims that Aristotle "says only that the theorizer may *perform* various virtuous actions" and that "Aristotle conspicuously avoids saying that his theorizer will *be* a virtuous person" (*Reason and Human Good*, p. 164). "This is easily understood," Cooper explains, "since it is clear that however often [the theorizer] may perform the just or the temperate or the liberal deed, anyone who organizes his life from the [strict] intellectualist outlook cannot care about such actions in the way a truly just or temperate or liberal man does" (p. 164). But unless one can find strict intellectualism elsewhere in Book X, this is not a plausible reading of the passage. The correct explanation of Aristotle's formulation is much simpler than the one Cooper offers. Aristotle says that the person who contemplates "chooses to do those things that are in accordance with virtue" (αἱρεῖται τὰ κατὰ τὴν ἀρετὴν πράττειν) because he is considering whether the person who contemplates will need very much external equipment and, as the immediately preceding passage makes plain, it is moral actions, not moral dispositions (ἕξεις), that require such equipment (1178a28–b3). Furthermore, it is Aristotle's view that an act cannot be just or temperate or liberal, except incidentally (κατὰ συμβεβηκός), unless it springs from a just or temperate or liberal character (II.4.1105a26–b9, V.9.1137a4–26).[50] Thus in order to choose to do those things that are in accordance with moral virtue one must possess the moral virtues.[51]

383

A.W.H. Adkins in a recent article concedes that the person who contemplates will on Aristotle's theory be a morally virtuous person: "[t]he *theoretikos* will indeed possess all the *aretai*. . . ."[52] But he remarks on the passage before us that Aristotle "does not tell us *when* [the *theoretikos*] chooses: he may well mean 'chooses when *theoria* is not available'" (p. 301). On Adkins' interpretation the author of this passage might without inconsistency condone the conduct of a man who refused to interrupt his theoretical activity in order to rescue a neighbor from a burning building. Thus Adkins believes the passage to be consistent with what I have called the *absolute priority* view—the view whose precept is: maximize theoretical activity first; then maximize moral activity. There are at least two reasons for rejecting Adkins' interpretation. First, Aristotle says that the person who contemplates, *qua* man, chooses to act in accordance with moral virtue. But a person is not a man—that is to say, a human being (ἄνθρωπος)—at one moment and at another not. He is a human being all of his life just as he is always an animal and always a living thing. Thus once the moral virtues are acquired he is *always* prepared to act in accordance with them. Secondly, possession of the moral virtues would seem to be inconsistent with their erratic exercise. The brave man defends his polis whenever the enemy attacks, not just at his convenience. Thus if the person who contemplates, *qua* man, chooses to act in accordance with bravery, he must always be prepared to sacrifice theoretical activity for battle. So this passage does not seem to be consistent with the absolute priority view. It seems better to take it as picking up the theme of the function argument, the centerpiece of Book I, that the various aspects of a person's total life—his life as a living thing, as an animal, as a man, and as a demigod—form a hierarchy with the higher aspects resting on and presupposing the lower.

If my interpretation is correct, Aristotle champions a single, consistent ideal of human happiness throughout the *Nicomachean Ethics*: one should seek to immortalize onself but only within the bounds of the life of practical wisdom and moral virtue.[53]

NOTES

[1] All Aristotelian references are to the *Nicomachean Ethics* unless otherwise identified.

[2] W. F. R. Hardie, "The Final Good in Aristotle's *Ethics*," *Philosophy* XL (1965):280; John M. Cooper, *Reason and Human Good in Aristotle* (Cambridge, Mass., 1975), pp. 99–100; Anthony Kenny, *The Aristotelian Ethics* (Oxford, 1978), pp. 203–06.

[3] J. L. Ackrill, "Aristotle on *Eudaimonia*," in *Essays on Aristotle's Ethics*, ed., Amélie Oksenberg Rorty (Berkeley, 1980), pp. 26–29. Reprinted from the *Proceedings of the British Academy*, LX (1974).

ARISTOTLE

⁴ In this paragraph I am following Ackrill's lead.
⁵ For the restriction see *De An.* II.2.413a31–32, 3.415a7–11.
⁶ For the equation of ζωή and ψυχῆς ἐνέργεια see I.7.1098a13.
⁷ Its ἔργον ἴδιον (*Pol.* II.5.1263a40) as distinct from its κοινὰ ἔργα (*G.A.* I.23.731a30–31).
⁸ See P. Glassen, "A Fallacy in Aristotle's Argument about the Good," *The Philosophical Quarterly* 7 (1957); and J. L. Ackrill, *Aristotle's Ethics* (New York, 1973), pp. 20, 244.
⁹ Most notably in *E.E.* II.1 especially 1219a35–39. See Cooper, *Reason and Human Good*, pp. 116–18.
¹⁰ For other illustrations of the distinction, see L. H. G. Greenwood, *Aristotle—Nicomachean Ethics Book Six* (Cambridge, England, 1909), pp. 46–47.
¹¹ οὗ ἄνευ οὐκ ἐνδέχεται, literally: "that without which it is not possible."
¹² "σοφία, while producing happiness, is identical with it: but πολιτική is to happiness as means to end," Alexander Grant, *The Ethics of Aristotle*⁴ (London, 1885), vol. II, p. 336.
¹³ See below.
¹⁴ See note 53 below.
¹⁵ See Ackrill "*Eudaimonia,*" p. 32; and Cooper, *Reason and Human Good*, pp. 149–50.
¹⁶ συμβλητός, compare *Pol.* III.12.1283a3 ff.
¹⁷ ὁ ἀπολαυστικὸς βίος, I.5.1095b17.
¹⁸ ὁ πολιτικὸς βίος, I.5.1095b18.
¹⁹ ὁ φιλόσοφος βίος, *E.E.* I.4.1215b1.
²⁰ ὁ γεωργικὸς βίος, *Pol.* I.8.1256b5.
²¹ ὁ στρατιωτικὸς βίος, *Pol.* II.9.1270a5.
²² See J. A. Stewart, *Notes on the Nicomachean Ethics of Aristotle* (Oxford, 1892), vol. II, pp. 443–45.
²³ This last life is not mentioned by Aristotle.
²⁴ For the divinity or quasi-divinity of νοῦς, see X.7.1177a13–17, b30–31 and *De An.* I.4.408b18–31.
²⁵ See the note to 1177a6–9 in R. A. Gauthier and J. Y. Jolif, *Aristote: l'Éthique à Nicomaque*² (Louvain, 1970).
²⁶ But for Aristotle, unlike Plato, life has three phases, not two: *work* (ἀσχολία) relieved by *play*, and *leisure* (σχολή). Play is for the sake of work, which is in turn for the sake of leisure (X.7.1177b4–6; *Pol.* VII.14.1333a30–36, 15.1334a14–16, VIII.3.1337b28–1338a1, 5.1339b15–17). See also Friedrich Solmsen's perceptive article "Leisure and Play in Aristotle's Ideal State," *Kleine Schriften* (Hildesheim, 1968), vol. II. Reprinted from *Rheinisches Museum für Philologie* CVII (1964).
²⁷ For the comparison of theoretical and practical activity, which runs throughout the argument, see 1177a21–22 (θεωρεῖν-πράττειν), a28–34 (ὁ σοφός versus ὁ δίκαιος, ὁ σώφρων, and so forth), b2–4, 16–24, 29; and in Chapter 8 see especially 1178b20–21.
²⁸ For the various formulations of Aristotle's conclusion see 1177a16–18, b24–26, 1178a7–8, b7–8, b32, 1179a31–32.

385

²⁹ ". . . la vie contemplative est pour Aristote un élément de la vie idéale, elle n'est pas, à elle seule, *toute* la vie idéale" (Gauthier and Jolif, *Aristote*, vol. II, p. 862). See also Stewart, *Notes*, vol. I, pp. 59–62; vol. II, pp. 443–45.

³⁰ It has often been pointed out that when Aristotle says that happiness requires a τέλειος βίος or a τέλειος χρόνος or a μῆκος βίου τέλειον (I.7.1098a18–20, 10.1101a8–16, X.7.1177b24–26), he must be using τέλειος in this third sense. If happiness can be lost and regained (1101a8–16), the μῆκος βίου τέλειον required for happiness must be somewhat less than the span of life from birth to death—the τέλειος βίος required for happiness cannot be a *complete* life. It seems rather to be a span of life that is sufficient to attain the τέλος of human life. See Stewart, *Notes*, and Gauthier and Jolif, *Aristote, ad loc.*

³¹ Cooper complains that the six reasons Aristotle gives at 1177a18–b26 do "not tend to show that [contemplative] activity would reasonably be pursued as a dominant end in anyone's life" even though, according to Cooper, this is just what Aristotle infers from them (*Reason and Human Good*, pp. 156–57). Cooper thinks, however, that the immediately succeeding passage, 1177b26–1178a22, contains a more intelligible reason for endorsing strict intellectualism (pp. 157 ff.).

³² ὁ πρακτικὸς νοῦς (*De An.* III.10.433a13–15).

³³ This possibility is suggested by Aristotle's use of τὸ διανοητικόν to describe it, διάνοια being Aristotle's generic term for thinking in general (see VI.2.1139a26–31 and *Met.* E.1.1025b25).

³⁴ ὁ θεωρητικὸς νοῦς (*De An.* III.9.432b26–28, 10.433a14–15).

³⁵ For a detailed analysis of the differences between the passage in Book X and the two in Book IX see the excellent discussion in Cooper, *Reason and Human Good*, pp. 169–75.

³⁶ See p. 368 above.

³⁷ See Daniel T. Devereux, "Aristotle on the Active and Contemplative Lives," *Philosophical Research Archives* III (1977):840–41.

³⁸ See p. 364-5 above.

³⁹ See D. F. Pears, "Aristotle's Analysis of Courage," *Midwest Studies in Philosophy* III (1978); and D. F. Pears, "Courage as a Mean," in *Essays on Aristotle's Ethics*, ed. Rorty.

⁴⁰ On τὸ καλόν as an end of action and τὸ αἰσχρόν as an object of avoidance, see III.7.1115b11–13, 23–24, 1116a11–12, 15; 8.1116a28–32, b2–3, 19, 30–31, 1117a8, 16–17; 9.1117b9, 14–15; 12.1119b16; IV.1.1120a23–24, 1121b4–5; 2.1122b6–7, 1123a24–25; IX.8.1169a21–22, 28, 32, 35; X.8.1178b13; and *E.E.* III.1.1229a2, 1230a29–33.

⁴¹ See I.1.1094a6–9 and III.9.1117b7–8. When Aristotle says in speaking of bravery that "it is not the case, then, with all the virtues that their exercise is pleasant, except in so far as one attains the end" (III.9.1117b15–16), the end in question is the external end. See also III.3.1112b33.

⁴² On Hector's motivation, see III.8.1116 a21–29.

⁴³ On this topic, see also the notes on 1139b1, 1176b7, and 1177b1–26 in J. L. Ackrill, *Aristotle's Ethics*.

⁴⁴ *Scil.* of the two pre-eminent human activities. *Happiness*, of course, is loved for its own sake.

ARISTOTLE

⁴⁵ *Aristotle's Ethical Theory*² (Oxford, 1980), p. 356.

⁴⁶ Aristotle's assertion that "from practical activities we gain more or less apart from the action" seems itself to be an overstatement, for there are actions such as bravely facing death from a terminal illness that have no external end but are performed entirely for their own sakes (see Pears, "Aristotle's Analysis," p. 274, and "Courage," p. 185).

⁴⁷ If it be objected that Aristotle, in giving his final account of happiness in X.6–9, seems to have forgotten his (implicit) distinction between an internal and an external end of action, the reply is that the internal end of action is alluded to twice in the course of these chapters: see X.6.1176b6–9 and 8.1178b12–13.

⁴⁸ See Ackrill, *Aristotle's Ethics, ad loc.*

⁴⁹ Stewart, *Notes, ad loc.*

⁵⁰ See p. 365 above and the note on 1137a11 in Stewart, *Notes.*

⁵¹ For further discussion of Cooper's interpretation of 1178b3–7 see Hardie, *Aristotle's Ethical Theory*², p. 422.

⁵² A. W. H. Adkins, "*Theoria* versus *Praxis* in the *Nicomachean Ethics* and the *Republic*," *Classical Philology* 73 (1978):301.

⁵³ On my interpretation, the superstructure view, which finds its full expression in X.7–8, is foreshadowed in Book I and developed in stages in the intermediate books. The ethical foundations of a life exemplifying this ideal are sketched in the books on the moral virtues (II–V) and on friendship (VIII–IX) and in the sections of Book VI on the practical intellect (VI.1–2, 4–5, 8–13); the intellectual superstructure of such a life is described in VI.3, 6–7.

In *The Aristotelian Ethics* Kenny argues that the three books shared by the *Nicomachean Ethics* and the *Eudemian Ethics* (*E.N.* V–VII = *E.E.* IV–VI) originally belonged to the *Eudemian Ethics*. One of his arguments is that the remarks on happiness in the common books fit the "inclusive, organic view of happiness" of the remainder of the *Eudemian Ethics* better than they fit the "dominant, intellectualist" view of Books I and X of the *Nicomachean Ethics* (pp. 190–214). Like Cooper, the kind of intellectualism that Kenny finds in X.7–8 is strict intellectualism: ". . . Aristotle's doctrine [in X.7–8] cannot be taken to be that there is a single happy life consisting primarily of the exercise of learning and secondarily of the exercise of the other virtues" (p. 209, n. 1). This argument is, of course, undermined if, as I maintain, the superstructure view rather than strict intellectualism is the doctrine of X.7–8.

In writing this paper I profited from a number of discussions with Fred Miller.

387

CHUNG-HWAN CHEN

Aristotle's Analysis of Change and Plato's Theory of Transcendent Ideas

I

JAEGER found evidence of Platonism in Aristotle's *Eudemus*, and commented that "at that time Aristotle was still completely dependent on Plato in metaphysics."[1] Further he discovered a fragment of Aristotle's *Protrepticus* (since then numbered 13[2]), and showed in detail that αὐτῶν θεατής there refers to Plato's Ideas.[3] Thus, for the first time in the history of the study of Aristotle it was asserted that there was a Platonic period in the development of his thought. Among the opponents to this view was I. Düring who wrote repeatedly to the effect "that Aristotle never accepted the theory of Ideas" of Plato.[4]

1. In discussing Düring's position Cornelia J. de Vogel reformulated his question by adding the word "transcendent" to make his meaning more explicit. Thus she asks: "Did Aristotle ever accept Plato's theory of transcendent Ideas?"[5] This addition is correct because Plato's Ideas, according to Aristotle in Book M of the *Metaphysics*, are the universals of Socrates made transcendent.[6] Since transcendence is the distinguishing mark of Ideas, "Plato's Ideas" implicitly means "transcendent Ideas."

2. She is also correct from a methodological standpoint in taking into consideration such matters as Aristotle's positive theory in the second book of the *Physics* when she discussed whether or not *Protr*. Fr. 13 contains Plato's theory of transcendent Ideas.[7] Since the question is Aristotle's acceptance or non-acceptance of Plato's theory of transcendent Ideas, it is unjustifiable from a methodological standpoint to limit oneself in discussing the problem to Aristotle's criticism of Plato and yet neglect the positive part

This paper was presented at the 1972 Boston meeting of the Society for Ancient Greek Philosophy and published in *Phronesis* vol. 20, no. 2 (1975):129–45; we thank the editors and Royal VanGorcum Company for permission to reprint.

Chung-Hwan Chen was Professor of Philosophy at the University of South Florida at the time of presentation of this paper; he has since retired to Oxnard, California.

of Aristotle's own thought. One should examine the constructive part as well as the destructive part to see whether or not there are any remnants of Plato's theory of transcendent Ideas contained in it, not just in any respect, but solely in respect of transcendence. Such a carry-over constitutes evidence of acceptance, while the inference from the unfavorable criticism to the rejection of the theory criticized is indirect and subject to erroneous inference in many ways, e.g., one may overlook the distinctions involved in Aristotle's discussion of the problem of χωρισμός. Let us consider the distinctions in question.

3. I have taken the term "transcendent Ideas" directly from de Vogel. The meaning of the phrase, however, requires elucidation in order to reach an unambiguous answer to the question proposed. I understand it in the following way, without assuming that de Vogel does too: "transcendent Ideas" is a translation of χωρισταὶ ἰδέαι. The original phrase was not Plato's but rather was coined by Aristotle. The linguistic basis of the coinage is most likely the passage in the *Parmenides*: χωρὶς μὲν εἴδη αὐτὰ ἄττα, χωρὶς δὲ τὰ τούτων αὖ μετέχοντα.[8] This is an extreme type of χωρισμός,[9] the reciprocal χωρισμός between Ideas and their particular instances. Plato's usual form, though not expressed in technical terminology, is, e.g., the opposition between τὰ ἴσα and αὐτὸ τὸ ἴσον with the stress laid on the χωρισμός of the Idea.[10] The παρά in a context like this *Phaedo* passage indicates transcendence. The Idea of the Equal transcends the corresponding instances of equality in the sense that it is separate from them. So do other Ideas.

This is one sense of "transcendent Ideas." Although it is the most prominent sense, and almost the only sense which is usually understood or stressed, there are two other senses which must be distinguished from it. E.g., when a carpenter looking to the Idea of Shuttle makes a shuttle,[11] the Idea transcends not only the wooden shuttle to be made (and even the one which has been made), but also the mind of the carpenter. This is the realism of Plato; the attempt in another passage to make Ideas subjective is immediately refuted.[12] This is the second sense of "transcendent Ideas": Ideas transcend the human mind.

There is still a third sense. According to the Platonic story of "creation" in the *Timaeus*, God created the world looking to the intelligible pattern.[13] Since a παράδειγμα necessarily implies χωρισμός, there is another sense of "transcendent Ideas": they transcend the divine mind.

But if, when one discusses whether Aristotle ever accepted Plato's transcendent Ideas, he keeps in view only these three senses, it will be far from sufficient. The problem of χωρισμός for Aristotle was very complicated. He distinguished three main types of χωρισμός (designated χωριστὸν ἁπλῶς, χωριστὸν λόγῳ, and χωριστὸν νοήσει, the

ESSAYS IN ANCIENT GREEK PHILOSOPHY

expressions for the first two being again various).[14] If "transcendent" is an appropriate translation of χωριστός, it is appropriate for the first type only. The present paper will be limited to the first type of χωρισμός since that will be enough to accomplish its purpose and to take all the three types into consideration would far surpass its scope.

Even within this limitation one has to pay attention to three other points in Aristotle's treatment of the problem of χωρισταὶ ἰδέαι or χωριστὰ εἴδη. One must on each occasion specify the following points in the given context: (1) what that is which is separate (τί χωριστόν), (2) from what it is separate (τίνος χωριστόν), and (3), how it is separate (πῶς χωριστόν). The three senses of transcendence in Plato's theory all fall under point (2),[15] but they do not coincide completely with it. There are also further distinctions among the τίνων in the sense of "what those things are from which the particulars are separate."

4. From the foregoing considerations it follows: (1) In order to prove the thesis that Aristotle never accepted Plato's theory of transcendent Ideas, one has to show that wherever in the *Corpus Aristotelicum* the author is concerned with the problem of the χωρισμός of εἴδη (whether in the sense of Plato's Ideas or his own forms), he denies the χωρισμός absolutely or at least he does not affirm it even relatively. (2) In order to disprove the same thesis, one has to show that in at least one passage where Aristotle is concerned with the same problem (whether with regard to Plato's Ideas or his own forms) he does not deny the χωρισμός absolutely or at least affirms it relatively. By "absolutely" is meant "without regard to what those εἴδη are whose separation (χωρισμός) is in question, what those things are the separation from which is at issue and what are the ways in which the separation of the former from the latter is to be ascertained." By "relatively" is meant "with regard to the specification in each case." It is in terms of these methodological requirements that the present paper will evaluate Düring's thesis. Since (2) does not require an examination of the whole *corpus Aristotelicum*, I limit myself to those well-known passages where Aristotle analyzes change (γίγνεσθαι, γένεσις).

II

The distinction of ὄντα into categories is fundamental in Aristotle's metaphysics. According to the treatise *Categories* they are classified into four groups: (1) universals in the primary category, or the category of substance; (2) particular attributes in the secondary categories, the category of quantity, quality, etc. (3) universal attributes in the secondary categories; (4) the particulars in the primary category.[16] From the viewpoint of the *Catego-*

390

ries Platonic Ideas must be assigned to different categories. The problem of whether Aristotle ever did accept Plato's theory of transcendent Ideas should be considered in the light of these distinctions. First, we shall analyze his view on the χωρισμός of Groups 2 and 3 from primary substances.

1. In the *Categories* Aristotle teaches that members of all secondary categories, both universals and particulars, e.g., τὸ λευκόν and τὶ λευκόν are inherent in the primary substances. Since the *Categories* (if it is authentic) must be among his early writings, it seems that this theory of inherence favors the thesis that Aristotle never accepted Plato's theory of transcendent Ideas. But if one argues in this way, he proceeds to the conclusion too hastily. Even if the philological problems involved here are set aside,[17] this conclusion will still not follow. In the last section of *Cat.* 5 Aristotle points out the most distinguishing mark of substances, more exactly, the primary substance. The primary substance is the only entity which, being numerically one and the same, is capable of admitting contrary attributes, e.g., one and the same man becomes pale at one time and dark at another, bad at one time and good at another.[18] He does it by self-changing.[19] As he is bad, the quality φαῦλον is inherent in him, and the quality σπουδαῖον is apart from him. When he becomes good, the quality σπουδαῖον is in him, and the quality φαῦλον is apart from him.[20] This is a dynamic account of the relation of accidental attributes to a primary substance, supplementary to the foregoing static analysis. With this dynamic account in view, can anyone suppose that Aristotle absolutely denies the χωρισμός of σπουδαῖον, φαῦλον, etc., from the man who is bad, good, etc., at the time when he is such and such? Even if we look only to the result of the theory of inherence in the *Categories* without considering what is Aristotle's purpose there, we can at most say that Aristotle denies the χωρισμός of members of secondary categories from the primary substances only conditionally.

2. a. From here on through section 3 we shall analyze Aristotle's view on the χωρισμός of Group 1, more exactly, substantial forms in the primary category, from individual substances. We now turn to his *Physics*, and first consider its second book because de Vogel attaches considerable importance to "the theory of teleology in nature" in this book as decisive for the question of Aristotle's rejection of Platonic transcendent Ideas. She does not discuss this book in detail, but assumes the theory as well-known and uses it finally in an attempt to prove that αὐτῶν θεατής in *Protr*. Fr. 13 cannot refer to transcendent Ideas. Let us quote her own words: "The theory of teleology in nature" in *Phys*. II is "the theory of an immanent 'end,' which is realized in the natural objects, which is their 'essence' and their 'good'—this theory which for Aristotle took the place of Plato's theory of transcendent Ideas is already clear in the *Protrepticus*."[21] We shall omit the part of this

quotation which concerns the *Protrepticus* and concentrate on the teleology in nature in *Phys.* II.

First we have to ascertain what she means by "the theory of teleology in nature." If she means the theory which holds that the γένεσις of natural objects is telic, that is correct. However, Aristotle speaks not of "an immanent 'end' which is realized in the natural objects," but of "ends," one for each species. The generation of a human being has the εἶδος ἀνθρώπου and the generation of a horse has the εἶδος ἵππου for their respective ends, but there is no common "end" or εἶδος in the sense of that toward which (εἰς ὅ) the development of human beings, horses, etc., proceed.

This is a general explanation, but we need a more exact exposition of the theory of natural generation. For this purpose the following passage will serve as the basis of our interpretation: μέχρι δὴ πόσου τὸν φυσικὸν δεῖ εἰδέναι τὸ εἶδος καὶ τὸ τί ἐστιν; . . . μέχρι τοῦ τίνος [γὰρ] ἕνεκα ἕκαστον καὶ περὶ ταῦτα ἅ ἐστι χωριστὰ μὲν εἴδει, ἐν ὕλῃ δέ;[22] To know the form to the extent of knowing the end is justified by the frequent coincidence of formal, final, and efficient causes.[23] ταῦτα is not clearly explained by Ross; it refers to the end of generations of natural objects. In respect of their being forms[24] they are separate from the γιγνόμενα, i.e., from the substrata which undergo the processes of generation, but they are immanent in the bodies of the generators. The end of generation of a human being qua form is separate from him who has not yet come to be, but immanent in the male parent. Thus this passage denies the transcendence of the εἶδος ἀνθρώπου as the form of man from the male parent, but affirms that the εἶδος ἀνθρώπου as the end transcends that which is becoming but has not yet come to be. It must be χωριστὸν τοῦ γιγνομένου, for (to borrow a word from de Vogel) it is not yet "realized." If it were not χωριστόν, the γιγνόμενον would no longer be what it is; instead it would be a new human being. But, as a matter of fact, at the moment he is not yet there. How can it be in a thing which has not yet come to be or which does not yet exist?

To understand Aristotle's view more precisely, one must take into consideration the difference between actuality and potentiality. The form is potentially in, and actually transcends, the substratum, the γιγνόμενον, so long as the latter has not reached the end of the process of generation. Since for Aristotle actuality is prior to potentiality, the actual separation should be stressed rather than the potential immanence.[25]

The alternation of two kinds of status, χωρὶς εἶναι and ἐνεῖναι, of one and the same εἶδος as the τίνος and the τίνι vary is still clearer in the sentence following the above quotation: ἄνθρωπος γὰρ ἄνθρωπον γεννᾷ.[26] This sentence is best explained by a passage in *Met.* Z[27] where it is repeated in order to explain that φύσις in the sense of form[28] as the efficient cause of natural generation is the same φύσις in a different member of the same species (in the case of human generation the efficient cause is the form of man immanent in the male parent). In this passage the transcendence of efficient cause is not brought out as clearly as its immanence, but in *Met.* Λ both are equally clearly stated. ἐπὶ μὲν οὖν τινῶν τὸ τόδε τι οὐχ ἔστι παρὰ τὴν συνθετὴν οὐσίαν, οἷον οἰκίας τὸ εἶδος . . .[29] ἀλλ᾽ εἴπερ, ἐπὶ τῶν φύσει.[30] We ask: πῶς? Aristotle answers: τὰ μὲν οὖν κινοῦντα αἴτια ὡς προγεγενημένα ὄντα, τὰ δ᾽ ὡς λόγος ἅμα.[31] Efficient causes (the εἴδη) as they precede the final results of the process, the γεγονότα, are separate from the latter and as formal causes are at the same time with, i.e., immanent in, τὰ καθ᾽ ἕκαστον.

To sum up, concerning the εἶδος in the sphere of natural generation Aristotle's view is: (1) εἶδος in the sense of formal cause is immanent in its particular instances (τὰ καθ᾽ ἕκαστον), but not without qualification. It is immanent in those which are actually existent as such, but separate from those which are undergoing the process of generation and have not yet come to be. (2) As efficient cause it is (a) immanent in the generator as its form and (b) separate from (i) that which is undergoing the process of generation and (ii) that which is generated. (3) As the final cause, it is similar to the efficient with respect to its transcendence and immanence in (a) and (b) (i) but different from (ii), namely, it is immanent in the γεγονός as its form. In any case Aristotle's "theory of teleology in nature" did not take the place of Plato's theory of transcendent Ideas; both transcendence and immanence find their place side by side in this theory, though not without qualification in each case. A more adequate interpretation would be that Aristotle retains Plato's theory of transcendent Ideas with such modifications as the distinctions in the subject-matter itself require.

b. The primary substances in the *Categories* in fact comprise both natural and artificial objects, though no example of the latter is given there. (Such examples are abundant in other places in the Aristotelian corpus.) We may consider Aristotle's theory of *genesis* in the first book of the *Physics* to help us to understand his view on the problem of χωρισμός in the sphere of artificial production. According to the result of his analysis change is a process between contraries;[32] what changes is always coupled with one of the contraries at the *terminus a quo* and with the other at the *terminus ad quem*. It is never something simple, but always a duplex of ὑποκείμενον, and στέρησις or εἶδος.[33] In the case of the substantial change or "simple *genesis*," e.g., the building of a house, before the house is built its materials (ὑποκείμενον) such as bricks and stones lie asunder, and when it has been built they are arranged in such a way that the form of the house is embodied in it.[34] εἶδος taken together with στέρησις to form a contrariety in any kind of change is employed in a general sense; when it is used to refer to change in the primary category it has the narrow sense of substantial form.[35] So the form of house is inherent in the house built. That this is Aristotle's view is testified to by his describing the house as σύνθετον.[36]

However, we cannot infer from this that Aristotle here rejected Plato's theory of transcendent Ideas because—as Solmsen properly notes—here the problem of the status of the form, whether it is transcendent or immanent, is not even under discussion.[37] The theory as it stands deviates from Plato's theory of transcendent Ideas, but it was not meant to deny the Platonic theory.

Even if we ignore Solmsen's warning, another point must be taken into consideration: The establishment of inherence is ultimately based upon the acceptance of the γεγονός as a σύνθετον. Since that which changes is never a simplex, but always a duplex, then just as it is coupled with the form at the *terminus ad quem* of the process it is coupled with the στέρησις at the *terminus a quo*. That is, at this *terminus* the form transcends the substratum. Here in the sphere of *artefacta* as in the sphere of natural generation, transcendence and immanence, with the necessary modifications, are found side by side; one cannot conclude in simplistic fashion that Aristotle here either did or did not accept Plato's theory of transcendent ideas.

We must also ask how the form of a manufactured object as efficient cause is related to the τεχνικός. The relation is more complicated than that of the form as efficient cause of natural generation to the male parent. In a certain sense, it is true that in the one case as in the other the form is not transcendent. But the πῶς is different. The efficient cause of building a house is immanent in the house-builder not as his substantial form but as an art: the efficient cause of human generation is immanent in the male parent not as a τέχνη but as his εἶδος. Since art or science is an ἕξις, a quality, the form of the house[38] is immanent in the τεχνικός in the way that an accidental attribute is in an individual substance. This is still not the whole explanation of the relation between the form of an *artefactum* and the artisan; it is only the first half, and the second half still remains.

3. In order to complete the unfinished discussion, let us consider first a passage from *Met.* Z 7 and then in the following section we shall come to the *Protrepticus*. (This order should not be taken as having any chronological implications.) In the passage from *Met.* Z 7 Aristotle analyzes another kind of *artefacta*, namely, health. The production of health is a process consisting of two parts, the first of which is νόησις and the second ποίησις. The problem is how to restore health to the patient. The νόησις starts with the definition of health, the art of medicine, in the physician's mind. "Since *this* is health, if the subject is to be healthy, *this* must first be present, e.g.,

a uniform state of body, and if this is to be present there must be heat; and the physician goes on thinking thus until he reduces the matter to a final something" which he can do and then he does it.[39] Here the νόησις stops and the ποίησις begins. The second process runs in the direction opposite to the first process and ends in the presence of health in the patient's body. In the whole process of restoration of health the ποίησις depends upon the νόησις. So far this is the same as the conclusion we reached at the end of the previous section, i.e., the efficient cause of artificial production is the εἶδος ἐν τῇ ψυχῇ or the τέχνη.

The νόησις is strictly determined by the essence of health, whose definition is the medical art in the physician's mind, for if he deviates even a little in his thinking from the essence of health the actual health could not be produced in the body of the patient. The essence of health is the cause in the strict sense of the health which is restored;[40] if the medical art is said to be the cause, it is simply for the reason that the science works in virtue of its objective content, i.e., the essence of health. The essence of health as the object of knowledge transcends the mind of the physician.[41] It is an ὂν κυρίως, τὸ ἔξω ὂν καὶ χωριστόν.[42] Thus we are referred first from the ἰδέα τῆς ὑγιείας as a form of a quality to art or knowledge, and then from knowledge referred again to form as an ἔξω ὂν καὶ χωριστόν. The second reference is just the one Plato made in the refutation of a possible subjectivization of Ideas in the *Parmenides*.[43] In view of this similarity one can hardly say that Aristotle never accepted Plato's theory of transcendent Ideas.

What is true of the εἶδος of health is equally true of the εἶδος of house and the like. These are also ὄντα κυρίως, which do not depend on the knowledge of artisans, but rather the knowledge of the artisans depends on them. From this we can see quite clearly how the second reference is necessary in Aristotle's metaphysics. The knowledge of building a house or architecture as the efficient cause precedes the house to be built. Since knowledge is an ἕξις and house a substance it would follow that quality is prior to substance—and this is impossible according to Aristotle.[44] By the second reference the efficient cause is referred to the essence of house, essence being a substance. Thus the possibility of a contradiction to his substantio-centric metaphysics is avoided. The result is that the essence of house as efficient cause transcends the house to be built.

4. The *Protrepticus*, especially Fr. 13, is the passage most debated as far as the question "Did Aristotle ever accept Plato's theory of transcendent Ideas?" is concerned. A more detailed discussion of this fragment will be found elsewhere,[45] here we shall just make a general inference from Aristotle's analysis of ποίησις. The following points are agreed upon by all scholars: (1) In *Protr.* Fr. 13 Aristotle speaks about how laws should be

made. (2) Lawmaking is an imitation. (3) The original from which laws should be copied is not empirical laws. Parallel to the restoration of health, construction of a house or production of any artificial objects, it follows that the pattern of imitation must be, not a fiction of arbitrary thinking, but rather the nature of what is to be made so that the expected result will certainly follow. Then the patterns from which the laws as-laws-should-be are copied must be ideal patterns.[46] Their archetypical character implies their transcendence. Thus, what the philosopher or the true statesman looks to in making laws can be nothing else but Plato's transcendent Ideas.[47]

III

Before concluding this paper we wish to go a step further so as to see what was the chief difficulty Aristotle found in Plato's theory of transcendent Ideas and what he really did in his treatment of the problem of χωρισμός. This procedure will supply an additional explanation of *Protr.* Fr. 13.

In *Met.* A 9, which is the main source of Aristotle's criticism of Plato's metaphysics, he says: πάντων δὲ μάλιστα διαπορήσειεν ἄν τις τί ποτε συμβάλλεται τὰ εἴδη τοῖς ἀϊδίοις τῶν αἰσθητῶν ἢ τοῖς γιγνομένοις καὶ φθειρομένοις, for (1) they cause no change in the physical objects nor (2) help towards (a) the knowledge of these objects or (b) their being.[48] The reason for (2) is that Ideas are not forms immanent in physical objects. The reason for (1) is that Ideas are neither causes of the motion of heavenly bodies nor of the generation of perishable objects. The causes of change are God in the first case and the generator or artisan in the second. They are particulars; they are not Ideas. But, as we saw above, in natural generation the efficient cause should be extended further to φύσις, the form which is immanent in the generator; in artificial production the efficient cause is instead the Ideas (e.g., ἰδέα τῆς ὑγιείας) in the sense of the science which as a quality is immanent in the mind of the artisan. Except in the case of cosmic motions, the difficulties of Plato's theory all lie in the χωρισμός of the Ideas. This χωρισμός is an impossibility: ἀδύνατον εἶναι χωρὶς τὴν οὐσίαν καὶ οὗ ἡ οὐσία. Then Aristotle concludes with a rhetorical question πῶς ἄν αἱ ἰδέαι οὐσίαι τῶν πραγμάτων οὖσαι χωρὶς εἶεν;[49]

But why did Plato hold to the χωρισμός of Ideas? To answer this question we must begin with an analysis of Plato's Ideas. They are, using Aristotelian terminology, formal causes, the principles of particulars being so-and-so. Let us call this aspect of Ideas the aspect of essence.[50] τῷ καλῷ πάντα τὰ καλὰ καλά. Beauty itself is the cause of bodies, minds, institutions, etc., being beautiful, or the Idea of Equality is the cause of sticks and stones being equal. But there is no beautiful instance which is not also ugly; equal sticks and stones always fall short of the Idea of Equality. Ideas are perfect. This is another aspect of Ideas. Let this aspect be called the *aspect of ideal*. This double aspect is most obvious in the Idea of the Good, the chief Idea among all Ideas, which is itself the highest value and at the same time the ἀρχὴ ἀνυπόθετος of being and becoming.[51]

Plato was attracted by the fact that things are so-and-so, but no one of them is perfectly so-and-so. In order to explain this phenomenon he posited Ideas with the double aspect of essence and ideal. His explanation is the theory of μέθεξις. Particulars are so-and-so because they partake of the nature of their Ideas. E.g., equal sticks participate in the Idea of Equality; hence they are equal. Their participation, however, involves a limitation of their possession of the attribute of being equal to a certain extent and is, therefore, an approximation to the Idea; they can never reach its perfection. The approximation is due to the double aspect of the Idea. The aspect of essence makes them like the Idea, and the aspect of ideal keeps their likeness to the Idea from coinciding with the ideal perfection.

Although this double aspect explains certain facts, it fails to explain certain other facts. So far as the aspect of essence is concerned, the nature of the Idea is shared by the particular instances. The Idea cannot be apart from them. If it were not in them, they would not be what they are. So far as the aspect of ideal is concerned, the Idea cannot be reached by them; it must be apart from them. The difficulty of combining ἐνεῖναι and χωρὶς εἶναι is obvious in certain Ideas, e.g., in the Idea of Shuttle or Bed or the like. But Plato did not speak about these Ideas in detail; he was rather interested in such Ideas as Just Itself, Good Itself, Beauty Itself, etc., which are also ideals. Such a one-sided emphasis is quite understandable in terms of the origin of his Ideas in the objects of Socrates' definition which are τὰ ἠθικά.[52] Aristotle saw the difficulty and pointing, e.g., to a house, says: This house would not have come to be if the form of house were apart from it,[53] and we have already discussed his general formulation of the difficulty.[54] In cases like these Plato's theory must be modified.

Aristotle's modification was to separate the two aspects, retaining the aspect of essence for his substantial forms and leaving out the aspect of ideal.[55] Substantial forms can be reached by particulars; when they are reached, they are immanent in the actually existent particulars. E.g., this animal is either a man or not a man. If it is a man, there is no variation of his being more or less a man.[56] So long as the κύημα is undergoing the process of development, the form Man transcends it, or, more exactly, actually transcends it. As soon as it reaches the end of the process, it is actually so-and-so formed, i.e., the form is actually immanent in it. The transcendence refers to the γιγνόμενον; the immanence refers to the γεγονός. There is an alternation in terms of the end having or not having been reached, but there is no alternation of the end in terms of having been reached in a higher or lower degree since essence is divorced from value. The same is true of the forms of artificial objects. When Aristotle criticizes Plato's transcendent Ideas, he means that the exclusion of the aspect of ideal from the aspect of essence in the substantial forms is necessary.

There is another group of forms. They are Ideas of value. They are ideals and can only be approximated, never reached. Hence they are eternally transcendent. The objects which the philosopher or the true statesman beholds in *Protr*. Fr. 13 are such Ideas. That they are Ideas of value is evident from their status as standards of value judgments.[57] That they cannot be reached is clear from the fact that the good lawgiver does not look to the empirical laws for legislation. The reason for this is that no empirical laws reach the ideal perfection. They approach the ideal more or less; what most fully conforms to it is the best.[58] The aspect of ideal entails eternal transcendence. Here Plato's theory of transcendent Ideas as having a double aspect is perfectly correct; it needs no modification and Aristotle simply accepted it in *Protr*. Fr. 13.[59]

IV

1. We may sum up the results reached as follows:
   I. Ideas as universals in the secondary categories:
      They are inherent in this or that primary substance while their contraries are not (*Cat.*).
   II. Ideas as substantial forms in the primary category:
      1. as forms of natural objects:
         a. as formal cause: the εἶδος is
            (i) immanent in the generator;
            (ii) transcending the γιγνόμενον;[60]
            (iii) immanent in the γεγονός;
         b. as efficient cause:
            (i) immanent in the generator as its form;
            (ii) separate from
               (α) what is undergoing the process
               (β) the generated:
         c. as final cause:
            (i) immanent in the generator as its form;
            (ii) (α) separate from what is undergoing the process of being generated;
               (β) immanent in the γεγονός as its form (*Phys*. II, *Met*. Λ, Z);

2. As forms of artificial objects, e.g., house, parallel to 1. (*Phys.* I, *Met.* Λ, Z):
   a. with the exception that as efficient cause and as final cause the εἶδος is immanent in the τεχνικός as art or science in his mind (*Met.* Λ, Z);
   b. with the peculiarity that as essence of the *artefactum* it transcends his knowledge or skill (*Met.* Γ, E).

Appendix: as forms of nonsubstantial *artefacta*:
   a. as forms of physical qualities created by man, e.g., health; the same as 2;
   b. as forms of value: they transcend the particular instances and the minds of agents (*Protr.*).

Aristotle did not discuss the third type of transcendence of Plato's Ideas, (Ideas transcending God's mind). But his view may be obtained from *Met.* Λ: they are separated from God's mind in the sense that God does not think of them at all.[61]

2. The table shows clearly that in none of the passages discussed does Aristotle deny the χωρισμός of Ideas absolutely. He either does not deny it or denies it relatively and also affirms it relatively. Only a failure to analyze the problem will lead one to the proposition that Aristotle always accepted Plato's theory of transcendent Ideas or that Aristotle never accepted it. One is no more tenable than the other. The *A*-proposition is not made by anyone. The *E*-proposition is fought for by Düring. To disprove the *E*-proposition a single *I*-proposition is enough, and each of the cases discussed above provides the basis for an *I*-proposition. The historical truth is not what Düring supposes it to be, but rather that Aristotle accepted Plato's theory of transcendent Ideas with modifications as the distinctions in the subject-matter under discussion on each occasion required. In so far as Ideas were ontological forms they were modified. The modifications are seen in Pt. II, Nos. 1–3. In so far as Ideas of value were ideals, no modification was needed; Plato's theory was simply accepted (Pt. II, No. 4, Pt. III, the last paragraph).

NOTES

[1] *Aristotle*, trans. R. Robinson, 2nd ed. (1948), p. 53.

[2] This fragment (Iambl. *Protr.* 10) was not included in V. Rose's *Aristotelis qui ferebantur librorum fragmenta*; R. Walzer numbers it as Fr. 13 in his *Aristotelis Dialogorum Fragmenta* (1934). Sir David Ross includes it as Fr. 13 in his *Aristotelis Fragmenta Selecta* (1945).

[3] Jaeger, *Aristotle*, pp. 90–91, especially n. 2 on p. 91.

[4] Düring's other writings besides his *Aristoteles* (1966) are "Problems in Aris-

totle's Protrepticus," *Eranos* 52 (1954):130–71; "Aristotle in the Protrepticus," *Autour d' Aristote* (1955); "Aristotle the Scholar," *Arctos, Acta Philologica Fennica* (1954), pp. 61–77; "Aristotle on Ultimate Principles from 'Nature and Reality,'" *Aristotle and Plato in the Mid-Fourth Century* (1961), pp. 35–55.

⁵ *Archiv für die Geschichte der Philosophie* 47 (1965):261–98.

⁶ 4, 1078 b 30–32.

⁷ de Vogel, *Archiv*, pp. 181–84. My approval applies only to her method; with (1) her interpretation of *Phys.* II, (2) the application of her interpretation to *Protr.* Fr. 13, and (3) the inference on the question of the Platonic element in *Protr.* Fr. 13, I can in no way agree. For (1) cf. below II, 2a; my comments on (2) and (3) will be reserved for another occasion.

⁸ 130 b 2–3. Cf., e.g., *Met.* A 9, 991 b 1–3.

⁹ The word χωρισμός is translated into English usually as "separation." As a philosophical term used by Aristotle it indicates independence. Since he distinguishes χωρισμός into different types, the meaning of "independence" varies accordingly. For different types of χωρισμός see p. 389–390. The extreme type is the χωρισμὸς ἁπλοῦς. The word ἁπλοῦς indicates that this type of χωρισμός is the primary type. Aristotle understands the transcendence of Plato's Ideas in this sense.

¹⁰ *Phaed.* 74 a 9–12.

¹¹ *Crat.* 389 b ff.

¹² *Parm.* 132 b–c.

¹³ 28 e–29 a.

¹⁴ See H. Bonitz, *Index Aristotelicus*, p. 860 a 22 ff.

¹⁵ Plato did not make a distinction among Ideas with respect to χωρισμός; all of them are similarly transcendent.

¹⁶ *Cat.* 2, 1a 20–b 6.

¹⁷ The chief problem is whether Aristotle in the *Categories* purposely attacks Plato's theory of transcendent Ideas. We have no evidence to affirm this.

¹⁸ 4 a 10–21.

¹⁹ *Cat.* 4 a 29–34, b 2–4.

²⁰ We must note that there is an ambiguity and a difficulty here. It is ambiguous whether the quality in question is τὶ λευκόν or τὸ λευκόν or both indiscriminately. If it is τὶ λευκόν, it is a very inexact way of speaking to say τὶ λευκόν, the shade of paleness which a man had, is χωρίς from him when he has become dark, because it has ceased to exist. If it is τὸ λευκόν, there is no such difficulty because universals in the secondary categories are from the very beginning of the *Categoriae* said to be predicated of particulars in the same categories. If this shade of paleness perishes, τὸ λευκόν does not perish. If it did, how could it still be predicated of other shades of paleness? How could the latter still be such? It is not unlikely that this difficulty was the reason, or one of the reasons, why Aristotle later gave up the distinction between τὶ λευκόν and τὸ λευκόν, and the similar distinction in all secondary categories—or rather gave up the use of τὶ λευκόν and the like.

²¹ de Vogel, *Archiv*, p. 282.

²² 2, 194 b 9–13, Ross' reading.

²³ 7, 198 a 24–26, Ross' reading.

²⁴ 194 b 9–15 is a "difficile passage," as A. Mansion observes in his *Introduction à la Physique Aristotélicienne*, 2nd. ed., p. 204, n. 17. "The reading and punctuation of this sentence [194 b 10–11] were debated by the ancient commentators (See Ross *ad. loc., Aristotle's Physics*, p. 510–511) . . ." (F. M. Cornford's note to P. H. Wicksteed's edition and translation of *Aristotle's Physics*, vol. I, p. 125, *n.*d.). I accept Ross's reading and punctuation, but this does not remove all the difficulties. The clause καὶ περὶ ταῦτα ἅ ἐστι χωριστὰ μὲν εἴδει, ἐν ὕλῃ δέ (b 12–13) still needs explanation. What does ταῦτα refer to? What does εἴδει mean? The translations of R. P. Hardie and R. K. Gaye (*The Works of Aristotle*, vol. 2), H. Carteron (French translation), and W. Charlton (*Aristotle's Physics*, I, II) do not suggest any answer to the first question. Wicksteed translates it by "forms," Ross understands it the same way in his commentary (Aristotle's *Physics*, p. 510 and p. 351. If they are correct, the text would mean καὶ περὶ τὰ εἴδη ἅ ἐστι χωριστὰ μὲν εἴδει . . . this leads to the second question, what does εἴδει mean? εἴδει cannot refer to the same thing as εἴδη refers to. If it did, what could the whole expression mean? Ross interprets χωριστὰ εἴδει by "separable in thought," Wicksteed by "conceptually . . . detachable"; Charlton by "in account." It is true, of course, that Aristotle often uses the expression χωριστὸν λόγῳ. But in such contexts λόγος means a definition (cf., e.g., *Met.* H 1, 1042 a 28–29) which is objective, and not the same as "in thought," which is subjective. εἴδει is even further removed from the notion "conceptually." Aristotle's standing terminology for these English translations is rather νοήσει (e.g., *Phys.* II 2, 193 b 34). If these translators and commentators are correct, why should Aristotle have not written καὶ περὶ τὰ εἴδη ἅ ἐστι χωριστὰ μὲν νοήσει . . .? That would be his usual style and its meaning would also be clear. He had no reason to prefer the obscure expression to the clear one. εἴδει has an objective sense; it means in respect of species or form, in contrast to ἀριθμῷ (e.g., *Met.* Δ 9, 1018 a 6; cf. 6, 1016 b 31–32). E.g., two members of the same species, which have the same form, are ταὐτὰ εἴδει and ἕτερα ἀριθμῷ; two members of two different species, which have different forms, are ἕτερα εἴδει; one and the same individual is ἓν ἀριθμῷ.

In the clause in question εἴδει must mean the same as εἴδει in b 10 means, namely, "form." Then ταῦτα cannot refer to forms. Its meaning follows from the preceding clause b 11–12 with the supplementation as suggested by Mansion (*Introduction à la Physique*, p. 204, n. 17). It refers to τὸ τίνος ἕνεκα ἕκαστον, the ends of generations of natural objects. It may seem that εἴδει could have its usual meaning "in respect of species" because the τέλος of the generation of man and the τέλος of the generation of horse are separate in kind. But it cannot have this meaning here because in the context Aristotle does not stress the different kinds of species. From b 9 on he is speaking of the coincidence of formal and final causes. I understand the clause in question as meaning "*qua* forms they are separate"—but from what? From those whose ends they are, i.e., from the γιγνόμενα. (This type of χωρισμός is the χωρισμὸς ἐπὶ γενέσεως. For the terminology cf. *Met.* Γ 2, 1003 b 29.) But these ends in the sense of forms are immanent in the bodies of the generators.

²⁵ For the sake of convenience cf. *Met.* Θ 8; priority is not limited to the temporal (for the different senses of priority cf. *Met.* Δ 11). For the stress on actuality rather on potentiality, cf., e.g., *Phys.* II 1, 193 b 7–8.

²⁶ 194 b 13.

²⁷ 7, 1032 a 24–25.

²⁸ *Phys.* II 1, 193 a 30 ff.

²⁹ For the omission of 1070 a 14–15 cf. below n. 38 and Part II, sect. 3 of this paper.

³⁰ 1070 a 13–17.

³¹ 1070 a 21–22.

³² 5, 188 a 19–b 8. For the sake of brevity we may neglect the intermediate states.

³³ 7, 190 a 13–16, b 23–24, b 11–13.

³⁴ In general, see 190 b 9 ff. The example of οἰκία is mentioned in 190 b 8; εἶδος is mentioned in b 28 and μορφή in b 20.

³⁵ This sense of εἶδος is confirmed by the term μορφή in 190 b 20. For the sense of μορφή see *Met.* Z 8, 1033 b 6.

³⁶ *Phys.* I 7, 190 b 11.

³⁷ *Aristotle's System of the Physical World*, p. 86.

³⁸ *Met.* Λ 3, 1070 a 14–15. That the εἶδος of an *artefactum* is the τέχνη is also asserted in *Met.* Z 7. See the following section for the discussion of this passage.

³⁹ 1032 b 15 ff., Ross' translation.

⁴⁰ *Met.* Z 7, 1032 b 5–6, 11–14. ἰατρική is a λόγος, a λόγος τῆς ὑγιείας. This λόγος has an objective content, which is the essence of health. Therefore the ὑγίεια ἄνευ ὕλης is the cause of the ὑγίεια ἔχουσα ὕλην. For the relation of the medical art, the λόγος τῆς ὑγιείας, to its objective content, see the following note.

⁴¹ Cf. *Met.* Γ 5, 1010 b 30–1011 a 1. There Aristotle speaks of the priority of the ὑποκείμενα which cause sensation over the sensation. For the sensation is not of itself, but of the substrata. Parallel to this perceptual realism there is in his epistemology an intellectual realism. Intellectual knowledge like perceptual knowledge is an affection by the intelligible (*De an.* III, 4 429 a 13–15). In the case of ἰατρική, the art is determined by the essence of health. So the latter is τὸ αἴτιον τὸ ἀκρότατον of the restoration of health. For the concept of "the most precise cause" see *Phys.* II 3, 195 b 21–25, though there (for the sake of illustration) the ascent is only from the ἰατρικὸς to the art.

⁴² *Met.* E 4, 1027 b 31, K 8, 1065 a 24.

⁴³ 132 b–c.

⁴⁴ See, e.g., *Met.* Z 13, 1038 b 26–28. For the argument for the priority of substance, see Z 1, 1028 a 30 ff.

⁴⁵ In my *Sophia The Science Aristotle Sought* (Hildesheim, 1976).

⁴⁶ For the Platonic term παράδειγμα used by Aristotle in the same way to signify εἶδος, see *Phys.* II 3, 194 b 26.

⁴⁷ It is just impossible to interpret the objects the true statesman beholds in making laws "against the background of *Anal. Post.* A 2" (Düring, *Mid-Fourth*

Century, p. 48), for in that chapter Aristotle deals with the principles of demonstration, which can never be the originals of the laws of any state.

48 991 a 8–14.

49 991 b 1–3.

50 The term *essence*, τὸ τί ἦν εἶναι, is borrowed from Aristotle, but it is not an anachronism since the Aristotelian concept is traceable to Plato (cf. *Crat.* 368 a, d–e).

51 *Rep.* VI 511 b.

52 Cf. *Met.* A 6, 987 b 1–7, M 4, 1078 b 30–31.

53 *Met.* Z 8, 1033 b 19–21.

54 Pt. III, second paragraph.

55 In this way one group of Plato's Ideas, i.e., ontological Ideas, was turned into Aristotelian essences. By "separate" is not meant that the essence is not good, but that value does not belong to essence καθ' αὑτό although it does belong concomitantly.

56 *Cat.* 5, 2 b 26–27, 3 b 33–4 a 9.

57 Ross, *Fragmenta*, p. 48, lines 5–7.

58 Ross, *Fragmenta*, p. 49, lines 10–23, 8–9.

59 This interpretation is not incompatible with the general theory in the *Categories* that the universals in the secondary categories are immanent in the primary substances. There Aristotle does not have Ideas of value in view. This is evident from his regarding δικαιοσύνη as a διάθεσις (8, 10 b 30–32). His approach is ontological or psychological, but not from the view point of value.

One might object by pointing to the definition of moral virtue in *Eth. Nic.* as an ἕξις προαιρετική . . . II 6, 1106 b 36. But virtue as ἕξις is only one of its aspects, the ontological aspect; it still has another aspect, the aspect of value. The double aspect is most clearly seen in Aristotle's additional explanation given after the definition of moral virtue in order to prevent a possibly one-sided conception. He says διὸ κατὰ μὲν τὴν οὐσίαν καὶ τὸν λόγον τὸν τὸ τί ἦν εἶναι λέγοντα μεσότης ἐστὶν ἡ ἀρετή, κατὰ δὲ τὸ ἄριστον καὶ τὸ εὖ ἀκρότης (*Eth. Nic.* 1107 a 6–8).

60 For the distinction between δυνάμει and ἐνέργεια, see above p. 392.

61 9, 1074 b 23–27, 33–34.

DAVID E. HAHM

The Fifth Element in
Aristotle's *De Philosophia*:
A Critical Reexamination

TWENTY-FIVE years ago Paul Wilpert called for a thorough reexamination of our knowledge of the content of Aristotle's lost work *De Philosophia*. Expressing his reservations about the validity of our current reconstruction of the work, he wrote: "On the basis of attested fragments, we form for ourselves a picture of the content of a lost writing, and this picture in turn serves to interpret new fragments as echoes of that writing. So our joy over the swift growth of our collection of fragments is clouded by the thought that we are not thereby really nearing the original character of the work, but we are entangling ourselves ever more tightly in a picture we ourselves have created." As a corrective Wilpert called for a critical retracing of our steps since 1830 to establish a more secure reconstruction of this important lost work.[1]

Since then there have been numerous searching analyses of the ideas and fragments of *De Philosophia*, but at least one venerable old theory has escaped critical reappraisal: the theory that in *De Philosophia* Aristotle discussed his doctrine of a fifth element, i.e., his belief that the heavenly bodies are composed of an element distinct from the four earthly elements, earth, water, air, and fire. This theory has become so widely accepted that it has virtually become a fact.[2] When support is needed, most modern authors simply cite one or both of the two modern authorities on the early Aristotle, namely, W. Jaeger and E. Bignone.[3] The more meticulous restate the traditional evidence with complete confidence that this evidence proves their case. If Wilpert's hope for a firmly grounded reconstruction of the *De Philosophia* is ever to be achieved, one of the important *desiderata* today is a critical reexamination of the evidence for the fifth element in this work.

This paper was presented at the 1971 Cincinnati meeting of the Society for Ancient Greek Philosophy, and revised for publication in the *Journal of Hellenic Studies*, 1982. We thank the editors for permission to reprint.
David Hahm is Professor of Classics at The Ohio State University.

In modern discussions of the fifth element in *De Philosophia* two fundamentally different approaches can be discerned, one based on a passage in Cicero, and the other on the doxographic evidence. Let us begin with the approach based on Cicero *De Natura Deorum* 1.33 (= Arist. *De Phil.* fr. 26 Ross). Here Velleius, an Epicurean, is attempting to refute earlier views about the gods by showing how contradictory they are. He observes that in Book Three of *De Philosophia* Aristotle "sometimes assigns all divinity to mind, sometimes says the cosmos itself is god, sometimes places some other being in charge of the world and assigns to it such parts that it may regulate and preserve the movement of the cosmos by some kind of rolling, and sometimes, too, says that the *ardor* of the heaven is god." The crucial question is what Cicero meant by *ardor*. Jaeger, who is the chief advocate of this passage as evidence for the doctrine of the fifth element, comments, "Cicero translates 'ether' by *Caeli ardor*. This is usual, and the description of it as divine is further evidence that what is meant is Aristotle's hypothesis of ether as the fifth element. (Cf. Cic. *De Natura Deorum* I.14, 37; *ardorem, qui aether nominetur* to which Plasberg refers in commenting on our passage)."[4]

At first glance, Jaeger's comment seems plausible; but if we trace this interpretation of Cicero's statement back to its original scholarly setting, we can see why it must be tested before it can be accepted. Among Aristotelian scholars this interpretation goes back at least as far as J. Bernays, who in 1863 laid the foundations for the reconstruction of *De Philosophia*. Citing the parallel in *Nat. D.* 2.41 (*in ardore caelesti qui aether nominetur*), Bernays translates *caeli ardor* as "the heavenly fire-material, the ether."[5] Bernays, trying to establish that references in the extant works of Aristotle to *exoterikoi logoi* and *enkyklia philosophemata* were really references to the lost dialogues, was eager to find similarities between the fragments attributed to *De Philosophia* (like the passage from Cicero) and the extant works. Hence he had polemical reasons to welcome this interpretation of Cicero's statement.[6] Moreover, Bernays wrote before anyone came to suspect an evolutionary development in Aristotle's thought, and he shared the common tendency to synthesize and harmonize apparent discrepancies. Consequently, he was predisposed to see *caeli ardor* as a reference to the fifth element of *De Caelo*. But this interpretation was not originated by Bernays. By 1850 it was already entrenched among commentators on Cicero, as the influential commentary of G. F. Schoenmann shows.[7] Commentators on Cicero, both before and after Bernays, followed the good philological principle that an author should be allowed to interpret himself; so they looked to Cicero's discussions of Stoicism, where Cicero explicitly states that the *ardor* of the heavens is called *aether* (*Nat. D.* 1.37; 2.41; cf. 2.91–92). From this they reasoned (1) that *ardor* in 1.33 translates the Greek word αἰθήρ and

(2) that this Greek word refers to Aristotle's fifth element. Following these Ciceronian commentators Aristotelian scholars concluded that Aristotle promulgated the doctrine of the fifth element in *De Philosophia*.

Before we can accept this conclusion, however, we must ask whether the two premises are correct. There can be no doubt that the Stoics believed that the cosmos consists of only four elements and that the element of the celestial region is a subtle, fiery substance that can be called by various names, including *heat, fire*, and *ether*.[8] Thus when Cicero attributes to the Stoics the belief that both *ardor* and *aether* are legitimate names for the element of the heavens, we can accept this as a correct statement of Stoic doctrine. But can we infer from Cicero's statement of Stoic doctrine that it is a peculiarity of Cicero's Latinity to translate the Greek word αἰθήρ by the Latin word *ardor*? The evidence of *De Natura Deorum* suggests that we cannot. In *Nat. D.* 2.91 Cicero tells us that *aether*, like *aer*, had originally been a Greek word but had been taken over by the Latin language and was being used as a Latin word. He quotes a line from Pacuvius, in which Pacuvius provided his audience with a translation, which is perhaps a sign that the word was unfamiliar to them. But the word had also been used by Ennius in his *Euhemerus* (*apud* Lact. 1.11.63) and *Annales* (line 472); and in the century since Ennius and Pacuvius it must have become increasingly more common, at least in Latin poetry, so that Lucretius could use it frequently without any reservations to describe the celestial region.[9] Since Cicero admits the Greek word can be simply transliterated to form a Latin word *aether* and his usual practice is to use the established Latin philosophical vocabulary wherever possible, there is no reason to think he could ever translate the Greek term αἰθήρ with the Latin word *ardor*, a misleading word closely associated with heat and burning. Thus Jaeger's contention that *ardor* must be Cicero's usual translation for αἰθήρ cannot be maintained.

We might try to escape this conclusion by suggesting that Cicero was so imbued with the language of Stoicism that it made little difference to him whether he called the celestial element *ardor* or *aether*. But if his translation was so free, we cannot claim with any more certainty that he was translating αἰθήρ than that he was translating θερμότης or πῦρ. We are forced to conclude that we cannot really prove that Cicero used *caeli ardor* to translate the Greek word αἰθήρ, and the first step in the line of reasoning leading from Cicero's words to Aristotle's fifth element must be considered pure conjecture.

Nevertheless, let us temporarily assume that Cicero was translating the Greek word αἰθήρ. Does the presence of the term αἰθήρ in *De Philosophia* presuppose the presence of the fifth body? In *Cael.* 1.3.270b20–24 and *Meteor.* I.3, 339b21–27 Aristotle approves the traditional term αἰθήρ for the celestial element because its assumed etymology (from ἀεὶ θεῖν) suggests its eternal movement, but he himself does not use this term. He consistently calls it τὸ πρῶτον σῶμα (or στοιχεῖον), τὸ ἄνω σῶμα (or στοιχεῖον), τὸ ἐγκύκλιον σῶμα or some similar term referring to its position or movement. As a matter of fact, in the genuine treatises Aristotle rarely uses the term αἰθήρ except when speaking of Empedocles, Anaxagoras, or common usage. The only exception is *Phys.* IV.5, 212b20–22, where Aristotle gives the stratification of the cosmos: "The earth is within the water; the water within the air; the air within the ether; and the ether within the heaven; but the heaven is not in anything else." Here, when he does use the term *ether*, he does not use it of the fifth element, but rather of fire, a practice for which he chides Anaxagoras in *Cael.* 1.3.270b24–25; 3.3.302b4–5.[10] Perhaps we can infer that when Aristotle discovered the fifth element, he refrained from calling it *ether* because ether had always been associated with fire. In any case the occurrence of a Latin translation of the term αἰθήρ in Cic. *Nat. D.*1.33 is no guarantee whatsoever that Aristotle discussed his theory of the "first body" in *De Philosophia*.

To be sure, nothing prevents us from conjecturing that Cicero's Epicurean source read Aristotle's exposition of his newly discovered fifth element, perhaps without a name attached to it (just as in *De Caelo*), and then gave to it the name that had subsequently become common for this element. But this is no more likely than that the Epicurean reader saw Aristotle's enraptured discussion of celestial fire and gave to this the name *ether*. We could, if we like, even imagine that Aristotle himself called this fire *ether*. Nevertheless, the fact remains that we are left without evidence that in *De Philosophia* the element of the stars is a fifth element, distinct from fire, air, water, and earth.

Jaeger's proof for the fifth element in *De Philosophia* rested primarily on the words *ardor caeli*, but he found further evidence in Cicero's characterization of this element as divine (*deum*), and we may yet be able to discover in this description a proof for the presence of the fifth element in *De Philosophia*.[11] To do so, however, requires the supposition that whereas Aristotle could call the fifth element *divine*, he could not, or at least would be unlikely to, make that claim about the fire that constitutes the heavenly bodies in a four-element cosmology. That he could call the fifth element *divine* is clear enough, for he says that there is a substance "different from those here, more divine and prior to all these" (*Cael.* 1.2.269a30–32), and he calls the heaven a "divine body" (*Cael.* 2.3.286a10–12); but it is not so clear that he would have refrained from using the term *divine* of the celestial fire at an earlier time when he still agreed with the rest of mankind that the heavenly bodies are made of fire. The very fact that he called his newly discovered fifth element "more divine" (θειοτέρα) suggests that he could admit at least some lesser degree of divinity to the other elements. Moreover, he claims that all parts of the cosmos, including the lowest part, earth, share in the divine principle as far as they are able, though less directly than the first heaven (*Cael.* 2.12.292b21–25). For Aristotle to call the element of the heavens *divine*, even if he believed the heavens were composed of fire, does not seem to be incompatible with Aristotle's view of the role of divinity in the cosmos.

Furthermore, it was not unheard of to distinguish sharply between the creative heat of the heavens and ordinary fire. Xenophon deplores the insanity Anaxagoras showed in attempting to explain the phenomena of the heavens and in claiming that the sun is fire. He accuses Anaxagoras of utter ignorance in failing to observe the vast difference between fire and sunlight (*Mem.* 4.7.6–7). Xenophon clearly implies that the heat of the heavenly bodies is far superior to fire. Euripides had earlier gone so far as to use the term god (θεός) of the bright, celestial substance, the *aither* (fr. 941 Nauck). Aristotle himself, like Xenophon, distinguished two types of heat when he claimed that the heat in living things is more akin to the element of the stars and the heat of the sun than to ordinary fire (*Gen. An.* 2.3.736b33–737a7). Obviously, in talking of the celestial fire, Aristotle was not bound to treat it in the same way as ordinary fire. He could easily have assigned it a dignity far above that of the material substances we encounter in our immediate environment. Moreover, Plato was quite explicit in calling the fiery heavenly bodies *gods*, even though he could not refer to their constituent fire itself as *god* (*Tim.* 39e–40b; cf. *Leg.* 7.821b–c; 10.886d, 899a–b).

If in *De Philosophia* Aristotle distinguished the heat of the heavens from ordinary fire or talked of celestial heat as the material of the celestial gods, it is at least possible that he used the term *divine* of the celestial heat. Moreover, even if Aristotle himself did not call this element *divine*, but showed the same care as Plato and used the term *divine* only of the heavenly bodies composed of celestial heat, we cannot rule out the possibility that Cicero or his Epicurean source might have misquoted him slightly. Thus, although the characterization of the celestial substance as divine might at first glance seem to point more strongly to the fifth element than to fire as the substance of the stars, there are too many other possibilities for us to feel any security in resting a proof on Cicero's statement alone; and we are left without firm ground for the theory that Aristotle mentioned the fifth element in *De Philosophia*.

The alternative approach to the theory that Aristotle's *De Philosophia* discussed the fifth element is based on doxographic evidence. This approach occurs in so many variations that no single author will serve as spokesman.

In modern times Bignone gave this approach its biggest impetus, but it goes back at least as far as E. Heitz, who made the second big advance in reconstructing *De Philosophia* just two years after Bernays published his work.[12] Unlike Bernays, Heitz had no preconception that *De Philosophia* was doctrinally similar to the Aristotelian treatises. In an adumbration of Jaeger's evolutionary hypothesis, Heitz suggested Aristotle's early philosophy was still under Platonic influence. Hence he saw no justification for the attempts to explain away apparent differences between *De Philosophia* and the later works. In fact, he exploited these differences to add to our knowledge of the early works. His method was approximately as follows: If a later writer attributes to Aristotle any doctrine that cannot be found in the extant works, this writer has either misunderstood the extant Aristotle or has derived the doctrine from one of his lost works. It is obvious that as the probability of misunderstanding decreases, the probability increases that a given doxographical item goes back to the lost Aristotle. Since we can measure the probability of misunderstanding by an evaluation of the reliability of the doxographer and his sources and by the extent of consensus among witnesses, we can add somewhat to our knowledge of the lost Aristotle. To be sure, the doxographic approach initiated by Heitz is subjective and at best produces probability; but it has been widely accepted because it has achieved dramatic results, especially for *De Philosophia* Book III, where the general content (cosmology and theology) is established, but specific references are few.

Let us look specifically at the application of this approach to the fifth element. In the first place, there are a large number of references in later literature to a "fifth body" (πέμπτον σῶμα) or a "body moving in a circle" (κυκλοφορικὸν or κυκλοφορητικὸν σῶμα). A number of these are assigned to Aristotle, but not to any specific work; and a few say explicitly that Aristotle called this element the "fifth body" (*Aet.* 1.7.32; 2.30.6). Our first thought, of course, will be that all such references are derived from *De Caelo*. But closer examination shows that in *De Caelo* Aristotle never speaks of a fifth body and never uses the adjectives κυκλοφορικόν or κυκλοφορητικόν. Hence some scholars conclude that these doxographies must derive from some lost discussions that did use these terms.[13] Moreover, Cicero and the Clementine *Recognitions* say that Aristotle added to the traditional four elements a "fifth nature" or "class" (*quinta natura, quintum genus*), which constitutes the heavenly bodies and human souls (fr. 27 = Cic. *Acad.* 1.26; *Tusc.* 1.22, 41, 65–66; Clem. Rom. *Recog.* 8.15). This fifth nature is "without name" (ἀκατονόμαστον). In the extant works Aristotle neither says it is without name, nor does he say it is the substance of the soul. Therefore some conclude that these reports too go back to *De Philosophia*.[14]

Further confirmation for the presence of the fifth element in *De Philosophia* may be garnered by the same method. Cicero says

> Since some living beings are born on earth, some in water, and some in the air, it seems absurd to Aristotle to think that no living being is born in that element which is most fit for giving birth to living things. Moreover, the celestial bodies occupy the region of the ether. Since this is most subtle and is always lively and in motion, it is necessary that the living being which is born in it be endowed with the keenest sense and swiftest mobility. Therefore since the heavenly bodies are born in the ether, it is reasonable that sensation and intelligence be present in them. (*Nat. D.* 2.42)

Though this passage mentions ether, the presence of the word itself does not point to the fifth element, for the argument offers a series of only four elements. However, some of the variations of this argument preserve the same analogical reasoning and also make use of a series of five elements.[15] Taking all of these together, some have inferred that originally Aristotle used an analogical argument to prove that since there are living things in each of the four elements, there must be living things in the fifth, i.e., the heavenly bodies.[16] Since this argument is not found in the extant writings, it too must be from *De Philosophia*.

Once we are convinced that this method has proven the presence of the fifth element in *De Philosophia*, we may use it to add almost any reference to the ether or the fifth element, if not as a fragment, at least as an echo of Aristotle. As some writers have observed, either all the doxographies regarding the fifth element already assigned to *De Philosophia* can be considered misinterpretations of *De Caelo* or else all the remaining references to a fifth element will have to be considered, at least hypothetically, echoes of *De Philosophia*.[17] Every one that diverges from *De Caelo* may be adding to our stock of information on *De Philosophia*. This line of reasoning has produced a flood of alleged echoes.[18] Even the apparently generalized polemics of Epicurus as found in Lucretius V and elsewhere may be interpreted as directed against *De Philosophia*.[19]

In spite of the dangers of circular reasoning inherent in the doxographic approach, the method is valid if it is carefully applied. The key to its application is the careful and critical assessment of the accuracy of the doxographic accounts. Only when accuracy can be confirmed, can a doxographic account that deviates from the doctrine of the treatises be enlisted as evidence for Aristotle's lost works. Finally, after the reference has been reliably established as evidence for a lost work, we may attempt to identify the specific work to which it refers. This identification requires further careful analysis and rigorous demonstration of close logical affinity between the reference in question and a fragment explicitly attributed to that work by a reliable ancient witness.[20] Clearly, then, the entire process depends for its success on the evaluation of the accuracy of the doxographic accounts and of their relation to the extant treatises.

To test the validity of the doxographic approach to the theory that *De Philosophia* discussed the fifth element, we may begin with the terminology for the fifth element. The most important term in question is *fifth body*, a term obviously different from the one Aristotle uses in *De Caelo*, namely, *first body*. This discrepancy, at first sight, suggests that the doxographies were derived from a lost work, not from *De Caelo*. Yet, if we consider the question a little further, we cannot avoid backing off somewhat from our initial impression. The term *first body* implies a value judgment and is appropriate only for one who believes in the exalted value of this body, as Aristotle indeed did (cf. *Cael.* 1.2.269a18–32, b13–17). The term *fifth body* is an objective term; and, though it could be used by one who believes that the fifth element is best, in itself it merely describes an element of a cosmological system without judging it. This is precisely the term that one would expect to find preferred by a doxographer who grew up in a world that had to a great extent come to accept as canonical the four elements of Empedocles, Plato, and the very popular Stoics. Consequently, it is just as easy, if not easier, to explain the term *fifth body* as a doxographer's term rather than a term taken from a lost work of the young Aristotle.[21] Even Aetius' allegation that Aristotle himself called it "the fifth body" (Stobaeus, *Ecl.* 1.502) is insufficient evidence to establish the presence of the fifth element in a lost work, for the term *fifth element* was eventually accepted not only by doxographers and late commentators, but even by Aristotelians as a suitable term for the celestial element in *De Caelo* (cf. Xenarchus of Seleucia and Nicolaus of Damascus *apud* Simpl. *Cael.* 13.18; 20.12; 21.33 Heiberg). Confusion in the doxographic terminology is quite understandable.

Furthermore, even if the doxography is not in error, the most it can prove is that Aristotle used the term at some time in some work; the specific work cannot be determined.[22] In fact, if we had only the doxographies and none of Aristotle's actual works, we would have to conjecture the theory occurred in *De Caelo* or the *Physics*, since the one doxographic reference that mentions a source for the discussion of the "fifth body" (Aët.2.10, 3) attributes it to these works. Hence, we can only conclude that the term *fifth body* is a doxographer's term, not a term used by Aristotle himself; and it is no evidence at all that Aristotle discussed this subject in a lost work.

If the term *fifth body* cannot be used to prove that the doxographies go back to a lost work, the terms κυκλοφορικόν and κυκλοφορητικόν are of even less value, for in *De Caelo* Aristotle calls the celestial body τὸ ἐγκύκλιον σῶμα (*Cael.* 2.3.286a11–12, b6–7), τὸ κυκλικὸν σῶμα (*Cael.* 2.7.289a30) and even τὸ κύκλῳ φερόμενον σῶμα (*Cael.* 1.3.269b30). As long as doxographers were passing down a tradition rarely, if ever, checked against the sources, their terminology is no satisfactory indication of the terminology of the original source and hence no evidence for the source of the doxographic material.

The references of Cicero and the Clementine *Recognitions* (cited as *De Phil.* fr. 27 Ross) to a fifth, nameless nature, which serves as the common substance of the celestial bodies and human souls, or at least of the intellective faculty of the soul, present a somewhat different situation. Here it is not only the terminology (ἀκατονόμαστον) that appears to be absent from the treatises, but the very idea itself, that the soul consists of a substance as corporeal as the substance of the celestial bodies.[23] If Aristotle actually held this theory, its absence from the extant treatises virtually assures its presence in a lost work.

However, it is very difficult to reconcile a corporeal view of the soul with Aristotle's philosophy in general, even if we make allowance for development. Aristotle's earliest view of the soul as expressed in his dialogue *Eudemus* was that it was an incorporeal form (fr. 8 Ross), a view similar to that of Plato's *Phaedo*. Over the years his views changed, but nowhere is there the slightest suggestion that he ever departed from the basic Platonic position that the soul is incorporeal.[24] Now if we postulate a corporeal theory of soul in some lost work, we shall be faced with the problem of fitting a materialistic phase into the evolution of his theory of the soul. Shall we postulate a double change from immaterialist to materialist and back to immaterialist again? Or shall we assume that the fifth element is incorporeal and risk the problem either of harmonizing such a theory with *De Caelo* or of accounting for a change to the mature doctrine of *De Caelo*, where the element of the stars is considered corporeal?[25]

Such questions have caused a considerable amount of discussion and widespread doubt that Cicero's statements can be taken to refer to a belief that the soul consists of the fifth element. One alternative interpretation is that Cicero's fifth, nameless nature refers to some incorporeal entity, constituting the souls of both men and heavenly bodies.[26] If this is the case, Cicero's statements have no value for establishing the presence of the fifth element in any work. Alternatively, Cicero's references may reflect a misunderstanding of something in the extant treatises and therefore cannot be used as evidence for a lost work.[27] The much disputed question of Cicero's reliability and interpretation is too complex to be discussed here and need not be.[28] For even the possibility of alternative interpretations or of some form of misunderstanding undermines Cicero's value as a witness to the presence of the fifth element in *De Philosophia*. For Cicero's reference these possibilities are too many and too likely to be ignored. Finally, regardless of Cicero's reliability or the interpretation one gives his statements, there are no grounds for assuming this doctrine on the nature of the soul occurred in *De Philosophia*, rather than in another lost work.[29] The net result is that the testimony of Cicero and the Clementine *Recognitions* is all but useless as evidence for the presence of the theory of a fifth element in the lost *De Philosophia*.

The only way still to find a path from Cicero's testimony to the hypothesis that the fifth element occurred in *De Philosophia* is to claim that Cicero's knowledge of Aristotle came primarily from the lost published works. Then, regardless of the accuracy of the reported information, the mere mention of a fifth element, or perhaps even of a fifth "nature," may become evidence for the hypothesis that Aristotle presented the doctrine of the fifth element in some lost work like *De Philosophia*. This claim is based on the observation that Cicero was familiar with Aristotle's early published works and quoted them freely, but knew relatively little about Aristotle's treatises. This claim can also be buttressed by the once common hypothesis that Aristotle's treatises were virtually unknown up to Cicero's time. According to Strabo 13.1.54 (C608–609) and Plutarch *Sulla* 26.1–2, Aristotle's treatises were willed by Theophrastus to his student Neleus of Skepsis in Asia Minor. Neleus' descendants hid them in a cellar or cave to keep them from the book-collecting kings of Pergamum, until they were sold to Apellicon of Teos, a book collector who took them to Athens and perhaps tried to copy the mutilated text early in the first century B.C. When Sulla returned from his capture of Athens, he brought them back to Rome and added them to the growing book collections there.[30] These manuscripts may have contributed to a renaissance of Aristotelian studies in the first century B.C. The leader of this renaissance was Andronicus of Rhodes, who produced a new edition of the text and inquired into the logical order and content of Aristotle's treatises.[31]

There can be no doubt that after Andronicus, Aristotle's doctrine of the fifth element was well known in scholarly circles. During the Augustan Age a Peripatetic, Xenarchus of Seleucia, wrote a refutation of the doctrine based on *De Caelo* and entitled *Against the Fifth Substance*.[32] Nicolaus of Damascus, the philosopher-friend of Antony and Cleopatra, King Herod of Palestine, and the Emperor Augustus, summarized the doctrine of *De Caelo* for popular consumption in his compendium *On the Philosophy of Aristotle*.[33] Philo of Alexandria, the Jewish philosopher, discussed and sometimes used the doctrine of the fifth element.[34] Hence, in Augustan or post-Augustan sources knowledge of the fifth element or references to it by the terms *fifth substance* or *fifth body* need in no way be considered dependent on *De Philosophia* for lack of knowledge of *De Caelo*.

Prior to Andronicus, however, the doctrines of Aristotle's *De Caelo* were less accessible. Though we now know that Strabo's and Plutarch's assertions that the treatises were entirely unknown before Andronicus are exaggerations, a list of the works of Aristotle that seems to reflect the holdings either of the library at Alexandria or of the Peripatos about the end of the third century B.C., omits most of the physical and biological works, including *De Caelo*.[35] Whether this should be taken as evidence that the physical works were less widely available is still not certain.[36] We do know, however, that the Peripatetics after Strato (died ca. 270 B.C.) showed little interest in physical subjects until the renaissance in the first century B.C.[37] Thus it seems clear that even if Aristotle's books were available, the physical works were not much read.

Still it would be rash to conclude that all knowledge of Aristotle's physical doctrines during the second and early first centuries B.C. came from the published works. The treatises were available even at Rome for those ambitious enough to seek them out. Cicero himself is one who went out of his way to read at least some of Aristotle's treatises.[38] Cicero's knowledge of the fifth substance might even be interpreted as evidence that *De Caelo* was not totally unknown in his day. Moreover, Cicero's source for his knowledge of the fifth element may have been Antiochus of Ascalon, head of the Academy when Cicero visited Athens in 79 B.C., or Posidonius, whom Cicero must have met in Rhodes on the same journey.[39] The treatises could have been available in both places all along. In fact, by this time Apellicon had already brought the treatises from Skepsis to Athens, and it is not impossible that some scholars had seen the manuscripts themselves or a copy of them before Sulla carried them off. Furthermore, we must not forget that the history of philosophy, a subject begun by Aristotle and carried to great heights by Theophrastus and Eudemus, was never abandoned in the Hellenistic period. Though pursued with less understanding than Theophrastus had shown, this subject produced many biographies of philosophers, now known only by title, and also doxographies, of which even the authors and titles have been forgotten. That these doxographies existed can be deduced from the fact that this doxographical information survived into the early centuries of our era to be used by Diogenes Laertius and Aëtius. Hence, regardless whether Aristotle's treatises were easily available or inaccessible and regardless whether the Peripatetic school was interested in physical questions or not, it is likely that the main outlines of Aristotle's doctrine survived throughout the Hellenistic period and could find literary expression at any time. In fact, it appears that most of Cicero's information on Aristotle's physical philosophy comes from such handbooks, not from a personal reading of Aristotle's works.[40] Since Cicero made use of Hellenistic handbooks containing Aristotle's mature philosophy and also sought out Aristotle's unpublished treatises at Rome, his knowledge of Aristotle's doctrine of the fifth element is no proof that this doctrine was found in *De Philosophia*.[41]

One major doxographical reference remains, namely, Cicero *Nat.D.*

2.42 (*De Phil*. fr. 21a, Ross), where the Stoic Balbus appears to attribute to Aristotle the argument that since earth, water, and air are filled with living things, the occupants of the ether, that is, the celestial bodies, must likewise be living and endowed with swift movement and keen senses. Since this same analogical argument occurs with a series of five elements, it has been claimed that in the version of *De Philosophia* the celestial bodies consisted of the fifth element. On this theory the version in Cicero is a Stoic remodeling of Aristotle's version to bring it into line with the Stoic theory of four elements.[42]

A careful analysis of the surviving versions, however, shows that the same argument is being used for three different purposes. One set proves the divinity of the celestial bodies; another assumes that the celestial bodies are the living things in the ether and tries to prove that spirits must be present in the air; and the third proves that the universe is eternal. There is also a hybrid attempting to prove both the divinity of the stars and the existence of demons in the air.[43] Since the proof for spirits in the air and the proof for the eternity of the cosmos both assume the conclusion of the proof that the heavenly bodies are divine living beings, we are tempted to assign the origin of the "spirit" proof and "eternity" proof to a later period than the proof of the divinity of the stars. The five elements occur only in the "spirit" proof and the "eternity" proof, not in the presumably earlier proof of the divinity of the stars. From this we should conclude that a four-element proof for the existence of god was remodeled into the later proofs by someone who believed in the five elements. Such a hypothesis is at least as tenable as the hypothesis that the four-element "god" proof, the four- and five-element "demon" proofs, and the five-element "eternity" proof were all remodeled from Aristotle's five-element "god" proof. It is only by an exceedingly arbitrary choice of elements from here and there that the latter hypothesis can pretend to reconstruct Aristotle's original proof.[44] Thus we are faced either with admitting that Aristotle actually used a loose four-element proof as Cicero's Stoic asserts or with despairing altogether of reconstructing Aristotle's original argument. In either case, this fragment loses all value as proof for Aristotle's theory of the fifth element in *De Philosophia*.

In the last analysis all the doxographic accounts alleged to prove that Aristotle discussed the fifth element in *De Philosophia* fail to meet the crucial test. In every case the probability of misunderstanding, contamination by doctrines from the treatises, or deliberate adaptation, is far too high to recommend any of them as evidence for a lost work. Neither Cicero's *ardor caeli* nor the doxographic reports, taken singly or collectively, can be used to produce a well-founded proof for the theory that Aristotle discussed the fifth element in *De Philosophia*. Until further evidence is discovered, this venerable theory must be considered, at best, an unproven conjecture.

The evidence on the other side has now to be considered. We have just seen that Cicero *Nat.D.* 2.42 (= *De Phil.* fr. 21a), if it be taken as evidence for *De Philosophia*, speaks of a universe of four elements, with the heavenly bodies made of fire. We have also seen that *ardor caeli* in Cicero *Nat.D.* 1.33 (= *De Phil.* fr. 26), the fundamental passage for reconstructing Book III of *De Philosophia*, cannot be taken as evidence of the presence of the fifth element. The word *ardor* literally means "heat" and otherwise refers to celestial phenomena that are bright, if not hot (e.g., lightning, comets, and stars). If this reference points to anything, it points to the presence of a word like θερμότης or θερμόν in the Greek original. It may thus be a clue that Aristotle had not yet come to the conclusion that the element of the heavens is different from fire.

Slightly more valuable may be several passages from Philo that have been assigned to *De Philosophia* on the basis of their content.[45] In one passage Philo describes how a man viewing with awe the works of the cosmos comes to the conclusion that these are the works of god (*Leg. Alleg.* 3.97–99 [= *De Phil.* fr. 13]). Cicero *Nat.D.* 2.95–6 (= fr. 13) assigns such a proof for God's existence to Aristotle. Philo's account describes the cosmos region by region: the earth, the water, the air, and the heavens—a series of only four regions. Philo also records anonymously several proofs for the eternity of the cosmos, a subject that Simplicius (*In. Cael.* 289.1–15 [= fr. 16]) suggests was included in *De Philosophia*.[46] In one of these proofs Philo states that the four elements of men are borrowed from the cosmos and return to their natural places at death; but in the cosmos all four elements are already in their natural places, earth at the center, water spread over the earth, air in the region between water and fire, and fire in the highest region of all (ἀνωτάτω, *Aet. Mund.* 33 [= *De Phil.* 19b]). *Highest* cannot mean just under the fifth element because Aristotle is basing his argument on the fact that each and every one of its parts is in its natural place. His argument would be incomplete and seriously weakened if he failed to mention one of the elements, the element of the stars. Hence we can only conclude that the element of the stars is fire.[47]

Philo's evidence is important because Philo himself was undecided whether the cosmos consists of four or five elements and so seems to follow his source, with the result that he sometimes speaks in terms of a five-element cosmos and sometimes (more often) in terms of the Stoic four-element cosmos.[48] Hence we can be reasonably sure Philo has not altered his source on this point. Nor is there any evidence of Stoicism in his arguments to make us suspect that Panaetius, one of the few Stoics who believed the cosmos to be eternal, was an intermediary for this argument. Both arguments sound Aristotelian and the second one with its use of the idea of natural places and four elements is very close to *De Caelo* III–IV. Hence if these arguments are from *De Philosophia*, we have some grounds for suspecting Aristotle in this work had not yet come to the conclusion that the heavens consisted of an element different from fire.

In sum, it is surely significant that a critical analysis of the fragments attributed to *De Philosophia* is able to turn up several references to a four-element cosmology (with fire at the periphery), but not a single allusion to a five-element cosmology. Though it may be possible to explain away the references to a four-element cosmology as later, possibly Stoic, adaptations, such a procedure requires at least one indisputable reference to the presence of the fifth element in *De Philosophia*. Since no reference of this kind has yet been found, any attempt to explain away the references to a four-element cosmology must be deemed arbitrary and unconvincing. We are left, then, in the position of weighing what amounts to a very meager amount of evidence. The absence of any defensible evidence in favor of a five-element cosmology, combined with some hints of the presence of a four-element cosmology, lead to the inference that Aristotle probably did not introduce the fifth element into the cosmology of the *De Philosophia*. Though certainty on this question still remains beyond our grasp, the balance of evidence inclines in favor of the hypothesis that in *De Philosophia* Aristotle still believed the heavenly bodies to be composed of fire.

The consequences of this conclusion cannot be explored here in detail, but we can survey some of the subjects that will be affected. First of all, the fragments or witnesses used for reconstructing *De Philosophia* will have to be reconsidered. Cicero's references to a fifth nature or substance serving as the substance of souls and stars (= *De Phil.* fr. 27 Ross, Walzer) may now safely be discarded. Even if some true, early Aristotelian content may yet be distilled from these references, the sole justification for attributing this material specifically to *De Philosophia*, namely, the mention of the fifth element as the substance of the heavens, can no longer stand. Similarly, the many alleged echoes of the early Aristotle, based on mentions of the fifth element, may also be discarded.[49] On the other hand, Cicero's references to Aristotle in *Nat.D.* 2.42 and 44 may find their position as witnesses to *De Philosophia* somewhat more secure. One of the major problems of interpreting them as references to *De Philosophia* was harmonizing them with the five-element cosmology assumed for *De Philosophia*. If in *De Philosophia* Aristotle held a four-element cosmology, some of these problems disappear. There is still, of course, the very real problem of Stoic contamination in these passages, but at least one area of possible Stoic contamination, the four-element cosmology in *Nat.D.* 2.42, may now be given a different interpretation.[50] Rather than a Stoic modification of Aristotle, it may well be part of the grounds for the attraction the Stoics felt for these Aristotelian ideas. Moreover, the new interpretation that may be given to *Nat.D.*

2.44 increases the doctrinal divergence from *De Caelo* and thereby increases the probability of its originating in one of the lost treatises. This brings us to the interpretive consequences of a four-element cosmology in *De Philosophia. Nat.D.* 2.44 is probably the fragment most affected by the hypothesis of a four-element cosmology. In this passage the Stoic Balbus commends Aristotle for his idea that all things that are moved are moved either by nature, force, or will. The circular movement of the celestial bodies is not due to nature because nature causes motion either downward by weight or upward by lightness. Nor is this circular movement due to force, for there is no stronger force that could move them contrary to their nature. Therefore their movement is voluntary. In the past the apparent denial of natural movement to the heavenly bodies in *De Philosophia* faced interpreters who assumed a five-element cosmology with a dilemma. Either they had to search around for an explanation for the origin of the theory of the fifth element, which in *De Caelo* was deduced directly from the theory of natural movements.[51] Or they had to reconcile Cicero's statement with the celestial mechanics of *De Caelo* by qualifying and restricting its denial of natural movements to a denial only of the inanimate motion of weight and lightness.[52] A simple, straightforward interpretation of Cicero's statement is now possible on the assumption that the cosmos consists of only four elements and these move in accord with the theory of natural movements that is developed in *De Caelo* III–IV.[53]

According to this theory, there are only two natural movements, up and down. Elements displaced from their natural place will move either up or down until they again reach their natural place, where by nature they will rest. This does not mean they must necessarily remain at rest. It is possible that some things will be moved by some stronger force that pushes them either contrary to nature out of their natural place (as a ball thrown into the air) or not contrary to nature within their natural place (as a ball rolled along the ground). Then there is a third possibility, exemplified by a man walking along the ground. This is not natural movement; for man as a heavy, earthy thing, the natural movement would be downward toward the earth and would occur only if he were to fall from a height. Nor is this forced movement, like the movement of a man riding in a truck or a ball rolled on the ground. His walking motion must be voluntary, due to his own free will. So, too, if the heavenly bodies are made of fire, their natural movement would be upward toward the periphery, where we could expect them to rest. The fact that they are moving within their natural place proves that their motion is due to something other than nature. Since no external force is strong enough to move these most powerful, divine beings, we must conclude their motion is voluntary, of their own free will.[54] This interpretation, which is possible on the assumption that the stars are made of fire, is both a simpler, more natural interpretation of Cicero's words, and as we noted above, different enough from the theory of *De Caelo* to justify the claim that Cicero's words are a witness to a lost work.

Finally, a four-element cosmology in *De Philosophia* has significant consequences for the interpretation of the role of *De Philosophia* in Aristotle's philosophical career. Though there is not yet complete agreement on the chronological ordering of the various cosmological accounts in the treatises, the evidence suggests three phases in Aristotle's cosmological thought.[55] (1) The first phase is exemplified by *De Caelo* III–IV in which Aristotle constructed the universe of four-elements, earth, water, air, and fire, and worked out his theory of natural movements for these elements. At this time it seems he had not yet postulated the fifth element. (2) The second phase is defined by his extension of the system of natural movements to the heavens and the postulation of a fifth element that moves by nature in a circle and serves as the substance of the heavenly bodies (*De Caelo* I–II). (3) Finally a third phase is marked by a redirection of attention from the physical movement of the elements and heavenly bodies to atmospheric phenomena. This required a reinterpretation of the spheres of air and fire, which formerly found a place below the sphere of the fifth, celestial element. In *Meteorologica* these two spheres became a region occupied by a mixture of two exhalations (not elements) whose proportions vary with altitude in such a way as to approximate the spheres of air and fire without actually constituting separate elemental spheres. In this phase the heavenly bodies continue to be composed of the unique celestial element that we have been calling the fifth element.

As long as *De Philosophia* was believed to contain an account of the fifth element, it was extremely difficult to place it comfortably into this scheme. It had to follow the first phase because it already recognized the fifth element. But *Nat.D.* 2.44 implied significant differences from the view of phase 2. Regardless whether one opted for placing *De Philosophia* between phase 1 and phase 2 or for harmonizing the differences between it and the view of phase 2, some special pleading was necessary.[56] If, however, Aristotle still held a four-element cosmology in *De Philosophia*, the work fits comfortably into Phase 1. We may conclude that at this time he still accepted the Platonic scheme of four elements, but he was already developing his theory of natural movement to explain the movement of the elements to their natural places, the movement associated with the phenomena of weight and lightness. This he worked out in *De Caelo* III–IV. About this same time, he considered the movement of the heavenly bodies in *De Philosophia*. Here he presupposed his theory of natural movements; but, thinking only in terms of the linear movement of weight and lightness, he had to attribute the circular movement of the heavenly bodies to the free will that they possessed as divine, rational, ensouled beings. It was not until some time later, that is, in phase 2, as seen in *De Caelo* I, that Aristotle noticed it was possible to extend the theory of natural movements to the movement of the heavenly bodies by grounding the whole theory in geometry. The two basic kinds of lines, straight and curved, could then serve as models for two basic types of natural motion, linear and circular. This theory forced him to abandon his four-element cosmology and postulate for the heavens a fifth element, distinct from the other four, which move up and down in straight lines. Thus *De Philosophia* can be securely dated before *De Caelo* I and fitted into the evolution of his cosmological thought.

Furthermore, if *De Caelo* was indeed an early work, as is generally believed, we now have another piece of evidence that *De Philosophia* must have been among Aristotle's very earliest works.[57] Moreover, the four-element cosmology is additional evidence of its Platonic character; and even if a small item like this cannot settle the controversy whether Aristotle's thought became less Platonic or more so as he developed, it is one more factor that will have to be considered in evaluating Aristotle's development and the role of *De Philosophia* in that process.[58]

This has been no more than a sketch of some of the possible implications of the hypothesis that the fifth element did not make its appearance in *De Philosophia*. A full reevaluation of the content and significance of *De Philosophia* on the basis of a critical reappraisal of all the evidence for the work still remains a major *desideratum* of Aristotelian scholarship.[59]

NOTES

[1] P. Wilpert, "Die aristotelische Schrift 'Über die Philosophie,'" *Autour d'Aristote: Receuil d'études de philosophie ancienne et médiévale offert á A. Mansion* (Louvain, 1955), pp. 99–116 (quotation, pp. 102–03); cf. also "The Fragments of Aristotle's Lost Writings," in I. Düring and G. E. L. Owen, eds., *Aristotle and Plato in the Mid-Fourth Century*, Studia Graeca et Latina Gothoburgensia 11 (Göteborg, 1960), pp. 257–64. A similar concern in connection with specific problems has been voiced by others, e.g., A. Mansion, "L'immortalité de l'âme et de l'intellect d'après Aristote," *RPhL* 51 (1953):450 and P. Moraux, "Quinta Essentia," *RE* 47 (1963):1219.

[2] To my knowledge, the only published rejections of this assumption are W. D. Ross, *Aristotle's Physics* (Oxford, 1936), pp. 96–97, and D. J. Furley, "Lucretius and the Stoics," *BICS* 18 (1966):22–23; but neither has affected the state of the question. See, for example, the recent reconstruction by A. H. Chroust, "A Tentative Outline for a Possible Reconstruction of Aristotle's Lost Dialog *On Philosophy*," *AntCl* 44 (1975):553–69, esp. 561–63. One authority, B. Effe, *Studien zur Kosmologie und Theologie der aristotelischen Schrift "Über die Philosophie,"* Zetemata 50 (Munich, 1970):127–28, is so convinced of the truth of this assumption that he is prepared to doubt Cicero's reliability as a witness to Aristotle's *De Philosophia* on

the grounds that Cicero *Nat.D.* 2.42 does not acknowledge the existence of the fifth element.
   [3] Jaeger, *Aristotle: Fundamentals of the History of His Development* (Oxford, 1948), pp. 139, 142–54; E. Bignone, *L'Aristotele perduto e la formazione filosofica de Epicuro* (Florence, 1936).
   [4] Jaeger, *Fundamentals*, p. 139, n. 1. Bignone, *L'Aristotele*, vol. 2, p. 352, n. 1, accepts this interpretation of the passage but does not use it as a proof that the fifth element was discussed in *De Philosophia*. This approach is adopted as proof by a number of more recent writers, e.g., E. Berti, *La filosofia del primo Aristotele* (Padua, 1962), p. 369; A. H. Chroust, *Aristotle: New Light on His Life and on Some of His Lost Works*, vol. 2 (London, 1973), pp. 183–84 (originally published as "The Concept of God in Aristotle's *On Philosophy* [Cicero, *De Natura Deorum* I.13.33]," *Emerita* 33 [1965]:205–28); P. Moraux, "Quinta Essentia," pp. 1196–1209; J. Pepin, *Théologie cosmique et théologie chrétienne* (Paris, 1964), pp. 151–52; and W. Pötscher, *Strukturprobleme der aristotelischen und theophrastischen Gottesvorstellung*, Philosophia Antiqua 19 (Leiden, 1970):34, 41.
   [5] J. Bernays, *Die Dialoge des Aristoteles in ihrem Verhältniss zu seinen übrigen Werken* (Berlin, 1863), pp. 99–100.
   [6] For the polemical purpose of his work, see Bernays, *Die Dialoge*, pp. 30–42; cf. also Berti, *La filosofia*, pp. 19–21.
   [7] G. F. Schoenmann, ed., *M. Tullii Ciceronis: De Natura Deorum* (Leipzig, 1850, 1857, 1865, 1876), notes on 1.13.33. It should be noted that Jaeger cites Plasberg, a commentator on Cicero, to support his interpretation. The other major commentators on this work concur; cf. J. B. Mayor, *M. Tullii Ciceronis: De Natura Deorum*, vol. 1 (Cambridge, 1891), p. 122; and A. S. Pease, *M. Tullii Ciceronis: De Natura Deorum*, vol. 1 (Cambridge, Mass., 1955), p. 242.
   [8] Cf. H. von Arnim, *Stoicorum Veterum Fragmenta* (Leipzig, 1903–05), vol. 2, Fragments 413, 527, 555, 558, 580, cf. 434. The use of *fire* and *ether* as alternative names for the celestial element is stated explicitly by Diog. Laert. 7.137 (= von Arnim, vol. 2, fr. 580). In general, Stoic texts use *fire* and *ether* interchangeably.
   [9] Cf. J. Paulson, *Index Lucretianus* (Göteborg, 1911), s.v. *"Aether."* The meaning of the term in Lucretius is not completely clear, perhaps because the traditional elements play only a small part in the Epicurean system (cf. C. Bailey, ed., *Titi Lucreti Cari: De Rerum Natura*, vol. 3 [Oxford, 1947], pp. 1393–94). On the development of the Latin philosophical vocabulary before Cicero and Cicero's attitude toward and use of this vocabulary, see O. Gigon, "Cicero und die griechische Philosophie," in *Aufstieg und Niedergang der römischen Welt: Geschichte und Kultur Roms im Spiegel der neueren Forschung*, ed. H. Temporini, section 1, vol. 4.1 (Berlin, 1973), pp. 250–54.
   [10] The statement in the *Physics* presents some problems. It occurs in a chapter whose authenticity has been questioned (cf. P. H. Wicksteed and F. M. Cornford, *Aristotle: The Physics*, Loeb Classical Library [London-Cambridge, Mass., 1963], pp. 314–19). Furthermore, it is unclear whether by οὐρανός Aristotle means the universe as a whole, as the previous lines suggest (*Phys.* 4.5.212b17–20), or the heavenly region consisting of the spheres of the heavenly bodies, as a parallel passage in *Cael.* 2.4.287a32–b4 suggests. If οὐρανός means the universe as a whole,

the passage would seem to presuppose a four-element cosmology (cf. F. Solmsen, *Aristotle's System of the Physical World* [Ithaca, 1960], p. 301), and *ether* then refers to the celestial fire. If, on the other hand, οὐρανός means the heavenly region, the region of the celestial element, it probably presupposes Aristotle's standard five-element cosmology (cf. H. J. Drossaart-Lulofs, *Nicolaus Damascenus: On the Philosophy of Aristotle* [Leiden, 1965], p. 127). In that case *ether* refers to the sublunar element, fire. In either case, the word *ether* refers to fire, not to the fifth element.

¹¹ In this Jaeger is followed by Chroust. *New Light*, vol. 2, pp. 403–04, n. 78. 78.

¹² Bignone, *L'Aristotele*; E. Heitz, *Die verlorenen Schriften des Aristoteles* (Leipzig, 1865), pp. 179–89.

¹³ Cf., e.g., Heitz, *Die verlorenen*, pp. 185–86 and J. Pepin, *Théologie*, pp. 222–23. I have presented the proof in its bluntest form. It is usually toned down somewhat and qualified with a word like *probably*. For example, Pepin, after admitting these expressions could be derived from *De Caelo* by an imprecise doxographer, continues, "But nothing prevents us from supposing that these expressions in reality belong to an earlier state of his terminology." He then chooses the latter interpretation because Cicero's divergence from the extant treatises has convinced him that the doxographic tradition is inspired by *De Philosophia* as well as *De Caelo*. Jaeger, *Fundamentals*, p. 144, n. 2, uses the doxography only as evidence for Aristotle's terminology, since he has already accepted the presence of this element on the basis of the text of Cicero.

¹⁴ Cf., e.g., Heitz, *Die verlorenen*, pp. 186–88; and Pepin, *Théologie*, p. 223 and n. 2, for explicit discussion of attribution. Most writers, however, simply accept the attribution without discussion.

¹⁵ Philo *De Gig.* 2.7–8; *De Plant.* 3.12; *Aet. Mund.* 14.45 (collected by R. Walzer, *Aristoteles Dialogorum Fragmenta* [Florence, 1934], pp. 87–88 as *De Phil.* fr. 22). Cf. also Plato *Epin.* 984d–985b.

¹⁶ Jaeger, *Fundamentals*, pp. 143–46.

¹⁷ S. Mariotti, "Nuove testimonianze ed echi dell' Aristotele giovanile," *Atene e Roma* 42 (1940):56, n. 22; Pepin, *Théologie*, p. 223.

¹⁸ Cf. the list of the books and articles in Moraux, "Quinta Essentia," p. 1215 and Berti, *La filosofia*, pp. 103–07. The book by Pepin, *Théologie*, is another work in this vein. The method has even been applied to Aristotle himself to attribute *Cael.* 1.3.270b16–25 and *Meteor.* 1.3.339b19–30 to *De Philosophia* because these passages do not fit into their contexts very well (Effe, *Studien*, pp. 39–41).

¹⁹ Cf. Bignone, *L'Aristotele*, vol. 2, pp. 406–503. Bignone, p. 425 and n. 3, takes the term *ether* in Lucr. 5.128 and 143 as further confirmation of the presence of the fifth element in *De Philosophia*. He apparently has not noticed that in Lucr. 5.143 it occurs in a series consisting of earth, fire, water, and ether, and therefore more likely designates air than Aristotle's fifth element.

²⁰ Cf. Wilpert, "The Fragments," pp. 262–63.

²¹ Cf. H. J. Easterling, "Quinta Natura," *MusHelv* 21 (1964):79–80.

²² The doxographic tradition as a whole is drawn from too many Aristotelian sources to allow us to trace a given *placitum* back to a single work. H. Diels,

Doxographi Graeci (Berlin, 1929), p. 215, lists some of the references to extant treatises.

²³ The term *nameless* (ἀκατονόμαστον), which late doxographic accounts claim is Aristotle's own term for the substance of the heavens (cf., e.g., Clem. Rom. *Recogn*. 8.14 [=*De Phil.* fr. 27 Ross] and Psellus, *De Omnifaria Doctrina* 131 [p. 69 Westerink]), is itself as inadequate as the term *fifth body* for grounding the hypothesis that the fifth element was discussed in a lost work. Aristotle's noncommittal account of the traditional name *ether* and his explicit criticism of Anaxagoras' use of this term (*Cael*. 1.3.270b16–25), combined with his own preference for descriptive paraphrases rather than a single name, is sufficient to account for the doxographical term. Furthermore, it occurs only in the later doxographies and may well be influenced by the doxographies regarding the substance of the soul. In that event, the term loses its value as independent evidence for Aristotle's cosmological doctrine and must be taken as part of the doxography of Aristotle's doctrine of the nature of the soul.

²⁴ Cf. F. Nuyens, *L'évolution de la psychologie d'Aristote* (Louvain-Paris, 1948). The evolution of Aristotle's psychology has been the subject of much debate since Nuyens. For a brief survey, see W. Fortenbaugh, "Recent Scholarship on the Psychology of Aristotle," *CW* 60 (1967):318–20.

²⁵ These suggestions have been made in attempts to save Cicero's credibility. C. Lefevre, "'Quinta Natura' et psychologie aristotélicienne," *RPhL* 69 (1971):5–43, accepts the double change, whereas Pepin, *Théologie*, pp. 245–47 suggests that Aristotle regarded the fifth element as incorporeal. Pepin's suggestion, which cannot be proven for *De Philosophia* and flies in the face of *Cael*. 1.3, seems to be an act of desperation to save Cicero's reputation.

²⁶ Cf., e.g., Moraux, "Quinta Essentia," pp. 1213–26 and Easterling, "Quinta Natura," pp. 73–85.

²⁷ One possible ground for misunderstanding is that Cicero or his source learned that Aristotle considered the soul to be of a nature totally distinct from that of the four corporeal elements of the body (whether the view of the *Eudemus* or the view of the extant treatises that the soul is the first actuality of the body) and then mistakenly identified this nature with that of the element of the celestial bodies, which in the treatises is regarded as a fifth corporeal element distinct from the earthly four. If this misunderstanding did not afflict Cicero, it certainly did later writers. (For full discussion, see Easterling, "Quinta Natura," pp. 73–85; cf. also Effe, *Studien*, pp. 148–55; and Moraux, "Quinta Essentia," pp. 1213–24.)

Another possibility is that Cicero's statement reflects a distortion of the unique account of how faculties of soul are passed on to offspring (*Gen. An.* 2.3. 736b29–737a1; on this passage cf. F. Solmsen, "The Vital Heat, the Inborn Pneuma and the Aether," *JHS* 77 [1957]:119–23). Here Aristotle claims that the faculty of soul is "associated with (κεκοινωνηκέναι) a body that is different from and more divine than the so-called [four] elements," a body that he goes on to identify as "the pneuma . . . and the natural substance within the pneuma that is analogous to the element of the stars." He does not actually claim that the soul consists of pneuma or of the unnamed substance in the pneuma, but he does bring the soul into close association with it by saying it shares in (κεκοινωνηκέναι) this corporeal substance, and he clearly states that the unnamed component of the pneuma that is significant in the transmission of psychic faculties is analogous to the element of the stars. It would not be too difficult for a reader of this text to identify the soul with this unnamed substance in the pneuma and then go on to identify this substance with the fifth element that constitutes the heavenly bodies.

[28] For a summary of the controversy with relevant bibliography see Berti, *La filosofia*, pp. 359–99 and Chroust, *New Light*, vol. 2, pp. 194–205. To the works cited there add Pepin, *Théologie*, pp. 226–34; P. Moraux, *Aristote: Du Ciel*, Collection Budé (Paris, 1965), pp. li-lvi; E. Berti. "Studi recenti sul *Peri Philosophia* di Aristotele," *Giornale di Metafisica* 20 (1965):310–11; A. P. Bos, *On the Elements: Aristotle's Early Cosmology*, Bijdragen tot de Filosofie 3 (Assen, 1973):138–40; Lefevre, "'Quinta Natura'"; and A. H. Chroust, "The Akatonomaston in Aristotle's 'On Philosophy,'" *Emerita* 40 (1972):461–68.

[29] The *Eudemus* has frequently been suggested, e.g., by S. Mariotti, "La 'quinta essentia' nell'Aristotele perduto e nell'Accademia," *RivFilol* n.s. 18 (1940): 179–89; O. Gigon, "Cicero und Aristoteles," *Hermes* 87 (1959):143–62, esp. 153, 156 (= Studien zur antiken Philosophie [Berlin, 1972]:305–25, esp. 315, 318–19); "Prolegomena to an Edition of the *Eudemus*," in Düring and Owen, eds., *Aristotle and Plato*, p. 32; and A. Grilli, "Cicerone e l'*Eudemo*," *La Parola del Passato* 17 (1962):98–100.

[30] On the history of Aristotle's books, see I. Düring, *Aristotle in the Biographical Tradition* (Göteborg, 1957), pp. 393–95; A. H. Chroust, "The Miraculous Disappearance and Recovery of the Corpus Aristotelicum," *Class. et Med.* 23 (1962):50–67; and the thorough, fully documented discussion by P. Moraux, *Der Aristotelismus bei den Griechen*, vol. 1 (Berlin, 1973), pp. 3–44. The history of Aristotelianism in the first century B.C. is now fully discussed by Moraux, *Aristotelismus*, vol. 1; for a brief summary cf. J. Moreau, *Aristote et son école* (Paris, 1962), pp. 279–83.

[31] Cf. M. Plezia, "De Andronici Rhodii Studiis Aristotelicis," *Polska Ak. Archivum Filologiczne* 20 (Krakow, 1946); Düring, *Aristotle in the Biographical Tradition*, pp. 420–25; and Moraux, *Aristotelismus*, pp. 45–94. Whether Andronicus worked in Rome or in Athens and whether before or after the death of Cicero are matters of current debate (cf. Moraux, 45–58).

[32] See P. Moraux, "Xenarchos (5)," *RE*, Reihe 2, vol. 18 (1967):1423–26; *Aristotelismus*, pp. 198–206.

[33] This summary has been preserved in a Syriac translation, edited with an English translation and commentary by H. J. Drossaart-Lulofs, *Nicolaus Damascenus: On the Philosophy of Aristotle* (Leiden, 1965). For the life and philosophical activity of Nicolaus, see Drossaart-Lulofs, pp. 1–5, 20–23 and Moraux, *Aristotelismus*, pp. 445–50. For his summary of *De Caelo*, see Drossaart-Lulofs, pp. 82–87 and commentary, pp. 152–65, and Moraux, pp. 475–76. Unfortunately his summary of *Cael.* 1.1–2.1 is missing in the Syriac MS.

[34] *Quis Heres* 283; *De Plantat.* 3, cf. 12; *Quaest. Gen.* 3.6; 4.8; *Quaest. Ex.* 2.73. Philo himself seems to consider the question of the nature of the heavenly bodies insoluble (*De Somn.* 1.21–24). He uses both the Stoic view that the heavens consist of a special kind of fire (*Quis Heres* 133–36; *Mos.* 2.148) and the Peripatetic

view that they consist of a fifth element. For full discussion see J. Drummond, *Philo Judaeus: The Jewish and Alexandrian Philosophy in its Development and Completion* (London, 1888), pp. 1.273–79, and Moraux, "Quinta Essentia," pp. 1235–36.

[35] P. Moraux, *Les listes anciennes des ouvrages d'Aristote* (Louvain, 1951), has shown that the catalog of Diog. Laert. 5.22–27 goes back to the Hellenistic period. He conjectures that it represents the holdings of the Peripatetic library about 200 B.C. I. Düring, "Ariston or Hermippus?" *Class, et Med.* 17 (1956):11–21; *Aristotle in the Biographical Tradition*, pp. 67–69, 90–92 has pointed out weaknesses in Moraux's conjecture and argues again for the traditional ascription to Hermippus (third century B.C.). The question remains unsettled (cf. Moraux, *Aristotelismus*, p. 4, n. 2).

[36] Cf. Moraux, *Listes*, pp. 313–20; Düring, "Ariston," pp. 20–21; and *Notes on the History of the Transmission of Aristotle's Writings*, Acta Universitatis Goteburgensis 56 (1950): pt. 3, pp. 35–70, esp. 57–70.

[37] Cf. Moreau, *Aristote*, pp. 272–78, esp. 272; or K. O. Brink, "Peripetos," *RE*, Suppl. 7 (1940):931–38 for a survey of the Peripetos in this period. The problem of the decline of the Peripatos is discussed by J. P. Lynch, *Aristotle's School: A Study of a Greek Educational Institution* (Berkeley, 1972), pp. 135–62.

[38] The case for the availability of Aristotle's treatises apart from the manuscripts from Skepsis is convincingly presented by Moraux, *Aristotelismus*, pp. 3–44. The evidence for Cicero's access to the treatises is also collected and discussed by Moraux, pp. 33–41.

[39] G. Luck, *Der Akademiker Antiochos* (Bern—Stuttgart, 1953), pp. 36–40, finds Antiochus behind Cicero's statements about the fifth nature as the substance of the soul; and Düring, *Notes*, p. 60 suggests that Cicero may have learned about Aristotle in general from Posidonius and could have seen Aristotle's works in a library at Rhodes.

[40] See O. Gigon, "Cicero und Aristoteles"; "Cicero und die griechische Philosophie," pp. 240–50; and Moraux, *Aristotelismus*, pp. 41–43.

[41] Cf. Easterling, "Quinta Natura," pp. 73–85. Cicero's statements that the human soul or mind consists of some fifth substance embody an idea also attributed to Critolaus, a Peripatetic of the second century B.C. (Aet. 1.7.21; Tert. *De An.* 5.2; Macrobius *In Somn. Scip.* 1.14.20). This fact only compounds the problem. If this doxography is reliable, Critolaus could be the source, directly or indirectly, of the misinterpretation of Aristotle (Cicero knew and approved Critolaus' views on the virtue of the soul [*Tusc.* 5.51]). Or the doxographies could have confused Aristotle's view with that of Critolaus. Finally, the doxography may have misinterpreted Critolaus in the same way it did Aristotle.

[42] Jaeger, *Fundamentals*, pp. 143–46, cf. Chroust, *New Light*, vol. 2, pp. 186–87. Though Jaeger himself does not use this as proof or even confirmation for the presence of the fifth element in *De Philosophia*, his theory has become part of the overall reconstruction of the position of the fifth element in *De Philosophia* and must be dealt with in this context. On the possible source of the Stoic remodeling, see D. Hahm, *The Origins of Stoic Cosmology* (Columbus, Ohio, 1977), pp. 144, 176, n. 18, and 267–73.

[43] Proof for divinity of celestial bodies: Cic. *Nat.D.* 2.42; Sext. Emp. *Adv.*

ESSAYS IN ANCIENT GREEK PHILOSOPHY

Phys. 1.49; cf. Aët. 5.20.1. Proof for spirits: Philo *De Somn.* 1.135; *De Gig.* 2.7–8; *De Plantat.* 3.12; Apuleius *De Deo Socr.* 8.137; Plato *Epin.* 984d–985b. Proof for eternity of cosmos: Philo *Aet. Mund.* 14.45. Hybrid proof: Sext. Emp. *Adv. Phys.* 1.86. Cf. the discussion of K. Reinhardt, *Kosmos und Sympathie* (Munich, 1926), pp. 62–64.

⁴⁴ Cf. Reinhardt, *Kosmos,* pp. 62–86, esp. 62–68.

⁴⁵ For a full discussion of the attribution of these proofs to Aristotle, see Effe, *Studien,* pp. 7–17.

⁴⁶ Simpl. *In Cael.* 289.1–15 (= *De Phil.* fr. 16 Ross). Simplicius' evidence must be used with caution because he did not have firsthand knowledge of *De Philosophia.* Cf. H. Cherniss, *Aristotle's Criticism of Plato and the Academy* (Baltimore, 1944; New York, 1962), pp. 119, n. 7; 587; Cherniss, in *Gnomon* 39 (1959): 38–39; and L. Tarán, in *AJP* 87 (1966):467.

⁴⁷ Effe, *Studien,* pp. 19–20 tries to escape this conclusion by suggesting that Philo's version might here be assimilated to the Platonic and Stoic view or else that Philo might have drawn from a section of Aristotle that focused on the human body and simply failed to mention the celestial fifth element. Effe would treat this fragment like Cic. *Nat.D.* 2.42 (= *De Phil.* 21a) and explain away its four-element cosmology.

⁴⁸ See above, n. 34.

⁴⁹ Cf. above, n. 17 and 18.

⁵⁰ On the problem of Stoic contamination and Ciceronian distortion in these passages, see K. Reinhardt, *Kosmos,* pp. 61–92; Cherniss, *Aristotle's Criticism,* pp. 592, 595–602; Moraux, "Quinta Essentia," pp. 1213, 1223–24; A. H. Chroust, "Some Comments on Cicero, *De Natura Deorum* II.15.42–16.44: A Fragment of Aristotle's *On Philosophy,*" *Classical Folia* 29 (1975):103–13; and Hahm, *The Origins,* p. 176, n. 18.

⁵¹ For some of the attempts to find an alternative ground for postulating the existence of a fifth element, see Jaeger, *Fundamentals,* pp. 139 and n. 1; cf. 143, 153; and G. A. Seeck, *Über die Elemente in der Kosmologie des Aristoteles,* Zetemata 34 (Munich, 1964):122.

⁵² This is done by Berti, *La filosofia,* pp. 368–70; A. Graeser, "Zu Aristoteles περὶ φιλοσοφίας (Cicero, *Nat. deor.* II 16, 44)," *MusHelv* 27 (1970):16–27; Aristoteles' Schrift 'Über die Philosophie' und die zweifache Bedeutung der 'causa finalis,'" *MusHelv* 29 (1972):44–61, esp. 61; Effe, *Studien,* pp. 132–36, and Bos, *On the Elements,* pp. 48–49, 62–63, 99 and n. 34 (cf. 61, n. 90). Though each has a slightly different interpretation of Aristotle's view, all minimize the difference between the celestial mechanics of *De Caelo* and of Cic. *Nat.D.* 2.44. Proponents of this approach fail to notice that the closer the celestial mechanics of Cic. *Nat.D.* 2.44 approaches that of *De Caelo,* the less reason there is to attribute the reference to *De Philosophia* at all and the more likely it is to be a Stoic adaptation of *De Caelo.*

⁵³ The theory of natural movements is also found in the context of a four-element cosmology in Philo, *Aet. Mund.* 28–34, a passage that has been attributed to *De Philosophia* on other grounds (= fr. 19b, Ross; cf. above, n. 45). If this reference is, in fact, drawn from *De Philosophia,* we have further confirmation that in *De Philosophia* Aristotle held a theory similar to the one presented in *De Caelo* III–IV.

426

[54] Presumably this voluntary movement of the heavenly bodies is analogous to the movement of human beings discussed in *Mot. An.* 6–7.700b4–701b32. As men need sensation and intellect to perceive a goal and move toward it, so the heavenly bodies are endowed with sensation and intelligence (Cic. *Nat.D.* 2.42 [= *De Phil* fr. 21a]; cf. fr. 24), which they doubtless use for the same purposes. The difficult question whether the Prime Mover is involved cannot be discussed here; cf. Jaeger, *Fundamentals*, pp. 140–45; H. von Arnim, "Die Entstehung der Gotteslehre des Aristoteles," *SB Wien*, phil.-hist. Kl. 212.5 (1931):7–9 (= F. P. Hager, *Metaphysik und Theologie des Aristoteles*, Wege der Forschung 206 [Darmstadt, 1969]: 1–15); W. K. C. Guthrie, "The Development of Aristotle's Theology," *CQ* 27 (1933):162–71 (= Hager [above], pp. 75–95); *Aristotle: On the Heavens*, Loeb Classical Library (Cambridge, Mass.—London, 1939), pp. xxv–xxvii; W. D. Ross, *Aristotle's Physics* (Oxford, 1936), pp. 95–96; Cherniss, *Aristotle's Criticism*, pp. 591–602; Graeser, "Aristoteles Schrift," pp. 44–61; Chroust, *New Light*, vol. 2 pp. 180–84; and H. J. Easterling, "The Unmoved Mover in early Aristotle," *Phronesis* 21 (1976): 252–65.

[55] Cf., e.g., Solmsen, *Aristotle's System*, pp. 287–303, 397–98. The main point still at issue is whether *De Caelo* III–IV represents a view different from, and therefore earlier than, the view of *De Caelo* I. Solmsen, *Aristotle's System*, pp. 293–303, and Seeck, *Über die Elemente*, pp. 97–98, 123–26, have argued convincingly that in *De Caelo* III–IV Aristotle shows no knowledge of the fifth element and that these books, or at least the theories reflected in them, were originally conceived before *De Caelo* I. There is still, however, some support for the traditional view that *De Caelo* III–IV were written at the same time as *De Caelo* I, but with attention focused so rigidly on the sublunar world that these books make statements that are misleading and appear to preclude the existence of the fifth element (cf., e.g., Moraux, *Du Ciel*, pp. xxxviii and n. 4, cxxxv and n. 3; and Bos, *On the Elements*, p. 70). If the latter view is correct, the first phase will be reflected only in *De Philosophia*, rather than in both *De Philosophia* and *De Caelo* III–IV; the ultimate reconstruction of the evolution of Aristotle's cosmological thought will be unaffected.

It should be noted that on the basis of a subtle and painstaking analysis of the various discussions of elements in *Gen. Corr.* and *Cael.* Seeck has questioned whether the evolutionary model is a complete and sufficient explanation for the great variety of theories of elements he claims to have discovered in these two works. His chief grounds for doubt are some subtle problems he sees in the relation between the fifth element and the various theories of elements that he has identified in *De Caelo* III–IV. Nevertheless, Seeck has no doubt whatsoever that the fifth element is later than the theories of *De Caelo* IV (cf. esp. pp. 97–98, 123–26, 157). Hence his concerns about the theoretical sufficiency of the evolutionary model need not trouble us here.

[56] See the attempts cited in n. 51 and 52.

[57] For a discussion of the absolute date of *De Philosophia* see A. H. Chroust, "The Probable Date of Aristotle's Lost Dialogue *On Philosophy*," *Journ. Hist. Philos.* 4 (1966):283–91 (= *New Light*, vol. 2, pp. 145–58). Chroust concludes that it was most likely published before 347 B.C. He also conjectures it is later than

the *Protrepticus*, therefore after 350 B.C. I. Düring, *Aristoteles: Darstellung und Interpretation seines Denkens* (Heidelberg, 1966), pp. 49–50, on the other hand, prefers an earlier date, i.e., ca. 360–355 B.C. Since the relative order of *De Philosophia* and other early works is still an open question, it is preferable to set Plato's *Timaeus* (i.e., ca. 360 B.C.) as the *terminus post quem*, and consider any reinterpretation that brings *De Philosophia* closer to the *Timaeus* as support for an earlier, rather than a later, date within the period of ca. 360 to 347 B.C.

⁵⁸ Some of the significant contributions to this controversy are: Jaeger, *Fundamentals, passim;* P. Wilpert, "Die Stellung der Schrift 'Über die Philosophie' in der Gedankenentwicklung des Aristoteles," *JHS* 77 (1957):155–62; C. J. DeVogel, "The Legend of the Platonizing Aristotle," in Düring and Owen, eds., *Aristotle and Plato*, pp. 248–52; and Düring, *Aristoteles, passim*.

⁵⁹ I would like to thank Friedrich Solmsen, George Kerferd, and David Furley for reading and commenting on an earlier version of this paper. I have benefited greatly from their criticisms and encouragement.

PART IV

POST-ARISTOTELIAN PHILOSOPHY

DAVID KONSTAN

Problems in Epicurean Physics

S OME surprising and ingenious propositions have been attributed to Epicurus, and to some extent to Democritus, in modern interpretations of ancient atomic theory. These propositions betray a serious involvement by the atomists with the physical and philosophical implications of their doctrines on matter and the void. In place of commonsensical notions about small, hard bodies falling or knocking about in space, we now find such sophisticated ideas as quantized space and time, discontinuous motion, theoretical minima—ideas comparable in their subtlety to the Eleatic paradoxes, which, as it seems, they were intended to resolve.[1] The advantage of these new interpretations is that they render a more satisfactory account of difficult arguments and principles in the Epicurean texts, they place the atomists squarely in the tradition of ancient philosophy from Parmenides through Aristotle, and they reveal a degree of philosophical intelligence behind ancient atomism that makes it a stimulating subject for investigation. At the same time they raise new problems, inconsistencies, and paradoxes which demand still further analytical machinery for their solution. Not that there is any cause for consternation in this fact. Even the most refined theories of modern physics produce singularities, limiting cases, and other conceptual potholes where the structure breaks down. It is entirely to be expected that a deeper analysis of the premises of ancient atomism should uncover new dilemmas, which in turn make fresh demands on the theory. There is nevertheless the real danger that in pursuing such lines of speculation as far as possible, we may begin to lose touch with the ancient texts and wander about in intellectual regions which, however fascinating in themselves, have little or nothing to do with the thought of Epicurus and his followers. That is, even if the problems we discover are real ones for the theory, the Epicureans may have been unaware of them or unimpressed by them, and in either case may not have given them much thought. But sometimes engagement with the theoretical issues in their own right points to new

This paper was presented at the 1976 New York meeting of the Society for Ancient Greek Philosophy and published, revised and expanded, in *Isis*, vol. 70, no. 253 (September 1979): 394–418; we thank the editors and the History of Science Society for permission to reprint.
David Konstan is the Jane A. Seney Professor of Greek at Wesleyan University.

significance in familiar texts or brings together apparently unrelated propositions in such a way as to suggest strongly a coherent address to the problems posed. At all events, this is the method of exposition which I have adopted: to raise what seem to me problems and paradoxes in Epicurean atomism, to respond to them, as far as I can, using the intellectual apparatus of the ancient theory, and to indicate, where possible, how the texts support the reconstructions which I offer.

I. Collision

There are several words in the Epicurean texts which refer to the process of collision among atoms and the subsequent rebounds which are the exclusive form of interaction between the basic particles. In general these terms are forms or compounds of *kopē, krouō,* and *pallō*. The question I shall take up here is the nature of such collisions. We may begin by recalling Epicurus' conception of the nature of atomic motion, as summarized in David Furley's fundamental essay "Indivisible Magnitudes":

> Epicurus was unable to accept Aristotle's theory of continuity, because it involved the notion of potentiality and this was in conflict with his fundamental principles. Like Leucippus and Democritus, therefore, he felt it necessary to accept the existence of indivisible magnitudes. To avoid Aristotle's refutation, he postulated that his indivisibles should be minima—not points without magnitude, but units of minimum extension. . . .
>
> Epicurus was now faced with further complications. Aristotle had demonstrated that indivisible magnitudes *in motion* require the assumption of indivisible units of space, time and motion, and, further, that there can be no real difference of speed. Epicurus accepted these conclusions, and worked out a theory of motion which would incorporate these features and at the same time be consistent with phenomena.[2]

This theory held that "one unit of motion involves traversing one unit of space in one unit of time; and in this case (he agreed with Aristotle) it is *never* true to say 'it is moving' but only 'it has moved.'"[3]

The problem is this: according to Epicurus' theory there is no way in which two atoms can collide or, what amounts to the same thing, no way to define the difference between collision and mere contiguity of atoms. For purposes of illustration, let us imagine two cubical atoms, which we may represent in two dimensions as squares. Suppose that they are a distance of six minimum units of space apart and moving toward each other at a speed of one minimum unit of space per minimum unit of time. If we represent the moment at which they are six minima apart as T(1), then clearly at T(2) they will be four minima apart, each atom having moved a distance of one minimum toward the other. At T(3) we shall find them separated by a distance of two minima, while at T(4) they will have traversed these last two units and so be up against one another. What happens at T(5)? Each atom is presumably inclined to advance another minimum unit in the direction it has until then been traveling. However, this is plainly impossible, since each represents an impenetrable obstacle for the other. For them to continue to move as they had been, they will be obliged to overlap physically, and this would be inconsistent with Epicurus' conception of matter. But neither is it the case that one or the other atom can shove its opposite number out of the way, thereby reversing the other's course and proceeding along its own. This is because, over a minimum interval, there is no moving, only a condition of having moved, which describes the position of an atom at any moment with respect to the moment before. Each atom is not only blocked from completing its motion across the subsequent interval, it is prevented even from beginning it because there is no beginning to such an interval, either in time or in space: there is nothing smaller than a minimum.[4] How, then, does either atom affect the subsequent motion of the other?

The same question may be put in a slightly different way. Imagine two atoms adjacent to each other and moving at a uniform speed in the same direction. Their relative positions at T(1), T(2), . . . , will be identical: with respect to one another they are not moving at all. Returning now to our earlier pair, which had been moving toward each other, in what way can they be said to differ at time T(4), when they are side by side, from our latter pair at any of the moments T(1), T(2), and so on? Of course, we can say that at the moment before, their positions were different with respect to one another, but this fact will only be relevant if we can show that the condition of the pair of atoms at any preceding moment or moments is in some way necessary to a complete or adequate description of them at the moment T(4). We may note in passing that Newtonian mechanics is not subject to this embarrassment because motion at an instant is defined as the limit of motion over a finite interval. With the Epicurean theory, on the other hand, Zeno's paradox of the arrow, which the atomists thought they had abolished, seems to have crept back in, though in a different guise. True, it now makes perfect sense to say that at any moment an atom is not moving (without recourse to Aristotle's formula that at a given instant a body is neither moving nor not moving, since for Epicurean minimalism there are no Aristotelian instants), yet over successive instants it does move, or has moved. Instead, the problem becomes this: what is it that distinguishes a moving atom at a given moment from a stationary one? If nothing, then why does the moving atom continue to move (or the stationary atom remain at rest)?[5]

The answer, I believe, is given in the passage by Furley quoted above: all atoms move always at a uniform speed. There are no stationary atoms. The two approaching atoms, once they are alongside each other, must change course (or at least one of them must), since they cannot proceed further in the direction they had been traveling, and they may not cease from motion. It *is* essential to take into account the previous history of an atom in describing it at any given moment because only in this way can we know whether and how it is moving with respect to other bodies (or to some absolute point of reference). In any collisions the direction of this motion may change but not its quantity. On this model, the word *collision* seems inappropriate, although it does correspond well with the Greek terms *krouō*, "to knock," and *kopē*, "a blow." "Deflection" is a better expression. An atom, simply by being there, prevents the progress of any other, which since it must move, departs along some other trajectory.

We come now to the third stage of the argument: what evidence is there that Epicurus was aware of this problem in his theory, or of its solution? We may begin by examining closely the text of Epicurus at the point where he first discusses atomic collisions in *Letter to Herodotus* 43:

> κινοῦνταί τε συνεχῶς αἱ ἄτομαι τὸν αἰῶνα καὶ αἱ μὲν εἰς μακρὰν ἀπ᾽ ἀλλήλων διιστάμεναι, αἱ δὲ αὐτὸν τὸν παλμὸν ἴσχουσιν, ὅταν τύχωσι τῇ περιπλοκῇ κεκλιμέναι ἢ στεγαζόμεναι παρὰ τῶν πλεκτικῶν.

> The atoms move continually throughout eternity, and while some of them separate from each other to a great distance, others maintain their vibration, when they happen to be supported by their entanglement or closed in by tangled atoms.[6]

As always in Epicurus, there are problems with the text. In the first place, Usener indicated a lacuna between αἰῶνα and καί, explaining: "hiatum scholion intrusum procreavit, duplex enim motus distinguendus erat, is quo atomi pondere suo deorsum feruntur et is qui conlisione gignitur, qui nunc solus respicitur."[7] Bignone and Bailey put the lacuna after καὶ αἱ μέν, adding that the doctrine of the swerve must also have been mentioned here.[8] I see, however, no reason to assume that Epicurus must have introduced every kind of atomic motion in this paragraph. In the passage immediately preceding, the variety of perceptible phenomena is explained by the various shapes of the atoms. Epicurus then turns, not to motion as such, but to motion in compound bodies. For this we must know that the atoms are constantly moving: if they are not hindered, they will scatter widely, but if they are—and that is the main clause following the καί —they will continue to oscillate as they did (reading αὐτόν with the manuscripts, not αὐτοῦ or αὖ, suggested by Brieger and Usener, respectively[9]), since there will be nowhere else to go. Once we understand the connection between the necessary motion of the atoms and the process of collision or deflection, the sense of the passage as it stands is manifest.

Epicurus continues (Sec. 44):

ἤ τε γὰρ τοῦ κενοῦ φύσις ἡ διορίζουσα ἑκάστην αὐτὴν τοῦτο παρασκευάζει, τὴν ὑπέρεισιν οὐχ οἷά τε οὖσα ποιεῖσθαι· ἤ τε στερεότης ἡ ὑπάρχουσα αὐταῖς κατὰ τὴν σύγκρουσιν τὴν ἀποπαλμὸν ποιεῖ, ἐφ' ὁπόσον ἂν ἡ περιπλοκὴ τὴν ἀποκατάστασιν ἐκ τῆς συγκρούσεως διδῷ.

For the nature of the void which delimits each atom provides this, since it is unable to offer the resistance; and the solidity which belongs to them makes the rebound in the case of collision, to whatever distance the entanglement allows the separation from the collision.

The argument is straightforward. Atoms must move: if they meet no resistance, they simply advance as they were going; if they do, they move off some other way. We must beware of importing into ancient physics modern notions of billiard-ball mechanics, in which collisions involve transfer of energy or motion. There is no transfer in Epicurus' system; the source of motion is entirely within the individual atoms. Finally, Lucretius' description of the rebound strongly suggests a process of simple deflection: "it happens that suddenly they leap apart in different directions; nor is it surprising, inasmuch as they are absolutely hard in their solid weight [or mass], and nothing stands in their way from behind" (*fit ut diversa repente dissiliant; neque enim mirum, durissima quae sint ponderibus solidis neque quicquam a tergo ibus obstet*).[10]

Let us consider the reasoning behind Epicurus' claim that all atoms constantly move and move at the same speed. Furley has shown most persuasively the dependence of this part of Epicurus' theory upon Book Z of Aristotle's *Physics*. In a nutshell, Aristotle's argument is this. Partless entities must move in a jerk from one position to the next, or else they will be located at some moment partly in one place, partly in another, which contradicts the premise that they have no parts.[11] He goes on to argue that if time is continuous, so is space.[12] The proof is to consider bodies moving at different speeds; in a shorter interval of time, the slower must traverse a smaller interval of space, and we may contract the intervals indefinitely. Furley concludes then that Epicurus "accepted Aristotle's contention that faster and slower motion entails the divisibility of time and distance; he developed the theory that there are no real differences in the speeds of visible moving bodies."[13] Did Epicurus have no other choice? Surely he did: he could have assumed that atoms may linger two or more temporal minima in a given position before making the move to the next. Never, on this conception, could an atom be caught part way across a spatial minimum, which is the heart of Aristotle's criticism. If Epicurus did not elect this option, it was perhaps because there seemed to be no sufficient reason why an atom should take a longer or shorter time to prepare its leap into another place.[14]

But the real reason may be a simpler one: Epicurus admitted the uniform speed of the atoms because it was an essential premise in his theory, not least of all in the account of atomic deflections. Only with this premise could Epicurus explain the constant movement of atoms after collision. The postulate of uniform motion of atoms is, in fact, analogous to the modern concept of the conservation of energy, differing however in one crucial respect. Whereas the conservation of energy applies to a dynamic system of particles, in Epicurus' theory it is reduced to a property of each corpuscle individually. The absence of a notion of transferable energy, or of energy as a feature of a system, is a major weakness in Epicurean physics; but his principle of uniform atomic motion is, like the conservation of energy, a bastion against entropy, the final degeneration of all motions as a result of innumerable collisions. No further principle is required to explain the continuous and eternal activity of atoms in the universe.

II.   Contact

The reason why atoms deflect each other in collisions is that they are impermeable (see *Letter to Herodotus* 44, quoted above); in the punning phrase of Lucretius, "officium quod corporis exstat officere" (I 336–337). How is this impenetrability accounted for? Taking the atomists as a group, four kinds of reasons are indicated in our sources: smallness of the atoms, their partlessness, their hardness or solidity, and the absence of void in the basic particles. Furley has suggested that all four reasons may be attributed to Democritus.[15] Plainly, they fall into two pairs, smallness being a function of partlessness, while hardness is the condition of matter as such—this by definition—and only the presence of void makes possible the division of apparently solid objects. Furley puts the questions: "Why did Democritus stress the hardness and imperviousness of the atoms, and the fact that they contained no void, as causes of their indivisibility? He certainly did so; yet to meet the Eleatics' arguments it was a *partless* unit that was required, rather than a hard one." Furley finds the answer to this problem in *De generatione et corruptione* I 8.

> The Eleatics, says Aristotle, objected to the pluralists that if the universe is divisible in one place and not in another, this seems like a piece of fiction. Why should it be so? We have the atomists' answer in the hardness of the atoms. What *is*, they said, is indivisible (as the Eleatics claimed): each atom is absolutely solid, packed with being and nothing else. There is no void, or not-being, in an atom; hence nothing can penetrate it, so as to divide it. The universe as a whole is divisible, however, in the sense that there is a plurality of existents separated by void.[16]

I am afraid I do not follow Furley's reasoning here. All the atomists needed to answer the Eleatics' conundrum was to posit the reality of empty space. This of course violated the Eleatics' fundamental principle that not-being cannot be used in any way as an analytical concept, but the atomists' attitude on this point was *tant pis* for the Eleatics. With this postulate alone, Democritus could have concluded that the universe may be divided where there is void, but not where there are atoms, because the atoms, being partless, cannot be further reduced. The hardness of the atoms was necessitated by a different and quite simple requirement, namely, that atoms be incapable of occupying the same place at the same time. For there is nothing in the description of atoms as small or partless which precludes this. However, the postulate that atoms are indivisible because they contain no void is too strong for Democritus' purposes, since it gives us two different causes for the same phenomenon, one of them quite otiose. It would have been sufficient merely to posit the atoms' *apatheia;* to explain it involved Democritus in a redundancy.[17]

However the case may be with Democritus' theory, Epicurus decisively separated the two arguments when he lifted from the atom its status as minimum or partless entity, attributing this feature to his (presumably) novel concept of smallest bits (*elachista, minima*) which themselves cannot have an independent existence (hence cannot be atoms). The atom, then, became simply a body of whatever size (though in actuality limited to imperceptibly small magnitudes), defined by the absence of any admixture of void, in other words, an extended volume bounded by space. Moreover, the solidity (*pleres, stereotes, mestos* are words used in this connection by Epicurus) of the atom plays a quite distinct role in Epicurean theory from arguments centered on the properties of *minima*. Solidity is the basis for the ultimate physical stability of the universe, the fact that matter cannot wither away (a) to nothing, or (b) to units indefinitely small. The doctrine of minima, on the other hand, was addressed to rather different considerations, such as the discontinuous nature of space, time, and motion. It is this very distinctness which leads me to doubt Furley's attempt to fuse the two lines of reasoning in his analysis of Sections 56–57 of the *Letter to Herodotus*.[18] The passage reads:

πρὸς δὲ τούτοις οὐ δεῖ νομίζειν ἐν τῷ ὡρισμένῳ σώματι ἀπείρους ὄγκους εἶναι οὐδ' ὁπηλίκους οὖν. ὥστε οὐ μόνον τῆς εἰς ἄπειρον τομὴν ἐπὶ τοὔλαττον ἀναιρετέον, ἵνα μὴ πάντα ἀσθενῆ ποιῶμεν κἂν ταῖς περιλήψεσι τῶν ἀθρόων εἰς τὸ μὴ ὂν ἀναγκαζώμεθα τὰ ὄντα θλίβοντες καταναλίσκειν, ἀλλὰ καὶ τὴν μετάβασιν μὴ νομιστέον γίνεσθαι ἐν τοῖς ὡρισμένοις εἰς ἄπειρον μηδ' ἐ⟨πὶ⟩ τοὔλαττον. (56).

In addition, one must not imagine that there are infinitely many bits in a bounded body, even of indefinite size. So that not only must we eliminate division to infinity into ever smaller (parts), so that we do not make everything weak and, in our conceptions of aggregates, be compelled to crush and squander existing things into nothing, but also one must not imagine that in bounded bodies there is a way to pass to the infinite even (by dividing) into (continuous but nonvanishing) ever smaller (parts).

Furley proposed taking the phrase *tōi hōrismenōi sōmati* to mean the atom, and the *onkoi*, accordingly, as the parts of the atom. Krämer has since restated quite forcefully the reasons why it is preferable to interpret *sōmati* as referring to any bounded body and to understand *onkoi* in the usual sense of particles.[19] My point here is that the clause following *ou monon* ("not only") affirms the thesis which I labeled (a) above, while the clause following *alla kai* ("but also") has reference to thesis (b). Thesis (a) is taken as already demonstrated (as indeed it was, rather summarily, earlier in 39). Thesis (b) is argued in the following paragraph (57), in the claim that an infinite number of parts, however minuscule, must sum to an infinite volume.[20] Lucretius gives another argument for the proposition: if the atomic constituents of nature could be infinitely small, then it would be impossible to conceive how they might ever recombine into coherent objects on the perceptible or macrocosmic scale (III 551–564).

In Epicurus' theory, at least, the explanation of the impenetrability of the atom on the ground of the absence of void is in principle detachable from arguments concerning minima or partless entities. In the analysis presented in Sections 56 and 57, it is assumed that matter free of void is indivisible; the only thing at issue is how small are the units of pure matter in nature. The answer is, of course, that they are of finitely small size. Now one problem we might offer Epicurus' theory is the possibility that atoms are hollow, in which case they might be said to contain void but nevertheless present a solid and impenetrable surface. I suppose that Epicurus excluded this possibility, though it is not an important omission. It is an entirely different matter, however, with the following difficulty. Imagine once more two atoms in the shape of boxes, placed alongside each other, face against face, as at the moment of collision. Between the two atoms there is no void. How then can they be separated, if indeed bodies can only be divided by cutting along the space between them, solidity being nothing but the absence of this space?[21]

To this dilemma it might be objected that Epicurus took as axiomatic the fact that atoms could not change in any way save in position and orientation. But the inalterability of the atoms was presented as a consequence of their solidity, not as an additional premise. Again and again we are told that the two fundamental principles (*archai*) of the Epicurean philosophy of nature are matter and the void, from which all other properties follow. The atoms are distinguished precisely by the intervening stretches of emptiness. Thus Epicurus speaks of ἡ τοῦ κενοῦ φύσις ἡ διορίζουσα ἑκάστην αὐτήν ("the nature of the void discriminating each [atom]," Sec. 44). The testimony of Simplicius is unequivocal:

For they [the atomists] said that the principles were infinite in number, and supposed that they were atomic and indivisible and impassive because they were compact and did not partake of void; they said that division occurred according to the void in bodies, but these atoms, being separated from one another in the infinite void and differing in shapes and sizes and position and order, raced in the void, and, intercepting each other, they collide and some rebound wherever they chance to, while others are interwoven with each other. . . .[22]

Finally, a passage from Aetius: "It was called an atom not because it is smallest, but because it cannot be cut, being impassive and without a share in void."[23] I have quoted these representative citations in order to show that the Epicureans were at least aware that to explain imperviousness by the absence of void means also to define atoms by the fact that they are bounded by space rather than more matter. Continuous matter is indivisible, divisible matter is discontinuous. But when two atoms are in contact, they are no longer discontinuous; how is their boundary defined? To find an answer, it is necessary to re-examine the reasons why the Epicureans separated the issues of hardness and partlessness—in other words, to look again at the question of minimal parts. And that, of course, means Aristotle.

In his chapter "Aristotle's Criticisms and Epicurus' Answers," Furley demonstrates brilliantly how Epicurus' conceptions of atomic time and motion were responses to Aristotle's analysis of the doctrine of spatial minima. Further on, Furley observes:

But this still leaves it undecided why Epicurus chose to make his minimum units of extension into *parts* of atoms, and not into the atoms themselves. . . . I have not been able to find any direct evidence on this question; but it is possible to make a reasonable guess. Aristotle's careful analysis of the geometry of motion made it clear that the distance traversed by a moving body must be composed of indivisible minima, if there are indivisible magnitudes at all. So he made it necessary for Epicurus to consider, not merely the atoms, but the places successively occupied by moving atoms. It must then have become obvious that the units must all be equal (otherwise absurd consequences would follow, such as that an indivisible space was too small or too large for an indivisible atom to fit into it). But if this is so, then either all atoms must be equal in size, or else some atoms must occupy more than one unit of spatial extension. The first alternative, so Epicurus thought, did not square with the phenomena. So he adopted the second.[24]

I leave aside the question of Democritus' conception of space; if it differed from Epicurus', it must have been fairly primitive, as Krämer makes clear.[25] On the issue of parts, however, there seems to be an oversight in Furley's argument. For to prove that "some atoms must occupy more than one unit of spatial extension" does not entail that *no* atoms may be exactly one minimum in magnitude. But it is just this latter, stronger proposition which we need to demonstrate. This is not a casual distinction. For just as the essential difference between Democritus and Epicurus on the nature of the atom is that for Epicurus the atom had parts, so the essential difference between them on the nature of minimal or partless entities is that for Epicurus, they could never subsist independently but must always exist only as parts of larger bodies. Lucretius' phrase *minimae partes* is in no way redundant: they are not simply partless, they are less than wholes and thus inseparable in fact or in thought from the atoms they compose. Our question then is why did Epicurus add this feature to the definition of the minima?

I believe the answer is to be found, not in Aristotle's analysis of motion, but rather in his analysis of contact and continuity in the opening paragraph of Book Z of the *Physics:*

> If there is continuity and contact and consecutiveness, as was defined above—that continuous things have their boundaries in common, touching things have them together, and consecutive things have nothing of the same sort between—then it is impossible for continuity to be composed of indivisibles, for example the line out of points, if indeed the line is a continuous thing, and the point is indivisible. For neither are the boundaries of points in common [*hen*] (for of the indivisible there is not both a boundary and some other part), nor are the boundaries together (for there is no boundary at all of the partless thing; for the boundary is a different thing from that of which it is the boundary). Moreover, it is necessary that the points be either continuous or touching each other, for a continuous thing to be composed of them; and the same argument applies also to all indivisibles. They would not be continuous according to the argument just stated. For everything touches either whole to whole or part to part or part to whole. And, since the indivisible is partless, it is necessary that it touch whole to whole. But whole touching whole will not be continuous. For the continuous has one part here and another there, and is divided into parts that differ in this way and are separated in place. But neither will point be consecutive upon point, nor instantaneous moment upon moment, so that magnitude or time can be composed from these. For consecutive means that there is nothing of the same sort between them, but there is always line between points and time between moments. Furthermore, there would be division into indivisibles, if indeed each [i.e., time and the line] were divided into these things of which they are composed; but no continuities were supposed to be divisible into partless things. And there cannot be another type of thing between. So it will either be indivisible or divisible, and if divisible, either into indivisibles or into forever divisibles; and this is the continuous. Clearly, then, every continuity is divisible into forever divisibles; for if into indivisibles, it will be indivisible touching indivisible; for the boundary of continuous things is in common and touches.

In brief, Aristotle's argument is this: a continuous magnitude cannot be composed of discrete, consecutive elements because the discreteness violates the very meaning of continuity—that any two distinct points bound a segment of the continuum. On the other hand, it cannot be composed of either continuous or touching partless elements because partless elements cannot be either continuous or in contact; the reason here is that continuity and contact are defined as relations between boundaries, and partless things cannot have boundaries distinct from some remaining portion. Now it is very important to be clear about what Aristotle does and does not say here. He does not argue, for example, that points are not part of a line. Quite the contrary, the point is the boundary of the line, and Aristotle is explicit that the boundary is a part of the whole (objects touching part to part touch precisely at their boundaries). However, these parts cannot be construed as a collection of free-standing entities arranged side to side, simply because they have no sides. That is, the partless entity has no independent existence, but subsists only as a part (cf. *De anima* 431b15–17: "So one thinks of mathematical entities, which are not separated, as though they were separated, whenever one thinks of them").

Simplicius, in his commentary on this passage in the *Physics* (268 Usener), suggested (cf. ἴσως) that Aristotle's argument was directed against the early atomists and that Epicurus, in sympathy with the Democritean conceptions but daunted by the force of Aristotle's logic, abandoned partlessness as a cause of the atom's indivisibility, though he preserved Democritus' other premise, that of impassivity (*apatheia*) as the reason for this quality of matter. But how, in fact, would Aristotle's reasoning have told against Democritus' theory? If Democritean atoms were true minima, and if indeed he did not think it necessary to posit a granular conception of space as well, as modern analysts seem to agree, then in the Democritean system there were no physical continua, and therefore there was nothing for Aristotle's critique to challenge. But if we look, not to Aristotle's conclusion, but to the first stage or lemma of his theorem, we may discover the issue that troubled Epicurus. Aristotle seems to have shown that Democritus' atoms, being partless, could not touch each other except as whole to whole, which is to say by overlapping—which contradicted the principle of atomic impermeability.[26] And Epicurus found the solution to this problem, here as often elsewhere, by accommodating his materialist analysis entirely to Aristotle's requirements.

Epicurus, then, abandoned the notion of a self-subsisting minimum entity. Every actual body accordingly has parts, and among these parts may be included all surfaces, edges, and corners. Thus, the Epicurean atoms answer to all the conditions imposed by Aristotle's definitions of continuity and contiguity. Moreover, with the stipulation of minimum parts, Epicurus' atoms are impervious to Aristotle's whole argument for infinite divisibility in the passage cited. The only (but crucial) difference is that the extreme or limit is assumed to be an inconceivably small but nevertheless finite quantity, while for Aristotle the boundary is of zero magnitude in at least one dimension.

Furley, however, has charged Epicurus with one departure from Aristotle's analysis, a departure so serious as to suggest that Epicurus altogether abandoned the line of reasoning which Aristotle had developed. In Section 58 of the *Letter to Herodotus*, Epicurus is speaking of minimum parts in perceptible objects: "We examine these beginning from the first and not in the same (spot), nor touching parts to parts, but in their own nature as things that measure sizes, more of them measuring a greater thing and fewer of them a lesser." Furley remarks on this sentence: "Here Epicurus answers Aristotle with an echo of his own words. These indivisible units are ranged in order in the continuum, and their contact is neither of whole with whole (i.e., 'within the same area') nor of part with part." Furley goes on to observe: "But Aristotle said that contacts *must* be either of whole with whole or of part with part or of part with whole. Epicurus clearly envisages another possibility altogether. His indivisibles, he explains, are to be *units of measure*: that is to say, they are to have extension."[27]

If, of course, Epicurus was simply unimpressed by Aristotle's analysis and dismissed it casually with the suggestion that there was some other way in which partless entities may be arranged in a continuum, then the argument which I have been developing must collapse. To see that this is not the case, we may put the following question to Aristotle's theory: given that an extremity is part of a whole, how is it attached? The extremity itself has no parts, else there would be an infinite regression, each boundary defined by a further boundary. Thus, the extremity cannot be continuous or contiguous with the remaining substance; nor, clearly, will it do to suppose it divided from it by a stretch of some other kind of matter. The answer to this conundrum is that we are not required to explain the connection between body and surface in the same way that we must account for the contact between two discrete bodies because a surface can only be understood as a part; it is not and cannot be discrete. Because we cannot conceive of it as a discrete element, there is no sense in inquiring how it might abut another object. Similarly, Epicurus was not obliged to indicate how his minima, which were likewise inconceivable except as parts, were arranged in the larger mass; it was sufficient to say that they did not touch part to part, nor did they overlap.[28] Furley goes on to argue that by identifying the extremity with the indivisible part, the Epicureans "were then left without a word for the edges of the indivisible part; but the existence of its edges was a necessary consequence of their theory. . . ."[29] I can only say that the Epicureans did not, I am sure, believe that the minimum quantity had edges; else there was nothing to prevent its independent existence. Nor is there a hint in the texts of such a doctrine. Furthermore, Furley's suggestion that they "could have pointed out that the extremity is not a *part*," would not have commended itself to the Epicureans. Could it have worked for the minimum, it would have done for the atom, too. I suspect that the notion of a boundary that was neither a part of matter nor physically separable from it would have smacked too much of idealism for Epicurus' comfort.

I have been arguing that the chief reason why Epicurus defined his minima as always and essentially participating in some larger extended bit of matter was to solve the problem of contact among atoms, which is equivalent to the problem of boundary. I believe that a passage in the *Letter to Herodotus* tends to corroborate this point, if we read it correctly. Reasoning from the observation that sensible objects have perceptible but partless extremes, Epicurus affirms by analogy that the same must hold true for atoms:

> ἔτι τε τὰ ἐλάχιστα καὶ ἀμερῆ πέρατα δεῖ νομίζειν τῶν μηκῶν τὸ καταμέτρημα ἐξ αὐτῶν πρῶτον τοῖς μείζοσι καὶ ἐλάττοσι παρασκευά-ζοντα τῇ διὰ λόγους θεωρίᾳ ἐπὶ τῶν ἀοράτων.

> . . . further, it is necessary to think of the minimum and partless entities as the limits (or boundaries) of extended masses, providing of themselves the primary measure for greater and smaller things in the rational theory concerning invisible things.[30]

My translation of the phrase πέρατα τῶν μηκῶν follows Bailey and Krämer, but differs from Furley's version, which reads: "Further, we must take these minimum partless limits as providing for larger and smaller things the standard of measurement of their lengths . . ."; that is, Furley takes *elachista* and *amerē* as adjectives modifying the substantive *perata*, which serves as the subject of *paraskeuazonta* (a participial construction with *nomizō*, for which Furley gives a parallel in *Letter to Herodotus* 74, 3). Bailey's interpretation is, Furley contends, unnecessary and "makes poor sense, because we do not need at this stage to be *told* that the minima are limits or extremities,"[31] since this information had already been provided in Section 57:

> ἄκρον τε ἔχοντος τοῦ πεπερασμένου διαληπτόν, εἰ μὴ καὶ καθ᾽ ἑαυτὸ θεωρητόν, οὐκ ἔστι μὴ οὐ καὶ τὸ ἑξῆς τούτου τοιοῦτον νοεῖν καὶ οὕτω κατὰ τὸ ἑξῆς εἰς τοὔμπροσθεν βαδίζοντα εἰς τὸ ἄπειρον ὑπ-άρχειν κατὰ τοιούτου ἀφικνεῖσθαι τῇ ἐννοίᾳ.

> Since a bounded body has an intelligible extremity, even if it is not imaginable in itself, there is no way not to think of the same kind (of part) following this, and thus for one proceeding to the next in succession to be able to arrive in thought by such a method at infinity.

The passage is textually problematic, and its significance, moreover, depends in part on whether we agree with Furley that the reference is restricted to atoms and minima or with Krämer and others that it embraces all bounded bodies. Either way, however, it is not the case that Epicurus has already averred that the minima constitute boundaries; all that he has done is to assume that boundaries are not of no size, and that if bodies are composed of boundary-like parts, then an infinite number of them must generate a mass of infinite size.

Krämer, as I have indicated, keeps the phrase πέρατα τῶν μηκῶν as a unit but would understand the term *perata* not as boundary but as limit in size, that is, smallest magnitude: "Das gleiche gilt für den Ausdruck πέρατα, womit nicht etwa 'Grenzen' im Sinne von 'äussersten Gliedern,' sondern Grenz- und Grundwerte der Ausdehnung, d.h. letzte Elemente der (linearen) Erstreckung (τῶν μηκῶν) gemeint sind, die nicht weiter teilbar sind und so eine letzte Teilungs 'grenze' setzen."[32] But this not only renders the passage redundant, it also ignores the feature of Epicurus' thinking for which Section 57 does give evidence, that the concept of the minimum part is acquired through extrapolation from the notion of an extreme border, whether a surface, edge, or corner. For it is only at the boundary that we can actually grasp, whether visually or intellectually, the minimum quantity as a percept or idea, though at the same time there is no way to conceive of it apart from the substance it delimits. According to Epicurean theory, our experience of minima is as boundaries. Of course, minima serve several purposes in the system, such as units of measure (*katametrēmata*) and as the basis of the atomistic reply to the Eleatic paradoxes. But that the minimum could not subsist independently occurred to Epicurus not in those contexts, but in the investigation of atomic boundaries.

In the sentence following the one we have been analyzing, Epicurus concludes his argument. I borrow Furley's translation and also his emendation of *ta ametabola* to *ta metabola*: "For the similarity between them and changeable things is sufficient to establish so much, but it is impossible that there should ever be a process of composition out of these minima having motion."[33] Why is this process impossible? Not because minima would be incapable of motion, since, as we have seen, the only argument Aristotle levelled at this (presumably) Democritean conception of the atom was that it entailed the minimalization of space and time, and this Epicurus accepted. I suggest that the impossibility resides in the *symphorēsis*, the coming together, and that the reasons are precisely Aristotle's: free-standing partless bodies cannot meet because they are without surfaces.

I shall conclude my discussion of the present topic with a question to Epicurus' theory: does the analysis of atomic boundaries in terms of minimum parts account satisfactorily for the discreteness of adjacent atoms? On the whole, it would seem so. The surface of a particle is inseparable from and inconceivable without the rest. It can only be part of that to which it has always belonged. To put it another way, the relationship among minimum parts in an atom is fundamentally different from the relationship among atoms; the former constitute continuous matter, while the latter, precisely in that they have the distinct surfaces which minima lack, can be brought into contact but cannot merge into a common corpuscle. We must concede, however, that the argument for the indivisibility of matter can no longer rest solely on the absence of void. That formulation will have to be regarded as part of the heritage of Democritus, which continues to be valid for Epicurus only in the sense that there is no void internal to an atom; atomic boundaries, however, are defined by the principles explicated above. And we may add, indeed, that without the additional postulate of minimum parts, there is no way that Epicurus could have solved the problem of contiguity and discreteness. For without a deep structure to matter, it differs from space only as its complement. It is a purely geometrical conception: we may picture a plane of dark shapes against a light background; adjacent and continuous forms cannot be distinguished. With the Aristotelian concept of boundary, made physical by endowing it with actual if minimal extension in all dimensions, Epicurus drew the line that divided contiguous substance.[34]

We know, from Diogenes Laertius' *Life of Epicurus* (10.28), that Epicurus wrote two books entitled *On the Corner in the Atom* (Περὶ τῆς ἐν τῇ ἀτόμῳ γωνίας) and *On Contact* (Περὶ ἀφῆς). Is it too presumptuous to suggest that in these volumes Epicurus may have taken up in greater detail some of the arguments concerning boundaries and contact which I have considered here?

III. Weight

Plutarch, in *The Opinions of the Philosophers*, tells us: "these bodies (i.e., atoms) have the following three attributes, shape, size and weight. Democritus, indeed, mentioned two, size and shape; but Epicurus added weight to these as a third."[35] There is no doubt, of course, about Epicurus' position, but in the case of Democritus there is room for considerable controversy. On one hand, there are several other testimonies to the effect that Democritus did not acknowledge weight as one of the fundamental features of atoms.[36] On the other hand, Aristotle states explicitly that in the case of atoms Democritus held that weight varies directly with size, a relationship which does not hold for compound bodies because they contain greater or lesser quantities of void.[37] Moreover, Democritus certainly provided an account of the phenomenon of weight, of bodies relatively lighter and heavier, in the perceptible world. How is the conflicting evidence of our sources to be reconciled? David Furley, in a recent investigation of the atomists' theory of motion, describes the current consensus as follows: "Faced with this contradiction, modern interpreters have propounded a clever solution. So long as atoms are not involved in a cosmic vortex, they are weightless, and collision is the only factor that explains their motion. The vortex, however, drives *larger* atoms to the center, and this tendency to move toward the center is what 'weight' means. So," he adds wryly, "this cake can be had and eaten."[38]

As will shortly become clear, I do not myself believe that the notion of atomic weight functions in quite this way in the Democritean system, but before addressing the implications of this issue for Epicurus' concept of weight, I must consider Furley's claim, advanced in this same paper, that the vortex played no role at all in Democritus' account of why things fall. Furley puts forward two objections to the modern solution. The first is that vortices do not have a punctual center: "the center of a vortex is a line, not a point, and although it may account for the motion of bodies towards the central axis, it does not yield an explanation of why bodies should congregate at the midpoint of the central axis. . . ."[39] I believe that Furley is in error here. Vortices do indeed have an axis; this they have in common with the mere centrifugal rotation of a column of fluid. But vortices also have a vertical vector, which is much in evidence in the action of a tornado. In fact, the centripetal force in the vortex is inseparable from the vertical motion at the axis, for the mechanics of the vortex are based on a drag effect, in which the speed of rotation and therefore the centrifugal force at one end of the column is less than that at the other. The result of this differential is a rotary flow along the axis of the funnel, with dispersion of the fluid at one end and a pressure toward the axis at the other. Figure I illustrates both the horizontal and the vertical flow patterns of the vortex: Moreover, since a vortex necessarily occurs in a medium, the effects of floating and sinking, that is, of differential densities, will also play a part in the distribution of any particles within the swirl. Light particles may, for example, be scattered at the top of the column, while heavy ones are concentrated at the bottom; objects of the appropriate density and shape (flat and wide, say) may even float suspended for a while at some point along the axial center.[40] Thus the vortex is a fairly complex system and can provide a model for several different physical phenomena, including dispersal and congregation of particles, suspension at different levels along the axis, and vertical motion in the axial vacuum. In a cosmological theory it could serve quite nicely as an explanation both for the differential distribution of substances varying in size, shape, and density, and also for a downward tendency in particles at or near the axis of the whirlpool. We do not have the evidence, so far as I know, to reconstruct even the broad outlines of Democritus' theory concerning this process, but it

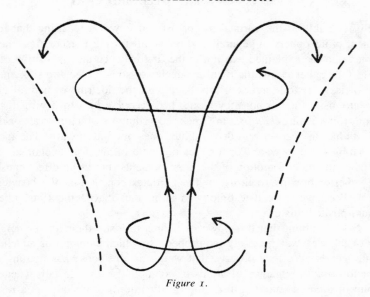

Figure 1.

is easy to imagine how a constant atomic rain could be invoked to explain why heavy objects are disposed to fall, or, when hurled upward, to slow down and ultimately reverse their course under such an imperceptible but massive bombardment.

Furley's second objection to the vortex theory is that "the Aristotelian view of weight as a tendency to move toward the midpoint of the cosmic sphere entails that the earth itself is spherical . . . , but Democritus believed the earth to be flat. . . ."[41] Here too, a clearer conception of the operation of the vortex provides us with a different image. An object caught at the bottom of an eddy is more likely to have the shape of a disk or drum; or perhaps we ought to imagine it resting like a metal plate on updrafts from below.[42] However this may be, I cannot agree with Furley that "the vortex seems totally inadequate to explain weight," and therefore I do not feel "forced back on the interpretation that weight, meaning a tendency to fall vertically, is a primary, irreducible property of the atoms." I continue to believe that it was an innovation of Epicurus to include weight in this sense among the fundamental attributes of the atom.

Before leaving Democritus' theory, however, we must examine one consequence of endorsing the role of the vortex: if the tendency of objects to fall—that is, the terrestrial effect of gravity—is to be ascribed to the action of the cosmic swirl, then what function is left to the category of weight in this system? I do not believe it is the case, as some have suggested, that weight is merely a redundant expression for a gravitational effect that is en-

447

tirely reducible to the vortical mechanism. It is worth recalling that for the ancient philosophers in general, and above all for the Presocratics, the phenomenon to be explained was not in the first instance the disposition of matter to fall; rather it was the twin tendencies of some objects to sink and others to rise. Aristotle attacked this issue with the doctrine of natural places. The atomists, though not they alone, had recourse to a theory of displacement or extrusion, *ekthlipsis* in Greek, according to which heavier or denser objects had the capacity to drive lighter ones out and upward. The fact that air bubbles rise in water, or tongues of flame in air, was explained, not in terms of the natural motion of the rarer elements, but as an effect caused by the superior downward thrust of the particles constituting the heavier medium. We have explicit testimony in Simplicius that Democritus, like Epicurus, posited this effect.[43]

Now I submit that this power of atoms to jostle their lighter neighbors out of the way was precisely the property to which Democritus attached the name *weight*. We may observe that weight in this sense has nothing whatever to do with tendency of atoms or compound bodies to fall; whenever a group of atoms is moving in a uniform direction and encounters a resisting surface or texture of corpuscles, the heavier (if they are atoms) or the denser (if they are compounds) will force their way further in the given line of progress and displace the lighter. To be sure, this process will only yield the regular contrariety of direction exhibited in the perceived motion of lighter and heavier substances when the random atomic movements are organized into a more or less uniform current, and such a current was assumed by Democritus to arise out of chance turbulences evolving into vortices. That is, the vortex is a necessary condition of the observed phenomena of displacement. But, in the first place, the vortex is not a sufficient condition: it must be supplemented by the power associated with weight. In the second place weight is not even a necessary condition for the formation of the vortex and the tendency of matter to fall. Against the hypothesis that Democritus saw any connection between weight and some privileged direction in the universe, I may add that I see no reason at all to suppose that according to his theory the vortices in different cosmoi necessarily had the same orientation.

Why did Democritus not elevate weight to the rank of one of the primary qualities of the atom, along with size and shape? Perhaps it was because weight was, for Democritus, simply a function of size,[44] which was certainly not the case for Epicurus. More likely, though, is the fact that weight could only manifest itself as a relation among atoms and under certain specified conditions; a single atom, considered in isolation, would present itself only as a geometric form. If this is so, then we can see that, at least with respect to the atomists, there was some justice in Aristotle's claim

448

that his predecessors had not accounted for weight as such, but only for the heavier and the lighter.[45] In the Democritean conception, it does not make sense to speak of the weight of an atom as such, but only with respect to other atoms heavier or lighter than itself.

In the physical theory of Epicurus, the role of *ekthlipsis* is every bit as important as it was for Democritus, if not more so. The pseudo-Plutarchan treatise *On the Opinions of the Philosophers* preserves a fairly detailed account of the distribution of the elements during the creation of the cosmos based entirely on the operation of this principle (308 Usener), and Simplicius too, as I have indicated above, makes clear the connection between weight and displacement in Epicurus' system.[46] Plainly, the Democritean concept of weight—that heavier, which is to say larger, atoms have the capacity to displace smaller and lighter ones—is essential also to Epicurus' view, and there can be little doubt that he simply adopted this function along with the doctrine of extrusion. Epicurus' own contribution was to make the category of weight serve a second purpose as well, that of accounting for the uniform flow of the atoms, without which it was impossible to explain the phenomena of sinking and floating.

For reasons that are still somewhat obscure to me, the vortex fell out of favor as a paradigm of the cosmological process in the time of Plato and Aristotle. I suspect that the vortex came to be considered a complex motion, which itself demanded an explanation in terms of simpler forces such as linear and rotary translation; in the pseudo-Aristotelian *Mechanica*, for example, the action of a vortex in collecting particles at the center (*meson*) is presented as a problem, and the solution is given in terms of circular motions (*Problem* 35, 858b3 ff.). Epicurus, at any rate, abandoned it as a cause of gravitational phenomena and posited in its place an inherent disposition of the atom to move in a single privileged direction. Such an assumption was undoubtedly facilitated by the doctrines of natural motion propounded by Plato and Aristotle, despite the great differences between the theories. In any case, Epicurus was also responsible (again, I am sure, under the influence of Aristotle) for assigning the name of weight to this power. At first sight this appears to be a perfectly reasonable move, but again I emphasize that two quite different concepts are cohabiting under the cover of a single term in the Epicurean interpretation. We are apt to overlook this because in the modern, Newtonian analysis of gravitational attraction the force varies directly with the mass of the bodies involved, and hence the same formula that defines the attraction also accounts for its greater magnitude in the case of heavier substances. There is no such relationship in the ancient system. As a property of the atom in itself, weight is only the tendency of atoms to move down in preference to some other direction. All atoms do this at a uniform speed, smaller and larger ones exhibiting no distinctions in this respect. Thus, if we look only to this feature, it cannot be said that weight implies any notion of heavier and lighter; it is an absolute property, not admitting of gradations. In the theory of extrusion, on the other hand, weight is a function of the size of the atom, and remains, as it was with Democritus, essentially a relative concept (cf. *Letter to Herodotus* 61).

It is worth noting that as an explanation of the observed phenomena of terrestrial gravitation, the Epicurean notion of atomic weight is not an obvious candidate. To say that all atoms fall uniformly downward does not explain why solid and liquid masses plummet to the earth, since the earth itself should, on this reasoning, be sinking as fast as any other body. The Epicurean explanation was that the earth's downward course is retarded by the resistance of a relatively thick or viscous atomic medium which surrounds it; the smaller, narrower objects on its surface more easily penetrate this fluid, which on the upper side of the disk may be recognized as the atmosphere. In this account, however, it seems that the Epicurean principle of *isotacheia* or uniform atomic velocity is a necessary premise, since it explains why the relatively compact aggregate of atoms that constitutes a cosmos—that is, the medium itself—must fall more slowly than free particles: collisions introduce a horizontal component to the atomic motions which reduces in a proportional degree the vertical or downward speed. I do not, however, know of any evidence that the Epicureans actually thought the problem through in this way.

I have argued that the Epicurean conception of weight may be understood as a disposition of the atoms to move in a privileged direction, which is defined as down. (Strictly speaking, I ought to discriminate between the two senses of weight in Epicurus' theory, gravitational and that relevant to extrusion of *ekthlipsis*; but in all that follows I shall be concerned only with the former quality, that is, with Epicurus' distinctive contribution.) Furley puts it well when he writes: "Epicurus defended and revised the Atomist theory of motion by introducing something like the concept of a vector."[47] But how did the Epicureans imagine this process to occur in the case of individual atoms? Commenting on Section 61 of the *Letter to Herodotus*, Furley explains it as follows:

> Two kinds of motion are mentioned here: motion downward, which is due to weight, and motion upward or sideways, which is due to collision. The last sentence of this passage may need explanation. Epicurus says that motion due to either one of these causes will go on at the same speed until it is countered. If it is downward motion, it can only be countered by collision with another atom coming up or across; if it is upward or sideways motion, it can be countered by collision or by the reassertion of weight. In the latter case one would expect a slow deceleration, followed by acceleration in another direction, but this is ruled out. Motion at full speed in one direction is

followed instantaneously by motion at full speed in the other direction. Of course, variations in weight must cause variations in motion (Arrighetti is right to stress this). Variations may be of two kinds, in direction or in distance. If a falling heavy atom collides with a light atom, then the heavy atom may perhaps be only *slightly* deflected, or else it may be turned directly about but move upward through only a few space units before its weight reasserts itself.[48]

The nub of the issue is the picture which Furley presents of the "reassertion of weight." The behavior of objects in the phenomenal world does, of course, provide a fair analogue to this description, although continuous deceleration to the apogee followed by gradual acceleration downward is a feature that is not preserved on the atomic scale.[49] As I suggested above in the case of Democritus, this behavior could be explained as a result of continual collisions between the rising object and the stream of descending atoms, here propelled by their own gravity rather than by the vortex. I do not know of any direct evidence that the Epicureans invoked this mechanism to explain the phenomenon of gravity, but there is a remarkable analogue to it in their theory of the operation of the magnet. Lucretius (VI 1022–1033) recounts how a magnet emits effluences, resembling simulacra, which have the power to scatter particles of air in the immediate neighborhood, thereby producing a partial vacuum. The result is a suction effect, which draws matter into the void. In the case of most substances this matter is provided by surface films which are detached from the main mass. But iron, a dense material whose atoms are tightly intertwined, does not release such laminae, and hence the entire lump is dragged toward the magnet. Of particular interest is the analysis of the suction in terms of atomic mechanics. A fraction of the particles on all surfaces of the iron object will at any given moment be moving outward from the center. In the direction of the magnet alone, however, they will meet no resistance because of the vacuum. This gives rise to a differential of forces along the axis between the magnet and the object; more atoms in the object are tending toward the source of attraction than away from it. To put it another way, it is air pressure, consisting in an inequality in the probability of atomic collisions on opposite faces of the object, which drives the iron to the magnet. To return to the problem of gravity, we can see how the tendency of atoms to descend would result in a differential vertical pressure in the atmospheric medium, which could be adduced to explain the observed deceleration of rising projectiles and acceleration of falling bodies.

But what about the reassertion of weight on the atomic level? In the first place, let us recall the mordant derision with which Cicero greeted the doctrine of the swerve, on the grounds that it was an arbitrary and uncaused occurrence.[50] Is it likely that Cicero and other critics of Epicurus would have passed over in silence the far more startling spectacle of an atom hurtling at full tilt upward, only to reverse itself for no apparent reason and at no fixed time or place in an equally precipitous descent? But this argument, which has the double fault of being both of the *eikos* form and *ex silentio*, will not bear much weight.

There is a text of Epicurus which suggests a different story. The last sentence of the passage from the *Letter to Herodotus* which, as Furley says, calls for explanation, reads as follows:

ἐφ' ὁπόσον γὰρ ἂν κατίσχῃ ἑκάτερον, ἐπὶ τοσοῦτον ἅμα νοήματι τὴν φορὰν σχήσει, ἕως ἀντικόψῃ ἢ ἔξωθεν ἢ ἐκ τοῦ ἰδίου βάρους πρὸς τὴν τοῦ πλήξαντος δύναμιν.

This is Furley's translation: "For as long as one of these two motions is in force the atom will move as quick as thought, until there is a counter-blow, either from something outside, or else from its own weight acting against the force of the object which hit it."[51] What is the meaning of the final clause? Usener excised it from the text as gloss, while other commentators, though not indulging in so drastic a revision, simply ignore its significance. Yet it suggests that the proper weight of an atom asserts itself only upon collision with another body. There seem to be two kinds of counterblows described here, one purely external (*exothen*), the other involving also the action of the atom's own characteristic weight (*ek tou idiou barous*).

I submit that for Epicurus all appreciable changes in the direction of atomic motion, including those which result in a downward course and occur under the influence of atomic weight, are consequences of atomic collisions (I leave aside the *clinamen* or swerve, which could not exceed a minimum unit of deviation). Accordingly we may interpret the gravitational property of atoms as a tendency to emerge from collisions in a preferred direction, a direction which is, by definition, down. It is important to be wary of carrying modern notions over into the analysis of ancient mechanics. I know of no evidence in Epicurus that even hints at a rule such as the conservation of momentum, which would entail that the direction of atomic rebounds bear some lawful relation to the shape of the particles and their direction of motion preceding the impact. Atomic collisions in the Epicurean system are in fact rather deflections; atoms blocked from proceeding in a given course by the presence of an opposing particle and under the necessity of maintaining an unvarying velocity simply take off in another direction. There is nothing to indicate that this is a determinate direction; nothing, that is, except the principle that the motion of an atom following a collision is most likely to be downward. The cause of this disposition is, I believe, what Epicurus called *weight*.[52]

The role of weight in the doctrines of extrusion and the fall of atoms does not exhaust the functions of the term in Epicurus' system. In the first part of this paper I examined the principle of isotachy, or the uniform speed of atoms. The inspiration for this concept appears to go back to Aristotle's analysis of minima, as Furley has shown. But while Aristotle may have persuaded Epicurus that quantum motion, if it exists, must proceed at a rate of one unit of space for every unit of time, he did not provide an argument to demonstrate that particles in such a spatial and temporal grid must move at all. We know from a report in Sextus Empiricus that Diodorus Cronus contemplated both still and moving minima.[53] Epicurus may have felt that some force was needed to explain why atoms may not be at rest. Or again, even if Epicurus believed that atoms could not vary from their natural velocity, he may nevertheless have wanted some power or impulse to account, albeit redundantly, for the drive that maintained their momentum. Certain passages in Lucretius point clearly to such a function, for example at the end of the first book (I 1077–1078): *nec quisquam locus est, quo corpora cum venere, ponderis amissa vi possint stare (in) inani.* "Nor is there any place at which, when bodies have arrived there, they can stand still in space, having lost the force of their weight." Again, at V 423–424, we have atoms *percita plagis/ponderibusque suis . . . concita,* "driven by blows and impelled by their own weight." Elsewhere: "all atoms must race along either by their own weight or by some chance blow from another" (*cuncta necessest aut gravitate sua ferri primordia rerum aut ictu forte alterius,* II 83–85; cf. also II 184–215). Weight is made responsible not only for the fact that atoms tend to plunge downwards rather than in some other direction, but also for the thrust that guarantees their motion.

There are two other testimonies concerning Epicurus' theory of weight that bear on this problem. The first is the passage in Plutarch's *On the Opinions of the Philosophers* in which is recorded the information that Epicurus added weight as a third atomic quality to Democritus' other two (275 Usener). The relevant lines read:

ὁ δὲ Ἐπίκουρος τούτοις καὶ τρίτον βάρος προσέθηκεν· ἀνάγκη γάρ, φησί, κινεῖσθαι τὰ σώματα τῇ τοῦ βάρους πηγῇ· ἐπεὶ οὐ κινήθησεται.

I translate literally: "But Epicurus added weight as a third to these; for he said it is necessary that bodies move by means of the blow of the weight, since they will not be moved [sc. by some other force or agency]." We may observe that for the word *plēgēi,* "blow," Usener substituted *holkēi,* "attraction" or "pull." This is consistent with his emendation of Section 61 of the *Letter to Herodotus,* but the manuscript text is confirmed by a passage in Cicero's *De fato,* which records the same formula:

. . . declinat, inquit, atomus. primum cur? aliam enim quandam vim motus
habebant a Democrito impulsionis quam plagam ille appellat, a te, Epicure,
gravitatis et ponderis.[54]

The genitives *gravitatis* and *ponderis* are clearly in parallel construction with
impulsionis and accordingly must likewise depend on *plagam*. The passage
may be rendered: "The atom, says he [Epicurus], swerves. In the first place,
why? For they had another kind of power of motion from Democritus,
which he calls 'the blow of collision,' and from you, Epicurus, the blow of
heaviness and weight." A few lines later in the same paragraph, Cicero
speaks of "the natural motion of the atom's own weight" (*naturalem sui
ponderis motum*). It is perhaps plausible to take the word *plaga* not as
"blow" in the sense of "collision," but rather more generally as "impact,"
which may be stretched to signify something like force. The "impact of
weight," Cicero would be arguing, is a sufficient cause of atomic motion,
and the doctrine of the swerve is supererogatory. Moreover, Simplicius tells
us in his commentary on Aristotle's *Physics* that "Democritus, calling the
atoms motionless by nature, says that they move by means of a blow"
(Δημόκριτος φύσει ἀκίνητα λέγων τὰ ἄτομα πληγῆι κινεῖσθαί
φησιν).[55] This would appear to support the view that Democritus used the
term *blow* in a technical sense to indicate an inherent force of propulsion
in the atom, and that Epicurus borrowed the usage but transferred its reference to his own enlarged concept of weight. But if the motive force indeed
resided in the atom, it is difficult to see in what sense the particles could
be described as "motionless by nature." The blow must pertain to an external agency, in which case it can denote nothing other than collision.
From the perspective of modern physics, energy may be transferred through
collisions, but not created thereby, so that the *plaga* will not explain how
naturally stationary bodies are kept in motion. Whether Democritus coped
with this question, it is impossible to say.[56] But if his *plaga impulsionis*,
"blow of collision" or "impact of impulsion," referred specifically to the
effects of an encounter between atoms, then it is reasonable to suppose
that the parallel expression for Epicurus, *plaga gravitatis et ponderis*, designated as well a collision through which the property of weight was actualized; and similarly for the passage from Plutarch.

The above interpretation of Cicero and Plutarch does not deny to weight
a role as the cause of atomic motion. Epicurus may have felt that weight was
responsible not only for the prevailing downward course of atoms, but also
for their restless activity, for the fact that they must move. When deflected
from the vertical by collisions, they presumably preserve the celerity of descent. But the same passages seem also to support the idea that the effect of
weight is bound in some way to atomic collisions. The simplest hypothesis
to account for this connection is that all gross variations in direction, includ-

POST-ARISTOTELIAN PHILOSOPHY

ing resumption of vertical descent by oblique atoms, depend on atomic encounters.

Is Epicurus' conception of weight a coherent one? Critics from antiquity onward have heaped scorn upon Epicurus for supposing that in an infinite homogeneous space one could rationally define the directions up and down. Consider the view of Felix Cleve, who writes: "Adopting Democritean atomism without real understanding and out of ulterior motives that have nothing to do with any genuine interest in natural philosophy, Epicurus just bowdlerizes the theories of Democritus." As a case in point, Cleve cites "Epicurus' assumption of atoms of different sizes that are 'falling' with equal velocity parallel 'downwards' (when there is not yet an earth, even!). . . ." While the tone is perhaps more vituperative than is customary in contemporary criticism, the point which Cleve makes is commonplace. Even so excellent a student of Epicurean physics as Jürgen Mau could say: "Im unendlichen Raum gibt es kein absolute Oben und Unten, demnach auch keine Mitte."[57]

I must insist that this kind of objection to Epicurus' doctrine of weight and cosmic orientation is really quite vacuous. Of course there is no top and bottom to an infinite universe. But the hypothesis that atoms tend to rebound preponderantly in a single direction, or even that they merely favor one direction slightly more than others, affords a perfectly rigorous and intelligible definition of a vertical orientation in space. The issue is entirely analogous to the modern theory of a distinction in nature between left and right (the abolition of parity): the spin of particles emerging from certain reactions does not exhibit the expected symmetry but rather a statistical preference for one direction over the other. The theory may of course be wrong, due to faulty measurements or invisible factors; but it is not nonsense. Similarly with Epicurus' doctrine: whatever its faults or virtues as an explanation of the phenomena of gravity and displacement, there is no problem whatsoever concerning the logical status of his fundamental premise of a directional vector in the universe determined by the preferential course of weighted atoms.

There may seem to be a difficulty, however, with the notion of absolute space, with respect to which all atoms are said to be in motion. In an unbounded universe, we are free to choose our frame of reference. There is no reason, for example, why we cannot imagine ourselves moving along with a free-falling atom; with respect to the coordinate system in which such an atom served as the origin, all atoms descending under the influence of weight would appear stationary, while rising atoms would appear to be ascending with twice the velocity that Epicurus assigns them. On this matter, two things may be said. First, there is no doubt that Epicurus believed intuitively in an absolute frame of reference, a fixed spatial grid, in terms of

455

which falling atoms had real motion and no atoms could be said to be at rest. This is not surprising. As Arnold Koslow has shown, Newton too held such a view, and it has persisted into this century. Koslow quotes H. Feigl, "Once (in 1920) I heard a disciple of Franz Brentano's—Oscar Kraus at the University of Prague—debate Einstein with great excitement. He maintained that the following was a synthetic *a priori* truth: 'If two bodies move relatively to each other, then at least one of them moves with respect to absolute space.' " Feigl goes on to remark that "this illustrates beautifully the intrusion of the pictorial appeal of the Platonic 'receptacle' notion of space or a confusion of a purely definitional truth (regarding three coordinate systems) with genuinely factual and empirically testable statements regarding the motion of bodies."[58]

The critique of the notion of absolute rest and motion is quite independent of relativity theory, although relativity theory is in fact incompatible with such an assumption. The second point is that the relativity of frames of reference introduces no practical difficulty into Epicurus' system. One may be tempted to suppose, for instance, that in the absence of a fixed frame it makes no sense to speak of atoms having uniform velocity, since, as we have seen, we may select another set of coordinates, in motion with respect to the first, in terms of which such a statement will be false. However, provided we do not contemplate a relativistic geometry, it suffices to assert that there exists some frame of reference in which all atoms are moving at uniform speed; we may call this the absolute frame.[59] Naturally I do not mean to imply that Epicurus contemplated such a view. I wish only to indicate that contrary to opinions of some impressive scholars, there is nothing incoherent or inconsistent in Epicurus' postulates concerning weight and motion in infinite space.

IV. Conclusion

The interpretations of Epicurean physics which I have proposed here, taking as my point of departure the work of Luria, Mau, Furley, and others, point to a coherent and consistent body of thought which we can justifiably call a scientific model of mechanics. To be sure, it is a very simple model, one which does not suggest new phenomena for observation or yield many falsifiable postulates about the natural world.[60] I am reminded of a model which Norbert Wiener devised to illustrate how highly complex social interactions can be produced in a system defined by a few elementary principles.[61] Imagine a collection of mechanical toys, little robots, which are programmed to move at a uniform speed and to change course whenever they encounter resistance. If they are placed in a confined space, or gathered in sufficient quantity to prevent the aggregate from quickly dispersing, it will be possible to observe highly intricate and infinitely varied encounters and combinations. If we were to build in also a preferred direction of motion (i.e., weight), allow for an imperceptible swerve now and then, endow the robots also with a short, jerky gait, and speed the whole process up fantastically, we would have a pretty fair approximation of the laws which govern the fundamental constituents of the Epicurean universe. I do not mean to disparage the theory by this homely analogy. Science strives to explain the multiplicity of phenomena through a few powerful premises. Moreover, we are familiar today with discontinuities in the behavior of subatomic entities, with particles that move necessarily at an enormous but uniform velocity, with differences in orientation grounded in nature, with essentially random processes, such as scattering, at the microscopic level, with infinitesimals and countable infinities, with the problem of defining the boundaries of elementary bits of matter. That is, the problems with which Epicurus wrestled, and the solutions which he propounded, were not inherently absurd. As it happens, Epicurus' theory does not describe satisfactorily any class of particles that are significant in nature, nor, we may add, is it likely to. But for its subtlety, sophistication, and boldness, it represents a major achievement in the history of mechanistic world models. Indeed, given the scant knowledge we have of the working principles of Democritus' system, it may be said that Epicurus' theory is the first such model we can satisfactorily identify and describe. It is yet to claim its rightful place in the history of science.

NOTES

[1] The origins of the atomistic theory, and its sources in the problems posed by Zeno, will be discussed only incidentally in this paper. There are three studies to be recommended to the reader who wants full information on these subjects: the pioneering work of S. Luria, "Die Infinitesimaltheorie der antiken Atomisten," *Quellen und Studien zur Geschichte der Mathematik* (B: Studien) (1932–1933), vol. 2:106–85; Jürgen Mau, *Zum Problem des Infinitesimalen bei den antiken Atomisten* (Berlin: Akademie-Verlag, 1954); David J. Furley, *Two Studies in the Greek Atomists* (Princeton: Princeton University Press, 1967), Study I: "Indivisible Magnitudes."

[2] Furley, *Two Studies,* pp. 128–29.

[3] Furley, *Two Studies*, p. 121.

[4] We may be struck here by the connection between the minimalist hypothesis and Zeno's paradox called the *dichotomy*, according to which a runner can never begin a race, having always to make first a motion half the size of any we may specify; cf. Furley, *Two Studies*, p. 70. Cf. also the paradox posed by Sextus Empiricus, *Adversus mathematicos* X 144–47. Sextus locates two particles nine (i.e., an odd number of) intervals apart and inquires what happens after four moments of time have elapsed. The atoms, each moving at the same speed, will be separated by a single interval. They cannot both advance a minimum unit nor meet halfway inside the

final interval; nor may one atom advance while the other remains still without violating the principle of uniform speeds.

⁵ Zeno's paradox of the arrow posed this dilemma: an arrow in flight cannot change its position in a single instant. Since at any instant it is at rest, it must be at rest at every instant. But this contradicts the premise that the arrow is in motion; see Furley, *Two Studies*, pp. 71–72. Aristotle's answer is that motion and rest are defined over a continuous interval of time, and therefore at an instant, while it is correct to say that an atom is not moving, it is not permissible to conclude that it is at rest; it is neither moving nor at rest. See *Physics* Z 3, 234 a–b.

⁶ Epicurus, *Letter to Herodotus* 43. All translations in the text are my own unless otherwise indicated.

⁷ "The interpolated scholium caused the lacuna. For a twofold motion ought to have been distinguished, that by which the atoms are borne downward by their own weight, and that which arises through collision, which is the only one considered here." Hermann Usener, *Epicurea* (Leipzig, 1887; reprint, Stuttgart: Teubner, 1966), p. 8, and corrigendum, p. lxxvii. Fragments cited from this fundamental collection will be identified by "Usener" following the number.

⁸ Cyril Bailey, *Epicurus* (Oxford: Clarendon Press, 1926). Ettore Bignone's textual criticisms are recorded in his translation, *Epicuro Opere* (Bari: G. Laterza, 1920).

⁹ A. Brieger, *Epikurs Brief an Herodot* (Halle: Program des Stadt-Gymnasiums, 1882); Usener, *Epicurea*.

¹⁰ Lucretius, *De rerum natura* II 86–88.

¹¹ Furley, *Two Studies*, pp. 111–14.

¹² This proposition is equivalent to the contrapositive, that if space is discontinuous, so is time. Aristotle in fact held that time is not an independent dimension but only a measure of motion (*Physics* Δ 11, 218b–19a), and Epicurus adopted the same position (*Letter to Herodotus* 72–73; cf. Lucretius I 459–63). On this account, the quantization of time would seem to follow necessarily from that of space. For if one assigned an infinitesimal temporal measure to motion over a finite interval, then over any finite stretch of time, however small, a moving body must cover an infinite distance.

¹³ Furley, *Two Studies*, pp. 119–21.

¹⁴ Cf. Alexander of Aphrodisias, quoted in Simplicius' Commentary on Aristotle's *Physics* IV 8, p. 679, 12 ff. Diels (*Commentaria*), who argues that the velocities of Epicurean atoms must be equal because there is no reason why they should be unequal (cited in S. Luria, *Democritus* [Leningrad: Nauka, 1970], Frag. 314). On the other hand, Gregory Vlastos, "Minimal Parts in Epicurean Atomism," *Isis* 56 (1965):139, points out the high status of the contrary principle in early atomism: that "every possibility is realized in nature unless there is a definite reason to the contrary." Epicurus had such a reason. (All references to the Greek commentators on Aristotle are to the Berlin edition, *Commentaria in Aristotelem Graeca*. Luria's Russian edition of Democritus will be cited by author's name, following the number of the fragment.)

¹⁵ Furley, *Two Studies*, pp. 94–99.

¹⁶ Furley, *Two Studies*, p. 99.

458

[17] See the objections to Furley's argument in Michael C. Stokes, *One and Many in Presocratic Philosophy* (Cambridge, Mass.: Harvard University Press, 1971), p. 232. Stokes concludes that the physical unsplittability of the atoms was intended to "answer Parmenides . . . , by denying atoms the power to come to be or pass away in the same physical way as physical aggregates of atoms." I am afraid I do not see how this argument avoids the redundancy.

There is a tradition that Democritus believed that atoms could be very large, even the size of the cosmos; see 207 Luria and A47 in H. Diels and W. Kranz, *Fragmente der Vorsokratiker,* 3 vols. (6th ed., Berlin: Weidmann, 1951; hereafter cited as DK). If this is credible, then the argument for indivisibility on the grounds of smallness or partlessness must go. I share Furley's skepticism (*Two Studies,* p. 96) in the matter of these gargantuan atoms, although I secretly wonder whether Democritus did not, at some point in his life, publish a book containing this and certain other extraordinary speculations which were not always compatible with the main lines of his theory. Luria's attempt to show ("Die Infinitesimaltheorie," pp. 172–80) that Democritus distinguished between minima and atoms is unconvincing (see Furley, *Two Studies,* pp. 97–99). Among other things, it is inconsistent with his own argument that atoms, inasmuch as they are partless, cannot touch each other (see Luria, pp. 154–56, and below, n. 22).

[18] Cf. esp. Furley, *Two Studies,* pp. 10–12.

[19] Hans Joachim Krämer, *Platonismus und hellenistische Philosophie* (Berlin: De Gruyter, 1971), pp. 237–39; cf. also Vlastos, "Minimal Parts," p. 123, n. 13.

[20] For the common supposition in antiquity that the sum of an infinite series is necessarily infinitely large, see Luria, "Die Infinitesimaltheorie," pp. 106–07. We may observe here that the issue of divisibility was always bound up closely with that of individuation in Greek thought. For Zeno, the fact that division, once begun, could reach no finite terminus, was part of an argument—according to Plato—that being is one and unchanging. For Democritus, atoms of minimum but finite size were the least bits into which nature might be resolved. Aristotle met the problem by the doctrine of potentiality, as Furley says (p. 128; quoted above), together with the theory of immanent forms: objects consist of only so many parts as are formally distinct and coherent; continuous homogeneous matter, while divisible, is one until divided. Perhaps something like this notion lies behind the curious proposition which Sextus attributes to the Stoics, that finite spans, such as a race course, are covered in a single movement (X 123–38).

[21] A version of this problem arises in a proof tendered by Giovanni Battista Benedetti (1530–1590), designed to refute logically the idea that bodies of different mass but identical substance fall at proportionally different rates. Benedetti connects two small equal masses by a line and argues that at their center of gravity, which lies on the midpoint of the line, is concentrated the mass of a body the size of both together. Hence the point must fall at the same rate as the larger mass. But each of the smaller, joined bodies will, on the Aristotelian hypothesis, fall at a lesser rate. In this, Benedetti discovers a contradiction and concludes that the rate of descent does not vary with mass. If I understand Benedetti correctly, the issue is really whether the line joining the bodies makes of them a single object with a center of gravity midway between them, or leaves them their individual identities, according to which

ESSAYS IN ANCIENT GREEK PHILOSOPHY

each should behave as an unattached entity. Thus the problem lies with the geometrical conception of matter, in which contact entails unity. Benedetti's paradox depends on holding simultaneously both conceptions. See Ch. 10 of his "Disputations
on Certain Opinions of Aristotle," in *Diversarum speculationum mathematicarum et
physicarum liber* (Turin, 1585), translated in Stillman Drake and I. E. Drabkin, *Mechanics in Sixteenth-Century Italy* (Madison: University of Wisconsin Press, 1969),
p. 206.

²² On Aristotle, *De caelo* A7 p. 242.18 ff. Heiberg (*Commentaria*, vol.
VII) = 284 Usener. Or Simplicius again on Aristotle, *Physics* (D6; 274 Usener):
"They said in fact there was such an interval, which, existing between bodies, does
not permit the bodies to be continuous, as the followers of Leucippus and Democritus said. . . ." Themistius' paraphrase of the same passage makes the same point:
"For these are the two types of arrangement of space, either that it is scattered among
the bodies, as Democritus says and Leucippus and many others and finally Epicurus
(for all these give the weaving in and about of void as the reason for the separation of
bodies), or that it is separate and compact in itself, surrounding the heavens. . . ."

²³ Aetius, 267 Usener. The problem is formulated with exemplary clarity by
Stokes in *One and Many*, pp. 228–33, e.g., p. 229: "Given an infinity of shapes,
some atoms ought to dovetail exactly. . . . Such a pair, when fitted, ought presumably to present the same solidity as a single atom." Stokes does not propose a solution, save by suggesting a motive for the oversight: "Atomist neglect of this by no
means obscure point is likely to be a symptom of their concentration on other matters, notably the permanence and indivisibility of the atoms." Lucretius too emphasized the complementarity of matter and void, each serving as the boundary of the
other; see esp. I 526–27, 454, 403–10, 958–67. It is worth observing that Lucretius
appealed to two different conceptions of space: a three-dimensional manifold corresponding to the space of geometry and a physical void, defined by the absence of
matter, which enters, together with matter, into the composition of compound bodies. Empty space (*vacuum inane*, Lucretius I 523) is not redundant but represents the
portion of the mathematical continuum not occupied by matter. See the excellent and
detailed analysis by Peter-Rudolf Schulz, "Das Verständnis des Raumes bei Luk-
rez," *Tijdschrift voor filosofie* 20 (1958):17–56.

²⁴ Furley, *Two Studies*, p. 129.

²⁵ Krämer remarks: "Der Atomismus gehört, sofern er nicht nur eine physi-
kalische, sondern auch eine ontologische Hypothese ist, seinem eleatischen Ursprung
nach ausschliesslich zu den *onta*, eben den Atomen. Der Raum der Geometrie, das
Leere, hatte daran als das *me on* per definitionem keinen Anteil" (*Platonismus*, p.
277). I cannot understand how Democritus could have responded to Zeno's paradoxes on motion if in fact he confined his minimalist doctrine to matter only, and I
am accordingly inclined to suppose, against the majority of scholars today, that he
conceived of space too as a quantized grid; see esp. Luria, "Die Infinitesimaltheorie," pp. 172–80, who minimizes, in this and other respects, the differences between Democritus and Epicurus.

²⁶ There are some hints in the ancient testimonies that Democritus was aware
that partless entities could not touch, and that accordingly he held that his atoms do
not strictly speaking ever come into contact with one another. The evidence is col-

lected in Luria, Frags. 236–37; e.g., Philoponus on *De generatione et corruptione* I 8, p. 158: "Democritus did not speak precisely of contact when he said that the atoms are in contact with one another . . . but rather what he called contact was the atoms being near one another and not standing very far apart." Also Simplicius on *De caelo* III 4, p. 609: "They [Democritus and Leucippus] said that these alone [i.e., atoms] were continuous; for the others things which seem to be continuous approach each other through contact. So that they also abolished division, saying that what seems to be division is really a dissolution of things in contact, and, as a result, 'neither do many things come from one,' they said, for the atom cannot be divided; 'nor from many one' that is truly continuous, but rather each seems to become one through the weaving together of atoms." Philoponus on *Physics* III 8, p. 494: "but according to the assumptions of Democritus this is what happens: the atoms borne along in the void are bounded, and, correspondingly, touch nothing." If the Democritean atoms were in principle prohibited from meeting each other, then their distinctness—the fact that they do not coalesce—and their impermeability would in fact follow from the premise that matter is defined by the exclusion of void, and that division can occur only where space intervenes. Luria himself adopted just this view of the Democritean atom ("Die Infinitesimaltheorie," pp. 154–56). It is perhaps more likely, however, that the Greek commentators on Aristotle were attributing retrospectively to the partless atoms of Democritus properties which they believed must pertain to them as a consequence of Aristotle's critique.

[27] Furley, *Two Studies*, p. 115.

[28] It is, of course, difficult to imagine how finite units, even if they are minuscule, should not stand in ordered succession; the more so since they are said to be *katametrēmata*, or measures, of all magnitude. It is tempting to speculate that the packing of matter inside the atom is of a qualitatively different order of density than that achieved when corpuscles are placed adjacent to one another, and that, accordingly, there is a sense in which void continues to intervene between contiguous atoms. If the Epicureans held such a notion, it would explain their continued appeal to the principle that atoms are demarcated by void and that division is possible only where void subsists. Tempting as it is, however, I cannot find any evidence for this conception in the texts. Lucretius too begins his argument for minima with the notion of boundary (*cacumen*, I 599), and informs us that the parts are arranged *ex ordine* (605) and *agmine condenso* (606). The latter formula, however, cannot be construed as a technical term for the packing of minimum parts inside the atom, since variations of it occur elsewhere in quite different contexts, e.g., *denso agmine* in VI 100 of clouds, or *condenso conciliatu* in I 575, II 100 of atomic clusters.

[29] Furley, *Two Studies*, p. 116.

[30] *Letter to Herodotus* 59. Text as in Furley and Krämer, except that I have preserved the *proton* of the MSS for *protōn*.

[31] Furley, *Two Studies*, p. 26.

[32] Krämer, *Platonismus*, pp. 247–48: quotation on p. 247. So too H. Von Arnim ("Epikurs Lehre vom Minimum," *Almanach der Wiener Akademie der Wissenschaften*, 1907), Bignone, and Bailey.

[33] *Two Studies*, p. 25.

[34] Other possible ways will no doubt suggest themselves to the modern analyst

by which to explain why Epicurean atoms should not unite on contact, even if we preserve as our solitary premise the rule that division may occur only in the interstitial spaces between material particles. E.g., the boundaries of atoms might be defined by infinitely various curves such that two atoms can meet only at a point (or at most a finite collection of points), with contact defined as contiguity along an extended area. Despite certain tantalizing hints, however, there is no evidence that Epicurus adopted this strategy.

³⁵ 275 Usener; DK 68 A47, cited as Aetius.

³⁶ Citations in DK 47; by implication also elsewhere, as in Aristotle *Physics* A 5 188a22 (DK 45): "Democritus says that there is the solid and void, of which the one is as being, the other as not being; further by position, shape and order"—no mention of weight; so also Cicero, *De natura deorum* I 26.73 (DK 51), *De finibus* I 6.17 (DK 56).

³⁷ Aristotle, *De generatione et corruptione* A 8 326a9; *De caelo* D 2 309a1, cit. DK 60. Cf. also Simplicius in Aristotle *Physics* VIII 9, p. 1318.33 ff., cit. DK 58; also DK 61.

³⁸ David Furley, "Aristotle and the Atomists on Motion in a Void," in *Motion and Time, Space and Matter*, eds. P. K. Machamer and R. J. Turnbull (Columbus: Ohio State University Press, 1976), p. 86.

³⁹ Furley, "Aristotle," p. 87.

⁴⁰ I am indebted for this description of the dynamics of the vortex to Steven Tigner, who summarized the basic principles in his article "Empedocles' Twirled Ladle and the Vortex-Supported Earth," *Isis* 65 (1974):440 (cited by Furley, "Aristotle," p. 98, n. 9). Tigner gave a much fuller account in an unpublished paper, "Vortex Action in Pre-Platonic Cosmology," in which he took as a point of departure Albert Einstein's "admirably brief and lucid explanation" of one kind of vortex in "The Cause of the Formation of Meanders in the Courses of Rivers and of the So-called Beer's Law," *Essays in Science* (New York: Philosophical Library, 1934), p. 86.

⁴¹ "Aristotle," p. 87.

⁴² Cf. Aristotle, *De caelo* D6 313a21 ff., cit. DK 68 A62.

⁴³ Simplicius on *De caelo*, cit. DK 61. The supposition in DK that Epicurus' position differed substantially from Democritus' because Epicurus ascribed uniform speed to the atoms seems unwarranted, since it is not clear that the relative velocity of the atoms has anything to do with the process of extrusion.

⁴⁴ See Aristotle, *De generatione et corruptione*, A8 326a9, *De caelo* D2 309a1, cit. DK 60.

⁴⁵ *De caelo*, D1 308a11. Furley, "Aristotle," p. 96, uses this remark of Aristotle's to a different effect, emphasizing Aristotle's phrase "*among things that have weight.*"

⁴⁶ The passages from his commentary on *De caelo* are quoted in 276 Usener.

⁴⁷ "Aristotle," p. 96; cf. also my article "Epicurus on 'Up' and 'Down' (*Letter to Herodotus* sec. 60)," *Phronesis* 17 (1972):269–78, esp. 274–75.

⁴⁸ *Two Studies*, pp. 122–23.

⁴⁹ The acceleration of falling bodies was a principle of Aristotle's theory of

weight and must have been obvious to the Epicureans as a law governing the rise and fall of macroscopic objects. Lucretius, in his argument for the existence of the swerve, explicitly contrasts the motion of atoms in the void, which move at uniform speed, with the behavior of ordinary bodies, which are capable of overtaking each other (II 225–42). It may be, however, that Lucretius is thinking here only of differences in velocity and not of acceleration; such differences were attributed to the resistance of the medium, i.e., air, whose effects varied with the weight, shape, and density of the falling object.

[50] Cicero, De fato 10.22, 20.46, etc., cit. 281 Usener.

[51] Two Studies, p. 122.

[52] It is possible too that the indeterminacy of the rebound may shed some light on the problem of the role of chance (tyche) in Epicurean philosophy.

[53] Sextus, Adversus mathematicos X 113–17; cf. Furley, Two Studies, pp. 133–34.

[54] De fato 20.46, cit. DK A47; 281 Usener.

[55] Simplicius in Aristotle Physics 42.10, cit. DK A47.

[56] On Democritus' conception of weight and its connection with atomic motion, see the discussion by W. K. C. Guthrie, A History of Greek Philosophy, vol. II (Cambridge: Cambridge University Press, 1965), pp. 400–04. Guthrie (p. 402) makes Cicero speak of "the force of gravity or weight" in De fato, which, for the reasons indicated in the text above, I regard as inexact.

[57] Felix Cleve, The Giants of Pre-Sophistic Philosophy, vol. II (The Hague: Martinus Nijhoff, 1969), p. 414; Jürgen Mau, "Raum and Bewegung: Zu Epikurs Brief an Herodot sec. 60," Hermes 82 (1954):20. Cf. also Schulz, "Das Verständnis," pp. 52–56.

[58] The essay by Feigl, "The Origin and Spirit of Logical Positivism," appears in The Legacy of Logical Positivism, Studies in the Philosophy of Science eds., F. Achinstein and S. Barker (Baltimore: Johns Hopkins Press, 1969), p. 7. Koslow's paper is "Ontological and Ideological Issues of the Classical Theory of Space and Time," in Machamer and Turnbull, Motion and Time (quoting Feigl on pp. 229–30).

[59] Cf. Albert Einstein and Leopold Infeld, The Evolution of Physics (New York: Simon and Schuster, 1966; orig. ed. Cambridge University Press, 1938), pp. 171–72: "What is meant by the statement that absolute and not only relative uniform motion exists? Simply that there exists one CS [coordinate system] in which some of the laws of nature are different from those in all others. Also that every observer can detect whether his CS is at rest or in motion by comparing the laws valid in it with those valid in the only one which has the absolute monopoly of serving as the standard CS. Here is a different state of affairs from classical mechanics, where absolute uniform motion is quite meaningless because of Galileo's law of inertia." The relevant law in Epicurus' theory is, of course, isotacheia, the uniform speed of all atomic particles. Schulz, "Das Verständnis," p. 56, asserts that Lucretius imagined the earth as the point of reference by which the descent of atoms is judged. This is impossible, since the earth too is falling, though not at atomic speed.

[60] Falsifiability (ἀντιμαρτύρησις) was the Epicurean's own criterion for postulates about the nature of atomic physics; see, most recently, the paper by Elizabeth

Asmis, "Epicurus' Scientific Method," circulated by the Society for Ancient Greek Philosophy for its meeting of December 1976. One clearly falsifiable conclusion from the Epicurean theory of gravity is the flat-earth hypothesis.

[61] The model which Wiener proposed was in fact somewhat more complex than the one I have suggested. See *The Human Use of Human Beings: Cybernetics and Society,* 2nd ed. (Garden City, N.Y.: Doubleday, 1954), p. 33.

JOHN M. RIST

Zeno and Stoic Consistency

I

Greek ethics is eudaimonistic," observed Max Pohlenz at the beginning of his account of the ethical theories of the Stoa;[1] and it is certainly true that, as Aristotle said,[2] εὐδαιμονία is regularly regarded by the Greeks as the moral good. But the Stoic version is rather complicated, and although some of the complications of their theory of the *telos* and *skopos* of the moral life have been sorted out, in particular by Rieth[3] and Long,[4] many problems remain, perhaps less in the work of Diogenes of Babylon and Antipater of Tarsus than among the earliest members of the school, indeed in Zeno himself. Part of the difficulty lies in the relation in the thought of Zeno between virtue and happiness, and an investigation of this relationship may conveniently begin with a passage which deals not with Zeno in particular, but with the Stoics in general. According to Stobaeus,[5] the Stoics were in the habit of saying that the *telos* is being happy (τὸ εὐδαιμονεῖν). To be happy is something with which we are satisfied; we do not use happiness as a means to achieving something else. Such a state consists in (ὑπάρχειν) living virtuously, living consistently (ὁμολογουμένως), and living naturally (κατὰ φύσιν). We are not told who specifically made these equations, though the impression we are left with is that all the Stoics would have accepted them. But the passage then goes on to say that Zeno defined happiness as a smooth flow of life (εὔροια βίου). Cleanthes, Chrysippus, and the rest accepted this definition,[6] but, says Stobaeus, they called happiness the *skopos*, while identifying the *telos* with "achieving happiness" (τὸ τυχεῖν τῆς εὐδαιμονίας).[7] The passage suggests that Cleanthes and Chrysippus (καίτοι γε λέγοντες) but not Zeno, distinguished between the ultimate target (*skopos*) of the moral life, and its immediate good or end (*telos*).[8] Has this distinction any philosophical significance? Does it give us any clue as to what *kind* of

This paper was presented at the 1973 St. Louis meeting of the Society for Ancient Greek Philosophy, and was published in *Phronesis* 22 (1977) 161–174; we thank the editor for permission to reprint.
John Rist is Regius Professor of Classics at the University of Aberdeen, Scotland.

moral system the Stoics offer us? There has been considerable interest in such matters recently.[9]

Perhaps we should begin with Zeno's concept of εὔροια. Happiness is a smooth flow. Presumably the man who is happy is never taken aback, never has to recast his priorities. He is above all consistent; his intentions and motives can be viewed as forming a coherent whole. According to Stobaeus,[10] Zeno also defined the end (telos) as living consistently, by which he meant living according to a single harmonious pattern. The reason he gave was that people who live otherwise, not consistently, but in conflict (μαχομένως) are unhappy (κακοδαιμονούντων). It is arguable that this is not only a deduction but an empirical appeal. For to suggest that those (and only those) in conflict are unhappy entails saying that the unhappy are in conflict and inconsistent. Thus unhappiness is a visible index of the quality (e.g., the degree of harmony) of our "inner life.[11] Such ideas enable the Stoics to avoid basing morals on an unjustifiable shift from statements of fact to statements of value. Everyone wishes to be happy, for God (divine reason) has ordained it so and "generated" us accordingly. Hence if people recognize that it is inconsistency which makes them unhappy, they will strive to avoid it. And for the Stoic an essential part of avoiding it is to recognize the rationality of moral obligations. My behaviour, for example, cannot be both consistent and dishonest. Therefore given my desire for happiness, it is rational to feel that I ought not to be dishonest.

Virtue regularly appears among the Stoics as either a "consistent disposition"[12] or more generally as some kind of condition of the ruling part of the soul (ἡγεμονικόν).[13] No one would dispute that the consistency in question, whether or not it was always consistency with "nature" in the sense of external nature,[14] is consistency within oneself. Plutarch attributes to the Stoics generally an account of virtue both as a disposition and power produced by reason, and as a consistent and steadfast reason itself,[15] and Cleanthes, in a poem, gives ὁμολογούμενον as one of a list of predicates of "the good"—which would certainly include the notion of the good for man.[16]

Let us go back to the passage of Stobaeus with which we began.[17] After identifying being happy as the end, Stobaeus tells us that the Stoics said that this "consists in" (ὑπάρχειν) living virtuously, living consistently, and living naturally. We notice that they did not simply identify virtue with happiness. But how are we to understand this concept of "consisting in"? Several other texts will help us out. Diogenes Laertius has the same sort of language, only with εἶναι ἐν instead of ὑπάρχειν ἐν: Happiness is in virtue.[18] According to Plutarch, Chrysippus expressed the relationship somewhat differently, though his formulation need not imply a different doctrine. Vice is the οὐσία, the "substance" of unhappiness[19]—and presumably therefore virtue is the substance of happiness. This does not seem to be a technical use of οὐσία or to point us to the Stoic doctrine of categories: probably all that Chrysippus wanted to say is that wherever you get vice, you get unhappiness, and therefore wherever you get virtue (= consistent behaviour) you get happiness. So when we read that for the Stoics virtues complete (ἀποτελοῦσι) happiness,[20] or that virtues produce happiness (ἀπογεννῶσι)[21] and compose it (συμπληροῦσι), since they are its parts, we need only conclude that nothing needs to be added, if virtue is present, for the achievement of happiness. Hence it is virtue and virtuous acts which are the necessary and sufficient conditions for happiness.[22]

So the Stoics are saying that virtue (consistency) always entails happiness but that the words "virtue" and "happiness" are not interchangeable. The doctrine was apparently unclear in antiquity. Lactantius misreads its implications in an interesting passage.[23] He comments rightly that without virtue no one can be happy. He concludes from this, again rightly, that a happy life is the reward of virtue. He further concludes, wrongly, that it is not the case that virtue is to be pursued for its own sake. But the conclusion does not follow. Happiness is elusive. Although it is a reward and a desideratum, it cannot be achieved if pursued directly. It is virtue that is to be pursued, and for its own sake.

We have glanced at the distinction between an end (telos) and a goal (skopos). Rieth drew attention to the relation between this distinction and that between what is αἱρετέον and what is αἱρετόν.[24] We notice that the -τέον forms of Greek verbs are used by the Stoics to express the obligation. Stobaeus again spells out the doctrine, which is presumably in a form elaborated by Chrysippus.[25] The distinction is between what is choiceworthy and what ought to be chosen. What ought to be chosen is "every beneficial action." Obviously happiness is not a beneficial action; it is activities which are virtues which are so to be described. Virtuous behaviour "ought to be chosen." Here again we are talking about the end (telos). The Stoics are not interested in saying that we ought to be happy; they are prepared to say, "We ought (given a desire for happiness) to act consistently."

We illuminate the problem still further by noting the distinction made by at least some of the Stoics, though not necessarily Zeno himself, between a τελικὸν ἀγαθόν and a ποιητικὸν ἀγαθόν.[26] Strictly speaking the Stoics prefer to call only virtue a good (and only vice an evil), but they often accept more normal sorts of language—only maintaining the caveat that they would limit the term good to virtue in any context where there is a danger of philosophical misunderstandings.[27] A passage where the wider use of "good" appears lists such things as "joy" and "sensibly walking about" as τελικὰ ἀγαθά. The point is that they are good for their own sake. On the other hand a friend or a sensible man is a "productive" good, that is he is the

467

means for goods to be secured. The virtues, in contrast to both of these, are both "productive" and "final" goods, that is, they are both ends in themselves and they are productive of something else, e.g., happiness. The passage goes on to say, as I have already observed, that the virtues generate happiness since they are its parts. Thus when all the virtues are present, happiness is present. The converse applies with vice and unhappiness.

Diogenes Laertius adds a further sublety.[28] He lists "actions in accordance with virtue" as τελικά and distinguishes them from virtue itself, which is τελικὸν καὶ ποιητικόν, as in Stobaeus. We should also notice that nowhere is *happiness* listed as a τελικὸν ἀγαθόν; this helps to confirm our view that happiness, though desirable in itself, is not to be sought directly. Virtue is to be contrasted with this: although it is productive (ποιητικόν) of happiness, it should not be sought merely for the sake of happiness, but also for its own sake. If it is not recognized as intrinsically good, it cannot be attained.

A recent critic, A. A. Long, seems to think that the Stoics rejected (or at least would not have accepted) Aristotle's view that self-interest is the primary or only moral motive.[29] It is not entirely clear what is meant in this context by a *moral* motive—we need to know whether a *moral* system should be defined in terms of its form or its content—though if Long means that the Stoics would reject the view that one should act well only, or largely, out of self-interest, he is correct, but misleadingly so. It is only when a man recognizes where his genuine self-interest lies that he is capable of being "moral" and of recognizing "moral" facts.

The Stoics say that virtue is sufficient for happiness (αὐτάρκης πρὸς εὐδαιμονίαν).[30] But it is not happiness we immediately strive for; it is a virtuous, that is, a consistent life. A conscious striving for happiness could be ineffective for two related reasons: it might inhibit the performance of those virtuous acts which are the only road to happiness, and it might be productive of a kind of behaviour which is in conflict with the development of our natural impulses. Originally these impulses are, as every student of Stoicism knows, associated with our recognition of what is "first suited" (οἰκεῖον) to every animal, namely, its own nature.[31] As has recently been pointed out,[32] the term *first* probably refers to temporal rather than logical priority. Now we find different things "suited" as we grow; our "first" impulses, however, are directed towards the preservation of the state we are in when we first acquire any kind of awareness of the external world, that is, at birth.[33] Presumably at this moment we are in some sort of "right" condition. Obviously in the strict Stoic sense we are neither virtuous nor happy. We are for the first time, however, presented with a hostile environment and we react accordingly,[34] satisfying so far as we may our instinct for self-preservation. Although as we grow our range of *oikeiosis* expands, and indeed, if we become wise, a desire for self-preservation will cease to be of overwhelming importance—the wise man may *choose* to sacrifice his own life—yet presumably the Stoics would have held that no "developed" impulses (i.e., impulses not present at birth, but developed as we grow towards maturity, physical and moral) should be given priority over earlier ones without good reason. Clearly in such a view of man the notion of consistent behaviour is maintained. A man should not abandon his life lightly, supported as it is by the instinct for self-preservation.

But new sound impulses and reactions are built on old, and we have to learn to adapt the old to the new. Presumably in an ideal world such adaptation would be simple and we should all develop into sages. Yet in fact from the very beginning there is the new factor of the external world. Corrupting influences from beyond the self impinge on our own individual nature, which *ceteris paribus* would develop via the "rationalizing" of the impulses to virtue and via the virtues to happiness. Before trying to understand, therefore, how the external world with its moral temptations can be reconciled with our own world, with the world governed by the instinct of self-preservation which we are given at birth, we have to determine the form in which these external dangers confront us. And the first form in which this occurs is the form of pleasure and pain. Diogenes Laertius has a passage in which the situation of the new-born human being is well summarized. Nature, he says, gives non-perverted points of departure (ἀφορμαί).[35] The rational animal is perverted either by the persuasiveness of external pursuits or by the communications of his companions. The image of perversion is notable. The Stoics seem to have compared bringing the soul from vice to virtue to straightening a bent stick.[36] Thus if a man lived aright from birth, he would start off right, as we all do, and maintain a consistent and straight path of virtue. He would therefore react to external stimuli in a consistent and coherent way. How does this work out in practice?

When Chrysippus—and it presumably is Chrysippus in the passage of Diogenes Laertius—says that we do not start perverted, he must mean that it is somehow right or sound for us to develop from our first *oikeiosis,* and to act in accordance with our instinct for self-preservation. In what sense is this right, unperverted, sound, or whatever? Nature gives us these starting points, we read, and this *cannot* refer to our own human nature, for it is a set of circumstances granted by "nature" whereby we are enabled to have a chance of survival in the world. Thus, at any rate for Chrysippus, our human first beginnings are in accordance with some sort of plan or design of nature—of the "designing fire" (πῦρ τεχνικόν). So when we are newborn, it must be assumed that our behaviour patterns are in accordance with the lawlike operations of nature as a whole, and are consistent with them. Now when we develop, if we are to be virtuous and consistent, our actions

469

must flow smoothly from our unperverted first beginnings—which means that our actions will themselves have to be consistent with the nature which gave us these first beginnings. So we can see why Cleanthes and Chrysippus argued that the *telos*—formula should be that we must live consistently with Nature, not merely that our lives should be internally consistent.

II

Diogenes Laertius not only tells us that Zeno referred to "living consistently with nature" but he gives us the source of this information, a book entitled *On The Nature of Man*.[37] Cicero, for what it is worth, agrees with this.[38] On the other hand Stobaeus gives what seems to be a fairly circumstantial but different view.[39] According to him Zeno had originally only spoken of internal consistency, but later thinkers, believing that *consistent* was an incomplete term and that we should be told with what we should be consistent, added that we should be consistent with nature. Cleanthes is specifically named as the first to have taken this step.

There has been a tendency to dismiss the reference to nature in Zeno, on the grounds that Diogenes is merely transferring a school commonplace to the founder. But the reference to the book *On The Nature of Man* makes it clear that Diogenes, or his source, had a specific text in mind. On the other hand the statement of Stobaeus that Cleanthes found the term *consistent* in some way incomplete has also to be taken seriously. The only solution which does justice to both sources is that Zeno spoke both of consistency with nature and of consistency with self, while Cleanthes thought that the second of these formulations was unnecessary, or imprecise, or misleading. Diogenes gives us the further information that Cleanthes thought that the nature in accordance with which we should live must be understood only as "universal nature" (κοινὴ φύσις),[40] and this can be understood as implying that our first impulses to self-preservation, those starting points on the road to virtue and happiness, are a gift of a power, i.e., Nature, which subsumes and indeed engenders the specifically human sphere.

Let us try to develop this theory of the roles of Zeno and Cleanthes. Why may Zeno have spoken now of living consistently with Nature, now simply of living consistently? Such accounts of the end, though not mutually exclusive, could well be given as answers to different kinds of philosophical questions. Talk about an internally consistent life could arise as a result of an ethical question; "consistency with Nature" should involve us with the grounds of ethics. Looking at this in another way, we might say that any questions about the end to which the answer "self-consistency" could be meaningfully given entail a further question about the kind of consistency required—to which the answer "consistency with Nature" might be given. We start off with the assumption that happiness is in some sense the goal. We are faced with trying to determine how such a goal may become a reality. What would be the natural way of looking at such a problem? In the first instance everyone would tend to look at it as a strictly ethical problem. And anyone thinking philosophically at the time when Zeno was first active would presumably look first to the kind of ethical answers available. According to Diogenes Laertius, whose testimony there is no reason to reject on such a point, Zeno was in some sense a pupil of the Cynic Crates.[41] And there is abundant evidence, particularly in his *Republic,* that the Cynic influence on his early thought was deep and persistent.[42] Zeno, of course, later broke with the Cynics on a number of issues, and one of the most important of these was his insistence that it is necessary for the wise man to know something of physics and logic as well as of ethics.[43] In his early days, Zeno was certainly writing with a more strongly Cynic flavour than he later thought desirable; his *Republic* is said by Diogenes to have been written when he was still a pupil of Crates.[44] So at a time when he has no use for physics we can well imagine Zeno defining the end as "living consistently" (that is, with no reference to nature—where a reference to nature would imply some kind of knowledge by the wise man of the laws of physics or of "natural philosophy"). Of course, the Cynics themselves frequently talk of nature, but the context is the old Sophistic antithesis between nature and convention[45] and has no significant connection with the use of the term by the Stoics to refer to natural philosophy. Thus for Zeno, when still largely in a Cynic context and thinking of ethics as the only necessary realm of thought for the wise man, to define the end as living in accordance with nature would be to point not to the factor of consistency with a more than moral Power in the universe, but to "living naturally" rather than "living conventionally." (Of course, it might well be the case that the consistent [Stoic] life would be unconventional, but in talking of consistency that is not the principal point a Stoic would want to make.)

Zeno's point in defining the end as a consistent life and in saying that a consistent life is a virtuous life and leads to happiness would be made within a purely ethical frame. It is the assumption of those working inside such a frame that happiness is the goal and that the content of virtue can be understood by right reason. Right reason, of course, must be consistent, for inconsistent reasoning can hardly be "right." It is the assumption of such a search for consistency that the original impulses of each man are sound *and intelligible* in themselves, and therefore that consistency with them in later thought and action will be sufficient for virtue. There is probably an echo of this attitude—together with its built-in ambiguities—in the remark of Cleanthes that all men have the starting points for *virtue* given by nature,[46] though he is using *nature* here in a way which (Stoically) does not make an obvious reference to the antithesis with convention.

It was, of course, the very issue of whether the ethical end could be determined by "ethical" reflection alone that seems to have been one of the causes of the antagonism to Zeno developed by his former pupil Aristo.[47] But Zeno had clearly seen further than the Cynics. Let us assume that he did define virtue, at some stage, as Diogenes says, as a consistent or harmonious life. The obvious question is, Consistent with what? In other words, is the predicate really elliptical, as Cleanthes seems to have thought? There seems no reason to doubt that Zeno's answer to this must have been "consistent with the natural behaviour to which our first impulses guide us." And this would put him right into a contemporary debate about what natural impulses are. In fact the best interpretation of why Zeno took up the study of "nature," of "natural philosophy" in the traditional pre-Socratic sense, would seem to be that he wished to find content for the formula that virtue is a consistent life. For one might admit that formula to be acceptable while disagreeing with Zeno about the nature of the consistency, if one took (for example) an Epicurean view of one's first natural impulses. In other words I should like to argue that Zeno was probably drawn to find an extra-ethical justification for his brand of ethics by those who could have accepted the importance of a consistent life. Such opponents might even have included Epicurus.

Epicurus could easily agree with the Cynics in distinguishing nature from convention, while still proposing a different account of "natural" behaviour. According to him pleasure is the first good we recognize when we are newly born: it is the beginning and end of the happy life.[48] Now it is generally agreed, and I would not want to dispute the view, that the majority of the evidence that refers to direct conflict between Stoics and Epicureans dates from a period later than the times of Zeno and Epicurus, but although these two may not have engaged in direct conflict, they certainly may have been dealing with the same issues—and coming up with conflicting answers. If one of the issues was, What is the nature of the first natural impulse? the answer to such a question would obviously predetermine the kind of *consistent* life a philosopher would come to advocate for adult human beings. And we have already observed that the question of the nature of natural things is raised by implication by the Cynics.

We know from a number of sources that Zeno was some kind of pupil of the Academic Polemo,[49] but Cicero provides us with the invaluable evidence that Zeno accepted Polemo's account of the "first-principles of nature."[50] This can only mean that it was Polemo who taught that the first natural instinct is to self-preservation, the theory which provided a basis for the Stoic account of *oikeiosis*, and which gave Zeno his opportunity to break with the Cynic view of nature. Perhaps Polemo was not the only person who held this theory—perhaps even Cicero's account is mistaken—but what really matters is that somewhere or other Zeno came across an account of nature which enabled him to develop his own particular version of the consistent life. For, as I have already indicated, to talk of consistency alone is to approach ethics in the way of a formalist: and no ancient theorist is a formalist. But when looking for a content for nature, Zeno desperately needed a context. The Cynics failed him almost completely here. Whatever they may have intended, we have ample evidence that for the Cynics the term *nature* is largely devoid of positive force. Natural behaviour seems consistently to be regarded as behaviour freed from conventional restraints. There are no specific and immediate goals in the Cynic freedom, the Cynic life according to nature; if a Cynic ethic had ever managed to exhibit consistency, it could only have been a consistent freedom *from* the constraints of society. There is no evidence that the Cynics added up their various freedoms *from* to amount to any kind of freedom *to*.

We have ample evidence that Zeno broke with the Cynic road of "morality alone"; his talk of "appropriate things" ($\varkappa\alpha\vartheta\acute{\eta}\varkappa o\nu\tau\alpha$)[51] joins with his uncynic approach to "natural impulses" to point to what Aristo abhorred: the wise man's study of physics. Physics not merely enabled Zeno to argue formally that consistency is necessary for virtue, and will bring happiness, but to show the nature of that consistency. In our terminology Zeno invoked extra-ethical factors to justify an approach to ethics, though, to avoid anachronism, we have to add that he was not conscious that this was what he was doing. In other words Zeno did not ask, How can I give point to the pursuit of consistency as an ethical end by the use of criteria not drawn from my own ethical system? Rather he seems to have asked, What is the nature of the first impulse with which my later life must be in harmony? This question is a non-ethical one in that it is value-free. It is simply a matter of finding the means to describe what nature has managed to give us.

The conclusion of all this must be that if Zeno did not speak precisely both of "living consistently" and "living consistently with nature," he must have described his ethical end in two different ways to which these different phrases could be properly applied—and therefore that since Diogenes Laertius attributes the second phrase to him, there is no good reason to reject it.

The only other question which should be treated briefly here is what it might mean for us to develop, to pass from infancy to manhood, while still living consistently with our first natural impulses. It is clear that from the time of Chrysippus the Stoics were in the habit of talking about different *oikeioseis*; from the *oikeiosis* to oneself at birth, there develop *oikeioseis* with different conditions in later life. As Kerferd puts it, "an organism seeks to preserve the constitution in which it is at the moment."[52] But our *oike-*

473

iosis not only reconciles us with ourselves; it helps to associate each man with his fellows. According to Hierocles, there is an *oikeiosis* with one's relations;[53] and there is no doubt that later Stoics extended *oikeiosis* to the human race in general.[54] Furthermore, as Porphyry puts it, "the followers of Zeno make *oikeiosis* the beginning of justice";[55] and this statement is confirmed by Plutarch who remarks more precisely that the parental instinct is "incomplete and not adequate" as a basis for justice.[56] Apparently Chrysippus expressly treated of the matter in his book *On Justice*.[57]

We may take it as certain that justice was derived from *oikeiosis* in the Stoa at least from the time of Chrysippus. To translate the first impulse to self-preservation into a deliberate intention to promote justice, of course, requires the use of the will and reason. The Stoics spoke of the intervention of *logos* as a craftsman.[58] The first *oikeiosis* is transformed by reason into an *oikeiosis hairetike*.[59]

Porphyry says that the "followers of Zeno" regard *oikeiosis* as the beginning of justice. Certainly Chrysippus seems to have done so, but the "followers of Zeno" could be a general term for Stoics and need not imply any real knowledge of whether Zeno himself thought along these lines. If the doctrine of *oikeiosis* grew up in the way we have suggested, in association with Zeno's liberation from the Cynics and indebtedness to Polemo, it would not originally have needed such wide ramifications. A feeling of endearment to oneself at different stages of one's life, and for one's family and friends might be adequate—and even more than adequate—for Zeno's purpose of providing the individual with a wider frame of reference and of associating human nature with Nature. Of course, as a man grows, his needs will change. Hence his consistent life must be determined in the light of the fact that men are not static beings, and that reason should more and more come to characterize them. However, it is not the same to say that *oikeiosis* will be extended beyond the self and its immediate surroundings, and that *oikeiosis,* as it widens rationally, will entail any kind of affection, let alone sense of justice, towards the whole human race. The Cynics think constantly of freeing oneself from conventional ties and the bond of society; the doctrine of *oikeiosis* is an attempt to understand the empirically observable instincts for self-preservation and the love for one's parents, and to use them to support the theory of natural bonds as distinct from bonds of convention. The question is how far did Zeno himself extend the ramifications of *oikeiosis*. And this entails the further question, With whom does the wise man feel akin? In his Cynic days, in the days of his *Republic*, Zeno would probably have said "Only with the wise."[60] But he was breaking with the Cynics and might have extended this. There is no answer in the sources. We simply do not know Zeno's attitude about the origin of a sense of justice towards those who are not to be counted among the wise. However, although Zeno's doctrine of *oikeiosis* may have been narrower than Chrysippus' (and possibly expansion took place even after Chrysippus), *oikeiosis* is *necessary* for Zeno, and it cannot therefore be only a doctrine in embryo in the founder of Stoicism.[61] The really fundamental principles of Stoicism cannot be stated without recourse to it.

Any Cynic could advocate a consistent life, for the description is purely formal. But one consistent life might be set against another, and Zeno's appeal to *natural* consistency prevents this, as well as showing exactly why virtue pays. The question could, of course, have been tackled in another way: Is there in fact more than one kind of *consistent* life?

NOTES

[1] M. Pohlenz, *Die Stoa*[3] (Götingen, 1964), p. 111.

[2] *N.E.* 1095 A 18–19.

[3] O. Rieth, "Über das Telos Stoiker," *Hermes* (1934):13–45.

[4] A. A. Long, "Carneades and the Stoic Telos," *Phronesis* 12 (1967):59–90.

[5] Stob., *Ecl.* II 77, 16 (= *SVF* III 16).

[6] Cf. Sextus Empiricus, *adv. Math.* 11.22 (*SVF* III 73); 11.30 (*SVF* I 554). For εὔροια as a time when the *daimon* in us is in harmony with the "will" of the director of the cosmos, see D.L. 7.88. But this cannot be used as evidence for Zeno himself.

[7] Cf. Rieth, "Über das Telos," pp. 24–26.

[8] For an assimilation of *skopos* as a kind of *telos*, see Stob., *Ecl.* II 76, 16 ff. (= *SVF* III 3).

[9] Cf. A. A. Long, "The Logical Basis of Stoic Ethics," *PAS* (1970):85–104; A. Graeser, "Zirkel oder Deduktion: Zur Begrundung der stoischen Ethik," *Kant-Studien* 63 (1972):213–24; "Zur Funktion des Begriffes 'Gut' in der stoischen Ethik," *Zeitschrift für philosophische Forschung* 26 (1972):417–25.

[10] Stob., *Ecl.* II 75, 11 (*SVF* I 179).

[11] For a similar Stoic attitude to the concept of "good" (as useful) see Graeser, "Zirkel oder Deduktion," p. 219, n. 17, correcting Long, "The Logical Basis," p. 98.

[12] D.L. 7.89 (*SVF* III 39) Cf. Sen., *Ep.* 31.8 (*SVF* III 200) *consonans sibi*.

[13] Sextus Empiricus, *adv. Math.* 11.22 (*SVF* III 75).

[14] Stobaeus suggests that the reference to nature was added by Cleanthes (*Ecl.* II 76, 3 ff. [*SVF* I 552]).

[15] Plut., *De virt. mor.* 441C (*SVF* I 202).

[16] Clem. Alex., *Prot.* 6.72 (*SVF* I 557).

[17] Stob., *Ecl.* II 77, 16 (*SVF* III 16).

[18] D.L. 7.89 (*SVF* III 39).

[19] Plut., *SR* 1042A (*SVF* III 55).

[20] D.L. 7.96 (*SVF* III 107).

[21] Stob., *Ecl.* II 71, 15 (*SVF* III 106).

[22] Stob., *Ecl.* II 77, 6 (*SVF* III 113).

[23] Lact., *Div. Instit.* 5.17 (*SVF* III 47).

²⁴ Rieth, "Über das Telos," p. 25.

²⁵ Stob., *Ecl.* II 78, 7 (*SVF* III 89).

²⁶ Stob., *Ecl.* II 71, 15 (*SVF* III 106).

²⁷ Plut., *SR* 1048A (*SVF* III 137).

²⁸ Cf. D.L. 7.96 (*SVF* III 107).

²⁹ Long, "The Logical Basis," p. 96.

³⁰ D.L. 7.127 (*SVF* III 49).

³¹ I still prefer συνείδησις in this passage (D.L. 7.85 = *SVF* III 82) despite the comments of H. S. Long, *A.J.P.* 92 (1971):749. Long seems to me to miss the point that the harder συνείδησις is too easily emended into συναίσθησις. The sense does not require the change.

³² G. B. Kerferd, "The Search for Personal Identity," *Bulletin of the John Rylands University Library of Manchester* 55 (1972):190–91. Cf. D.L. 7.85 (*SVF* III 178) and other references supplied by Kerferd.

³³ Hierocles, Ethische Elementarlehre (P. Berlin, 1780), ed. H. von Arnim, *Berliner Klassikertexte* 4 (Berlin, 1906), col. 6.23–24.

³⁴ See S. G. Pembroke, "OIKEIOSIS," in *Problems in Stoicism,* ed. A. A. Long (London, 1971), p. 146, n. 89 (with Philo, *de opif. mundi.* 161 [1, 56, 7 ff. Cohn]).

³⁵ D.L. 7.89 (*SVF* III 228).

³⁶ Cf. *SVF* III 489.

³⁷ D.L. 7.87 (*SVF* I 179).

³⁸ Cic., *De Fin.* 4.14.

³⁹ Stob., *Ecl.* II 134, 75 ff.

⁴⁰ D.L. 7.89 (*SVF* I 555).

⁴¹ D.L. 7. 2–3 (*SVF* I 1).

⁴² Cf. H. C. Baldry, "Zeno's Ideal State," *JHS* 79 (1959):3–15; J. M. Rist, *Stoic Philosophy* (Cambridge, 1969), pp. 64–67.

⁴³ Rist, *Stoic Philosophy*, pp. 71–76.

⁴⁴ D.L. 7.4 (*SVF* I 2).

⁴⁵ D.L. 7.38; 7.71.

⁴⁶ Stob., *Ecl.* II 65, 7 (*SVF* I 566).

⁴⁷ *SVF* I 351 and 353; J. Moreau, "Ariston et le Stoicisme," *REA* 50 (1948):43.

⁴⁸ *Ep. ad Men.* 128–29.

⁴⁹ D.L. 7.1 (*SVF* I 1); Strabo 13 p. 614 (*SVF* I 10).

⁵⁰ Cic., *De Fin.* 4.45 (*SVF* I 198).

⁵¹ D.L. 7.2 (*SVF* I 1).

⁵² Kerferd, "The Search," p. 191; cf. Sen., *Ep.* 121, 15–16.

⁵³ Hierocles, P. Berlin 1780, col. 9. 3–4; Cf. *Anon. Comm. on Theaet.* (P. 9782), *Berliner Klassikertexte* 2, eds. Diels and Schubart (Berlin, 1905), cols. 7.28; 8.5–6.

⁵⁴ Cic., *De Fin.* 3.63 (*SVF* III 340).

⁵⁵ Porphyry, *De Abst.* 3.19 (*SVF* I 197).

⁵⁶ Plut., *De Amore Prolis* 495 B (Cf. *Soll. An.* 962A). Cf. S. G. Pembroke, "OIKEIOSIS."

[57] Plut., *SR* 1038B (*SVF* II 724).

[58] D.L. 7.86 (*SVF* III 43).

[59] Kerferd, "The Search," p. 191; Hierocles, col. 9.5–8; *Anon. Comm.* col. 7.40.

[60] See O. Murray, Review of Baldry, *Unity of Mankind, C.R.* 80 (1966):369.

[61] Rightly, Kerferd, "The Search," p. 178, and S. G. Pembroke, "OIKEIOSIS," pp. 114–15 against Brink, "Οἰκείωσις and Οἰκειότης: Theophrastus and Zeno on Nature and Moral Theory," *Phronesis* 1 (1956):141 ff. Brink rightly emphasizes the role of Polemo (against Pohlenz) but neglects the problem of Cynicism.

JOSIAH B. GOULD

The Stoic Conception of Fate

"Under an accumulation of staggerers, no man can be considered a free
agent."

The Old Curiosity Shop, chapter 34

"But it's Destiny, and mine's a crusher!"

Ibid., chapter 50

RISTOTLE maintains in his *Nicomachean Ethics* (1139a13–14;
1140a31– 32) that no one deliberates about things which cannot be
otherwise. The notion of that which cannot be otherwise (*to
adunaton allōs echein* [or alternatively] *to mē endechomenon allōs
echein*), used by Aristotle to demarcate a certain class of events or things, is
perhaps an illuminating one with which to begin a characterization of the
Stoic conception of fate. We first encounter the notion as it appears in Stoic
philosophy in Chrysippus' *On Nature:* "No individual, not even the least of
them, can come to be otherwise than in accordance with common nature and
in accordance with the *logos* of common nature" (Plutarch, 1050A). The notion appears again in a comment by Servius on a passage from Virgil's *Ae-
neid* (iv. 696). Having given as an example of a certain kind of fate the
proposition that Pompey will triumph three times, Servius remarks: "The
fates determine through him that wherever he may be he will triumph three
times, and it cannot turn out otherwise (*nec potest aliter evenire)*" (*SVF* II
958). The Stoic theory of fate, then, maintains that for any event you care to
choose (Grumach, 38–39), a description of that event may be substituted in
the following sentence-frame (with appropriate tenses provided) and yield a
true statement, "_____ not _____
otherwise." For example, take the event of Sirhan Sirhan's having shot Robert Kennedy; according to the Stoic conception of fate, Sirhan Sirhan could
not have acted otherwise. Or, consider the event of my writing these words
(or that of your reading them); on the Stoic theory, I cannot fail to be writ-

This paper was presented at the 1970 Philadelphia meeting of the Society for Ancient
Greek Philosophy and published in the *Journal of the History of Ideas*, vol. 35, no. 1
(1974):17–32; we thank the editors for permission to reprint.

Josiah Gould is Professor of Philosophy at the State University of New York at Albany.

ing them; I cannot be doing something other than writing them. Or, choosing at random some description and supposing that it is going to be the description of some actual event, say, an earthquake in Santa Cruz in 1975, the Stoic would say of it that it cannot fail to occur; and that that is what it means to say of it that it cannot be otherwise.

It might be objected that I am doing violence to the words I have quoted from Chrysippus' *On Nature,* on the ground that the notion *cannot happen otherwise than in accordance with something* is less restrictive than the notion *cannot happen otherwise (full stop),* and that I have been treating the first as though it were the second. A boy who cannot act otherwise than in accordance with his mother's wish that he go home after school may go home on a bicycle, in a car, or on foot; but if the same boy cannot do otherwise than *whatever* he is doing after school, then if he is walking, one cannot say of him that he might have gone in a car or on a bicycle. That the distinction underlying this objection does not apply to the Stoic conception of fate will become evident on understanding that, according to the Stoic view, *nothing* which occurs can happen otherwise. Showing that this is so involves a consideration of the Stoic treatment of causality; and this is appropriate, for the notion of causality is at the heart of the Stoic conception of fate.

In the Stoic view, nothing happens "without a cause, but rather in accordance with antecedent causes" (*SVF* II 912). The principle of causality is set forth most straightforwardly by Chrysippus, whose position is paraphrased by Plutarch. Chrysippus is arguing against some philosophers who maintain that there is in the ruling part of the soul an adventitious movement which can by itself provide an inclination in one direction when the soul might otherwise be stuck on "dead center." Plutarch's words are:

Against them Chrysippus, by way of reply, on the ground that they are laying violent hands on nature with an uncaused phenomenon, sets forth in many places as examples the die, the balance, and many of the things which cannot receive falls and inclinations sometimes in one way and sometimes in another without some cause or difference which comes about either entirely in them or in the things outside; for what is uncaused and spontaneous is entirely non-existent; but in these things imagined by some and called adventitious impulses unseen causes are at work underneath, and we are oblivious to the fact that they are leading impulse to the one or the other side. . . . Of the things said often by him these are the best known. (Plutarch, 1045B–C)

The feature of causality which Chrysippus is obviously stressing in this passage is its universality. Nothing, absolutely nothing, lies outside its domain. An uncaused occurrence was viewed by the Stoics as the destruction of an otherwise unified cosmos (*SVF* II 945). And since the chain of causes was thought by the Stoics to be the substance of fate (*SVF* II 945), to say that nothing can be otherwise than in accordance with fate is to say that nothing can be otherwise than in accordance with antecedent conditions. Again, to stress the universal domain over which the Stoic principle of causality was thought to range, the last statement means that if you take *anything at all,* then there are certain antecedent conditions which determine it cannot be otherwise. The Stoic conception of fate, then, involves the thesis of determinism.[1]

That the Stoics should have set forth this extraordinary thesis is remarkable. For, leaving aside the not unimportant point that the thesis may be false, the Stoics were not only flatly contradicting what had been significant insights by Plato, Aristotle, and Epicurus into the nature of human action, they were also flying in the face of a distinction plainly presupposed by fourth-century juries in the trials of persons indicted for homicide (at least in Athens). I wish first of all briefly to substantiate this claim, and then I shall try to make evident the crucial move made by the Stoics, which, in fact, if not in intent, must have made their otherwise highly para-conventional position seem plausible to themselves, and evidently to others, but not to everyone.

No Greek philosophers before the Stoics developed a universal determinism, or if, as in the case of Democritus, this thesis appears, its implications for the freedom of the will and morality seem not to have been drawn (Adkins, chapters V and VI and p. 324; Huby, *passim;* Stenzel, 295–96, 297). To the Greek the mind seemed immune from any conceivable law of causality which might regulate events in the realm of nature (Pohlenz, i. 104). Plato evinces this view in two passages, and the second of them will prove to be peculiarly appropriate when I turn to consider further the Stoic position, ostensibly a highly paradoxical one in the light of Greek intuitions about responsibility. In one of these passages (*Phaedo* 98E5–B6), where he distinguishes between necessary conditions and causes, Plato has Socrates say that he is in prison because he chose to be, on the ground that this was the best thing for him to do, and not because of the disposition of nerves, bones, and other such parts of his body. If one takes seriously Socrates' remark that it is to things of the latter sort to which most people apply the name *cause,* then clearly what Plato is doing is distinguishing choices by human beings from causes as ordinarily conceived (or denominated). In another passage Plato states explicitly that while fate provides the consequences or the consequent locale appropriate to various states of character, men themselves are the causes of the kind of persons they become. Since it will be important later to show wherein the Stoic account of human agency differs from that of Plato, I quote the passage I have in mind:

> The causes of the formation of character God turned over to the wishes of each of us. For as one desires and as is the character of the man, such gen-

erally everyone of us almost always becomes. . . . And so all things which share in soul change, and they possess in themselves the cause of their change, and as they change they are moved in accordance with the order and law of fate. (*Laws* 904B8–C9)

Here, then, Plato sets forth in fairly straightforward language the proposition that character formation is exempt from whatever causal nexus governs other things. When the Stoics affirm that one and the same causality, common nature, or fate ranges over everything, they must have meant to include character formation. How did they justify taking a position flatly contradictory to that of Plato on this matter and, in my view, to the truth?

As for Aristotle, a writer with whose works the Stoics must have been familiar, it is well known that, in his view, (i) all things happen by nature, by reason (art or skill), or by chance, and (ii) that he makes a distinction between things which are in our power and things which are not (*EN* 1113b5–1117a8 *passim*); and that in conjunction with this distinction he appears to have held that character formation is one of the things in our power, i.e., that men are responsible for the kinds of persons they become or are (*EN* 1114a3–21). There are difficulties in Aristotle's position (Hardie, 175–76) to which I shall come; for now it is germane merely to remind ourselves that a philosopher of considerable stature who had died only a generation before the first Stoic began teaching at Athens, in his doctrine restricted the domain of nature in such a way that virtue, vice, and character formation generally stand, in one respect at least, outside it. The Stoics take a contrary view. Why? How did they justify to themselves and others the denial of a philosophical view which seems so eminently to have encapsulated the experience of the Greeks?

In connection with that experience it ought to be stated that the Athenian homicide law in the fourth century made a distinction between intentional and unintentional homicide, a distinction which is incompatible with the metaphysical thesis of determinism. The places where the two kinds of homicide were tried were different and the penalties for unintentional homicide were less severe than those for intentional homicide (MacDowell, 45, 117). A number of subtle questions arose over the determination of the class to which a given case of homicide belonged (MacDowell, 58–69), but the existence of the two classes is all that is to the point for my purpose, and that is attested. But this fact suggests that either the Stoics with their conception of fate were, in the face of experience and philosophy, being plainly perverse or that they must have thought that they had a way to square their conception of fate with the traditional notion that men are responsible for their characters and therefore for some of their deeds.

To forestall the thought that perhaps the tradition changed radically between the fourth and third centuries, I only need allude to the Epicureans who, as is well known, introduced a radically *ad hoc* assumption into Democritean metaphysics in order to provide a theoretical basis for their conviction that the mind is not compelled in its decision-making activity by factors extraneous to itself (Lucretius ii.251–93; Furley, 166).

Needless to say, the Stoic conception of fate hardly seemed plausible to all men. Holders of rival views are reputed to have said:

> If Chrysippus thinks that all things are moved and governed by fate and that the courses of fate and their turns cannot be changed or surmounted, then the faults and misdeeds of men ought not to cause anger or to be referred to themselves and their wills, but to a certain imperious necessity which stems from fate; and this is the mistress and arbiter of all things, by which everything which will happen must happen; and for this reason punishments of criminals have been established unjustly, if men do not come to their evil deeds willingly, but are led to them by fate. (*SVF* II 1000)

How did the Stoics shore up their conception of Fate so as to make it provide an answer to such attacks as this one and to make it seem plausible to so many men for so many years (Tarn, 3, 325)?

The Stoics adhered to their conception of fate, which, as has been seen, involves the notion of determinism, and at the same time sought to remain faithful to the traditional and philosophical intuitions that a man is responsible for some of his actions, by assuming that responsible decision making is itself an element in the deterministic system of fate (Bréhier, 187). In other words, they too, like their predecessors and contemporaries among philosophers and jurors, felt strongly that some things are "in our power," and that men make effective choices after deliberating. The problem was to do justice to this sentiment or insight and at the same time to maintain a conception of fate which involves the notion of determinism. As for its solution, the evidence seems to show that the Stoics tried to make decision making itself a part of the universal domain over which fate, in their view, ranged. That this was the solution adopted by the Stoics and what meaning the solution has, I now try to show (1) by introducing some supporting fragments, (2) by pointing out that a roughly Aristotelian theory of action breaks out within the Stoic system, which is what we should have anticipated if the Stoics had meant for fate to embrace even a man's deliberated-upon and then chosen acts, and (3) by showing that Alexander of Aphrodisias, one of Aristotle's most respected commentators and a man who knew Stoicism well and was himself influenced by its doctrines (Pohlenz, i.358; Verbeke, 81), so interpreted Stoic fatalism, as is evident in his recommended revision of it, which was that fate be restricted so as to range over nature alone.

I now introduce some fragments from which one might better understand in what sense the Stoics subsume responsible decision making under the decrees of fate. Consider, first of all, this report from Alexander of Aphrodisias:

> For they [the Stoics] assume the position that fate uses all the things which have occurred and are occurring in accordance with fate with a view to the unhindered activity of the things which occur by its agency as each of them has come to be and is naturally constituted, a stone as a stone, a plant as a plant, and an animal as an animal, and if as an animal, then as something which is motivated by impulses. . . . (208, 3–7)

From this statement it is clear that fate is not a causal chain working through some one part of nature but is rather operating through all its parts, that it employs even the impulses of animals for its own ends. The sense of the doctrine is that fate is not impeded by but is rather able to exploit the impulsive nature of animals (including human beings, of course). From another report, this one by Origen, one gains some impression as to how fate was thought to achieve this:

> For animate things are moved from themselves when a presentation arises in them and calls forth impulse; and again in some of the animals presentations occur and call forth impulse, the impulse belonging to a movement of nature which has been presentationally arranged, as in a spider a presentation of weaving occurs and an impulse towards weaving follows—its presentational nature in an orderly way having called it forth towards this, and since there is nothing else along with its presentational nature, the animal obeys—and in the bee [this presentation calls forth the impulse] towards making wax. In the case of the rational animal, however, there is reason [logos] in addition to the presentational nature, which judges the presentations, rejecting some and letting in others, in order that the animal may be guided in accordance with them. (*SVF* II 988)

The impulses of the animal are moved by fate either directly, as in the case of bees and spiders, or indirectly, as in the case of man. How *logos* functions in the case of the human animal is, of course, a process requiring further elucidation, but now I wish only to emphasize the comprehensive nature of fate, for it has emerged as embracing both the merely impulsive movements of animals and the impulsive-reflective movements of human beings. This is stated rather succinctly in the following statement from the Placita of Aëtius: ". . . fate is an ordered interweaving of causes, in which interweaving there is also the cause within us, so that some things are fated, others are not fated" (*SVF* II 976). The inference is, of course, that of Aëtius, and would have been denied by the Stoics. What is clear, I trust, is that the Stoics regarded "the cause within us" not as either competing with or cooperating with fate, but as a part of the network of causes constituting fate.

The notion that fate works through deliberate decisions seems to lie behind the Stoic conception of "condestinate" facts (*confatalia*). This is the idea that some events can occur only if they occur in tandem with other events. For example, a man cannot win a wrestling match unless he wrestles with someone. Or a man cannot have a child unless he mates with a woman. (No attempt seems to have been made here to distinguish between logically conjoined ideas and law-like conjunctions of events. See *SVF* II 956–58 for these and other examples.) Some events, we are told in another place, have been fated to occur only along with willingness and effort on our part (*SVF* II 998; Zeller, 171).

Finally, I introduce a rather long fragment from Chalcidius' commentary on the *Timaeus*, for it expresses the all-encompassing nature of fate in the Stoics' conception of it and also brings out nicely how fate was believed to lie behind the thoughts and decisions of human beings:

> Therefore the Stoics say if god knows all things from the beginning, before they occur, not only celestial happenings, which are governed by a felicitous necessity of everlasting bliss, as though by a certain fate, but also these our thoughts and wills, and if he knows also that uncertain nature and governs things past, present, and future, and this from the beginning, and god cannot fail, then certainly all things have been disposed and decreed from the beginning, those which are said to have been placed in our power as well as those which are said to be fortuitous and to have been subjected to fortune. Moreover, since all these things, already for a long time, have been decreed, they conclude that everything which happens happens by fate. Also laws, exhortations, reproofs, and each kind of teaching are of this sort—all are ruled by conditions predisposed by fate; when, if to him to whom something has been decreed to happen, then, at the same time this has been decreed—that it must happen through his deed and intercession; for example, if safety for someone at sea is about to be accomplished, it will not happen to him in any other way than through the navigator guiding the ship, or if [security] is about to come about for some city, it is because it will employ good laws and customs, as this had to come about for Sparta through the laws of Lycurgus. Similarly, if someone is about to be just, the education of his parents is a help to him in taking hold of justice and equity in conduct. (*SVF* II 943)

An example, which I extrapolate from this fragment, will perhaps make clear how in my view the Stoics tried to incorporate into their conception of fate the notion of responsible action supposed by Athenian jurors, affirmed by Plato and Epicurus, and developed and emphasized by Aristotle. Consider the case of a man who is trying to decide whether or not to start smoking. Any such case is, of course, rather complicated and a careful analysis of it along Aristotelian lines would require much more space than I can give it here. The only point, however, that for my purposes needs to be stressed is that, in Aristotle's eyes, the man's beginning or failing to begin to smoke is a genuine alternative which hinges only on the man's decision. It is a case in which in an authentic way what he does is up to the man. If he decides to start smoking, he will start; and if he decides not to start smoking, he will not start. Neither of these alternatives has, in Aristotle's view, been laid down in advance to occur, either with or apart from the man's decision. The man himself is a true starting point of some of his actions. The Stoics, on the other hand, as is evident from the Chalcidius fragment just quoted, would maintain that the man was already destined either to start smoking or not to start, but to do neither of these apart from deliberation and choice. If, say, he were destined to start smoking, then beginning to smoke would be one term in a "condestinate" fact, the other term of which would be deliberation and then assent to the idea of smoking. To generalize, one might say that, while for Aristotle everything which occurs comes about by nature, by reason (or art), or by chance (*Phys.* 198a9–13; *Meta.* 1032a12–13, 1065 b3–4, 1070a6–7) with no generically higher category to umbrella over these, for the Stoics everything which happens comes about by the agency of fate *working through* nature and reason (there is, of course, no place for chance in the Stoic system). This, in fact, is about the doctrine Chalcidius in a slightly different way ascribes to the Stoics in the passage quoted above; for when alluding to the things which have been disposed and decreed from the beginning, he mentions "those which are said to have been placed in our power" (Aristotle's reason or art), and "those which are said to be fortuitous" (Aristotle's chance and spontaneity).

The second major consideration I offer in support of my interpretation of the Stoic conception of fate is that if, indeed, the Stoics did encompass within their theory the traditional view of man as a responsible agent, then we ought to find reappearing in their theory distinctions and difficulties connected with the notion of responsibility advanced by earlier thinkers such as Aristotle. And the confirmatory evidence consists of Stoic fragments which show that some things were thought to be in the power of the agent (and some not), and that the human agent was thought to deliberate and decide before acting. The Stoics were also able to, indeed, bound to give an answer to the question which Aristotle faced squarely momentarily, but then dodged, namely, is the agent himself responsible for the formation of his own character or for the final condition of his own character? The answer they gave seems to me to be fatal, but I am not as interested in showing that as I am in stressing that the question to which it was an answer had raised its head, and that the question arose just because the Stoics had taken over lock, stock, and barrel the Aristotelian analysis of responsible decision making by human agents. Now to the evidence for this.

Aristotle makes use of the distinction between "things in our power" (τὰ ἐφ' ἡμῖν) and "things not in our power" (Τὰ οὐκ ἐφ' ἡμῖν) (*EE*

1226a23–1226b9; *EN* 1113b2–1115a3) in conjunction with his discussion of the voluntary and involuntary, and in particular to drive home the points that deliberation and choice are concerned with things in our power while wish isn't necessarily, and that generally the moral virtues and vices are in our power inasmuch as the ends and means involved in their cultivation are in our power. If the Stoics continued to have Greek intuitions about human responsibility, as I am maintaining they did, then we should expect to find this distinction breaking out in their discussions as well. And this expectation is not disappointed.[2] As an example, consider the argument, reported by Cicero (*De Fato* xvii. 40–41), made against the Stoics that if all things happen by fate, then desire and assent are not in our power, to which Chrysippus replied by first making a distinction in kinds of causes (to which I shall recur) and then insisting that desire and assent would not be in our power (*in nostra potestate* = ἐφ' ἡμῖν) if everything happened in accordance with one kind of cause; but that since this is not the case, desires and assents are things in our power (see also II, 976, 977). That the Stoics claimed some things to be in our power and that they connected this with a manifestation of fate is apparent in the irate perplexity of Alexander of Aphrodisias over their doctrine (*SVF* II 979, 984, 1005, 1006); for he is concerned just over the fact that "they [the Stoics] say that those things which occur by fate through the animals are in the power of the animals" (182, 12–13). Finally, there is an argument used by the Stoics and interesting in its own right, which shows that even though the Stoics objected to one way of regarding "things in our power," they nonetheless adopted the conception. Indeed, their zeal to reject this particular interpretation of it, one which possibly would have produced an inconsistency in their system, shows how bent they were on maintaining within the scope of their own philosophy the distinction between things in our power and things not in our power. The argument, reported by Alexander (196,24–197,3), goes as follows:

> If, they [the Stoics] say, those things are in our power, the opposites of which we are also capable, and in reference to things of this sort there exist praise and blame, exhortations and hinderings, punishments and rewards, then the existence of wise men and the possession of virtues in those who have them will be impossible, because they can no longer acquire the vices opposed to their virtues, and similarly neither can vices exist in bad men, for neither in them can virtues opposed to their vices any longer be acquired; but it is absurd to deny that virtue and vice are in our power and that praise and blame come about in regard to them. Therefore, what is in our power is not of this sort.[3]

Needless to say, the attempt to keep the distinction of things in our power and things not in our power under the same tent with fate generated problems, and I intend to notice some of them presently, but for now my aim is only to substantiate the claim that the Stoics appropriated the distinction between things in our power and things not in our power, thereby making their doctrine seem more plausible to themselves and others.

That the Stoics believed, like Aristotle, that the human agent deliberates and decides before assenting or acting is perhaps already evident, since, of course, deliberation and assent were thought to be the cardinal instances of things in our power. But, to reinforce this, I cite one or two additional fragments. First of all, there is the report by Origen (*SVF* II 988) to which I have already alluded; from that it is clear that the human agent, in the Stoics' view, examines presentations critically; and it is said explicitly that what is good and what is best provide the starting points for his deliberation. Also in the king/messenger model used to explicate their empirical theory of knowledge, a point set forth is that the ruling part of the soul (the king) scrutinizes critically each of the messages conveyed to it by the senses (II 879; Gould, 51–66). This seems to imply that some deliberation occurs before the mind assents to the messages brought it by the senses.

Another circumstance which lends confirmation to my thesis that the Stoics adopted the Aristotelian theory of responsible agency is the appearance in their doctrine of the same difficulty which had afflicted the Aristotelian theory. For Aristotle, a man is a responsible agent because, although the ends he pursues are determined by the kind of person he is, the kind of person he is depends on himself. At least in the beginning it is up to him; once his character has become formed, he can no longer change it, or, at the very least, it is enormously difficult. Here Aristotle is speaking explicitly of bad states of character, but he would in consistency be bound to say the same of good states of character.[4] His argument hinges upon his fundamental doctrine that "the beginning is in the agent or in the power of the agent" (*EN* 1114a19). Aristotle, on being pressed further about the relation of ends pursued to states of character, begins by entertaining the hypothesis that each man is a cause [*aitios*] of his own state of character, and concludes with the weaker affirmation that "we ourselves are somehow contributing causes [*sunaitioi*] of our states of character" (*EN* 1114b1–24; Hardie, 175–80). It is as though the consequences of his own remarks elsewhere about the importance of good upbringing (*EN* 1095b4–6; 1179b20–1180a24) were dinning in his ears; and hence the compromise.

Now notice how and why this problem breaks out for the Stoics. The Stoics, too, acknowledged the differences in human character and the influence of these differences on goals pursued and decisions made (*SVF* II 951). In fact, the point of their frequently used cylinder analogy was to illustrate and stress the role of human character in what happens. A moving, cylindrically shaped object has received its initial impetus from outside, but the kind of movement that ensued on the beginning push was something which depended on the shape of the object itself (*SVF* II 1000). The moral to be drawn, according to the Stoics, is that while a man in any given situation is evidently affected by external forces, what then happens is something to which his own condition or his own character is a contributing factor. So far, the Stoics seem to be riding on Aristotelian wheels. It is no surprise, then, when we hear of men "bad, useless, harmful, and reckless," who claim that they ought to be tolerated and heard after they've been caught in wrongdoing, men who "have recourse to the necessity of fate, as if in the asylum of some shrine, and say that the terrible things which they have done are not to be attributed to their own rashness, but to fate" (*SVF* II 1000). In other words, the Stoics, having appealed to character, as had Aristotle, must now, again like Aristotle, confront the challenging question: But is a man himself responsible for his own character? I wish in the last part of this paper to discuss the answer given by the Stoics to this fundamental question, for it is here that a crucial difference between the Stoics and Aristotle breaks out and it is also here that we come upon an interesting philosophical impasse. For now, the point I want to emphasize is that the problem about responsibility for character did, in fact, arise within Stoic philosophy, and that it did so because the Stoics had after all tried to remain faithful to the intuition, avowed by jurists and philosophers, that men are responsible for some of their actions.

Thirdly, my interpretation gains some support from the attitude Alexander of Aphrodisias takes up towards the Stoic conception of fate. It will be remembered that on my view the Stoics wanted fate to encompass both those things which according to Aristotle happen by nature and those which happen by reason. Alexander has no doubts about the existence of fate, but he wants to know what it is and—very important for my purposes—what the extent of its domain is (165, 23–24). In the early chapters (2–6) of his work, *On Fate*, Alexander explicates the Stoic conception of fate by considering into which of the four classes of Aristotelian causes it is to be placed. He concludes that fate belongs in the class of final causes (169, 2–3), and then continuing, writes,

> And since of the things which happen for the sake of something, some happen in accordance with reason and others happen in accordance with nature, either one must place fate in both sub-classes so as to say that all occurrences happen in accordance with fate, or in one of them. (169, 3–6)

It is, of course, the Stoics who have made fate cover both sub-classes and Alexander's remarks make it clear that in his view the Stoics ought in their conception of fate to have restricted its domain. He argues that things which occur in accordance with reason do so because the person who does them also has the power of not doing them; and he applies the same remark to things which are produced by the arts, thus exhibiting his judgment that Stoic fate has invaded the domain described variously by Aristotle as "things which happen in accordance with art" (*Meta.* 1032a12–13) and "things which happen in accordance with reason" (*Phys.* 198a9–13; 196a6–12). Alexander's next point shows that, while in his view the Stoics may think they have intelligibly appropriated the Aristotelian distinction "things in our power" and "things not in our power," they in fact with their doctrine of fate have made the former a null class, a point he argues at length at a later stage in his treatise (181,7–188,1). He writes here, drawing the conclusion which defines the area of his agreement with the Stoics,

> If those things in our power are those over the carrying out or not carrying out of which we seem to be in positions of authority, and of these it is not possible to say that fate is a cause nor that there are any beginnings and extrinsic antecedent causes of the absolute occurrence or non-occurrence of any of them (for nothing would any longer be in our power, if things happened in that way), then the remaining alternative is to say that fate is in the class of things which happen by nature, because fate and nature are the same thing. (169, 15–19)

I don't think I could state any more plainly than Alexander himself has that, in his view, the Stoics in their conception of fate sought to encompass kinds of occurrence formerly distinguished by Aristotle. Alexander introduces the point exclusively for polemical purposes, and that is another matter. My point is that his interpretation lends some weight to my own—that the determinism involved in the Stoic conception of fate seemed less obnoxious because the Stoics along with their conception of fate (in fact, by means of it) had sought to remain faithful to intuitions and distinctions about human responsibility held by ordinary Athenians and set forth by philosophers like Aristotle. Alexander's argument which tries to disarm the Stoic conception of fate by introducing the distinction between reason (*logos*) and nature (*phusis*)—a distinction which, of course, the Stoics would not have accepted (Verbeke, 80 n. 23)—included the notion of an "antecedent intrinsic cause." And his argument also goes to the heart of a difference between the Stoics and Aristotle by touching upon the notion of a person as a beginner or initiator of action. In concluding my remarks on the Stoic conception of fate I want to show how the Stoics appealed to a distinction in kinds of causes in their answer to challenges about human responsibility, to draw some contrasts with Aristotle, and finally to lay out some perplexities in regard to the idea of human responsibility which, in my view, the Stoic conception of fate raises.

As I indicated earlier, the Stoics in attempting to reconcile their conception of fate with the notion of human responsibility, have recourse to a distinction in kinds of causes. Chrysippus, for example, maintained that if all things happen by fate, this certainly follows, that all things happen in accordance with antecedent causes, but yet not in accordance with first and perfect causes (*principales et perfectae*), but in accordance with auxiliary and proximate causes (*adiuvantes et proximae*). If these themselves (the latter) are not in our power, it does not follow that desire also is not in our power. But this would follow if we were to say that all things occur in accordance with perfect and first causes, because since these causes would not be in our power, neither would desire be in our power. (*SVF* II 974)

From another part of this same fragment, a passage from Cicero's *De Fato*, it appears that what the Stoics called an auxiliary and proximate cause is what we should regard as a necessary condition, although I cannot believe that the Stoics held all antecedent causes to be merely necessary conditions. Their view was, in my judgment, rather that in events where the assents and desires of human agents are not concerned, all "antecedent causes" are necessary and sufficient conditions. But where the assents and desires of human agents are concerned, the "antecedent causes" are necessary, but not sufficient, conditions. To put the matter briefly, assent requires a presentation of some sort, but a presentation is not sufficient to produce assent (*SVF* II 974).

There is an interesting contrast to be drawn here with both Plato and Aristotle. Notice first that in the Socrates prison scene (*Phaedo* 99A–B) what Plato regards as a necessary, but not a sufficient, condition for human assent and what most men call *cause* he will not call a cause of any kind; the Stoics, adherents of universal causality, call these necessary conditions *causes,* but causes of a special kind. Aristotle was able to classify his kind of occurrences (by nature, by reason, and by chance) into one or the other of the categories in his framework of causes. Nature and reason are final causes (*Phys.* 199b29–34); chance is an efficient cause (*Phys.* 198a2–3). Had the Stoics made use of Aristotle's categories, they would have called *assent* something which falls under reason and therefore a final cause. I make no conjectures here as to why the Stoics did not make use of the Aristotelian classification of causes.[5]

I turn now to a problem which has arisen several times during the course of this paper, namely, how the Stoics dealt with the question, Is a man himself responsible for his character? I have noticed the difficulties that arose for Aristotle in his attempt to deal with this question, and I have observed that it looks as though the problem arose for the Stoics as well. I might emphasize at this point how important it is that the Stoics had to be prepared with an answer to this question and how natural it was that their frequently used cylinder analogy invited the question. For the point of the cylinder analogy, it will be remembered, was that, even though the original impetus to move was received from outside, the quality of its subsequent motion was something to which the shape of the cylinder itself contributed. If a man, then, is to be held responsible for his action, as the Stoics believed ought to be the case, then they must be prepared to state the sense in which he is accountable for his "shape," i.e., his condition or character. There are three fragments (*SVF* II 937, 951, 1000) which help us both to see the answer the Stoics tried to give to this question and also the answer they were obliged to give. From *SVF* II 1000 it looks as though the Stoics maintained that the "inclinations of the mind" have either been "formed by nature from the beginning healthfully and usefully" or they are "savage, ignorant, and crude" and they either can or cannot be reinforced by the "supports provided by good occupations." And, as a consequence of the "natural and necessary connection of things," good characters will prosper and bad characters will not be "free from crimes and errors." The lesson of *SVF* II 951 also appears to be that it is not in men's power whether they are dissolute, irascible, cruel, arrogant, keen-witted, or dull-witted; and generally here the Stoics appear to be acknowledging that character is the result of natural causes. Plutarch is a hostile witness in regard to the Stoics, but his inference, which is a part of *SVF* II 937, is, I fear, valid, and indeed the only one possible given the Stoic fatalistic premises. Complaining that Chrysippus is giving license to vice by placing it under the aegis of necessity and Zeus, Plutarch quotes Chrysippus and then draws the inference:

> "For since common nature extends into all things, it will be necessary that everything whatsoever which happens in the universe and in any whatsoever of its parts happen in accordance with that and its reason one after the other in an unimpeded manner; on account of the fact that there is nothing outside which will impede its rule, nor is any of its parts disposed in such a way that it will be moved or constituted otherwise than in accordance with common nature." Now what are the conditions and movements of the parts? It is obvious that vices and illnesses are conditions, avarice, love of pleasure, love of fame, cowardice, and injustice; and acts of adultery, theft, betrayal, murder, and parricide are movements. (*SVF* II 937, Plutarch, 1050C–D)

And, surely, in respect of the question as to who is responsible for the formation of a man's character, this is the only answer to which the Stoics are entitled. The ultimate responsibility lies with fate.

Perhaps if I briefly describe a tack the Stoics might have taken, but didn't—one which is consistent with if, indeed, not entailed by their principles—it will be more clear that they sought to be faithful to Greek intuitions about human responsibility in spite of the fact that this was disallowed, in the ultimate analysis, by their conception of fate. The *logos* or reason of common nature was thought by the Stoics to be an immanent force present in all things in different forms; in men it manifests itself as reason (in contrast, say, to its manifestation in inanimate objects in which it is present as a cohesive force holding the body together [*SVF* II 473; Gould, 111]). This *logos* is a single power the freedom of which is conceived in terms of being unimpeded. Nothing stands in its way. Rather than speaking of some things as being in our power, the Stoics might have held that all things are in our power, since "we" collectively help to constitute the *logos* of common nature or fate, and nothing can occur otherwise than in accordance with that. The Stoics, in fact, come close to taking this line when they use as a model of fate the chariot with the dog tied on behind (*SVF* II 975). Its point, of course, is that if the dog moves along willingly with the chariot, the going will be easy; but if it resists, it will be dragged. Nothing can oppose fate. The Stoics did not push this model nor hold consistently to the view that it illustrates. To have done so would have been to do violence to those experiences of deliberating, making decisions, making excuses, praising and blaming, to which the Stoics wished to do justice as much as Plato, Aristotle, and Epicurus had. But when they upon challenge had to square their avowals of human responsibility with their conception of fate, the task proved impossible.

My conclusion is that when the Stoics were pressed on the question whether a man is responsible for his character, their finally negative answer was entailed by the notion of determinism, which is involved in their conception of fate. But it isn't at all clear to me that one can on some metaphysical thesis other than determinism avoid an impasse when one tries to justify an affirmative answer to this question. For example, consider Aristotle's notions about character formation. Aristotle's sample case is the man who "perhaps is a person of a sort not to take care" (*EN* 1114a3–4) with the tacit suggestion that the sort of person he is is not something for which he himself is responsible. He might argue that his character was a product of genetic and early environmental conditioning. Aristotle apparently held that a man is able to change his character. But notice the kind of regress that Aristotle's position on this matter involves. Consider the case of an irascible man who wants to reform his character. Of what sort is *this* character who wants to change the irascible character? If it is the irascible character working on itself, and the man is not responsible for having become an irascible person, then neither is he responsible for this attempt to change his character. And if it is some character other than the irascible character, we have to ask who is accountable for *that* character, and we are off on a regress which either is endless or it ends at the genes and early environment; in neither case can we conclude that the agent in question is responsible.[6] In other words, attempts to make the agent responsible for the reformation of his character are no more successful than those to make him responsible for the original formation of his character.

The Stoic conception of fate is one with which the notion of human responsibility is incompatible. It is to the credit of the moral sense of the Stoics, if not to their sense for consistency, that they tried with great vigor to sustain the intelligibility of such notions as praise, blame, excuse making, and human responsibility within their system. And it may have been some comfort to realize (as perhaps some of them did) that it is exceedingly difficult not to run into an impasse when trying to give a theoretical account of human responsibility. Is it possible at all to give such an account? If it is, neither hard determinists, soft determinists, simple indeterminists, nor agency theorists (for example, Aristotle) have shown it to be so. If, then, the Stoics suffer embarrassment in this regard, they are hardly alone.

NOTES

[1] ". . . in the case of everything that exists, there are antecedent conditions, known or unknown, given which that thing could not be other than it is. That is an exact statement of the metaphysical thesis of determinism" (Richard Taylor, *Metaphysics* [Englewood Cliffs, N.J., 1963], p. 34).

[2] This is the reason why I am inclined to agree with the general point of view which informs Rist's recent book on Stoic philosophy, namely, that "the thought of the post-Aristotelian schools is frequently grounded on philosophical problems bequeathed to them not by the Presocratics or even by Plato but by Aristotle and his followers" (page 1). I think, however, that Rist's interpretation of Stoic fate as "what will be will be" (127, 129) is mistaken, and I say why in a review of his book (*Journal of the History of Philosophy* [Jan. 1971]:81–86).

[3] This kind of consideration may have been in the wings when Aristotle, reporting an opinion at *EN* 1137a15–19, writes: "For just this reason men think that to be unjust is no less a mark of the just man, because the just man would be not less but even more capable of doing each of these things; for he could have sexual intercourse with a woman and inflict a blow on someone; and the courageous man could drop his shield, turn about, and flee in some direction or other." Aristotle replies that these things have not merely to be done, but to be done with the appropriate state of character, and the suggestion is that it would be difficult or impossible for a just man or a courageous man to change his character on the spot.

[4] *Supra,* n. 3.

[5] The Stoics themselves had a classification of causes more elaborate than that invoked to solve the problem cited in the text above (*SVF* II 346, 351, 354), and they also conceived a cause as being a body (*SVF* II 336). I am not familiar with any studies which compare the Stoics' classification of causes with that of Aristotle. Such a study might throw additional light on the differences in the accounts the two schools give of human responsibility.

[6] I first came upon an argument very like this one in the section on free will in Wallace I. Matson, *The Existence of God* (Ithaca, N.Y., 1965), pp. 164–65.

BIBLIOGRAPHY

Adkins, Arthur W. H. *Merit and Responsibility*. Oxford, 1960.

Alexander Aphrodisiensis. *De Fato*. In *Scripta Minora*. Edited by Ivo Bruns (Supplementum Aristotelicum, vol. II, part 2). Berlin, 1892.

Bréhier, Emile. *Chrysippe et L'Ancien Stoicisme*. Paris, 1951.

Cicero. *De Fato*. Translated by H. Rackham. (Cambridge, Mass.: Loeb Classical Library, 1948).

Furley, David J. *Two Studies in the Greek Atomists*. Princeton, 1967.

Gould, Josiah B. *The Philosophy of Chrysippus*. Albany, 1970.

Grumach, Ernst. *Physis und Agathon in der Alten Stoa*. Berlin, 1932.

Hardie, W. F. R. *Aristotle's Ethical Theory*. Oxford, 1968.

Huby, Pamela. "The First Discovery of the Freewill Problem." *Philosophy* 42 (Oct. 1967):353–62.

Lucretius. *De Rerum Natura*. Vol. I. Edition by Cyril Bailey. Oxford, 1947.

MacDowell, Douglass M. *Athenian Homicide Law in the Age of the Orators*. New York, 1963.

Matson, Wallace I. *The Existence of God*. Ithaca, N.Y., 1965.

Platonis Opera. Burnet, John, ed. Vols. I and V. Oxford, 1901, 1907.

Plutarch, *De Stoicorum Repugnantiis*. In *Moralia*. Vol. VI, Fasc. 2, 2nd ed. Edited by Max Pohlenz and R. Westman. Leipzig, 1959.

Pohlenz, Max. *Die Stoa*. Geschichte einer geistigen Bewegung. 2nd ed., 2 vols. Göttingen, 1959.

Rist, J. M. *Stoic Philosophy*. Cambridge, 1969.

Stenzel, J. "Das Problem der Willensfreiheit in Platonismus." *Antike* 4 (1928): 293–313.

Arnim, Hans von., ed. *Stoicorum Veterum Fragmenta*. Vol. II. Leipzig, 1903. (= *SVF*).

Tarn, W. T. *Hellenistic Civilisation*. 3rd ed., rev. by author and G. T. Griffith. London, 1952.

Taylor, Richard. *Metaphysics*. Englewood Cliffs, N.J., 1963.

Verbeke, Gerard. "Aristotélisme et Stoicisme dans *De Fato* d'Alexandre d'Aphrodisias." *Archiv für Geschichte der Philosophie* 50 (1968):73–100.

Zeller, Eduard. *Die Philosophie der Griechen in ihrer geschichtlichen Entwicklung*, Dritter Teil, Erste Abteilung. 5 Aufl. Darmstadt, 1963.

RICHARD T. WALLIS

Plotinus and
Paranormal Phenomena

HE present paper, I should make clear at the outset, is intended primarily for classicists who are not specialists in Neoplatonism and will therefore tell experts in Plotinus little of which they are not already well aware. Its purpose is to explain Plotinus' views on a subject that finds itself, perhaps surprisingly, once again of some contemporary interest, and where misunderstandings and emotionally toned judgments are only too easy. It will be concerned as much with the reasons underlying Plotinus' beliefs as with those beliefs themselves, and in particular will show how his views on paranormal phenomena spring naturally from some of the most fundamental principles of his whole philosophy.

It need hardly be said, though it is a consideration more widely observed in theory than in practice, that in considering Plotinus or any thinker of the past, we must observe two basic principles. First we should ask his questions and not ours; in other words we should not allot him marks for his supposed rationalism in terms of some eighteenth- or nineteenth-century criterion, but rather ask what it was reasonable for him to believe in the light of contemporary attitudes and of the evidence available to him. Secondly we must consider the whole of what he has to say and try to determine the general principles running through it, not simply extract a few accessible phrases and hope that they will do instead. Thus the common statement that Plotinus regards the stars as signs, not as causes, is based on a careless reading, out of context, of the opening words of the treatise II. 3, *On Astrology*,[1] and cannot be reconciled with a careful study of the whole of that treatise or of Plotinus' other discussions in Chapter 5 and 6 of the early work III. 1 *On Fate* and in the concluding section (IV. 4. 30–45) of the great work *On The Soul*. There are also odd little chapters or isolated remarks scattered throughout the *Enneads* that present a viewpoint apparently more or less at variance with his considered position, while there is reason to sup-

This paper was presented at the 1973 St. Louis meeting of the Society for Ancient Greek Philosophy and has not been published previously.
Richard Wallis is Associate Professor of Classics at the University of Oklahoma.

pose that his oral teaching contained even greater oddities.[2] Thus the chapter II. 9. 14, with its attack on the Gnostics' use of incantations and their demonic theory of disease, has a somewhat more "rationalistic" ring than is usual with Plotinus; conversely, on a more "superstitious" level there are the chapter IV. 7. 15, on oracles from the dead, which so upset Bréhier[3] and the references to anthropomorphic daemons that crop up at various points.[4] Here, since space is limited, I propose, with one exception, to ignore such passages and to concentrate on Plotinus' general attitude.

If then, with this caution in mind, we seek to determine Plotinus' attitude to astrology, the paranormal phenomenon to which he devotes most space, we may note, first, that he was commonly regarded in antiquity as an opponent of astrology and, secondly, that this did not mean then quite what it would now.[5] For, first, total denial of astrological doctrine was normally confined to the most determined materialists and skeptics, whose influence by the third century A.D. was virtually negligible, and, secondly, the motives of astrology's opponents were rarely what we should consider scientific, prompted as they largely were by the desire, on the one hand, to preserve human free will and, on the other, to defend particular theological views. Thus Christian attacks on astrology were greatly influenced by its association with pagan cosmic religion. But if, ignoring this question of motive we ask simply what it was reasonable for Plotinus to believe, we may observe that astrology, and paranormal phenomena in general, had the sanction of most of the greatest scientists of the immediately preceding centuries (such as Ptolemy and Galen) and seemed supported by abundant empirical evidence. Thus Plotinus refers as matters of general acceptance to the possibility of divination,[6] the influence of the heavens on terrestrial phenomena (III. 1. 5. 1–15, IV. 4. 31. 8–15) and the remarkable properties of stones and herbs (IV. 4. 35. 69–70). Perhaps even more important for him, the influence of the heavens, especially the sun, on physical phenomena on earth, was supported by Aristotelian authority,[7] and from here it was a natural step to the acceptance of such less scientific notions as the moon's supposed connection with kleptomania (cf. III. 1. 2. 4–5); similarly the view that the stars influence man's lower soul and the events of his physical life could be derived from the Timaeus (where the younger gods were identified with the heavenly bodies) and from the Myth of Er's account of the Spindle of Necessity (II. 3. 9 and 15). Hence it would have been no more reasonable for Plotinus to reject such phenomena than for a modern philosopher, with no special scientific training, to reject Evolution or Relativity. Any doubts he might have had were likely to be quenched by his belief that he had himself on one occasion been the victim of a magical attack (V. P1. 10. 1–13). Hence, while certain individual cases might be called into question, the reality of such phenomena as a whole seemed beyond reasonable doubt.

This brings us to the most individual feature of Plotinus' own approach: its extreme generality. A modern investigator of psychic phenomena will normally proceed by first assembling alleged cases of such phenomena, then examining their authenticity; finally, if he is bold enough, he may propound a theory to explain them. A roughly similar procedure, though using much less rigorous criteria, was followed by the Stoics, with their collections of case histories of allegedly fulfilled prophecies,[8] echoed in Cicero's *De Divinatione*. By contrast Plotinus shows no interest in the truth or falsity of such individual cases; instead he proclaims his willingness to accept such phenomena as are commonly admitted, provided they admit a rational explanation,[9] and proceeds to frame a general theory that will explain as many, or as few, of them as subsequently turn out to be justified. His procedure in fact has strong resemblances to Hume's attempt to frame a single decisive argument to demolish any case of an alleged miracle that either has been produced or ever can be. Yet, while Plotinus may be thought wise, in the light of our earlier remarks, to have confined himself to general principles, his generality even so goes far beyond what would appear necessary. Thus Hume in the second part of his famous essay does in fact proceed to apply his principle to some alleged cases of miracles, both ancient and modern. Similarly while Sextus Empiricus in his attack on astrology (*Adv. Math.* V) refers to the alleged influence of "Saturn" or "the Moon," Plotinus simply refers to the view of "one star as operating by cold and another by liquid fire."[10] In fact, of course, such extreme generality was a characteristic of his mind and exhibits itself in similar form in his attacks on contemporary Gnostic and Middle Platonic views, where his concern is not at all with the individual authors or systems in question but solely with the general principles they represent[11]; hence the difficulty modern scholars have found in identifying his sources and opponents.

Next to the generality of Plotinus' discussion its most striking point is perhaps the small number of phenomena he examines. If such isolated references as those noted earlier are excluded, his concern is almost entirely with three of them, astrology, the object of several discussions already listed, magic and, a phenomenon not generally included in this class, petitionary prayer, both the latter two being dealt with in the latter part of the treatise *On The Soul* (IV. 4. 30–45). By contrast there is no more than a brief allusion to "natural mantic," the soul's alleged ability to foresee future events in dreams or prophetic ecstasy and even less reference to most other phenomena.[12] The reason for Plotinus' concentration on the three phenomena mentioned is, of course, their special relevance to his metaphysical and religious concerns, especially the two noted earlier. Admittedly Plotinus' conception of free will, like that of many other philosophers, is very different from the popular one[13]; what is, however, of fundamental importance for him is that man's essential self belongs to the intelligible order and is therefore free from any determinism imposed by the sensible world or the fate governing it. On the theological side there was the need to safeguard Plato's basic principles that the gods are never responsible for evil (*Rep*. II. 379–80) and are free from change (*Rep*. II. 380–81), in particular that they cannot be moved by prayers or sacrifices (*Laws* X. 905–07). These points acquired special importance for Plotinus in the light of the need to defend the world-soul and celestial gods against the Gnostics' charge that they are evil or that their knowledge, at best, is inferior to that attainable by man. These considerations are clearly paramount both in Plotinus' discussions of astrology and in his examination of prayer. Thus at the start of the latter three problems are set out. First the fact that many prayers are answered only after a long time would seem to imply that the gods have memory (IV. 4. 30. 14 ff.); but this in Plotinus' view is impossible, both because memory constitutes an inferior way of knowledge compared with pure intuitive insight and because memory of this world would involve an interest in the world on the gods' part similar to that which causes the fall of the human soul.[14] Secondly, and even worse, many prayers are for evil things; but gods can give only good (IV. 4. 30. 5 ff.). Finally there is the problem posed by theurgy, the attempt to invoke and manipulate divine powers by ritual magic, with its implication that the gods are subject to human constraint and that "even the whole heaven can be bewitched by men's audacity and art" (IV. 4. 30. 28–30); it was a primary concern for Plotinus' successors, whether their acceptance of theurgy was partial (as with Porphyry) or total (as with Iamblichus), to show that their views did not involve unacceptable consequences of this kind.[15]

Similar concerns are uppermost in Plotinus' critique of astrological doctrine, which seems in its contemporary form to have come under heavy Gnostic influence. Armstrong, in his introduction to II. 3, lists among Plotinus' objections, in addition to the charge that they exaggerate the stars' causality, the points (1) that they make the stars evil and the cause of evil to men, (2) that they make them changeable and subject to variations of mood, and (3) that they regard them as acting independently and capriciously instead of following the rational and orderly direction of Universal Soul.[16] With regard to the first point Plotinus observes that to conceive the stars as harmful beings who have never harmed them is to charge them with acting in a manner unworthy even of decent men, let alone gods; indeed it is doubtful whether even bad men would act in such a way, unless they expected some profit from so doing.[17] As for the idea that the stars derive sexual pleasure from driving human beings to adultery, it is simply absurd (II. 3. 6. 1–4). Equally absurd is the anthropomorphic view that the stars change from good to evil according to whether they see each other or not, or that such changes depend on whether they are rising or setting or pass from day into night; for such terms have meaning only in relation to the earth, not for the stars themselves.[18] Hence both Plotinus' general metaphysical views and detailed arguments of this kind require the rejection of any such view of the nature of the stars' causality.

There is, however, another way of conceiving that causality which is no less repugnant to Plotinus' basic principles, and that is to conceive it in materialist or corporealist terms. Against this Plotinus argues, first, that the idea that the stars operate through cold or moisture is inconsistent with the true view of them as composed of pure fire; secondly, that material causation could not in fact produce all the effects the stars are supposed to produce. We may indeed suppose that the stars influence man's bodily constitution and thereby affect his lower, irrational soul, but the effect of such influence would be severely limited and could scarcely produce all the variations in character the astrologers allege. And how in any case could they cause lucky or unlucky events, such as noble birth or the discovery of a treasure?[19] In fact, however, there is no more reason to suppose the stars to be causes of all they indicate than are the birds from whose observation diviners draw omens,[20] and there are some events that they indicate of which they obviously *cannot* be the cause, namely, those, like noble ancestry, whose roots lie in the past (II. 3. 14. 2–4, III. 1. 5. 41–53.). Similarly the Aristotelian principle that the sun and the heavens contribute to the birth of living beings also severely limits their influence; the sun does not produce a horse but merely gives something thereto (II. 3. 12). The stars are thus only one of many causes, hereditary and environmental, whose relative importance in determining a being's nature requires careful investigation,[21] a view in support of which Plotinus quotes the stock examples of beings born at the same time with totally distinct characters and destinies (III. 1. 5. 5–9). The most important restriction on the stars' causality, however, will become clear if we examine the world-view in terms of which Plotinus regards astrology and other paranormal phenomena as finding their explanation.

The answer, in Plotinus' view, lies in an adaptation to his own system of the Stoic doctrine of "cosmic sympathy," the view that the sensible universe constitutes "one living creature embracing all living creatures within it, and having one soul reaching to all its parts, insofar as each thing is part of it" (IV. 4. 32. 4–7). There is thus a network of invisible psychic forces linking everything within the cosmos, each of whose parts, like those of any other living being, may exercise a sympathetic effect on, or itself react in sympathy with, any other part (II. 3. 7, IV. 4. 32). Similarly, just as a man's character, or the state of his liver, may be inferred from his eyes, so one part of the cosmos, such as the stars, may indicate what is happening in another part (II. 3. 7. 4–10). Thus even when the stars are not causes, they may be signs, they are like letters for those to read who can.[22] For just as other living things develop from a seed according to the natural law governing their development, so the universe is governed by a single directing principle, the Universal Logos, which is the source of its activities and brings them into harmony with one another. Hence the interactions between its parts may be compared to the movements of a dancer, whose limbs move in perfect coordination at each step under the direction of the single rhythm governing the whole dance (IV. 4. 33). Thus any accusation that the stars act at random falls to the ground, since their actions spring not from their individual will, but from their being parts of the universal organism, and hence follow the direction of the Universal Logos (II. 3. 6. 10–20).

Paranormal phenomena in Plotinus' view provide empirical confirmation that the doctrine of cosmic sympathy, like those of the unity of all souls and the organic nature of the sensible cosmos, on which that doctrine depends, is correct.[23] But he is equally emphatic that without it even the ordinary phenomena of sense-perception would be impossible (IV. 5 passim). Most important is the fact that the doctrine is a necessary consequence of his view of reality as a hierarchy of degrees of unity, in which the sensible world's organic unity constitutes the best possible imitation, on its own level, of the unity-in-diversity of the intelligible cosmos.[24] Hence on two vital points Plotinus transforms the Stoic theory to accord with his own metaphysics. First of all the interaction between the world's parts should not be conceived, as the Stoics conceived it, in crudely mechanistic or corporealist terms.[25] What determines the sympathetic reaction between one part and another is not, Plotinus maintains, a matter of far and near, but of like and unlike; action may take place between two parts separated by vast physical distances and without affecting intervening objects in any way (II. 4. 32. 13–25). Similarly a medium between the eye and its object is necessary only incidentally, to ensure that both form part of the same psycho-physical world organism: sight depends not on the transmission of an image through a medium, but on a sympathetic reaction of the object and the organ of vision (IV. 5. 2–3). Whether such effects are beneficial or harmful depends on whether the nature of the recipient is in harmony with that of the agent; hence evil effects are due, not to the stars' deliberate intention, but to the individual's inability to receive their gifts in their pure state. But, in any case, since both giver and recipient fall under the direction of the Universal Logos, such evil is so only for the part; viewed in the context of the whole universe—and here Plotinus agrees completely with the Stoa—there is nothing evil or unnatural, though the conditions of the physical world do not always permit each of its members to have what it would like.[26]

The second fundamental point on which Plotinus corrects the Stoics is that in his view each individual is subject to the Fate governing the sensible world only insofar as he is part of that world. But, as we have seen, the higher souls of both men and gods belong to the intelligible order. Hence the latter, living wholly by their higher souls, are at all times totally free from the network of forces governing this world; man, on the other hand, has to choose whether to live by his true self or to submit to his lower being and thereby subject himself to the domination of Fate.[27] It is true that his higher soul, in her descent, has joined herself to the harmony governing the sensible order and that even her acts are therefore indicated by the stars; this is possible since, deriving as they do from the same intelligible source, all souls are ultimately one (IV. 3. 8. 1–4, 12. 12–30). But as long as man remains on that level, the stars are only signs for him, and no more. This Plotinus takes as Plato's meaning in the *Timaeus* and *Republic* X, and especially of the famous remark in the latter that "virtue has no master."[28] The consequences of this view for the divine souls will become clear if we examine Plotinus' treatment of magic and petitionary prayer.

These phenomena Plotinus regards as similarly explicable by the magician's learning to apply the same psychical forces as are already naturally operative within the physical world. The magician's power, he once again stresses, depends on his situation within that world and his ability to adapt himself to its forces so as to draw on them. For instance there is a natural magical attraction which leads men to fall in love, and love-magic involves simply a skillful application of the forces it involves (IV. 4. 40). Once again, however, the power of magic extends only to men's body and lower soul. Hence even the sage is not immune to a magical attack on his body or lower soul; he may, for instance, fall sick or even face the danger of death, and have to resort to counter-spells to repulse the attack.[29] But his true self remains immune, and contemplation, the soul's inner self-concentration, secures his essential being against attack; conversely the man whose goal is action in the external world has already yielded to that world's beauty and thereby succumbed to its magical spell (IV. 4. 43–44). It is easy, reading such passages, to dilute Plotinus' references to "magic" into a mere metaphor. This, however, is a mistake parallel to the view, which he rejects, that the stars' power over men resides only in their beauty, not in the stars themselves or their groupings (IV. 35. 57 ff.). Plotinus recognizes the efficacy of the incantations and gestures used by the magician (IV. 40. 21 ff.), as also of the stones and herbs he employs (IV. 35. 69–70). Hence the paradox of his position. It is true that falling victim to magic is in his view no more mysterious than falling in love or the emotional appeal of a piece of music (IV. 40. 24–26),[30] but this is because in his view the sensible world, penetrated as it is with magical forces, is already a more mysterious place than the ordinary man believes it to be. Hence the man who pursues action for its own sake is already a victim of the same forces as a magician would use against him. The title "paranormal phenomena" is thus misleading; the trouble is that the common man admires only what is unfamiliar and fails to see the same powers as operative in the everyday things he takes for granted. Similarly, being unwilling to recognize that *soul* and *life* admit of degrees, he regards only beings that visibly live and move as alive. Yet, if he conducted a proper philosophical inquiry, he would see that the activities of supposedly inanimate things, such as the burning of fire, are inexplicable without the power of a sustaining and governing soul (IV. 4. 36. 15 ff., 37. 1 ff.). Here is yet another of the dominant themes running through Plotinus' whole philosophy. On the one hand, here, as elsewhere, he shows himself determined on a rational explanation of phenomena; yet this in its turn he regards as possible only by totally overthrowing the common-sense view of the world.

Petitionary prayer, for Plotinus, is only one application of magic among many. Just as one string may vibrate in harmony with another, so prayer may evoke a sympathetic response from the world-soul or the lower soul of one of the celestial gods (IV. 4. 41). Hence, if we describe them as "hearing" the prayers addressed to them, we should be clear that this involves a mere automatic response on their part without will or awareness (IV. 4. 26. 1–4). Similarly there is no reason why prayers should not be answered only after a considerable time, without our having to ascribe memory to the gods (IV. 4. 43. 11–12). The stars' attention is wholly concentrated on their higher soul's contemplation of the intelligible world, while their lower soul is wholly free from the passions that perturb men, since the body they govern is either (in the case of the stars) composed of a purer substance than ours or (in the case of the world) all-containing and without external wants or dangers, and hence admits of automatic control, without deliberate, conscious attention.[31] Hence, if there is any place in Plotinus' thought for any form of divine grace, this does not involve change or deliberate intent on the gods' part. For both men and gods the only worthy object of contemplation is the intelligible world; hence the only prayer worthy of the philosopher is the soul's silent concentration upon that order.[32] This is why Plotinus ranks petitionary prayer on such a relatively low level and exempts the gods from any conscious concern with it; as Bréhier observes: "jamais le culte n'a été plus extérieur, plus réduit à son côté matériel que dans sa doctrine."[33] On such an explanation it is clearly no more remarkable that wicked men's prayers should be answered than that they should draw water from streams or use any other natural force; but since the world is subject to divine law, they will subsequently have to pay for their sin (IV. 4. 42. 14–19). What is especially noteworthy is the contrast not just with popular religious ideas, but with the Stoics' continual stress on the deliberate and anthropocentric nature of divine benevolence. Thus, whereas they had seen divination as one of the most obvious benefits bestowed on man by God, for

Plotinus the stars are fully occupied with their own business, and the possibility of astrological divination is merely a necessary but incidental and unintended consequence of their movements.[34] Similarly that procreation can occur unintentionally and without awareness is for Plotinus a sign that the gods' gifts may be similarly unintended (IV. 4. 37. 21–25); Seneca, on the other hand, while admitting that we owe gratitude to our parents whether they intended to beget us or not, denies emphatically that the gods can have failed to intend the good they do us (*De Benef.* VI. 23). The contrast speaks for itself.

Finally, that theurgy can in Plotinus' system play no part in the soul's return to the intelligible order is clear from the fact that its operations, like those of any form of magic, must remain confined within the sensible cosmos. We have already remarked Plotinus' indignation at the theurgists' claim to command the world-soul; but the Gnostics' boast that their spells have power even over the intelligible beings arouses even greater resentment on his part (II. 9. 14. 1–11). The episodes from Porphyry's biography that have sometimes been taken as showing that Plotinus himself practiced magic have been fully dealt with by Armstrong[35] and need no treatment here. A careful reading of them will show that, while Plotinus may not have disapproved of ritual worship for others, he saw no need to engage in it himself; that, while he permits the sage to use magic for the limited practical purpose of self-defense, this has nothing to do with theurgy; and, while he was on one occasion persuaded to attend an evocation of his guardian daemon (which turned out to be a god), the only daemon that really interested him was the metaphysical conception of the daemon as an inner psychological principle. This is the subject of the treatise III. 4, *On Our Guardian Daemon*, which Porphyry claims was inspired by the event in question; if so, Plotinus will have astutely seized the occasion to turn his pupils' attention away from popular religion toward philosophy.

There is, however, one chapter from the earlier part of the treatise *On the Soul* (IV. 3. 11), which appears to accord theurgy at least a qualified respectability and which, since it has often been overlooked, is worth discussing even in violation of our earlier injunction against giving too much weight to isolated paragraphs. Here Plotinus remarks that "the ancient sages," who sought to secure the gods' presence in shrines and statues, considered the nature of the universe and realized that Soul would be easy to attract if a suitable receptacle were prepared for her (IV. 3.11.1–8). In seeking to tone down the passage's theurgic implications, Dodds notes Plotinus' further remark that what is needed is a representation suitable "in any way" (IV. 3.117. τὸ ὁπωσοῦν μιμηθέν), which, he claims, "seems to involve denying any specific virtue to magical rites of consecration."[36] But, as we have seen, while Plotinus may be taken here as denying that such rites are always necessary, our other evidence shows clearly that he did believe in their efficacy. And that special rituals and ritual objects were in fact used in the construction of such images is clear from our ancient evidence, such as the Hermetic *Asclepius'* defenses of the Egyptian image cult (paras. 23–24, 37).[37] That the cult of magical images in fact originated in Egypt is accepted by Dodds himself,[38] and there is a strong resemblance between the reference here to the "ancient sages" and that at V. 8. 6. 1 to the "Egyptian wise men."

Admitting then the theurgic reference of the passage, we may see in it a much more tolerant attitude, at least to magic of this kind, than appears in the latter part of IV. 4, with its implication that magic constitutes a distraction for the philosopher that is at best superfluous for him and at worst a danger. On the other hand not even in IV. 3. 11 is there any hint that theurgic ritual plays any part in the philosopher's ascent and here, as elsewhere, the powers invoked by the theurgist do not go beyond the level of soul. Hence in the debate as to the value of theurgy Plotinus would here be on the side of Porphyry against Iamblichus; more precisely, Porphyry, in framing his view of theurgy as an easier first step for the average man, took care not to depart from his master's metaphysical views.[39] On the other hand, a follower of Iamblichus could note the implication of the latter part of IV. 3. 11 (8–26) that the divine intelligences are indirectly present in their statues through the intermediary of their respective souls in the same way that the solar intelligence is indirectly present in the physical sun through the intermediary of its own soul, and might wonder whether, if Plotinus had developed this idea, the difference between him and Iamblichus might turn out to be mainly one of emphasis. Yet not merely would the difference of emphasis even so remain fundamental; as has been shown elsewhere it rests upon profound metaphysical differences between Iamblichus and his predecessors regarding the relation of the several orders of Reality to one another, and especially regarding the status of the human soul. Furthermore a reply to the charge that the theurgists claim to subject the gods to human constraint was possible only in the light of Iamblichus' new stress on the role in theurgy of divine grace, a concept present only in embryo, if at all, in Plotinus.[40] What IV. 3. 11 does seem to show is that Porphyry's advocacy of ritual as an easier way for those unable to pursue philosophy directly is far less un-Plotinian than has often been supposed and may perhaps have had Plotinus' tacit approval, or even encouragement. If so, not merely would Plotinus have been in no danger of departing from his own principles; he would have gone a long way toward removing one of his system's greatest weaknesses.

POST-ARISTOTELIAN PHILOSOPHY

NOTES

¹ II.3.1.1–3: Ὅτι ἡ τῶν ἄστρων φορὰ σημαίνει περὶ ἕκαστον τὰ ἐσόμενα, ἀλλ᾽ οὐκ αὐτὴ πάντα ποιεῖ, ὡς τοῖς πολλοῖς δοξάζεται, εἴρηται. . . . The erroneous interpretation is maintained even by a scholar of the calibre of E. R. Dodds; cf. *Pagan and Christian in an Age of Anxiety* (Cambridge, 1965), p. 15.

² This is observed by J. M. Dillon in "Iamblichus' Criticisms" (paper presented to the Society for Ancient Greek Philosophy, 1972). Iamblichus *De An.*377.9 ff, cited by Dillon, is especially remarkable.

³ Cf. É. Bréhier, ed. and trans., Plotinus, *Ennéades* (Paris 1924–38), tome IV, p. 188; for another view cf. Richard Harder, trans., *Plotins Schriften* (Hamburg, 1956–71), *ad loc.*

⁴ II.1.6.54, III.5.6–7, IV.3.18.22–4, IV.4.43.12–16.

⁵ As in the sixteenth century "with the learned and the studious the question was not so much whether astrology was true, but whether all of it were true," Sir Charles Sherrington, *Man on His Nature* (Cambridge, 1941), p. 59. Similarly those who have read, e.g., W. R. Inge's praise of Christianity for its opposition to astrology (*Philosophy of Plotinus* [New York, 1923], I. p. 51) may be somewhat startled by the amount of astrological lore that medieval Christians in fact accepted. For Plotinus as an opponent of astrology, cf. Firmicius Maternus, *Mathesis* IV.11–14, quoted by Paul Henry, *Plotin et l'Occident* (Louvain, 1934), pp. 31–34.

⁶ That the Epicurean system does not admit the possibility of divination is in his view strong evidence of that system's falsity (III.1.3.13–17).

⁷ Cf. Aristotle *Physics* II.2, 194b13; *De Gen. et Corr.* II.10, whose views are echoed at *Enn.* II.3.12.3 ff.

⁸ On these cf. E. R. Dodds, "Supernormal Phenomena in Classical Antiquity," reprinted in his *The Ancient Concept of Progress* (Oxford, 1973), p. 159; on the poor quality of this evidence by modern standards, cf. Dodds, *Ancient Concept*, p. 183.

⁹ IV.4.31.29–32: νῦν δὲ τὰ πᾶσιν ἢ τοῖς πλείστοις συγχωρούμενα ἐάσαντες οὕτως ἔχειν, ὅσα διὰ λόγου φανεῖται, πειρατέον λέγειν τὸν τρόπον. . . .

¹⁰ Cf. II.3.5.1 ff., IV.4.31.32 ff. The main exceptions are II.3.6.1, where the names *Ares* and *Aphrodite* have special reference, and the very doubtfully authentic section II.3.12.12 ff., an apparent reply to II.3.5.

¹¹ Cf. the remark by Henri Puech (in E. R. Dodds *et al.*, *Les Sources de Plotin* [Geneva, 1960], p. 181) on the extreme generality of Plotinus' anti-Gnostic polemic and the problems it poses.

¹² For natural mantic cf. III.1.3.15–16. There may be an allusion to telepathy at IV.9.3.6–9; cf. Dodds' discussion in *Ancient Concept* p. 165, n. 8; on the Neoplatonists' general lack of interest in telepathy, cf. Dodds, *Ancient Concept*, pp. 165–166.

¹³ Cf. my discussion, R. T. Wallis, *Neoplatonism* (London, 1972), pp. 63–64.

¹⁴ Cf. my *Neoplatonism*, pp. 79–82. The problem is discussed in relation to the human soul in IV.3.25–IV.4.5; for the divine souls cf. IV.4.6–17.

¹⁵ Cf. Wallis, *Neoplatonism*, pp. 110, 121–122.

[16] Cf. A. H. Armstrong, *Plotinus, with an English Translation*, vol. 2 (Loeb, Cambridge, Mass., 1966) p. 54.

[17] II.3.1.6 ff., 2.16–21, IV.4.31.48–57.

[18] II.3.1.12–24, 3–4, 5.6–10, etc.; III.1.6.11–18.

[19] II.3.2.1–16, III.1.6.1–11, IV.4.31.32–48.

[20] II.3.3.27–8, III.1.5.33–37, 6.23–24.

[21] II.3.13–14, III.1.5.20 ff., IV.3.7.20–31.

[22] II.3.7.4–6, 20–23, III.3.6.17–22.

[23] In addition to the passages so far noted, cf. also IV.9.3.1–9.

[24] Cf. Wallis, *Neoplatonism*, pp. 69–71.

[25] For Neoplatonic criticisms of Stoic mechanism cf. *SVF* II.342–43; the crudity of the Stoic view of divine agency is also brought out by Epictetus I.14 and the Stoic-influenced *De Mundo*.

[26] II.3.11, IV.4.32.23 ff., 38.19–24, 39.18–28, 41.8–15.

[27] II.3.9–10, III.1.8–10, III.3.6, IV.4.34, etc.

[28] *Rep.* X.617e3, quoted II.3.9.17, IV.4.39.2.

[29] IV.4.43.1–11. Whether these "counter-spells" are only a metaphor for the soul's power of contemplation, as A. H. Armstrong suggests (*Phronesis* I.1 [1955]: 76), must remain doubtful. In any case there is surely no suggestion, as Armstrong implies, that they are used to repel a magical attack on the sage's *higher* soul; for Plotinus is emphatic that the higher soul, especially that of the sage, is immune to magic; this is why the sage cannot fall victim to love-spells (IV.43.5–7). The counter spells are rather to repel an attack on his irrational element (IV.4.43.7–8). Admittedly, there is a difficulty in that Plotinus seems to say that philtre-love requires the consent of the higher soul, which would contradict his other statements about magic, but his reasoning may be: (a) such love requires the consent of the level on which a man lives; but (b) in the case of the sage this is the rational soul, which can never yield to magic; hence (c) such love is impossible for him. In any case, the sage's higher soul is even here clearly stated to be unaffected.

[30] Cf. also the echoes in the passage of Plato's condemnation of the effects of art on the irrational soul. For Plotinus' view of magic, cf. also II.3.15.13–17, IV.9.3.1–6.

[31] Cf. IV.4.35.38 ff., 37.18 ff., 40.27 ff., 42.1 ff.; on the difference between divine and human souls cf., e.g., II.9.2, IV.3.4.21 ff., IV.8.2, etc.

[32] Cf. IV.9.4.6, V.1.6.8, V.8. 9. 13.

[33] É. Bréhier, Budé *Plotinus*, IV p. 53.

[34] For the Stoic view cf., e.g., Cicero *De Div.* I.38.82; for Plotinus cf. II.3.3.25–28, 9.34–39, III.1.6.18–24, IV.4.39.13–18; with these passages contrast especially Seneca *De Benef.* VI.20 ff.

[35] A. H. Armstrong, "Was Plotinus a Magician?" *Phronesis* I.1 (1955) 73–79, opposing P. Merlan, "Plotinus and Magic," *Isis* XLIV (1953) 341–48; cf. Armstrong's further remarks Armstrong, ed., *Cambridge History of Later Greek and Early Medieval Philosophy* (Cambridge, 1967) 207–09. For the relevant episodes, cf. V.P.l.1.10.

[36] E. R. Dodds, *The Greeks and the Irrational* (Berkeley, 1951) p. 306, n. 83; cf. A. Smith, *Porphyry's Place in the Neoplatonic Tradition* (The Hague, 1974) p.

127, n. 8.; on the other side see Ficino's interpretation of the chapter, discussed by Frances Yates, *Giordano Bruno and the Hermetic Tradition* (London, 1964) pp. 64 ff.

[37] Dodds, *Greeks and Irrational*, pp. 292–95.

[38] Dodds, *Greeks and Irrational*, p. 293.

[39] Cf. Wallis, *Neoplatonism*, pp. 109–110.

[40] For the difference, cf. Wallis, *Neoplatonism* pp. 118–123, and E. R. Dodds, *Proclus, Elements of Theology* (Oxford, 1963) p. xx.

JOHN M. DILLON

Metriopatheia and *Apatheia*: Some Reflections on a Controversy in Later Greek Ethics

I

L ATER Platonic theory on the passions faced considerable problems, largely inherited from Plato himself. The master had in various places in his dialogues given occasion for rather different doctrines, or at least varieties of emphasis, in this area. From a dialogue such as the *Phaedo* one could derive the doctrine that the passions were to be extirpated root and branch from the soul of the wise man. The passage of the *Theaetetus* (176A ff.) advocating *likeness to god* as the purpose of life could be taken as implying the same view. On the other hand, in the *Republic* and the *Timaeus* all three parts of the soul are accorded their due place, and there is no question of abolishing the passionate element, simply of controlling it. In such a passage as *Polit.* 284E ff., Plato actually seems to propound the doctrine of *virtue as a mean* in the Aristotelian sense, implying that passions are bad only as excesses that require moderating, or "measuring," by logos. Again, in *Laws* I, 631B ff. the distinction between *divine* and *humann* goods (goods of the soul as opposed to goods of the body and external goods) finds a definite place for such lower goods, if only an inferior one, and these goods are inseparable from the passions.[1]

Let us first briefly recall the positions which form the basis for the controversy, as propounded by their originators. In the *Nicomachean Ethics* Book II, as we know, Aristotle puts forward a theory of virtue as a mean, which involves it in being, as set out in Chapter 5 (1105b19 ff.), a *hexis* imposing a correct measure upon *pathe*, which, left to themselves, would tend to irrational excess. On the other hand, for Zeno of Cition and his immediate successors (*SVF* I 205 ff.), all pathos was an irrational movement of the

This paper was presented at the 1978 Vancouver meeting of the Society for Ancient Greek Philosophy and has not previously been published.
John Dillon is Regius Professor of Greek at Trinity College, Dublin.

soul , a *hormē pleonazousa*, an "excessive impulse," which must simply be removed from the soul of the wise man. The passions in question are chiefly four: desire, fear, grief, and pleasure.

The question necessarily arises as to what is left to the soul, and it has been variously answered. There are, after all, two possibilities. Either the wise man is to be seen as a sort of yogi, totally impervious to normal human impulses, or we must redefine what it is to be *rationally* affected by events. The former alternative does seem to have been attractive to certain Stoic "heretics" such as Ariston, but orthodox Stoicism, as represented by Chrysippus, and—it seems probable to me—by Zeno himself, did not intend to impose upon the Wise Man total impassivity.

This involves us with the theory of the *eupatheiai*,[2] and thus brings us to the point at which the Stoic and Aristotelian positions require considerable powers of discrimination to distinguish, powers not granted, it seems, to many of the Platonist writers who have come down to us. The theory of *eupatheiai* in its explicit form seems to be the creation of Chrysippus, but Zeno is on record as making the remark (*ap.* Seneca, *De Ira* I 16, 7) that "in the soul of the Wise Man, even when the wound (of the passions) is healed, a scar remains. He will feel therefore certain suggestions and shadows of passions, though he will be free of the passions themselves." Whether or not the latter remark is that of Zeno or of Seneca himself, the point is clear enough. The wise man will experience *something*, and it is not a passion.[3] Whether or not Zeno conceived a name for it, he stated the position. The only respect in which Chrysippus is reported as differing with him on this question (Galen, *De Hipp.* V 429, p. 405 Mu. = *SVF* III 461) is that Chrysippus held the passions to be actually "judgments" (*kriseis*), while Zeno held that they were disturbances in the soul that arise after (some) judgments.

We see here, I think, Chrysippus pressing the Stoic position to its logical conclusion. Zeno is trying to separate off the purely intellectual element in, say, a decision in the mind of the wise man arising from righteous indignation, from any trace of emotion that might supervene upon that. Chrysippus sees this as illogical; there is only one element operating in the soul (the *hēgemonikon*); it is illegitimate to break down certain of its *kriseis* into two operations. Some *kriseis* of the wise man cannot be performed without some emotion, however rational. Such an emotion cannot be a *pathos*, since that is essentially irrational, and thus unworthy of the wise man. Let us therefore propound a new term, *eupatheia*, for this inevitable accompaniment of certain judgments. There will be *eupatheiai* answering at least to three of the four *pathē*—"joy" (*chara*) to pleasure, "willing" (*boulēsis*) to desire, and "caution" (*eulabeia*) to fear (*SVF* III 431, 437, 438). Only to Grief was Chrysippus unwilling to allow any rational equivalent, though later Stoics seem to have recognized a permissible "nibbling" or "gnawing" at the soul (*dēgmos*, e.g., Cic. *Tusc. Disp.* III 83), to match *lypē*.

II

With the development of the doctrine of *eupatheiai* in its full form, the positions of the two schools seem to come, on the practical level at least, dangerously close.[4] The Stoic sage is not, after all, a totally passionless yogi. He begins to appear very much like the well-moderated Aristotelian gentleman. What then does this great controversy amount to, and, in particular, what did the Platonists make of it? That is the proper subject of this paper. Let us take a few significant passages, and analyse them.

I begin with Antiochus of Ascalon, as reported by Cicero.[5] Antiochus was a thoroughgoing Stoic sympathizer both in physics and in ethics (though he felt that Zeno and his followers had rather gone out on a limb in denying all place in rational life to the "lower" goods, sc. the goods of the body and external goods.[6]) Here is how Cicero makes Antiochus' mouthpiece, Varro, present Zeno's position in the *Academica Posteriora* (I 38):

> Also, whereas they (sc. the Old Academy, with Aristotle and Theophrastus) did not remove emotion out of humanity altogether, and said that sorrow and desire and fear and pleasure were natural, but curbed them and narrowed their range, Zeno held that the wise man was devoid of what he termed "these diseases"; and whereas the Ancients said that these emotions were natural and non-rational, and placed desire and reason in different parts of the soul, he did not agree with these doctrines either, for he thought that even the emotions were voluntary and were experienced owing to a judgement of opinion, and he held that the mother of all the emotions was a sort of immoderate intemperance (a rendering, no doubt, of *hormē pleonazousa*).

Antiochus here presents a strong antithesis between the two doctrines, ignoring the subtlety introduced by the doctrine of *eupatheiai*. He himself, on Cicero's evidence, seems to have been in sympathy with the Stoic position. In an admittedly polemical passage of the *Acad. Pr.* (II 135–36), Cicero presents Antiochus as adhering to the Stoic line on extirpation of the passions, and reproaches him for importing into the "Old Academy" an *atrocitas* foreign to it. But Antiochus was, as we know, wedded to the doctrine that there was no essential difference between the Old Academy (including the Peripatos), and the Stoics (except in this matter of the self-sufficiency of virtue), so that he must in fact have made some satisfactory equation in his own mind between Aristotelian moderation of the passions and the Stoic *eupatheiai*. This equation, if indeed he made it, may be regarded as the beginning of a long-standing confusion in later Platonism as to what the opposition to the Stoic ideal was about. The main element in the opposition, plainly, is the contrast between the Stoic belief in a unitary soul, which should be dominated by logos, and in which anything irrational must be a perversion (*diastrophē*) of logos (cf. *SVF* I 208), and the Platonic-Aristotelian bipartite or tripartite soul. If one does not postulate an irrational part of the soul, as the Platonists did (and as, later, Posidonius, among the Stoics, came to do[7]), then the phenomenon of *pathos* becomes extremely troublesome. There can be no "moderate" form of it. One cannot be partly or moderately irrational, rather as one cannot be half pregnant. The logos is the guiding principle within the soul, and it is the only principle, since the soul is unitary; either it is perverted, or it is not. It cannot be in full or partial control of some other "irrational" element within the soul.

The issue, then, would seem to turn on how one views the structure of the soul. The Stoic position derives with rigid logic, as did all their positions, even the most paradoxical, from their basic premises, in this case the unitary nature of the soul. The Platonists recognized this in theory, as we see Antiochus doing here, but the traditions of ancient polemic, even in the philosophical schools, were such that in practice the Peripateticisers among them are frequently to be found attacking the Stoic position without any apparent regard for its theoretical underpinnings—simply appealing to the "facts" of human nature. Here is a passage from Plutarch's *Consolation to Apollonius* (102CD)—admittedly a rhetorical rather than a strictly philosophical work—which serves to state the Peripatetic polemical position well enough:

> The pain and pang felt at the death of a son has in itself good cause to awaken grief, which is only natural, and over which we have no control. For I, for my part, cannot concur with those who extol that harsh and callous indifference (*apatheia*), which is both impossible and unprofitable. For this will rob us of the kindly feeling which comes from mutual affection and which above all else we must conserve. But to be carried beyond all bounds and to help in exaggerating our griefs I say is contrary to nature and results from a perverted opinion (*phaulē doxa*) within us. Therefore this also must be dismissed as injurious and depraved and most unbecoming to rightminded men, but a moderate experiencing (*metriopatheia*) of grief is not to be disapproved.[8]

Plutarch here provides us with a useful contrast between *apatheia* and *metriopatheia*, borrowing the Stoic doctrine of passion as a perverted opinion to characterize *excess* in passion, rather than passion as a whole, and concentrating on the one passion, grief, of which the Stoics admitted no rational equivalent. The important question of the structure of the soul, however, is something that he does not touch upon.

Perhaps the most important surviving document in this controversy, on

the other hand, is another work of Plutarch's, this time a philosophical treatise, his essay *On Moral Virtue*. This constitutes the best defense of the
Platonist-Peripatetic position against Chrysippus that has come down to us,
and I propose to concentrate on it in my examination of the nature of the
controversy.

Plutarch begins by defining the subject matter of moral virtue (*ēthikē
aretē*) as having as its 'matter' (*hylē*), the passions, and as its form (*eidos*)
the reason (*logos*), thus presenting to us forcibly the image of form being
imposed on a matter external to it, and even antithetical to it. He recognises
as a possible question whether the passionate part itself has a *logos* (440D),
but he takes as a basic premise that there can be no talk of *ēthikē*, as opposed to *theorētikē, aretē* without the postulation of some such passionate part of the soul distinct from the rational part. He thus rejects at the outset the premises on which the Stoics base their doctrine.

In his doxography of previous opinions, however, he does state clearly
the Stoic position (441C):

> Yet all these men agree in supposing virtue to be a certain disposition of
> the governing portion (*hēgemonikon*) of the soul and a faculty engendered
> by reason, or rather to be itself reason which is in accord with virtue and is
> firm and unshaken. They also think that the passionate and irrational part
> of the soul is not distinguished from the rational by any difference or by its
> nature, but is the same part, which, indeed, they term intelligence and the
> governing part; it is, they say, wholly transformed and changes both during
> its emotional states and in the alterations brought about in accordance with
> an acquired disposition or condition (*hexis* or *diathesis*) and thus becomes
> both vice and virtue; it contains nothing irrational within itself, but is called
> irrational whenever, by the over-mastering power of our impulses, which
> have become strong and prevail, it is hurried on to something outrageous
> which contravenes the convictions of reason. Passion, in fact, according to
> them, is a vicious and intemperate reason, formed from an evil and per-
> verse judgment which has acquired additional violence and strength.

This position seems to Plutarch repugnant to common sense. Is not one of
the basic facts of our psychic life the struggle between what one should do
and what one would? His most effective argument invokes the difference between moderation and continence (445B ff.), which, he claims, could not be
made unless there were in fact two opposed elements within our souls,
which are now overcome the one by the other, now locked in combat. The
whole essence of *enkrateia* and *akrasia* is surely the imperfect domination of
one of these elements by the other. Chrysippus is in fact involved in maintaining very much the position of Socrates before him and is open to the
same kind of criticisms.

Plutarch here appeals to the fact of human existence. How is Chrysippus to answer him? His position must be, surely, that no action, in the sense of conscious or purposive action, could take place without a decision to act, and the only element in us that can make a decision is the "ruling part," the *hēgemonikon*. The *hēgemonikon* may act as a result of extensive, rational deliberation, or in accordance with an impulse of some sort or other, and the impulse may well prove stronger in moving the *hēgemonikon* then the set tled attitude resulting from previous deliberations—as in the case where one decides to have another drink, though one "knows," on the basis of previous experience, that this action is dangerous or will have unpleasant consequences. To say here that desire is overcoming reason is superficially plausible, but in fact it misdescribes what takes place and merely shifts the difficulty to another quarter. In fact one makes a *decision* to have another drink, and this is essentially the same sort of mental act as would be the decision not to have another drink. The mind, or soul, directs the limbs (by activating the *pneuma*) either to reach out for a glass, or to get up, excuse oneself, and leave the room. Those who have emancipated themselves from the idea of a mind at all can rephrase this in suitably Rylean terms, but the essential similarity of the two actions is not altered.[9]

And further, Chrysippus might say, what if we do postulate this other element, warring against the reason, and all too frequently winning? How does that solve our problems? We must then explain how *it* acts, and what its relation is (abandoning Platonic imagery of spatially distinct parts of the soul as poetic fancy) to the so-called rational part of the soul.

Well, says Plutarch in reply, what then do we envisage happening in a state of *akrasia*, this being the most difficult situation to explain? Here above all we have a sensation of two warring principles. If there is after all only one principle, what is it that is warring?

> For those who assume that the *hēgemonikon* becomes now desire, and now that reason (*logismos*) which is opposed to desire, are in the same position as those who assume the hunter and the beast to be not two, but one and the same body, which, by a change, is now the beast and now becomes the hunter. (447C)

Eloquently put, Chrysippus might say, but not really compelling. In talking of the hunter and the beast, you are already assuming two antithetical elements in the soul, which is just what I am concerned to deny. Is there after all anything stranger about *akrasia* than about the purely rational process of changing one's mind on a question of science or philosophy, on a reconsideration of the evidence, or on the acquisition of new evidence?

Yes indeed, says Plutarch (447D). In the latter case, the intellectual part of the soul is not opposing itself, but on receiving new impulses, in the form of new evidence, or new views of the evidence, assents to the new impulses.

In the former case, on the other hand, the evidence remains the same, and the intellect assents to it, but yet the individual acts contrary to this assent.

> In such cases the senses make the decision, since they have contact with both (sc. reason and passion); and if, in fact, one gains the mastery, it does not destroy the other, but forces it to comply and drags it along resisting. For the lover who admonishes himself uses reason against his passion, since they both exist at the same time in his soul, as it were pressing with his hand the other member, which is inflamed, and clearly perceiving that there are two distinct forces and that they are at variance. (448B)

But this, replies Chrysippus, is surely rubbish. First of all, purely intellectual changes of mind are not as unequivocally dispassionate as all that. Life would be rather less troublesome than it is if that were so. In fact, one often clings tenaciously to settled convictions long after the evidence has made them rationally untenable. Secondly you are disregarding the fact that even the lover, in throwing prudence to the winds and climbing up the drainpipe, is making a *decision*, and a decision is a rational activity. The senses do not make decisions; the senses only *sense*. What is this other decision-making entity? No, there is only one mind. Sometimes, through bed conditioning, it assents to impressions that it should not assent to, and this is what we have to try to prevent by philosophical argument and training. It is not a question of taming a beast; it is a question of preventing the dislocation (*diastrophē*) of the mind as a whole.

The fact is that Plutarch, despite the lucidity and eloquence of his presentation, does not really come to grips with this problem. He cannot seem to take the notion of a unitary soul seriously. When he turns to discuss the doctrine of *eupatheiai* (449A ff.), he can only view this as a piece of Stoic casuistry, inventing high-sounding terms to disguise the fact that they recognize the passions after all. At 450C, he triumphantly quotes Chrysippus against himself:

> In his work *Peri Anomologias*, Chrysippus has said: "Anger is a blind thing: often it prevents our seeing obvious matters, and often it obscures matters which are already apprehended (*katalambanomena*)"; and, a little further on, he says, "For the passions, when once raised, drive out the processes of reasoning and all things that appear otherwise than they would have them be, and push forward with violence to actions contrary to reason. . . ."
>
> And again, Chrysippus proceeds to say that every rational creature is so disposed by nature as to use reason in all things and to be governed by it; yet often reason is rejected when we are under the influence of some other more violent force. Thus in this passage he plainly acknowledges what conclusion is to be drawn from the difference which exists between passion and reason. (450CD)

We are glad to have these extracts from Chrysippus' work, but beg leave to dispute that they prove what Plutarch wants them to prove. Of course Chrysippus recognizes the existence of what are commonly known as passions, and that all too frequently what is commonly known as passion overcomes reason. Plutarch is surely missing the point. All Chrysippus wishes to maintain is that whatever impulse is dominant, it is the *hēgemonikon* that must assent if an action is to result. This is precisely why the passions are so dangerous. They cannot be confined in a dungeon below stairs, and chastised repeatedly to keep them moderate. If they are around in the soul at all, they are necessarily right in the center of things, twisting the ruling element in their direction. Nor does Chrysippus wish to deny that even the wise man will be affected. Some sense-perceptions, and the assents to them, are inseparable from such affections (*propatheiai*), and there is nothing wrong with that, so long as the reason is in command of them. Plutarch reports Stoic doctrine as follows (449B): "*Eupatheia* arises when reason does not destroy the emotion, but composes and sets it in order in the souls of temperate persons." He states it, however, in such a tendentious way as to suggest that the Stoics in fact recognize a passionate element in the soul. What he might more properly have said was, e.g., "*Eupatheia* arises (in the soul of the wise man) when reason deliberates about some thing which has value relative to us" (cf. *SVF* III 118–21).

What we find, then, in Plutarch (and in other Platonists of the period, such as Taurus, Albinus, and Apuleius, and in such a Platonist-influenced thinker as Philo of Alexandria) is a remarkable unwillingness or inability to comprehend what the Stoic position was. Only so can Plutarch alternately represent Chrysippus as advocating total insensibility, *and* think that he is convicting him out of his own mouth when he catches him talking of anger overcoming reason. Only so can Taurus (*ap*. Gellius *NA* I 26) contrast Stoic "insensibility" (*analgēsia*) with Platonic-Peripatetic "moderation" in the matter of the control of anger. Only so can Philo comfortably make a distinction between *metriopatheia* as being proper to the man of median virtue, who is still improving (the *prokoptōn*, symbolized by Aaron), and *apatheia*, which is proper to the achieved sage (symbolized by Moses, *Leg. All.* III 129–32), as if the two concepts could be accommodated on a sliding scale. Plainly Philo is here taking *apatheia* as being a truly yogic ideal and is quite missing the significance of the great debate.[10]

To return to our starting point, then: the controversy about *metriopatheia* and *apatheia*, which generated such heat in later Greek philosophy, is properly one between the concept of a bipartite or tripartite soul, in which the lower part of parts can never be eradicated—at least while the soul is in the body—but must constantly be chastised, and that of a unitary one. Of course, a Stoic *eupatheia* comes out in practice as being very similar to a properly moderated Platonic-Aristotelian pathos, but that, as we have seen, is irrelevant to the main point.

The incomprehension on the part of Platonists as to what the argument was really about is remarkably analogous to a similar incomprehension in ancient sources, drawn attention to not long ago in an excellent article by Michael Frede,[11] about the true difference between Stoic and Aristotelian logic. Platonists such as Albinus, Apuleius, or Galen[12] are quite prepared to use both side by side, entering into discussion as to which was the more basic, but not seeming to be much concerned about the difference between a logic of propositions and a logic of terms. In each case, one is tempted to wonder if something was obvious to them that we are missing, but on the face of it one can only wonder at these blind spots.

NOTES

[1] Plotinus draws attention to this apparent tension in Plato's thought in a somewhat different context, at *Enn.* IV 8, 2.

[2] For good discussions of the Stoic doctrine of the passions and, of *eupatheiai*, see J. M. Rist, *Stoic Philosophy* (Cambridge, 1969), ch. 2, pp. 25–36, A. A. Long, *Hellenistic Philosophy* (New York, 1974), pp. 175–78, and F. H. Sandbach, *The Stoics* (New York, 1975), pp. 59–68.

[3] There is another thing that the wise man may experience, with which we are not now concerned but which should be noted. That is what were later, at least, termed *propatheiai*. These are the instinctive feelings, preliminary to a passion proper, which result automatically from certain *phantasiai*. Seneca, *De Ira* II 1–4 has a good discussion of these, which he terms *nec adfectus, sed principia proludentia affectibus* (II 2). Cf. also Aulus Gellius *NA* XIX 1, 14 ff., where the doctrine is traced back to Chrysippus from Epictetus. This, however, does not seem to be what Zeno is talking of here, but rather of something "remaining."

[4] I quote Sandbach, *The Stoics*, p. 63: "The distinction (sc. between *apatheia* and *metriopatheia*), although justified, can be exaggerated. The Stoic passion is an excessive uncontrolled drive, due to an overestimation of indifferent things, but there is also a correct drive towards these same things. The moderate passion of the Peripatetic is a correct feeling and so could perhaps not be regarded by a Stoic as a passion at all."

[5] On Antiochus, see further J. M. Dillon, *The Middle Platonists* (Ithaca, N.Y., 1977), ch. 2.

[6] E.g., Cicero *De Finibus* IV, 20 ff.

[7] Cf. I. G. Kidd, "Posidonius on Emotions," in *Problems in Stoicism*, ed. A. A. Long (London, 1971), pp. 200–15.

[8] The translations of Plutarch here are borrowed from the Loeb translators, Babbitt (for *Cons. ad Apoll.*) and Helmbold (for *Virt. Mor.*), though with modifications where they do not attain the required degree of accuracy.

[9] Cf. J. M. Rist, *Stoic Philosophy*, ch. 14: "The Unity of the Person"—a most useful discussion.

[10] Elsewhere, we may note, Philo is prepared to commend *metriopatheia* as opposed to *apatheia* as an ideal even for the sage. At *Abr.* 256–57, for example, he praises Abraham, on the loss of his wife Sarah, for "neither fretting beyond measure, nor showing a complete lack of emotion (*apatheia*), but choosing the mean rather than the extremes, and trying to moderate his passions (*metriopathein*)," a position concordant with that of Plutarch.

[11] "Stoic vs. Aristotelian Syllogistic," *Archiv f. Gesch. d. Philos.* 56 (1974): 1–32.

[12] E.g., Galen, *Inst. Log.* p. 17, 13 f. Kalbfleisch; Apuleius, *Peri Herm.* cf. 13. (I accept this work as genuine, regarding the arguments against this as less than cogent, but its authenticity does not greatly affect the point I am making.)

Index of Proper Names

Index of Topics

INDEX OF TOPICS

Chariot and dog analogy, 492
Choice, 482, 484
Chorismos, 389ff
Chorus of Thinkers, 131f, 134
Chresimon (useful), 132, 134
Christians, 496
Cicero's knowledge of Aristotle, 405ff, 412ff, 418f
Civil disobedience, 149, 152
Clines, 341
Cloak (*tribon*), 132, 134
Coherence, 210
Collision of atoms, 395ff
Collision of atoms, and weight, 413ff
Comedy, 129, 131, 133, 137f, 169f, 190, 194ff, 199ff
Comic poets, 180
Common opinions (*endoxa*), 376
Component v means, 368
Condensation, 14f
Condestinate facts, 483f
Conjecture (see *doxa*), 96, 98
Constitution in Parmenides (see Nature), 49
Constitution, true and perverted, 354f
Constitutions, collection, 357
Constitutions, taxonomy of, 354ff
Contact, of atoms, 398–407
Contemplation (*theoria*), 364, 371f, 374, 375, 382
Continuity, 403
Continuity, diachronic and synchronic, 341
Cosmic sympathy, 499f
Cosmogony, 7, 11, 16
Cosmology, 42, 279, 404ff
Courage, 205
Cross-reference, as substitute for argument, 109–111, 116f
Cylinder analogy, 487, 490

Daemons, 192, 496, 503
Daimonion, 171
Definition. *See acriby*
Degree of necessity, 348
Degrees of Reality, 42, 52, 63, 65ff, 237
Deliberation, 303–308, 312, 313ff, 482, 484ff
Demiurge, 245
Democracy, 153
Democritean metaphysics, 482
Desire (*epithymia, orexis*), 214, 310ff, 317, 319, 485, 489
Determinism, 480ff, 492
Dialectic, 168, 178, 203, 211f, 253
Dialogue form, 177
Dianoia, 179, 209
Diatribe, 168

Dichotomists, 346
Dikaiosyne (justice), 163, 167
Dine, Dinos, 3–19 passim, 131, 135, 138, 143
Dionysia, 129, 131, 137
Direction (in the universe), 416
Discontinuity (space and time), 395
Disease, 317
Divided Line, 179, 252
Divination, 502f
Divisibility, 83
Division, method of, 181
Doing (*praxis*), 376, 380, 383
Doxa (opinion), 279, 282–289, 297f
Doxographies of Aristotle, 408ff
Drama, and Plato, 158, 160
Drama, 134f, 178
Dramatic chorus, 134f
Dreamed theory in Tht, 264–279
Drug, 114
Dualizing, 342, 359
Dynamis (potentiality), 344
DNA, 343

Earth, 4f, 12f
Ecological niche, 356
Education. *See paideia*
Egyptian cult, 504
Eide (forms), 280–283
Eidolon, 97ff
Eidos (form, species), 340ff, 392ff
Eikasia, 210
Einai, vital use of, 63
Eleatic Stranger, 181
Element (*stoicheion*), 73–76, 265–269, 271, 174
Elenchus, 149, 152
Elephant, 350
Emotion, 303–308, 312–317
Enaima/anaima, 346
Endurance, 206
Energy, 398
Enkrateia, 512
Enuma Elish, 17
Ephorate, 359
Epic and logos, 159f, 167
Episteme (knowledge), 199f, 279–282, 285, 289–293, 297f
Epistemological priority, 235ff
Epithymia (desire), 192
Eros (love), 192f, 200
Eros, god, 192
Eros, praise of, 187f, 191f
Erotesis, 168f
Essence, 237ff, 396
Essentialism, 341ff

528

531

Index of Passages Cited

INDEX OF PASSAGES CITED

180 Es73c1 v2   AAM-1993
050101 000

Essays in ancient Greek philos

0 0003 0174218 5

Lyndon State College